# INSCRIPTIONS FROM
# BURIAL GROUNDS OF THE
# NASHAWAY TOWNS:

Lancaster, Harvard, Bolton, Leominster, Sterling
Berlin, West Boylston, and Hudson
MASSACHUSETTS

Compiled By

THE LANCASTER LEAGUE

OF HISTORICAL SOCIETIES

Esther K. Whitcomb, editor

HERITAGE BOOKS, INC.

Published 1989 By


HERITAGE BOOKS, INC.
1540E Pointer Ridge Place, Bowie, Maryland 20716
(301)-390-7709

ISBN 1-55613-221-2


A Complete Catalog Listing Hundreds of Titles on
History, Genealogy & Americana
Free on Request

# TABLE OF CONTENTS

# FOREWORD

Settled on land bought from the Nashaway Indians in 1642 as the Nashaway Plantation, and incorporated in 1653, the Town of Lancaster was the first town in Worcester County. After the massacre in King Philip's War, Lancaster was without a white inhabitant for several years. Resettlement began about 1679 to 1680, partly on second division land which became the towns of Harvard and Bolton.

In time, ten towns evolved from the original purchase and the "Additional Grant." Each town established a burial ground and, as the need arose, others.

Over the years, many gravestones have met with disaster, natural deterioration, the freezing and thawing of New England winters, acid rain, and, more recently, vandalism and theft. It seemed that something should be done to at least preserve the inscriptions for future generations. The Lancaster League of Historical Societies has copied the inscriptions of all the stones in their towns up to 1850 with a scattering up to the middle of the present century. A cemetery that was not started until 1850 was not done at all. This should be a valuable tool for genealogists in the future.

We have been aided financially by the following to whom we wish to express our gratitude: The Arts Lottery Councils of Bolton, of Sterling, of West Boylston and the Arts Lottery Council administered through the Mayor's Office of Cultural Affairs of Leominster. We wish to thank Mrs. Isabelle Fry Sawyer of Durham, New Hampshire for a donation in memory of the Fry family of Bolton.

Esther K. Whitcomb, editor
Barry W. Eager
Evelyn Hachey
Ruth Hopfmann
Barbara Dudley
Grace Klar
Alfred Braga

# LANCASTER – THE OLD BURIAL FIELD

The founders of the Town and their descendants (during the 17th century at least) buried their dead without formal services, following the custom of the Puritans in England; and perhaps a plot of ground for the family graves was sometimes selected within the home lot or orchard. Early in this century, ancient graves were visible near the sites of both the Roper and the Prescott garrisons. But in the infancy of the Nashaway Plantation, land adjoining the Meeting House was set apart for common use as a "burying place." The practice of marking graves by inscribed headstones probably did not begin until after the resettlement, one apparent exception being that of Mrs. Dorothy Prescott, who died in 1674. The oldest date now to be found is that over the grave of the first John Houghton--1684. For half a century, all memorial stones were but fragments of slate riven from some ledge, or rough granite slabs, upon which unskilled hands rudely incised name and date--the latter being often upon a foot-stone or on the back of the head-stone. Many of the older inscriptions are illegible to most eyes. In his *History of Lancaster*, Reverend A.P. Marvin has given a plan of this ancient burial place, upon which the marked graves are located and numbered, and has added literal copies of the epitaphs.

WILDER, Andrew d 28 Dec 1764 in 56y
  Andrew s/o Andrew & Elizabeth d 4 Sept 1741
  Ruth d/o Andrew & Elizabeth d 19 Jan 1753 ae 8y
  Joseph s/o Andrew & Elizabeth d 15 Aug 1755 ae 3y
  Deborah d/o Andrew & Elizabeth d 22 Aug 1755 ae 11d
PHILLIPS, John d 23 Nov 1776 ae 56y
  John s/o John d 29 Oct 1776 ae 5y
  Samuel s/o John d 2 Nov 1776 ae 3y
  Rebecca d/o John d 26 Oct 1776 ae 22m
ROBBINS, Edward d 9 Oct 1791 in 78y
  Bathsheba w/o Edward d 16 Oct 1805 in 86y
PHILLIPS, John d 31 Jan 1763 ae 70y
  Lydia d 31 May 1760 ae 29y
  Rebecca d 14 July 1775 ae 53y
  Jonathan d 20 July 1780 ae 44y
  Jotham s/o Edward & Bathshebe d 24 Nov 1762 ae 17y 7m
    24d
WATERS, Jacob d 15 Dec 1714 ae 65y 7m
WYMAN, Ephraim d 17 Feb 1780 in 30y

Nathaniel d 15 Dec 1801 ae 55y
WHITNEY, Mary w/o Jonathan d 12 Jan 1778 in 34y
WYMAN, Nathaniel d 5 June 1776 in 58y
   Mary w/o Nathaniel d 8 May 1759 in 37y
   Submit w/o Nathaniel d 25 Nov 1804 in 74y
   Elizabeth d/o Abijah & Abigail d 20 July 1766 ae 11y 10m
BENNIT, John d 30 Dec 1748 ae 29y 11m 10d
   Bathsheba w/o Capt John d 7 Feb 1762 ae 67y
   John d 5 June 1761 ae 68y -- Capt
   Samuel d 6 July 1742 in 77y
MOORE, Mary d 26 Sept 1705
SERS, Anna
GODFREY, Levi s/o Salmon & Rebecah d 3 May 1789 ae 7m 8d
CLARK, Mathew d 9 July 1760 in 56y
   Mary d/o Mathew d 27 Jan 1749 in 9y
   John s/o Mathew d 15 May 1751 ae 3wks
   Mathew s/o Mathew d 24 July 1750 in 9y
   Sarah d/o Mathew d 6 Oct 1758 in 3y
WILDER, Martha w/o Gardner d 7 Mar 1764 ae 27y
   Gardner s/o Gardner & Martha stillborn 17 Sept 1761
BUSS, John d 30 Apr 1734 ae about 55y
   Hannah w/o John d 14 Mar 1738 in 56y
LOCKE, Mary w/o William d 17 Nov 1796 in 50y
WILDER, Rebecca w/o Joseph Esq d 10 Sept 1789 in 80y
LOCKE, James d 19 Mar 1772 in 33y
   Samuel d 13 Apr 1775 in 73y
   Josiah d 16 May 1769 ae 33y
   Esther d/o Josiah & Esther d 25 Mar 1768 ae 6m 1d
   Abel s/o Josiah & Esther d 13 Oct 1766 ae 2m 1d
WILDER, Rebeccah d/o Ephriam & Lucretia d 14 May 1766 ae 8m 7d
LOCKE, Abel s/o Josiah & Esther d 6 May 1765 ae 3m 20d
WARNAR, John d 27 Mar 1776 in 41y
WILDER, Oliver  d 16 Mar 1765 in 71y -- Col
   Mary w/o Col Oliver d 15 June 1748 in 53y
HARRINGTON, Timothy s/o Rev Timothy & Anna d 16 June 1749
     ae 7m 25d
   Anna w/o Rev Timothy d 19 May 1778 ae 62
   Rev Timothy ae 80 4th Pastor of Church in Lancaster
HOUGHTON, Abigail w/o Henry ae 30 1711
   Hasadiah d/o Henry & Abigail d 1711 ae 2y 2m
HASKELL, Henry d 1 Apr 1779 in 73y
SWAN, John d -- --- ---- ae 3-1/2y
CARTER, Mary w/o Ephraim d 30 May 1738 in 21y
OSGOOD, Elizabeth w/o Joseph d 9 Oct 1755 in 34y
WHITING, Rev John 2nd minister killed by Indians 11 Sept
   1697. This stone replaces one broken & Decayed. Set
     by Town 1878.
HOUGHTON, Henry s/o Henry & Abigail d -- --- 1702 ae 1y 6m
   ---- s/o of Henry & Abigail d -- ---- 1708 ae 6wk
   John d 29 Apr 1684
   Abigail d/o JMH

PRENTICE, Stanton MD d 1 Dec 1769 ae 58y
SWAN, Ebenezer d 22 Aug 1750 ae 42y
GARDNER, Rev Andrew d 26 Oct 1704 in 30y
PRENTICE, Rev John Pastor of Church d 6 Jan 1747/8 ae 66y
   Mary w/o Rev John d 9 Mar 1717/18 in 37y
   Mercy w/o Dr Stanton d 26 Oct 1756 in 40y
   Thomas s/o Dr Stanton & Mercy d 2 May 1752 ae 6y 7m
   Thomas s/o Dr Stanton & Mercy d 17 Aug 1745 ae 3y 10m 19d
   Mary d/o Dr Stanton & Mercy d 23 May 1749 ae 1y 3m
   Daniel s/o Dr Stanton & Mercy d 21 Sept 1756 ae 5y
   Mercy d/o Dr Stanton & Mercy d 6 Oct 1756 ae 2y
   Mercy d/o Dr Stanton & Rebecca d 12 Jan 1759 ae 3m
   Peter s/o Dr Stanton & Rebecca d 1 July 1766 ae 5y 6m
CARTER, Susannah d/o Dr James & Susannah d 28 July 1795 ae
    2y 17d
SAWYER, Thomas d 1 Mar 1760 ae 22y 9m 27d
   Eunice w/o Bezaleel d 4 Mar 1712 ae 26y
   Also her dead born infant
   Bezaleel d 25 Aug 1760 ae 75y 3m 12d
T W, T W,
CARTER, John s/o John & Abigail d 18 Oct 1739 ae 1y 9m 9d
   Elisha s/o John & Abigail stillborn
   John s/o Lt John & Abigail d 21 Dec 1746 in 5y
   Abigail d/o Lt John & Abigail d 25 Dec 1746 in 7y
   John d 8 May 1766 ae 53 -- Col
TOWNSEND, Caleb
CARTER, Ruth w/o Capt Thomas d 25 Dec 1739 ae 55y 7m 16d
   Thomas d 31 Mar 1737 ae 55y -- Capt
   Samuel d 22 Aug 1738 in 61y
TEMPLE, Elizabeth w/o Isaac d 27 Aug in 78y
BALLARD, Josiah Jr d 17 Sept 1771 in 22y
BOWARS, John d -- ---- 1718
NICHOLS, Roger d 3 June 1765
BALLARD, John s/o John & Anna d 7 Nov 1789 in 6y
   John s/o Thomas & Abigail d 3 Mar 1792 ae 4m 10d
   John s/o Thomas & Abigail d 20 Aug 1794 ae 19m 20d
KENDALL, Thomas s/o Thomas & Abigail d 25 Aug 1756 in 1y
GOSS, Jonas s/o Daniel & Eunice d 27 May 1774 ae 3d
   Anna d/o Daniel & Eunice d 17 Jan 1779 ae 3y 8m 19d
WILDER, Ephraim d 13 Dec 1769 in 94y -- Capt
   Elizabeth w/o Capt Ephraim d 28 May 1769 in 89y
WILDER, Ephraim Jr d 7 Mar 1770 in 63y -- Capt
   Anna w/o Capt Ephraim d 16 Oct 1778 in 67y
GATES, Anna w/o Capt Hezekiah d 23 Apr 1779 ae 70y
HOUSE, Joseph d 9 July 1756 in 61y
   Elizabeth d/o Joseph & Lydia d Oct 1739 in 14y
THURSTON, Nancy d/o Peter & Dorothy d 25 Sept 1778 in 5y
GATES, Hezekiah d 27 June 1777 in 73y -- Capt
HOUGHTON Rebeckah w/o Philimon d 15 Feb 1766 ae 26y
   Rebeckah d/o Philimon & Rebeckah d 5 July 1765 ae 1y 5m 5d
PAGE, Martha w/o Levi d 16 Apr 1785 in 28y

ATHERTON, David s/o Amos & Elizabeth d 4 July 1769 in 14y
HARRISS, Edmond d 10 Dec 1726 in 53y
   Elizabeth w/o Edmond d 31 Jan 1755 in 73y
   Amos d 4 Apr 1713 ae
MARSH, Hon Elisha d 25 July 1784 ae 71y of Walpole NH
WILLARD, Samuel d 20 Nov 1752 in 63y -- Col
GATES, Wilder s/o Thomas & Abigail d 2 July 1766 ae 1m 2d
   John s/o Thomas & Abigail d 24 Nov 1785 in 7y Their
      third only son
   Anna d/o Thomas & Abigail d 27 Nov 1785 in 16y
THURSTON, Thomas s/o Capt John & Becca d 14 Dec 1785 ae 2y
     5m 8d
GATES, Lucy d/o Capt Thomas & Abigail d 19 July 1797 in 33y
FAIRBANK, Elizabeth w/o Dea Cyrus d 1 Oct 1778 in 39y
   Lucy w/o Dea Cyrus d 16 Sept 1776 ae 36y 8d
   Ephraim her son stillborn 1 Sept 1776
   Dea Cyrus d 28 Feb 1801 ae 63y
   Jonas d 4 Nov 1792 in 89y
RUGG, Isaac d 14 Oct 1758 in 38y
FAIRBANK, Thankful w/o Jonas d 13 May 1795 ae 81y
   Lucy d/o Cyrus & Lucy d 1 Mar 1764 in 3m
   Anna d/o Cyrus & Lucy d 17 July 1769 ae 3m 8d
   Sally d/o Cyrus & Lucy d 9 June 1790 in 18y
   Anna d/o Cyrus & Lucy d 31 Mar 1773 ae 2y 7m 20d
   Jabez d March 1758 ae about 84y -- Lieut
   Mary w/o Jabez d -- March 1718 ae 42y
   Elizabeth d/o Jabez d 11 May 1755 ae 80y 7m
   Grase
   The Dafter of Joseph Fairbank
DUNSMOOR, William Esq d 20 May 1784 in 51y
   John s/o William & Hannah d 29 Oct 1756 ae 1y 8m
SAWYER, Darius d 13 Aug 1789 in 69y
   Deborah d/o Darius & Daborah d 16 Dec 1765 ae 21y 9m
DUNSMOOR, John MD d 7 Dec 1747 in 45y
   Eunice d/o Dr John d 9 Sept 1745 in 3y
   Olive d/o Dr John d 19 Sept 1745 in 8y
   John s/o Dr John d 26 Sept 1745 in 5y
PHELPS, Sylvester s/o Joel & Prudence d 7 Apr 1765 ae 2y 1m
ALLEN, Ebenezer d 9 July 1770 ae 94y
   Sarah w/o Ebenezer d 15 June 1755 in 71y
PHELPS, Phinehas s/o Dr Phinehas & Sarah d 12 Dec 1784 in 19y
   Phinehas MD d 12 Aug 1770 in 37y
GOSS, Philip d -- May 1698
FAIRBANK, Jonathan d 11 Sept 1697
   Grace d/o Jonathan d 11 Sept 1697
   Hannah d/o Jonathan d 11 Dec 1704
   Jonas s/o Jonathan d 13 Sept 1697
SAWYER, Amos d -- --- 1768
   Abigail w/o Amos d 20 Nov 1753 ae 65y 7m 13d
ALLEN, Thomas s/o Amos & Rebecca d 23 Jan 1793 ae 5y 7m 16d
PRESCOTT, John d 11 Oct 1749 in 77y

Dorothy w/o John d 28 Sept 1749 in 73y
John d 1 Apr 1791 in 79y
Mary w/o John d 20 Oct 1788 in 66y
Experience dasesed this life
WILLARD, Abijah Jr s/o Capt Abijah & Elizabeth d 12 Dec 1749
     ae 10m
   Elizabeth w/o Capt Abijah d 6 Dec 1751 in 29y
   Catherine w/o Levi Esq d 10 Jan 1791 ae 56
   Levi Esq d 11 July 1775 ae 48y
   John d 1 May 1775 ae 17y
   Katharine d/o Capt Levi & Katharine d 3 Dec 1759 ae 5m 14d
   Theodorah d/o Capt Abijah & Anna d 14 Oct 1756 ae 9m
   Elizabeth d/o Capt Abijah & Anna d 6 Oct 1756 in 3y
SAWYER, Thomas d 12 Sept 1706 about 90y
   Mary w/o Lt Moses d 12 Apr 1774 in 33y
   Thomas d 5 Sept 1736 in 89y
   Joseph d 10 July 1737 in 55y
   Sarah w/o Joseph d 7 Mar 1717/18 ae 37y
BEMAN, Priscilla w/o John d 6 Aug 1729 in 73y
   John d 15 Jan 1739/40 in 90y
PRESCOTT, Sarah d 14 July 1709 ae about 63y
   Mary d 23 Feb 1718
   John Prescott ?Desased (in 1681) 1681
   Dorothy d/o John & Dorothy d 27 Mar 1713 ae 7y
   Dorothy w/o Jonathan d -- --- 1674
WILDER, Deborah w/o Hon Joseph d 20 Apr 1773 in 65y
   Peter s/o Hon Joseph & Deborah d 1 July 1762 ae 19y
   John Twin to Peter d -- --- ---- on the day of his birth
SAWYER, Martha w/o Paul d 10 May 1794 ae 31y
FLETCHER, Hannah w/o John d 10 Apr 1737 in 52y
LOCKE, Rebecca w/o James d 9 Mar 1769 in 28y
JOSLIN, Martha w/o Nathaniel d 13 Feb 1768 in 37y
   Joanna w/o Capt Peter d 24 Sept 1717 in 44y
   Dorothy d/o Peter & Joanna d 20 Apr 1732 in 18y
   Hannah w/o Capt Peter d 14 Aug 1739 in 71y
RUGG, Rebekah d/o John & Lydia d 6 July 1747 ae 2y 9m 27d
VOSE, Ann Austin w/o Peter Thacher d/o Hon John Sprague
     1776-1834
   Peter Thacher b Milton 4 Sept 1769 - 4 Mar 1851
   Francis Henry s/o Peter & Ann 25 Aug 1816-22 July 1841
   Samuel Sprague s/o Peter & Ann d Mar 1826 ae 27y
   Edward Henry s/o Peter & Ann d 23 June 1810 ae 3y
SPRAGUE, Hon John Esq Chief Justice d 28 Sept 1800 ae 61
   Katharine w/o Hon John d/o Richard Foster Esq d 5 May
     1787 in 49y
   Samuel John AM s/o Hon John & Katharine d 10 Sept 1805 in 26y
SAWYER, Amos s/o Amos & Prudence d 1 Nov 1792 ae 3y 2m 5d

## THE OLD-COMMON BURIAL GROUND

When in 1706, after long debate, the third Meeting House was built far from the old site, upon the east side of the river, a suitable lot of land across the highway near it was given to the Town for burials by Captain Thomas Wilder, second of the name. The donor's grave is the oldest in the enclosure, the date of which is known. Inscriptions prior to 1850, beginning with those of the Wilder family are as follows--the first given being upon a cenotaph of modern erection.

WILDER, Thomas from Lancaster England came to Lancaster
      Massachusetts 1 July 1659 d 23 Oct 1667
   Thomas d 7 Aug 1716 ae about 70y -- Capt
   Hon Joseph Esq d 29 Mar 1757 ae 74y
   Lucy w/o Hon Joseph d 13 May 1763 ae 84y
   Caleb d 19 June 1776 ae 59y -- Col
   Abigail w/o Col Caleb d 1 Oct 1804 ae 92
   Abigail Smith d/o Caleb & Abigail d 8 Sept 1778 ae 32
   Sarah d 31 Aug 1819 ae 66y
   Levi d 5 Jan 1793 ae 42y
   Prudence w/o Josiah ae 33y 1m with 4 of their children
      Rufus Martha Josiah Sarah  All died by fire 23 Jan 1739
   James d 13 May 1739 in 59y -- Col
   Abigail w/o Col James d 18 Sept 1761 ae 80y
   Josiah Esq d 20 Dec 1788 in 45y
   Titus s/o Thomas & Susannah d 1 May 1749 ae 25y 4m
   Jonathan d 13 Jan 1836 ae 80y
   Ruth Prescott w/o Jonathan d 19 Nov 1826 ae 69y
   David s/o Lt Jonathan & Ruth d 29 Jan 1786 ae 4y 4m
   John s/o Lt Jonathan & Ruth d 25 Jan 1786 ae 3y 3m
   Asaph d 8 July 1747 ae 23y 7m 12d
PHELPS, Zipporah w/o John formerly w/o Asaph Wilder d 20
      June 1758 ae 34
WILDER, Hannah d/o John & Sarah d 30 Sept 1723 in 16y
   Ebenezer d 25 Dec 1745 in 65y
   Mary w/o Ebenezer d 6 Jan 1733/4 ae 54y 9m 22d
   Anna w/o David d 20 Sept 1744 in 35y
   Eunice w/o David d 17 Feb 1750/1 in 30y
   Josiah s/o Capt James & Martha d 4 Apr 1736 ae 5m 16d
   Manasseh s/o Capt Ephraim & Anna d 17 Dec 1741 in 4y
   Ephraim s/o Capt Ephraim & Anna b&d 17 June 1732
   Katharine d/o Capt Ephraim & Anna d 21 Dec 1741 in 7y
   Anna Maria d/o SVS & Electa d 20 June 1834 ae 18m
   Sampson Vryling Stoddard s/o SVS & Electa d 20 Feb 1832
     ae 3y 8m
   Sarah Vryling Stoddard d/o SVS & Electa d 23 July 1823 ae 23m
   Francina Melanie d/o SVS & Electa d in Paris 20 Mar 1818 ae 8m
WILLSON, Rhoda d/o Benjamin & Rebecca d 1 Aug 1732 in 15y
   Nathaniel d 19 Aug 1778 in 67y -- Capt
   Jeremiah d 22 Mar 1743 in 77y
WHETCOMB, Josiah d 21 Mar 1718 in 80y

David d 11 Apr 1730 in 62y
Mary w/o David d 5 Jan 1733/4 in 67y
Hezekiah d 6 May 1732 in 51y
WARNER, Rebekah d/o John & Sarah d 30 Mar 1718 ae 20
WILLARD, Dorothy d/o Lt Nathanial & Elizabeth d 25 May 1765
    ae 2y 2m 17d
  Wright s/o Aaron & Mary d 28 Mar 1754 ae 8y 24d
  Dorothy d/o Aaron & Mary d 28 Mar 1754 ae 11y 18d
  Elizabeth d/o Aaron & Mary d 25 Sept 1746 ae 11y 10m 25d
  Mary w/o Aaron d 27 Apr 1767 ae 63y 2m 8d
JOSLYN, Martha w/o Capt Peter former w/o Josiah Wheeler d 21
    May 1748 in 69y
WHEELER, Josiah d 8 Dec 1738 in 64y
WOODBERRY, Rebecca d/o Samuel & Rebecah d 25 Feb 1815 ae 24y
WHITING, Timothy d 12 Jan 1826 ae 67y
  Abigail w/o Timothy d 1 Oct 1798 ae 39y
  Lydia w/o Timothy d 15 Jan 1851 ae 75y
BUTLAR, Olive d 24 Feb 1822 ae 59y
CHASE, William J s/o Charles & Ruth d 23 May 1806 ae 9m
  Albert R s/o Alanson & Maria d 4 Apr 1825 ae 8m
  Amia Ann d 4 Feb 1831 ae 21y
CARTER, Mary w/o Capt James d 18 Apr 1795 ae 66y 15d
  James d 15 July 1800 ae 79y -- Capt
  Prudence w/o Capt James d 10 Jan 1747 ae 19y 3m 16d
CARLETON, Mary Louisa d 22 Jan 1837 ae 16y
  Mary w/o Moses d 7 May 1832 ae 32y
  George Henry s/o Moses & Mary d 8 Sept 1829 ae 4y
  Theodore s/o Moses & Mary d 23 Oct 1823 ae 1y
  Mary w/o Moses d 7 Feb 1816 ae 23y
  James s/o Jonathan d 29 June 1819 in 12y
CLEVELAND, Mary w/o William d 7 May 1815 ae 36y
  Joseph Hiller s/o William & Mary d 28 June 1817 ae 3y
HILLER, Joseph Esq d 9 Feb 1814 ae 66y
EMERSON, Moses d 22 Oct 1822 ae 48y
  Judith Kelley d 5 Dec 1798 ae 23y
  Sally Carleton d 16 Oct 1808 ae 29y
  Lydia Carleton d 13 Jan 1813 ae 32y
  Eunice Wright d 27 Sept 1844 ae 58y
  Hazen d 4 Apr 1807 ae 3y
  Sally C d 26 Nov 1817 ae 3y
  Moses K d 27 Oct 1825 ae 27y
  Francis P d 24 Aug 1835 ae 25y
FIFE, Deliverance w/o William d 4 Nov 1750 ae 37y 10m 4d
  William d 5 May 1790 in 74y
  Abigail w/o William d 30 Apr 1790 in 69y
  Joseph d 3 Nov 1810 ae 22y
FALLAS, Charity w/o William d 29 Oct 1786 in 65y
FARNWORTH, Ephraim d 18 Feb 1737 in 35y
FAIRBANK, Jonathan s/o Jonathan & Thankful d 14 Sept 1741 in 2y
  Martha w/o Silas d 8 Dec 1849 ae 68y
  Silas d 26 Aug 1847 ae 67y

FLAGG, Hannah w/o Gershom d 13 Oct 1784 ae 73y
FAULKNER, Paul d 9 Feb 1841 ae 75y
   Abigail F w/o Paul d 23 Sept 1811 ae 42y
   Hannah w/o Paul d 4 Oct 1817 ae 46y
   Eunice w/o Paul d 5 Oct 1846 ae 62y
   Emily w/o Horace d 24 Aug 1825 ae 22y
GOOS, John d 5 Oct 1747 in 30y
GOSS, John d 24 Mar 1843 ae 73y
   John Jr s/o John & Mary W d 13 Jan 1828 ae 23y
   John s/o John & Mary W d 1 Oct 1803 ae 1y 7m 22d
   Joseph s/o John & Mary W d 16 Aug 1801 ae 1y 10m 2d
   James s/o John & Mary W d 30 Dec 1800 ae 3y 18m 2d
HOUGHTON, Dinah d/o Jonas & Mary d 23 Sept 1723 ae 12y 5m
   Jonas d 20 Sept 1723 ae 60y 5m
   Mary w/o Jonas Sr d 31 Dec 1720 in 60y
   Jonas d 15 Aug 1739 in 57y -- Capt
   Josiah d 29 Sept 1723 ae 24y 11m
   Ephah d/o Lt Jonathan & Thankful d 27 Sept 1729 ae 2y 3m
   Mary d/o Ens Jacob & Mary d 30 Aug 1736 ae 3y 10m 29d
   John d 5 Apr 1724 ae 51y -- Lieut
ALBERT, Mary w/o Daniel d 23 Oct 1726 in 25y
   Levinah d/o Jonathan & Mary d 5 July 1738 in 5y
   Silance d/o Jonathan & Mary d 4 Sept 1728
   Rebeckah w/o Jacob d 22 Oct 1752 ae 80y 10m 29d
   John Esq d 3 Feb 1736/7 in 87y
   Mary w/o John Esq d 7 Apr 1724 in 76y
   William d 15 July 1743 ae 48y 2m 20d
   Robart d 7 Nov 1723 in 65y
   Ebenezer d 13 Oct 1723 in 24y
   Esther w/o Robart d 13 Jan 1740/1 in 82y
   Rufus  28 Nov 1796 - 31 May 1846
   Martha P w/o Rufus 12 June 1803 - Dec 17 1835
HOUGHTON, Simon of Weare NH d 7 July 1814 ae 41y
   Martha w/o Simon d 3 Apr 1823 in 73y
   Simon d 25 Mar 1814 in 77y
HOOKER, Thomas d 18 Sept 1768 in 79y -- Lieut
HOLT, Uriah d 24 Aug 1741 ae 40y 2m 10d
JENKS, Phebe w/o William d 11 Oct 1822 ae 88y
   Mary d 17 May 1817 ae 44y
KNIGHT, Sarah w/o Daniel d 30 Apr 1722 in 38y
MARSHALL, George s/o George & Eunice d 17 May 1847 ae 18m
MOORS, Joseph s/o Dea Joseph & Rebeckah d 25 Oct 1746 ae 3y
     6m 28d
   Rebekah d/o Dea Joseph & Rebeckah d 22 Sept 1746 ae 1y 7m 10d
   Rebekah d/o Dea Joseph & Rebeckah d 26 June 1740 in 6y
   Cathorign d/o Dea Joseph & Rebeckah d 23 June 1740 in 2y
   Ephraim s/o Dea Joseph & Rebeckah d 15 June ae 7y 6m 22d
   Hannah d/o Dea Joseph & Rebeckah d 17 June ae 3y 1m 7d
   Jacob s/o Dea Joseph & Rebeckah d 18 June ae 11y 8m 6d
   Lucy d/o Dea Joseph & Rebeckah d 7 Oct 1744 ae 3y 6m 15d
   Lucy d/o Dea Joseph & Rebeckah d 22 Aug 1740 in 14y

MOORE, Harriet d/o Henry & Achsah d 8 Apr 1826 ae 14m 14d
ROBERTSON, David Steuart s/o John Esq d 21 July 1849 in 30y
QUINCY, Ann w/o Josiah Esq d 17 Feb 1805 ae 80 of Braintree
PAYNE, Eloise Richards d 3 July 1819 ae 31y
PACKARD, Eliza Quincy d/o Rev Asa d 18 Nov 1816 ae 24y
   Ann Guild d/o Rev Charles d 28 Apr 1846 ae 10wks
   Ann Marsh d/o Rev Asa d 6 June 1796 ae 5y
PHELPS, John d 14 Jan 1776 in 28y
   Sally w/o Aaron d 12 Apr 1794 ae 36y
   Peter d 7 Mar 1847 ae 72y
   Abiel S d 15 Oct 1825 ae 14y
PLUMMER, Charles s/o Farnham & Nancy d 25 May 1818 ae 9m
   Thomas s/o Farnham & Nancy d 2 Oct 1814 ae 5m
   Thomas s/o Farnham & Nancy d 12 June 1808 ae 9m at Beverly
PRIEST, John d 29 Sept 1756 in 75y
   Anna w/o John d 3 Apr 1751 in 67y
   Jonathan s/o John & Anna d 23 Apr 1738 ae 12y 7m
   Abigail d/o John & Anna d 25 Sept 1723 in 17y
RICHARDSON, Charlotte d/o Ephraim & Eunice d 13 Nov 1827 ae 15y
STOW, Abigail H w/o Luke d 15 Feb 1847 ae 54y
   Luke d 19 Aug 1846 ae 49y
SAWYER, John d 2 Oct 1731 in 43y
   Sarah d/o John & Ruth d 21 Dec 1717
   Dinah w/o Seth d 25 Oct 1727 in 23y
   Elias d 20 Nov 1752 in 63y
   Moses d 24 Nov 1739 ae 27y 2m 29d
   Thomas d 29 Nov 1752 ae 63y
   Lydia w/o Elijah d 5 May 1799 ae 72y 6m 1d
   Elizabeth w/o Thomas d 14 Feb 1799 in 34y
   Amos d 13 June 1821 ae 68y
SAFFORD, Elizabeth w/o Thomas d 11 Mar 1818 ae 49y
   Thomas d 20 June 1825 ae 59y
   Catharine d/o Thomas & Elizabeth d 4 July 1798 ae 15m
TOWNSEND, Joshua d 20 Jan 1790 in 90y born in Boston
   Elizabeth w/o Joshua d 8 Feb 1779 in 76y


## THE MIDDLE CEMETERY

In May 1798 a committee elected to procure and lay out new burial grounds bought of Reverend Nathaniel Thayer and Honorable John Sprague one acre and twenty-four rods of land lying in a rectangular form, sixteen rods in length on the highway, and eleven and one-half rods in width. According to their report, they "agreed to pay Mr Thayer fifty dollars on his executing a deed to Mr. Sprague of the Gore of Land between the old and new burying fields, which he agrees to receive in exchange for what the Town will have of him, and each of them giving a deed to the Town agreeably to the plan." In 1842, this field being crowded with graves, about one-half acre was added to it on the west end by purchase of the widow of Nathaniel Thayer DD; and space for two tiers of lots along the whole front was gained by enclosing common land on the highway, removing therefrom the hearse-house and Town pound, which for many years had been obtrusive features of this locality. The following is a carefully revised transcript of all inscriptions in this populous field bearing dates earlier than 1850.

ALLEN, Lucy w/o Samuel d 13 Oct 1847 ae 80y 9m
ANDREWS, Annis w/o Samuel d 25 Jan 1845 ae 81y
    William B d 1 Apr 1833 ae 44y
ALLEN, Abel s/o Samuel & Lucy d 4 Apr 1800 ae 3y 5m
    Samuel s/o Samuel & Lucy d 21 Jan 1807 ae 8y
ANDREWS, Elizabeth d/o Ferdinand & Elizabeth d 13 Jan 1831
    ae 6m
BURDITT, Sarah B w/o John d 17 Mar 1832 ae 47y
    Franklin C s/o John & Sally d 24 Nov 1837 ae 2y
    F Wentworth s/o John & Sarah d 18 June 1849 ae 21y
    Charles A s/o Thomas & Sarah d 21 Feb 1842 ae 6m
BEAMAN, Joseph d 7 Apr 1813 ae 72y
    Hannah d 29 May 1835 ae 99y
BURDITT, Nathan
    Margaret w/o Nathan d 16 Sept 1845 ae 59y 6m 19d
BELL, Rhoda P w/o William d 18 Feb 1847 ae 48y
BOWMAN, Samuel W s/o Jonathan & Sarah d 7 Apr 1846 ae 4m 5d
BALLARD, William A s/o William & Elsey d 27 Oct 1848 ae 25y
BUTTRICK, Ann Elizabeth d/o Jonathan & Charlotte d 3 Nov
    1847 ae 11m
BANCROFT, Luther T s/o LT & SJ d 24 Apr 1846 ae 22m
    Luther T d in Boston 29 June 1844 ae 26y
BENNETT, Salome Pratt w/o John d 1 Apr 1845 ae 26y
    John s/o John & Salome d 16 Mar 1846 ae 1y 22d
BANCROFT, Ann w/o Lorey F d 12 May 1846 ae 27y
BARRETT, Lydia d/o Joseph & Lucy d 14 Sept 1831 ae 2y 2m 28d
BRUCE, Jonathan d 20 Jan 1832 ae 69y
    Catharine w/o Jonathan d 20 Feb 1824 ae 56y
BRAGG, Horatio C s/o Capt Ebenezer & Martha d 7 Dec 1826 ae 16m
BILLINGS, Alonzo s/o Josiah & Nancy d 28 Mar 1825 ae 36hrs
    Hannah w/o Josiah d 6 Aug 1822 ae 39y
    Josiah d 23 May 1843 ae 60y
BURPEE, Lydia w/o Martin d 23 Mar 1817 ae 29y
BRIDGE, Sarah d/o Josiah & Eirene d 11 May 1814 ae 3m
BRIGHAN, Lucy w/o Jotham d 20 Dec 1830 ae 71y
BRADLEY, Franklin s/o RM & MP d 9 May 1838 ae 5y
    Robert M d 15 Nov 1842 ae 48y
BOWERS, Rebecca w/o Capt Josiah d 30 Nov 1836 ae 85
    Josiah d 22 Aug 1836 ae 84y -- Capt
BALDWIN, Lucy w/o Oliver d 30 July 1720 ae 45y
BLISS, Martha Jane d/o Cyrus & Susan d 11 July 1839 ae 9m
BARNARD, Winsor s/o Winsor & Phebe d 9 Apr 1835 ae 2y
    William d 4 Nov 1834 ae 20y 9m
    Caleb s/o Winsor & Phebe d 4 Nov 1816 ae 3m
    Jonathan d 5 Mar 1824 ae 60y

Benijah s/o Jonathan & Annas d 4 Oct 1805 ae 7y 21d
Julia d/o Jonathan & Annas d 5 Sept 1805 ae 1y 9m 8d
Jonathan s/o Jonathan & Annas d 12 Feb 1799 ae 3y 2m 20d
BALLARD, Sophronia w/o Eliphas d 18 May 1849 ae 75y
Anna G w/o Eliphas d 22 June 1818 ae 32y
Sally d 25 Mar 1841 ae 60y
Josiah s/o Jeremiah & Rebeckah d 10 June 1804 ae 25y
Rebecca w/o Jeremiah d 2 June 1800 ae 52y
Jeremiah d 2 Oct 1838 ae 86y
Dea Josiah d 6 Aug 1799 in 78y
Sarah w/o Dea Josiah d 31 Mar 1799 in 74y
Thomas d 1 Jan 1838 ae 76y
Abigail w/o Thomas d 20 Aug 1843 ae 75y 4m
Sophia d/o Thomas & Abigail d Sept 1799 ae 4y 8m
Lucy d/o Thomas & Abigail d 19 Aug 1799 ae 2y 9m 9d
Abigail d/o Thomas & Abigail d 25 Aug 1799 ae 9m 13d
BATES, Nancy w/o Stephen Esq d 1 Oct 1821 ae 33y at Dunstable NH
BALLARD, John d 9 Sept 1826 ae 66y
Anna w/o John d 1 Mar 1808 ae 49y
Charles d 1 Apr 1807 ae 21y
Molly w/o John d 8 July 1819 ae 53y
Henry d 12 Jan 1830 ae 36y killed in felling a tree
John Augustus s/o Henry & Abigail d 31 May 1830 ae 6y
Sarah Elizabeth d/o Henry & Abigail d 19 Feb 1841 ae 14y
Nancy Whitney d 19 Mar 1810 ae 3 wks
Sarah Augusta d 15 Jan 1811 ae 14 hrs
Nancy d 27 Jan 1811 ae 26y
BRIDGE, Henry d 31 Oct 1824 ae 30y
Abigail 10 Oct 1820 ae 22y
Abigail w/o William d 13 Aug 1810 ae 41y
BENNETT, Catherine w/o Luke d 4 Oct 1814 ae 24y
Elisha d 14 Aug 1801 ae 46y
BRIDGE, George s/o Charles & Sophia drowned 25 Dec 1844 ae
10y 10m
Franklin s/o Charles & Sophia d 6 May 1844 ae 17m 24d
Caroline d/o Charles & Sophia d 31 Aug 1841 ae 1y 6m 5d
Susan w/o Charles d 19 Feb 1825 ae 35y
Solomon d 24 Sept 1829 ae 27y
James d 18 Mar 1846 ae 53y
BALL, Emily S d/o Levi & Lucinda 17 June 1840 – 17 June 1845
BENNETT, Nancy d/o Nathan & Eunice d 21 Jan 1802 ae 5y 1m 12d
BROWN, Mary d/o Capt John & Polly d 7 Jan 1809 ae 22m
Infant d/o Capt John & Polly d 5 Apr 1809 12hrs
CARTER, H Emma d/o Granville & Martha d 29 Aug 1848 ae 13m
CHANDLER, Benjamin d 24 Feb 1847 ae 79y
Julia Louisa d/o Benjamin & Elizabeth d 8 May 1842 ae 19y
CARR, Dolly H d/o John & Mary d 1 Mar 1847 ae 23y
Attosa d 20 Nov 1848 ae 27y
CUMMINGS, Anna Maria d/o Dr Wright & Mary 6 Mar 1828 –
20 Nov 1848
CARTER, MAR Bragg w/o WC d 28 July 1844 ae 24y

Polly W w/o Oliver 2nd d 28 Feb 1842 ae 27y
CHILDS, Jane Augusta d/o Isaac & Polly d 22 Apr 1848 ae 20y
    Mary d/o Isaac & Polly d 14 July 1836 ae 15y
    James s/o Isaac & Polly d 22 Feb 1822 ae 3y 2m
    Isaac d 23 Feb 1840 ae 65y
    Sarah d 17 Oct 1815 ae 34y
COLBURN, Elijah d 17 Oct 1849 ae 78y
    Sally w/o Elijah d 9 Feb 1831 ae 53y
CARTER, Rebecca W d/o George & Nancy d 18 Sept 1842 ae 7m
    Horatio d 6 Sept 1833 ae 37y
    Emily w/o Oliver d 17 Mar 1835 ae 68y
    Oliver d 18 May 1842 ae 84y
CONQUERETTE, Mary d 7 Feb 1840 ae 81y
CARTER, John d 19 Nov 1815 ae 65y
    Martha w/o John d 30 July 1838 ae 83y
    John d 6 Aug 1841 ae 63y
    Tempe w/o John d 31 Aug 1826 ae 43y
    Marietta d/o Cephas & Abigail d 17 June 1847 ae 13y
    Cephas d 29 Sept 1842 ae 52y
    Sally w/o Thomas d 1 May 1845 ae 86y
    Thomas d 1 Feb 1823 ae 70y
    Nancy d/o John 3rd & Betsy d 22 Nov 1832 ae 21y 7m
    John 2nd d 3 July 1830 ae 48y
    Betsy w/o John 2nd d 28 Dec 1815 ae 31y
    Ephraim d 19 May 1798 ae 55y -- Capt
    Abigail w/o Capt Ephraim d 16 Nov 1804 ae 56y
    Mary w/o Capt Ephraim d 22 June 1826 ae 55y
    Ephraim d 31 Aug 1827 ae 54y -- Capt
    Solomon d 8 Nov 1829 ae 56y
    Elizabeth w/o Solomon d 26 July 1843 ae 56y
    Lucy w/o Solomon d 5 Apr 1813 ae 35y
    Calvin MD
    Sally Perry w/o Calvin d 30 Apr 1840 ae 56y 4m
    James s/o Calvin & Sally d 20 Mar 1830 ae 17y
    Marianne Augusta d/o Calvin & Sally d 17 Jan 1835 ae 17y 4m
    Martha Lincoln d/o Calvin & Sally d 20 Mar 1822 ae 2y
    Two Infants d -- ---- 1807 & -- --- 1822
    Martha Lincoln d 30 Apr 1847 ae 23y 8m
    Susanna d/o James & Sarah d 29 Mar 1805 ae 8m 6d
    Ens James d 12 Mar 1814 ae 33y
    James MD  9 Nov 1753 - 17 Jan 1817
    Susanna Kendall w/o James 9 Nov 1755 - 30 Apr 1837
    Newall s/o Dr James 9 Sept 1796 - 7 Sept 1838
COREY, Rebecca d/o Stephen & Triphena d 19 Apr 1810 ae 24y
DIVOLL, William d 18 Nov 1849 in 50y
DANFORTH, Lucy w/o Elias d 25 Dec 1843 ae 50y
    Sarah Ann d/o Elias & Lucy d 23 Nov 1847 ae 26y
DICKENSON, Lemuel d 10 July 1826 ae 36y
DEAN, Emily w/o John d 29 June 1834 ae 35y
    Charles s/o John & Emily d 18 Sept 1832 ae 3m
    Sarah B d/o John & Emily d 2 June 1834 ae 9m

DAMON, Rebecah w/o Samuel d 4 Apr 1844 ae 86y
  Abigail w/o Samuel d 8 Oct 1826 ae 74y
  Samuel d 1 June 1845 ae 89y
  Abraham s/o William & Abigail d 29 Sept 1825 ae 21y 8m
  Margaret Ann d/o Jonas M & Margaret d 18 Sept 1840 ae
    1y 3m 23d
  Margaret w/o Jonas d 22 Sept 1842 ae 33y 6m 4d
DANFORTH, Sarah w/o Dr F d 19 Apr 1814 ae 79y
  Sarah d 4 Sept 1832 ae 76y
DAVIS, Walter Austin s/o Austin & Sally d 15 Mar 1844 ae 5 1-2y
  Emma d/o Hollis & Hannah d 6 Oct 1847 ae 6y 4m
EMERSON, Phebe w/o Elias d 16 Dec 1840 ae 72y
  Elias d 16 June 1835 ae 76y
  Joseph d 9 May 1803 ae 81y
  Phebe w/o Joseph d 19 Jan 1811 ae 81y
EDGERTON, Benjamin d 1 Apr 1806 in 45y
  Maryann d/o Benjamin & Sarah d 1 May 1807 ae 2y 11m 14d
EAGER, Sarah A d/o Farwell & Althina d 27 Nov 1840 ae 18y
  Caroline d/o Farwell & Althina d 2 Dec 1842 ae 21y
EATON, Nathaniel d 24 Feb 1826 ae 82y
  Lucy w/o Nathaniel d 11 Feb 1847 ae 96y
FARNSWORTH, Catharine M w/o Andrew d 19 Sept 1847 ae 30y 4m
    10d
FARWELL, Mary w/o James d/o Elias & Phebe Emerson d 9 Jan
    1849 ae 55y
FOSTER, Benjamin d 10 May 1826 ae 42y
FLETCHER, Mary w/o Rufus d 30 Aug 1808 ae 42y
  Thomas d 23 June 1832 at Boston ae 22y
  Mary w/o Dea Joel d 1 Apr 1837 ae 74y
  Martha d 29 May 1829 ae 26y 29d
  Hannah Fosdick w/o Timothy d 14 Aug 1832 ae 75y
  Timothy Esq d 17 Mar 1823 ae 72y
  Joshua d 14 Nov 1814 ae 90y
  Mary w/o Joshua d 25 July 1813 ae 86y
  Dorcas w/o William d 21 May 1844 ae 75y
  Roxanna d/o William & Dorcas d 22 Oct 1805 ae 21d
  Joshua d 4 July 1844 ae 61y
  Joseph Warren s/o Joshua & Nabby d 11 May 1816 ae 2y 6m
  Julia Maria d/o Joshua & Nabby d 2 May 1819 ae 2y 1m 11d
  Martha Celestine d/o Joshua & Naby d 7 July 1837 ae 6y 11m
FALES, Jeremiah d 22 Apr 1848 ae 69y
  Amy w/o Jeremiah d 23 Nov 1849 ae 67y
  Sophia d/o Jeremiah & Amy d 17 Mar 1836 ae 12y
  Warren d 4 Apr 1848 ae 34y
FITCH, Johnnie s/o George & Sophronia d 17 Oct 1843 ae 4y 7m
  Torrey d 4 Sept 1843 ae 48y
  Two infants d 15 June 1828 & 20 June 1829
FULLER, Franklin W 1842-1845
  George W 1835-1836
  Francis F 1830-1832
  Ephraim H 1833-1833

13

Abigail L 1829–1829
Francis F 1822–1829
Susan w/o Ephraim 1798–1829
Ebenezer W 1769–1841
FAIRBANK, Jonas d 6 Apr 1826 ae 51y -- Capt
Elizabeth w/o Jonas d 9 Apr 1818 ae 70y
Mary w/o Cyrus d 13 Dec 1827 ae 63y
Jonas d 7 July 1829 ae 86y
Cyrus d 30 Apr 1835 ae 68y
FAY, Nancy F w/o Josiah d 7 July 1845 ae 52y
FISHER, Jacob Esq d 2 June 1843 ae 75y
Nancy w/o Jacob Esq d 15 Apr 1822 ae 50y
Betsy w/o Jacob Esq d 6 Nov 1837 ae 57y
Elizabeth d/o Ephraim & Sarah d 1 Dec 1831 ae 11m
Sophronia d/o Ephraim & Sarah d 13 Apr 1834 ae 11m
Charles s/o Ephraim & Sarah d 4 Apr 1836 ae 8m
FARNSWORTH, Edward E s/o Asa D & Betsy d 22 Oct 1837 ae 10wk
James s/o Benjamin 2nd & Dorcas d 11 June 1822 ae 9m 25d
FLAGG, Josiah Esq b Boston 12 Nov 1760 d Lancaster 11 Feb 1840
Dolly w/o Josiah 6 Nov 1766 – 1 June 1835
FRENCH, Fidelia w/o Seth d 14 May 1843 ae 49y
FARNSWORTH, Sally w/o Benjamin d 1 Feb 1844 ae 68y
Benjamin d Aug 1830
GOULD, Lydia d/o Benjamin & Sarah d 17 Aug 1841 ae 5y
GOODSPEED, Elizabeth d/o Capt Daniel & Elizabeth Rugg d 28
Dec 1830 ae 57y
GOSS, Jonas d 18 Oct 1840 in 61y
Judith d/o Jonas & Judith d 21 Aug 1807 ae 4m
Ebenezer s/o Jonas & Judith d 15 Dec 1817 ae 4y 6m
Nancy d/o Jonas & Judith d 25 Jan 1831 ae 12y 2m
Daniel d 10 Dec 1809 ae 69y -- Capt
Eunice w/o Capt Daniel d 7 Jan 1813 ae 66y
Daniel Jr d 11 June 1841 ae 81y 11m -- Capt
GOSS, Henry Lawton s/o Henry & Sarah d 2 Sept 1830 ae 16m
GOULD, William Jr d 21 Feb 1840 ae 56y
Elizabeth w/o William d 3 Mar 1839 ae 84y
William d 7 Nov 1834 ae 80y
GODDARD, Eber d 26 May 1835 ae 67y
GILSON, Martha Ann d/o Varnum & Martha d 23 Nov 1828 ae 3m
Varnum d 6 Oct 1828 ae 23y
GOSS, Rebecca w/o Capt John d 27 Jan 1827 ae 43y
GATES, Abigail w/o Capt Thomas d 5 Sept 1810 ae 70y
Thomas d 27 Dec 1814 ae 79y
GOODWIN, James d 8 Sept 1831 ae 90y
Bathsheba w/o James d 7 Jan 1814 ae 70y
John d 1 Sept 1812 ae 69y
Rebecca d 7 Feb 1839 ae 62y
Bathsheba d 11 June 1833 ae 22y
Harriet M d 6 Feb 1836 ae 20y
GOULD, Marshall E s/o James & Harriet d 24 Aug 1845 ae 5y 10m
Edward E s/o James & Harriet d 5 Feb 1839 ae 1y

14

Infant s/o James & Harriet d 21 Apr 1836 ae 2d
HUNT, Otis Jr s/o Otis & Arrethusa d 3 July 1804 ae 1y 8m 13d
   Maria d/o Otis & Arrethusa d 27 Feb 1809 ae 2y 4m 2d
HOWARD, Elizabeth w/o George W d 2 June 1837 ae 27y
   Sarah M w/o George W d 7 Sept 1830 ae 39y
   Asa W s/o George & Sarah d 27 July 1843 ae 28y
HARRIS, Emory d 31 Dec 1838 ae 50y
   Hezediah w/o Emory d 11 Jan 1820 ae 26y
   George s/o Emory & Hezediah d 12 Oct 1838 ae 23y
   Eliza H d 28 Mar 1843 ae 22y
   Asahel d 14 Jan 1844 ae 50y  -- Capt
HOLMAN, John d 6 Dec 1827 ae 33y
   Nancy W w/o John d/o Robert & Betsy Townsend d 25 Jan
      1827 ae 29y
HASKELL, John E s/o John & Sarah d 3 Feb 1836 ae 21m 3d
HOSLEY, David death by fall of a Frame 5 July 1802 ae 59y
   Luceba w/o David d 14 Jan 1834 ae 72y
HOLLAND, Elizabeth d 18 Oct 1847 ae 22y
HOUGHTON, Elijah d 7 July 1810 ae 82y  -- Capt
   Mary w/o Capt Elijah d 21 May 1818 ae 82y
   Oliver d 20 Sept 1836 ae 70y
   Abigail w/o Oliver d 4 Feb 1837 ae 66y
   Salmon d 28 May 1844 ae 63y
   Lucy w/o Salmon d 12 Sept 1831 ae 46y
   Frances w/o Salmon d 11 Sept 1839 ae 32y
   Salmon J s/o Salmon & Frances d 26 Aug 1839 ae 1y 10m
HASTINGS, Sarah Abby d/o Samuel & Olive d 13 Mar 1841 ae 7y
   10m
HOUGHTON, Benjamin d 4 May 1837 ae 73y  -- Capt
   Lydia w/o Capt Benjamin d 8 Aug 1825 ae 54y
   Lydia d/o Capt Benjamin & Lydia d 13 Sept 1826 ae 21y
HAWKES, John d 8 Oct 1847 ae 74y
HALE, Rebecca w/o CB d 20 Feb 1849 ae 29y
HILDRETH, Nancy w/o Richard d 20 Nov 1819 ae 32y 6m
   Ezekiel s/o Richard & Nancy d 26 Jan 1820 ae 6m
HASTINGS, Thomas s/o Benjamin & Experience of Sullivan NH
      drowned 4 July 1813 ae 28y
   Benjamin Jr s/o Benjamin & Experience of Sullivan NH
      drowned 4 July 1813 ae 16y
HOOPER, Emily w/o Edward d 26 Jan 1849 ae 35y
HOWARD, Parney d/o Sidney & Sally d 18 Mar 1847 ae 27y
HOUGHTON, Mary M d/o Phineas & Allice d 2 Mar 1829 ae 2y
JONES, Solon s/o Aaron & Sally ae 2y
   Mary Ann d/o Aaron & Sally ae 11y
   Edwin s/o Aaron & Sally ae 2y
   Benjamin F s/o Aaron & Sally ae 20y
   Aaron d 23 Sept 1839 ae 72y
   Sullivan s/o Moses & Submit d 18 July 1832 ae 25y
   Moses d 5 Dec 1829 ae 60y
   Submittee w/o Moses d 19 Dec 1836 ae 36y
JOSLYN, Samuel d 15 Feb 1826 ae 88y -- Capt

Abigail w/o Capt Samuel d 8 Aug 1814 ae 65y
Mary w/o Nathaniel d 18 Feb 1825 ae 88y
Nathaniel d 28 May 1806 ae 78y
Peter d 20 June 1802 ae 26y
Jonas d 5 Aug 1838 ae 64y
JONES, Marcus L s/o Luther & Charlotte d 11 Oct 1842 ae 14y
Sarah J d/o Luther & Charlotte d 23 Oct 1826 ae 1y 1m
KEYES, Sarah J d/o Amasa & Sally d 12 Sept 1817 ae 5y 2m
Amasa d 7 Oct 1826 ae 53y
KNIGHT, Sophia M d/o Charles E & Catherine d 26 Dec 1828 ae
6m 10d
Nathaniel E s/o Charles E & Catherine d 7 Mar 1828 ae
6y 2m
James M s/o Charles E & Catherine drowned 26 Sept 1823 ae 6y
Sally w/o Charles d 1 June 1813 ae 34y
Patty d/o Manesseh & Hannah d 29 Jan 1802 ae 22y
Manasseh d 28 Sept 1814 ae 63y
LUND, Eveline B w/o Mark d 16 May 1846 ae 29y
Charles B s/o Mark & Eveline d 7 Apr 1846 ae 4m
LOW, Edgar s/o Henry & Mary d 17 Aug 1849 ae 5y
Nathaniel d 29 Apr 1827 ae 63y
Annes w/o Nathaniel d 11 Mar 1821 ae 49y
Polly d/o Nathaniel & Annes d 15 Sept 1805 ae 6y
Saxon s/o Nathaniel & Annes d 16 Sept 1805 ae 6m
Rufus s/o Nathaniel & Annes d 14 Oct 1824 ae 19y
Almira d 17 Apr 1830 ae 24y
Mary E d/o Anson & Emeline d 31 Aug 1848 ae 8m
LOCKE, Jonathan d 13 Aug 1814 ae 66y
Jonathan d 26 Jan 1839 ae 61y -- Maj
Mary w/o Maj Jonathan d 4 July 1849 ae 67y
LINCOLN, Chloe w/o Jacob d 10 July 1829 ae 63y
Cummins d 5 Jan 1822 ae 24y
LITCH, Washington s/o John & Lydia d 11 Aug 1798 ae 22y
LAWRENCE, Sally w/o Edmund d 6 July 1849 ae 52y
LYON, John d 3 Jan 1836 ae 61y
Sally w/o John d 28 Dec 1844 ae 69y
Martha Ann d/o John & Sally d 13 Nov 1821 ae 4y 7m
LEACH, Abigail w/o Eliab d 4 Dec 1835 ae 27y
LEE, B s/o B & L d -- --- ---- ae 1m
LINCOLN, Caleb d 21 Oct 1825 ae 52y
LEACH, Rebecca w/o Joseph d 28 Apr 1810 ae 39y
Susannah w/o Joseph d 31 Dec 1800 in 34y
Collins s/o Joseph & Susannah d 28 Sept 1789 ae 18m
LAUGHTON, Martha B d/o John & Nancy d 28 May 1849 ae 19y
Mary Ann d/o John & Nancy d 9 Aug 1842 ae 21y
John Jr s/o John & Nancy d 18 Sept 1841 ae 21y
LEWIS, William d 9 Oct 1836 ae 24y
LAUGHTON, Artemas d 15 Mar 1825 ae 39y
Lucy Ann d/o Stephen & Clarissa d 22 Sept 1822 ae 13m
Ephraim s/o Stephen & Clarissa d 14 Sept 1820 ae 22m
MAYNARD, Abigail d/o Joseph & Anna d 28 Dec 1829 ae 15y

Caroline E d/o Joseph & Anna d 30 Mar 1831 ae 11y
MOORS, Edward A s/o Jeremiah & Mary d 24 July 1847 ae 15m
   Margaret Ann d/o Jeremiah & Mary d 9 Sept 1848 ae 26d
MAYNARD, John Harrison s/o John & Mary d 25 Sept 1847 ae 3y 10m
   Erastus Henry s/o John & Mary
MILLER, Oscar M s/o Charles & Matilda d 14 Jan 1844 ae 4y
MATTHEWS, Ann w/o David d/o J & P Winditt d 3 Nov 1840 ae 25y
MANNING, Lucy w/o Dr Samuel d 4 Oct 1817 ae 38y
   Rebecca Pratt d/o Dr Samuel & Lucy d 30 July 1816 ae 2y 3m
MUNROE, Aaron d 17 Jan 1825 ae 69y
MALLARD, Maryann d/o Abraham & Sally d 17 Apr 1808 ae 2y 6m
   James s/o James & Betsy d 11 Jan 1810 ae 11m 21d
   James s/o James & Betsy d 10 Aug 1813 ae 2y 5m 26d
MILES, Catherine d/o Thomas & Ruth d 24 Jan 1832 ae 21y
   Ruth w/o Thomas d 19 Oct 1841 ae 67y
MAYNARD, Mary E d/o Joseph & Betsy d 27 Jan 1841 ae 23y
   Alvira d/o Joseph & Betsy d 19 May 1836 ae 28y
   John Esq d 21 Jan 1823 ae 70y
   Martha w/o John Esq d/o Maj Gardner Wilder d 19 Feb 1836 in 69y
MILLER, Joseph T d 17 Feb 1827 ae 31y
MCLALLEN, William d 19 Oct 1822 ae 55y
MANLEY, Sarah d 11 Sept 1833 ae 84y
NOURSE, Fordyce d 6 Aug 1848 ae 39y
NOWELL, Elizabeth A d/o Wm & Elizabeth d 28 May 1847 ae 21y
   John William s/o Wm & Elizabeth d 9 Mar 1832 ae 3y 15d
   Elizabeth A d/o Wm & Elizabeth d 8 Apr 1826 ae 2y 3m
   William Nichols s/o Wm & Mary d 12 June 1843 ae 5y
NEWMAN, Gowen B d 9 Dec 1833 ae 64y
   Lucy w/o Gowen d 2 June 1842 ae 71y
   James Homer d in Savannah 24 June 1822 ae 24y
   Caroline M d 29 Mar 1845 ae 29y
NEWHALL, Patty w/o Pliney d 18 Jan 1810 in 23y
   Infant d Jan 1810 ae 15d
OSGOOD, Jonathan d 10 Jan 1847 ae 71y
   Almira d/o Jonathan & Anna d 15 July 1845 ae 39y 8m
   Mary N w/o Dea Peter d 11 June 1847 ae 50y
   Abigail C d/o Dea Peter & Mary d 17 Oct 1843 ae 17y
   Martha W d/o Dea Peter & Mary d 29 Aug 1832 ae 9m
   Joel d 7 Nov 1821 ae 75y
   Lucretia w/o Joel d 28 Mar 1846 ae 91y
   Jonathan d 14 July 1808 ae 59y
   Nahum d 18 Feb 1815 ae 36y
   Ephraim d 16 Mar 1834 ae 76y
PITTS, Lucinda w/o James d/o Hervey Burditt d 23 Oct 1848 ae
      30y 3m
POIGNAND, David b in Island of Jersey 12 Jan 1759 d
      Lancaster 28 Aug 1830
   Delicia Amiraux 17 Dec 1764 – 30 Sept 1833
PLANT, Delicia Amiraux d/o Samuel & Delicia d 26 Jan 1834 ae
      2y 20d
PHELPS, Julia L d/o Joel & Lorinda d 10 Mar 1846 ae 17m

Meriel d/o Ephraim & Dolly d 15 Aug 1819 ae 12y 7m
PEASLEE, Moses d 8 May 1823 ae 36y
PRATT, Emily w/o Eben d/o Joseph & Betsy Rice d 10 July 1839
    ae 42y
  Emily F d/o Joseph & Emily ae 2y
PHELPS, Robert d 9 June 1834 ae 66y
PEACOCK, Elizabeth d 9 Sept 1813 ae 56y
PITTS, Betsy S w/o Hiram W d/o James Burditt d 12 May 1843
    ae 29y
  Lewis Hiram s/o Hiram & Betsy d 7 Sept 1843 ae 4m 15d
  James d 13 Jan 1835 ae 52y
PRESCOTT, Abigail w/o Jabez d/o Thomas Gates d 4 Oct 1827
    ae 59y
PLUMMER, Abigail w/o Farnham for w/o Henry Ballard d 5 Feb
    1842 ae 42y
PUFFER, Abigail w/o Nathan d/o Samuel & Abigail Wilder
    Joslyn 1774 – 1802
PHELPS, Mary E d 26 Jan 1848 ae 22y
  Henry d 18 Aug 1826 ae 30y
  Joseph d 8 May 1830 ae 33y
  Mary Ann d 11 May 1833 ae 20y
  Hezekiah d 25 Dec 1833 ae 36y
  Mary d/o Sylvester & Esther d 22 May 1814 ae 20d
  Father d Oct 1848 ae 80y
  Mother d June 1857 ae 83 1/2y
  Mary w/o Abijah d 2 Mar 1831 ae 59y
  Abijah d 23 June 1829 ae 74y
REED, Mary Elizabeth 19 Apr 1839 – 20 Oct 1840
  George Francis 13 Feb 1841 – 6 Feb 1846
RUGG, Sarah Wilder d/o Samuel & Sally d 23 Feb 1846 ae 45y
RICHARDSON, David d 5 Apr 1818 ae 30y
ROBBINS, Prudence d 14 Dec 1845 ae 90y
RAND, Lucy w/o Nathaniel d 3 Nov 1826 ae 37y
  Harry s/o Nathaniel & Lucy d 10 Mar 1816 ae 6y 6m
  Nancy Elizabeth w/o Nathaniel d 29 Mar 1838 ae 42y
  Ellen Maria d/o Nathaniel & Nancy E d 7 Nov 1835 ae 4m
RICE, Mary Ann d/o Joseph & Betsy d 13 May 1825 ae 20y
RUGG, Betsey w/o Ephraim d 28 Nov 1846 ae 66y
  Ephraim d 20 Oct 1836 ae 57y
  Elizabeth w/o Capt Daniel d 8 Apr 1834 ae 88y
  Daniel d 11 Apr 1830 ae 87y -- Capt
  Prudence d 16 Mar 1838 ae 77y
  Stephen d 23 Dec 1834 ae 78y
  Joel I s/o Joel & Bathsheba d 1 Jan 1847 ae 28y
  Rebekah w/o Isaac d 1 Jan 1847 ae 79y
  Abijah d 12 Feb 1816 ae 65y
  Susanna w/o Abijah d 11 Jan 1832 ae 77y
  Isaac d 1 Apr 1813 ae 67y
  Aaron d 6 July 1810 ae 50y 11m
  Bathsheba w/o Joel d 13 Nov 1832 ae 42y
  Joel d 17 Sept 1836 ae 48y

Mary d/o Joel & Bathsheba d 2 Apr 1838 ae 24y
Francis s/o Joel & Bathsheba d 21 Nov 1839 ae 7y
Lucy d 10 Aug 1805 ae 22y
Elisha d 7 Jan 1805 ae 49y  -- Capt
Abel d 14 Feb 1843 ae 91y
Katharine d 2 Nov 1843 ae 84y
Hannah Jones w/o Abel d 27 Mar 1836 ae 38y
Martin d 4 Sept 1819 ae 15m 15d
Addison E s/o James & AML d 20 Feb 1847 ae 15m
Submit w/o James d 1 Sept 1830 ae 38y
ROSS, Josiah s/o Seth & Abigail d 22 Oct 1814 ae 27y
SAWYER, Mary w/o Daniel d 31 Dec 1848 ae 64y
SAFFORD, Sarah Julia d/o Charles & Julia d 22 June 1847 ae 4m
SAWYER, Thomas d 10 June 1846 ae 49y
SARGENT, Martha A d/o Merick & Rebecca d 26 Sept 1849 ae 1y 2m
Julia Ann d/o Curtis & Huldah d 30 Oct 1847 ae 1y 8m
Winfield P s/o Curtis & Huldah d 10 Jan 1849 ae 3m
STRATTON, Lydia Ann d/o George & Lucinda d 23 June 1849 ae
1y 3m 19d
SAWYER, Henry H s/o Ezra & Eliza d 30 Jan 1842 ae 18y
Francena d/o Elias & Nancy d 2 Sept 1833 ae 11m 19d
Frederick H s/o Elias & Nancy d 9 May 1834 ae 20m 21d
Abby B d/o Elias & Nancy d 3 Oct 1842 ae 18y
Louisa A d/o Elias & Nancy d 8 Jan 1844 ae 16y
CHANDLER, Mary Ann w/o James d/o Elias & Nancy Sawyer d 8
Jan 1846 ae 25y
SAWYER, Elias d 16 Jan 1849 ae 57y
Nancy w/o Elias d 16 Dec 1849 ae 57y
SMITH, Sally w/o Howell d 20 Oct 1849 ae 59y
SAWYER, Eben d 23 Oct 1822 ae 25y
SWEETSER, Jacob d 23 Jan 1823 ae 76y
Margaret w/o Jacob d 9 July 1838 ae 85y
Margaret d 6 Mar 1840 ae 53y
SOLLENDINE, Deborah w/o Manasseh d 9 Oct 1827 ae 46y
STEARNS, Eli 12 Nov 1757 - 7 Mar 1825
Mary Whitney w/o Eli 14 Jan 1767 - 24 May 1828
Augustus d 27 Sept 1811 ae 4y
SANFORD, Garry C d 23 Oct 1847 ae 32
SAWYER, Sarah E d/o Charles & Eliza d 23 Apr 1827 ae 3y 8m
Charles F s/o Charles & Eliza d 8 May 1831 ae 4y 3m
Martha S d/o Charles & Eliza d 28 Nov 1831 ae 6y 8m
Sarah E d/o Charles & Eliza d 17 Sept 1832 ae 3y 4m
---- ch/o Charles & Eliza d 4 Dec 1834 ae 4d
Symmes 10 Oct 1842 - 21 June 1844
SAFFORD, Mary w/o George d 19 Feb 1831 ae 36y
STEVENSON, Lydia w/o Martin d 5 June 1840 ae 72y
Martin d 20 Mar 1839 ae 73y
SAWYER, Lucy Ann d/o Silas & Sally d 28 Oct 1829 ae 4y 3m
Francis A s/o Silas & Sally d 19 June 1846 ae 23y
Moses d 12 Mar 1831 in 67y
Elizabeth w/o Moses d 20 Nov 1849 ae 80y 8m

SMITH, Moses d 4 Feb 1812 ae 72y
   Abigail w/o Moses d 26 Jan 1812 ae 70y
   Moses Esq d 27 June 1835 ae 58y
   Charles Henry s/o Moses Esq & Sarah d 3 Apr 1812 ae 10m 18d
STREETER, Eliza H w/o Vernis d 15 Oct 1845 ae 36y
STEARNS, Daniel d 30 June 1818 ae 74y
   Deborah w/o Daniel d 10 Oct 1834 ae 78y
SAWIN, Ellen C d/o Aaron & Phebe d 23 Nov 1840 ae 2y 4m
SARGEANT, John d 21 Dec 1802 ae 80y
   Hannah w/o John d 26 Aug 1799 ae 77y
   Aaron d 5 Feb 1801 ae 36y
STEPHENSON, Lydia d 5 Aug 1827 ae 28y
SAWYER, Moses d 5 Oct 1805 Our Grandfather
   Elizabeth w/o Moses d 21 Apr 1844 ae 94y Our Grandmother
SARGEANT John d 1 Apr 1822 ae 73y
   Ann w/o John d 17 Feb 1837 ae 74y
   Seth d 28 Nov 1830 ae 77y
   Elizabeth w/o Seth d 24 May 1837 ae 74y
STEDMAN, Christopher E s/o William & Almy drowned at sea
        9 Aug 1809 ae 17y
   Mary Ann d/o William & Almy d 1 Aug 1807 in 13y
   William Jr s/o William & Almy d 16 Apr 1810 ae 11y
   N Thayer a Tomb
TURNER, Lurenia J d/o SH & BT Turner d 19 June 1842 ae 3y 7m
   Charlotte E d/o SH & BT Turner d 29 Jan 1845 ae 4y 2m
THURSTON, Charles F s/o Silas & Parney d 3 Feb 1847 ae 20y
      6m 10d
   Josephine d/o JG & HL d 15 Oct 1832
TIDD, Elizabeth d 14 Jan 1844 ae 88y
   Joel d 20 July 1825 ae 40y  WAR OF 1812
   George C d 8 Nov 1834 ae 41y
TUTTLE, George C d 8 Nov 1834 ae 41y
TOWNSEND, Martha w/o William d 29 Dec 1846 ae 62y
   Martha d/o William & Martha d 14 Dec 1842 ae 23y
TUTTLE, George -- Capt
   Eunice Emily w/o Capt George d 5 Feb 1847 ae 38y
   Lydia B d/o George & Eunice E d 30 Mar 1834 ae 13m 22d
THURSTON, Peter d 9 Dec 1824 ae 56y
   Sallie w/o Peter d 21 Jan 1832 ae 73y
   Dorothy w/o Peter Sr d 20 Dec 1831 ae 92y
   Gates d 12 Feb 1816 ae 51y
   Elizabeth w/o Gates d 14 Sept 1848 ae 86y
   Henry d 30 Sept 1842 ae 50y  -- Capt
TOWNSEND, Robert d 1 Sept 1826 ae 66y
   Betsy w/o Robert d 12 July 1826 ae 55y
   Henry d 22 Nov 1822 ae 29y
   Almira w/o Capt Warren d 12 Feb 1835 ae 31y
   Abigail H d/o Capt Warren & Almira d 11 Sept 1831 ae 5y 6m
TAYLOR, James Newhall d 14 Oct 1843 ae 4y 8m
   Susan d 1 Feb 1834 ae 8d
THURSTON, Caroline M w/o Wilder S d 2 Nov 1849 ae 25y

Ann M w/o Wilder S d 14 Dec 1846 ae 29y
Russell Gates s/o Wilder S & Ann d 17 Apr 1841 ae 10m
Rebekah w/o Capt John d 9 May 1801 ae 39y
John d 7 Dec 1838 ae 84y -- Capt
Mary Ann d/o John & Lucy d 27 Nov 1835 ae 19y
Lucy w/o John Jr d 2 July 1827 ae 32y
TYLER, Mary w/o Benjamin d 19 Mar 1839 ae 36y 10m
Eliza w/o Benjamin d/o Rosewell Hubbard d 15 May 1835 ae 40y
TOWNSEND, Caroline P w/o John d 5 Mar 1840 ae 36y
John d 2 July 1815 ae 42y
Ruth w/o John d 14 Dec 1825 ae 50y
Elvira d/o John & Ruth d 7 Jan 1826 ae 14y
TOWER, Asahel d 3 Aug 1833 ae 73y -- Capt
Meliscent w/o Capt Asahel d 20 Sept 1820 ae 59y
UPTON, Phebe w/o Joseph d 11 June 1812 ae 33y
WILDER, Mary M w/o Daniel K d 24 Nov 1842 ae 39y
WINCHESTER, Sarah d/o Samuel & Sarah d 23 Oct 1846 ae 18y
WALLACE, Cleora Ann d/o David & Sarah d 1 Apr 1848 ae 9y
WOODS, Henry s/o Matthew & Charlotte d 12 Sept 1849 ae 4y 7m
WINDITT, Sarah d/o John & Phebe d 24 Sept 1846 ae 22y
Mary E d/o JW Jr & ME d 23 Nov 1858 ae 12y
Sarah A d/o JW Jr & ME d 11 Aug 1846 ae 1y
WARD, Samuel 25 Sept 1739 - 14 Aug 1826
Dolly 16 Sept 1745 - 31 Dec 1818
Samuel Jr -- ---- 1769 - 29 Nov 1800
Sarah Hall -- ---- 1793 - 27 June 1826
Lucretia Murray -- June 1762 - 30 Aug 1836
WAITE, George s/o Joel & Deborah H d 8 Nov 1842 ae 13y
WILDER, Jonas d 15 Nov 1845 ae 58y
GOSS, Sarah E w/o Jonas d 28 Jan 1845 ae 24y
WHIPPLE, Hannah d 12 July 1844 ae 70y
WILDER, William d 20 Mar 1816 ae 61y
Sophia w/o Elijah d June 1822 ae 30y
Joseph d 23 Aug 1841 ae 55y
WARNER, Sally d/o Nathaniel & Polly d 24 Mar 1818 ae 18m
Asa d 31 Dec 1816 ae 67y
WHITNEY, Abigail H d/o Robert & Betsy Townsend d 24 Sept
1823 ae 27y
WHEELER, Amos Augustus s/o Amos & Prudence d 16 May 1818
ae 7wk
Roxanne d/o Amos & Prudence d 30 Apr 1822 ae 15m 8d
WILDER, Lusena w/o Ebenezer d/o Moses & Betsy Sawyer d 25
June 1825 ae 37y
Joel d 19 Oct 1847 ae 70y
Sophia w/o Joel d 21 Feb 1844 ae 64y
Susanna w/o Calvin d 24 Mar 1847 ae 73y
Calvin d 5 Apr 1832 ae 59y
Martha w/o Samuel d 13 Nov 1814 ae 72y
Samuel d 3 Nov 1827 ae 81y
WILSON, Eliza Ann w/o Col John d 14 July 1842 ae 30y
WILDER, Francis s/o Volney & Charlotte d 20 Aug 1843 ae 11m

21

Edward s/o Volney & Charlotte d 25 Aug 1843 ae 11m
WILLARD, Mary w/o Abijah Esq d 16 Dec 1807 ae 77y
WALES, Elizabeth w/o Joseph Esq d 19 Aug 1822 ae 61y
WILDER, Lydia w/o Daniel d 18 July 1825 ae 47y
   James d 22 Dec 1834 ae 40y
WELLINGTON, Ann Maria d/o Capt Thomas & Lucy d 1 June 1839
   ae 5y 3m
WADE, Charlotte O d/o Snell & Deborah d 8 Apr 1838 ae 3y 6m
WHITMAN, Davis d 24 Apr 1844 ae 81y 11m
   Hannah w/o Davis d 25 May 1836 ae 70y 7m
WALTON, George Henry s/o Jotham & Eliza d 9 July 1834 ae 26y
WILDER, Ephraim s/o Luke & Mary d 12 Sept 1818 ae 2y 8m
   Holman s/o Luke & Mary d 20 Jan 1807 ae 2y 8m
WILLARD, Jerome d 30 Sept 1846 ae 12y
   Amasa d 10 Nov 1842 ae 71y
   Fanny w/o Amasa d 8 July 1812 ae 29y
   Betsy d/o Simon & Elizabeth d 19 Apr 1799 ae 15y 22d
   Simon d 9 Jan 1825 ae 97y
WILDER, Sally w/o John d 28 Nov 1815 in 46y
   Rebekah d/o John & Sally d 25 Apr 1832 ae 16y 6m
   Enos d in NY 19 Oct 1844 ae 39y
   Lydia w/o Josephus d 23 Jan 1835 ae 23y
WHITING, Orpha w/o Col John d 10 Mar 1837 ae 78y
   John d 3 Sept 1810 ae 50y -- Col buried at Washington DC
   Fabius d 16 May 1842 ae 50y -- Maj
   Julia d/o Col John & Orpha d 2 July 1817 ae 30y
WILDER, Dea Joel d 2 May 1837 ae 70y
   George W s/o Charles J & Eliza C d 10 Mar 1843 ae 10wk
   Joel Thomas s/o Charles J & Eliza C d 24 Aug 1844 ae 3y 8m
WHITE, Dea Joseph d 1 July 1806 ae 55y
   Dea Samuel F d 15 Mar 1843 ae 50y
   Elizabeth d/o Dea SF & EG d 19 Jan 1847 ae 14y 9m
WHITTEMORE, Asa Dunbar s/o Nathaniel & Lydia d 21 Feb 1808
   ae 23y
   Nathaniel d 3 Jan 1822 ae 80y 6m
   Amelia w/o Nathaniel d 18 Apr 1834 ae 45y
   Mary w/o Nathaniel d 15 Aug 1828 ae 49y
   Mary M d/o Nathaniel & Mary d 16 June 1819 ae 5y 6m
   Nathaniel Jr s/o Nathaniel & Mary d 14 Dec 1831 ae 15y
WHITE, Sarah Emory d/o EH & SS d 15 Nov 1842 ae 3d
   Lucy C d 10 June 1829 ae 24y
   Joseph C killed by a tree 28 Jan 1825 ae 16y 1m
   Abel d 30 July 1844 ae 64y 8m
WILDER, Gardner Esq d 26 Nov 1809 ae 70y
   Catherine w/o Gardner d 23 Sept 1845 ae 93y
WHITNEY, Jonathan d 30 Nov 1802 ae 66y
   Lucy w/o Jonathan d 11 Oct 1817 ae 74y
   Ephraim d 6 Sept 1842 ae 62y
   Jonas d 14 Jan 1846 ae 74y
   William s/o Zaccheus & Fanny d 4 Oct 1823 ae 15m
WYMAN, Dea Benjamin d 30 Dec 1826 ae 61y

Martha Joslin d 4 May 1806 ae 40y
Jonas d 14 Jan 1846 ae 74y
William s/o Zaccheus & Fanny d 4 Oct 1823 ae 15m


## NORTH BURIAL GROUND

At a Town Meeting in April 1800, the fourth article of the warrant was: "to consider the expediency of appropriating a certain piece of land at the north part of the Town, where a number of persons are buried for the purpose of a burying field." A committee to whom the matter was entrusted, with full powers to act, reported the following May that they had "received a quitclaim Deed of Mr. Elijah Wiles of 112 Rods of Ground, being 16 Rods in length bounding on the Road leading by Col. Henry Haskell to Harvard, and 7 Rods deep." The deed found in the Town's archives, however, is dated February 20, 1805, whereby Elijah Wilds conveys to the Town 144 rods of land, measuring 8 rods along the highway, and 18 rods in depth. In the public burial place thus established are numerous graves mostly undistinguished by monuments.

ALEXANDER, Rebecca w/o Nathaniel d 7 Nov 1843 ae 61y 6m
BLANCHARD, Elizabeth d/o William & Elizabeth d 19 Dec 1807
     ae 10m
  William d 13 Nov 1818 ae 56y
BACON, Jacob R d 3 Nov 1845 ae 25y
BARRETT, Reuben Jr d 26 July 1816 ae 34y
  Moses d 4 Aug 1846 ae 62y
  Rebecca d 27 Sept 1847 ae 85y 4m
  Samuel P d 23 Sept 1847 ae 29-1/2y
BUTLER, Nancy d/o Samuel & Nancy d 11 July 1827 ae 20y 4m
  Samuel d 27 Mar 1828 ae 44y
  Nancy w/o Samuel ? 11 Aug 1849 ae 64y
  Sally d/o Samuel & Nancy d 25 Dec 1831 ae 20y
  Sarah w/o Abel 16 Mar 1800 - 14 July 1830
BARNES, Jeremiah d 27 July 1845 ae 34y
COWDRY, Ruthy w/o Isaac d 19 Jan 1828 ae 50y
COOK, Aaron Jr s/o Aaron & Betsy d 3 July 1803 ae 2y 4m
  Harriot d/o Aaron & Betsy d 12 Oct 1807 ae 12y
  Betsy d/o Aaron & Betsy d 20 Feb 1830 ae 33y
  Aaron d 20 Oct 1845 ae 74y
  Elizabeth w/o Aaron d 17 Jan 1842 ae 67y
  Susan d/o Aaron & Elizabeth d 17 Feb 1844 ae 26y
CUTLER, Rebeckah w/o James d 9 July 1840 in 69y
DYAR, Susan w/o Jeremiah d 16 Feb 1824 ae 47y
FARWELL, Ann Elizabeth d/o Capt Joseph & Sarah d 31 Aug 1842
     ae 17y 2m
  Sarah w/o Leonard d 1 June 1809 in 51y
  Leonard 2 Oct 1760 - -- Oct 1822 ae 62y
  Mary w/o Lucius L d 7 Nov 1845 ae 30y
  Mary I d/o Lucius & Mary d 5 Aug 1846 ae 9m 4d

HASKELL, Elias d 2 July 1811 ae 76y
JOHNSON, Luther d 22 Apr 1822 ae 33y
   Aaron d 6 Feb 1820 ae 79y
   Sewell s/o Calvin & Abigail d 22 Nov 1845 ae 28y
   Abigail w/o Calvin d 13 Feb 1845 ae 54y
   Harrison d 13 Oct 1842 ae 28y
MORSE, William Gibbs s/o Joseph & Lucy d 6 Mar 1832 ae 7y
NICHOLS, Abijah s/o Joseph & Anna d 19 Aug 1801 ae 23y
SANDERSON, Elisha d 14 Mar 1843 ae 81y
   Mary w/o Elisha d 18 Dec 1829 ae 63y
   Martha d/o Elisha & Mary d 1 Mar 1829 ae 20y
THOMAS, Anna w/o Dr Joshua d 18 June 1799 ae 47y
   Joshua 14 Mar 1745 - 4 Feb 1831
   Mary w/o Joshua d 25 May 1808 ae 67y
WORSTER, Mary d/o Samuel & Rebecca d 10 Oct 1815 ae ?
   Elizabeth d/o Samuel & Rebecca d 31 May 1818 ae 1y 8m
WILLARD, Sarah w/o William d 2 June 1803 in 36y
   Paul Esq d 2 Aug 1817 ae 52y
   Martha w/o Paul d 22 May 1808 in 34y
   Mary d/o Paul & Martha d 4 Oct 1803 ae 2y 1m
   Lucia d/o Paul Esq d 14 Nov 1818 ae 15y
   Dexter s/o Paul Esq d 6 July 1810 ae 17y
   Sarah F w/o Dr Amory 6 Feb 1787 - 9 July 1834
   S Josephine d/o Dr A & SF 24 Jan 1825 - 24 Apr 1830
   Luke d 17 Sept 1813 ae 20y
   William d 18 May 1837 ae 70y
   Lucy w/o William d 27 June 1819 ae 41y
   Benjamin d 11 June 1847 ae 37y
   Mary Ann w/o Benjamin d 20 Feb 1847 ae 41y
   Abigail w/o Benjamin d 12 Oct 1848 ae 74


## LANCASTER - SHIRLEY SHAKER BURIAL GROUND

The burial ground of the Shirley Shaker Community, while close to the buildings there, was not in Shirley but was actually over the line in Lancaster. The Shirley Shakers merged with those of Harvard in 1908 and very few members were buried in Shirley after that date.

The early stones were rough slate cut from a quarry nearby. After 1860 marble was used. The last burial in this graveyard was Eldress Josephine Jilson in 1925.

Two years later, the individual stones were all removed on the orders of the Shaker Central Ministry at Hancock, Massachusetts and a single monument was erected in their place. On it is the following inscription:

Erected by the United Society of Shakers to Honor the Memory of Members Interred in this Lot 1792-1925.

The above information is from *The Shaker Holy Land* by Edward R. Horgan, Harvard Common Press 1987.

*Shirley Shaker Burial Ground in Lancaster*

In 1927 the individual stones were removed by order of the Shaker Central Ministry and the monument pictured above was erected in their place. Sketch by Lee Tavares from photo by Edward Horgan.

BROCKLEBANK, M d 30 July 1838 ae 85
KILBURN, L d 24 Mar 1835 ae 88
BURT, O d 24 Nov 1834 ae 19.
BARRETT, R d 5 Dec 1833 ae 82
GROVER, d 12 Oct 1832 ae 22
WILLARD, N d 12 July 1832 ae 80
OSGOOD, E d 1831 ae 82
BROCKLEBANK, Asa -- --- 1831 ae 59
HAYWARD, M -- --- ----
WILD, E -- --- ----
PRATT, P -- --- ----
WARNER, P -- --- ----
KINNEY, S -- --- ----
OSGOOD, M d 3 Dec 1834 ae 87
SAFFORD, Sarah d 24 Jan 1838 ae 75
WARNER, Percis d 28 Dec 1836 ae 72
TEMPLE, J d 30 July 1834 ae 80
PRIEST, E -- --- ----
PIERCE, E -- --- ----
ROBBINS, R d Mar 1822 ae 65
HAYWARD, L d Mar 1822 ae 75
BURT, B d -- --- 1820 ae 81
EDMANDS, S -- --- ----
LYON, M d 9 Jan 1834 ae 73
BECKWITH, A d -- --- 1812
WILDS, I d 13 Sept 1817 ae 65
PERSONS, George d 11 Sept 1841 ae 17
HAMMOND, G d 29 Nov 1835 ae 76
BARRETT, S d 1 Sept 1835 ae 83
WORSTER, A d 5 May 1835 ae 88
PREVOT, Ellin G d 17 Feb 1848 ae 26y

25

ABBOTT, B d -- --- 1840 ae 38y
CLARK, S d -- --- 1840 ae 21y
WHEELOCK, A d 28 Sept 1838 ae 89y
PROUTY, M d 16 Mar 1833 ae 31y
WILLIAMS, R d 8 Nov 1829 ae 56y

There were many more stones marked only with initials which are not included in the above list.

Edward R. Horgan copied from the Western Reserve Library the following list of deaths of the Shirley Shaker Community. Used by permission of Mr. Horgan.

BURNS, ---- Sally d 24 Aug 1848 ae 80y
HOLT, Susanna d 19 Oct 1848 ae 85y
CLARK, William d 6 May 1849 ae 71y 8m 22d
CROUCH, David d 28 Aug 1849 ae 97y
HAMMOND, Joseph d 16 Sept 1849 ae 60y
WARNER, Francis d 15 Apr 1850 ae 81y 2m
LYON, Lucy d 18 June 1851 ae 27y
NEWHALL, Elmira (?) d 19 July 1851 ae ?y
WHITTEMORE, Susanna d 29 Sept 1854 ae 86y 7m
COOLIDGE, Culy d 28 Mar 1855 ae 82y ?m
PURRINGTON, Anna (?) d -- May ---- ae 7y ?m
AGER, ---- Polly d 24 June 1856 ae 76y
CARLTON, Elmira d 23 Apr 1859 ae 32y consumption
GODFREY, Lucy d 4 Oct 1857 ae 75y
HATCH, Olive d 23 Mar 1858 ae 84y
LYON, Hanna d 12 Apr 1858 ae 73y
COOK, Abigail D d 16 June 1858 ae 62y
PROUTY, ---- d 5 July 1860 ae ?
----, Susanna d 18 Aug 1862 ae 43y
----, Daniel d 30 Nov 1862 ae 60y 6m 21d
JONES, David d 9 Aug 1863 ae 83y
GODFREY, ---- Annie C d 17 May 1864 ae 54y 1m 3d
----, Chloe d 20 June 1864 ae 82y 7m 2d
OSGOOD, Relief d 22 Nov 1866 ae 88y 4m 7d
RICHARDSON, Isadora d 17 May 1868 ae 11y 8d
----, d 28 Aug 18-- ae?
NUTTING, Jonas d 26 Aug 18-- ae 71y 4m 19d
BURNS, Mary Ann d -- Mar 1875 ae 53y 4m
PEARSON, Julia E d 25 July 1875 ae 38y 1m ?d
BODGER, ---- Parmelia d 15 Apr 1876 ae 74y
BOWER, ---- Elizabeth d 13 Mar 1879 ae 62y 6m
MORSE, Mary R d 3 July 1879 ae 30y 1m 3d
GODFREY, Eldress Lucretia M d -- Mar 1880 ae 71y 4m
---- d 25 Apr 1881 ae 75y 2m
BOLTON, Edward ---- d 25 Apr 1881 ae 75y 2m
WHITNEY, Abraham d 9 Aug 1882 ae 97y 4m
WETHERBEE, William ---- d 14 Mar 1886 ae 70y 1m 26d
PARSONS, Leander A d 12 Apr 1887 ae 75y 6m 27d
BABBITT, ---- Abbott ---- Cora Bell d 27 May 1887 ae 11y 9m

26

## HARVARD CENTER BURIAL GROUND

Harvard became a town on 30 June 1732. In February 1733 the Town petitioned the proprietors of Lancaster for a piece of land still in the hands of the proprietors after four divisions. As it was brushy, rocky and ledgy, almost worthless for farming, nobody wanted it. The proprietors were glad to oblige. The tremendous task of clearing it was, thereupon, undertaken as soon as weather permitted, both by men and oxen. The Meeting House was built, first occupied 10 October 1733, and shortly after a "burying place" was surveyed and accepted by the Town. The committee had chosen the southwest corner of the Meetinghouse Plain, as the Common was then called.

An old road laid out in 1717 coming down from the Bare Hill settlement in a fairly straight line divided the Common here, forming the eastern bound and separating the new graveyard from the rest or southeastern part of the Common; this land was later given to Harvard's second and third ministers, Joseph Wheeler and Daniel Johnson. The southern and western bounds separated it from lands in private ownership not then occupied. The northern bound was, of course, the rest of the Common.

It is not ideal ground, as it is ledgy, and in some parts, sloping so that the lots have to be levelled.

Inscriptions copied by Elvira L. Scorgie.

KINGMAN, Ebenezer d 25 Mar 1788 ae 77y 2m 2d
   Content w/o Ebenezer d 29 Aug 1791 ae 71y 7d
DARBY, John d 25 Sept 1811 ae 72 -- Lt
   Dinah w/o Lt John d 6 Oct 1822 ae 80
MERRIAM, Sarah d/o Wm & Fanny Lewis d 23 Sept 1830
SPRAGUE, Sam'l d 16 Mar 1828 ae 57
   Lydia w/o Sam'l d 21 Aug 1863 ae 84
   Laura d/o Sam'l & Lydia d 20 Oct 1826 ae 14y 6m
CHAFFIN, Gladwin d 10 Feb 1813 ae 44
   Eunice w/o Gladwin d 13 Jan 1813 in ye 49y
MYCALL, Mary w/o John Esq d 8 Apr 1804
WHEELER, Levi s/o Joseph & Mary d 8 Mar 1781 ae 16m 14d
PARK, John s/o Thomas & Rosannah d 24 Aug 1806 in ye 21y
   James s/o Thomas & Rosannah d 9 Apr 1793 in ye 23y
   Margaret d/o Thomas & Rosannah d 1 Nov 1795 in ye 21y
   Thomas s/o Thomas & Rosannah d 16 Aug 1803 in ye 27y
   Thomas d 8 June 1806 ae 61

Rosannah w/o Thomas d 28 Oct 1812 ae 69
EMERSON, Sarah d/o Peter & Mary d 23 Mar 1800 in ye 19y
    Hannah d/o Peter & Mary d 28 Jan 1798 in ye 21y
BAILEY, Lucy d/o Peter & Mary Emerson d 14 Aug 1853 ae 81
STOW, Benjamin d 28 Feb 1813 ae 55 SAR
WETHERBEE, Sally d/o Benjamin Stow d 15 Jan 1879 ae 93
STOW, Abigail w/o Benjamin Stow d 15 Jan 1879 ae 32y ?-m
    Benjamin D 18 June 1790 in ye 72y
    Dorcas w/o Benj d 15 Jan 1801 ae 73
PRIEST, Jacob d 11 Sept 1858 ae 73
    Sally w/o Jacob d 2 Feb 1871 ae 83
    Oliver s/o Jacob & Mary d 11 Dec 1791 ae 1m 10d
    Mary w/o Jacob d 7 Nov 1791 ae 33y 19d
    Jacob d 14 Dec 1836 ae 79
    Rhoda w/o Jacob d 12 Apr 1848 ae 84
    Sarah d/o Capt Philemon & Lois d 2 Mar 1800 ae 21
    John s/o Capt Philemon & Lois d 1 July 1824 ae 33
    Lois w/o Capt Philemon d 9 Jan 1802 ae 44
    Philemon d 24 Feb 1837 ae 84   -- Capt  SAR
LAWRENCE, Betsy w/o Abijah d 9 Jan 1860 ae 82
DAVIS, Flint d 8 May 1812 ae 54y 5m
    Abigail d/o Flint & Abigail d 29 Oct 1800 ae 5y 6m
HILL, Sam'l  d 21 Sept 1797 in 63y -- Capt
GOLDSMITH, Rachel w/o Richard d 11 Aug 1812 ae 38y 11m
    Richard d 11 May 1836 ae 72y 7m
    Salla d/o John & Moriah d 13 Jan 1805 ae 12y 2m 13d
    John d 22 Sept 1798 ae 28y 5m 5d
    Sarah w/o Richard d 24 Sept 1811 ae 71y 2m 16d
    Richard d 12 May 1824 ae 85y 4m
    Timothy d 26 Jan 1819 ae 52
    Sherman s/o Richard & Sarah d -Jan 1796 ae 23
KIMBALL, Nahum s/o Benjamin & Nancy d -Dec 1798 ae 4y
    Benjamin Esq d 30 Apr 1830 ae 78
    Nancy w/o Benjamin Esq  d 17 Oct 1839 ae 84
DUSTIN, Alexander s/o Alexander & Sophia d 21 Mar 1809 ae
    2y 2m 19d
BARNARD, George Edward d -- --- 1825 in 36y
    Daniel s/o Lt Sam'l & Hannah d 4 Oct 1799 ae 14y 29d
    John d 2 Apr 1818 in 27 y
    Hannah w/o Sam'l d 5 Dec 1822 ae 59
    Samuel d 26 Jan 1831 ae 71
WILLARD, Robert d 1 Apr 1826 ae 6m
    Francis H d 10 Aug 1838 ae 3m
    Alfred R d 8 Nov 1924 ae 91y 2m 4d
    Mary B w/o Alfred R d 17 Aug 1885 ae 51y 3m 5d
    Robert d 21 Dec 1890 ae 92y 4m
    Sally d 20 Oct 1823 ae 27 y
    Nancy B d 11 Oct 1878 ae 71y 1m 11d
HOUGHTON, EW d 15 Nov 1899 ae 75  CW
    Caroline L w/o EW d 4 May 1861 ae 32y 5m
    Ella G d 24 Feb 1861 ae 8y 5m

Walter E d 17 Apr 1861 ae 3y 7m
George Robert d 12 May 1861 ae 1y 2m
WETHERBEE, George W d 29 Apr 1858 ae 29y
WRIGHT, Nancy S w/o Isaac d 28 Nov 1867 ae 37y 6m
    Isaac F d 29 Aug 1905 ae 81y 7m 8d
FISHER, Mary H w/o Rev George & d/o Elisha Fiske d 29 Apr
      1852 ae 50y 6m
    Geo Rev Pastor of Harvard Evangelical Congregational
      Church d 6 Sept 1853 ae 56y 10m
    Charles Luther d 12 Feb 1835 ae 5m
    Elizabeth S d 2 Mar 1860 ae 31y 9m
HOLMAN, Francis Eugene s/o Eliakim & Lucinda d 5 Jan 1888
      ae 58y
    Margaret Stebbins w/o FE d 11 Mar 1889 ae 49y
    Harry Atherton s/o FE & MS d 12 Feb 1857 ae 2y
    Grace & Alice Twins d Aug 1860 ae 7m
    Eliakim A MD d 22 Jan 1869 ae 69y 9m  CW
    Lucinda w/o Dr EA d 29 May 1857 ae 54y
    Francis Eugene d 1 Dec 1828 ae 2m
    Sophia Whitcomb d 27 June 1846 ae 2y 6m
    Susan C d/o Dr EA d 29 May 1869 ae 55y 3m
BULL, Trumball 1807-1878
    Abby Wetherbee w/o Trumball 1822-1867
    William Albert 1854-1855
    Annie Francis 1861-1862
    Joseph s/o Trumball & Abby 1864-1864
    Julia Gertrude 1859-1865
    Abby Delia 1858-1877
WHITNEY, Solon W 1851-1909
    Harriet E Bull w/o Solon 1850-1926
    Harriet E Wetherbee Clark 1819-1868
    Sarah A Bull 1841-1875
    Bertha Laura Bull 1871-1878
HARLOW, William d 27 Oct 1877 ae 59y 3m 13d
    William 1789-1810
    Phebe K d 29 May 1855 ae 30
    Sarah R d 30 Nov 1902 ae 77y 2m
    Abbie R Fletcher d 30 Dec 1902 ae 75y 10m
    MOTHER d 3 May 1876 ae 82y 7m Miriam A
    FATHER d 24 July 1875 ae 85y 3m Ellis
WHITING, William H d 3 Aug 1900 ae 46y 3m 28d
    Dorcasina B d 13 Apr 1854 ae 28
HARLOW, Ada F w/o George H 11 Nov 1853 - 24 Oct 1931
    George H 10 Dec 1851 - 2 Oct 1935
    Anna E d 9 June 1907 ae 68y 2m 17d
    P Holden d 23 Aug 1890 ae 75y 8m 9d FATHER
    Nancy H d 25 Jan 1883 ae 68y 6m MOTHER
    Susie M d 27 d 1871 ae 24y 8m
    Mary W d 12 Apr 1865 ae 8y 3m 20d
    Charles E d 2 Mar 1864 ae 23y 3m 24d  CW
    John B d 3 Sept 1931 ae 77y 2m 7d

Carrie S w/o John B 10 Apr 1866 – 21 June 1941
Pauline 5 May 1894 – 17 Nov 1957
Adeline S 21 July 1848 – 20 June 1942
BACON, Samuel d 23 Apr 1868 ae 75
Nancy F d 15 June 1824 ae 30
Alma E d 15 Aug 1879 ae 87
Lucia H d 26 Dec 1850 ae 23
Sophia A d 25 Oct 1850 ae 59
Luther Austin s/o SN & SE 9 Apr 1857 – 31 May 1857
EATON, Jacob S MD d 5 Sept 1888 ae 83y
Alma E Tyler w/o Dr JS d 21 Nov 1899 ae 84y 10m
ROYAL, Austin G s/o Dr HB & AT d 25 Feb 1896 ae 5m 19d
POLLARD, Albert d 23 Aug 1859 ae 53
Susan w/o Albert d 22 Oct 1857 ae 36
HARROD, William H d 28 Jan 1880 ae 87
Rebecca w/o William H d 4 June 1864 ae 65
Fredric A s/o Wm & Rebecca d 14 Oct 1824 ae 1y 6m
Fredric s/o Wm & Rebecca d 30 Mar 1834 ae 8m 22d
Edward H s/o Wm & Rebecca d 28 May 1838 ae 8m 18d
Noah d 8 Apr 1820 ae 56  -- Capt
Eusebia w/o Capt Noah d 8 Oct 1847 ae 84
DUDLEY, John d 16 May 1861 ae 65y 7m
Sally Emerson w/o John d 18 Mar 1872 ae 70
Harriet R d/o John & Sally d 15 May 1853 ae 19y 7m
DAVIS, Phineas d 12 Aug 1831 ae 65
Lydia w/o Phineas d 19 Oct 1953 ae 83
KNOWLTON, George d 2 Aug 1870 ae 32y 1m 25d
Mary E Rand w/o George d 1 July 1876 ae 31y 10m 19d
PEARSON, Eliphalet Rev Dr 1752-1826
P Holyoke 1740-1783
S Bromfield 1757-1831
BLANCHARD, IHT Rev 1797-1845
Margaret Bromfield w/o Rev IHT Blanchard d/o Rev
Eliphalet Pearson 10 Nov 1787 – 29 Nov 1876
ABBOT, Mary Holyoke P 1783-1829
PEARSON, Edwin A 1789-1853
Abigail B 1793-1794
Henry B Esq d 29 June 1867 ae 72
Mary E McFarland w/o Henry 1814-1887
DODGE, ---- d/o Lt Isaac & Elizabeth 1882-1882
SAFFORD, Ward d 1 Dec 1820 ae 73  SAR
Priscilla w/o Ward d 29 Aug 1822 ae 75
RANDALL Ruth d 13 Mar 1809 ae 59
SAFFORD, Martha w/o John d 30 Apr 1807 ae 90
John d 2 June 1782 in 74y
CONN, Mary w/o George d 19 May 1783 ae 70y
WHITNEY, Isaiah d 26 Sept 1812 ae 31
Ruth d 4 Jan 1815 ae 29
George d 6 May 1819 ae 30y 4m 21d
Daniel d 10 Nov 1834 ae 37y 7m 28d
Amos d 15 Dec 1838 ae 43y 9m

CROOKER, Peleg d 3 Jan 1783 in 49y -- Capt
WHITNEY, Francis s/o Isaiah & Mary d 19 Apr 1805 ae 26
    Amos s/o Isaiah & Mary d 11 Sept ae 3y 6m 11d
    Isaiah d 15 Jan 1841 in 86y
    Mary w/o Isaiah d 5 Dec 1843 in 88y
    Abraham d 10 May 1784 ae 75y 3m 9d
    Sarah w/o Abraham d 4 July 1800
HINDS, John d 9 Jan 1812 ae 49  SAR
    Elizabeth w/o John d 3 July 1860 ae 87
SAWYER, Alma d/o James & Naomi d 7 Oct 1826 ae 5wk
FAIRBANK, Eliza d/o Joseph & Betsy d 10 Sept 1808 ae 14m
WHITNEY, Henry s/o Israel & Phebe d 1 Sept 1808 ae 2y
FARWELL, Clarisa d/o Capt John & Arathusa d 2 Feb 1804
        ae 8m 4d
WHITNEY, Luke s/o Dea Israel & Naby d 2 May 1795
        ae 2y 2m 24d
    Israel  16 Apr 1776 - 17 June 1843
    Henry s/o Israel & Phebe d 1 Sept 1808 ae 2y
    Caroline W d 16 Sept 1846 ae 34y
    Hannah w/o Lt Israel d 14 Aug 1788 ae 34y
    Israel Dea d 20 Dec 1826 ae 75y 5m 15d
    Abigail w/o Dea Israel d 13 Sept 1844 ae 85
    Luther d 12 Mar 1871 ae 81y 1m 7d FATHER
    Malinda Wetherbee w/o Luther d 3 May 1847 ae 53 MOTHER
EMERSON, Peter d 16 May 1821 ae 93  SAR
    Mary w/o Peter d 10 Feb 1828 ae 88
    Jacob d 21 Oct 1850 ae 86
    Dorothy w/o Jacob d 13 Mar 1853 ae 74 y 8m
BAILEY, Betsy w/o Levi d 6 Nov 1853 ae 76
PRIEST, Andrew d 18 Apr 1892 ae 75y 1m 17d
    Sarah A w/o Andrew d 7 June 1879 ae 52y 5m 7d
    Benjamin J 1855-1930
    Sara C 1855-1933
    Sarah E d/o Andrew & SA d 3 Sept 1834 ae 15m
SAWYER, Agatha H w/o Josiah d/o Moses Gardner Jr d 11 June
        1828 ae 19y 3m
BOWLES, William d 19 Oct 1799 in 26y
    Anna d/o Wm & Sarah d 24 Jan 1797 in 17y
    Nathaniel s/o Wm & Sarah d 3 Feb 1793 in 21y
    Stephen s/o Wm & Sarah d 3 Feb 1793 ae 4y
    Elizabeth d/o Dea Wm & Sarah d 9 Jan 1793 ae 20
    Mary d/o Dea Wm & Sarah d 25 Nov 1792 ae 27
    John s/o Dea Wm Bowles d 28 Sept 1795 ae 32
    Sarah w/o Dea Wm d 11 Nov 1798 in 57y
    William Dea d 11 July 1796 in 59y
WHITNEY, Isaac d 10 Mar 1856 ae 81
    Mary Hill w/o Isaac d 31 Aug 1828 ae 53
    Hannah Haskell w/o Issac d 2 Aug 1868 ae 80
    Claricy d/o Dea Isaac & Lucy d 8 Sept 1796 ae 10m 10d
    Isaac Dea d 28 Apr 1815 ae 66y 2m
MEAD, Samuel Dea d 1 June 1814 ae 90y 5m

Hannah w/o Dea Sam'l d 23 Sept 1808 ae 85y 7m
WHITNEY, Lucy w/o Dea Isaac d 31 Dec 1837 ae 82
BROOKS, Betsy d/o Sam'l & Betsy d 19 Aug 1797 ae 18m
TYLER, Moses d 6 Oct 1817 ae 86
   Mary w/o Moses d 23 Oct 1838 ae 80
   Moses d 30 June 1843 ae 86  SAR
TURNER, Elisha s/o Capt Prince & Rebecca d 5 July 1797 in 3y
   Betsy d/o Capt Prince & Rebecca d 10 July 1797 in 5y
   Prince d 29 Mar 1800 in 47y -- Capt
   Rebecca w/o Capt Prince d 3 June 1838 ae 80
BURGES, Mary d 10 Sept 1803 ae 2y 2m 14d
   Nancy d/o Ephraim & Mary d 9 Jan 1834 ae 11w
   Marret d 17 July 1834 ae 70
   Sarah w/o Marret d 18 Sept 1849 ae 87
   Josiah d 17 May 1845 ae 51
   Abigail d 21 June 1880 ae 84
   Loami d 16 Mar 1825 ae 55
   Moranda d/o Laomi & Sarah d 18 Sept 1803 ae 2y 5m
   Ebenezer d 20 Dec 1807 ae 92
   Ephraim d 20 Jan 1885 ae 78y 2m
   Hannah Hazen w/o Ephraim d 23 Oct 1881 ae 77y 4m
WILLARD, Charles A s/o Ebenezer & Susan d 17 Mar 1815 ae 5m
   Nellie P Rich w/o Ephraim d 24 Dec 1884 ae 70
BARNARD, Benjamin d 25 Jan 1815 in 77y
   Mary w/o Benjamin d 18 May 1810 in 69y
ATHERTON, Charles d 30 May 1840 ae 49y 3m 18d
   Annes w/o Charles d 12 Apr 1880 ae 88y 3m 26d
BURGES, Rachel w/o Ebenezer d 29 May 1812 ae 85
HOUGHTON, Benjamin s/o Peter & Mercy d 20 July 1860 ae 63
   Betsy W w/o Benjamin d 2 Nov 1881 ae 80
   Peter d 10 May 1830 ae 67
   Mercy W w/o Peter d 25 Aug 1845 ae 82
   Abel s/o Peter & Mercy d 28 Oct 1815 ae 17
   Henry B s/o Benjamin & Betsy d 16 July 1861 ae 33
BARNARD, Joseph s/o Reuben T & Eliza Robinson d 8 Apr 1835
     ae 1y 7m
STONE, Maria d/o Joseph & Rachel d 11 Nov 1829 ae 20
FARWELL, John d 8 Aug 1824 ae 46 -- Capt
   Arathusa w/o Capt John d 23 July 1836 ae 52
BRIDGE, Isaac d 16 Sept 1833 ae 63
   Elizabeth w/o Isaac d 12 Oct 1833 ae 63
BLANCHARD, Abel d 9 Mar 1826 ae 73
   Lucy w/o Abel d 5 Feb 1836 ae 74
CONANT, Abigail d/o Levi & Abigail d 26 Jan 1826 in 26y
   Sewall 1798-1843
   Abigail D 1774-1843
   Levi 1767-1842
WILLARD, Charles d 16 Aug 1882 ae 86y 9m
   Martha w/o Charles d 16 Mar 1851 ae 51y 11m
   Clarissa Malvina d/o Charles & Martha d 17 Jan 1846 ae 8y
   Sarah E d/o Charles & Martha d 9 Sept 1831 ae 4y 2m

Charles A d 26 Nov 1859 ae 36y 6m
BLANCHARD, Betsy d 25 Nov 1850 ae 68
HINDS, Pamelia w/o Henry d/o John & Abigail Blanchard
    Charles Henry s/o Henry d Mar 1835 ae 1y 6m
MILES, Nancy Maria d/o Wm & Betsy d 26 Aug 1837 ae 13m
REED, Levi d 22 May 1837 ae 44
    Sophia d/o Jonathan & Lois d 28 June 1830 in 22y
    Lois w/o Jonathan d 9 Jan 1834 ae 64
GILBERT, Abigail w/o Jude d 22 Oct 1837 ae 88
DADMUN, Charles Ruggles 1830-1905
    Charlotte Haskell w/o Charles R 1847-1936
    Mary Hannah 25 Feb 1835 - 21 Dec 1901
    William d 10 Nov 1841 ae 47
    Joanna w/o Wm d 13 Nov 1867 ae 75
BURNHAM, Moses d 16 Nov 1842 ae 69y 8m
    Hannah w/o Moses d 5 Jan 1876
POLLARD, Nathan s/o Thad & Submit d 14 Nov 1796 ae 4y 7m 28d
    Nabby d/o Thad & Submit d 20 Jan 1790 ae 17m 22d
    Eusebia d/o Thad & Submit d 23 Mar 1790 ae 21y 3m 15d
    Submit w/o Thaddeus d 26 June 1790 ae 41y 1m 17d
    Thaddeus d 3 Sept 1803 ae 57  -- Capt  SAR
GARDNER, Sally B w/o Jerome d 18 Feb 1818 ae 21y 5m
    Moses d 8 Dec 1810 ae 24y 5m 14d
    Moses d 30 Dec 1812 ae 49y 2m 15d  -- Capt
    Agatha w/o Moses d 6 Sept 1824 in 61y
HAPGOOD, Mary d 26 Sept 1803 ae 2y 8m
    John Jr d 5 Oct 1803 ae 5y
    George d 16 Sept 1808 ae 4y 1m
    John Dea d 24 Apr 1859 ae 87y 10m
    Mary d 4 Mar 1866 ae 89y 3m
    Andrew s/o John & Mary d 28 Sept 1832 ae 23y 6m
    Peter D d 20 Mar 1863 ae 58y 11m
    Mary w/o Peter d 12 Nov 1898 ae 85y 6m
ATHERTON, Philemon d 21 May 1826 ae 55
    Elizabeth w/o Philemon d 30 Oct 1854 ae 78
    Martha w/o Philemon d 21 Oct 1804 ae 21 d/o Rev George
       & Aseneth Robinson
    Oliver d 29 May 1813 ae 92
    Rachel w/o Oliver d 18 Aug 1813 ae 83
ROBINSON, George Rev d 25 Sept 1847 ae 92
    Roxalania d/o Rev George d Sept 1808 ae 25
HARLOW, William s/o Ellis & Sarah d 25 Jan 1810 ae 11y 3m 23d
    Ellis d 7 Nov 1827 ae 63  -- Capt
    Sarah w/o Capt Ellis d 11 Jan 1844 ae 78
    Charles d 30 May 1840 ae 39
    Dorcasina w/o Charles d 25 Oct 1837 ae 32 buried under
       North Church Boston
    Charles Ellis d 1 Aug 1832 ae 1y 6m buried Copps Hill
    Sarah Ann d 7 Feb 1837 ae 2y 1m buried Copps Hill
    Sarah Ann d 9 Oct 1838 ae 11m 14d buried Hanover
WILLARD, Maria P w/o WB d 17 Apr 1864 ae 48

Eliza S d/o WB & AW d 6 Aug 1863 ae 18y
Susanna A d/o WB & AW d 6 Apr 1830 ae 21m
WB d 28 Feb 1891 ae 89y 1m
Abiah W w/o WB d 20 Aug 1862 ae 59
Luther s/o WB & Abiah 10 Nov 1836 – 1 Oct 1920
Ellen R Dudley w/o Luther 30 Sept 1839 – 29 Dec 1920
Luther D s/o L & ER d 16 Mar 1863 ae 16m
WILLARD, Eleanor B w/o Abel d 21 Aug 1856 ae 86
  Abel d 6 Oct 1840 ae 77
HAPGOOD, Shadrach d 21 Jan 1853 ae 69y 1m  –– Maj
  Nancy w/o Shadrach d 16 Oct 1849 ae 63y 5m
  Shadrach d 20 Jan 1818 in 71y  SAR
  Elizabeth w/o Shadrach d 30 Aug 1816 ae 76
SPRAGUE, Nathan d 5 Apr 1817 ae 44
LEACH, William S Rev d 31 Mar 1871 ae 67
  Joanna P w/o William d 12 Apr 1871 ae 62d
FAIRBANK, Jabez d 11 Mar 1813 ae 44y 7m 15d
WILLARD, Salley w/o Levi d 19 Apr 1842 ae 72y 8m
  Levi d 28 June 1847 ae 72
  Joseph d 22 Sept 1812 ae 84y 3m 25d
  Elizabeth w/o Joseph d 13 Nov 1803 in 70y
  Joseph d 18 Jan 1823 ae 62  –– Capt
  Susan w/o Joseph d 19 Apr 1840 ae 78
  Joseph d 21 Apr 1859 ae 75
  Abigail w/o Jospeh d 13 Mar 1880 ae 96y 10m
  Sarah Wetherbee w/o Joseph K d 5 Feb 1903 ae 84y 3m
  Joseph Kendall d 5 Dec 1900 ae 79y 4m 14d
SHERMAN, Sarah E w/o Alfred d 30 Mar 1854 ae 24y 3m
  Lydia Ann d/o Alfred & Sarah d 9 Aug 1854 ae 7m 25d
MAYNARD, Jonah d 21 Oct 1785 in 29y
HUSE, Enoch Jr d 31 May 1813 ae 52y
DYER, Lucy w/o Jeremiah Dyer formerly w/o Enoch Huse d 14 Feb
    1846 ae 70
HUSE, Enoch d 27 Apr 1821 ae 88
  Rebecca w/o Enoch d 20 Oct 1816 ae 80
  John D d 6 Aug 1840 ae 84
  Rebecca w/o John D d 14 Sept 1869 ae 103y 2m 12d
  Stephen s/o John D & Rebecca d 17 May 1822 ae 20y 5m
  John s/o John & Rebecca d 14 Jan 1808 ae 11y 2m
  Charlotte d/o John & Rebecca d 18 Jan 1808 ae 9y 3m
  Esther W w/o Enoch d 19 Oct 1833 ae 21y 5m
ROBBINS, Charlotte w/o Daniel d 29 Sept 1842 ae 32y 4m
ATHERTON, Caroline w/o Otis R d 26 Apr 1858 ae 54
  Otis R d 10 Nov 1859 ae 55
MANNING, Hannah w/o Theophilas d 9 Oct 1813 ae 31
TAYLOR Solomon d 27 Jan 1812 ae 55  –– Lt
  Daniel s/o Lt Solomon & Anna d 25 Aug 1813 ae 21
HAPGOOD, Jabez d 12 Aug 1860 ae 78y 10m
  Susannah w/o Jabez d 19 Feb 1851 ae 69y 6m
  Lucy d 27 Sept 1959 ae 36
  George d 21 Nov 1878 ae 68y 11m 9d

Cleora w/o George d 13 May 1850 ae 39y 7m 24d
Elizabeth d 2 Jan 1897 ae 85y 1m 18d
WHITNEY, Lydia H Hapgood w/o Luke d 17 Apr 1898 ae 78y 9m
HARTWELL, George d 26 Mar 1885 ae 54
Margaret A w/o George d 21 Feb 1897 ae 65
Susan w/o Josiah d 19 Mar 1881 ae 74y 6m
Josiah d 19 Sept 1851 ae 52y 8m
GAMAGE, Ellen C d/o Josiah & Susan Hartwell 1848-1927
GETCHELL, William 1829-1910
Sarah Hartwell w/o William Getchell 1834-1922
Frederick s/o William & Susan 1858-1922
HAPGOOD, Henry d 1 Apr 1879 ae 71
Matilda w/o Henry d 11 July 1888 ae 67y 7m
Charles H d 7 July 1913 ae 72y 9m  CW
Augusta P d 17 June 1929 ae 85y 8m
DWINELS, Edwin d 12 Mar 1839 ae 25
Sarah d 16 Feb 1840 ae 21y 8m
Jerome d 17 Jan 1861 ae 48y 1m
Mary A d 3 Mon 1871 ae 56y 5m
Sarah E d/o Jerome & Mary d 15 Mar 1865 ae 18y 9m
SYMONDS, Bowman d 26 Jan 1837 ae 23
Jonathan Esq d 31 Oct 1830 ae 75  SAR
Jane B Nutting w/o Jonathan Esq d 14 Apr 1872 ae 86y 9m
Hannah w/o Jonathan Esq d 25 July 1805 ae 42
Jonathan B d 13 Oct 1820 ae 20
BARNARD, Francis d 18 Apr 1838 ae 65
Sally w/o Francis d 13 May 1852 ae 76
Mary H d/o Francis & Sally d 10 Aug 1801 ae 2y 9m
David d 14 Dec 1828 ae 63
Mary w/o David d 5 Apr 1844 ae 76
FARNSWORTH, Lydia d/o Samuel & Lydia d 10 Nov 1812
    ae 1y 7m 25d
Lydia w/o Samuel d 24 July 1863 ae 70
Samuel d 17 July 1846 ae 58y 25d
WHITNEY, Isaac d 12 Apr 1825 ae 64
Susanna w/o Isaac d 11 Nov 1845 ae 81
CONANT, William d 14 Apr 1872 ae 80
Susan d 5 Sept 1862 ae 71
Betsy w/o William d 17 Sept 1840 ae 48
NEWELL, Adeline w/o NN d 9 Sept 1866 ae 53y 2m 18d
Norman N d 7 July 1880 ae 65y 8m 15d
DOWNING, Sally M d 8 May 1817 ae 19
HASKELL, Josiah W s/o Jacob & Susan d 17 Mar 1817 ae 2y 6m
Sally Preston w/o Jacob d 29 Dec 1812 ae 43
FREEMAN, Olonzo s/o David & Mary P d 25 Feb 1808 ae 2m
---- d 1 Jan 1809
HUBBARD, Calvin P killed at San Pedro CA 27 Apr 1863 ae 37
HASKELL, Sally w/o Jacob d 23 Jan 1811 ae 42y 2m
ATHERTON, William d 13 Apr 1867 ae 21y 9m  CW
Oliver H 1809-1898
Adeline 1812-1893

BEARD, Susan d 24 Mar 1885 ae 94y 11m 5d
   Eldad s/o Jonathan & Abigail d 10 Jan 1847 ae 53
   Ezra K d 9 Oct 1873 ae 85y 10m
   Judith d/o Jonathan & Abigail d 26 May 1817 ae 21
   Jonathan Jr s/o Jonathan & Abigail d 1 Feb 1813 ae 27
   Jonathan d 27 May 1843 ae 87y 11m  SAR
   Abigail w/o Jonathan d 22 Feb 1857 ae 98y 3m 13d
WILSON, Lucy w/o James d 29 Oct 1851 ae 75y 10m
HAMLIN, Africa d 15 May 1824 ae 41
   Sophronia d/o Africa & Lydia d 9 Feb 1818 ae 5y
STETSON, Thomas d 28 Nov 1820 ae 68  -- Capt
   Elizabeth w/o Capt Thomas d 20 Oct 1836 ae 81
   Jane d/o Thomas & Elizabeth d 17 Jan 1818 ae 22
   Sarah A d 16 Nov 1849 ae 70
BURGESS, Asa d 5 July 1888 ae 93y 3m 1d
   Lydia W w/o Asa d 9 June 1858 ae 66
   Jane Maria d/o Asa & Lydia W d 8 May 1847 ae 18y 8m 8d
   Lydia Ann d/o Asa & Lydia W d 25 May 1846 ae 12y 2m 27d
   Asa Simeon d 12 Sept 1911 ae 86y 5m 6d
   Sylvia P w/o Asa S d 15 Feb 1850 ae 20y 5m 3d
   Abigail w/o Asa S d 12 Oct 1864 ae 34
   Frank A s/o Asa & Abi d 15 Mar 1862 ae 5m 8d
BAGSTER, Mary J d/o Thomas & Sophia C d 4 Aug 1864 ae 1y 6m 14d
FARR, Asa 12 Dec 1783 - 5 June 1854
   Maria w/o Asa d 17 June 1875 ae 87y
   Francis s/o Asa & Maria d 12 Oct 1826 ae 10m
   Ezannah d/o Asa & Maria d 16 Oct 1811 ae 8m
LANE, Edwin d 27 Jan 1876 ae 53y 7m
   Jane W w/o Edwin d 10 Oct 1897 ae 79y 11m
COOLIDGE, Mary W d 14 Dec 1874 ae 77y 3m
CONANT, Sherman G d 22 Oct 1849 ae 43
   Maria w/o Sherman d 18 Mar 1848 ae 41y 5m
   Ellen Sophia d/o Sherman & Maria d 5 Aug 1847 ae 10y 10m
WILLARD, Howland d 28 July 1893 ae 91y 7d
   Melissa O d 5 Dec 1888 ae 83y 2m 9d
   Melissa A d 3 Sept 1843 ae 16y 2m 23d
     Also four infant children
   Alpheus R d 30 Dec 1871 ae 40y 8m 13d
   Augusta M Farwell w/o Alpheus 1 July 1831 - 2 July 1908
MONROE, John d 28 Oct 1866 ae 48y
   Eliza A w/o John d 8 July 1895 ae 67y 7m
   Delia C d/o John & Eliza A d 4 Mar 1880 ae 29y 10m 14d
   Joseph d 25 July 1847 ae 73y
   Polly d 25 Oct 1841 ae 57
   Joseph s/o Joseph & Polly d 9 Dec 1855 ae 50y
HAPGOOD, John d 16 Feb 1886 ae 78y 10m 28d
   Mary Ann w/o John d 11 Mar 1868 ae 58y 13d
   Clara C d/o John & Mary A d 12 Dec 1931 ae 80y 4m
RAND, Josiah d 26 June 1890 ae 80y 11m 21d
   Clarissa B w/o Josiah d 28 June 1871 ae 58y 3d
DANIELS, Sarah A d 20 Feb 1869 ae 29y 2m 22d MOTHER

Ella D d 7 Oct 1888 ae 23y 2m 9d SISTER
James R 1817-1902
M Josephine 1835-1909
FALES, George G d 14 Sept 1854 ae 32
   Louise J w/o George G d 19 July 1884 ae 57
   Ellen Louise d 3 Nov 1861 ae 10y
TORREY, Roger Clapp d? 14 June 1892
STONE, Samuel F 1812-1898
   Sarah Robinson w/o Samuel 1817-1864
   Mary Godfrey w/o Samuel 1817-1896
MANN, Sarah w/o William d 22 Jan 1813 in 51y
TUCKER, Joshua d 18 July 1833 ae 83
   Elizabeth w/o Joshua d 3 Sept 1827 ae 73
PIERCE, John d 12 Sept 1828 ae 69
   Dinah w/o John d 12 June 1825 ae 52
   Eliza d/o John & Dinah d 16 June 1818 ae 18y 2m
SAMSON, Thomas H d 8 Aug 1839 ae 31y
   James Manning s/o Abisha & Mehitable d 8 Jan 1831 in 10y
   Eleanor d/o Abisha & Mehitable d 30 Mar 1819 in 3y
   Eleanor w/o Abisha Pastor Baptist Church Harvard
      d 15 Feb 1813 in 34y
HILDRETH, Carrie w/o EN 18 Mar 1853 - 15 June 1895
TURNER, Luther d 17 Jan 1832 ae 57
   Abigail d 3 Sept 1844 ae 66
   Harriet w/o Luther G d 16 Feb 1838 ae 33
   George d 16 Sept 1821 ae 31
WILLARD, ---- s/o Capt George & Hannah d 10 Oct 1820 ae 3m 5d
BURGESS, Isaac d 14 Sept 1840 ae 40
   Roxalana w/o Isaac d 22 Nov 1837 ae 32 ?repeat?
CROUCH, Enoch d 23 Sept 1855 ae 71 ?repeat?
   Sarah w/o Enoch d 21 Aug 1874 ae 85
LANE, Benjamin R d 7 Aug 1840 ae 36
HARRIS, Frederick W s/o Joel & Mary d 10 Feb 1817 ae 27 1m 22d
BARBER, Darius s/o Daniel & Rebecca d 3 Apr 1816 ae 4y
FAIRBANKS, Amos d 25 Mar 1837 ae 65
   Rebecca w/o Amos d 15 Oct 1863 ae 86
KNIGHT, Lucy Whitney w/o John Knight d 3 Dec 1858 ae 81y 5m
   John d 3 May 1852 ae 83y 9m
   Relief Phelps w/o Jonathan P d 1 Apr 1902 ae 75y 3m
   Jonathan P d 21 Feb 1891 ae 67y 11m
   Hannah E w/o Jonathan P d 27 Oct 1846 ae 22
TURNER, Ellen P d 12 Nov 1874 ae 21y 8m
   Oliver W d 18 July 1879 ae 69y 3m
   Rebecca Harrod w/o Oliver W d 10 Feb 1911 ae 90
   Edward O d 3 July 1885 ae 36y 2m
   Adeliza Atherton w/o Edward O 1849-1934
CROUCH, Harriet C d 18 Oct 1857 ae 47
WHITCOMB, Hannah w/o Leonard d 18 Sept 1844 ae 67
HILDRETH, Augustus S 26 Oct 1822 - 12 May 1900
WILLARD, Hosea 2nd d 3 Mar 1848 ae 42y 6m
   Lucy Melvina d/o Hosea & Alice d 19 Apr 1842 ae 1y 9m 19d

PARKER, Granville M d 10 Sept 1871 ae 54y 3m
   Lydia w/o John d 20 Apr 1867 ae 84y 7m 20d
   John d 11 July 1851 ae 76
   Lucy w/o William d 29 Mar 1864 ae 67
   William d 1 June 1883 ae 80y 1m 25d
GODFREY, Zechariah T d 26 June 1867 ae 57
   Amelia S w/o Zechariah d 11 Oct 1849 ae 43
   George E R d 20 Dec 1856 ae 12y 4m 20d
WARNER, Caleb d 28 Nov 1815 ae 36y
   Betsy d 24 Jan 1813 ae 1y 3m 22d
   Caleb Jr d 19 Sept 1888 ae 74y 5m
   Catherine B w/o Caleb d 24 June 1892 ae 74y 3m
   Louisa d 21 Feb 1869 ae 62y 2m 21d
FAIRBANK, Edwin Symonds s/o George C & Lucy A d 7 July 1872
     ae 1y 6m
   Harry Gardner s/o George C & Lucy A d 13 July 1870
     ae 1y 1m 17d
   Ellen Louisa d/o George C & Lucy A d 9 Oct 1861 ae 8y 6m
   Walter H d 27 May 1857 ae 27y 3m 19d
   Clark d 7 May 1885 ae 84y
   Jane S d 24 Feb 1874 ae 67y
FARNSWORTH, Abel d 15 Sept 1861 ae 81y 3m
   Caroline C d 2 Apr 1831 ae 2y
   Lucy w/o Abel d 10 Nov 1876 ae 86y 8m 2d
   Rebecca d 11 Sept 1874 ae 57y 3m 4d
   William A 17 Mar 1826 – 16 Dec 1895
WETHERBEE, Arne d 23 Mar 1862 ae 69y 2m
   Mary w/o Arne d 12 June 1882 ae 89y 7m
FARR Lucia E d 4 Jan 1890 ae 49y 11m 2d
WILLARD, Clarence C R 5 Mar 1867 – 7 Aug 1896
   Josiah R 4 May 1832 – 9 Mar 1909
WORCESTER, Ann E 30 Dec 1838 – 6 Feb 1862
FARR Martha E 8 July 1844 – 10 Dec 1826
   George R 4 Sept 1860 – 20 Feb 1861
WORSTER, George 1811–1891
   Mary Senter w/o George 1806–1877
WILLARD, Hosea 16 Apr 1800 – 17 Jan 1884
   Nancy w/o Hosea 16 Apr 1795 – 8 Aug 1879
HUSE, Mary B w/o Denison d 23 Oct 1844 ae 42y 1m
   James W s/o Denison & Mary B d 4 June 1841 ae 15
HOUGHTON, William d 30 Dec 1852 ae 46
   Hannah w/o William d 2 Nov 1890 ae 87
   Abraham d 4 Nov 1844 ae 67
   Elizabeth w/o Abraham d 3 June 1873 ae 94y 10m
OTHELLO, Othello – faithful friend of Henry Bromfield came
   from Africa c 1760 d 1818 ae about 72
CHACE, Maria Louisa d -- --- 1848 ae 25y
   Ellen Bridges d -- --- 1848 ae 23y
   Mary d -- --- 1867 ae 39y
   Sarah d 25 Aug 1877 ae 50y 4m
   Charles Deacon 1797–1894

Mary w/o Deacon Charles d 18 June 1880 ae 82y 6m
Elizabeth d 10 Jan 1888 ae 58y 10m
LAWRENCE Sarah Jane d/o Kimball & Sarah d 9 Nov 1829 ae 5y 6m
Caroline d/o Kimball & Sarah d 12 June 1831 ae 4y 7m 16d
Kimball d 10 Dec 1884 ae 85
Sarah Pinder w/o Kimball d 3 July 1883 ae 84
Mary Pinder d 3 Apr 1884 ae 82
BATEMAN, George Henry s/o Jonas & Harriet d 11 Jan 1860
ae 27y 10m 17d
Harriet F d/o Jonas & Harriet d 25 Oct 1853 ae 38y 9m 22d
Francis A s/o Jonas & Harriet d 3 Jan 1852 ae 21y 6m
Silas C s/o Jonas & Harriet d 1 Aug 1846 ae 22y 8m 27d
John F C s/o Jonas & Harriet d 16 Jan 1843 ae 17y 4m 11d
Charles C s/o Jonas & Harriet d 30 Oct 1841 ae 25y 6m 13d
Sarah E d/o Jonas & Harriet d 23 June 1840 ae 6y 10m
George s/o Jonas & Harriet d 26 June 1831 ae 2y 11m 19d
Mary d/o Jonas & Harriet d 26 Dec 1836 ae 6m 2d
Andrew P s/o Jonas & Harriet d 29 Mar 1837 ae 18y 11m 8d
Harriet w/o Jonas d 2 Aug 1837 ae 41y 7m 4d
Jonas d 15 Mar 1852 ae 60y 10m
William F d 31 Jan 1877 ae 56y 11m
Louisa H w/o William F 17 Feb 1828 – 10 June 1910
Frederick William s/o WF & LH 17 Dec 1853 – 2 Sept 1948
Carleton B s/o WF & LH d 14 Sept 1863 ae 8m
Eliza Abiah d/o WF & LH d 14 Sept 1863 ae 8m
Ellen Clara d/o Horatio & Clara M d 1 Aug 1847
ae 1y 11m 12d
GROVER, Hiram S 16 Dec 1828 – 20 Jan 1906
Martha L d 15 May 1869 ae 20y 10m
Olive M d 18 May 1868 ae 23
Charles H d 4 Nov 1858 ae 28y 5m
Benjamin d 28 Mar 1858 ae 24y
Caroline W d 2 June 1854 ae 15y 8m
Charlotte Ann d 30 Aug 1840 ae 5m 16d
William d 1 Oct 1847 ae 5m 9d
Charles W d 24 June 1851 ae 44y 10m
Mary w/o Charles W d 16 Nov 1871 ae 65y 5m
THOMPSON, Herbert U s/o William JB & Eliza E d 28 Jan 1853
ae 3m
DOLBY, Sherman W d 22 Apr ae 26
WILLARD, Mary E d/o William & Rebecca d 23 Mar 1841 ae 3y 7m
Sarah B d/o William & Rebecca d 3 Apr 1828 ae 2y 2m
Rebecca w/o William d 27 May 1880 ae 78y
William d 31 Mar 1879 ae 83y 6m
BRADFORD, Winslow s/o Winslow & Luzana d 25 Sept 1853 ae
5wk 4d
FARNSWORTH, Mehitable w/o Ira d 11 Aug 1857 ae 62y 10m 6d
Ira d 6 Sept 1869 ae 46y 8m 24d
BARNARD, Emory L d 21 Apr 1835 ae 18
Emory Esq d 30 Sept 1868 ae 74
Susan G w/o Emory d 8 Mar 1853 ae 58

39

Harriet VA w/o Emory d 9 Feb 1862 ae 59
Albert Willard d 5 Nov 1850 ae 27
Ann Willard d 18 Sept 1848 ae 7wks
Josiah d 26 June 1858 ae 42y
SAFFORD, Martha Ann d 9 July 1878 ae 53y 5m
Augustus d 17 Mar 1894 ae 69
WOOD, Benjamin 1799-1877
Tryphena 1798-1836
Abigail H 1827-1859
Benjamin Lewis 1824-1895
Eliza E 1818-1912
B L -- --- ---- CW
CLEVERLY, Rachel d 11 Mar 1851 ae 73
KNIGHT, Amanda d 22 Nov 1880 ae 59y 8m 21d
Heman d 1 July 1827 ae 47y 7m 12d FATHER
Nabby Turner w/o Heman d 7 Nov 1846 ae 69 MOTHER
WARNER, Edwin S s/o W & C Warner d 19 Apr 1854 ae 2y 1m 9d
Harriet S w/o W & C Warner d 12 Jan 1857 ae 1y 3m 2d
KNIGHT, Mary d/o Jesse & Sally 25 Sept 1814 - 7 Aug 1875
Sarah H d/o Jesse & Sally 23 Jan 1812 - 17 July 1881
Rachel B d/o Jesse & Sally 7 June 1807 - 7 Feb 1892
Jesse 26 May 1771 - 19 Apr 1822
Sally w/o Jesse 11 Feb 1773 - 17 Apr 1846
GERRY, George 15 June 1798 - 3 Jan 1854 -- Capt
Sabra w/o George 28 Oct 1804 - 18 Aug 1884
Jesse K s/o George & Sabra 19 Jan 1824 - 27 Nov 1827
Sabra A d/o George & Sabra 21 Feb 1827 - 15 May 1861
KITTREDGE, Julia w/o William d 27 Mar 1822 ae 36
PAGE, Susan L w/o DO d 10 Sept 1891 ae 72y 2m 16d
WILLARD, Ephraim S d 7 Feb 1873 ae 70y 8d
Betsy R w/o Ephraim S d 5 Nov 1853 ae 43
Abbie Sophia d/o Ephraim & Betsy d 19 Oct 1845 ae 8wks
Emeline Augusta d/o Ephraim & Betsy d 24 Jan 1846 ae 2y 5m
Ithamar d 23 July 1871 ae 79
Gardner s/o Ithamar d 1 Apr 1837 ae 1y 6m
Lucy w/o Capt Ithamar d 1 Sept 1865 ae 70
GRANT, L A -- --- ----
S Augusta Hartwell w/o LA Grant d 27 Jan 1859 ae 23
HARTWELL, Daniel d 9 Apr 1884 ae 84
Sarah C w/o Daniel d 13 Apr 1867 ae 65y 7m
FAIRBANK, Jacob d 5 July 1831 ae 69
Sarah w/o Jacob d 25 Dec 1878 ae 79
TAYLOR, Mercy Taylor d 5 May 1832 ae 39
Sarah Taylor d 30 May 1832 ae 18
Phineas d 23 Dec 1866 ae 77
BACON, Samuel A 1842-1905
Elizabeth George 1827-1901
Sarah 1842-1921
Hezekiah 1797-1864
Mary w/o Hezekiah 1794-1836
Elizabeth C w/o Hezekiah 1801-1856

Lydia L d/o H & M Bacon 1823-1844
Elizabeth D d/o H & M Bacon 1831-1857
J Willard 1826-1913
Caroline Elizabeth 1827-1904
Lizzie d/o JW & CE d 1862 ae 4wks
CUMMINGS, Thomas 1805-1885
   Mehitable T 1806-1892
   Sarah T Wetherbee 1780-1866
   Charles H 1834-1893
   Helen S 1839-1902
   Emma 1858-1858
   FLT ---------
HARTWELL, David W 1814-1901
   Abigail T w/o David 1814-1858
   Lucinda 2nd w/o David W 1821-1898
   David 1850-1850
   Daniel 1856-1859
   Lucy E 1855-1859
   Lucinda F 1852-1859
   Ethan 1861-1864
   Abigail P 1846-1898
WHITNEY, Samuel 1821-1895 FATHER
   Sarah T Gardner w/o Samuel 1824-1897 MOTHER
   Ruth d/o Samuel & Sarah 1864-1864
   Estella G Scattergood d/o Samuel & Sarah 1851-1890
   Jerome G s/o Samuel & Sarah 1855-1904
   Clara Sophia d/o Samuel & Sarah 1857-1914
LAMB, Mary Gardner 24 Oct 1838 - 4 July 1916
   Charles Francis 15 Mar 1838 - 1 June 1922
GARDNER, Andrew d 6 Apr 1850 ae 61
   Eliza H w/o Andrew d 22 Dec 1856
   Francis H s/o Andrew & Eliza d 9 Mar 1837 ae 17y 4m
   Walter L d 8 Nov 1822 ae 49y 10m 8d
   Sally T 25 Sept 1797 - 13 Nov 1887
   Jerome d 22 Nov 1858 ae 66
   Walter L d 18 Oct 1830 ae 7y 7m 21d
   Clarissa d 5 Aug 1901 ae 74y 5m 29d
FAIRBANK, Margaret Blanchard 24 Dec 1828 - 15 June 1874
WILLARD, Frederick A 1823-1888
   Sarah 1825-1868
   Luther R 1887-1888
   Mary G 1835-1902
   Arabella 1838-1901
   Luther 1780-1856
   Mary Davis 1798-1854
   John B 1822-1900
   Luther Jr 1827-1836
   Mary 1830-1833
MUNROE, Ephraim MD d 8 Dec 1795 in 51y
   Mercy w/o Dr Ephraim d 10 Nov 1788 in 36y
BATEMAN, Elizabeth w/o Jonas d 19 Feb 1798 in 62y

FAY, Warren s/o Rev Warren & Betsy d 28 Apr 1816 ae 5m
WILLARD, Lemuel Dea d 11 Mar 1821 ae 69  SAR
    Nabby w/o Dea Lemuel d 8 June 1842 ae 79y
KITTREDGE, Thomas MD d 6 Sept 1809 ae 26y
KEEP, Jabez d 19 Aug 1774 ae 68y 4m 28d -- Capt
BEMIS, Stephen Rev d 11 Nov 1828 ae 54 Pastor of
    Congregational Church in Harvard 12 years
    Sophronia Chapin w/o Rev Stephen d 10 Sept 1804 ae 28
    Susan Chaplin w/o Rev Stephen d 5 Oct 1810 ae 30
    Rejoice Wetherbee w/o Rev Stephen d 29 Jan 1856 ae 76
HOUGHTON, E H ---------
    Lathrop s/o ---- d 2 Oct 1813 ae 1y
BEMIS, Abigail w/o William d 25 Dec 1823 ae 83
WILLARD, Nabby d/o Simeon & Elizabeth d 9 Sept 1779 ae 4y
    Simeon d 9 Apr 1777
SAWYER, Manasseh d 27 May 1856 ae 88
    Mercy w/o Manasseh d/o Dea Samual Meed d 20 Feb 1849 ae 80
    Manasseh Jr s/o Manasseh & Mercy d 5 Oct 1826 ae 35y 2m
TURNER, Simeon d 27 Nov 1802 in 85y -- Capt  SAR
    Bethia w/o Simeon d 13 Jan 1773 in 50y
FULLER, Lemuel MD d 11 Feb 1864 ae 51
    Catherine w/o Dr Lemuel d 11 Apr 1898 ae 84
GROSVENOR, Lucy d/o Rev Ebenezer & Elizabeth d 8 Feb 1795
        in 29y
    Nancy d/o Rev Ebenezer & Elizabeth d 22 Sept 1798 in 16y
    Ebenezer s/o Rev Ebenezer & Elizabeth d 15 May 1788 ae 20
    Ebenezer Rev d 28 May 1788 ae 49 Pastor of
        Congregational Church in Harvard 6 years
WHITNEY, Oliver Dea d 16 Apr 1802 in 71y
    Abigail w/o Dea Oliver d 8 Nov 1804 ae 73
POLLARD, Ephraim d 15 Apr 1799 in 32y
    Rachel w/o Ephraim d 10 Aug 1793 in 28y
    Thomas 25 Nov 1794 - 21 Apr 1845 -- Maj
    Walter d 5 Feb 1790 ae 80 -- Capt
    Dorothy w/o Walter d 22 June 1791 ae 76
    Patty w/o David d 18 Sept 1802 ae 61
    Thaddeus d 29 Oct 1826 ae 71 -- Capt
    Mary d 5 Nov 1847 ae 86
LAUGHTON, Jeremiah Dea d 11 Aug 1775 ae 49y 11m 27d
    Olivea d/o Dea Jeremiah & Rachel d 25 Nov 1768 ae 6y
    Rachel w/o Dea Jeremiah d 28 Oct 1810 ae 83y 10m
    John d 28 May 1791 ae 35y 10m 28d
    Sarah w/o Dea John d 4 Feb 1772 ae 90y 11m 24d
    John Dea d 5 Mar 1768 ae 86y 1m 17d
POLLARD, ---- ch/o Dea Luke & Becky d 30 Mar 1802 ae 1d
    Mary d/o Dea Luke & Becky d 3 Mar 1804 ae 11m 3d
    ---- ch/o Dea Luke & Becky d 5 Mar 1805 ae 6d
    Luke s/o Dea Luke & Becky d 21 Oct 1806 ae 28d
    Julia Ann d/o Dea Luke & Mary d 16 Apr 1831 ae 6y 5m 16d
    Becky w/o Dea Luke & d/o Jonathan Whitcomb Esq d 10 Apr 1811
        ae 32

Luke Dea d 6 Jan 1866 ae 93
Mary w/o Dea Luke d 16 Dec 1865 ae 76
Horatio d 21 Feb 1890 ae 68
Henry d 14 Jan 1852 ae 41
Olivia d 11 Nov 1890 ae 80
Frank B 1863-1934
Mary G d 19 July 1924 ae 78
Sara E 1848-1955
S Estelle 1842-1935
F Ellery 1853-1938
Luke d 22 Jan 1906 ae 92
Susan T d 7 Mar 1839 ae 23
Charles H d 5 Dec 1838 ae 13m
Elizabeth d 1 June 1887 ae 64y

STONE, Charles Newton s/o Isaac & Lucy d 30 July 1838 ae 5y
Charles Timothy s/o Isaac & Lucy d 21 June 1843 ae 4y
Issac N d 4 Oct 1870 ae 70
Lucy D d 14 Aug 1846 ae 45
Cynthia D d 6 Jan 1854 ae 56
Benjamin d 1 July 1912 ae 78
Emeline w/o Benjamin d 11 Apr 1888 ae 57

BLOOD, Mary E d/o Alfred & Catherine d 26 Jan 1903 ae 60y
Emma Maria d/o Alfred & Catherine d 11 Oct 1847 ae 11m
Henry Albert s/o Alfred & Catherine d 25 Oct 1847 ae 3y
Herbert Eugene s/o Alfred & Catherine d 4 May 1852 ae 8m
Alfred S d 8 Apr 1887 ae 69
Catherine S d 14 Sept 1893 ae 77

PARKHURST, Theophilas d 9 Nov 1827 ae 77
Sophia d 11 Feb 1870 ae 78
Sophia d 26 May 1826 ae 5y

WALKER, Harriet d 1 Sept 1856 ae 57

BIGELOW, Jason d 17 Aug 1854 ae 67
Sarah d 24 Dec 1857 ae 63
Sarah E d 8 June 1826 ae 7y

PARK, William d 7 Aug 1854 ae 75
Abigail d 27 May 1863 ae 79
Maria Stetson d/o William & Abigail d 22 Dec 1815 ae 1y
Stuart James s/o William & Abigail d 25 June 1821 ae 1y
William s/o William & Abigail d 28 June 1821 ae 3y
Susan Hayward d/o William & Abigail d 26 July 1821 ae 5y
Thomas s/o William & Abigail d 31 May 1831 ae 2y
Hannah Fisher d/o William & Abigail d 3 June 1831 ae 5y

WALKER, Samuel S d 18 Nov 1846 ae 50
Mary F w/o Samuel S d 7 Aug 1851 ae 53y 3m

PAGE, Nathaniel d 14 Dec 1819 ae 51
Anna w/o Nathaniel d 16 July 1821 ae 49

WHITNEY, Daniel H d 26 Apr 1874 ae 49
Susan H w/o Capt Aaron d 19 Sept 1848 ae 63
Sally w/o Capt Aaron d 9 June 1814 ae 32
Sally d/o Capt Aaron & Sally d 31 Aug 1815 ae 1y 3m 3d
Aaron d 29 Mar 1864 ae 86 -- Capt

Sarah d/o Capt Aaron & Susan d 25 Dec 1817 ae 8m
Abel s/o Capt Aaron & Susan d 25 Nov 1840 ae 11y
WHITCOMB, Sarah F w/o Charles d 14 Jan 1848 ae 24y 6m
POLLARD, Abner d 26 Mar 1858 ae 82
Asenath w/o Abner d 3 May 1864 ae 80
Asenath Alma d/o Abner & Asenath d 8 Apr 1820 ae 3y 2m 6d
Margaret d/o Abner & Asenath d 31 Aug 1840 ae 19y
Franklin s/o Abner & Asenath d 8 Nov 1837 ae 26y
Abner Jr s/o Abner & Asenath d 2 Nov 1844 ae 29y
PRIEST, Jacob 3rd s/o Jacob Jr & Sally d 22 Feb 1836 ae 11m
Zimri s/o Jacob & Rhoda d 24 Sept 1831 ae 30y 8m 4d
DAVIS, William 8 Sept 1790 – 6 Jan 1880
Eunice w/o William 8 Jan 1791 – 2 Nov 1828
Hannah J w/o William 21 Feb 1803 – 11 Apr 1848
Hosea s/o William & Eunice 28 Mar 1821 – 25 Apr 1826
Rebecca T d/o William & Eunice 1 May 1818 – 15 Dec 1839
FULLER, Eliza H Davis w/o Daniel Jr 22 Sept 1819 – 20 Apr 1841
KNIGHT, Abidan d 3 Nov 1841 ae 60
Sally w/o Abidan d 14 Jan 1822 ae 40
GERRY, Caleb S d 23 Apr 1885 ae 70y 6m
Elizabeth R w/o Caleb S d 25 Aug 1843 in 25y
Sarah B w/o Caleb S d 6 Feb 1894 ae 76y 11m
Ella E d/o CS & SB d 11 Mar 1852 ae 3y 2m
Elbridge d 31 Dec 1881 ae 22y 5m 22d
BARNARD, Phineas Dea d 11 Oct 1865 ae 91
Betsy W d 3 May 1825 ae 50
Sarah B d 23 May 1860 ae 85
WHITNEY, Richard d 28 Sept 1835 ae 82y 7m  SAR
Mercy w/o Richard d 15 Aug 1836 ae 81y 6m
JACKSON, Ann d 8 Aug 1844 ae 59
FARNSWORTH, Betsy d 10 Feb 1864 ae 82y 8m
William d 2 Nov 1828 ae 48  -- Capt
William d 27 Oct 1827 ae 23
DAVIS, Drusilla d 19 May 1850 ae 58y 10m 8d
WHITNEY, Anna Danforth d/o Aaron & Anna d 21 Jan 1846
    ae 79y 2m 3d
Lucy w/o Abel d 1 Dec 1864 ae 82y 11m
Abel Esq 17 Feb 1786 – 30 May 1853
Sarah w/o Aaron d 10 Apr 1820 ae 73
Aaron d 13 Apr 1817 ae 77  SAR
Anna w/o Aaron d 16 July 1772 ae 30y 11m 27d
Moses s/o Aaron & Anna d 25 Apr 1773 ae 11m 21d
Jonas d 18 Sept 1770 ae 71y 7m 7d
Miriam d/o Jonas & Zebudah d 30 Apr 1775 ae 22y 8m 11d
Jonas d 23 Dec 1781 in 65y
Salmon d 11 Aug 1844 ae 84
Hepzibah w/o Salmon d 6 Dec 1850 ae 89
JOHNSON, Daniel Rev d 23 Sept 1777 in 30y Pastor of Church
    in Harvard – Died in Continental Army  SAR
Daniel s/o Rev Daniel & Betsy d 16 Nov 1776 ae 4y
WILLARD, Betsy d/o Timothy & Elizabeth d 3 Sept 1779 ae 1y

9m 27d

ATHERTON, George d 17 Feb 1875 ae 77
　Mary w/o George d 8 Mar 1886 ae 81
GALE, Absolom B d 16 Jan 1915 ae 100y 1m 16d
　Louisa Farwell w/o AB Gale d 22 June 1860 ae 33
　Ellen A w/o AB Gale d 16 June 1880 ae 47y 2m 17d
HUTCHINS, William d 7 Mar 1772 in 77y -- Ensign
　Bethia w/o William d 21 Oct 1758 in 59y
POLLARD, David d 5 Jan 1860 ae 75y 5m
　Susan R w/o David d 4 Oct 1859 ae 87y 7m
　Alfred H s/o David & Susan d 10 Mar 1834 ae 1y 3m
　Josiah d 27 Dec 1855 ae 29y 4m
　Frank Eugene d 19 Mar 1856 ae 3y
　Mary d 30 Aug 1865
　　ae 31y 8m 9d
KEYS, Martha A Pollard d 11 Dec 1905 ae 76y 4m
DAVIS, Abigail w/o Eleazer d 29 July 1762 ae 58y 11m 13d
　Sarah w/o Eleazer d 3 Feb 1746 ae 31y 9m 23d
　Eleazer d 26 Mar 1762 ae 59y 10d
FARWELL, Abby Maria d/o John & Emeline d 26 Feb 1835 ae 4m 11d
　Mary Emeline d 12 June 1872 ae 36y 8m
　Sarah H d 18 Oct 1927 ae 86
　John d 16 Nov 1880 ae 71y 2m
　Emeline w/o John d 5 Nov 1895 ae 83y 2m
　John d 8 Aug 1824 ae 46　-- Capt
　Arathusa w/o Capt John d 23 July 1836 ae 52
　Maurice s/o William & Arathusa d 13 Apr 1878 ae 1y 1m
ATHERTON, Peter Esq d 13 June 1764 in 60y
　Experience w/o Peter Esq d 14 Nov 1775 in 64y
　Elizabeth w/o Peter d 10 June 1793 ae 62
DABY, John d 6 Jan 1769 ae 80y 11m
　Elizabeth w/o John d 9 Sept 1767 in 62y
　Hannah w/o John d 17 Nov 1744 ae 58y 5m
HASKELL, Eunice d/o Moses & Anna d 16 July 1782 ae 28y
PERKINS, Enoch d 20 Apr 1880 ae 83y 3m 5d
　Mary w/o Enoch d 24 Dec 1837 ae 35y 1m 10d
　Francis s/o Enoch & Mary d 14 Nov 1830 ae 7d
　Mary Adeline d/o Enoch & Mary d 2 Apr 1863 ae 29
　Julia A d 5 Feb 1881 ae 43y 3m 28d
ATHERTON, James H 1826-1908
　Arathusa F w/o James H 1832-1900
　Fred A 1833-1903
　David d 17 Mar 1831 ae 74
　Esther d 3 Mar 1852 ae 88
　Ebon d 31 Jan 1856 ae 67
　Lucy d 1 Nov 1869 ae 75
　William M d 13 Feb 1845 ae 26
ROBINSON, George C d 18 May 1888 ae 69y 6m
　Abby D w/o George C 10 Nov 1817 - 23 Apr 1866
WETHERBEE, Stillman d 14 Oct 1871 ae 69y 5m 11d
　Elizabeth Sargent w/o Stillman d 28 Oct 1878 ae 76y 14d

SARGENT, Angeline E d 26 June 1901 ae 84y 7m
GREEN, Simeon d 20 Mar 1908 ae 83y 9m 20d
   Susan Elizabeth d 25 Feb 1906 ae 78y 11d
   Lizzie Etta 1861-1944
HAPGOOD, Charles D 31 Mar 1898 ae 79y 5m 22d FATHER
   Elizabeth Bennett w/o Charles d 24 Mar 1897 ae 78y 9m
      MOTHER
   Mary Josephine d 19 Sept 1872 ae 15y 9m 15d
   Adella -- --- ----
   Mary -- --- ----
   Susie -- --- ----
   Ella -- --- ----
FORBUSH, Jonathan s/o John & Eunice d 26 May 1777 ae 20y 1m 26d
   John d 6 Dec 1775 ae 65y 23d
   Eunice w/o John d 14 Mar 1788 ae 74y 5m 14d
   Rachel d 6 Feb 1808 ae 70y 28d
   Molly d 8 Oct 1822 ae 74y 7m 1d
   Lucy d 5 Dec 1822 ae 70y 6m 19d
   Samuel d 31 May 1827 ae 73
   Mary w/o Samuel d 26 Mar 1813 ae 59
SMITH, Samuel d 15 Jan 1842 ae 63
WHITNEY, Cyrene Adelia d/o Nathan & Nancy d 6 Oct 1835 ae
     13m 13d
POLLARD, Frances C d/o Otis & Catherine d 19 Aug 1852 ae 22y 2m
   Mary A d/o Otis & Catherine d 15 Jan 1856 ae 18y 4m
SAWYER, Luke d 9 Nov 1863 ae 64y 11m
   Achsah d/o Luther & Achsah d 27 Apr 1823 ae 23y
   Abner s/o Luther & Achsah d 17 Jan 1814 ae 3m 8d
   Luther d 5 Sept 1834 ae 61
   Achsah w/o Luther d 18 Apr 1852 ae 78y 6m
   Sophia d 15 Aug 1879 ae 75y 7m
   Nahum d 4 Apr 1882 ae 76y 10m
   Cephas d 23 Nov 1888 ae 78
   Jabez d 6 Jan 1891 ae 71y 11m
HAYDEN, Benjamin d 6 Feb 1851
   Ruth d 19 Aug 1851 ae 84
   Fanny d 19 Sept 1860 ae 70
HOUGHTON, Thomas d 28 July 1862 ae 76y 2m
   Polly w/o Thomas d 1 Jan 1877 ae 87y 10m
   Hiram d 2 Jan 1853 ae 39
   ---- 1837
DeFOREST, Eleanor M d 28 Mar 1911 ae 73y 1m
LAWRENCE, Alvarus d 9 Oct 1891 ae 77y 9d
   Delia Maria w/o Alvarus d 13 Feb 1861 ae 47y 6m
   Francis s/o Alvarus & Delia d 26 Mar 1858 ae 22y 1m
ATHERTON, Martin d 21 Mar 1816 ae 22y 8m 10d
   Mary d/o David & Esther d 6 July 1801 ae 4m 4d
HERSEY, Charles d 12 Apr 1862 ae 68
   Emila w/o Charles d 24 Mar 1867 ae 72
ATHERTON, Joseph d 5 Dec 1789 in 61y
   Sarah w/o Joseph d 27 Mar 1813 ae 86

WETHERBEE, Ethan d 21 May 1840 ae 67
  Betsy w/o Ethan d 12 Sept 1817 in 37y
  Catherine d/o Ethan & Betsy d 6 Mar 1816 ae 1y 6m 13d
  Nahum d 28 Jan 1851 ae 49
GREEN, Martha w/o Dr Peter d 6 June 1770 in 25y
WILLARD, Tarbell d 7 Oct 1805 ae 86y 17d
GOLDSMITH, Theodore d 22 Mar 1859 ae 83y 7m
  Mercy w/o Theodore d 31 Oct 1850 ae 71y 9m
  Charles Theodore s/o Charles & Mercy d 10 Nov 1850 ae 20y
MAYNARD, Charles d 8 Mar 1862 ae 47
  Mercy w/o Charles d 18 Nov 1889 ae 72y
LOVERING, Jonas 1807-1893
  Rebecca H 1814-1896
  Anna H 1840-1857
  Charles G 1856-1859
  Laura H 1857-1859
  Electa C 1838-1913
  George W 1844-1929
WILLARD, John Jr s/o John & Ann d 16 May 1739 ae 23y
ATHERTON, Joseph d 16 Aug 1735 in 43y -- Ensign
HAPGOOD, Shadrach d 6 Oct 1782 ae 77y 11m  -- Lieut
  Elizabeth w/o Lt Shadrach d 30 Nov 1808 in 95y
  Asa s/o Lt Shadrach & Elizabeth d 16 Aug 1743 ae 3y 2m 2d
FAY, Mary E d/o John & Betsy A d 28 Aug 1846 ae 23
  John d 26 Aug 1863 ae 77y 10m
  Betsy w/o John d 9 July 1834 ae 44
GATES, Abraham s/o Jonathan & Mary d 1 Nov 1770 ae 2m 6d
DABY, Asa d 10 Aug 1813 ae 46
  Mary Symonds d 23 Dec 1815 ae 57
  Asa Whitcomb s/o Asa & Lurena d 5 Oct 1822 ae 7w
  Judith w/o Simon d 28 Feb 1809 ae 74
  Simon d 18 Dec 1802 in 85y
  Esther w/o Simon d 18 Oct 1769 ae about 52
FARNSWORTH, Nathaniel d 12 Sept 1811 in 60y  SAR
  Eunice w/o Nathaniel d 6 Aug 1799 in 79y
  Nathaniel d 7 Mar 1784 ae 20
WILLARD, Joseph d 30 July 1761 ae 76
  Elizabeth w/o Joseph d 23 Dec 1763 ae 72
  William d 17 Mar 1797 ae 84y 6m
  Ellen w/o William d -- --- ---- ae 81y 4m 9d
ALLEN, Edward M 22 Feb 1839 - 28 Oct 1862
PROCTOR, Job s/o Jonathan & Elizabeth d 7 Oct 1751 ae 21y 1m 14d
  Amos s/o Jonathan & Elizabeth d 5 Sept 1749 ae 10y 14d
WHITNEY, J Milton d 5 Nov 1888 ae 72y 5m 15d
  J Milton d 18 Aug 1862 ae 41y 6m 13d
  Mary P Sherman ?illegible ae 63y 8m 7d
HASKELL, Mary w/o Dea Joseph d 23 Feb 1744 ae 43y 9m
PARKHURST, Silas d 12 Sept 1811 ae 77
  Sarah d 28 Mar 1787 ae 46
  Fanny d 4 Apr 1866 ae 84
FARWELL, John d 17 Apr 1816 ae 87

Sarah w/o John d -- --- 1761
Eunice w/o John d -- --- 1769
Lydia w/o John d -- --- 1772
Sarah w/o John d -- --- 1810
Luther d 13 Jan 1873 ae 85
Bethia W d 6 Mar 1874 ae 91
HOLDEN, Betsey d/o John Farwell d 1 June 1860 ae 94
FARWELL, David d 7 May 1839 ae 83  SAR
Hannah d 12 Feb 1795 ae 39
John s/o David & Hannah -- --- ----
Sarah d/o David & Hannah -- --- ----
Daniel s/o David & Hannah -- --- ----
John s/o David & Hannah -- --- ----
Sally d/o David & Hannah -- --- ----
Sewall s/o David & Hannah -- --- ----
Stedman s/o David & Hannah -- --- ----
---- ch/o David & Hannah -- --- ----
GOULD, Joseph d 15 Jan 1809 ae 76
Jane w/o Joseph d 10 June 1834 ae 98
BURNS, Martha w/o John d 13 Aug 1793 ae 96
WILLARD, Artemas s/o Wm & Patience d 6 Aug 1803 ae 12y 6m
GATES, Elizabeth w/o Ens Jacob d 24 Jan 1742 ae 39y 9m 15d
HOUGHTON, Sarah w/o Capt Cyrus d/o Capt Isaac & Submit Gates
d 9 Oct 1851 ae 80y 19d
Jacob d 22 Aug 1769 ae 81y -- Ensign
Isaac d 30 Oct 1796 in 68y  -- Capt  SAR
Submit w/o Capt Isaac d 23 Feb 1813 ae 73
Nabby d/o Isaac & Submit d 19 Apr 1811 in 29y
Isaac s/o Isaac & Submit d 9 Nov 1852 ae 75y 5m
DAVIS, Alfred s/o William & Rebecca d 29 Aug 1846 ae 35
Alvin s/o William & Rebecca d 26 Sept 1813 ae 2y 1m
William d 22 July 1833 ae 72
Rebecca w/o William d 9 Nov 1860 ae 89y 8m
STONE, Anna d/o Oliver & Moriah d 25 Feb 1749 ae 7y 9m 12d
Moriah w/o Oliver d 13 June 1754 ae 32y 11m 20d
Eunice d/o Simon & Eunice d 7 June 1752 ae 12y 1m 25d
Ephraim s/o Simon & Sarah d 16 June 1754 ae 18y 5m 14d
Simon Dea d 22 Oct 1746 ae 60y 9m 21d
Sarah w/o Dea Simon d 30 May 1767 in 78y
WILLARD, Mary w/o Joel d 28 July 1801 ae 30
HASKELL, Mary w/o Col Josiah d 5 Jan 1798 ae 53
Josiah Esq d 19 May 1819 in 82y
DAVIS, Daniel s/o Aaron & Ruth d 10 Dec 1771 ae 10d 9h
John d 29 Jan 1768 in 70y
FAIRBANK, Joseph Jr d 12 May 1784 ae 40y 5m 18d
WHITNEY, Cyrus d 24 Aug 1847 ae 76
Mary d 19 Nov 1857 ae 78
Isaac d 19 Mar 1869 ae 45
WRIGHT, Dorcas w/o Isaac F d 16 Dec 1898 ae 74y 1m 7d
WHITNEY, Isaiah d 30 June 1867 ae 51y 9m
Mary w/o Isaiah d 13 July 1889 ae 67

Isaiah d 23 Feb 1817 ae 83  SAR
Percis w/o Isaiah d 5 July 1812 ae 76
Lauretta d 3 Nov 1842 ae 32
MUSSEY, Emily d/o I & P w/o Chas Mussey d 5 Dec 1874 ae 33
Minnie d/o Emily & Charles d 28 Mar 1873 ae 2y 5d
Eddie s/o Emily & Charles d 31 Aug 1875 ae 11m
WHITNEY, Joseph Addison d 10 Feb 1847 ae 44y 3m 17d
Charles L  1851-1922
Harry M 1845-1902
Carrie W Wright w/o Harry M 1867-1915
STONE, Ame w/o Dr Ephraim d 9 Aug 1839 ae 77
PARKER, Norman F 1852-1921
Mary w/o Norman F 1851-1926
TAYLOR, Mary w/o Dr John d 29 Nov 1764 ae 27y 9m 22d
SAWYER, John s/o John & Mary d 17 Aug 1739 ae 16y 10m 10d
WORSTER Rebackah d/o Jonathan & Rebackah d 13 May 1739
         ae 5y 3m 12d
Jonathan s/o Jonathan & Rebackah d 8 May 1739 ae 2y 1m 14d
Mary d/o Jonathan & Rebackah d 1 Nov 1736 in the 2y
Jonathan s/o Jonathan & Rebackah d 10 Oct 1746 ae 3y 10m 4d
John s/o Jonathan & Rebackah d 26 Oct 1746 ae 5y 7m 18d
Jonathan d 12 Apr 1754 ae 46y 5m
Rebekah w/o Jonathan d 20 Jan 1772 in 58y
RUSELL, Deborah w/o Amos d 14 Sept 1745 ae 17y 11m 28d
WHITNEY, Solon Franklin 1831-1917
Lottie C Wilder 1832-1898
Sarah Louisa d 6 May 1854 ae 20
Mary Louisa d 6 Oct 1829 ae 9m
Frances Alice d 27 Aug 1839 ae 17m
Harriet Lucy d 15 May 1844 ae 8m
Charles Edward s/o Benjamin F & Louisa d 8 Feb 1872 ae 31y  CW
Benjamin Franklin 23 Mar 1804 - 15 Dec 1885
Louisa w/o B F 17 May 1808 - 6 Jan 1887
LAWRENCE, Lucy d -- --- 1795
Eliza d 2 Oct 1804 ae 16m
Stephen Jr d 12 July 1813 ae 9y
Henry d 7 Feb 1829 ae 39
Lucy Folger d 9 May 1845 ae 24
Rhoda d 8 June 1877 ae 76
Stephen d 23 Apr 1828 ae 64
Lucy B d 2 Sept 1821 ae 38
Deborah W d 27 Sept 1827 ae 42
Esther W 21 Nov 1824 - 22 Mar 1896
William d 2 July 1855 ae 36
Mary H d 13 Aug 1876 ae 56
WHITCOMB, Sally M d/o William & Sarah d 13 Jan 1808 ae 23
SAWYER, Abigail d/o Joseph & Abigail d 15 May 1740 ae 4y 15d
Joseph d 9 May 1775 in 66y
Abigail w/o Joseph d 30 Mar 1793 in 85y
Lemuel d 31 Oct 1809 ae 64y
WHEELER, Deliverance s/o Thomas Jr & Mary d 7 Oct 1748

ae 3y 6m 9d

FAIRBANK, Little Eddie's grave -- --- ----
   Little Henry's grave -- --- ----
   Sophia no inscription
   Rachel Sophia w/o Omar d 6 June 1880 ae 52y 6m 25d
   Omar d 26 Aug 1891 ae 69y 26d
   Jonathan d 8 Sept 1840 ae 82 GRANDFATHER
   Hannah w/o Jonathan d 19 Sept 1849 ae 86 GRANDMOTHER
   Artemus d 22 July 1874 ae 86y 8m FATHER
   Rachel Houghton w/o Artemas d 22 Apr 1870 ae 76y 7m
HASKELL, Abigail w/o Dea Joseph d 27 Jan 1775 ae 71y 2m
   Joseph Dea d 7 Aug 1791 in 93y
HOYT, John d 30 Sept 1857 ae 59y 11m buried at Sea
   Elizabeth T d 30 Nov 1883 ae 75y 2m 8d
   Abbie d/o John & Elizabeth T d 6 Oct 1865 ae 18y 10m
WETHERBEE, Jonathan d 9 Apr 1860 ae 78
   Mary G w/o Jonathan d 26 Mar 1874 ae 89
   Jonathan d 23 June 1811 ae 63 -- Col SAR
SPRAGUE, Lowell d 19 Feb 1883 ae 91y 11m FATHER
   Elizabeth Hartwell w/o Lowell d 13 May 1882 ae 89
WHITNEY, Simon s/o Simon & Mary d 8 Dec 1792 ae 15m
LAWRENCE, Phebe d/o Abel & Phebe d 31 Oct 1756 ae 2y 6m
   Tryphena d/o Abel & Phebe d 12 Nov 1756 ae 7y 20d
SAWTELLE, Susan w/o JD d 16 Oct 1883 ae 68y 4m
HOUGHTON, Elijah d 20 July 1819 ae 80 SAR
   Mercy w/o Elijah d 11 Jan 1817 ae 73
WARNER, Elizabeth d/o Capt Ephraim & Mercy d 16 Sept 1816
     ae 6y 5d
   Elizabeth w/o Phinehas d 25 June 1834 ae 92
   Ephraim d 17 June 1851 ae 77y 2m 1d -- Capt
FAIRBANK, Joseph d 6 Feb 1826 ae 50
   Betsy w/o Joseph d 14 Apr 1844 ae 61
   Nahum d 31 Dec 1877 ae 73y 8m 24d
   Jane K Ballentine w/o Nahum d 26 Mar 1900 ae 79y 4m 20d
   Warren N DDS d 17 May 1885 at Asheville NC ae 30y 5m
FROST, Mary w/o Artemas 5 Nov 1802 – 26 June 1882
   Artemas 22 Feb 1803 – 10 Nov 1848
MAYNARD, Annie R Frost w/o Wm M 2 Sept 1838 – 10 May 1922
FROST, Scripture d 4 July 1824 ae 65y 8m
   Sarah w/o Scripture d 22 Mar 1841 ae 74
   Scripture Jr d 16 Nov 1835 ae 38y 1m
   Thomas S 17 Oct 1797 – 11 May 1879
   Mercy Sawyer w/o Thomas S 26 Dec 1798 – 11 Sept 1876
   Nathanael S d 3 Jan 1825 ae 1y 1m
   Marcia d 12 Oct 1830 ae 4m 7d
   Manassah S d 18 Sept 1833 ae 2y 8d
   Laura Ann d 27 Feb 1835 ae 2m 13d
   Ann Maria 4 Sept 1836 – 13 Sept 1908
WARNER, Aaron d 7 May 1821 ae 40
   Lucinda w/o Aaron d 7 July 1853 ae 73
FAIRBANK, Cyrus s/o Joseph & Mary d 3 Sept 1736 ae 10y 3m

Elizabeth d/o Joseph & Mary d 19 Nov 1736 ae 2y 19d
SAWYER, Caleb d 12 Feb 1755 ae 98y 10m 2d
   Sarah w/o Caleb d 15 Nov 1751 in 90y
   Seth d 29 Mar 1768 ae 63y 2m 29d
SYMONDS, Jonathan d 24 Jan 1770 in 55y
FULLAM, Sarah w/o Lt Elisha d 15 May (illegible)
HUNT, Samuel d 4 July 1775 in 68y
   Tabitha w/o Samuel d 2 Nov 1762 in 68y
SCOTT, Mary w/o Abraham d 13 Dec 1810 ae 70
HASKELL, Samuel d 13 Oct 1770 ae 55y 29d
   Sybel w/o Samuel d 9 July 1799 in 77y
   Henry d 17 Apr 1739 about 62y
   Ruth w/o Henry d 16 June 1749 about 67y
ROBINS, James s/o Capt Benjamin & Lydia d 25 Sept 1794 ae 5m 23d
   Suky d/o Lt Benjamin & Lydia d 5 May 1791 ae 10d
   James s/o Capt Benjamin & Lydia d 13 Sept 1794 ae 2y 2m 24d
   Sally d/o Capt Benjamin & Lydia d 25 May 1797 ae 18y 5m
SAMPSON, Stephen
SEARS, Hulda d 5 Aug 1866 ae 71
STONE, James s/o James & Deborah d 21 May 1789 ae 40
   James d 24 June 1788 ae 60y 10m
   Deborah w/o James d 2 Nov 1774 ae 46y 33d
HASKELL, Samuel -- --- ---- (Footstone?)
   Sarah d/o Samuel & Ruth d 1 July 1800 ae 7y 3m
WHITCOMB, Sarah w/o James Jr d 3 Oct 1766 in 23y
   Molley d/o Lt James & Lucy d 15 Oct 1778 ae 5y 4m 15d
HOUGHTON, Olive d/o Asa & Elizabeth d 22 Oct 1757 ae 4y 7m 20d
   Asa s/o Asa & Elizabeth 1 Aug 1756 - 8 Aug 1756
   Jonathan s/o Asa & Elizabeth d 13 Oct 1750 ae -
RAND, Silas s/o Jonathan & Abigail d 26 Dec 1736 ae 11y 9m 26d
FAIRBANK, Mary w/o Joseph Jr d 26 Aug 1748 ae 25y 10m 17d
   Joseph d 28 May 1802 in 80y -- Capt
   Abigail w/o Capt Joseph d 12 Apr 1798 ae 76y 10m 6d
   Thomas s/o Capt Joseph & Abigail d 10 Oct 1756 ae 5y 11m
   Ephraim s/o Capt Joseph & Abigail d 15 Oct 1756 ae 2y 11m 17d
WORSTER, John s/o Jonathan & Rebekah d -- Aug 1755 in 4y
   Lemuel s/o Jonathan & Rebekah d 20 Apr 1773 in 20y
RUSSEL, Parker s/o Jason & Elizabeth d 16 Nov 1750 ae 4y 6m
   Parker s/o Jason & Elizabeth d 7 May 1745 ae 3y 10m 16d
BIGELOW, Elizabeth w/o Rogers d 14 May 1802 ae 49
PRIEST, Hannah w/o Gabriel d 15 Sept 1810 ae 51
WETHERBEE, John d 30 May 1746 ae 44y 11m 4d
   Micah s/o John & Anna d 10 Sept 1756 in 12y
   Anna d/o John & Anna d 22 Sept 1756 in 15y
PEARCE, Gad s/o William & Marcy d 19 July 1739 ae 2y 2m 9d
CLARK, Hannah d/o Judah & Eunice d 18 July 1739 ae 4y 5d
FAIRBANK, Joseph Dea d 6 Dec 1772 in 79y
   Mary w/o Dea Joseph d 14 Nov 1791 ae 91y 11m 6d
WHITNEY, Asena d/o Cyrus & Asena d 4 Nov 1800 in 8m
   Asena w/o Cyrus d 22 Mar 1800 ae 27y
GUTTERSON, Lucy w/o Jacob d 24 Mar 1830 ae 25

---- c/o Jacob & Lucy d 7 Mar 1830
SAWYER, Wesley s/o Jonathan & Mary d 2 Dec 1809 ae 2y 1m 27d
    Mary d/o Jonathan & Mary d 17 Jan 1802 ae 1y 11m 4d
    Jonathan Jr s/o Jonathan & Mary d 8 Jan 1802 in 6y
    Caleb d 30 May 1829 ae 31 killed while blasting rock
    Jonathan d 9 Sept 1817 ae 47
    Mary w/o Jonathan d 10 Oct 1854 ae 81y 10m
    Caleb d 5 June 1820 ae 83   -- Lt  SAR
    Sarah w/o Caleb d 19 Aug 1825 ae 84
HOUGHTON, Thomas d 9 Mar 1764 ae 67y 11m 9d
    Moriah w/o Thomas d 2 May 1798 ae 91y 10m
PRIEST, Jonathan d 4 Nov 1849 ae 54
    Sophia w/o Jonathan d 13 Sept 1888 ae 82
    Elizabeth d/o Jonathan & Sophia d 20 Apr 1839 ae 3y
    Edward H d 20 Aug 1845 ae 5y
    Henry A d 8 Nov 1847 ae 3m
    John F d 19 Mar 1873 ae 34y 6m  CW
    Mary E d 22 June 1924 ae 82
    Caroline S d 28 Nov 1926 ae 82
FARNSWORTH, Jerome 14 Apr 1816 - 24 Feb 1903
    Lydia 31 Oct 1819 - 31 Dec 1906
    Jerome Jr 10 Dec 1844 - 19 Sept 1864
HILDRETH, Amos d 30 Sept 1872 ae 79
    Lydia & Lucy b 28 Feb 1852 d 26 Sept & 13 Sept 1852
    Mary d 14 Oct 1901 ae 81
    Dolly d 28 Dec 1878 ae 87
    Susan d 12 Feb 1851 ae 67
HAYDEN, Susan P 22 June 1839 - 31 July 1912
    Levi d 27 Mar 1877 ae 84
    Sally w/o Levi d 22 May 1836 ae 46
    Frances J d/o Levi & Susan d 13 Aug 1848 ae 7y 5m 11d
    Lewis T d 9 Jan 1853 ae 35
WATSON, Sarah w/o Alexander d/o Levi & Sally Hayden
    d 8 May 1855 ae 39
WHITNEY, Betsy d 18 Aug 1836 ae 62
PATTERSON, Lemuel d 11 Nov 1828 ae 69
    Susan w/o Lemuel d 30 May 1825 ae 67
    Asa s/o Lemuel & Susan d 6 Feb 1812 ae 24
BURT, William d 4 June 1811 ae 81  SAR
    Hannah w/o William d 13 July 1821 in 82y
    John s/o William & Hannah d 29 Aug 1775 ae 7y 8m
    Molly d 12 Sept 1849 ae 84
BRIDGE, John A d 2 Feb 1853 ae 51y 5m
    Polly d/o Ebenezer & Annis d 21 June 1788 ae 16m 26d
    Ebenezer d 28 Apr 1807 ae 45
    Annes S w/o Ebenezer d 28 Dec 1851 ae 87
TURNER, Horatio s/o Luther & Abigail 26 Feb 1806 - 23 Nov 1838
WETHERBEE, Julia Ann d/o Ezra & Rachel 7 Sept 1808 -
    24 Jan 1834
    Zophar d 29 Nov 1889 ae 85y 4m 19d
    Sarah Coolidge w/o Zophar d 4 July 1900 ae 90y 1m

Ezra Z d 13 Dec 1863 ae 28y 4m
Ethan D d 8 Dec 1851 ae 2m 10d
Ezra d 10 June 1849 ae 77
Rachel d 21 May 1813 ae 33
Sally d 15 Nov 1875 ae 91
Rachel d 13 Oct 1817 ae 4y
Francis W d 17 Apr 1878 ae 53y 7m
DABY, Adeline d 16 Sept 1831 ae 26
HOMER, Harriet F d/o Jacob & Sarah Wetherbee d 16 Aug 1894
   Sarah L 1838-1912
GARDINER, Mary P 26 Jan 1846 - 21 Feb 1937
BEAN, Javan E 12 Oct 1847 - 15 July 1898
WHITCOMB, Sarah w/o Abel d 20 June 1772 ae 22y 4d
   Lois d/o James & Hannah d 16 May 1739 ae 8y 3d
   Lydia d/o James & Hannah d 24 Apr 1739 ae - illegible
   Peter s/o James & Hannah d 16 Apr 1739 ae 5y 8m 24d
   Mary d/o James & Hannah d 25 Nov 1736 in 8y
BIGELOW, Daniel d 23 Apr 1802 ae 25
BOWERS, Joel d 29 Dec 1886 ae 67y 3m FATHER
   Charlotte A w/o Joel d 4 Mar 1882 ae 60y 4m 19d
   Lucy Ann 1850-1929
WHITNEY, Joshua s/o Caleb and Anes d 24 Jan 1750 ae 3wk 4d
PRIEST, Hazadiah d 19 July 1736 in 19y
   Elizabeth w/o Daniel d 6 Sept 1737 in 53y
FAIRBANK, Cyrus s/o Phinehas & Sarah d 5 Oct 1746 ae 5y 6m 13d
   Manasseh s/o Jabez & Keziah b 3 Oct 1767 d 3 Oct 1767
   Mary d/o Jabez & Keziah d 11 Oct 1777 ae 5y 5m 20d
   Jabez d 18 May 1774 ae 30y 2m 10d
SAWYER, Relief w/o Caleb d 2 Dec 1764 ae 24y 10m 20d
WHITNEY, Jonathan s/o Hezekiah & Lucy d 5 May 1776 ae 1y 2m
   Sarah d/o Dea Jonathan & Alas d 26 Dec 1746 ae 6y 6m 26d
   Jonathan Dea d 8 Nov 1773 ae 78y 3m 12d
   Alice w/o Dea Jonathan d 19 May 1792 ae 92y 2m
PARK, Benjamin K d 2 Dec 1840 ae 34
   Sally d/o William & Eunice d 29 July 1835 ae 34
   Andrew s/o John & Nabby d 12 Sept 1810 in 3y
   Nabby w/o John d 8 Dec 1819 ae 34y
   ---- Inf/ d d 10 Dec 1819 ae 3d
   Eunice w/o William d 20 July 1850 ae 90y 5m
   William d 9 Feb 1827 ae 77
   Andrew s/o John & Jane d 6 July 1775 Continental
      Service ae 18 y 1m 17d  SAR
   John d 20 Sept 1768 ae 67y
   Jane w/o John d 6 Feb 1800 in 87y
NEELAND, Merriam w/o Joseph d 15 Mar 1763 in 54y
BRIDGE, John H d 12 Sept 1896 ae 77
   Thomas H s/o Ebenezer & Susan d 7 Aug 1842 ae 24y
   Abigail C d 5 Aug 1868 ae 64
   Susan Hartwell w/o Ebenezer d 30 June 1834 ae 43
   ---- d May 1824
   Ebenezer d 31 Aug 1858 ae 69y 11m

Mehitable w/o Ebenezer d 2 Jan 1817 in 31y

---- Inf/ch/o Ebenezer & Mehitable d 26 Aug 1816

BEAN, Spencer D d 23 July 1898 ae 71y 2m 23d

   Mary S w/o SD d 18 Apr 1871 ae 42y 4m

   Willie Louis s/o SD & Mary S d 6 July 1872 ae 8y 9m 14d

FARNSWORTH, Edwin A s/o Mark & Laura d 30 Sept 1870 ae 24d

PRIEST, Rachel d 17 May 1737 in 81y

WARNER, Aaron s/o Samuel & Hannah d 12 Oct 1746 ae 24y 8m

   Samuel d 17 July 1744 in 39y

   Charles d 25 Mar 1792 in 39y

   Hannah w/o Samuel d 22 Apr 1775 in 98y

FAIRBANK, Mercy d/o Lt Amos & Lucy d 1 Nov 1784 ae 18y 7m

   Amos Dea d 14 Jan 1809 ae 71

   Lucy w/o Dea Amos d 12 Nov 1767 ae 28y 12d

KNIGHT, Levi s/o Nathan & Susannah d 17 Sept 1807 in 22y

HALE, Mary d/o Benjamin & Mary d 12 Apr 1782 ae 19y 4m 6d

   Benjamin d 20 Sept 1771 in 43y

PRIEST, Sarah d/o John & Mary d 7 Jan 1772 ae 10m 27d

   Mary d/o John & Mary d 9 June 1767 ae 2y 4m

   Calvin s/o John & Mary d 9 Oct 1762 ae 3wk 4d

   Mary d/o John & Mary d 20 Sept 1756 ae 1y 27d

   ---- Inf/s/o John & Mary d 19 July 1749

   Sarah w/o John d 6 Dec 1744 ae 24y 7m 19d

   ---- ch/o John & Sarah d 4 Dec 1744 ae 1d

   John d 4 Apr 1772 ae 54y 4m 2d

   Mary w/o John d 17 June 1772 ae 43y 4m 18d

   Relief d/o John & Mary d 11 Sept 1794 ae 26y

   Jabez s/o John & Mary d 23 Dec 1789 ae 25y 10m

WHITNEY, James d 15 July 1816 ae 57

   Rachel w/o James d 14 Apr 1803 ae 42y 8m 7d

   Lucy w/o James d 13 Jan 1810 ae 32

   Hannah d/o Richard & Mary d 12 Oct 1767 ae 4y 11m 26d

   Richard d 4 May 1798 in 73y

   Mary w/o Richard d 18 Feb 1804 ae 81y 1m

   Jacob d 12 Apr 1864 ae 87

   Mercy F d 9 July 1822 ae 36

   Hannah d 24 May 1838 ae 44

   Elizabeth d 24 Feb 1870 ae 77

   Martha Ann d 7 Dec 1829 ae 18

   Reuben d 4 Feb 1823 ae 60

   Lucy w/o Dea Reuben d 17 Nov 1843 ae 80

UPHAM, Lysander 1820-1891

   Mercy F w/o Lysander 1822-1903

HOUGHTON, Edward Warren 1829-1912

   Francena E W 1828-1892

   Anna Gertrude d/o E W & Francena 1864-1911

HILL, John d 11 Apr 1832 ae 70

DAVIS, Henry d 28 Oct 1881 ae 82y 3m

   Hannah Giles w/o Henry d -- ---- 1897 ae 93

WILLARD, Elliott s/o Abel & Ellen drowned 6 July 1884
     ae 14y 9m 22d

Abel 1841-1921
Ellen M Davis w/o Abel 1848-1921
William B 1877-1913
WHITTEMORE, Raymond G s/o Henry & Florence 1903-1913
KITTREDGE, Floyer MD d 1 June 1878 ae 64 -- Surgeon CW
Sally T M w/o F C d 3 Apr 1892 ae 90y 2m 4d
Sarah Frances 1836-1920
COLE, Martha d/o Jonathan & Judith d 23 Nov 1746 ae 20y 20d
Judith w/o Jonathan d 1 Nov 1746 ae 46
Jedediah s/o Jonathan & Judith d 21 Oct 1746 ae 9y 7m 11d
Mary d/o Jonathan & Judith d 22 Oct 1746 ae 3y 25d
WHITNEY, Elias s/o Lt Elijah & Rebbeca d 12 Apr 1775
        ae 14y 9m 21d
Elijah d 19 Feb 1755 ae 47y 6m 14d -- Lt
WILLARD, Hosea Edwin d 1 Nov 1898 ae 75y 4m
Esther C w/o HE 3 Aug 1830 - 11 Apr 1903
HOUGHTON, Henry d 24 Dec 1777 ae 73
Elizabeth d 10 Nov 1779 ae 82
RUGG, Abigail w/o Abram d 20 Sept 1746 ae 31y 1m 19d
Relief d 30 Sept 1746 ae 11m 14d
HAZARD, James T s/o Allen & Martha 24 Mar 1883 - 21 Jan 1894
Tower 1820-1897
Catherine F w/o Tower 1824-1911
Martha A d/o Tower & Catherine 1863-1945
Allen H h/o Martha d -- --- 1858
Lucy W d/o Allen & Martha 1881-1918
Warren T S s/o WT 1883-1884
Winfield s/o RB 1884-1884
CONANT, Lydia w/o Reuben d 25 Aug 1831 ae 69
WHITNEY, Jonathan 20 May 1782 - 16 Nov 1848
Mehitable w/o Jonathan 12 Aug 1795 - 9 May 1871
Agnes d/o Caleb & Agnes d 13 Jan 1758 ae 1y 8m 22d
Everlina d/o Levi & Sarah d 9 Sept 1838 ae 26
Levi d 29 Feb 1853 ae 35y
Hannah 1853-1933
Hazel 1908-1911
William 1859-1936
STONE, Mary w/o Micah d 21 Aug 1764 ae 26y 1m
BLOOD, Lucy A w/o Heman L d 16 Mar 1865 ae 46y 4m
Lyman R killed 18 Oct 1863 ae 15y 8m CW
Heman L s/o Heman L & Lucy A d 7 Nov 1839 ae 2y 3m 27d
BRUCE, Ezra T d 24 Nov 1897 ae 86y 10m 6d
Paulina C w/o Ezra T d 10 Jan 1892 ae 78y 6m
George H s/o Ezra T & Paulina C d 9 Feb 1854 ae 13y 10m
DYAR, Charles H d 12 Aug 1834 ae 3wk
Albert A d 12 Aug 1905 ae 76y 10m CW
Albert F d 18 Nov 1871 ae 68y 4m CW
Mary w/o Albert F d 3 Aug 1834 ae 30y
Arethusa P w/o Albert F d 21 Aug 1881 ae 76y 8m
Arethusa W d/o Albert & Arethusa d 27 Dec 1836 ae 3m
John F s/o Albert & Arethusa d 9 Feb 1838 ae 4wks

Guildford D s/o Albert & Arethusa d 14 June 1846 ae 7y
Charles G s/o Albert & Arethusa d 27 June 1848 ae 8m
Louisa d/o Albert & Arethusa d 24 July 1929 ae 89y 4m 10d
EDGERLY, Mary w/o Addison d 2 May 1879 ae 83y 3m
Edward Gardner s/o Addison & Mary d 28 Jan 1836 ae 5m 5d
George G s/o Addison & Mary d 22 July 1857 ae 20 1m 15d
Abigail w/o George G d 21 Oct 1868 ae 89y 3m 17d
George d 22 Sept 1856 ae 19y 9m 22d
THORNTON, Olive D 23 Sept 1803 - 30 June 1877
WRIGHT, Julian A d 30 May 1851 ae 10m 12d
Frederick M d 17 Aug 1856 ae 6m 28d
BUTTERFIELD, Emeline 1850-1930
Addie 1858-1859
Mother 1826-1913
Father 1817-1905
DUDLEY, Zaccheus d 29 Nov 1819 ae 74
SAWYER, Manassah d 24 Dec 1808 ae 78  SAR
Lydia w/o Manassah d 31 Mar 1805 ae 74
HOUGHTON, Elijah s/o Thomas & Betsy d 7 Apr 1822 ae 24y 9m
WILLARD, Augustus G d 24 May 1885
CRAGGS, William 1843-1895
Annie 9 --- 1912
NEAL, Annie Craggs 1881-1949
BROWN, Hepzabeth d/o Dea Caleb & Elizabeth d 4 July 1766 in 29y
Caleb Dea d 3 Nov 1758 in 62y
BURGESS, William s/o Ebenezer & Hannah d 18 Sept 1748
        ae 3y 2m 25d
PARKER, Augustus D 7 Dec 1847 - 30 July 1915
Mary Edna Willard w/o Augustus 1854-1953
Mabel L 1876-1894
Eva B ---------
Orville C ---------
Blanche W ---------
CATE, Eben 1832-1906
Sophia w/o Eben 1837-1880
Emma E w/o Eben 1868-1938
Charles G 1871-1877
HALL, William s/o John & Sarah d 15 Apr 1781 ae 1y 9m 17d
Sally d/o John & Sarah d 24 Aug 1778 ae 3y 3m 24d
Timothy d 13 Sept 1751 ae 32y 7m 10d
BARNARD, Benjamin d 24 Oct 1794 in 79y
Lucy d/o Benjamin & Lucy d -- --- 1752 ae 9y 2m 11d
Jotham d 17 Apr 1808 ae 64
Lucy w/o Jotham d 22 June 1839 ae 89
Lucy d 24 Jan 1850 ae 76
FAIRBANK, Phinehas Dea d 22 Aug 1800 in 82y
Sarah w/o Dea Phinehas d 1 July 1809 ae 87
BARNARD, Benjamin d 1 June 1857 ae 80
Jemima w/o Bemjamin d 28 July 1863 ae 73y
Rebecah d/o Benjamin & Jemima d 5 Nov 1817 ae 3y 6m
Levi d 25 Jan 1886 ae 64

Ephraim Jr s/o Ephraim & Hannah d 27 June 1795 ae 23y 4m
Hannah w/o Ephraim d 4 Oct 1777 in 28y
WETHERBEE, Josiah d 5 Apr 1783 in 77y

## TOMBS BETWEEN THESE TWO SECTIONS

WHITNEY, Susan d/o Richard & Sally d 7 Jan 1810 ae 1y 9d
WOOD, Francis d 28 Feb 1838 ae 36
   John H d 26 Mar 1824 ae 12
   Harvey d 23 Aug 1884 ae 79
   Mary w/o Harvey d 23 Apr 1879 ae 70
   John d 19 July 1832 ae 60
   Louise w/o John d 24 Mar 1838 ae 65
   Timothy d 18 July 1801 ae 51
   Elizabeth w/o Timothy d 10 Sept 1796 ae 50
DAVIS, Jonas d 30 May 1764 in 37y
KNIGHT, Daniel d 18 Oct 1760 ae 33y 5m
HILL, John d 30 May 1764 ae 27y 3m 10d
GEARY, Nathaniel d 29 Jan 1791 in 59y
   Susannah w/o Nathaniel d 2 Dec 1836 ae 95y
WHITTEMORE, Nathaniel d 31 Jan 1769 ae 70y 20d
FARNSWORTH, Asa D 1809-1892
   Betsy S w/o Asa 1807-1882
   John A 1846-1885  CW
   Sarah F Cunningham w/o John 1847-1936
HALL, William H Corp s/o Henry & Jerusha killed 12 May 1864
     ae 21  CW
   Henry M d 24 Sept 1894 ae 76
   Jerusha Smith w/o Henry d 16 Aug 1887 ae 84
SAMPSON, John d 29 Apr 1759 ae 69y 7m 1d
PIERCE, Jonathan s/o Jonathan & Sarah d 19 Oct 1759 ae 11m 19d
   Sarah w/o Jonathan d 3 Mar 1771 ae 36y 23d
NURSE, Daniel s/o Francis & Nabby d 11 Aug 1804 ae 10m 12d
PUFFER, Molly d/o Jonathan Jr & Abigail d 8 May 1776 ae 1y 4m 22d
   Jonathan d 2 Sept 1789 ae 36y -- Lt
   Jonathan d 1 Nov 1782 ae 71y
DUDLEY, Deborah 1821-1872
   Silas 1824-1908
PARKER, Lottie D d/o Oliver & Essie d 15 JUne 1878 ae 6m 15d
WILLARD, Willie s/o JO & EED Parker 15 May 1879-31 May 1901
   Grace M d/o JO & EED Parker 12 Dec 1885 - 7 Sept 1904
PARKER, J Oliver 15 Apr 1844 - 28 Dec 1907 FATHER
   Esther E Dudley w/o J Oliver Parker 3 Aug 1848 -
     30 Dec 1926 MOTHER
DICKENSON, John W 23 Dec 1835 - 28 June 1882  CW
   Harriet A w/o John W 3 Apr 1842 - 8 Feb 1929
   John W s/o John & Harriet 22 Sept 1872 - 6 July 1938
WARNER, John 1789-1875
   Sally Gould w/o John 1798-1874
   Eliza d/o John & Sally 1821-1838
   Benjamin F s/o John & Sally 1844-1848

John s/o John & Sally d 10 Oct 1834 ae 7m 14d
BLOOD, Nancy M w/o Oliver d 18 Sept 1841 ae 25
SIBLEY, Henry C 9 Mar 1843 - 8 Mar 1918
   Clark Rev 30 Oct 1800 - 23 Mar 1853
   Jerusha Adams w/o Rev Clark 22 Apr 1809 - 3 May 1897
   Ellen Amelia 5 Sept 1839 - 5 Apr 1901
   Emily Adams 27 Apr 1846 - 1938
   Ann Adelia 14 Nov 1835 - 13 Sept 1854
   Amelia 29 Mar 1838 - 2 Sept 1838
DAVIS, Cummings E 1816-1896
   Caroline S 1814-1839
   Mary Davis Stone 1787-1877 MOTHER
CUMMMINGS, Joseph d 5 Feb 1841 ae 61
CARTER, Joseph d 22 Mar 1857 ae 56
   Betsy C w/o Joseph d 13 Sept 1843 ae 37
   Charles A s/o Joseph & Betsy C d 21 July 1851 ae 20
   Ella A d 15 Jan 1851 ae 1y 6m
WHITNEY, Charlotte d/o Luke & Abigail d 4 June 1862 ae 19y
     9m 23d
   ---- d/o Luke & Abigail d 22 Feb 1865 ae 4y 4d
   Luke d 11 July 1884 ae 68y 8m 28d
   Abigail Knight w/o Luke d 20 Apr 1881 ae 62y 11m 16d
   Charlotte M Turner w/o Luke d 13 June 1840
     ae 23y 4m 3d
   Horatio Turner s/o Luke & Charlotte d 7 Nov 1872 ae 32
     CW
NEWMAN, Nancy d 9 Nov 1849 ae 69
   Robert E d 17 Nov 1861 ae 60
   Abigail w/o Robert E d 30 Sept 1887 ae 73y 14d
   Mary Homer d/o Robert & Abigail d 31 July 1836
   Abby Davis s/o Robert & Abigail d 2 Feb 1842 ae 4
PARKER, Margaret w/o Moss d 24 May 1750 ae 77y 12d
HAMMOND, Elmira A d/o David & Elmira d 23 June 1890 ae 64y
     4m 11d
   David 17 Oct 1796 - 1 Jan 1889 FATHER
   Elmira 16 Feb 1805 - 24 Aug 1883 MOTHER
   John s/o SH & HL d -- --- ---- ae 17y 9m 22d
   Lizzie d/o SH & HL d 12 Feb 1884 ae 17y 6m 21d
   Ruby L d/o SH & HL d 23 Sept 1876 ae 15y 6m 21d
   Simon H 31 Mar 1830 - 6 Nov 1885
MERIAM, Frances 18 Aug 1818 - 27 Nov 1886
   William d 3 Apr 1782 ae 49
   Sarah 8 Jan 1808 - 21 Feb 1847
   Jonas 6 Nov 1773 - 19 Feb 1848
   Rachel 2 Jan 1778 - 26 May 1825
CONANT, Sarah d/o & Huldah (illegible)
WORSTER, Nancy w/o Samuel d 21 Sept 1776 ae 24y 8m 21d
BURT, George E ---- - 1908
   Emeline E 1828-1904
   Daniel ---- - ----
   Adeline ---- - ----

Eva ---- - ----
WHITNEY, Eva H Burt w/o George F July 1842 - Oct 1900
BAILEY, Daniel Aug 1822 - Nov 1889
   Adeline C Burt w/o Daniel July 1842 - Oct 1898
HASKELL, Flora Burt w/o Joseph E May 1840 - Oct 1870
ADAMS, Jonathan d 14 June 1831 ae 46
   Alice w/o Jonathan d (illegible) ae 76
STACY, E Waldo killed 6 May 1864 ae 22y Battle of the
      Wilderness CW
   Lucy W w/o Nathaniel d 23 Aug 1883 ae 66y 6m
   Nathaniel d 25 Nov 1868 ae 66y 6m 9d
HAPGOOD, J Gardner 1855-1932
   M Adelaide w/o JG 1857-1926
WHITNEY, Mary Jane d/o William F and Jane J d 1 Dec 1840 8 wks
HASKELL, Charles H 19 Dec 1818 - 27 Apr 1886
   Eleanor B 10 Jan 1824 - 9 Aug 1881
   Charles C 11 Feb 1852 - 26 Feb 1854
BARNARD, Abner d 23 Dec 1906 ae 84y 10m 9d CW
   Asenath F w/o Abner d 8 Mar 1856 ae 24y 17d
   Rebecca E w/o Abner d 20 July 1915 ae 84y 11m 6d
   Benjamin Keep d 14 Jan 1900 ae 81
   Mary Hager d 12 Nov 1906 ae 84
   Charles Wesley d 13 Feb 1873 ae 17y
   Charles s/o Benjamin K d 5 Oct 1845 ae 11m 24d
SAVAGE, Sarah Barnard Puffer Savage 20 Dec 1848-14 July 1924
PUFFER, William A d 30 Dec 1887 ae 49y 5m
TURNER, Thomas J 2 Jan 1804 - 2 Aug 1870
   Abbie D Newman w/o Thomas J 23 Aug 1806 - 10 Jan 1879
   T Jackson s/o TJ & DN 21 Nov 1829 - 20 Dec 1830
HASKELL, Edward d 3 Sept 1869 ae 42
   Judith B d 25 May 1898 ae 81y 11m
   Elvira d 25 Jan 1874 ae 53y 6m
   Lucius s/o Asa & Cynthia d 18 Jan 1828 ae 22
   Edward s/o Asa & Cynthia d 22 June 1817 ae 3y 6m
   Asa d 24 Feb 1858 ae 78
   Cynthia w/o Asa d 24 June 1878 ae 94y 1m 3d
   Asa s/o James & Anna d 22 Nov 1777 ae 24y 2m
   James d 11 Mar 1827 ae 86
   Lydia w/o James d 22 Feb 1817 ae 72y 22d
GERRY, John d 18 Nov 1847 ae 74
   Sally d 20 Apr 1808 ae 33
   Rebecca d 26 Apr 1858 ae 69
   Fisher d 31 Dec 1818 ae 10m
   Luther T d 18 Feb 1826 ae 16y
   Susan R d 26 Aug 1855 ae 30
   Ward S d 10 Jan 1881 ae 76y 6m
WHITNEY, Sarah w/o Josiah d 21 Apr 1773 in 39y
RAND, Jonathan Jr d 16 Aug 1827 ae 25y 5m 15d
TAYLOR, Ephriam s/o Charles & Mercy d 7 Sept 1778
   Israel Esq d 2 Sept 1779 ae 69y 3m
REED, Israel d of small pox 19 Mar 1822 ae 54

Thomas R d 13 May 1841 ae 46
WOOD, Charles P MD 5 Mar 1824 – 11 July 1881
STEELE, Elizabeth G w/o A Steele 12 Apr 1804 – 28 Mar 1877
MOTHER
   Ab--- 1 May 1803 – 28 Dec 1878
STACY, George d 18 Oct 1844 ae 24
   John d 3 Sept 1840 ae 83 -- Capt SAR
BLANCHARD, Nathaniel d 10 Jan 1864 ae 39
   Edward s/o John & Abigail d 23 Oct 1837 ae 18
   Abigail d/o John & Abigail d 27 Nov 1837 ae 21
   John d 12 Apr 1842 ae 55
   Abigail w/o John d 5 Sept 1833 ae 39
EMERSON, William 1811–1895
   Abigail Knight w/o William 1809–1845
   William B s/o William & Abigail 1844–1845
   Sarah A d/o William & Abigail 1842–1845
   Catherine R d/o William & Abigail 1840–1845
   Alfred B s/o William & Abigail d -- --- 1838
   Harriet E Porter 1824–1902
   Abigail R 1852–1854
   Frederick B 1861–1861
   Arthur L 1865–1875
   Edward P 1849–1909
LAWRENCE, John K d 9 Mar 1851 ae 38y 4m
PATCH, Andrew Warren 2 Oct 1850 – 17 Apr 1925
   Adelbert H s/o Andrew & Maria M d 19 Dec 1859 ae 4y 7m
   John Herbert s/o Andrew & Maria d 11 Aug 1854 ae 1y 10m 28d
   Maria Mead 7 Sept 1827 – 24 Nov 1905
   Andrew 6 July 1819 – 2 July 1880
GRAY, Bella 1 Nov 1834 – 9 Sept 1836
   Charles Francis 19 Oct 1850 – 17 July 1851
   Emma Cleone 2 Mar 1843 – 15 May 1863
NOBLE, Gideon C 6 June 1803 – 6 Sept 1879
   Nancy Perkins 26 Oct 1807 – 19 Oct 1875
   Matthew 22 Nov 1773 – 29 Aug 1861 FATHER
WARNER, Zopher d 24 Jan 1894 ae 69y 9m 13d FATHER
   Sarah I w/o Zopher 5 Nov 1886 ae 47y 6m 10d MOTHER
FARMER, Emroy 1816–1877
   Sophia Raymond w/o Emroy 1817–1901
   Warren A 1841–1841
   Mary A P 1845–1847
   Almeda P 1853–1858
   Ella C 1849–1912
   Luke W 1849–1922
   Elizabeth w/o Luke 1868–1935
   Martha d 2 Jan 1892 ae 67y 3m
   Mary d 3 Jan 1892 ae 67y 6m
SAVAGE, Virginia 1860–1946
   Frederick 1858–1947
LAKEMAN, Mary w/o Ebenezer d 22 Nov 1866 ae 73y 6m
RICHMOND, Sally w/o Capt Sylvester d 19 May 1818 ae 35

TYLER, Abigail w/o Ellis d 20 Oct 1816 ae 65
   Ellis d 26 Apr 1817 ae 43
   James R d 4 Apr 1906 ae 85
   Edward d 26 Dec 1823 ae 47  -- Capt
   John MD d 8 Feb 1844 ae 25
WARNER, Abigail w/o Elias d 16 Nov 1835 ae 73y 7m 4d
PRIEST, Jeremiah d 28 Dec 1781 ae 60y 8m
KENDALL, Enoch d 13 Oct 1835 ae 40
   William s/o Enoch & Fanny d 2 July 1829 ae 2y 2m 2d
   Luke d 30 Aug 1832 ae 23y 8m 28d
   Sybel w/o James d 4 Oct 1831 ae 29y
   ---- Inf/d 11 Oct 1831 ae 16d
ADAMS, Joseph S d 19 June 1876 ae 71y 7m 12d
   Nancy W w/o Joseph S d 17 Mar 1877 ae 70y 4m
   Sarah w/o Joseph S d 15 Sept 1839 ae 32y 6m 15d
   Sarah Adeline d/o Joseph & Sarah d 8 Sept 1839 ae 4wk 3d
   Sarah Adeline d/o Joseph & Sarah d 13 Dec 1852 ae 8y 10m 20d
HILL, Augustus Granville d 14 Jan 1877 ae 73
   Martha Sawyer w/o AG d 31 July 1837 ae 29
   Oliver d 3 Mar 1847 ae 75  -- Capt
   Mary Goldsmith w/o Oliver d 4 Aug 1853 ae 76
   Sherman G d 15 May 1838 ae 39
SAWYER, Seth A s/o Luke & Mercy B d 6 Oct 1855 ae 6y 23m
   Martyn A s/o Luke & Mercy B d 18 Aug 1849 ae 4y 7m
   John P d 15 Aug 1849 ae 2y 9m
   Mary L H d/o Luke & Mercy d 30 July 1843 ae 5y 8m
   Caroline L d/o Luke & Mercy d 18 July 1843 ae 8m
   Mercy B w/o Luke d 12 Aug 1849 ae 38y 8m
   Luke d 17 Apr 1870 ae 60y 6m
HAYDEN, James N s/o Edmund & Charlotte d 16 Sept 1845 ae 10m 2d
HOUGHTON, Miriam d 5 July 1880 ae 62y 6m
   Lucinda 1838-1908
BOWERS, Rebeckah w/o Capt Joel d 14 --- 1868 ae 78y 2m
   Joel d 6 Mar 1851 ae 62  -- Capt
   Francis d 28 Sept 1867 ae 33y 11m
   Cephas H 19 Oct 1816 - 22 Aug 1901
DADMUN, Abbie A Haskell w/o James F d 8 July 1939 ae 95y 7m
   James F d 17 Feb 1873 ae 33y 11m  CW
   Elizabeth F w/o James F d 21 May 1866 ae 26y 5m
   Addie Sophia d/o JF & EF d 26 Apr 1866 ae 14d
FARR, Francis Esq d 16 Sept 1819 ae 66  SAR
   Sarah d 3 June 1830 ae 82
   Francis d 22 Feb 1799 ae 17
   William d 13 Sept 1819 ae 21
   Thomas d 12 Jan 1840 ae 54
   Jonathan Rev d 3 June 1844 ae 54
   Sarah d 22 Apr 1859 ae 66
   Lydia d 22 June 1892 ae 96
HASKELL, Joseph F d 10 June 1864 ae 21y 10m 4d  CW
   Elizabeth F w/o Adolphus 25 Feb 1812 - 10 May 1900
   Adolphus 24 Feb 1811 - 22 Nov 1898

GERRY, Nathaniel d 21 Apr 1822 ae 54y
 Betsy d June 1838 ae 70
 Elbridge G s/o Nathanial & Betsy d 10 Jan 1811 ae 7y 7m
FARNSWORTH, Abel d 19 Jan 1800 ae 70y
 Elizabeth d 13 Apr 1811 ae 67y
SAWYER, Jonathan d 9 Sept 1865 ae 76y
 Adaline d 3 Sept 1864 ae 58
 Eliza d 28 May 1818 ae 24
 Jonathan s/o Jonathan & Eliza d 26 Sept 1844 ae 26
 Rebecca d/o Jonathan & Eliza d 8 Aug 1817 ae 1m 5d
 George L 15 May 1839 - 29 Dec 1896
 Marcia Frost w/o George L -- Nov 1837 - 24 Dec 1924
 Elmer J s/o GL & MF d 28 May 1869 ae 7y 4m 3d
 Lucy F w/o Arad d 20 Dec 1879 ae 71y 7m
 Arad d 24 May 1878 ae 69y 10m
 Guy F s/o Alfred & Emma d 26 Jan 1885 ae 10y 3m
 Emma w/o Alfred A 26 May 1851 - 10 Sept 1924
 Alfred A 12 Sept 1849 - 12 Aug 1906
 Leroy F 1873-1956
FAIRBANKS, Joel W 30 July 1889 ae 79y 3m
 Elizabeth B w/o JW d 9 Oct 1888 ae 76
 G d 30 Sept 1858 ae 22
 Ellen J d 30 Aug 1845 ae 4y
 Albert W d 30 Sept 1873 ae 21y 7m
 Thomas d 13 Feb 1813 ae 48y
 Lydia d 2 Sept 1863 ae 94y
 Levi d 5 Feb 1813 ae 15
 Clark d 28 Oct 1824 ae 17y
 Jonathan H s/o Jonathan & Sally d 16 Mar 1840 in 15y
 Hannah w/o Jonathan d 3 Mar 1819 ae 24
 Hannah d/o Jonathan & Hannah d 26 Apr 1818 ae 1y 5m
 Jonathan Dea d 3 Oct 1881 ae 92y 9m
 Sally w/o Jonathan d 25 Feb 1876 ae 87y
 Margaret B d 15 June 1874 ae 46
LAWRENCE, Benjamin d 5 July 1767 ae 53
 Benjamin d 26 Aug 1775 ae 23
HARTWELL, Nathan d 8 Dec 1768 in 49y
 Mary w/o Nathan d 21 Oct 1800 ae 77
PRIEST, David s/o Philemon Jr & Ann d 7 Apr 1815 ae 2y 1m
POLLARD, Sally d/o David & Patty d 7 May 1783 ae 2y 3m
ADAMS, Susannah w/o William d 22 Nov 1818 ae 35
WARNER, Calvin d 8 May 1853 ae 64y 4m 13d
 Lydia w/o Calvin d 1 July 1879 ae 91y 3m 21d
LAKEMAN, Eben H 1826-1911 CW
 Selenda S w/o Eben H d 8 Jan 1880 ae 45
 Lindie A 1864-1952
HAMLEN, Asia s/o Capt Eleazar & Sarah d 2 Nov 1778 ae 4y 5m 21d
 Sarah w/o Eleazar d 15 Nov 1788 ae 45y
WRIGHT, Joseph d 27 Mar 1880 ae 71
BROWN, George W ---- - ----
 Belinda S w/o George d 4 Nov 1854 ae 37

STEARNS, Jonas d 21 April 1839 ae 52y
    Anna d 24 Jan 1861 ae 75y
    Winslow B d 1 Mar 1855 ae 24y
    Abby E d 14 Aug 1857 ae 28
GOODRIDGE, Asaph d 16 Jan 1843 ae 32
    Lavinia w/o Asaph d/o Joel & Rebecca Bowers d 4 Sept 1837 ae 25
RAYMOND, Charles d 1 Nov 1842 ae 43
    Mira W Dwinell w/o Charles d 29 Aug 1883 ae 79
    Stillman W d 12 Aug 1850 ae 25
ROBINS, Caroline d 29 Mar 1819 ae 3
SKILLINGS, William P 26 Feb 1831 – 12 Dec 1883
    Adelma Beane s/o WP & JG d 25 June 1870 ae 1y 1m
DADMUN, Elizabeth Jane d/o Joseph & Elizabeth d 6 Sept 1870
        ae 10m 12d
    Polly A w/o Joseph d 9 Apr 1841 ae 39
    Elizabeth Bigelow w/o Joseph 1810–1896
    Joseph 3 Mar 1800 – 14 Oct 1891
HAPGOOD, Sally w/o Joel d 19 Jan 1820 ae 27y 3m 26d
    Joel d 28 Sept 1855 ae 67
    Charlotte Mead w/o Joel d 17 July 1884 ae 92y 6m 25d
HOUGHTON, Elizabeth d/o John & Esther d 20 Sept 1771 ae 1y
        1m 26d
    Eunice d/o John & Esther ---- – ----
    John d 9 Aug 1819 ae 81 -- Lt SAR
    Esther w/o John d 28 Apr 1817 ae 77
WHITNEY, Joseph s/o Abraham & Rebekah d 16 May 1799 ae 4y
        4m 10d
    Abel s/o Abraham & Rebekah d 2 Dec 1799 ae 8y 1m 11d
    John d 10 Feb 1813 ae 28
    Josiah d 26 Feb 1813 ae 31
    Abraham d 26 Aug 1833 ae 84
    Rebekah w/o Abraham d 27 Aug 1838 ae 81y
    Nancy d 9 Jan 1856 ae 69y 8m
    Mary d 6 Feb 1864 ae 64
    Simon d 29 Apr 1859 ae 72y 1m
    Eliza d 2 Sept 1883 ae 80
POLLARD, Sarah d/o James & Molly d 7 Apr 1788 ae 1y 3m 18d
    James s/o James & Molly d 19 July 1779 ae 12y 6m
    Israel s/o James & Molly d 1 Jan 1788 ae 19y 5m
KITTREDGE, S Augusta d 29 Dec 1859 ae 30y 11m
    Catharine A d 11 Oct 1836 ae 6m
    John W d 25 Feb 1853 ae 38
WILLARD, Susan M w/o Ebenezer C d 23 Oct 1848 ae 26
    Frances M d 24 Sept 1848 ae 4y 2m
    Henry C d 11 Aug 1848 ae 1y 9m
SAWYER, Mary d/o AJ & HWC d 26 Aug 1853 ae 10wk 5d
    Wilbur F d 22 Oct 1899 ae 63y 6m
    Abbie G Smith w/o Wilbur d 6 Apr 1918 ae 72y 8m
    Augustus J d 27 Dec 1881 ae 65y 8m 13d
    Hannah Coolidge w/o AJ d 5 July 1882 ae 59y 3m 21d
HOSMER, Samuel d 10 Sept 1884 ae 75y 6m 23d

Sally B w/o Samuel d 4 June 1878 ae 60y 7m 11d
Sylvanus G s/o Samuel & Sally d 13 Nov 1845 ae 3y 5m
Myra E H 1850-1916
DICKENSON, Samuel d 29 Nov 1841 ae 88  SAR
Lois w/o Samuel d 23 Sept 1829 ae 74
Lois Emeline d 14 Dec 1859 ae 30y 7m 18d
Samuel W d 5 Feb 1901 ae 77
Lizzie J d 8 June 1872 ae 27y 6m 4d
Lois d 22 June 1878 ae 9y 14d
Henrietta H d 11 Jan 1840 ae 7y 10m twin
Harriot C d 25 Jan 1845 ae 10y 10m twin
---- Inf/s/o Willard & Lois d 2 Mar 1834
Sally Gibson d 17 Mar 1832 ae 54
Damaris d Oct 1784 ae 3y 3m
Willard d 26 Dec 1851 ae 65
Lois w/o Willard d 11 Aug 1875 ae 77y 7m
WHITNEY, Wetherbee d 14 Oct 1775 ae 29y 5m
WARNER, Aaron d 12 Feb 1777 ae 25y 7m
Sarah d/o Samuel & Hannah d 6 Mar 1777 in 65y
Dorothy w/o Nathan d 31 Mar 1777 in 65y
Nathan d 9 Jan 1792 in 82y
ROBINS, Peter s/o Jacob & Anna d 20 Mar 1776 ae 5y
Susannah d/o Jacob & Anna d 12 Mar 1776 ae 3y 3m 5d
Ephraim Whitcomb s/o Jacob & Anna d 25 Mar 1776 ae 13m 5d
Jacob d 25 Nov ---- in 50 y -- Lt
Anna w/o Lt Jacob d 4 June 1816 in 84y
Augustus MD 17 Oct 1805 - 13 Sept 1855
Juliana W w/o Augustus 21 Sept 1803 - 23 Oct 1888
Olive S 6 July 1839 - 15 Feb 1915
Olive w/o Jacob d 13 Aug 1853 ae 84y
WILLARD, Alonzo 8 July 1824 - 29 Aug
Sarah Esther 22 Aug 1831 - 6 Jan 1891
Adelle Gerry s/o 10 May 1855 - 21 Nov 1887 SISTER
Carrie Ellsworth 2 May 1861 - 18 June 1885
HOUGHTON, Jerusia K d/o Levi & Anna d 3 Oct 1830 ae 2y 5m 10d
WARNER, Lovisa w/o Luke d 23 Nov 1844 ae 46
Luke d 12 June 1838 ae 42y 7m
Albert d 24 Oct 1854 ae 26y 8m
Zerviah d/o Calvin & Anna d 30 June 1817 ae 18y 7m 25d
WOOD, Maranda w/o Emory d 5 Feb 1838 ae 29
Emory d 11 Nov 1868 ae 65y 4m 13d
Mary E w/o Emory d 17 Mar 1880 ae 70y 4m 11d
WILLARD, Christopher d 21 Nov 1910 ae 91y
REED, Charles F d 28 Mar 1879 ae 33y 2m 4d
Etta H w/o Charles F d/o CL & MH Willard d 29 Oct 1876
ae 26y 17d
WILLARD, Dorcasina d/o CL & MH d 21 Feb 1861 ae 6y 10m 25d
Andrew L s/o CL & MH d 21 Aug 1850 ae 16m 11d
ROBBINS, Henry d 13 Feb 1877 ae 65y 11m
Sally M w/o Henry d 10 Oct 1867 ae 55
John d 19 Aug 1837 ae 61

Lucy Whitney w/o John d 7 Oct 1867 ae 85
Lucy d 22 Sept 1808 ae 3y 4m
Martha d 28 Sept 1800 ae 1y 7m
HOSMER, Eli d 11 Feb 1876 ae 81
Olive R w/o Eli d 30 May 1835 ae 36
Lucy w/o Eli d 6 Mar 1909 ae 99y 11m 24d
Eli W d 4 July 1913 ae 77y
S Augusta d 16 Feb 1943 ae 95y 8m 11d
WHITNEY, Simon d 1 Oct 1818 ae 48 -- Capt
Mary w/o Capt Simon d 26 May 1840 ae 68
MEEDS, Lydia Priest d/o Reuben & Lydia d 16 Oct 1824 ae 13y 8m
FROST, Lydia Farmer w/o Reuben Meed d 6 Mar 1858 ae 75
MEED, Reuben d 2 Mar 1815 ae 32
RANDAL, Sarah d/o Stephen & Sarah d 21 Mar 1776 ae 3y 14d
David s/o Stephen & Sarah d 18 Mar 1776 ae 5y 29d
FAIRBANK, Lydia d/o Phinehas & Sarah d 1 Oct 1782 in 22y
DICKINSON, Mary w/o Francis d 13 Apr 1796 ae 40y 3m 6d
Mary w/o Francis d 27 Jan 1820 in 65y
Francis 20 Sept 1746 - 18 Feb 1825
BROWN, Mary w/o Stephen B d/o Francis & Mary Dickenson
d 15 Mar 1843 ae 44
WILLARD, Julia A d 13 Aug 1901 ae 74y 3m
Susan M d 12 Dec 1912 ae 80y 5m
Mary J d 10 May 1886 ae 56y 3m
Ebenezer d 4 Jan 1878 ae 86y 9m -- Capt
Susan w/o Ebenezer d 29 Feb 1876 ae 84y 11m
Charles A s/o Ebenezer & Susan d 17 Mar 1815 ae 5m
GREEN, Andrew Fairbank d 31 Dec 1899 ae 76
-- A w/o Andrew d 31 Jan 1890 ae 59
Warren H 1852-1915
Catherine A w/o Warren H 1856-1933
Ethel A d/o Warren & Kitte d 1 Mar 1892 ae 14y 6m 15d
HARROD, James d 3 Jan 1905 ae 75y 15d
Mary R w/o James d 19 Aug 1886 ae 48y 7m 15d
READ, Abigail d 16 Nov 1821 ae 61y 6m 27d
WOOD, Lucy d/o Eliphalet & Abigail d 5 Nov 1800 ae 32y 4m 11d
Abigail w/o Eliphalet d 25 Jan 1780 in 48y
Eliphalet d 16 Apr 1817 ae 87y 8m 17d
Mary w/o Eliphalet d 15 Jan 1829 ae 86
FORBUSH, John D 31 Jan 1838 ae 74y
HARROD, James 1829-1905
Mary E w/o John 1838-1886
OAKS, Lavinia d 6 July 1880
SANDERSON, Isaac d 17 Feb 1835 ae 57y
Eunice w/o Isaac d 8 Dec 1860 ae 75y 7m
PRIEST, Rhoda d 16 Aug 1880
CHAPMAN, Lucy d 13 Feb 1882
CALLAHAN, Michael d 30 Mar 1880
TURNER, Washington d 14 Feb 1890
BUTTRICK, William d 20 Mar 1844 ae 52y -- Col
NURSE, Stillman d 11 Oct 1853 ae 52y 6m

ELLIS, Joseph S Rev d 19 June 1842 ae 30y
WOOD, Nabby w/o Jabez d 6 June 1865 ae 86y 6m
   Jabez d 16 Mar 1850 ae 75
   Fanny d/o Jonathan & Caroline d 7 Jan 1860 ae 1y 24d
   Jonathan d 8 June 1880 ae 64y 8m
   Caroline w/o Jonathan d 10 Aug 1889 ae 64y 9d
   Maria d/o Jonathan & Caroline d 3 July 1884 ae 34y 8m
WORCESTER, Sally w/o Job d 22 Feb 1849 ae 63
FULLER, Newell d 18 Apr 1863 ae 68y 2m
   Rebecca Jane d 1 Sept 1847 ae 1y 28d
   Harriet Newell d 7 Sept 1847 ae 5y 3m
COOK, Hannah 20 Jan 1775 – 7 Dec 1846
   Roger 20 Dec 1781 – 10 Mar 1855
BULL, Eliza M d/o Merrit & Hannah 20 Sept 1802 – 11 Oct 1846
   Sidney H 18 Feb 1806 – 7 Aug 1889
   Louisa H w/o Sidney 10 Nov 1806 – 18 Dec 1844
   Mercy Sawyer w/o Sidney 6 June 1812 – 5 June 1901
   Abbie L d/o Sidney & Mercy S 2 May 1854 – 10 Nov 1870
TAYLOR, Lucy Jane d/o William & Mary d 12 Nov 1845 ae 19
   Mary W w/o William d 11 Mar 1882 ae 80y 9m
   William d 29 Aug 1890 ae 90y 8m
DUDLEY, Silas
   Stilman s/o Silas d 27 May 1858 ae 32y 6m
   Charlotte W w/o Silas d 23 Nov 1894 ae 88y 10m 17d
   Martha L d/o Silas & Charlotte d 7 Nov 1845 ae 1y 5m
HYNES, Franklyn M 1883–1925
   Christie Sawyer w/o Franklyn
KENNY, Mary F d 10 Mar 1964 ae 46y 9m
FORBUSH, Alice d 17 July 1862 ae 79y 23d
   John d 1 Sept 1849 ae 68
WHITNEY, Mercy d 3 Aug 1851 ae 49
   Marshall d 22 July 1882 ae 73
   Caroline W w/o Marshall d 16 Sept 1846 ae 34
   Charles H s/o Marshall & Caroline d 31 Aug 1846 ae 1y 10m
   Henry B s/o Marshall & Maria S d 19 Oct 1861 ae 22d
   Maria S d 7 Mar 1899 ae 75
   John Marshall MD d 16 Aug 1864 ae 22y 48d
   Simri d 19 Sept 1870 ae 75
   Adeline w/o Simri d 8 Jan 1892 ae 79
   George B d 22 July 1851 ae 16y 7m
   Adeline P d 13 Aug 1859 ae 17y 8m
   Reuben F d 11 Dec 1845 ae 2y 3m
   Reuben Dea d 1 Jan 1868 ae 84
   Milly w/o Dea Reuben d 17 Dec 1876 ae 92y 7m
HARROD George 1835–1907
   Ann Maria w/o George 1935–1917
   Charles E 1862–1865
WITHINGTON, Josiah 1819–1910
   Isabelle w/o Josiah 1819–1901
   Sarah Jane d/o Josiah & Isabelle 1847–1850
   Samuel 1797–1888

Belinda 1792–1879
WILLIS, Daniel d 24 Jan 1865 ae 59
  Maria Whitney w/o Daniel d 20 Feb 1896 ae 88
  Abbie H d 11 Aug 1847 ae 1y
  Josephine R d 10 June 1853 ae 2y
  Albert E d 27 Aug 1855 ae 19y
  George W d 12 Sept 1862 ae 18 in Military Hospital  CW
  Victoria A d 24 Apr 1923 ae 73
  Marilla E d 21 July 1929 ae 87
HAPGOOD, Charles Butler 21 Aug 1858 – 27 Apr 1943
  Fannie Augusta Foster w/o Charles B 20 Dec 1860 – 2 Aug 1902
  Warren E 15 Nov 1881 – 21 Mar 1907
HASKELL, Sarah d 26 June 1874 ae 96
  Eliza d 5 Dec 1843 ae 41
  Emma Josephine d/o George & Catherine d 23 Sept 1863 ae 15y
  Eugene Ormond s/o George & Catherine d 7 Sept 1846 ae 2m
WETHERBEE, Katrina d/o Sylvanus & Lucy H d 14 July 1847 ae 2m
  Sylvanus 4 Oct 1804 – 3 Nov 1855
  Lucy w/o Sylvanus 12 June 1805 – 27 Mar 1883
PRIEST, Philemon d 10 Apr 1860 ae 74
  Ann P d 22 Oct 1861 ae 78
  Ellen E d/o Philemon Jr & Eliza d 24 July 1847 ae 2y 24d
  Philemon d 3 July 1885 ae 69y 5m
  Eliza S w/o Philemon d 1 Feb 1899 ae 82y 7m
SAVAGE, Frederick S 1858-----
  Susan J Clark w/o Philemon 1860–1944
  Walter W 1887–1889
  Harold G 1899–1900
NORCROSS, Alma d/o HN & MA d 23 Oct 1884 ae 8m
HAPGOOD, Jonathan Fairbank 15 Jan 1814 – 29 Aug 1878
  Susan Wetherbee w/o Jonathan 26 Nov 1822 – 28 Feb 1842
  Dolly Mosman w/o Jonathan 29 Sept 1822 – 4 Jan 1894
  Theodore Goldsmith 1850–1851
  Hiram 1848–1861
  Martha Ann 1862–1862
  Mary Elizabeth 1853–1869
  Sarah Mosman 1852–1870
  Theodore Goldsmith 1860–1883
FARWELL, Andrew d 11 June 1873 ae 58y 7m 9d
  Mary R Fisher w/o Andrew d 6 July 1912 ae 87y 11m 17d
  Alice E d 30 Dec 1854 ae 1y 6d
  Harriet N d 23 Mar 1926 ae 69y
PARKER, Harriet F w/o William A d 20 Feb 1870 ae 37y 8m 8d
HILL, John d 26 Apr 1835 ae 49y 6m
  Betsy w/o John d 21 Mar 1839 ae 49y 1m
PARKER, William A 1832–1904
  Emma J Weld w/o William 1849–1926
  Ethel 1885-----
WILDER, Charlotte w/o George d/o Dr Samuel & Seraphinia
      Young d 6 Feb 1840 ae 26
  Seraphinia d/o George & Charlotte d 6 Feb 1840 ae 7y

YOUNG, Samuel s/o Dr Samuel & Seraphinia d 23 Oct 1832 ae
    21y 7m
  Samuel MD d 30 Mar 1845 ae 63y 7m FATHER
  Seraphinia w/o Samuel d 29 Dec 1871 ae 85y 9m MOTHER
JOY, Hiram d 5 Jan 1882 ae 78
  Seraphinia P d 28 Feb 1882 ae 72y 5m 22d
WHITNEY, James L d 29 Aug 1882 ae 65y 6m 27d
  Elizabeth w/o JL d 10 June 1863 ae 44y 11m 10d
  Ann w/o JL d 22 Aug 1913 ae 81y 11m 1d
  Richard Dea d 1 Oct 1865 ae 81y 6m
  Sally w/o Dea Richard d 19 July 1875 ae 88y 9m
  Susan d/o Dea Richard & Sally d 7 Jan 1810 ae 1y 9d
PRIEST, Milly d/o Dea Richard & Sally Whitney d 8 Feb 1846 ae 23
WHITNEY, Hiram d 6 July 1879 ae 64y 3m 25d
  Sophia A w/o Hiram d 9 Nov 1859 ae 42y 3m 9d
  Martha A w/o Hiram d 14 Feb 1884 ae 53y 1m 28d
  Susia L d/o JL & A d 11 Oct 1867 ae 4m 22d
BARNARD, Levi d 31 Jan 1883 ae 82y 3m
  Charlotte w/o Levi d 13 Nov 1889 ae 89y 5m
  Elizabeth w/o Charles P d 22 Jan 1892 ae 56
  Charlotte E w/o Charles P d 30 Mar 1853 ae 21y 6m
DAVIS, H Fessenden 14 July 1827 - 11 July 1903
  Hulda P w/o HF 22 Jan 1831 - 13 Dec 1903
WRIGHT, Eliza A W w/o John R d 7 Mar 1852 ae 24y
BARNARD, Ephraim d 11 Apr 1883 ae 78y 23d
  Dorothy F w/o Ephraim d 30 July 1854 ae 50y 7m
  Augustus E s/o Ephraim & Dorothy d 26 June 1853 ae 20y 7m
  Waldo G s/o Ephraim & Dorothy d 19 Oct 1870 ae 22y 10m 8d
WHITCOMB, Vandola E d 16 Aug 1906 ae 76y 6m 25d
  Emeline Barnard w/o Vandola 1835-1922
BARNARD, Our baby Alice d 16 June 1868 ae 11m
  Antoinette d -- --- ---- ae 71y 9m
  Luther A 17 Nov 1867 ae 29
TAYLOR, John H d 21 Aug 1875 ae 33
  Ella A d 17 July 1881 ae 29y 21d
OLWELL, Mary P 1860-1930
  Martha L Taylor w/o Philip 1839-1926
CHILDS, Ames F s/o Noah & Ann d 8 Dec 1829 ae 9wk 2d
CILLEY, John Emery s/o John B & Mercy A d 24 May 1842 ae 5y 3m
  Josephine d/o John B & Mercy A d 1 Dec 1844 ae 14wk
TAYLOR, William d 20 Sept 1860 ae 81y 7m 10d
  ---- d 26 May 1870 ae 89y 7m (illegible)
  Zopher 9 Mar 1810 - 12 June 1897
  Eunice w/o Zopher 29 Oct 1819 - 22 Sept 1901
  Maria w/o Zopher d 12 June 1845
  Ellen Elizabeth d/o Zopher & Eunice d 4 Sept 1848 ae 16m 28d
  Maria Nourse d 6 Aug 1854 ae 21y
GERRY, John d 20 Oct 1856 ae 50y 7m
  Sally Knight w/o John d 6 Apr 1904 ae 91y 4d
WILLARD, Warren O 1840-1923
  Helen M Gerry w/o Waren O 1855-1910

GERRY, Sarah Elizabeth d/o John & Sally d 26 Mar 1852 ae 19y 1m
CHASE, George H 1837-1913
   Adeline Gerry w/o George H 1837-1909
   Walter ---------
   Paul d 9 Dec 1868 ae 3d
   Parker d 4 Oct 1870 ae 6m
   Annie d 15 June 1875 ae 8m
SAVAGE, William H 1831-1916 Co G 1st US Artillery  CW
   Annie W Thacher w/o William d 15 July 1892 ae 57y
   Charles T d 5 Nov 1879 ae 83 -- Capt
BROWN, Reuben 1808-1876  -- Capt
   Clarissa P Shannon w/o Reuben 1805-1886
   Reuben F 1836-1839
   William H 1840-1856
   Mary Brown Houghton 1844-1903
   Ellen Brown Winde 1838-1918
HOLMAN, Silas W d 18 Dec 1855 ae 41
   Nancy T w/o Silas W d 11 Mar 1853 ae 41y
   Charlotte Louisa d/o Silas & Nancy d 19 Feb 1852 ae 3y 5m
   Charlotte Louisa d/o Silas & Nancy d 16 Sept 1849 ae 4y 5m
   Jonas s/o Emory & Lucy d 16 May 1843 ae 19
   Roxana d 23 Nov 1846 ae 28
BARNARD, John 1846-1921
   Maud 1870-1871
WOODWARD, Esther MD d/o John 1874-1962
PECKHAM, Horace L 1827-1895
   Betsy Houghton w/o Horace 1827-1858
   Chandler Adams 1861-1863
   Horace Lyman 1865-1883
HOUGHTON, Samuel W d 26 July 1870 ae 48y 6m 4d
   Harriet A w/o Samuel W d 3 Mar 1875 ae 50y 10d
   Ida d/o Samuel & Harriet d 14 Dec 1872 ae 16y 1m 12d
   Elizabeth Violetta d/o Samuel & Harriet d 22 Oct 1851 ae 13m
   Ellen Maria d/o Daniel P & Lucy M d 28 June 1871 ae 15y
   Daniel P d 20 Oct 1866 ae 46
   Abby G w/o Daniel P d 16 July 1845 ae 22
   Mary Carrie d/o Charles W & Sally d 3 Mar 1861 ae 6y 2m
   Francis A d 5 May 1915 ae 70y 11m
   Charles W d 7 Mar 1895 ae 78y 4m
   Sally H w/o Charles W d 23 Jan 1877 ae 54y 3m
   Mary w/o Daniel P d 8 Jan 1853 ae 30
   Mary Ellen d/o Daniel P & Mary d 19 Jan 1854 ae 3y 7m
   Daniel d 7 Jan 1866 ae 76
   Betsy Wetherbee w/o Daniel d 31 Oct 1887 ae 91y 11m 21d
DICKSON, Walter E d 20 July 1872 ae 41y 7d  CW
   Catherine Houghton w/o WE d 30 Nov 1917 ae 87y 6m 15d
   George H d 11 Oct 1861 ae 1y 10m 11d
   Susan E d 1 Mar 1863 ae 1y 5d
   Sarah E d 14 Sept 1872 ae 3m 28d
CARR, Lyman d 7 Oct 1880 ae 82y 4m
   Lucy w/o Lyman d 15 Sept 1844 ae 47

LAWRENCE, Jonathan 21 May 1809 – 22 May 1889
   Sarah A Williston w/o Jonathan d 2 Dec 1901
   Katherine L 1846–1935
   Lucinda Maria -- --- ---- ae 1y 6m
   Charles Allen -- --- ---- ae 7y 3m
HARDY, Carrie w/o ES d 25 Jan 1885 ae 31y 11d MOTHER
LAWRENCE, Rollin H s/o CH & SS d 5 Sept 1853 ae 1y 1m 21d
   Abbott s/o CH & SS d 19 Apr 1860 ae 10y 6m 19d
   Susie J d/o CH & SS d 22 Sept 1864 ae 4y 11m 1d
   Horace R s/o CH & SS d 18 Oct 1864 ae 9y 4m 7d
   Horace A 17 July 1866 – 24 Nov 1884
FAIRBANKS, John O 8 Mar 1868 –23 Dec 1887 BROTHER
   Addison 1829–1908
   Emeline Talmage w/o Addison 1836–1874
   Emma Della 30 Jan 1874 – 19 Oct 1874
LAWRENCE, Rhoda Wood w/o Abraham d 15 Apr 1872 ae 88y
   Oliver W d 27 Nov 1815 ae 1y
   George E d 13 Apr 1831 ae 7y
   Bradley V d 23 Mar 1831 ae 5y
   Abraham d 26 Aug 1863 ae 81
BALDWIN, William CW
HARTONE, Harry
SAUNDERS, Washington d 23 Feb 1900
PECKHAM, Samuel H 1837–1916
   Honora Hayden w/o Samuel 1836–1902
   Alfred N s/o Samuel & Honora d 11 Mar 1865 ae 1d
   Nellie O d/o Samuel & Honora d 5 May 1871 ae 7m 17d
HAYDEN, Warren d 25 June ae 51y
   Sarah w/o Warren d 15 Aug 1856 ae 41
CRAGGS, James 5 May 1839 – 19 Feb 1902   FATHER
   Elizabeth E w/o James 16 June 1851 – 17 July 1899
   Mary Ann d 28 Dec 1901 ae 65y
   John R d 3 Feb 1903 ae 14y 7wk
FREEMAN, Nathan B d 17 Oct 1879 ae 76y 3m  FATHER
   Jane A d 4 Jan 1888 ae 70
   Mary Jane d/o NB & JA d 18 Nov 1855 ae 10m 5d
   George F d 24 Feb 1854 ae 4y 5-1/2m
   Frank G d 22 Feb 1854 ae 3y
FOSTER, John W 1863–1882
   Thomas R 1868–1902
   Albert E 1874–1889
   Henry -- --- 1826
   Catherine L w/o Henry 1838–1889
   Maria L 1862–1878
   Emma J 1866–1866
LAWRENCE, Laura Ann d/o Andrew & Laura Ann ae 9y 3m
   Lewis D s/o Andrew & Laura Ann d 28 June 1854 ae 19m
CROUCH, George 20 Oct 1810 – 1 Apr 1884
   Lucinda E w/o George 22 Feb 1818 – 9 Aug 1906
NOYT, Jennie M d 17 Mar 1909
WEBB, James A 1 Feb 1834 – 9 Oct 1901

JONES, James d 5 May 1889 ae 78
   Samantha w/o James d 9 Oct 1859 ae 49
HARDY, Emerson G d 16 Nov 1870 ae 67
   Eliza B w/o Emerson d 17 Jan 1877 ae 71y 6m 13d
   Charles O d 21 Mar 1866 ae 23  CW
   Sarah E d/o Emerson & Eliza d 30 Sept 1877 ae 46y 10m 15d
   Albert E d 13 Dec 1910 ae 66y 1m 14d  CW
   Sarah W w/o Albert d 10 Mar 1875 ae 26y 5m
HARTSHORN, Stephen M 1824-1904
   Fanny E 1840-1923
   Nellie T 1860-1932
HOUGHTON, Samuel M 14 Sept 1854 - 17 June 1918
   Carrie w/o S Herbert d/o S & MA Fletcher d 10 Feb 1882
      ae 19y 10m
FLETCHER, Annie M adpt d/o Martha Fletcher Feb 1882 - Aug 1900
   Bertie s/o Albert d 2 Sept 1870 ae 7m 25d
   Martha Wright d 14 Sept 1916 ae 81y 9m 18d
   Samson d 5 Apr 1884 ae 54y 5m 12d
PATCH, John W 1822-1856
   Mary Haskell w/o John 1823-1904
   John W 1847-1913
   Abbie S Rahn w/o John 1851-1919
   Albert B 1850-1881
   Clarence M 1876-1901
WHITNEY, Francis W d 24 Aug 1825 ae 17y 6m
   Phinehas s/o Isaiah & Lydia d 4 Oct 1810 ae 17m
   Hannah d/o Isaiah & Lydia d 8 Feb 1812 ae 3m
BOWLES, Josiah d 29 Mar 1799 in 22y
BLOOD, Frankey C s/o Charles & Harriet d 18 Sept 1859 ae 2m 23d
STONE, William MD d 20 May 1842 ae 59y
   Hannah w/o William d 4 Dec 1845 ae 58y
   Eliza d/o Hannah & William d 4 Aug 1843 ae 11y 8m
   Elisha D d 13 Jan 1904 ae 75y 10m 13d
   Sophia w/o Elisha d 22 Sept 1912 ae 84y 9m 19d
   Agnes M d/o ED & Sophia d 8 Sept 1857 ae 9m
   Joseph C d 11 Jan 1886 ae 60y
   Emeline E w/o Joseph C d 7 July 1896 ae 70y
   Louis C s/o JC & EE d 17 Apr 1889 ae 24y
WILLARD, Mary G 1835-1902
   Arabella 1838-1901
ROYAL, Herbert B MD 24 Sept 1863 - 14 Sept 1949 Graduated
      Bowdoin; for 60 years practicing physician in Harvard
PECKHAM, Samuel H 1837-1916
PRIEST, J Rogene 1880-1947
   Francis W d 24 Aug 1825 ae 17y 6m


## THE TOMBS


Tomb #1 - DABY
   Asa d 14 Feb 1887 ae 89y 5m

Lurenia d 14 July 1837 ae 35
Abbie d 5 May 1846 ae 39
Adeline d 16 Sept 1831 ae 25
Lucy H d 7 Apr 1869 ae 62
Ethan d 2 Feb 1876 ae 76y 11m

Tomb #2 - HERSEY
  Thomas d 10 May 1839 ae 70
  Hannah w/o Thomas d 30 Dec 1858 ae 83
  ---- d 5 Oct 1858 ae 62

- NASON
  Maria d/o Seth & Nancy d 13 Aug 1821 ae 4y
  Seth d 17 Jan 1862 ae 90y 2m 15d
  Nancy w/o Seth d 22 Jan 1862 ae 81y 2m 15d

Tomb #3 - PRIEST
  Jabez d -- --- 1844

- FAIRBANK
  John d -- --- 1828

Tomb #4 - HASKELL

Tomb #5 - NOURSE
  David d 5 Sept 1827 ae 65
  Lois Brown w/o David d 22 Oct 1852 ae 84
  James R ?2? 29 Dec 1888 ae 93y 2m 19d
  Lucy Forbush w/o James R d 18 Nov 1832 ae 23
  John d 1 Jan 1833 ae 26y 8m 5d
  Harry d 5 May 1838 ae 29y 6m
  Mary Ann w/o John Whitney d 11 June 1851 ae 37y 4m 9d
  David Jr d 16 June 1878 ae 79y 5m 24d

Tomb #6 - WHITCOMB
  John Post d 1 Nov 1815 ae 62y
  Hannah d 23 Oct 1827 ae 75y
  Reuben d 16 Apr 1863 ae 94
  Mercy d 1 Feb 1849 ae 74
  John P d 21 Apr 1847 ae 50
  Louisa D d 13 Aug 1862 ae 57
  Reuben Jr d 18 Apr 1861 ae 58
  Abby F d 15 Feb 1880 ae 16
  Son s/o R & AF d 29 Aug 1832 ae 3d

Tomb #7 - HOUGHTON
  Betsy W d 27 Feb 1860 ae 93y 11m
  Mercy W French d 4 Oct 1874 ae 7y 8m
  Cephas d 13 Aug 1881 ae 89
  Sarah W d 18 June 1882 ae 85y 4m
  Sarah E d 20 Mar 1840 ae 20y

George Emery drowned 17 May 1824 ae 1y 6m

Tomb #8 – Unmarked

## SHAKER CEMETERY

Copied by Elvira L. Scorgie.

ROW 1 (right rear)

| | | |
|---|---|---|
| BABBIT, Polly | d 12 May 1868 | ae 68 |
| RAYMOND, Elizabeth D | d 6 Jan 1867 | |
| MITCHELL, Eliza | d 3 July 1856 | ae 28 |
| MAYO, Anna D | d 22 June 1858 | ae 79 |
| CHURCH, Sarah A | d 26 Dec 1854 | ae 32 |
| COLBURN, Mary F | d 2 Mar 1853 | ae 17 |
| HAMLIN, Rebecca | d 29 May 1854 | ae 55 |

Interred here in 1844 when bones were discovered when the cart house was moved:

| | |
|---|---|
| KEEP, Phebe | d 25 Aug 1783 |
| WORSTER, Mary | d 1 May 1790 |
| COOPER, Eleanor | d Oct 1790 |
| WILLIAMS, Hannah | d Oct 1790 |

| | | |
|---|---|---|
| WINCHESTER, Elhanan | d 20 Sept 1810 | ae 90 |
| WOOD, Rachel | d 4 June 1810 | ae 75 |
| WILLIAMS, Elizabeth | d 19 May 1809 | ae 67 |
| COOPER, Sarah | d 9 April 1807 | ae 92 |
| GRACE, Sarah | d 28 Jan 1806 | ae 24 |
| COOPER, Francis | d 27 Nov 1805 | ae 51 |
| SHATTUCK, Thomas | d 27 Jan 1803 | ae 77 |
| SHATTUCK, Elizabeth | d 7 Oct 1798 | ae 72 |
| WILLIAMS, Hannah | d 10 July 1798 | ae 12 |
| MIXTER, Elizabeth | d 25 Dec 1797 | ae 56 |
| POWERS, Miriam | d 23 July 1796 | ae 74 |
| ADAMS, Rachel | d 21 June 1796 | ae 70 |
| BEMIS, Sarah | d 26 May 1795 | ae 75 |
| KEEP, Ruth | d 19 Apr 1794 | ae 23 |
| LATHE, Eunice | d 27 Jan 1794 | ae 60 |
| CROUCH, David | d 20 July 1793 | ae 68 |

ROW 2

| | | |
|---|---|---|
| FAIRBANKS, Nancy S | d 28 Feb 1880 | ae 72 |
| SARGENT, Sarah | d 18 Jan 1876 | ae 88 |
| FOSGATE, Mary | d 28 Sept 1871 | ae 80 |
| BLANCHARD, Asenath | d 21 Sept 1871 | ae 65 |
| REUSE, Lissie | d 6 Dec 1884 | ae 39 |

| | | |
|---|---|---|
| CARR, Evangeline | d 7 Dec 1854 | ae 2 |
| DUNHAM, Elizabeth | d 19 Oct 1854 | ae 90 |
| COOPER, Abigail | d 23 Aug 1816 | ae 90 |
| WILLIAMS, Deborah | d 8 Dec 1815 | ae 66 |
| TURNER, Ezra | d 3 Nov 1815 | ae 76 |
| CLARK, Mercy | d 23 Oct 1815 | ae 81 |
| DABY, Susannah | d 11 Feb 1815 | ae 66 |
| CROUCH, Mary | d 14 Dec 1814 | ae 89 |
| STANHOPE, Abigail | d 23 Aug 1814 | ae 65 |
| | | |
| JEWETT, Mary | d 17 Aug 1814 | ae 71 |
| PRESCOTT, Bethia | d 6 Oct 1813 | ae 84 |
| CROUCH, Elizabeth | d 7 Oct 1813 | ae 62 |
| PHINNEY, Elizabeth | d 19 Sept 1813 | ae 89 |
| BABBITT, Abigail | d 21 June 1813 | ae 89 |
| CLARK, Lucy | d 13 Mar ---- | ae 43 |
| DWINELL, David | d 19 Jan 1812 | ae 70 |
| LATHE, Ezra | d 8 Feb 1807 | ae 67 |
| STEVENS, John | d 28 Jan 1807 | ae 80 |
| BABBIT, Abiather | d 16 Nov 1806 | ae 90 |

ROW 3

| | | |
|---|---|---|
| TEMPLE, Abigail | d 24 June 1866 | ae 72 |
| EDSON, Relief | d 16 Jan 1866 | ae 96 |
| ATHERTON, Sylvia | d 1 Jan 1866 | ae 65 |
| ALDEN, Sophronia | d 12 Nov 1864 | ae 75 |
| HALL, Hannah | d 1 Feb 1864 | ae 63 |
| ROBBINS, Sally | d 10 Sept 1819 | ae 15 |
| ROBBINS, Sarah A | d 31 Dec 18 | |
| KNOWLES, Lucy | d 16 Feb 1853 | |
| ROBBINS, Ruth | d 8 Feb 1853 | ae 79 |
| PRATT, Sarah | d 2 Aug 1852 | ae 57 |
| JONES, Sarah Elizabeth H | d 26 Aug 1851 | ae 53 |
| MASON, Sarah | d 9 Mar 1851 | ae 84 |
| EDSON, Polly | d 8 Mar 1851 | ae 48 |
| BABBITT, Susan | d 25 May 1848 | |
| HANNUM, Sarah | d 3 July 1845 | ae 85 |
| WINCHESTER, Bathsheba | d 29 Sept 1841 | ae 66 |
| LYSCOM, Phebe | d 26 May 1837 | ae 38 |
| SPARROW, Mary | d 12 Nov 1837 | ae 17y 8m |
| ROBBINS, Rebecca | d 31 Aug 1834 | ae 86 |
| LATHE, Anna | d 25 May 1932 | ae 91 |
| CROUCH, Elizabeth | d 3 Apr 1832 | |
| BLOOD, Kezia | d 3 Mar 1832 | |
| PRATT, Cynthea | d 26 May 1830 | ae 31 |
| WYTHE, Eunice | d 16 Jan 1830 | ae 75 |
| KEEP, Phebe | d 22 July 1826 | ae 88 |
| DODGE, Delighteth | d 4 May 1826 | ae 11 |
| ROBBINS, Azana | d 8 Feb 1826 | ae 10 |
| BABBITT, Elizabeth | d 10 Aug 1825 | ae 69 |

| | | |
|---|---|---|
| HAMMOND, Mary | d 10 Dec 1824 | ae 79 |
| EDDY, Hannah | d 2 Jan 1823 | ae 78 |
| ALLEN, Abigail | d 20 Oct 1622 | ae 80 |
| STERNS, Ruth | d 15 Sept 1822 | ae 91 |
| JEWETT, Sarah | d 20 July 1822 | ae 66 |
| PERRY, Mary | d 22 Nov 1821 | ae 83 |
| CROUCH, Mehitable | d 16 Mar 1821 | ae 41 |
| WINCHESTER, Lydia | d 3 Feb 1820 | ae 86 |
| ROBINSON, Elizabeth | d 2 Oct 1819 | ae 79 |

ROW 4

| | | |
|---|---|---|
| GILLETTE, Lottie Tremper 1860 – 1929 | | |
| WALKER, Annie L | d 27 Apr 1912 ae 61y 7m 28d | |
| GROVER, Elizabeth E | 11 Sept 1826 – 20 Jan 1909 | |
| HATCH, Olive | 5 Sept 1808 – 11 Oct 1908 | |
| WALKER, Catherine | d 10 Sept 1894 ae 75y 9m 24d | |
| CARR, Martha Ann | d 23 Aug 1894 | ae 72 |
| HART, Harriet P | d 27 Nov 1891 | ae 57 |
| PRATT, Mahaleth | d 13 June 1891 | ae 80 |
| PRIEST, Charlotte | d 25 May 1891 | ae 90 |
| SEARS, Elizabeth | d 28 Apr 1890 | ae 91 |
| ROBBINS, Mary | d 7 July 1889 | ae 89 |
| GIDDINGS, Susan | d Apr 1887 | ae 85 |
| NILES, Sophia S | d 29 Apr 1887 | ae 62 |
| HALL, Betsy M | d 12 Jan 1884 | ae 61 |
| BATHRIC, Eunice | d 24 June 1884 | ae 89 |
| KENDALL, Susan G | d 9 May 1882 | ae 75 |
| HAMMOND, Lucy A | d 19 May 1881 | ae 83 |
| DERING, Marcy A P | d 9 Apr 1881 | |
| PARSONS, Ann E | d 3 Oct 1877 | ae 49 |
| LOCKE, Belle Florence | d 14 Oct | ae 21 |
| WHISKINS, William | d 10 Mar 1874 | ae 74 |
| FOSGATE, Luke | d 26 Nov 1875 | ae 86 |
| MYRICK, Jesse | d 10 Apr 1872 | ae 92 |
| RICH, Obediah | d 19 May 1870 | ae 70 |
| PARKHURST, Eliza E | d 4 Apr 1867 | ae 57 |
| ELLSWORTH, Henry | d 29 Oct 1866 | ae 57 |
| MARROW, Hugh | d 16 Oct 1841 | ae 37 |
| EDSON, Hiram | d 26 May 1837 | ae 27 |
| EDSON, Charles | d 7 May 1835 | ae 30 |
| OWEN, Samuel | d 17 Sept 1833 | ae 27 |
| GODDEN, Henry | d 18 Sept 1830 | ae 94 |
| EDSON, Hosea | d 5 Aug 1829 | ae 96 |
| WYETH, Joseph | d 13 Oct 1837 | ae 85 |
| ROBBINS, Silas | d 13 Mar 1825 | ae 79 |
| HAMMOND, Thomas Sr | d 28 Oct 1824 | ae 81 |
| MUNDAY, William | d 19 July 1822 | ae 84 |
| PERRY, John | d 20 Dec 1819 | ae 86 |
| ALDEN, Barzilla | d 9 Nov 1819 | ae 21 |

ROW 5

| | | |
|---|---|---|
| HILL, Mary R | d 7 Mar 1903 | ae 86 |
| BABBBIT, Eliza | d 21 Feb 1900 ae 92y 9m 14d | |
| FOSTER, Maria | d 9 Sept 1897 ae 75y 4m 26d | |
| NEWTON, Ezra B | d 23 Apr 1896 ae 101y 2m | |
| McGOODEN, Susannah | d 15 Apr 1890 | ae 95 |
| DAVIDSON, William | d 22 Aug 1891 | ae 77 |
| PERSONS, Matilda S | d 25 Feb 1890 | ae 88 |
| COOK, Henrietta | d 10 June 1889 | ae 59 |
| CHANDLER, Olive F | d 8 Mar 1887 | ae 93 |
| KELLEY, Mary A | d 7 Oct 1886 | ae 32 |
| CHANDLER, Mary | d 17 May 1885 | ae 79 |
| CLARK, Lucy G | d 1 July 1884 | ae 80 |
| CLOUTMAN, John | d 10 Sept 1883 | ae 75 |
| KNOWLES, Betsy | d 4 Oct 1882 | ae 80 |
| FLOYD, Mary | d 18 June 1880 | ae 29 |
| WHITING, Sarah | d 17 May 1880 | ae 75 |
| SPARROW, Martha H | d 11 Sept 1877 | ae 63 |
| MILLER, Emma | d 19 Dec 1875 | ae 11 |
| PERSONS, Elizabeth | d 8 Sept 1874 | ae 72 |
| MEEHAN, Sally | d 19 Apr 1874 | ae 75 |
| JONES, Robert | d 20 Oct 1866 | ae 79 |
| RICH, Isaac | d 14 May 1866 | ae 76 |
| GROSVENOR, Augustus H | d 9 Sept 1864 | ae 57 |
| PHELPS, Joshua | d 5 Mar 1864 | ae 69 |
| HURD, William | d 15 Feb 1861 | ae 28 |
| MANCHESTER, William H | d 18 May 1858 | ae 40 |
| YOUNG, Stephen | d 27 June 1856 | ae 41 |
| PARKER, Joseph | d 28 Nov 1854 | ae 49 |
| BABBITT, Henry S | d 7 Feb 1853 | ae 17 |
| BROWN, George W | d 29 Jan 1852 | ae 18 |
| TEMPLE, Silas | d 9 May 1852 | ae 77 |
| PATCH, David | d 19 Sept 1848 | ae 41 |
| WOODSOME, Luther | d 25 Apr 1846 | ae 33 |
| WINCHESTER, Benjamin | d 24 Aug 1845 | ae 85 |
| ROBBINS, Daniel M | d 5 Apr 1844 | ae 38 |
| BLOOD, Samuel | d 23 Jan 1844 | ae 94 |
| GROVER, William | d 19 Apr 1843 | ae 21 |

ROW 6

| | | |
|---|---|---|
| CROUCH, Martha | d 12 Jan 1875 | ae 66 |
| HAMMOND, Thomas | d 21 Nov 1880 | ae 89 |
| SWAZEY, Joseph | d 24 Mar 1877 | ae 59 |
| ORSMENT, John Jr | d 21 Mar 1877 | ae 76 |
| LEONARD, William | d 23 Jan 1877 | ae 74 |
| MYRICK, Daniel | d 30 June 1868 | ae 53 |
| SPARROW, Godfrey | d 29 Mar 1865 | ae 80 |
| MYRICK, Isaac | d 12 Sept 1859 | ae 70 |
| TENNY, Moses | d 31 Aug 1857 | ae 46 |

| | | |
|---|---|---|
| GROSVENOR, Ebenezer | d 18 Dec 1854 | ae 76 |
| ROBBINS, William | d 12 Feb 1853 | ae 17 |
| CHANDLER, Jonathan | d 11 Aug 1852 | ae 76 |
| MYRICK, Joseph M | d 14 Mar 1849 | ae 45 |
| ORSMENT, John Sr | d 14 Oct 1848 | ae 71 |
| KENDELL, Nathan | d 11 Mar 1845 | |
| CROUCH, Caleb | d 2 Jan 1841 | ae 73 |
| WORSTER, Abijah | d 10 Jan 1841 | ae 96 |
| ROBINSON, Oliver | d 29 Dec 1838 | ae 72 |
| MYRICK, Jesse | d 23 Nov 1837 | ae 27 |
| CROUCH, Jonathan | d 8 Feb 1837 | ae 79 |
| BRIDGES, Jonathan | d 23 May 1839 | ae 75 |
| HAMMOND, Bennjamin F | d 12 Oct 1828 | ae 25 |
| FROST, Joseph | d 18 Dec 1827 | ae 70 |
| DOLIVER, Timothy | d 17 July 1839 | ae 10 |
| KENDALL, William | d 8 Nov 1827 | ae 12 |
| BABBITT, Seth | d 25 Nov 1826 | ae 69 |
| THOMAS, George W | d 7 July 1825 | ae 19 |
| WARNER, Levi | d 29 June 1825 | ae 64 |
| ROBBINS, Thomas | d 10 Jan 1820 | ae 19 |
| BLANCHARD, Seth | d 26 Jan 1868 | ae 84 |

ROW 7

| | | |
|---|---|---|
| McLEAN, Almyra E | 1842 – 1923 | |
| GREEN, Ellen | d 20 Mar 1915 | ae 71 |
| GREEN, Louisa E | d 25 Aug 1914 | ae 90 |
| WOOD, Maria M | d 10 Mar 1914 | ae 95 |
| MAYER, Philip J | 22 Nov 1809 – 1 Dec 1898 | |
| BULLARD, Marcia M | d 7 May 1899 ae 76y 10m 26d | |
| HALL, Catherine | d 1 Dec 1890 | ae 77 |
| MYRICK, Elijah | d 9 Feb 1890 | ae 67 |
| ATHERTON, Simon T | d 7 Oct 1888 | ae 85 |
| OSGOOD, Abigail | d 9 Mar 1866 | ae 78 |
| MAYNARD, Betsey | d 8 Feb 1875 | ae 67 |
| BRIDGES, Hannah | d 13 Jan 1875 | ae 95 |
| CROUCH, Martha | d 12 Jan 1875 | ae 66 |
| JEFFERSON, Sarah | d 14 Nov 1874 | ae 18 |
| KELLEY, Charles N | d 2 Nov 1866 | ae 14 |
| WOOD, Charles H | d 30 Jan 1866 | ae 15 |
| HALL, William | d 25 Jan 1865 | ae 13 |
| TOMPKINS, Lemuel | d 2 May 1860 | ae 65 |
| CROUCH, Moses | d 30 Mar 1887 | ae 86 |
| MAYO, Joseph | d 20 Dec 1852 | ae 81 |
| MYRICK, Samuel H | d 5 Feb 1852 | ae 32 |
| COOPER, Solomon | d 24 Dec 1819 | ae 75 |
| WINCHESTER, Frederick | d 1 Oct 1818 | ae 17 |
| JEWETT, Aaron | d 6 Feb 1886 | ae 15 |
| JEWETT, Abel | d 9 Dec 1859 | ae 82y 9m |
| EDDY, Abiather | d 7 Feb 1816 | ae 70 |
| WARNER, Elijah | d 17 July 1814 | ae 51 |

| | | |
|---|---|---|
| FRIZZLE, Solomon | d 15 July 1814 | ae 58 |
| JEWETT, Daniel | d 26 Dec 1813 | ae 32 |
| FROST, Mary | d 30 Nov 1801 | ae 34 |
| DARNUM, Asa | d 2 Oct 1796 | ae 43 |
| KEEP, Elizabeth | d 13 Oct 1796 | ae 27 |
| WARNER, John | d 4 July 1834 | ae 76 |
| KENDALL, Mother Hannah | d 18 Aug 1816 | ae 55 |
| RAND, Eleazer | 9 Nov 1808 | ae 45 |
| TIFFANY, Daniel | d 25 Sept 1793 | ae 25 |
| BLANCHARD, Grove B | d 23 Apr 1880 | ae 82 |

ROW 8

| | | |
|---|---|---|
| NILANT, Nathaniel | d 7 Dec 1920 | ae 73 |
| McKNIGHT, Stephen | d 20 Apr 1914 | ae 84 |
| HALL, Helen H | d 12 June 1880 | ae 21 |
| CHANNEL, Susan L | d 5 May 1880 | ae 71 |
| KING, Caroline L | d 18 Nov 1878 | ae 78 |
| ORSMENT, Nancy | d 17 Apr 1874 | ae 71 |
| McINTOSH, Lucy | d 3 Oct 1872 | ae 90 |
| ROBBINS, Anna | d 1 May 1882 | ae 80 |
| KENDALL, Sarah | d 8 Feb 1852 | ae 93 |
| BLANCHARD, Abigail | d 25 July 1844 | ae 89 |
| DODGE, Sarah | d 7 May 1841 | ae 92 |
| HASKINS, Mary C | d 8 Oct 1840 | ae 36 |
| COOPER, Deliverance | d 9 Jan 1840 | ae 86 |
| DRAPER, Martha | d 17 Nov 1838 | ae 71 |
| ROBBINS, Sarah Ann | d 17 Sept 1838 | ae 21 |
| BARRETT, Sarah | d 1 Dec 1832 | ae 62 |
| WILLARD, Bethiah | d 17 Mar 1832 | ae 74 |
| LYSCOM, Sarah | d 29 Oct 1830 | ae 29 |
| FARR, Mary C | d 2 Nov 1828 | ae 47 |
| WHITTEMORE, Deliverance | d 12 Feb 1827 | ae 56 |
| CROUCH, Mary E | d 5 Apr 1826 | ae 63 |
| COX, Lydia | d 7 June 1825 | ae 58 |
| WINCHESTER, Elvira | d 11 May 1824 | ae 25 |
| ROBBINS, Sally | d 10 Sept 1818 | ae 15 |
| HILDRETH, Lucy | d 22 Aug 1814 | ae 26 |
| TRASK, Selah | d 9 Aug 1814 | ae 17 |
| KILBURN, Anna | d 6 June 1813 | ae 31 |
| KEEP, Sarah | d 27 Nov 1809 | ae 46 |
| KEEP, Rachel | d 5 Mar 1822 | ae 49 |
| BRIDGES, Persis | d 19 Oct 1803 | ae 24 |
| HAMMOND, Sarah | d 19 July 1848 | ae 84 |

ROW 9

| | | |
|---|---|---|
| BABBITT, Betty | d 22 May 1865 | ae 34 |
| CHANDLER, Desire | d 13 May 1865 | ae 92 |
| BLANCHARD, Olive | d 21 Dec 1863 | ae 81 |
| GROSVENOR, Mary | d 10 Dec 1863 | ae 77 |

| | | |
|---|---|---|
| BABBITT, Tabitha | d 10 Dec 1853 | ae 71 |
| BABBITT, Hannah | d 17 Oct 1852 | ae 86 |
| THOMAS, Sarah | d 31 Mar 1843 | ae 73 |
| LYON, Molly | d 27 Mar 1843 | ae 92 |
| HAYNES, Amanda | d 25 May 1840 | ae 26 |
| FLETCHER, Elizabeth | d 6 Nov 1839 | ae 84 |
| ORSMENT, Margaret | d 27 Jan 1839 | ae 25 |
| HAMMOND, Mary A | d 29 Sept 1838 | ae 43 |
| BABBITT, Abigail | d 3 Mar 1837 | ae 23 |
| JEWETT, Elizabeth | d 23 Sept 1838 | ae 82 |
| PERHAM, Dolly | d 23 Aug 1838 | ae 66 |
| COOPER, Bulah | d 22 June 1837 | ae 82 |
| ROBBINS, Sarah | d 7 Mar 1835 | ae 73 |
| CROUCH, Sarah | d 10 Dec 1833 | ae 83 |
| PROCTER, Rebecca | d 20 Nov 1833 | ae 68 |
| WINCHESTER, Polly | d 31 Mar 1825 | ae 14 |
| CAPEN, Harriet | d 20 Oct 1822 | ae 11 |
| CLARK, Hannah | d 20 Dec 1820 | ae 14 |
| WINCHESTER, Susan | d 23 May 1820 | ae 17 |
| CHANDLER, Rebecca | d 19 May 1820 | ae 13 |
| CHANDLER, Betsey | d 3 May 1820 | ae 11 |
| HILL, Roxalana | d 27 May 1871 | ae 82 |
| BRIDGES, Rachel | d 13 Mar 1819 | ae 61 |

ROW 10

| | | |
|---|---|---|
| BABBITT, Mary | d 25 Sept 1861 | ae 58 |
| WINCHESTER, Elizabeth | d 16 Feb 1861 | ae 81 |
| BABBITT, Anna | d 6 Feb 1861 | ae 88 |
| GOODING, Margaret | d 3 Aug 1860 | ae 43 |
| SPARROW, Betsy F | d 24 Feb 1880 | ae 32 |
| PARKHURST, Mary M | d19 Aug 1858 | ae 22 |
| MYRICK, Elizabeth | d 4 Aug 1855 | ae 71 |
| CHANNEL, Mary | d 24 June 1855 | ae 91y 9m |
| WILDS, Eunice | d 25 May 1855 | ae 83 |
| SHERER, Mary C | d 17 Feb 1855 | ae 8 |
| LOOMIS, Sally | d 29 Sept 1854 | ae 52 |
| WINCHESTER, Selah | d 20 May 1854 | ae 42 |
| ORSMENT, Anna | d 30 June 1851 | ae 69 |
| ADAMS, Elmira | d 23 Dec 1850 | ae 32 |
| MYRICK, Eliza | d 3 Feb 1850 | ae 44 |
| MYRICK, Susan K | d 18 Jan 1849 | ae 41 |
| BLANCHARD, Jemima | d 31 Dec 1847 | ae 89 |
| PRIEST, Charles F | d 9 Mar 1842 | ae 37 |
| FARRAR, Martha | d 19 July 1844 | ae 72 |
| HILL, Minerva | d 24 June 1844 | ae 32 |
| MYRICK, Lucy | d 19 May 1844 | ae 28 |
| CROUCH, Patience | d 29 Aug 1843 | ae 77 |
| BARRETT, Maria | d 22 June 1871 | ae 87 |
| MYRICK, Sally | d 18 June 1842 | ae 23 |

JEWETT Sarah          d 20 July 1822          ae 67
WHITON Henry L        d 26 June 1893

## JONATHAN AND REBECCA WORSTER

### by Elvira L. Scorgie

Jonathan Worster was born in Bradford 1 December 1707, the son of Ebenezer and Experience (Locke) Worster. The various Town clerks have at least five ways of spelling his surname, but Jonathan spelled it as above. The family moved to Littleton in 1723, where in the course of time he married Rebecca--the time, place, and maiden name of the bride is unknown. His first child, Mary, was born there 18 June 1732. The second child, Rebecca, is registered in Harvard as born in February 1733/34. She was baptized in Harvard 10 February 1733/34. It would seem, therefore, that Jonathan came to Harvard early in 1734 or before. The death of Mary, the first child, is not recorded either in Littleton or Harvard. From her gravestone we learn that she died 10 August 1734. Though her parents were living in Harvard, she is buried in the Old Burying Ground at Littleton Common.

As Jonathan had bought the quarrying rights of Pin Hill Quarry, all the stones in the Center Cemetery from 1734 to the time of his death in 1754 are the work of his hands or from his shop. With one exception the design is exactly the same on all stones--a pear-shaped death's head with little round circles for eyes, straight line for a nose, and two horizontal lines for a mouth. The oldest existing stone is that of Ephraim Stone, who died 16 June 1734 ae 18y 5m 14d. This may well be the first as well as the oldest stone. There had been several burials before this, but none of the graves now have markers, and their location is unknown. It is estimated that there are today over a hundred unmarked graves. There may be some significance in the fact that Ephraim's father was one of the most prominent men in the new Town. Simon Stone led the Groton contingent in the struggle for a new town, and was appointed by the General Court to call the first Town Meeting where he was chosen Moderator and voted Selectman. He was also deacon in the Church. He would have wanted his son to have a proper headstone.

Rebecca Worster was only thirty-seven years old when her husband died. She had borne him twelve children, six of whom had died in early childhood. Of the six still living, Moses, age fifteen, was the oldest. While he was then too young to take charge of the business, he was of great help to his mother when he was older. Nevertheless, she determined courageously to carry on assisted by her husband's apprentices and other employees. She did not of course go out herself with sledge hammer and wedge, but oversaw the work and kept the accounts. Ten year old Rebecca probably took over most of the house work, with Lois, aged seven, doing what she could. Children were supposed to be self-reliant in those days. The three younger boys were Ebenezer, age five; John, three; and Lemuel, age one. John died the next year. Lemuel died at age twenty after his mother's death.

As Moses reached manhood, he did more and more of the actual stonecutting; but he wanted to marry Sarah Witt, which he did in 1769, leaving town shortly after that to start his own business. Two stones of his in Boxborough are entirely different from those of his father. They represent a human being, male or female as the case may be, looking out of a window probably meant for the door of a tomb. Thomas Park had a similar device but there is no indication that he ever saw any of Moses Worster's work. There is none in Harvard.

Jonathan Worster's own stone is unique. It is twice as broad as any of the others and must have been specially quarried. The last Worster stone in Harvard is dated 1767.


## THE WILLIAM PARK FAMILY OF GROTON

### by Elvira L. Scorgie

Four generations of the Park family of Groton carried on an active stone carving, stone cutting, and stone quarrying business for many years. Evidence of their work can be found on gravestones in Groton, Harvard, and other towns in the vicinity.

The first of the family, William Park, came to Westford from Glasgow, Scotland, where he had been born in 1705. He came to this country alone, no doubt to establish himself before sending for his wife, Anna, and the rest of the family. One married son, John, was employed in Scotland by the Duke of Argyle, possibly as a stone mason.

William went first to Westford in the early 1760's, but he was warned out* as a single man who might become a Town charge. This was a routine custom. It absolved a town of any liability, but was rarely carried out. William took it seriously, however,and proceeded to Groton where he spent the rest of his life. He died 17 June 1788 at age 83.

By 1767, all of his family, including John and his wife, had arrived in Groton. It is likely that William was a stone mason as well as a stone carver. He is believed to have built a stone house of one room in the south part of Groton, now Ayer. This house, which is no longer standing, was situated on Park Street, named for him and his family.

William Park's stones were quite different from those of Worster. Instead of the death's head, he carved an unpleasant looking human head, rather small and wizened. There may be a few of his stones in Harvard and there are several in Fairview Cemetery in Westford.

* An early law of the colony prohibited anyone settling in a town until he had obtained permission from its Selectmen. This was to keep out criminals and it also kept out those who had no property, who might become town charges. If anyone neglected to apply to become a citizen and was "warned out," he could go to its Selectmen, explain his circumstances, the fact that he had a profitable trade, and get permission to remain. A vagrant, an idle or disreputable person, would be sent back from whence he came.

The early stone cutters never spoke of the stones as slate, which geologically-speaking, they are not. They are metamorphic rock, transformed under tremendous pressure and heat from primordial lake mud bottom to its present form. To the stone cutters, slate was something used in school on which to do sums, etc. In the middle of the last century they avoided circumlocution by calling it blue-stone. However, the word "slate" is now in common use and recognized by the dictionary.

## WILLIAM PARK'S SONS

**John Park:** John came to Groton from Scotland with his wife and children in 1756 and joined his father and the other members of the family. Presumably he had fulfilled his obligations in the Duke's service by that time.

Because there are so many stones in the Center Cemetery in Harvard with John's pattern carved on them, it seems unlikely that one stonecutter working only part-time on gravestones could have produced them all. It would seem more likely that they are the work of the firm of Park and Daniel Hastings, using John's pattern. His pattern is not unlike those of his father but the head has been refined to represent a more human and dignified portrait.

The early stone cutters did not sign their names to the stones, but there is one stone, that of Israel Taylor, Esq. who died in 1779 and whose estate paid "J Park" for the stone. Unfortunately, the marker is so encrusted with lichen that the inscription is almost illegible.

John Park died in 1793 as the result of an accident during the building of the jail at Amherst, New Hampshire.

**Thomas Park:** John's brother, Thomas, the youngest child of William, was born in Glasgow in 1745. He too came to Groton in 1765, entered his father's stone cutting works as an apprentice, and remained in his employ. He married Rosannah Conn in Harvard in 1768. Sometime after 1784, he moved to Harvard.

Thomas's original work was portrait heads. A very fine specimen is that of Martha, wife of Deacon Peter Green, holding her stillborn baby in her arms. She is pictured as rising from the tomb. His usual pattern was of the same type, but simpler, depicting the deceased, head and neck only, seemingly looking out of a window. Probably the window was also meant to represent the door of the tomb. His gravestone for his mother-in-law is of this type and there are others.

Thomas Park must have had a very fine reputation as a stone cutter, as he was chosen by the Town of Lexington to carve and install a suitable monument on the Green in honor of the battle fought there 19 April 1775. Thomas was himself a veteran of that memorable day.

Thomas Park died 8 June 1806. Of his eleven children, only three daughters and one son, William, also a stone cutter, survived him. He is buried in Center Cemetery in a grave marked with a simple but impressive stone, which is blue-stone, and unusually lovely .

# WILLIAM PARK'S GRANDSONS

**William Park 2nd:** Thomas Park (of the portrait heads) had one son, William Park 2nd, who continued in the family business. William had many business interests, but his ability as a stone cutter was evident in a monument he carved for his parents. He was born in Groton in 1779. During his time the method of sawing stones was invented, and he employed this method in his early stones, sawing against the grain.

Besides the monument for his parents, there is a stone he made for his brother-in-law, Isreal Reed, who died of small pox. This is mentioned in Harvard town reports. Later in his career he started using the popular urn and willow design. Not all of the numerous examples in the Harvard Cemetery are by Park, nor are they of Harvard slate.

**John Park Jr.:** Although a member of the family firm, John Jr. has as yet not been identified as a stone cutter. He lived and died in Groton, having come as a very young child with the family from Scotland in 1765 to join his grandfather, William. It is John Jr.'s son, John Park 3rd, who represents the fourth generation of the Park family as a gravestone carver. John 3rd is recorded as working as a stone cutter in Groton.


## JOHN PARK OF HARVARD

### by Elvira L. Scorgie

John Park, born 22 August 1782, was the son of William and Eunice (Stone) Park, and grandson of John and Jane (Park) Park, who came from Londonderry, New Hampshire to settle in Harvard. The compiler of the Park genealogy was unable to find any connection of this family to that of William Park of Groton. Neither John's father nor his grandfather were stonecutters, so probably no connection exists.

As John refers to himself as a stone cutter, he must have followed that trade. He may have worked in marble, which was just coming into vogue, but the Town records for the year ending 7 March 1831 state that John Park was paid $13.00 for "stone monuments" for the Common. This suggests that he had the quarry rights at that time, as a late survey refers to them as blue-stone.

John's oldest son, Benjamin Kimble Park, worked in both slate and marble. The second son, Rufus, designates himself as a blacksmith, but one marble stone in the Old Common Cemetery in Lancaster marked R. Park must be his. With the introduction of marble, the custom arose for the stone cutter to sign his name on the stone. John's son by his second wife was also a stone cutter but did not work locally.

## THE OLD SOUTH BURIAL GROUND

Bolton was incorporated in 1738 and on 17 March 1739 at a Town Meeting "it was put to vote whether the Town would chuse a committee to provide a Burying Place in Bolton." It passed in the affirmative and John Moor Jr., Wm. Pollard, and Benj. Atherton were chosen to be that committee. The problem was solved by the gift of a piece of land from his farm by William Sawyer, whose gravestone bears the earliest date of any in the Burial Ground.

We have looked for a deed from William Sawyer to the Town of Bolton, but there is none at the Registry of Deeds. It appears he must have given the land verbally.

This Burial Ground, when it was first laid out, was not on any Town road, although South Bolton Road now runs in front of it. Coffins were probably borne to the grave by friends and neighbors of the deceased, who thereby earned the name "bearers."

At present there are 279 stones in this Burial Ground of which thirty-eight are Revolutionary soldiers and two are Civil War soldiers. There were once many more, now gone. Everywhere may be seen the slight mounding of graves.

As this was the only graveyard in Bolton for eighty years, most of the Revolutionary soldiers who died in Bolton must have been buried here.

*Slate Stone for William Sawyer 1740/41*
Mr. Sawyer gave the land for the Old South Burial Ground from his farm and was the first to be buried there.

An addition to this Burial Ground in 1871 made it a total of 7 1/2 acres. This additional land is in use today as the Town Cemetery.

There is one tomb facing the road at the SW corner of the Burial Ground. It is marked:

C. G. & L. MOORE

1853

Inscriptions copied 1986 by Esther Whitcomb and Kathleen Long.

SAWYER, Hooker d 19 Nov 1771 in ye 27 yr of his age
   Eunice d/o Hooker & Relief d 22 Aug 1771 in 4th y
   Mary d/o H & R d 20 Aug 1771 in 3rd y
POLLARD, Achsah w/o Thaddeus d 18 Feb 1826 ae 47y
ATHERION, Eliakim d 24 Dec 1786 in 44th y  REV
POLLARD, Amory d 6 Sept 1844 in 74th y
   Lois w/o Amory d 20 June 1837 ae 62y
   Phebe w/o Amory d 6 Mar 1799 in 24th y
GODDARD, William s/o James & Hannah d 14 Jan 1762 in 4th y
   Jacob s/o James & Hannah d 7 June 1757 in 6th m
LONGLEY, Robert d 10 Aug 1802 ae 70y -- Col  REV
   Anna w/o Robert d 10 Dec 1815 ae 78y
   Becke d/o Col R & A d 11 July 1787 ae 22y
   Tille s/o Col R & A d 17 Aug 1790 ae 18y
HOLMAN, Amory s/o Silas & Elizabeth d 10 July 1794 ae 1y 3m
   Horatio s/o Silas & Elizabeth d 10 Apr 1809 ae 2y 4m
   Oliver s/o Oliver & Katharine d 10 Dec 1801 ae 2y 4m 7d
   Katharine w/o Oliver d 2 Apr 1804 ae 25y
   Eunice w/o Jonathan d 1 Oct 1824 ae 57y
FAIRBANKS, Charlotte d/o Phineas & Charlotte d 3 Sep 1817 in
   19th y
SAWYER, Elizabeth w/o Thomas d 28 May 1761 in 59th y
   Thomas d 31 Mar 1797 in 87th y  REV
   Mary s/o Thomas d 3 Oct 1800 in 81st y
WHITOMB, Asa s/o Lt Asa & Sarah d 21 Sept 1796 ae 1y 6m 21d
   Silas w/o Lt Asa & Sarah d 9 Apr 1795 ae 7y 6m 8d
HOLMAN, Abigail w/o Lt Abraham d 30 Aug 1777 in 40th y
   Abraham d -- Nov 1782 ae L11 (52)  REV
WHITCOMB, John d 3 Dec 1798 ae 38y  REV
   Azuba w/o John d 2 July 1838 ae 77y
HOLMAN, Abigail w/o Abraham d -- Mar 1811 ae 49y
   Abraham Jr d 15 May 1805 ae 42y
   Abraham 3rd d 18 May 1815 ae 31y
WHITCOMB, Mary w/o Jonathan d 22 Nov 1852 ae 88y
   Jonathan Esq d 14 Feb 1830 ae 80y  REV
   Sophia d/o Jona & Mary d 23 Mar 1834 ae 28y
   Susannah Bond w/o Isaac d/o Jona Whitcomb Esq d 31 Mar 1828
     ae 29y
   Francis s/o Jona & Mary d 5 May 1827 ae 30
   Elizabeth d/o Jona & Achsah d 13 Nov 1815 ae 24

Henry G s/o Jona & Mary d 13 Oct 1806 in 6th y
BLANEY, Sarah w/o Ambrose d 19 July 1814 ae 33y
BROOKS, Sarah former w/o Col Asa Whitcomb d 8 Aug 1849 ae 81y
WHITCOMB, Asa d 13 Jan 1806 ae 40y -- Col REV
    Nabby d/o Capt Silas & Lucy d 26 May 1816 ae 20y
    Silas s/o Capt Silas & Lucy d 15 May 1803 ae 2y 2m
    John s/o Capt Silas & Lucy d 5 Mar 1795 ae 1y 4m
CHAPLIN, Harriat w/o Wm d 13 Mar 1818 ae 24y
    William B d 16 Dec 1847 ae 59y
    Sarah L w/o Wm d 29 Sept 1868 ae 70y
WOODBURY, Hannah d/o Thos & Marcy d 12 Aug 1802 ae 2y 3m 12d
CHAPLIN, Charles F s/o Wm & Sarah d 1 Mar 1828 ae 3w
    Abigail S d/o Wm & Sarah d 20 Apr 1823 ae 13m
HOUGHTON, Hepzibah d 7 May 1807 ae 66y
    Lucy w/o Jacob d 29 Mar 1804 ae 46y
    John d 23 Oct 1769 ae 57y
WHITCOMB, Hepzabah w/o Simon Whitcomb former w/o John
    Hoghton d 24 Jan 1796 ae 79y
    Achsah w/o Jonathan d/o Ephm Fairbank Esq d 5 Jan 1796 ae 45y
    Becke w/o John Esq d 3 Feb 1804 ae 76y
    John Esq d 17 Nov 1785 in 73rd y REV
    Mary w/o John d 3 Feb 1743/44 in 26th y
HAPGOOD, Marcy w/o Nath'l d 1 Oct 1774 in 79th y
    Nathaniel d 26 Aug 1758 in 62nd y
GATES, Sarah w/o Paul d 6 Feb 1745 ae 16y 1m 16d
WHITCOMB, Ruhamah d/o Josiah & Ruhamah d 19 Dec 1749 in 15y
    Josiah s/o J & R d 1 Aug 1747 ae 8y 7m 21d
    Thomas s/o J & R d 20 July 1747 ae 1y 11m 26d
    Elizabeth d/o J & R d 19 July 1747 ae 18y 7m 17d
    Ruhamah w/o Dea Josiah d 13 Dec 1754 ae 48y
    Dea Josiah d 2 Jan 1771 in 70th y
    Doritha w/o Dea Josiah d 17 Oct 1803 in 96th y
WHITCOMB, Paul d 15 Mar 1802 in 70th y -- Capt REV
    Rebecca w/o Capt Paul d 13 July 1835 ae 92y
    Silas d 20 Dec 1809 ae 49y -- Capt REV
    Lucy w/o Capt Silas d 15 Dec 1852 ae 87y
    Francis d 21 Oct 1855 ae 48y
    Elizabeth d 22 Jan 1871 ae 61y
    Clarissa d 18 Sept 1871 ae 74y
    Sally d 26 Sept 1890 ae 88y
    Rebecca d 21 Apr 1904 ae 104y 4m 25d
JEWETT, Eunice d/o Benj & Olive d 17 Oct 1817 ae 3y 7m
TOWNSEND, Alfred s/o James & Sarah d 20 Feb 1816 ae 16y
    Lucinda d/o James & Sarah d 13 Feb 1816 ae 9y
    Olive w/o James d 8 June 1838 ae 89y
    James d 11 June 1801 in 68th y REV
MERRIAM, Amos d 5 May 1786 in 71st y
    Hannah w/o Amos d 17 Apr 1811 in 89th y
WHETCOMB, Lucy w/o William d 12 Sept 1773 in 25th y
TOWNSEND, Hannah w/o James d 7 Apr 1777 in 34y
NURSE, Samuel d 8 May 1790 ae 75y -- Capt REV

Elizabeth w/o Capt Sam'l d 14 Oct 1751 ae 30y
Abigail w/o Capt Sam'l d 9 Sept 1820 ae 86
Daniel d 10 Mar 1805 in 26th y
Hezediah w/o John d 9 Jan 1785 in 40th y
Calvin d 7 Sept 1816 in 38th y
Luther s/o Jona & Ruth d 17 Nov 1801 in 21st y
Hannah w/o Jona Jr d 21 Aug 1809 ae 37
MOORE, Marshall s/o Luther & Ruth d 21 Sept 1832 ae 21y
MOORE, Hannah w/o Henry d 23 Mar 1798 ae 20y 1m 25d
NURSE, Sophia d/o Jona & Ruth d 19 July 1795 in 3rd y
Eunice d/o Jona & Ruth d 6 Sept 1787 ae 3y 6m
MOOR, Achsah w/o Peter d/o Jona Whitcomb Esq d 7 Nov 1803
ae 26y
Peter d 3 May 1800 in 27th y
Eliza & (illeg) ch of Levi & Betsy d -- --- 1803
WHITCOMB, David d 30 Aug 1778 ae 29y 6m 12d REV
Jonathan d 7 Oct 1743 ae 41y 5m 15d
MOORE, Isaac d 19 Jan 1759 in 40th y
SAWYER, William d 3 Feb 1740/41 in 62nd y
Hannah d/o Peter & Sarah d 26 Oct 1802 ae 9y 5m 8d
MOORE TABLE STONE - Abraham MD d 7 Mar 1803 ae 55y
REV also
Mrs Sarah w/o Dr Abraham d 5 Jan 1898 ae 54y
MOORE, Jonadab s/o Abraham & Silence d 2 May 1760 ae 18y 9m
Sarah d/o Abraham & Silence d 21 June 1768 ae 18y 5m
Silence w/o Abraham d 8 May 1794 in 75th y
Abraham d 10 Nov 1773 ae about 57y
Hannah w/o Jonathan d 1 Mar 1765 ae 87y 11m
Jonathan d 6 Feb 1741/42 ae about 74y
Jacob d 5 June 1852 ae 41y
HOUGHTON, Dea Jonas d 21 Nov 1801 ae 73y REV
Lucy 2nd w/o Dea Jonas d 15 Apr 1794 ae 44y
Rebecca w/o Dea Jonas d 20 Mar 1772 ae 43y
Sarah d/o Jonas & Rebecca d 29 Jan 1760 ae 4y 3m 3d
Jaazaniah d 22 Feb 1828 ae 74 y
Eunice w/o Jaazaniah d 18 May 1813 ae 52y
Phineas d 26 Nov 1764 in 40th y
Eunice w/o Phinehas d 9 Jan 1756 in 27th y
WHITCOMB, Richard d 9 Oct 1810 ae 54y REV
Hannah w/o Jonas d 27 June 1796 ae 70y
Jonas d 31 Dec 1792 ae 69y REV
Sarah w/o Jonas d 25 Oct 1748 ae 26y 11m 6d
HOUGHTON, Lewis d 8 Mar 1864 ae 36 CW
Martin d 19 June 1833 ae 55y 7m -- CAPT
Polly w/o Capt Martin d 2 Apr 1823 ae 45y
also 4 children of above deceased
WOODBURY, Edeth d 22 Dec 1808 ae 60y
Samuel d 24 July 1814 ae 90y REV
Edeth w/o Samuel d 15 May 1797 ae 74
Thomas d 11 May 1820 ae 54y
Mercy w/o Thomas d 13 June 1836 ae 65

William 15 Aug 1763 – 21 July 1850 ae 87  REV
Eunice w/o William d 23 Oct 1817 ae 47y
BAILEY, Lusinda w/o Benj'd 9 Nov 1821 ae 52y
Benjamin s/o Benj & Lusinda d 15 Aug 1820 ae 16
SAWYER, Betty d 16 Feb 1830 ae 63y
DRAPER, Eunice d/o Sam'l & Sarah d 26 Jul 1801 ae 2y 3m 26d
JEWETT, John d 8 Feb 1802 ae 52y  REV
Eunice w/o John d 31 Dec 1843 ae 91y
Lydia d 24 Feb 1850 ae 68y
Sarah d/o John & Eunice d 10 Aug 1830 ae 50y
MOOR, Ruth w/o Phineas d 30 Oct 1849 ae 87y
SAWYER, Lucy d/o Capt Elijah & Lucy d 10 Jan 1827 ae 29y
Dea John d 30 May 1812 ae 64y 1m 19d  REV
Mary w/o Dea John d 8 Nov 1795 ae 45y
Rhoda w/o Dea John d 26 Sept 1801 ae 47y
WHITNEY, Elijah d 18 May 1866 ae 85y
Alice d 9 May 1860 ae 72y
Sarah w/o Elijah d 3 Oct 1812 ae 59y
Elijah d 6 Jan 1834 ae 79y
Samuel d 29 July 1868 ae 90
Lois w/o (illegible – died illegible)
HOLT, Thomas d 29 Sept 1808 ae 60y  REV
Mary w/o Thomas d 18 Jan 1801 ae 55y
MOORE, Phineas d 15 Dec 1839 ae 88y  REV
Sarah w/o Phineas d 2 Sept 1826 ae 75
RICHARDSON TABLE STONE – A table stone slate top brick base on
large mound possibly a tomb or crypt
Achsah d/o Caleb & Elizabeth d 27 Sept 1783 ae 34y
Elizabeth w/o Caleb d 25 Dec 1783 ae 68y
Joshua d 21 May 1793 ae 81y  REV
Lydia w/o James d 17 Dec 1796 ae 69y
James d 21 Nov 1799 ae 76y  REV
Elizabeth Ruggles w/o Robert of Boston d 15 May 1784 in 43rd y
SAWYER, Hannah w/o William d 18 June 1747 ae 34y
COBURN, William d 25 Mar 1876 ae 63y
Catherine w/o Wm d 2 Mar 1852 ae 36y
SAWYER, William s/o David & Lavinia Sawyer adopted s/o
William & Catherine Coburn d 16 Feb 1848 ae 2y
KEYES, James d 29 Sept 1746 ae 76y 16d
Hannah w/o James d 19 Mar 1742 ae 73y 9m
WHITNEY, Rhoda w/o John d 28 Oct 1832 ae 30y
FAIRBANK, Dea Jabez d 24 Apr 1782 ae 88
Hepzibah w/o Dea Jabez d 26 Apr 1789 in 89th y
Ephraim Esq d 18 Nov 1799 in 75th y  REV
SAWYER, Levi s/o Dea Josiah & Mary d 9 Feb 1765 ae 3m
MOOR, John d 27 July 1740 ae about 79y
PATCH, Eliza d/o Joshua & Rebecka d 18 Apr 1795 ae 9m
HOUGHTON, Sanderson d 24 Nov 1799 ae 83y  REV
Joseph d 7 Nov 1847 ae 75y
Henry d 17 Dec 1756 ae 80y 9m 11d
Joseph d 27 Nov 1788 in 69th y

Susannah w/o Joseph d 19 Sept 1809 in 70th y
NURSE, Rachel w/o (illeg) d 10 May 1751 ae 23y
MOORE, Caleb Esq d 24 Oct 1826 ae 58y
    Achsah w/o Caleb d 15 Jan 1831 ae 55y
    Joshua d 14 Nov 1819 ae 20y 3m
    Achsah d/o Caleb & Achsah d 30 Sept 1833 ae 17y 7m
    James Richardson s/o Caleb Esq d 8 Dec 1825 ae 21
    Lydia Richardson d 10 June 1840 ae 32y 3m 14d
    Charles d 3 May 1876 ae 64y
    Christopher C d 4 Jan 1892 ae 81y
WEST, Mary d 5 Nov 1751
    Ann d 6 Apr 1757 in 73rd y
HOUGHTON, Anna w/o Henry d 14 Feb 1747/48 in 66th y
GREENLEAF, Dolly d/o Calvin & Becke d 8 Feb 1776 ae 6y 5m 6d
    Sarah d/o Calvin & Becke d 18 Sept 1775 ae 1y 9m 7d
    Becke d/o Calvin & Becke d 11 Sept 1776 ae 11y 3m 1d
    Asa s/o Calvin & Becke d 12 Oct 1778 ae 14d
    John s/o Dr Daniel & Silence d 2 Aug 1744 ae 2m
HOLMAN, Nathaniel d 14 Jan 1805 ae 70y  REV
HOUGHTON, Abigail formerly w/o Nath'l d 13 July 1819 ae 80y
HOLMAN, Levi s/o Nath'l & Abigail d 22 Aug 1796 in 20th y
ATHERTON, Benjamin d 15 Apr 1786 ae 84y 11m 26d  -- Capt
    Eunice w/o Capt Benj d 27 May 1792 ae 82y
GREENLEAF, Daniel Jr MD d 18 Jan 1777 ae 44y  REV
    Daniel MD d 18 Aug 1785 ae 82y 8m
    Silence w/o Dr Dan'l d 13 May 1762 in 60th y
    Calvin d 12 Aug 1812 in 75th y  REV
    Becke w/o Calvin d 4 Sept 1787 ae 41y 8m 20d
    Moses d 12 Aug 1865 ae 79y
    Experience w/o Moses d 28 Dec 1829 ae 39y
    Laban d 9 July 1874 ae 52y 9m
    Lorin d 15 Oct 1844 ae 20y
BARRETT, Sarah w/o Levi d 28 July 1818 ae 28y
HASTINGS, Mary A d 16 Apr 1884 ae 85y
    Deborah A d 3 June 1863 ae 63y
    Mary d 6 Apr 1823 ae 62y
    William d 16 Dec 1836 ae 72y  REV
GIBBS, Sarah d/o Hezekiah & Elizabeth d 6 Feb 1776
    ae 26y 6m 16d
SOUTHWICK, Silas d 24 Aug 1854 ae 42y
BRUCE, Sarah w/o William d 28 May 1821 ae 86y
HOLMAN, Asa d 28 June 1846 ae 69y
    Becca w/o Asa d 12 July 1835 ae 53y
HOUGHTON, Thomas d 2 July 1863 ae 82y
    Asenath w/o Thos d 28 Dec 1821 ae 37y 10m 7d
    Damforth s/o Thos & Asenath d 29 May 1806 ae 1y 1m 6d
    Anne - rest chipped off
WHITNEY, Milley d 27 June 1763 ae 86y
BENDER, Sarah w/o Peter former w/o John Whitney d 16 Dec 1840
    ae 86y
WHITNEY, John d 25 Apr 1802 ae 55y  REV

Isaiah d 19 Mar 1835 ae 61y
Susannah d 20 Nov 1810 ae 42y
MERRIAM, Phebe w/o Simon d 2 May 1815 in 62nd y
HAYNES, Nathan s/o Sam'l & Rebeckah d 1 June 1805 ae 9m 12d
Samuel d 12 Sept 1829 ae 56y
Rebecca w/o Sam'l d 21 Nov 1842 ae 62y
COTTING, Martha w/o Daniel former w/o Aaron Brown d 31
Jan 1821 ae 72
MOULTON, John s/o Aaron d 8 Apr 1790 ae 14y 9m
NEWTON, Olive M w/o Francis M 1853-1936
Francis M 20 Feb 1842 - 26 July 1889  CW
RAY, David d 4 Aug 1794 ae 33y 8m 12d  REV
HASTINGS, Submit w/o John d 31 Oct 1816 ae 72y
WELSH, Jonas d 30 Nov 1840 ae 87y -- Capt  REV
JEWETT, Keziah d 20 July 1797 ae 39y
Oliver d 22 Aug 1829 ae 82y 6m  REV
Sarah w/o Oliver d 9 Dec 1830 ae 81y
CROSSMAN, Ellen Maria d/o John & Evelina d 19 Sept 1841 ae 5m
OSBORNE, Thomas d 13 Sept 1810 ae 75y  REV
BROWN, Samuel MD d 16 Jan 1805 ae 36y
Arad s/o Sam'l & Abigail now w/o Thos Osborne
d 9 Oct 1798 in 16th y
CLARK, Samuel B d 17 Aug 1858 ae 47y 11m
Arad d 21 Sept 1817 ae 19y
Elizabeth D d 21 July 1866 ae 58y
Elizabeth w/o Peter d 5 Sept 1869 ae 91y
CHAMBERLAIN, Lucretia w/o Wilder d 14 Jan 1784 ae 21y 8m 10d
Nathan s/o Wilder & Lucretia d 10 Sept 1783 ae 8m 16d
POLLARD, Curtis d 20 July 1829 ae 50y -- Capt
Lucy w/o Capt Curtis d 26 Sept 1846 ae 56y
Luke d 15 Aug 1860 ae 50y
Sarah d/o Capt C & L d 24 Aug 1858 ae 44y 10m
Asaph A s/o Capt C & L d 13 May 1830 ae 13y
Abijah d 14 Jan 1816 ae 69y
Hannah w/o Abijah d 5 Sept 1805 ae 51y 8m 2d
Experience w/o Wm d 18 May 1785 ae 77
William d 28 May 1762 ae about 65y
POLLARD, Oliver d 18 July 1812 ae 84y 9m
Mary w/o Oliver d 2 Sept 1813 ae 73y 6m
Jonas s/o Oliver & Mary d 5 Oct 1775 ae 3y
Rebeckah d/o Oliver & Mary d 5 Oct 1775 ae 1y
Ann d/o Oliver & Mary d 9 Oct 1775 ae 11y
Mary d/o Oliver & Mary d 17 Oct 1775 ae 15y
Stephen s/o Oliver & Mary d 10 May 1776 ae 6y 9m
Stephen s/o Oliver & Mary d 25 Sept 1777 ae 1y 11m
Mary d/o Oliver & Mary d 4 May 1783 ae 2y
Jonas d 12 June 1848 ae 70y
Sarah w/o Jonas d 28 Nov 1845 ae 64y
MOORS, Eunice w/o Thomas d 14 Dec 1852 ae 69y
Mary Ann, d/o Thos & Eunice d 2 Oct 1838 ae 33y

Rev. Thomas Goss - Inscription translated from the Latin A slate table stone about six feet by three feet on a brick foundation. No other stones close to it:

> Sacred to the memory of Rev Thomas Goss, A.M.; Pastor of the church among the Boltonians, who, for upwards of thirty nine years having exercised the sacred office, departed this life January 17th 1780, in the 63d year of his age. A man adorned with piety, hospitality, friendliness, and other virtues; somewhat broken in body but endowed with wonderful fortitude; he was the first among the clergy in these unhappy times to be grievously persecuted for boldly opposing those who were striving to overturn the prosperity of the churches, and for heroically struggling to maintain the ecclesiastical polity which was handed down by our ancestry. Friends erected this monument.

## THE OLD SETTLERS' TOMB

On West Pond Farm is an ancient tomb which has been viewed by students from several universities and by antiquarians who place the date of its building prior to the incorporation of Bolton. It is the so-called Corn Hill type of tomb, which dates around 1700. This tomb has been open for many years and is now empty.

However, many years ago, on its shelves were several coffins, originally painted red, which had crumbled and pulled apart at the corners. The bones, which could be seen inside the coffins, were white and bleached. It has been said that this tomb was constructed by the Sawyer family, and that John Sawyer, aged twenty-one, is interred there; but that theory will hardly hold in face of the fact that Benjamin Sawyer bought the place in 1791, at which time no tomb was mentioned in the deed. Benjamin's son, John, lived to a ripe old age, and John's son, John F., died in 1898, age seventy-three. Both are buried in the Sawyer lot in the Pan Burial Ground.

It is now thought that this may have been a community tomb in the early 1700's. A number of families lived along the Bay Path, Long Hill; in its east and northeast parts this was part of what became Bolton. The nearest graveyard was on the Old Common in Lancaster, and in winter that must have been an impossible journey over icy paths and through deep drifts. Perhaps the old tomb was used when the weather prohibited the long trip to Lancaster.

## OLD FRY BURYING GROUND

This yard, not visible from the road, is at the top of a little knoll, walled in, with a chain across the entrance. It is perhaps one-fourth or one-third acre. A number of Friends or Quaker families lived in this area of the Town and this yard was near their first Meeting House. We do not know when it was first used, but the land was deeded to "The People called Quakers" by John Fry and Rachel, his wife, in

1779. The Quakers did not believe in the use of "graven images" and there were only eight stones, placed there many years after it was first used.

The Town, at the request of the Quaker Meeting, took over this graveyard as a family lot in 1926 to receive perpetual care.

Inscriptions copied 1985 by Esther Whitcomb and Kathleen Long.

SMITH, David d 6th m 14th 1827 ae 42
  David A d 3rd m 21 1829 ae 2 (one stone for both)
  Richard R d 12th m 23rd 1858 ae 41
CUTTING, Leonard d 23rd June 1850 ae 45
EARLE, Our Mother Matilda Earle survivor of two husbands
  Israel Chase & Clark Earle d 1st m 10th 1843 ae 73y 1m 24d
FRY, Thomas d 3rd m 25 1839 ae 48y 9m
  Jonathan d 5th m 8th 1844 ae 62y
  Amy d 10th m 2d 1850 ae 64y
  Jesse Eddy s/o Thomas & Mary E d 9th m 6 1822 ae 14m
  Mary Ann d/o Thomas & Mary E d 1st m 9 1828 ae 12y 7m

## THE PAN BURIAL GROUND

By 1820 the Old South Burial Ground had hardly any more space in it and the Town voted to purchase land for two more graveyards. On 6 May 1822 a piece of land on the Great Road one mile east of the Meeting House containing one acre 208 rods was bought from Oliver Barrett for one hundred dollars. A small piece of land was added at the western end about 1860. It is the width of one double lot and as deep as the rest of the burial ground.

A stone wall along the road and at the west end of this burial ground is a thing of beauty. Hand-wrought iron hitching rings are set into the front wall. The large double wrought-iron gates were made by Captain Oliver Sawyer. The Town paid him fourteen dollars for them. Although extremely heavy, they swing on their pintles at the touch of a finger. The small gate appears in the 1863 Town Report as an expense of $36.03 with no mention of to whom it was paid.

Seven tombs were built at the east end of the burial ground facing the Great Road. On each heavy iron door is the date 1839 and the name of the owner. These are: I. Allen, Gardner, Amory Holman & Samuel Kendall Holman, Jonathan Nurse, Caleb Nourse, Abram Holman & Nathan Brooks, J. & N. Sawyer.

Inscriptions copied 1986 by Esther K. Whitcomb.

POWERS, Frank A 1880-1973
  Edith w/o Frank 1884-1968
  Helen D w/o A H Nourse 2 Aug 1877 - 27 Apr 1909
  Amos H 1847-1933
  Ellen Carpenter w/o Amos H Powers 1842-1931
CARPENTER, Diana W w/o David d 2 Oct 1890 ae 85

David d 1 Aug 1880 ae 87
ROBINSON, William W   Co B 44 Reg MVM 1837-1922  CW
    Fannie H Wife 1839-1924
HOUGHTON, T J 1832-1905
    Sarah E 24 Mar 1804 - 4 June 1898 MOTHER
    Sherman W 31 July 1807 - 10 Feb 1894 FATHER
BAILEY MONUMENT - Rev Ira Bailey d 5 July 1884 ae 59
    Sarah E w/o Rev Ira d 11 Dec 1889 ae 56
    Luther W Houghton d 3 Apr 1875 ae 65
    Sophronia w/o Luther d 23 July 1883 ae 70
HOUGHTON, Emma J w/o Andrew J 1838-1865
BOWMAN MONUMENT - Jonathan Bowman 1805-1867
    Sarah B w/o Jonathan 1810-1886
    John W Houghton 1838-1906
    Clara E w/o John 1842-1932
    Herbert L 1869-1915
    Elsie G 1876-1941
PIERCE MONUMENT - Lucy S Pierce d 17 Dec 1893 ae 54y
    Lucy S Pierce d 4 Sept 1863 ae 11m
    Fred A Cutler d 13 Mar 1883 ae 22y
WOOD, Roxana S w/o John H d 16 Nov 1877 ae 65y 3d
    John H d 21 Sept 1859 ae 54
NOURSE, Delia S d/o E & L d 22 May 1871 ae 36y
    Mrs Lucretia w/o Franklin d 2 Oct 1841 ae 26y
SAWYER, Capt Oliver d 23 Mar 1836 ae 52y
    Azuba w/o Capt Oliver & formerly w/o Abraham Holman
        d 4 June 1839 ae 55
NEWTON, Prudentia d 21 March 1874 ae 87y 6m
    Edward S d 25 May 1879 ae 37y 1m 13d
    Charles E d 21 Dec 1922 ae 76y 11m 12d
    Reuben d 4 Feb 1896 ae 78y 6m
    Emily S w/o Reuben d 15 Dec 1874 ae 59y 5m
BRIGHAM, Legrand L 1850-1929
    Addie L 1851-1941
SAWYER, Daniel d 4 Nov 1847 ae 66
    Rachel w/o Daniel d 12 Nov 1843 ae 60
    Abigail w/o Calvin d 26 Nov 1839 ae 87
SAWYER MONUMENT - John Sawyer d 3 Mar 1872 ae 78y
    Abigail w/o John d 1 Oct 1859 ae 58y
    Henrietta H d/o J & A d 22 July 1874 ae 23y
    James M d 7 Oct 1864 ae 30y
    Charles A d 11 Nov 1865 ae 37y
    John F d 7 Nov 1882 ae 57y
    Achsah d 22 Aug 1904 ae 77y
    Charles J 1866-1943
    Nellie F w/o Charles 1863-1940
    Lucy H d 22 July 1936 ae 67y
    H Mabel Windram 1871-1915
    George d 2 Aug 1876 ae 76y 6m
    Sarah Whitney w/o George d 27 Mar 1836 ae 36y
    Abigail G Shedd w/o George d 19 Jan 1840 ae 30y

Mary E Wilson w/o George d 1 Feb 1857 ae 41y
ADAMS, Oliver 1791-1839 -- Col
   Zilpah Sawyer w/o Col O Adams 1795-1852
   Amy 1764-1852
SAWYER, Joseph d 12 Mar 1828 ae 72y REV
   Ruth w/o Joseph d 10 June 1830 ae 67
GATES, David d 15 Apr 1839 ae 54
DEXTER, James M 1811-1854 FATHER
   Elizabeth A 1811-1892 MOTHER
   Sarah E d/o J & E d 7 Sept 1859 ae 15y
   Ann Maria d/o J & E d 9 Mar 1841 ae 2y 9m
NOURSE, Rufus C 1862-1934
   Bertha E Morgan w/o Rufus
   Carlton H their son 1898-1898
BROWN, Abijah 31 July 1830 - 10 Mar 1903
   Lucy A 9 Oct 1831 - 21 Jan 1911
   Elmer E 15 Oct 1861 - 9 Sept 1862
   Gladys M 26 Aug 1864 - 6 Oct 1865
BAKER, Thomas G 16 Jan 1802 - 19 Dec 1857
   Sally 13 Sept 1802 - 24 Aug 1886
WHITCOMB, Horatio F s/o Abel & Sophia d 25 Sept 1823 ae 13m
   Abel d 16 June 1841 ae 82y
   Elizabeth w/o Abel d 21 June 1849 ae 88y
   Sophia w/o Abel d 16 Nov 1852 ae 60y
   Abel d 14 March 1866 ae 84
OSBORNE, Susannah T d 10 Apr 1844 ae 50y
WARNER MONUMENT - Elias Jr 7 Oct 1785 - 10 July 1872
   Mary Ann Lawrence w/o Elias d/o Abijah Lawrence
      18 Feb 1805 - 14 July 1846
   Martha M 18 Jan 1837 - 9 June 1853
   Mary A 25 May 1839 - 18 Nov 1839
   Mary Ann 9 Sept 1840 - 25 Sept 1840
   George H 18 May 1846 - 19 Sept 1846
   Quincy A 5 Nov 1826 - 5 Apr 1834
   Roena B Warner Smith 30 Sept 1830 - 16 Apr 1881
   Susan C Warner Wright 4 June 1832
   Sarah J Warner Houghton 29 June 1834 - 15 Mar 1888
   Sarah J w/o Geo H S Houghton d 15 Mar 1888 ae 53y
WOODBURY, Inf/o ---- William & Harriet d 14 June 1828
ADAMS, John Quincy d 25 Apr 1837 ae 6y 6m
   Frances Ame d 22 Sept 1838 ae 14y 4m
   Children of Oliver & Zilpah
SAWYER, William Corey s/o Geo & Sarah d 29 Aug 1829 ae 6m
HOUGHTON, Edward E d 1882 ae 36y
DEXTER, Ann Maria d/o James & Elizabeth d 9 Mar 1841 ae 2y 9m
HOUGHTON, William d 26 July 1850 ae 81
   Lucy w/o Wm d 13 June 1841 ae 55
   ---- Ellen d 5 November 1853
HOLMAN, Betsy d/o Silas & Betsy d 12 May 1825 ae 38y 3m
WHITMAN, Rev Nathaniel 25 Dec 1785 - 29 Oct 1869 ae 84y
   Sarah H 1 May 1791 - 18 May 1841 ae 50

Abbie Pollard his wife d 4 June 1892 ae 75y 5m
DWINNELLS, Horace s/o Benj & Mary Ann d 22 Sept 1828 ae 18m
   Frances A d/o Asa P & Anna d 21 July 1853 ae 9y 8m 24d
ELLINWOOD, Nathan d 4 Sept 1847 ae 75y 9m 3d
   Sarah w/o Nathan d 8 Oct 1842 ae 76y 6m 24d
BURNAM, Lemuel Jr d 28 April 1838 ae 24y
   Lemuel d 13 Feb 1852 ae 85y  REV
   Sarah w/o Lemuel d 12 Mar 1854 ae 77y
   Lucinda d 20 May 1874 ae 75y
   Roxanna W w/o Reuben d 9 Nov 1867 ae 62y
WHITE, Mary Ann 18 Jan 1809 – 2 Aug 1879
SPARHAWK, Thomas s/o Dexter & Calphurna d 8 Feb 1849 ae 7w
   Harrietta d/o Dexter & Calphurna d 9 July 1848 ae 5y
   William E s/o Dexter & Calphurna drowned 26 July 1850
      ae 19y 9m
BLOOD, Augustus d 9 Jan 1901 ae 73y 5m 13d
   Caroline A w/o Augustus d 4 May 1877 ae 45y 10m 28d
BROWN, Rev Warren d 5 Dec 1862 ae 24y 4m 15d
RICE MONUMENT – George A s/o AA & EJ d 20 Sept 1844 ae 9m
   Frederick A s/o AA & EI d 25 Sept 1849 ae 1y 13d
   Mary E d/o AA & EJ d 16 Aug 1855 ae 4d
   Mother AT REST
   Husband GONE HOME
   Mary L w/o H Frank 1853–1935
   H Frank 1843–1913
   E Maud Rice 1886–1943
   Harold F Rice 1881–1963
WOODBURY, Susan w/o Wm d 7 Feb 1863 ae 78y 10m
CARR, Sarah d 7 July 1889 ae 92y 1m
BRYANT, Amos d 7 May 1897 ae 79y 4m 8d
   Sarah S w/o Amos d 26 Dec 1845 ae 23y
   Sarah C w/o Amos d 15 July 1891 ae 79y 10m
   Ida E d/o Amos & Sarah C d 23 May 1882 ae 16y
   Emma R w/o Irvin Putnam d 30 Oct 1881 ae 23y
   Mary H d/o Amos & Mary I d 4 July 1871 ae 15y
   Geo Albert s/o Amos & Sarah ae 16m
HOUGHTON, George W 1830–1906
   Abbie F Draper 1838–1863
   Adelaide E Dudley 1845–1928
   Flora Gertrude 1863–1863
   Grace Inez 1865–1865
   George Harriman 1867–1868
WHITCOMB, Abel d 17 Oct 1900 ae 84y 10m 11d
   Sarah M w/o Abel d 28 Mar 1883 ae 61y 6m 10d
   George William d 8 Dec 1843 ae 1m 2d
   Adella Asenath d 26 Oct 1857 ae 1y 7d
   Martha L 20 Oct 1846 –23 Apr 1917
THAXTER, Warren P 1846–1935
   Sophia H w/o Warren 17 Apr 1924
HOWE, Francis d 19 Dec 1896 ae 65y 4m 28d
   Sophia w/o Francis d 13 Sept 1878 ae 48y 4m 23d

Lovilla S d/o Francis & Sophia d 21 May 1870 ae 24y 5m 15d
Freddie d -- May ---- (illeg)
Moses d 20 Nov 1866 ae 74y
Eunice B w/o Moses d 19 Aug 1882 ae 84y
Lillie & baby
BROWN, Lewis B 26 Nov 1815 - 8 Feb 1869
Nancy w/o Lewis B 27 June 1827 - 8 July 1889
Charles H 7 Sept 1850 - 17 Aug 1865
Lillie A 1 Jan 1859 -23 Jan 1880
children of Lewis B and Nancy Brown
DUNN, Lucas d 17 Oct 1834 ae 38
BROWN, Josiah Jr d 31 Mar 1837 ae 37
HOUGHTON, Eunice w/o Thomas d 15 June 1881 ae 80y 8m 13d
CLARK MONUMENT - Phineas 8 May 1797 - 6 Aug 1867
Clarissa P w/o Phineas 30 June 1800 - 30 Aug 1885
Francis A 29 June 1838 - 18 Nov 1857
Anna 19 Feb 1829 - 3 June 1837
Mary E 4 March 1831 - 12 Feb 1895
Clarissa P 2 Dec 1824 - 23 March 1895
Mary J d/o Jonathan & Sarah d 29 Sept 1876 ae 12y 2m
Sarah J w/o Jonathan P d 22 Aug 1870 ae 25y
Jonathan P d 27 Aug 1887 ae 64y 10m 18d
WHEELER, Anna d/o Sam'l & Anna 10 Nov 1794 - 22 May 1875
Jonathan d 2 Sept 1858 ae 58y
Anna w/o Samuel d 12 April 1848 ae 79
Samuel d 18 Nov 1830 ae 65
BROWN, Jerusha D w/o Thos H & d/o Caleb & Dolly Wheeler
d 3 Feb 1864 ae 48y 6m
GOSS, Joseph F d 24 Apr 1853 ae 36y
SAWYER, A D d 10 Dec 1875 ae 55
Ann Genette w/o A D d 10 Mar 1852 ae 27
Francis W s/o A D & A G d 29 Aug 1853 ae 1y 7m
WHEELER, Dolly M d/o Caleb & Dolly d 10 May 1845 ae 26
Caleb d 21 Dec 1875 ae 84y 5m
Dolly w/o Caleb d 8 Feb 1881 ae 87
WHITCOMB, Frank H 4 Sept 1846 - 16 Feb 1901
Carrie S 13 Sept 1850 - 20 June 1894
Frank Oscar 27 Aug 1867 - 10 Mar 1869
Mary Agnes 28 Feb 1875 - 11 Apr 1884
WHITCOMB, Maria M d/o Asa & Adeline d 15 May 1856 ae 4y 2m 9d
Adeline A w/o Col Asa d 16 Mar 1892 ae 78y 7m 5d
Caroline w/o Col Asa d 22 June 1833 ae 30y
Col Asa d 4 Apr 1868 ae 68y 8m
TAYLOR, Burgess d 10 Sept 1882 ae 66y 5m  CW
Mary Frances w/o Burgess 1837-1911
Laura Ann w/o Burgess d 14 July 1853 ae 17y 8m
Laura A                    Hattie T
Flora A                    Bertha C
HOUGHTON, Cephas d 12 Oct 1865 ae 71
Mary d 21 Dec 1863 ae 46
MASON, Nathaniel W 17 May 1833 - 30 June 1907  CW

Mary A 22 June 1838 – 23 Oct 1911
MINER, Aurilla 5 Mar 1868 – 12 Dec 1940
   Arthur B 21 Aug 1866 – 11 Apr 1949
   Alvin B 1888–1889
BRUCE, Ella B 27 Nov 1873 – 29 Apr 1941
WHITTAKER, Gordon -- --- ----
   Genevieve w/o Gordon -- --- ----
BRIDGES, James d 17 Dec 1861 ae 81y
DOW, Cora -- --- ----
   Maria C 1845–1927
   James G 1849–1918
WHITCOMB, George L 1870–1950
WHITCOMB, Boulder ----
KIMMENS, Erma Alice 5 Jan 1892 – 18 Jan 1892
   Ruth Persis 26 Oct 1905 – 23 Nov 1905
   Charles L 29 Sept 1867 – 23 Dec 1929
   Persis E Bolster w/o Chas 14 Aug 1870 – 6 Feb 1956
WHITCOMB, Charles d 16 Sept 1860 ae 33y
   Luke d 10 Aug 1860 ae 38y
   Nancy w/o Luke d 7 Aug 1831 ae 42y
   Luke d 1 Sept 1876 ae 84y 10m
WHITCOMB MONUMENT – Edwin A 24 July 1807 – 20 Dec 1872
   Persis H w/o E A 12 Feb 1811 – 26 Aug 1854
   Joseph 30 Mar 1830 – 6 May 1910
   Mary Gardner 1 Jan 1848 – 13 Dec 1915
   Mary G 1843–1844
   Charles H 1845–1850
PROCTOR, Emery A 1860–1916
   May H w/o E A 20 Oct 1858 – 21 Jan 1907
   Ruby E 21 May 1884 – 13 Feb 1903
   Lutie E 22 Sept 1891 – 1 May 1897
CONNELL, John E 28 Dec 1892 – 9 Sept 1897
EMMES, Stephen s/o John & Esther d 23 Aug 1826 ae 16
   (Illegible – same style stone as above)
PARKER MONUMENT – Amos M D d 24 Oct 1861 ae 84y
   Elizabeth w/o Amos d 12 Jan 1864 ae 88y
   Elizabeth L B d 1 Apr 1882 ae 72y
   Louisa Jane d 1 Aug 1900 ae 88y 7m
BLOOD, Samuel d 15 Aug 1831 ae 85y  REV
   Lucretia w/o Samuel d 10 Oct 1827 ae 75y
BROOKS, Mary O w/o Nathan d 6 Aug 1845 ae 43y
OSBORNE, Elizabeth W 27 June 1808 – 25 Jan 1898
   Rebecca (Illegible) -- --- ----
   Abigail d/o Ephraim & Dolly d 27 July 1829 ae 24y
   Thomas s/o Ephraim d 23 Aug 1823 ae 19y
   Ephraim d 17 April 1832 ae 59y
   Dolly w/o Ephraim d 31 Dec 1827 ae 55y
HILDRETH, Julia Ann d/o Joseph & Persis d 8 Sept 1831 ae 8y
   Joseph S d 1 Dec 1829 ae 29y
   Adaline d/o Timothy d 2 Oct 1831 ae 31y
   Abigail d/o Timothy d 18 Oct 1829 ae 43y

Hannah w/o Timothy d 4 Jan 1826 ae 68y
STRATTON, Nahum 30 Mar 1811 – 30 Oct 1895
    Elizabeth w/o Nahum d 25 Dec 1838 ae 26
SWIFT, Caroline d 22 May 1882 ae 72y 11m 20d
SAWYER, Lucy d 27 July 1871 ae 97y 7m 22d
STRATTON, Mary Harlow d 25 Dec 1836 ae 27y
    Isaac d 27 Jan 1836 ae 21y
    Dolly d 10 Jan 1836 ae 19y
    Children of Isaac & Mary Stratton
ALLEN TOMB – Rev Isaac 31 Oct 1771 – 18 March 1844
GARDNER TOMB – Theodore 20 Dec 1809 – 9 Apr 1895
    Lucy Anne w/o Theo 22 May 1807 – 11 Oct 1878
    Charles T 1 Nov 1836 – 30 Dec 1851 d at sea
    Stephen P d 11 Oct 1841 ae 75y
    Achsah w/o Stephen P d 30 Dec 1837 ae 63y
    Sarah E Jones d/o S & A Gardner d 8 Oct 1844 ae 36y
HOLMAN TOMB – Amory Holman   Samuel Kendall Holman
NOURSE TOMB – Dea Jonathan d 9 Aug 1859 ae 83
    Mary w/o Jonathan d 2 Sept 1851 ae 70
    Howard d 8 April 1858 ae 38
NURSE TOMB – Caleb
HOLMAN & BROOKS TOMB
    Abraham Holman   Nathan Brooks
J & N SAWYER TOMB – TABLESTONE OVER TOMB
    Joseph Sawyer d 15 Aug 1865 ae 78y
    Abigail Bender w/o JS d 12 Oct 1856 ae 69y
    Joseph Henry d 19 July 1866 ae 36y
    Nathan Corey d 16 Nov 1853 ae 76
    Eunice Sawyer wife d 5 Dec 1856 ae 73
    Amory Pollard s/o N & L d 20 May 1860 ae 26
NOURSE MONUMENT – Caleb 1805–1884
    Orissa 1808–1859
    Barnard 1772–1851
    Hannah 1776–1856
    Rufus C 1830–1862
    Abby A 1831–1885
    Edward R 1854–1874
    Caleb E  In Texas  1867
    Hattie M  In Texas  1867
    Rufus  In Maryland  1825
SAWYER MONUMENT – Levi MD 6 Oct 1785 (error) – 16 Mar 1844
    Hannah his wife 5 Aug 1797 – 21 Nov 1824
    Alice J 1848–1854
    Minnie L 1861–1866
    George W 1851–1927
    S Konisky 1821–1902
    Sarah B 1826–1905
BARRETT MONUMENT – Oliver d 17 Jan 1859 ae 78
    Lucy w/o Oliver d 10 Nov 1874 ae 88
    Lucy d 14 Aug 1816 ae 3y
    John d 7 Sept 1818 ae 2y

Asa d 26 Nov 1823 ae 7y
Roswell d 30 Oct 1889 ae 69y
Sarah J w/o Roswell d 20 June 1897 ae 78y
Joel Sawyer d 10 Sept 1897 ae 92y
Sarah w/o Joel d 27 Dec 1891 ae 85
Jabez d 27 Nov 1873 ae 57
Helen w/o Jabez d 11 Mar 1897 ae 56
Jabez d 2 Oct 1845 ae 1d
Hellen M d 5 May 1859 ae 16y
Frank J d 13 Oct 1880 ae 32y
Ellen E w/o Frank d 21 Mar 1920 ae 71y
Frankie & Bertie inf/children F J & E E Barrett
Ella V d/o Roswell & Sarah J d 8 Oct 1940 ae 81y
WETHERBY, Reuben d 5 June 1837 ae 64
Rebeckah w/o Reuben d 19 Apr 1847 ae 72
Europe d 20 May 1852 ae 47
WILDER, Mary H w/o Isaac A d 23 May 1860 ae 55
Becca w/o Moses d 16 Mar 1865 ae 84
Moses d -- --- 1852 (broken)
Lucinda w/o Abraham d 8 Jan 1835 ae 32y
WHITCOMB, Joel d 2 July 1842 ae 75
Abigail w/o Joel d 10 May 1843 ae 77
DAKIN, Joel 1791-1877
Betsy w/o Joel 1796-1874
POWERS, Henry R s/o A R & E d 7 Mar 1877 ae 16y 9m 28d
Hattie J d/o A R & E d 7 Nov 1856 ae 2y 10m 21d
Aaron R 23 Sept 1832 - 29 Apr 1905
Elizabeth Proctor 11 June 1826 - 15 June 1894
Charlie A d 1 Apr 1868 ae 5w 4d
PROCTOR, Amos d 22 Apr 1900 ae 85y 11m
Rebecca M w/o Amos d 27 Dec 1858 ae 50y 8m
Jemimah K w/o Amos d 16 Aug 1863 ae 38y 4m
Adelaide R w/o Amos P & d/o J E & J K Bradford d 30
    Apr 1863 ae 16y
BRADFORD, Frank d 8 July 1876 ae 25y 7m 9d
HOUGHTON, Joseph d 7 Dec 1832 ae 60y 2m 8d
Mary w/o Joseph d 30 July 1834
B S Co K  Mass RIF  -- Sgt  CW
NOURSE, Dea Jonathan d 24 July 1827 ae 78y  REV
Ruth w/o Dea Jonathan d 16 Dec 1841 ae 92y
Sarah Ann d/o Silas & Sarah d 30 Dec 1834 ae 13y 4m
Charles Edwin s/o Silas & Sarah d 5 Feb 1852 ae 15y 6m
Silas Martin s/o Silas & Sarah d 23 Jan 1853 ae 22y 6m
Sarah w/o Silas d 9 Nov 1860 ae 64y
Silas d 31 Mar 1864 ae 77y 7m
Calvin d 31 July 1863 ae 46y
Mary Rebecca w/o Calvin d 12 June 1846 ae 24y
Lucy Maria w/o Parkman d 7 Mar 1851 ae 35y
Samuel d 11 Jan 1875 ae 85y 6m
Sarah w/o Samuel d 17 May 1868 ae 75y 9m
Mary E d/o Sam'l & Sarah d 31 Aug 1850 ae 18y

Sarah d 23 Sept 1847 ae 17y
Fanny W d 29 May 1848 ae 32y
Harriet S w/o Waldo d 3 Oct 1841 ae 23y
BARNARD, Mary Eliza w/o Joel d 28 Sept 1879 ae 53y
NEWTON, Hannah Ann w/o Orien H d 7 Apr 1830 ae 21y
Sarah 23 Dec 1816 - 9 Jan 1891
Haven d 24 Apr 1847 ae 73y
Betsy w/o Haven d 18 July 1840 ae 58y
HOWE, Charles A 4 Mar 1840 - 19 Nov 1903  CW
Maggie A 13 Nov 1840 - 27 Jan 1929
COOLIDGE, William d 15 Mar 1826 ae 72y  REV
COLBURN, Nathaniel 1776-1866
Abigail 1781-1868
CASWELL, Frances C 1835-1933
Father - Elcanah 1800-1887
Mother - Catherine C 1805-1896
Charles Augustus s/o C & E d 26 Feb 1837 ae 4y 11m
SPARHAWK, Mary Abbie d/o E & C Caswell w/o Rufus S d 9 May
1856 ae 26
Rufus S 1832-1860
HAYWARD, Amos d 7 Apr 1862 ae 74y
Sally w/o Amos d 7 Apr 1870 ae 73
NO NAME - American Legion Marker
NOURSE, Asa W 1825-1900
Priscilla H w/o Asa 1839-1920
BURGESS, Nathaniel d 25 Nov 1852 ae 60y
Eunice w/o Nath'l d 23 Dec 1860 ae 48y
Josiah Nelson s/o N & E d 6 Oct 1837 ae 7m 8d
SAWYER, Sarah w/o Peter d 28 Nov 1838 ae 85
Peter d 18 Oct 1840 ae 77
DOW, Ruth Day 1909-1972
William H 1857-1944
Ella Powers w/o W H d 5 Jan 1891 ae 32y 3m 5d
WILLIAMS, Esther P 1886-1961
SAWYER, Joshua d 5 July 1854 ae 66y
Esther C w/o Joshua (Illegible)-- --- ----
Susan w/o J E d 14 Dec 1894 ae 78y 3m
Elbridge d 15 July 1896 ae 79y 9m
WOODBURY, Hope D 18 Apr 1896 - 18 Oct 1955
Frederick A 23 July 1865 - 10 Feb 1920
Julia A d 4 Apr 1897 ae 63y 3m 13d
BAILEY, Betsy B w/o Dexter d 12 May 1876 ae 64y 9m
Dexter d 6 Mar 1893 ae 84y 4m 6d
Andrew d 11 June 1834 ae 22y
Orson d 18 Apr 1834 ae 31y 6m
Eliza Sophia d/o Orson & Eliza d 11 May 1832 ae 8m 11d
PATRICK, Eliza B d 10 Oct 1871 ae 65y
Samuel d 6 Mar 1851 ae 55y
Henry d 3 Dec 1842 ae 6y
PROCTOR, Joel 13 Feb 1820 - 22 Oct 1899
Pamelia A w/o Joel d 22 July 1890 ae 63y 1m

ROBERTS, Polly w/o Aaron Roberts d 5 May 1871 ae 87y
POWERS, Pamelia w/o John d 31 Aug 1871 ae 74y
   Dea John d 20 Jan 1875 ae 71y
HOWE, Adeliza B d/o Nahum & Sarah d 11 Apr 1844 ae 5y 11m
   Susan E d/o Nahum & Sarah d 25 Apr 1844 ae 3y 3m
DONNALLY, Felix drowned 22 June 1823 ae 36
BALCOM, Lyman H 1819–1895
   Electa W w/o Lyman 1826–1917
   Ezra A 1863–1924
   Evelyn S 1866–1949
   Charles B 1848–1907
   Emma F w/o Chas 1850–1931
   Edgar P s/o C & E 1872–1943
   Sara E Stoughton 1876–1965
   Edmund W 1854–1854
   Mary E 1856–1856
   Francis L 1859–1860
   Eliza 1809–1859
SETZER, Judith Ann 1946–1948
RAMSEY, Burl 1905–1960
BARRY MONUMENT – Benjamin W A d 19 Jan 1868 ae 26y
   Simeon Chamberlin d 15 July 1883 ae 74y
   Sarah w/o Simeon d 19 Mar 1870 ae 63y
   Jane w/o Simeon 1811–1895
HILDRETH, J H  Co I 22nd Mass Infantry  CW
HOWE, Susan d/o Jonas & Lydia d 28 Jan 1831 ae 23y 9m
BIGELOW, W H MD d 12 Dec 1874 ae 52y 8m 17d  CW
   Letitia w/o Dr W H d 14 Feb 1870 ae 42y 2m 7d
   James G s/o Dr W H & L d 31 Oct 1872 ae 19y 9m 21d
   Mary Alice d/o Dr W H & Letitia d 6 Jan 1942 ae 83y
BELL, James d 25 Jan 1864 ae 72y 10d
   Rebecca Weston w/o James d 27 Apr 1883 ae 82y 6m
HURLBUT, James D d 26 Dec 1887 ae 83y  CW
   Lucy S w/o James 1849–1927
   Cora A Jacobs 1882
DAKIN, Joseph H 1854–1887
   Herbert J 1885–1973
BALCOM, Henry L 1852–1933
   Rebecca P 1843–1937
BAGLEY, Lizzia S d/o Curtis & Sarah d 29 Nov 1869 ae 27
WHEELER, Gertrude E d/o J K & H A 3 Jan 1875 – 28 July 1956
   Rosella E d/o J K & H A 11 Dec 1872 – 19 Dec 1951
   W K 4 Sept 1850 – 20 Oct 1945
   J K d 2 May 1928 ae 92y
   Harriet A w/o J K d 19 July 1906 ae 66y
   Abigail K w/o Sam'l d 15 Dec 1872 ae 72y
   Samuel d 12 Dec 1876 ae 79y
   James Lincoln s/o J K & H A d 8 Mar 1868 ae 2y 9m

# THE WEST BURIAL GROUND

On 6 May 1822, the same day that the Town of Bolton bought the Pan Burial Ground, they also bought one acre 80 rods on Green Road. This land was purchased from Thomas and Silas Welsh for one hundred dollars. A small part of the back of this burial ground had never been taken as lots, and in recent years the Cemetery Committee has laid out a small number of lots there.

There are a number of large imposing monuments in this burial ground.

Inscriptions copied 1986 by Esther K. Whitcomb and Kathleen Long beginning west of the driveway.

WELSH, Guildford s/o Thos & Zilpah Welsh d 16 June 1831 ae 5y 3d
    Sophia Ann d/o Thos & Zilpah Welsh d 25 Aug 1830 ae 8m 15d
    Silas Jr s/o Silas & Rebecca d 1 Jul 1832 ae 15m 20d
MORSE, Susannah w/o Benj d 29 June 1835 ae 72
    Benjamin d 22 Feb 1844 ae 80y 11m  REV
    Benjamin d Lancaster 26 Jan 1880 ae 83y 9m
    Sally d 15 Feb 1880 ae 87y
    Lydia d 3 Feb 1883 ae 75y
    Eliza d 2 Oct 1887 ae 85
BIGELOW, William d 6 Oct 1826 ae 81  REV
    Nancy B d/o Wm & Hannah d 3 Sept 1847 ae 56
NOURSE, Maria A w/o Andrew L 14 Mar 1803 – 19 Oct 1846
    Andrew L d 18 Nov 1919 ae 76y  Co 1 5th Reg Ma Inf  CW
    Luther d 20 Apr 1891 ae 82y 18d
    Elizabeth w/o Luther d 14 May 1874 ae 64y 4m
    Susan d/o Luther & Elizabeth d 30 Nov 1872 ae 33y
WHITNEY MONUMENT
    David s/o David & Betsy d 7 Mar 1816 ae 17y
    David d 17 Sept 1838 ae 77  REV
    Betsy w/o David d 4 Jan 1843 ae 77
    Joseph d 11 Apr 1878 ae 75y 8m  -- Capt
    Eliza H w/o Capt Joseph d 14 Mar 1887 ae 80
    Anna E d/o Joseph & Eliza d 29 June 1917 ae 73
    Emma d/o Joseph & Eliza d 13 Sept 1898 ae 52
    Martha d/o Joseph & Eliza d 10 May 1886 ae 37
    David s/o Joseph & Eliza d 18 Aug 1872 ae 31
LIPPITT, Lydia w/o J M d 25 June 1871 ae 36y 8d
CRAGG, Richard 1857-1932
    Georgia Baker 1880-1924
    Sarah Ann 26 Dec 1852 – 2 Oct 1915
ATHERTON, Edward F d 27 Sept 1865 ae 14y
    Mary w/o Franklin d 11 Jan 1879 ae 60y
    Franklin d 7 Feb 1866 ae 50y
WHITCOMB, Reuben M 1838-1916
    Henrietta w/o Reuben M 1848-1908
    Hattie May d/o Reuben & Etta M d -- --- 1891
    Catherine w/o Charlie d 17 Aug 1866 ae 90y 2m 19d

REED, Rachel d 26 Mar 1858 ae 76y
  Sarah Sawyer w/o Wm d 15 Mar 1889 ae 67y
  William d 26 Mar 1858 ae 76y
  Sabra w/o Elihu d 23 Feb 1848 ae 61y
  Elihu d 27 Aug 1863 ae 79y
  Rachel w/o John d 10 Apr 1845 ae 94y 9m
  John d 9 Feb 1835 ae 80y  REV
NOURSE, Martha Pierce w/o Charles W d 21 July 1873 ae 26y 21d
PIERCE, James d 30 Dec 1872 ae 71y 3m 20d
  Martha W w/o James d 21 Jan 1888 ae 78y 9m 27d
TOWNSEND, Hannah d 21 Sept 1889 ae 85y 1m 17d
  James d 5 May 1886 ae 88y 5m 1d
  Nancy d 20 Dec 1858 ae 80
  James d 30 Sept 1841 ae 74y
  Sarah d 4 Jan 1841 ae 65
WOODBURY MONUMENT – Lorenzo b 16 May 1806 – d 7 Oct 1882
  Emorancy Bates w/o IW 26 Aug 1801 – 27 Jan 1844
  Sarah Tufts w/o IW 5 June 1812 – 10 Jan 1894
  Luke d 1 July 1890 ae 97y 9m 9d
  Sally Conant d 30 Dec 1832 ae 34y
  STW
  HUSBAND
  EBW
  Olive B w/o Israel d 18 June 1872 ae 69y 3m
  Eunice Farnsworth d 27 Nov 1843 ae 47y
GRASSIE MONUMENT – George B 1825–1895
  Eliza A H w/o Geo B 1831–1920
  Elizabeth d/o Geo & Elizabeth d 19 Oct 1857 ae 28
  Elizabeth Field w/o Geo b Feb 20 1796 –– ––– ––(illeg)
  Sibby Ann w/o Alexander d 10 Feb 1854 ae 32y
FLOYD, Emma P 1840 – 1940
LYMAN, Sarah M 1844 – 1907
  Mary W 1869 – 1953
  Alfred 1834 – 1914
BILLINGS, Benjamin M d 25 Feb 1902 ae 89y 5m
OSGOOD, Emily C d/o Wm & Susan d 4 Oct 1851 ae 5y 2m
CUMMINGS, Charles F d 8 Mar 1852 ae 26y
COFFRAN, Joseph d 25 Mar ae 17y 7m
HOUGHTON, Frank E killed (illeg) ae 20y 8m Battery L 1st Reg
    US Army  CW
  Silas d 10 July 1872 ae 72
(ILLEG), 2 on 1 base Suffer Little Children
NOURSE, Arthur Henry 6 July 1877 – 28 Aug 1961
  Maude A Boothby 2 Apr 1884 – 14 Dec 1957
CROOK, Elizabeth Boothby 16 Nov 1892
NOURSE, Ralph B    29 June 1915
  Mary E 26 Feb 1934
CUTTING, Surepta w/o George d 13 Oct 1863 ae 54y
  George d 28 May 1863 ae 55y
MOORE, Cornelius d 13 Apr 1852 ae 79y
  Hannah d 19 July 1851 ae 78y

DWINELS, Jared d 22 Oct 1860 ae 49y 9m 4d
LUMSDEN, Francis d 20 Jan 1825 ae 58 Native of Edinburgh
    Scotland -- Capt
BALL, Edward E s/o Emerson & Sarah d 1 Mar 1853 ae 10m
  Francis A s/o Emerson & Sarah
  Sarah E d/o Emerson & Sarah
  Abby A d/o Emerson & Sarah
  Charles E s/o Emerson & Sarah d 31 May 1847 ae 1y 10m
  Albert W s/o Wm & Elizabeth d 8 Oct 1853 ae 10y 3m
KING, Asenath w/o Isaac d 18 Feb 1842 ae 53
CARRUTH, John E d 7 Sept 1875 ae 32 a VET of Co C  CW
PALMER, Edward T d 18 Dec 1868 ae 25y 3m 15d  Co  G  36th  Reg
    MVM - CW
NOURSE, (no other cutting)
PHILLIPS, Ruth W Schoellkopf w/o Philip Phillips 30 Nov 1899 –
    20 Nov 1961
FULLER, Judy
CARVILLE, Margaret F 1848-1911
MERRIAM, Asaph 20 March 1792-19 Sept 1868
WHITE, Charles H 1835-1903
  Marietta E 1832-1899
  Fred W 1868-1908
HIGGINS, Robert F 1906-1973
  Albert F 1883-1969
TOMBS, Lewis d 19 Nov 1827 ae 53
  Polly w/o Lewis d 17 July 1849 ae 69
FARNSWORTH, Lewis H d 12 Mar 1890 -- -- (illeg)
  Lydia B w/o Franklin 17 Sept 1807 - 20 Aug 1894
  Franklin d 22 Jan 1845 ae 32
  Charles L d 26 Apr 1840 ae 6y
  Lewis F d 5 June 1854 ae 18y
  Charles C d 6 May 1860 ae 18y
  Abigail w/o Obidiah d 26 Nov 1849 ae 60y 10m
FAIRBANK, Ephraim d 17 July 1849 ae 83 -- Capt REV
BRIGHAM MONUMENT - William M 1854-1932
  Mary C K 1856-1931
  Helen M 1884-1933
  William H 1885-1956
  George H 1825-1910
  Anna W 1827-1912
  George L 1859-1925
  Jennie M 1871-1913
ROSS MONUMENT - William age 88  REV
  Abigail d ae 70
  William Jr d 27 Jan 1829 ae 85 error in age on stone
  Charles P s/o Wm Jr & Deborah d 8 Nov 1822 ae 6y 8m
  Rebecca w/o David d -- --- 1809
  Ellen M -- --- ----(illeg)
NOURSE, Sarah D 1810-1879
HOWARD, Hannah 1845-1895
NURSE, Stephen d 31 May 1826 ae 62

1/ JONATHAN JEWETT 1835
2/ SAMUEL S HOUGHTON 1835
3/ IM & A WOODBURY's TOMB AD 1836
4/ ERECTED by SANFORD HOUGHTON 1848
HOUGHTON MONUMENT (above Tomb)
   Jonas d 1847 ae 87y -- Maj REV
   Eunice w/o Jonas d 1 Dec 1842 ae 78y
   Emily w/o Sanford d 3 Nov ae 42y
   Silas A s/o S & E d 24 Mar 1835 ae 2y
   Jonas s/o S & E d 20 Sept 1845 ae 2y
   Sanford d 21 Dec 1876 ae 72y 10m
   Lucinda H Jacobs d 18 Aug 1874 ae 76y 11m
5/ C A WHEELOCK 1866
WOOD, Charles 3 Jan 1809 - 29 Apr 1898
   Hannah w/o Charles 25 Aug 1806 - May 1869
HOUGHTON, Jonas s/o Maj Jonas & Eunice d 9 Mar 1804 ae 4y 1m
HAVEN, Dea Richard d 2 Nov 1855 ae 85y
   Sally w/o Richard d 7 Dec 1843 ae 69y
PRIEST, Sarah -- --- ----(illeg)
HAYNES, Samuel S d 24 Jan 18-6 ae --
   Caroline w/o Sam'l S 16 --- 1882 ae 76y
ATHERTON, Benjamin d 27 Feb 182- ae 22y s/o Benj & Lucretia
   C Lowell s/o Benj & Lucretia d 29 Dec 1834 ae 21y
   Lucretia d/o Benj & Lucretia d 18 Jan 1826 ae 29y
   Lucretia w/o Benj d 15 Nov 1834 ae 63y
   Benjamin d 7 Feb 1826 ae 56
HOUGHTON, Azor s/o Timothy & Olive d 22 Feb 1825 ae 25y 4m
   Oren s/o Timothy & Olive d 4 May 1828 ae 26y 11m
WOOD, Mary Ella d/o Henry & Hattie d 26 Jan 1874 ae 4m 29d
   Alice May d/o Henry & Hattie d 11 Feb 1877 ae 4m 29d
HAVEN, Lucy d/o Jubal & Nancy d 12 Apr 1829 ae 4d
   Horris s/o Jubal & Nancy d 12 Sept 1829 ae 2y 6m
BARNES, Joseph P s/o S & C d July 1845 ae 15m
   Adelaide A d/o S & C d July 1845 ae 4y
HOWARD, Job d 1 Oct 1844 ae 86 -- Capt REV
   Hannah w/o Capt Job d 1 Jan 1848 ae 84
   Barnard d 27 Mar 1816 ae 33
   Ann d/o Barnard & Hannah d 9 May 1816 ae 13m
   Hannah w/o Barnard d 1 Feb 1855 ae 68
   Dea Levi d 24 Feb 1875 ae 86y
   Mary w/o Dea Levi d 1 Oct 1865 ae 77
PAINE, Chester 1885-1981
   Helen L 1885-1965
   Winthrop s/o Chester & Helen 13 Mar 1915 - 13 Mar 1915
MOORE, Henry O d 22 Sept 1857 ae 19y
   Freeman B 1804-1882
   Lucy Lawrence w/o Freeman 1830-1883
JEWETT, Caroline A Moore d 21 Dec 1868 ae 26y 5m 9d
NEWTON, W E 1838-1913

M J 1849–1908
LAWRENCE, Abijah d 28 Nov 1856 ae 79y
   Millicent w/o Abijah d 17 Aug 1847 ae 71y
   Abijah Jr s/o Abijah & Millicent d 3 Jan 1833 ae 21y 6m
SMART, ---- (illeg)
   Little Haynie s/o HM & RH d 9 June 1851 ae 5y
HOWARD, Rachel d/o Dea Levi & Mary d 27 Jan 1821 ae 4y
   Amasa s/o Dea Levi & Mary d 9 July 1830 ae 21m
   Agnes ----(illeg)
FAIRBANK, Phineas d 9 Sept 1843 ae 69y
   Phineas J d 13 Feb 1879 ae 71y
   Susan Robinson w/o Horatio d 1 Oct 1843 ae 30y
   Waldo s/o Horatio & Susan d 14 Mar 1840 ae 4y
BARNARD, Joab 12 May 1793 - 24 Oct 1871
   Abigail w/o Joab 10 May 1801 - 22 Jan 1871
   Joel 12 May 1793 - 4 July 1871
   Mary w/o Joel 15 June 1796 - 26 June 1876
ROWE, Edith S 1876–1926
   Everett B 186B–1939
   Miriam Brownold 1907–1969
   Catherine Davison 1913-----
   Helen Woodbury 1897–1980
   Eliot E 1901–1957
   Susan Goodrich 1901-----
RICHARDS, Gerald R 1901–1978
   Florence E 1905–1981
HOUGHTON MONUMENT - Quincy A 1826–1907
   Rebecca A G w/o Q A 1827–1911
   Joseph Osgood s/o QA & RA d 16 Oct 1873 ae 16y 4m
   Josephine A w/o G B Fletcher 1863–1903
   Sarah d/o QA & RA 1852–1932
   Daniel W s/o QA & RA 1855–1936
FLETCHER, Sydney R 1894–1974
   Ruth 1899-----
HANSCOM MONUMENT (no cutting)
FYFE MONUMENT - William E 1837–1899
   Mary J 1839–1916
   William d 18 Feb 1854 ae 64y
   Sarah w/o Wm d 3 Oct 1862 ae 61y
   Joseph E d 28 Oct 1849 s/o Wm & Sarah
   Francis A 14 July 1842 s/o Wm & Sarah
   William D 28 Nov 1835 ae 76  REV
   Patience d 31 Oct 1830 ae 73
   Helen L Plummer 1888–1977
   John R Dwelley 1883–1955
   Josephine Plummer w/o JRD 1892–1945
   Sarah A w/o AG Rivers d 17 Apr 1870
WHEELER, Frank A 1857–1947
   Jennie S w/o FA 1854–1922
   Florence A 1883–1968
HOLMAN, Jonas W d 24 May 1885 ae 79y

Abigail w/o Jonas d 19 Mar 1873 ae 61y
Susan d/o Jonas & Abigail d 5 Feb 1855 ae 18y
HOUGHTON, Sanderson d 26 Feb 1833 ae 65y
Dea Henry d 1 Feb 1838 ae 64
Rhoda w/o Henry d 4 Jan 1890 ae 80
WOOD, Henry   Co I 5 Mass Inf  CW
Hattie A w/o Henry 1 Mar 1849 - 19 Oct 1896
ROSS, Maria H w/o B A Ross d 30 May 18-- (illeg)
CAMPBELL, Carl Albert 24 May 1897 - 19 Sept 1954 --Pvt  WWI
Harlan 1924-1939
Margaret E 1902-1966
WHITMAN, Susanne 10 Mar - 11 Mar 1961
KNIGHT Carter d 1 Dec 1831 ae 76y  REV
HOUGHTON, Stephen d 3 Dec 1866 ae 63
Julia A w/o Stephen d 12 Mar 1884 ae 83y 5m
Cephas s/o Josephas & Ann d 26 May 1837 ae 2y
POWERS, Lorenzo J 1846-1924
Louisa Houghton w/o Lorenzo 1847-1896
PIERCE, S H 1820-1896
Helen B w/o SH 1834-1906
Charlotte S 1822-1864
William S 1851-1901
---- Robert L s/o Alexander & Janette d 1 Jan 1855 ae 22y 4m 10d
4 MARBLE MARKERS - ----
Eva                  Ida May          (Illeg)                    Elmer
NEWTON, Horatio 9 Nov 1807 - 31 Aug 1893
Rebecca Barrett w/o Horatio 26 Mar 1819 - 25 Dec 1897
George B 1842-----
Helen C 1847-1881
Emma F 1856-1948
Henry B 1849-1933
Mary L Sampson w/o Henry B 1856-1903
Mary L d/o HB & ML 1898-1914
Fidelia 1845-1934
Mercy S Soule 1835-1926
Grace M Powers 1882-1964
Baby Keizer 1924
PIERCE, James W 1839-1902
Annah L 1839-1919
Bertie ----
Ralph s/o Warren & Amy
HICKS, Jesse B 1873-----
Frances V w/o Jesse 1866-1944
John S Veal 1896-1964
SPRAGUE, Walter L 1872-1939
Mary E Blood w/o Walter 1870-1959
SMITH, Helen R 1923-1975
EDES, Francis C 1853-1942
Catherine O w/o FC 1856-1940
Edward L 1881-----
Miriam B Sprague w/o EL 1897-----

McDONALD, Carrie A w/o JB 1877-1899
ROBINSON, Arna W d 25 Oct 1927 ae 80y 5m
   Lucy A w/o Arna d 9 Aug 1876 ae 24y 2m
   Myra W w/o Arna d 10 Oct 1921 ae 71y 11m
   Edna L d 3 Feb 1958 ae 71y 4m
   William A 1873-1949
CLARK, Robert F 1865-1934
   Ella F Robinson w/o Robert 1871-1959
   Emma C d/o Robert & Ella 17 Sept 1890 - 23 Apr 1899
   Lucy Ellen d/o Robert & Ella 17 June 1902 - 25 Dec 1925
GARDNER, Joseph H 22 Feb 1826 - 8 Apr 1884
   Harry C 31 Oct 1850 - 12 Jan 1893
MOORE, Helen F d 2 Mar 1830 ae 11y
ROBINSON, G W 1839-1911
   Mary E w/o GW 1839-1905
   John E 1876-1956
JEWETT, Henry 1819-1884
   Mary C 1824-1899
   Mary w/o M Houghton d 23 Apr 1894 ae 86y
RICHARDSON, Elizabeth G 1853-1905
POLLARD, Otis d 16 May 1885 ae 82y 1m
   Catherine w/o Otis F d 3 May 1885 ae 77y 9m
   Otis F d 19 Jan 1929 ae 89y 4M
   Anna L w/o Otis F d 12 Aug 1899 in 56 yr
ROBINSON, William d 2 Aug 1888 ae 78y 10m 6d
   Anna Gates w/o Wm d 30 Nov 1894 ae 86y 6m 6d
WELSH, Mary d/o Thos & Lovisa d 25 Nov 1824 ae 18y
   Silas d 14 Feb 1831 ae 40
HAYNES, John C ----(illeg)
   Elizabeth w/o HF 1828-18--
   Henry F 1826-1912
   Mary E d/o Francis & Mary d 25 Feb 1897 ae 64y  CW nurse
   Mary w/o Francis d ----(illeg)
   Charles D s/o Henry & Elizabeth d -- April 1868 ae 15y


## FRIENDS or QUAKER BURIAL GROUND

In 1844 James N. Fry and his wife, Ruth, deeded to the Society of Friends a plot of land, .6 of an acre in size on Berlin Road, to be used as a burial ground. There are no more lots to be obtained there, although an occasional burial is made in a family lot.

Many of the verses were written by the Rustic Bard, Amos Collins, although the only one actually bearing his signature is the one on the gravestone of his son, Abel Collins, age eighteen, who died in Andersonville Prison during the Civil War.

About 1960, Frederick B. Evans, a native of Bolton, had a granite marker set into the front wall of this Burial Ground. The inscription on it reads: "Society of Friends Burial Ground." Mr Evans' grandparents, Josiah and Elizabeth Babcock Evans, are buried in this yard.

Perhaps an explanation is in order for the dates on the gravestones in the Quaker Burial Ground. The Quakers did not use the names of the months or days of the week which had been evolved from the names of ancient gods. They preferred to say "1st day" for Sunday and "3rd of 7th month" instead of July 3rd. Not all of the inscriptions were done in this manner, but it should be borne in mind that this was the custom.

Inscriptions copied 1986 by Esther Whitcomb and Kathleen Long.

WHEELER, Caroline A d/o Henry H & Abbie d 3 Apr 1862 ae 1y
    11m 16d
SOUTHWICK, Jerusha B w/o JD ae 52y 10m
  Jonathan D 29 Apr 1831 - 9 Oct 1902
WHEELER, Abigail d 8th m 3rd 1852 ae 49y 11m
  Asa W d 21 5th m 1862 ae 66
  Mary T w/o Asa passed to Summerland 2 4th m 1883 ae 86
  Asa A d -- --- ----(illeg) ae 86
GOLDSMITH, Hannah w/o Perley Dunsmore 6 Oct 1803 - 29 Jul 1896
PAINE, Mary w/o Tyler d 20 Oct 1862 ae 34y 7m
WHEELER, Frederick W 1837-1924
  Adeline Kent w/o Frederick 1844-1878
WOOD, Ruth F w/o William E d 12 mo 20 1845 ae 24y
  Mary d/o Wm E & Ruth F d 9 mo 17 1861 ae 18y 4m 4d
WHEELER, Merriam w/o Thos W d 29 Nov 1901 ae 89y 1m
  Thomas W d 6 June 1885 ae 70y 6m 10d
SOUTHWICK, George M d 3d m 5 1846 ae 21y
  Stephen S d 6th m 28 1849 ae 68y
  Mary w/o Stephen S d 13 Feb 1874 ae 89
WHEELER, Roena d 7 Mar 1927 ae 88y
  William W 1812-1888
  Sabra w/o Wm 1811-1895
  Louisa d/o Wm & Sabra 1847-1939
  Hannah d/o Jonathan d 7th m 22 1846 ae 63
  Buffum W d 4th mo 13th 1873 ae 78y 10d
HOLDER, William P 1816-1899
  Hannah S 1829-1899
  Lois W 1822-1848
  Lunette E 1861-1923
  Ruth w/o David d 8mo 31st 1881 ae 86y 3m 12d
  Geo W s/o Wm P & Lois W Holder d 8mo 6th 1851 ae 5y
  Issac B s/o Wm P & Lois W Holder d 3mo 31st 1852 ae 8y
  Christopher s/o Wm & Lois -- ---(illeg) 1856
KIMMENS, John d 6mo 20th 1852 ae 52y 10m 16d
  Dinah H d 12mo 5th 1871 ae 74y 21d
WHEELER, Jane F w/o Reuben d 3mo 3 1873 ae 48y 4m 14d
  Reuben A d 9mo 11th 1896 ae 68y 2m 23d
  Sarah H w/o Francis A & d/o Nath'l and Mary E King d 24
    Dec 1859 ae 27y 4m
  Francis A 1835-1909
  Jennie H Manchester w/o F A Wheeler 1839-1874
BABCOCK, Josiah d 3d mo 17th 1851 ae 77y 7m

Elizabeth w/o Josiah d 5th mo 15 1859 ae (illeg)
Josiah C d 6th mo 7 1852 ae 29y 3m
Maria M d 3rd mo 27 1875 ae 56y 3m 12d
Elizabeth w/o Amos Evans Jr d 10mo 18th 1855 ae 38y 11m
SOUTHWICK, Stephen H d 30 Dec 1860 ae 33y 9m
Sophia H w/o Stephen H d/o Paul & Sophia Whitcomb d 22 June 1855 ae 28y
MERRILL, Mellissa w/o J D d 26 Aug 1893 ae 74y 4m
John D d 30 Oct 1885 ae 89y 5m
WHEELER, Jonathan d 3mo 5th 1845 ae 25y
SOUTHWICK, Willard d 22 Feb 1877 ae 60y
MERRILL, Mary Hattie d/o John D & Mellissa d 22 May 1862 ae 5y 5m
RANDALL, Joseph d 21 June 1857 ae 69y
Mary A w/o Joseph d 18 Jan 1891 ae 89y
Stephen A 1843-1905
Martha T w/o Stephen 1848-1932
Ruth W d/o Stephen & Martha d 31 May 1891 ae 11y
Baby s/o Stephen & Martha b & d 31 Mar 1877
Reuben d 12 mo 15th 1857 ae 59y
Sarah E d 5mo 23rd 1865 ae 60y
HOLDER, Rachel F w/o Joseph d 13 of 12th mo 1846 ae 46y
Deborah D w/o Joseph d 24 8th mo 1851 ae 16
Joseph d 7th mo 3rd 1867 ae 82
David G d 4th mo 3rd 1886 ae 76
ALDRICH, Marilla d 5th mo 5th 1859 ae 30y 3m 2d
WHEELER, Elizabeth d 2 Oct 1858 ae 50y 9m 17d
Miriam d 9th mo 6th 1863 ae 75y 6m
Daniel d 1st mo 7th 1853 ae 76y
Abigail d 5th mo 21 1875 ae 92y 4m 18d
BARTLEY, A Elmira d 21 Feb 1895 ae 68y
Marble - (illeg)
WHEELER, Thomas A 1st mo 10th 1825 - 7th mo 31st 1904
Susan C 3rd mo 5th 1828 - 8th mo 4th 1866
Hannah D 11th mo 15th 1843 - 5th mo 21st 1931
Jesse A 4th mo 13th 1875 - 1st mo 13th 1959
Lilla G 8th mo 23d 1877 - 11th mo 16th 1934
Elwood O 17 Feb 1877 -18 Oct 1965
Bessie M 27 Apr 1884 - 11 Feb 1974
Chester M 25 Aug 1912 - 28 Feb 1979
Thomas A 1904-1977
Mary B w/o Jarvis d 29 Sept 1889 ae 82y
Jarvis d 2nd mo 11 1865 ae 59y 10m
BLANCHARD, Emma A 1857-1920
WHEELER, Marilla Emora d/o JD d 1855 ae 1y 19d
Jonathan F 1816-1902
Jemima D 1830-1910
Jonathan d 3rd mo 30 1851 ae 64
Phebe K w/o Jonathan d 8th m 15 1806 ae 62y
WALCOTT, Mary B w/o Joshua B d -- --- ----(illeg)
Joshua B d 25 Nov 1885 ae 29y 9m

FRYE, Mary E w/o James N d 8th mo 8 1854 ae 30y
  James N d 9th mo 30th 1854 ae 30y
FAULKNER, Mary w/o Emory Jr d 3 Dec 1861
FRY, David A d 11mo 21 1854 ae 42y 8m 24d
  Sarah Howard w/o David A 1828-1890
  Baby 1894-1895
RANDALL, Joseph J 1861-1901
  Anna A 1861-1906
BLISS, Lydia Elizabeth d/o Roswell & Lydia d 2d mo 21 1851 ae
    18y
  Minerva Chadwick d/o Roswell & Lydia d 13 Sept 1856 ae 38y
KENDALL, Mary W w/o Otis A Kendall d/o R & L Bliss 20 May 1857
    ae 33y 10m
BLISS, Roswell d 4th mo 30 1869 ae 78y 1m 15d
  Lydia d 1st mo 15 1872 ae 76y 7m 6d
WHEELER, Betsy Jones w/o John Wheeler d 7 Feb 1872 ae 66y
    9m 19d
  John d 13 June 1856 ae 59y 11m 26d
  Amasa J Gilbert d 11 Nov 1837 ae 7y 8m 18d
  Mary Lovisa d 26 Feb 1841 ae 3y 27d
  Albert Buffum d 2 Feb 1841 ae 9mo 22d
JACOBS, Rachel F w/o Ira Jacobs d 2 May 1879 ae 49y 1m 16d
GATES, Calvin d 5th mo 1847 ae 84y
  Lydia w/o Calvin d 11th mo 19th 1865 ae 92
BABCOCK, Elizabeth Walcott w/o David d 5mo 15 1888 ae 79y 11m
    26d
  David d 12mo 4th 1891 ae 86y 9m 21d
  Nathan b 30 Dec 1830 d 23 Aug 1925
  Sarah W w/o Nathan d 10th mo 22 1888 ae 50 3mo
DAVIS, William d -- --- ----(illeg)
RATHBUN, (broken)
  Francis E s/o Solomon & Hannah d 10th mo 9 1848 ae 1mo 24d
  Hannah M D w/o Solomon d 5th mo ae 36y
  Solomon H d -- --- 1871 ae 65y
  ------- d 10th mo 5 I846 ae 12d
BROWNELL, Lizzie A 1856-1925
DOW, Alfred 1851-1935
  Alice M w/o Alfred 1851-1927
  Mary A 1881-1937
  Susan L 1877-1973
  Alfred W 1875-1941
  Hanna E w/o Alfred W 1872-1919
  Irene J d/o A & H 1912-1912
KIMMENS, Amos P 9-12-1817 - 2-16-1898
  Nancy A w/o Amos d 8mo 26th 1849 ae 36
  Joanna H w/o Amos 9-27-1826 - 8-11-1907
BABCOCK, Charles J 1891-1985
  Marjorie J 1899-1981
COLLINS, Lucy F w/o Amos W d 3mo 21st ae 58y 1m 2d
  Abel J d Andersonville Ga 11mo 4th 1861 ae 18y 6m
DOW, Greeley 1817-1907

Lydia B Holder w/o Greeley 1825-1914
George E 10 Dec 1854 - 28 Feb 1917
Alice L w/o George E Nov 1863 - 26 Sept 1923
Ruth N d/o Geo & Alice 2 July 1893 - 2 July 1977
BABCOCK, Katie E w/o Jesse W d 15 June 1882 ae 38y 4m 25d
Jesse W 1845-1913
Ellen E w/o Jesse 1857-1953
Bessie E d/o Jesse & Ellen 1889-1892
WEST, Howard E 1868-1891
Annie G 1870-1954
Harry A 1891-1973
FRY, James N d 1st mo 2nd 1869 ae 88
Ruth w/o J N d 1st mo 27th 1875 ae 87
BRUCE, Mary O w/o Simeon d 18 Aug 1858 ae 26y 6m
COOLEDGE, Charles Edward s/o Silas & Judith d 19 July 1849 ae
11y 11m
Albert d 2mo 2 1850 ae 2y
FATHER 1800-1840
MOTHER 1805-1883
OSGOOD, Martha B d/o D & S d 11 Nov 1849 ae 19
Sarah H d/o D & S d 4th mo 29th 1855 ae 16y 5d
Daniel d 1st mo 25th 1857 ae 54Y 9m
Sarah H w/o Daniel d 4mo 2d 1866 ae 62y 6mo
Daniel L s/o D & S d 10th mo 20th 1859 ae 20y 11m
COOLIDGE, Lucy J 1841-1911
Abigail S w/o Silas d 20 Nov 1877 ae 82y 6m
WHEELER, Miss Elonor E d/o Aaron & Mariam d 3 June 1851 ae 18y
Franklin G s/o A & M d 26 July 1858 ae 23y 4m
FAY, Baxter d 4th mo 28 1853 ae 75y
JACOBS, William 1902-1984
Urena R w/o William 1909-----
George C 1899-1958
George E 1858-1915
Gertrude 1894-1929
Arthur 1897-1935
Helen C 1870-1941
George S 1833-1918
Caroline w/o Geo S 1837-1872
WRIGHT, Hattie L w/o Edward E ---------


## SMALL POX BURIAL GROUND

There were once two small pox burial grounds in Bolton, but the bodies in one were moved long ago to a family lot in the Pan Burial Ground. The other one, on Sugar Road near the bridge over Route 495, contains only one grave, a father and his four year old daughter buried together. It is surrounded by four granite posts with chains between.

It is believed there were many other burials of small pox victims of which we know nothing. These may have been in the orchard, the garden, or on some sightly knoll near the house and, lacking a gravestone, there is now no sign of any grave.

HATCH, John P d 19 Oct 1845 ae 42y 8m 15d
   Rebecca B d/o John & Eliza d 18 Oct 1845 ae 4y 8m 11d d

## CEMETERIES OF LEOMINSTER

### Old Burial Grounds

According to traditions before Leominster was incorporated in 1740, some of the early settlers began to use for a burial place a tract of land offered by Jonathan Wilson. His farm was located on the easterly side of Main Street at the junction of Day Street near number three school house in North Leominster.

Among the families using that burial ground were the Wilsons, Joslins, and the Wilders. A native of the neighborhood remembered that in the early 1860's there were more than twenty-five headstones in various condition; the broken ones were taken up when the hay was cut, some were thrown in a swamp hole, others were removed a few at a time before the land was plowed in 1868. An effort to perserve the burial ground was made by Major Elias Joslin, but the descendants of the other families did not respond to his appeal, and all outward traces of the burial ground disappeared.

In 1893, a broken headstone discovered near the site was placed in the Museum of the Leominster Public Library. It contained the following inscription: "here lies ye body of Jonathan Wilson ye son of Mr. Jonathan and Hepsebah Wilson who died November ye 18, 1736 aged 2 years 3 months and 9 days." After the 1936 flood, the gravestone was removed from the Library Museum and given to the Cemetery Commission for Pine Grove Cemetery.

On May 6, 1912 a monument with the inscription: "this Stone erected by Leominster Historical Society marks the site of the first burial ground in Leominster." On October 23, 1968, the Leominster Historical Society granted the City of Leominster permission to move the monument a short distance for reasons of safety to school children.

With the loss of this burial ground in Leominster and others throughout the Commonwealth, a law originating in 1880 (Chapter 114 Section 14 of the General Laws of Massachusetts) is directly concerned with preserving the historical assets of cemeteries. To further protect early cemeteries another law was enacted in 1902 (Chapter 114 Section 18 of the General Laws). Another law (Chapter 272 Section 73) imposes a substantial fine or prison term for destroying or removing memorials of the dead.

Pine Grove Cemetery is located on the easterly side of Main Street, adjacent to the Old Training Field (Carter Park). This area was the center of Leominster in our early history. According to the Proprietors Records, Volume 3 1701-1783, a meeting was held October 12, 1742:

> 3 1y     To see if the propriety will give a piece of
>        land near the Leominster Meeting hous for a
>        Biering Place
> 3         Voted to give a piece of land in ye place
>        praid for for a convenient Biering place to
>        ye east of Leominster Meeting Hous.
>                     Jacob Houghton, Clerk

The first Meeting House (1742-1775) stood here, and the first school house built in 1749 was next to the Meeting House. Many of our early settlers and their families were buried here, as well as Revolutionary War Soldiers, Veterans of the War of 1812, and Veterans of the Civil War. The last burial in Pine Grove Cemetery was that of Miss Emma C. Moore, Leominster Historian who was laid to rest in the family plot on June 13 1937.

A white picket fence enclosed Pine Grove Cemetery for many years, later being replaced by a stone wall which incorporated three earlier granite tombs at the Main Street entrance.

In 1936, with the help of W.P.A. Funds, private donations, and hundreds of volunteer hours from friends and members, Mrs. Frederick F. Johnson (Pearle W.), Regent and Historian of the Capt. John Joslin, Jr. Chapter, Daughters of the American Revolution chaired a Pine Grove Cemetery project. At that time, a place in the cemetery was set apart, and Bronze Plaques laid in Concrete noting the unknown but proven graves of the following veterans:

Elias Joslyn Jr. War of 1812
Jotham Bennet - Oliver Carter - Silas Carter - Edward Fuller - Ephraim Johnson - Luke Johnson - Josiah White Jr. and James Wilder all Veterans of the Revolutionary War. The cemetery was inventoried, landscaped and put in fine condition.

Inscriptions copied by Evelyn B. Hachey.

ABBOTT, Ella Olivia d/o James P & Sara S d 3 Dec 1810
     ae 2d (D-30)
   Ellen Sarah d/o Samuel & Abigail d 23 Mar 1833 ae 24y
     3m (D-30)
ADAMS, Emma d 1822 ae 2y (J-34)
   Oliver Ellis s/o Col Oliver & Silpah d 16 July 1822 ae 2y 5m
   Windsor s/o Benjamin & Emma d 1839 ae 9m (J-33)
ALLEN, David d 9 Nov 1857 ae 81y -- Capt War of 1812 (F-29)
   Elizabeth d/o David & Sarah d 10 Nov 1843 ae 23y (F29)

Sarah K d 17 Dec 1846 ae 43y (D-19)
Sarah w/o David Allen d 11 Nov 1862 ae 83y (F-30)
Sarah d/o David & Sarah d 8 Nov 1828 ae 18y (F-29)
ANDERSON, JG d -- --- ----   Co H 57 Mass Inf  CIV (I-29)
   Robert d 21 Jan 1854 ae 25y (I-29)
BAKER, Elizabeth Woodbury w/o Reuben d (K-20)
   Reuben b 8 Feb 1755 d 29 Sept 1834 ae 79y  REV
     Battle of Bunker Hill Wounded (K-29)
BALCH, Dorcas A d/o Er & Susan d 25 Dec 1827 ae 4m 10d (J-4)
   John H s/o Er & Susan d 17 Apr 1821 ae 2m 10d (J-4)
BALL, George s/o Micah d 15 Sept 1812 ae 4m (0-15)
BARKER, John d 11 July 1829 ae 42  -- Col
BARTLETT, Luther d 15 Oct 1838 ae 51y War of 1812 (I-34)
BENNETT, John d 21 Oct 1806 ae 52y REV (U-6)
   Nathan s/o John & Bathsheba d 18 Apr 1760 ae 38y
BIGELOW, Abijah s/o Abijah & Hannah d 17 Apr 1817 ae 3y
     2m 13d (0-16)
   Nancy w/o Isaac d 4 June 1823 ae 40y (B-24)
BOUTELL-BOUTELLE, Abigail wid/o James d 15 Sept 1845 ae 75y
   Artemas s/o Col Timothy & Rachel d 20 Nov 1799 ae 18y (M-21)
   Dorothy d/o John & Dorothy d 14 July 1827 ae 23y (I-16)
   Dorothy wid/o John d 10 Feb 1824 ae 62y (I-16)
   Eliza A d/o William & Martha d 4 Aug 1834 ae 9y
   Enock d 5 Apr 1816 ae 40y (M-20)
   George W s/o William & Martha d 29 May 1832 ae 3m
   James d 26 Sept 1822 ae 69y (M-14)
   James d 11 Oct 1791 ae 66y (L-15)
   James d 22 Aug 1752 ae 53y (T-5)
   John d 1837 ae 74y (I-16)
   Josiah s/o James & Abigail d 3 Sept 1827 ae 15y (L-13)
   Judith wid/o James d 28 May 1791 ae 91y (T-5)

Loring s/o Col Timothy & Rachel d 4 July 1791 ae 18y 4m
7d (M-20)
Martha Jane d/o William & Martha d 2 Aug 1834 ae 1y
Philinda T s/o William & Martha d 24 Aug 1839 ae 7m
Rachiel wid/o Col Timothy d -- --- ---- (M-21)
Relief d 18 Nov 1824 ae 64y (L-16)
Sarah d 1793 ae 46y (M-14)
Sarah F d -- --- ---- (M-20)
Timothy d 7 June 1849 ae 34y (M-21)
Timothy s/o Maj Timothy & Rachel d 9 Feb 1778 ae 8y (M-20)
Timothy T d 25 May 1810 ae 70y REV (M-20)
William d 8 Apr 1797 ae 69y REV (I-16)
BOWERS, Jerahmeal d 5 Oct 1795 ae 67y REV
Mary Houghton wid/o Jerahmeal d 17 May 1811 ae 81y
Phebe 2nd w/o Samuel d 13 Oct 1847 ae 76y (-24)
Rebekah w/o Samuel d 15 Oct 1806 ae 49y (I-24)
Samuel s/o Samuel & Rebekah d 25 Aug 1800 ae 20y
Samuel d 23 Mar 1823 ae 70y (I-24)
BRABOOK, Charles s/o Ezra & Elizabeth H d 9 July 1838 ae 8y
Elizabeth H w/o Ezra H d 30 May 1841 ae 33y (F-33)
Hollis s/o William & Joanna b 23 Sept 1830 d 9 July
1838 ae 8y (F-32)
Joanna w/o William d 4 June 1833 ae 43y (F-32)
Levi s/o William & Joanna b 14 Nov 1813 d 21 Sept 1818
ae 5y (F-32)
Nancy d/o William & Joanna b 23 Apr 1808 d 5 Aug 1820
ae 12y (F-32)
Sophia d 1869 ae 77y (J-24)
William d 22 May 1841 ae 60y War of 1812 (F-32)
BEARNARD, Alfred d 1837 ae 13y (E-15)
BRIGHAM, Elizabeth wid/o Joel d 6 Sept 1846 ae 87y (I-21)
Joel d 24 June 1813 ae 58y (I-21)
Sally d/o Joel & Elizabeth d 16 Oct 1796 ae 2y (I-21)
BROWN, Abigail S w/o Timothy d 10 Jan 1838 ae 30y (H-20)
BURDETT, BURDIT, & BURDITT, Abigail w/o John d 8 Mar 1830 ae
78y (M-11)
Betsey w/o Hervey d 10 May 1836 ae 49y
Edwin J s/o Nathan & Mary E d 30 Aug 1840 ae 1y (N-10)
James d 1881 ae 92y War of 1812 (K-14)
John d 19 Dec 1843 ae 97y REV (M-11)
Lucinda w/o James d 23 Apr 1818 ae 22y (K-14)
Lydia w/o Phinehas S d 31 July 1825 ae 24y (K-15)
Mary Elizabeth w/o Augustus P d 14 Aug 1849 ae 26y (K-9)
Mary T w/o James d 15 Dec 1826 ae 33y (K-14)
Polly d 1871 ae 75y (K-14)
Sarah Jane d 1850 ae 20y (L-15)
William s/o John & Abigail d 6 Feb 1813 ae 26y (N-11)
BURRAGE, Abigail w/o Thomas d 9 Feb 1862 ae 89y (A-25)
Asenath w/o John d 11 Mar 1824 ae 31y (A-24)
Caroline d/o Deac William d 22 Oct 1826 ae 21y (E-21)
Dana Bassett s/o William & Roxanna d 28 Apr 1843 ae 7y

12d (D-20)

Henry Augustine s/o Deac William & Roxanna d 16 Apr
    1838 ae 5y (E-21)

Henry Waldo s/o Deac William & Roxanna d 19 Mar 1841 ae
    11m 19d (E-20)

Joseph s/o William & Phebe d 31 Oct 1803 ae 23y (T-8)

Mary Jane d/o William & Roxanna d 1851 ae 22y (E-20)

Molly w/o Deacon William d 17 Dec 1820 ae 52y

Patty d/o William & Phebe d 30 Ot 1807 ae 21y (N-8)

Phebe wid/o William d 25 May 1822 ae 82y (N-9)

Polly d/o Deac William & Mary d 10 Dec 1817 ae 23y (E-21)

Roxana w/o Deac William d 17 Oct 1858 (E-20)

Sarah d/o William & Phebe d 18 Sept 1806 ae 23y (N-8)

Thomas d 11 Oct 1828 ae 65y (A-25)

William s/o William & Phebe d 9 Aug 1844 ae 76y (E-21)

William Sr d 23 Oct 1820 ae 89y  REV (N-9)

BUSS, Asaph C s/o Asaph & Elizabeth d 23 Apr 1838 ae 7w (K-17)

Elizabeth T w/o Asaph E  d 31 Mar 1838 ae 25y

Ephraim s/o John & Sarah R d 5 Oct 1880 ae 78y (K-5)

John d 31 Oct 1845 ae 86y  REV (J-4)

John Jr d 24 Sept 1824 ae 40y  --Maj (J-4)

Mary E d/o Maj John & Elizabeth d 10 Jan 1829 ae 9y 6m
    (J-4)

Polly d/o John & Sarah R d 3 June 1860 ae 60y (K-5)

Prudence w/o Stephen d 6 Apr 1789 ae 67 (W-2)

Sarah d/o John & Sarah d 24 Dec 1790 ae 4y 9m (J-4)

Sarah R w/o John d 27 June 1852 ae 91y (J-5)

Stephen d 9 Apr 1790 ae 72y  REV (X-2)

BUTLER, Abijah Dea d 19 Jan 1822 ae 71y  REV (Q-15)

CARTER, Abel d 26 July 1844 ae 64? (D-16)

Alfred s/o Josiah & Prudence d 4 Oct 1825 ae 25y (I-9)

Alvah Whitcomb s/o John & Anne d 26 July 1797 ae 10m (J-6)

Anna d 1851 ae 71y (E-20)

Anna Burrage d 1851 ae 73y (L-30)

Asa d 24 Jan 1822 ae 51y (0-19)

Asaph s/o Oliver & Bulah d 23 Dec 1776 ae 19y  REV (P-19)

Bartimus d 1879 ae 79y (N-29)

Beaman s/o Capt Nathaniel d 31 Aug 1799 ae 6y (G-20)

Bedah w/o Oliver d 1 Mar 1777 ae 58y (P-20)

Benjamin d 16 Mar 1850 ae 80y (L-30)

Betsy w/o Capt James d 20 Apr 1844 ae 72y (D-21)

Betsey d/o James & Betsy d 2 Nov 1820 ae 22y (D-21)

Betsey d/o John & Anna d 23 Apr 1859 ae 69y (K-7)

Betty d 15 Jan 1811 ae 57y (P-19)

Caroline w/o James H d 15 Feb 1887 ae 83y (B-21)

Charlotte S d -- --- ---- ae 8y (N-8)

Catherine Addia d/o James H & Caroline d 27 Aug 1838 ae
    3y 6m (B-21)

Demaris w/o Jonathan d 6 July 1820 ae 74y (B-18)

Dorothy d/o Nathaniel & Eunice d 11 Sept 1799 ae 5y (E-20)

Dorothy w/o Capt Nathaniel d 25 Jan 1789 ae 47y (G-20)

Edwin d 1816 ae 19y (E-8)
EL d 1857 ae 33y (E-20)
Elisha s/o Capt Nathaniel d 1 Sept 1799 ae 9y (G-20)
Elizabeth wid/o Phinehas d 7 Mar 1843 ae 67y (F-26)
Emma w/o James H d 3 Nov 1822 ae 25y (B21)
Ephraim Deacon d 7 May 1817 ae 69y REV War of 1812 (F-10)
Esther d/o Oliver & Beulah d 3 Feb 1777 ae 22y (F-19)
Eunice w/o Nathaniel d 23 Jan 1820 ae 45y (E-19)
Granville d -- --- ---- ae 1y (N-25)
Henry W d 30 Dec 1876 ae 71y (D-21)
---- Inf/o William & Betsey d 26 Jan 1827 ae ? (M-29)
Jacob d 24 Aug 1835 ae 72y (M-29)
James d 28 May 1853 ae 84y -- Capt (D-21)
James H d 13 Mar 1871 ae 77y (B-21)
Joanna w/o Deacon Ephraim d 13 June 1803 ae 55y (F-10)
Jonathan d 9 Mar 1824 ae 56y (B-17)
Jonathan d 19 Mar 1799 ae 87y --Lieut REV (I-6)
Joseph W d 31 July 1839 ae 82y 9m REV
Josiah d 13 Feb 1812 ae 85y --Col (I-10)
Josiah d 19 July 1827 ae 78y --Maj REV (I-9)
Julia N d/o James & Betsey d 13 Mar 1822 ae 5y (D-21)
Louisa w/o Samuel d 16 May 1848 ae 40y (M-28)
Lucy w/o Abel d 26 May 1846 ae 64y (D-17)
Lucy d/o Ephraim & Joanna 20 Jan 1894 ae 8y (G-10)
Martha d/o Deacon David & w/o John Jr d 13 Mar 1808 ae
    27y (K-6)
Mary relict/o Deacon Ephraim d 9 Nov 1819 ae 61y (F-6)
Mary Elizabeth inf/o William & Betsey d 26 Mar 1828 (M-29)
Mary Jane d 1891 ae 65y (N-29)
Mary Johnson w/o Jonathan d 19 Jan 1846 ae 71y (B-18)
Mary S d/o James H & Caroline b 17 Mar 1840 d 21 May
    1882 ae 42y (B-21)
Nathaniel Jr d 13 Mar 1812 ae 76y -- Capt REV (C-20)
Nathaniel d 20 July 1787 ae 79y REV (U-8)
Nathaniel d 1850 ae 79y (E-19)
Oliver d 1822 ae 2y (B-19)
Oliver d 11 Sept 1790 ae 75y REV (P-20)
Orville G s/o Bartimus & Sophia d 23 Oct 1849 ae 14y (N-28)
Phineas d 2 Mar 1843 ae 84y REV (F-26)
Pricella w/o Oliver Jr d 10 Mar 1777 ae 38y (G-34)
Prudence wid/o Josiah d 21 Sept 1849 ae 86y (I-10)
Prudence d 24 Jan 1799 ae 3m 20d (I-9)
Rachel w/o Jacob d 20 Aug 1830 ae 59y (M-30)
Rebecca w/o Thomas d 15 May 1836 ae 58y (M-28)
Ruth w/o Joseph W d 20 Dec 1850 ae 72y
Samuel M d 1889 ae 83y (M-28)
Sarah w/o Asa d 13 Mar 1833 ae 47y (D-16)
Sewell s/o Asa & Betty d 21 Aug 1821 ae 33y (D-16)
Sophia d/o Phineas d 26 Feb 1803 ae 57y (N-28)
Tabitha w/o Col Josiah d 27 June 1810 ae 81y (I-9)
Thankful w/o Nathaniel d 5 Dec 1755 ae 41y (U-8)

Thomas d 28 May 1773 ae 35y (P-20)
Thomas d 19 Nov 1848 ae 73y (M-28)
William s/o Nathaniel Jr & Eunice d 25 Aug 1799 ae 3y (E-20)
CHASE, Betsey w/o Joshua d 28 Aug 1812 ae 24y (K-13)
   George d 9 Aug 1841 ae 46y (O-7)
   Joshua d 4 July 1815 ae 31y (K-13)
   Lois w/o Moses d June 1872 ae 74y (E-33)
   Maria w/o Metaphor d 17 Feb 1841 ae 79y (O-7)
   Metaphor d 14 Apr 1806 ae 45y --Col REV (O-7)
   Moses d 4 July 1850 ae 70y (E-34)
   Sarah d/o Joshua & Betsy d 1812 ae 5m 18d (K-12)
   Sophronia w/o George d 27 Dec 1838 ae 46y (O-7)
   Stephen d 6 Oct 1819 ae 71y REV (K-13)
CHESMORE, Almira w/o Daniel d 25 Dec 1887 ae 79y (B-29)
   Daniel d 15 June 1886 ae 83y (B-29)
   Francis A d 1861 ae 20y (B-29)
   Mehitable w/o Daniel d 8 July 1844 ae 42y (B-29)
   Thomas H d 17 Sept 1842 ae 11y (B-29)
COLBURN, Abigail w/o Oliver d 10 May 1859 ae 59y (A-33)
   Anna Darby w/o John b 1741 d 1803 (D-22)
   Betsey w/o Joseph d 26 Sept 1867 ae 83y (D-22)
   Caroline Matilda d -- --- ---- ae 4m
   Charles S s/o Joseph & Relief d 14 Jan 1825 ae 22m (D-22)
   Deborah H w/o Elisha d 30 Oct 1856 ae 81y (A-30)
   Elisha d 21 Dec 1831 ae 64y (A-30)
   John b 1738 d 1827 REV (D-23)
   Joseph h/o Betsy d 15 Jan 1857 ae 77y 3m (D-22)
   Lorenzo Theodore s/o Oliver & Abigail d 28 July 1841
     (A-34)
   Mother d 1881 (A-33)
   Oliver d 15 Nov 1868 ae 69y (A-33)
   Relief w/o Joseph d 29 May 1826 ae 46y (D-22)
   Sarah Ann d/o Chas d 8 Aug 1828 ae 3y (D-28)
COLLINS, Dorcas w/o Daniel d 22 Nov 1845 ae 63y (N-10)
   Hannah wid/o Jedidiah d 8 Dec 1803 ae 89y (C-14)
   James d -- --- 1839 ae 17y (N-9)
   Jedidiah d 22 Sept 1791 ae 78y (G-13)
CONANT, Reverand Abel d 6 Dec 1836 ae 43 (A-32)
   Antonette d/o Rev Abel & Rebecca d 5 Apr 1839 ae 10y (A-31)
   Joseph d 26 June 1859 ae 78y (H-14)
   Joshua s/o Joseph & Patience d 14 Feb 1813 ae 21d (H-13)
   Maria R d/o Rev Abel & Rebecca d 12 July 1865 ae 40y (A-31)
   Patience w/o Joseph d 20 May 1845 ae 63y (H-14)
   Rebecca w/o Rev Abel d 1 Aug 1884 ae 86y (A-32)
COOK, Calvin B d 7 Feb 1875 ae 68y (D-8)
   Miriam w/o Calvin B d 9 Dec 1892 ae 84y (D-8)
   Theodore s/o Calvin & Meriam d 15 Apr 1831 ae 5m 11d (D-8)
COOLIDGE, Anna w/o Elisha d 5 July 1821 ae 32y (L-5)
   Elisha d 29 Apr 1841 ae 72y (D-3) Eliza d/o Elisha &
   Eliza d/o Eliza & Rebekah d 18 Oct 1819 ae 19y (L-4)
   Martha wid/o Elisha d 14 Nov 1868 ae 81y (L-4)

Mary Ann d/o Elisha & Anna d 30 July 1838 ae 25y (L-4)
Rebecah w/o Elisha d 30 May 1807 ae 29y (L-4)
CUMMINGS, Abigail w/o Jonathan d 10 May 1868 ae 85y (J-16)
Emeline d/o Jonathan & Abigail d 1 Apr 1813 ae 3y (J-15)
Jonathan 8 Feb 1822 ae 46y (J-16)
Rufus K d 29 Mar 1866 ae 52y (J-15)
Timothy S s/o Jonathan & Abigail d 31 Aug 1836 ae 19y (J-16)
DABY, Anna w/o Deliverance d 3 Jan 1799 ae 50y
DARLING, Cassius Augusta s/o Joseph & Mary d 15 Apr 1840
ae 12y (F-11)
Charles s/o Joseph & Mary d 30 Apr 1836 ae 1m (F-11)
Granville s/o Joseph S & Mary d 1832 ae 14m (F-12)
Joseph d 6 Apr 1808 ae 45y REV (F-12)
Joseph Frank s/o Joseph S & Mary M d 24 Aug 1849
ae 1y (F-11)
Joseph Granville s/o Joseph & Mary M d 8 Mar 1830
ae 7m (F-12)
Joseph S d 10 Mar 1833 ae 80y
Mary M w/o Joseph S d 25 Mar 1857 ae 50y (F-11)
Mary Richardson d/o Joseph & Mary d 1826 ae 2d (F-12)
DAVIS, Nancy NST w/o William d 5 Jan 1837 ae 41?? (M-4)
DERBY, Albert G s/o Haskell & Eliza d 22 Aug 1846 ae 3m (H-15)
Edmund s/o Joshua & Olive d 9 July 1820 ae 2y (H-10)
Eliza w/o Haskell d 23 Aug 1846 ae 36y (H-15)
Joshua d 3 Dec 1845 ae 68y (H-10)
Sarah d/o Joshua & Olive d 13 Oct 1814 (H-10)
DEXTER, Ebenezer d 22 Jan 1850 ae 74y (N-24)
John d 15 June 1827 ae 87y (L-11)
Martha w/o John d 6 May 1836 ae 77y
William s/o William & Betsey d 14 June 1804 ae 25y (K-16)
DIVOLL, Abagail d 16 Aug 1827 ae 62y (A-19)
Alfred B s/o Briant & Tabitha d 19 Aug 1839 ae 3m 16d (H-34)
Elizabeth w/o John d 1812 ae 77y (A-20)
Frances d/o Levi & Francis D d 1875 ae 63y (A-20)
Frances D w/o Levi Jr d 6 Apr 1873 ae ? (A-20)
John d 30 Aug 1814 ae 86Y (H-21)
John d 1 Dec 1842 ae 80y REV (K-9)
Levi d 29 Jan 1888 ae 76y (A-20)
Levi Jr d 24 July 1824 ae 36y (A-20)
Luke d 27 Nov 1826 ae 58y (F-27)
Oliver d 6 Dec 1822 ae 63y REV (A-19)
Rebecca w/o John 13 Mar 1838 ae 68y (K-9)
Sophronia d 13 Aug 1824 ae 7y (A-20)
DODGE, Lucy w/o Thomas d 17 Mar 1845 ae 62y (K-34)
Thomas d 9 Aug 1840 ae 75y (K-33)
DUNNELL, Luther s/o Soloman & Hannah d 30 June 1808 ae 16y (K-4)
ELLENWOOD, Arah d 13 Jan 1848 ae 45y (D-28)
Ellen L d/o Arah & Eliza P d 15 Mar 1842 ae 4m 2d (D-28)
Emily M d/o Arah & Eliza P d 1848 ae 8y (D-28)
Frances d/o Arah & Eliza d 24 Apr 1847 ae 7w (D-28)
Luicrelia w/o Arah d 15 Jan 1833 ae 41y (D-28)

ESTERBROOK, Mehitabel w/o Gen Nathaniel C d 2 Feb 1842 ae
    49y (B-28)
EVANS, John s/o Nathaniel & Mary d 5 July 1777 ae 23m (Q-19)
    Samuel d 9 Dec 1812 ae 69y (L-7)
FAIRBANK, Elijah d 14 Sept 1803 ae 68y  REV  (I-6)
FISK, Jonas d 4 Nov 1799 ae 57y (M-11)
    Louisa w/o James d 15 Nov 1832 ae 26y (F-29)
FOLLANSBEE, Mary d 3 Sept 1824 ae 33y
FULLER, Edward d 3 Mar 1783 ae 21 (S-16)
FULLUM, Elizabeth w/o Jacob d 5 Feb 1818 ae 67y (D-24)
    Jacob d 20 Oct 1833 ae 84y  REV  (D-24)
    Rebekah d 22 Apr 1865 ae 86y (D-24)
GARDNER, Anne d/o John & Elizabeth d 8 Sept 1823 ae 11y (G-15)
    Catherine b 23 Oct 1775 d 8 Dec 1863 (F-15)
    Caroline d/o John & Eliza d 10 Dec 1800 ae 3m
    Clarinda d/o John & Eliza d 29 Dec 1811 ae 4y (G-15)
    Elicia d/o Francis & Sarah b 7 Dec 1773 d 30 Oct 1851 (F-15)
    Elizabeth d/o Francis & Sarah d 11 Mar 1849 ae 82y 9m
        15d (F-16)
    Elizabeth w/o John Esq (G-16)
    Elizabeth G d/o John Esq d 1814 ae 44y (G-16)
    Francis Rev 2nd Minister b 29 Feb 1736 d 2 June 1814 ae
        79y (F-17)

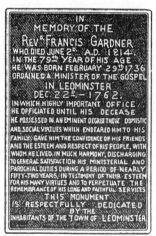

Henry d 28 May 1831 ae 24y (G-16)
John s/o Rev Francis &  Sarah b 1768 d 1856 ae 88y (G-16)
Joseph s/o Francis & Sarah d 25 Mar 1777 ae 1m (O-16)
Lucinda d/o Francis & Sarah d 14 Apr 1826 ae 43y (F-16)
Sarah w/o Rev Francis b 1769 d 15 Aug 1852 ae 74y (F-17)
Susanna d/o Francis & Sarah b 21 Nov 1769 d 2 Nov 1852
    ae 82y (D-25)
GATES, Ann Maria d/o Carter & Anna d 4 Mar 1854 ae 21y (D-25)

Ann Mariah d/o Carter & Ann d 17 Oct 1831 ae 1y (D-24)
Anna w/o Carter d 5 Feb 1852 ae 58y (D-25)
Artemus C s/o Carter & Anna d 20 Dec 1838 ae 11m (D-24)
Carter s/o Jonas & Mary d 2 July 1846 ae 55y (D-25)
Charles s/o Elias & Mary d 20 Jan 1839 ae 17y (H-25)
Elias d 24 Oct 1823 ae 26y (G-23)
Gardner R s/o Jonas J & Martha d 18 July 1846 ae 20y (K-31)
Henry d 21 July 1870 ae 53y (D-3)
James C s/o Carter & Anna d 21 Dec 1851 ae 30y (D-25)
Jonas d 25 July 1839 ae 83y  REV  (G-23)
Jonas Jr d 23 Sept 1834 ae 45y  War of 1812 (D-30)
Lois w/o Jonas d 11 Nov 1848 ae 72y (G-24)
Luke 31 May 1833 ae 44y  -- Capt  (E-23)
Lydia d/o Reuben & Marcy d 11 Mar 1806 ae 36y (G-16)
Marcy w/o Reuben 10 Mar 1796 ae 72y (R-17)
Martha d 20 May 1862 ae 69y (K-13)
Mary w/o Jonas d -- --- ----
Mary C d -- --- 1811 ae 11w (E-23)
Molly d 2 Apr 1813 ae 54y (O-16)
Polly w/o Luke d 20 Nov 1811 ae 24y (E-24)
Reuban d -- Mar 1787 ae 70y (R-17)
Sarah E d/o Carter & Anna d 31 Dec 1849 ae 31y (D-25)
Sophia d/o Silas & Vashti d 16 Aug 1822 ae 18y (H-24)
Vashti wid/o Silas d 25 July 1807 ae 40y (J-10)
GIBSON, Adelia M d/o Bezaleet & Lucinda d 21 Apr 830 ae 1y (I-25)
Avery s/o James & Lucy P d -- --- ---- (G-28)
Charles A s/o James & Lucy P b 1827 d 1908 (G-28)
Ellen d/o James & Lucy P b 1836 d 1923 (G-28)
James b 1796 d 1854 (G-27)
Lucy P w/o James b 1801 d 1880 (G-28)
GLOVER, Betsy w/o William d 17 Mar 1874 ae 83y (E-29)
Mary Ann d/o William & Betsy d 1 Mar 1842 ae 28y (E-29)
William d 1864 ae 71y (E-29)
GOODRIDGE, Lois d 3 Sept 1834 ae 71y (H-13)
GOODWIN, Susan w/o John d 18 Mar 1825 ae 28y (D-6)
Susan E d/o John & Susan d Oct 1824 (D-26)
GOWING, Esther wid/o Doct? Thomas d 7 Feb 1812 ae 74y (G-12)
Thomas Doct d 22 Mar 1800 ae 63y  REV (G-12)
GRAHAM,  Warren s/o Samuel & Asenath d 17 Sept 1836 ae
        22m (K-32)
GROUT, Charissa A d/o Charles & Lucinda d 23 May 1836 ae 16y
        (D-33)
Charles d 1876 ae 67y (D-34)
Eliza P d 1903 ae 77y (D-33)
Louisa E b 1837 d -- --- ----
Lucinda d 1873 ae 79y (D-34)
HALE, Calvin d 20 Dec 1841 ae 80y  -- Capt  REV  (H-19)
Catherine wid/o Oliver d 16 July 1821 ae 89y (T-11)
Eleanor d/o Samuel & Hepzibah d 13 Feb 1822 ae 26y (F-17)
Elias s/o Samuel & Hepzibah d 1 Aug 1798 ae 3y (F-17)
Eliner w/o Samuel d 7 Mar 1794 ae 67y (F-18)

Elizabeth w/o Thomas 21 July 1820 ae 60y (G-19)
Esther d/o Samuel & Hannah d 23 Aug 1789 ae 2d (R-19)
Father d -- --- ---- (H-33)
Hannah w/o Samuel d 22 Aug 1789 ae 38y (P-19)
Hepzibah w/o Samuel d 10 May 1827 ae 68y (F-18)
Mary d -- --- ---- (H-33)
Mother d -- --- ---- (H-33)
Oliver d 7 May 1799 ae 78y -- Capt REV (S-10)
P c/o Oliver & Sarah d -- --- ---- (H-19)
P c/o Oliver & Sarah d -- --- ---- (H-18)
Polly c/o Oliver & Sarah d -- --- ---- (H-19)
Sally w/o Calvin d 28 Mar 1846 ae 67y (H-19)
Samuel d 13 June 1834 ae 86y (F-18)
Samuel d 4 July 1794 ae 86y (F-10)
Sarah w/o Capt Oliver d 14 Apr 1756 ae 35y (at her left
      side lies 4 of her children) (S-10)
Sarah c/o Oliver & Sarah d 19 Oct 1756 (H-18)
Sintha d/o Calvin & Phebe d 1 Sept 1799 ae 1y 3m 24d (H-33)
Thomas d 3 Apr 1808 ae 71y  REV (C-19)
HALL, Abigail w/o Bailey d 17 Feb 1843 ae 71y (D-16)
   Bailey d 13 Jan 1839 ae 77y (D-16)
   Eliza b 17 May 1796 d 15 Dec 1881 ae 85y (D-16)
HARBACK, Elizabeth w/o Thomas d 22 Sept 1880 ae 81y (F-7)
HARVEY, John P d 16 July 1823 (A-21)
   Sally R d 18 June 1869 (A-21)
   Sarah Ann d/o John & Sally b 1813 d 1905 (A-21)
HAWKS, Mary w/o Benjamin d 9 Apr 1820 ae 57y (She has the
      remains of children deposited in this burying ground)
      (M-10)
HAYDEN, Daniel b 1764 d 1824 ae 60y (He was a soldier in the
      army of the Revolution at the age of 15  His grandson
      Frederick who died in 1825 is buried here too) REV (K-26)
HEALD, Ann A b 1834 d 1909 ae 75y (L-31)
HENDERSON, John d 16 May 1821 ae 69y (J-9)
   Margret w/o John d 28 Aug 1816 ae 69y (J-9)
HILLS, Albert s/o Charles & Betsy Buss b 1827 d 1844 (D-12)
   Belinda b 1794 d 1814 ae 20y (M-22)
   Betsey relict of Smith Hills d 16 Dec 1828 ae 59y (N-24)
   Betsey d 20 Oct 1830 ae 19y (M-22)
   Betsey Buss w/o Charles b 1790 d 1853 ae 63y (D-11)
   Betsey M d/o Smith & Betsey d 3 May 1799 ae 13m (M-22)
   Charles b 1786 d 1851 (D-11)
   Charles A s/o Charles & Betsey Buss b 1819 d 1825 (D-12)
   Christinia d/o Charles & Betsey Buss b 1826 d 1826 (D-12)
   Dennis s/o Smith & Betsey d 21 Sept 1799 ae 3y 7m 7d (M-23)
   Dolly B w/o Capt Thomas d 12 Sept 1836 ae 48y (D-33)
   Dorothy B d/o Charles & Betsey Buss b 1816 d 1817 (D-11)
   John  d 29 May 1848 ae 81y -- Capt  (I-11)
   Josephine A d/o Thomas & Nancy W d 6 Sept 1907 ae 68y (D-32)
   Josiah J d 29 Aug 1879 ae 77y (N-24)
   Nancy W w/o Capt Thomas d 11 Apr 1887 ae 83y (D-32)

Sally w/o John d/o Josiah & Elizabeth Carter d 12 Feb
  1814 ae 43y (I-11)
Smith b 30 Sept 1768 d 23 Sept 1816 ae 52y (N-24)
Thomas d 2 Apr 1851 ae 67y -- Capt War of 1812 (D-33)
Volney s/o Capt John & Sally d 30 Aug 1803 ae 2y (I-11)
HOUGHTON, Abigail d 1876 ae 79y (E-26)
  Calista w/o David d 26 Sept 1828 ae 29y (F-28)
  David d -- --- 1867 ae 74y (F-28)
  Ebenezer d 16 Aug 1826 ae 73y REV (E-27)
  Emme w/o Ebenezer d 28 June 1831 ae 62y (E-27)
  Gershom d 3 April 1757 ae 66y (He build first home -
    1725) (W-3)
  Laura H d 16 Nov 1893 ae 85y
  Loenza d 1871 ae 63y (E-27)
  Louisa d 1893 ae 85y (E-27)
  Mary d/o Ebenezer & Emme d 28 May 1812 ae 9y (Q-14)
  Mary J w/o William A d 16 July 1864 ae 48y (E-27)
  Polly d 23 Feb 1872 ae 63y
  Sally d 1852 ae 61y (E-26)
JOHNSON, Amelia d/o Jonas & Prudence b 1792 d 11 July 1792
    ae 6m (F-8)
  Artimas R s/o Ephraim & Jane d 24 Mar 1837 ae 22y (D-15)
  Belinda H d 1 Oct 1874 ae 74y (A-25)
  Benjamin d 3 Mar 1836 ae 76y REV (K-32)
  Betsey w/o Benjamin d 9 Jan 1853 ae 87y (K-32)
  Charles S s/o Josiah & Belinda d 21 Sept 1832 ae 13m (A-26)
  Emily Porter d -- --- 1851 (G-25)
  Ephraim d 1 Dec 1864 ae 93y (D-15)
  Huldah w/o Joseph d 21 Aug 1851 ae 85y (H-25)
  Jane w/o Ephraim d 26 Apr 1849 ae 73y (D-25)
  John P s/o Levi & Sophronia d 22 Jan 1828 ae 18d (G-25)
  Jonas d 9 Apr 1828 ae 32y (F-8)
  Jonas d 23 July 1823 ae 66y (F-8)
  Joseph d 18 Apr 1815 ae 55y REV (L-24)
  Josiah d 16 May 1836 ae 38y (A-25)
  Jotham d 6 Sept 1815 ae 61y (E-7)
  Levi d 29 Oct 1866 ae 75y (G-26)
  Mary d/o Jotham & Sarah d 6 Jan 1815 ae 15y (E-6)
  M d -- --- 1866 ae 75y (1-17)
  Mary W d/o Josiah & Belinda d 14 May 1828 ae 9d (A-26)
  Nathan d 4 Oct 1771 ae 49y (Y-4)
  Nathan Jr d 14 Oct 1775 ae 22y REV (V-4)
  Prudence w/o Jonas d 18 Jan 1812 ae 39y (F-8)
  Sally Ann b -- --- 1811 d -- --- 1871 ae 60y (P-22)
  Sarah w/o Jotham & d/o Rev Francis Gardner d 25 Apr
    1838 ae 75y (E-7)
  Sarah Adelia d/o Levi & Sophronia d 19 Sept 1832 ae 2y
    (G-25)
  Sophia d/o Benjamin & Rhoda d 8 Nov 1853 ae 62y (K-31)
  Sophrona w/o Levi d 16 Nov 1833 ae 40y (G-26)
JONES, Amasa d 13 June 1828 ae 63y (F-26)

Amasa s/o Amasa & Pattie d 6 Dec 1867 ae 57y (F-25)
Frederick d 16 July 1824 ae 39y -- Capt  War of 1812 (A-25)
Martha w/o Amasa d 27 Sept 1841 ae 79y (N-13)
Martha w/o Samuel d 19 Aug 1841 ae 87y
Phebe d 12 Dec 1850 ae 61y (N-13)
Sally w/o Capt Frederick W d 23 Aug 1859 ae 71y (A-4)
Samuel d 11 July 1847 ae 86y REV (N-13)
JOSLIN, Abigail R d/o Calvin & Patience d 30 June 1831 ae
11y (S-13)
Betsey d -- --- 1799 (F-12)
Betsey w/o Joel d 19 Oct 1845 ae 56y (B-5)
Calvin d 26 Jan 1864 ae 82y (R-12)
Caroline d 4 Sept 1823 ae 17y (S-13)
Elias d 11 Dec 1824 ae 61y -- Capt  War of 1812 (F-12)
George W s/o Elias & Elizabeth d 29 Oct 1835 ae 3y (H-13)
James d 11 June 1824 ae 77y REV (J-7)
Joel d 28 Dec 1840 ae 56y -- Col  War of 1812 (B-5)
John d 6 Sept 1810 ae 75y -- Capt  REV (S-12)
John s/o James & Mary d 18 July 1845 ae 63y (J-7)
Joseph d 18 Aug 1829 ae 86y --Lieut  REV (S-21)
Lorin s/o Capt Elias & Prudence d 26 Nov 1799 ae 2y (F-12)
Luke d 24 Sept 1824 ae 53y -- Col  (F-24)
Mary w/o James d 1793 ae 49y (J-7)
Mary d -- --- 1871 ae 50y (J-10)
Patience w/o Calvin d 22 July 1869 ae 85y (S-12)
Peter d 18 Apr 1759 ae 94y -- Capt (R-13)
Polly w/o William d -- --- 1808 ae 20y (J-10)
Priscilla wid/o James d 17 July 1830 ae 81y (J-8)
Prudence wid/o Elias d 16 Jan 1848 ae 79y (F-13)
Sally w/o Luke d 18 Feb 1831 ae 29y (F-25)
Sarah w/o Lieut Joseph d 28 Aug 1810 ae 69y (S-21)
William s/o Capt Elias & Prudence d 27 May 1795 ae 4y (F-12)
KENDALL, Abel Deacon b 13 Nov 1770 d 13 Aug 1846 ae 75y (D-19)
Annas w/o David d 5 Apr 1777 ae 27y (R-17)
Claressa 2nd w/o John Jr d 18 Aug 1814 ae 26y (G-18)
David d 16 Sept 1825 ae 76y REV & War of 1812 (R-17)
Elizabeth Bennett wid/o Jonas b 12 May 1732 d 15 Apr
1825 ae 92y 11m (F-9)
Hanna 3rd w/o John Jr d 10 Nov 1818 ae 29y (G-18)
Jonas d 22 July 1799 ae 79y REV (F-19)
Lucy d 28 Nov 1799 ae 40y (F-8)
Luke s/o David & Annas d 4 Sept 1777 ae 2y 2m (R-16)
Polly w/o John Jr d 25 Dec 1808 ae 23y (G-17)
Prudence w/o David d 8 Feb 1822 ae 71y
Sarah w/o Deacon Abel b 7 Feb 1770 d 11 Oct 1819 ae 49y
(D-12)
KNIGHT, Daniel d 27 Oct 1767 ae 78y (W-2)
LAMB, Charles Albert s/o Albert & Adeline d 6 Apr 1837 ae 2y
6m
LEGGATT, Elizabeth Dorothy Evered d/o Capt Thomas & Mary
d 4 Aug 1766 ae 7m (O-18)

Mary consort of Capt Thomas & d/o Honorable Charles
   Morris Esq of Halifax d 26 Feb 1766 ae 23y (Q-17)
LELAND, John d 14 Jan 1789 ae 76y  -- Lt  (J-7)
LINCOLN, Abigail F wid/o Capt Thomas d 10 Oct 1837 ae 65y (F-28)
   Augusta d/o William & Tabitha d 10 Sept 1825 ae 9y 7m (E-21)
   David s/o William & Relief d 16 Aug 1781 ae 3y (P-14)
   David d 13 Sept 1777 ae 1y (P-14)
   Elizabeth 2nd w/o Mark d 13 Aug 1799 ae 59y (N-19)
   Elizabeth d/o Mark & Mary d 16 Oct 1815 ae 57y (N-19)
   Ephraim d 11 Sept 1843 ae 80y  REV (J-15)
   Eunice w/o Ephraim d 8 Jan 1813 ae 45y (J-15)
   Laura d/o Ephraim & Eunice d 1819 ae 24y (J-15)
   Lydia wid/o Capt Luke d 30 Oct 1899 ae 89y (P-14)
   Lydia d/o William & Prudence d 9 Oct 1777 ae 3y (P-16)
   Lydia d 16 June 1846 ae 66y (P-15)
   Mark d 10 Oct 1798 ae 66y  REV  (N-20)
   Martha R d/o Ephraim d 12 Oct 1849 ae 52y (J-15)
   Mary 1st w/o Mark d 29 Sept 1777 ae 40y (N-20)
   Mary w/o Ephraim d 9 Mar 1864 ae 86y (F-12)
   Mary Ann d/o William & Tabitha b 3 Aug 1806 d 4 Sept
      1906 ae 100y (E-22)
   Prudence w/o William d 1772 ae 26y (V-2)
   Prudence d/o Lieut William & Tabitha d 12 June 1799 ae
      1y 1m 18d (E-21)
   Relief w/o William d 29 Oct 1786 ae 39y (P-15)
   Sarah w/o William d 17 Feb 1835 ae 89y (P-15)
   Sarah d -- ---1865 ae 53y (E-22)
   Susan d 11 Nov 1862 ae ? (J-14)
   Tabitha wid/o William d 12 Feb 1849 ae 76y (E-22)
   Thomas d 10 May 1835 ae 67y -- Capt (F-28)
   William s/o William & Prudence d 28 Dec 1846 ae 77y (E-22)
   William  d 22 Feb 1814 ae 76y --Lieut  REV (P-15)
   Zadock d 18 Dec 1822 ae 49y (D-14)
LITCHFIELD, Galen L d 9 Oct 1837 ae 26y (B-15)
   Leonard d 9 Nov 1833 ae 50y (B-15)
   Mary d 2 Feb 1884 ae 65y 4m (B-15)
   Polly w/o Leonard d 28 June 1868 ae 86y (B-16)
   Silas H d 16 Dec 1838 ae 22y (B-15)
LONGLEY, Albert d 30 Oct 1901 ae 75y (A-17)
   Asa d 21 May 1881 ae 85y -- Col (A-16)
   Henry W s/o Asa & Mary d 22 Dec 1823 ae 3y (A-16)
   Mary C w/o Col Asa d 20 Feb 1874 ae 77y (A-16)
LOW, Betsey w/o Edward d 12 Dec 1846 ae 93y (N-24)
   Edward d 14 Feb 1823 ae 79y (N-24)
   Nabby d/o Edward & Rachel d 27 Apr 1777 ae 9m 10d (N-23)
   Rachel w/o Edward d 13 Apr 1792 ae 43y (N-24)
   Tristrom s/o Edward & Rachel d 13 Oct 1782 ae 12y (N-23)
   Tristrom s/o Edward & Rachel d 11 May 1810 ae 25y (K-17)
LYON, Josiah d 15 July 1826 ae 78y (B-29)
   Julius P d 24 Jan 1836 ae 47y (b-29)
   Polly w/o Julius d 21 Apr 1828 ae 38y (B-30)

Sarah w/o Josiah d 27 Apr 1829 ae 76y (B-29)

MAY, Dennis s/o Willim & Harriet d 28 Feb 1857 ae 24y (J-21)

    Emmerline S s/o William & Harried d 18 Mar 1849 ae 23y
        (J-21)

    Esther w/o Jacob d 21 Jan 1838 ae 69y (I-22)

    Harriett w/o William d 18 Mar 1872 ae 72y (K-22)

    Jacob d 22 June 1856 ae 87y (I-22)

    William d 11 June 1843 ae 47y (K-21)

MAYNARD, John d 27 Sept 1853 ae 82y (N-28)

    Joshua s/o Elijah d 26 May 1840 ae 21y (N-25)

    Sophia w/o John d 11 Sept 1834 ae 53y (N-28)

McCONNOR, Abiah w/o James d 13 Sept 1789 ae 45y (N-5)

MELVIN, Lucy D b 1801 d 1879 (A-19)

MERIAM & MERRIAM, Amos d 28 Sept 1830 ae 38y  War of 1812
        (I-18)

    Amos d 6 Mar 1818 ae 78y -- Lieut  REV (J-19)

    Clarissa w/o Luther d 8 May 1861 ae 80y (I-19)

    Delia w/o Nathan d 28 Nov 1850 ae 82y (D-33)

    Elizabeth w/o Lieut Amos d 20 Aug 1816 ae 69y (J-19)

    Elizabeth d 30 July 1808 ae 29y (J-18)

    Jonathan d 16 Apr 1853 ae 82y (B-19)

    Jonathan Jr s/o Deacon Jonathan & Polly d 25 Feb 1832
        ae 24y (B-19)

    Luther S d 17 Nov 1875 ae 65y (H-18)

    Mary d/o Deacon Jonathan & Polly d 28 Sept 1821 ae 20y
        (B-19)

    Polly w/o Deacon Jonathan d 23 Oct 1856 ae 86y (B-19)

    Rachel J d 1 July 1869 ae 63y (I-17)

MOORE, Elizabeth Wood w/o Marius b -- --- 1822 d -- --- 1899
        (B-27)

    Emma C d -- --- ---- (B-27)

    Levi Deacon d 4 Fan 1812 ae 52y (J-12)

    Marius H b -- --- 1814 d -- --- 1905 (B-26)

    Parney relict of Deacon Levi d 1 Oct 1820 ae 57y (K-12)

    Wilbur E d -- --- ---- (B-27)

MORSE, Joseph d 29 July 1834 ae 51y (B-14)

    Susan w/o Joseph d 20 MLay 1837 ae 52y (B-14)

MURDOCK, Edward F s/o Albert H & Charlette D d 12 Feb 1852
        ae 2y (H-28)

    Laura Jane d/o Abel & Margarette d 6 Aug 1827 ae 18m
        (H-26)

NEWHALL, Asa J  d 1 June 1880 ae 77y (G-32)

    George W s/o Asa J & Mary M d 20 Oct 1838 ae 10y (G-33)

    Jane J w/o Asa J d 18 Aug 1895 ae 88y (G-32)

    Mary M w/o Asa J d 17 Sept 1850 ae 46y (G-33)

    Michael Esq d 17 Sept 1812 ae 73y REV (G-14)

    Susanna wid/o d 24 Sept 1799 ae 82y (G-14)

NICHOLS & NICKOLS, Artemas J s/o John & Thirza b -- --- 1842
        d -- --- 1881 (L-31)

    Bartimas s/o Ephraim & Betsy d 3 Sept 1822 ae 3y (A-20)

    Betsy w/o Ephraim d 31 Jan 1824 ae 36y (A-21)

Charles C s/o Col Israel & Esther b -- --- 1821
    d -- --- 1903 ae 82y (D-30)
Desire w/o Israel d 8 Sept 1803 ae 75 (I-11)
Edmund H s/o Col Israel & Esther Gowing b -- ---1807
    d -- --- 1874 (D-29)
Eleanor B d/o John & Thirza  b -- --- 1831 d -- --- 1839
    (L-31)
Emily d/o Levi & Eleanor d 3 Aug 1817 ae 18y (D-8)
Ephraim d 28 May 1823 ae 45y (A-21)
Esther d/o Col Israel & Esther Gowing b -- ---1813
    d -- --- 1844 (D-29)
Esther Gowing w/o Col Israel b -- --- 1778
    d -- --- 1852 (D-28)
Harriet d/o Col Esrail & Esther Gowing b -- --- 1815
    d -- --- 1884 (D-29)
Israel b -- --- 1778  d -- --- 1828  -- Col
    War of 1812 (D-28)
Israel T s/o Col Israel & Esther Gowing b  -- --- 1810
    d -- --- 1869 (D-29)
Israel Esq d 12 Oct 1802 ae 81y  REV  (I-12)
John b 11 Oct 1802 d 4 June 1877 (L-31)
John S s/o Levi & Elinor d -- --- 1817 ae 19y 11m (L-31)
Laura d/o Col Israel & Esther Gowing b -- --- 1801
    d -- --- 1851 (D-29)
Levi d 19 Aug 1818 ae 54y  REV (D-8)
Mary d/o Col Israel & Esther Gowing b -- --- 1818
    d -- --- 1835 (D-30)
Ruth w/o William d 11 Nov 1811 ae 55y (I-12)
Thirza w/o John b -- --- 1802 d -- --- 1885 (L-31)
Thomas s/o Levi & Eleanor d 22 July 1817 ae 19y
    War of 1812 (D-8)
Thomas G s/o Col Israel & Esther Gowing b -- --- 1803
    d -- --- 1829 (D-29)
William d 11 Dec 1835 ae 85y  REV  (I-12)
William A s/o Col Israel & Esther Gowing b -- --- 1805
    d -- --- 1858 (D-29)
NURSE, George Francis s/o Francis & Sally d 26 Jan 1830 ae
    2y (G-29)
Nabby w/o Francis d 6 Jan 1845 ae 68y (G-29)
OSGOOD, Andrew M s/o Merick R & Nancy d 6 Nov 1844 ae 13y
    (B-30)
Nancy w/o Merrick d 20 Jan 1843 ae 36y (B-31)
Merick R d -- --- ---- (B-30)
OTIS, Henry d 10 Feb 1834 ae 37y (I-30)
Mabel w/o Paul d 6 Apr 1855 ae 70y (I-31)
Paul s/o Stephen & Rachel d 24 Sept 1849 ae 78y (I-30)
PARK, Eliza d/o Capt Richard & Betsy d 20 Apr 1812 ae 4y 2m
PARKER, Abigail relict of Willard d 5 Aug 1858 ae 90y (H-11)
Hepsibah R d/o James & Lydia d 29 Jan 1845 ae 42y (O-27)
James s/o James & Lydia d 19 Dec 1831 ae 31y (O-26)
J S s/o Lydia Parker Putnum d 10 Mar 1826 ae 10y

Lydia w/o Capt James S d 8 Apr 1840 ae 74y (O-27)
Willard d 13 Jan 1827 ae 51y (H-11)
Willard Jr s/o Willard & Abigaild 17 Oct 1811 ae 2y (H-11)
William s/o James & Lydia d 2 Dec 1845 ae 38y (O-27)
*PATTERSON, John d 28 Mar 1859 ae 70y (D-24)
PERKINS, Benjamin d 9 Oct 1834 ae 86y (I-12)
   Lydia consort of Benjamin d 25 Mar 1804 ae 56y (I-12)
PERRY, Catherine d/o Icabod & Hannah d 23 June 1793 ae 5y (G-8)
   Delia J d/o William & Sophia K d 21 Dec 1822 ae 7m (B-22)
   Elizabeth d 7 Mar 1836 ae 50y (G-8)
   Evelina Parker d 13 Jan 1890 ae 8y 6m 2d (D-33)
   Hannah d 10 Oct 1858 ae 64y (G-9)
   Hannah w/o Ichabod d 25 Apr 1847 ae 84y (G-8)
   Henry d 27 Apr 1885 ae 81y (D-34)
   Ichabod d 4 Dec 1825 ae 71y  REV  (G-8)
   Jane Eliza d/o Martin & Elizabeth d 21 Nov 1832 ae 8m (G-8)
   Josephine d/o Henry & Evelina d 25 Feb 1838 ae 3y (D-33)
   Lavina d/o Ichabod & Hannah d 17 May 1811 ae 21y (G-8)
   Simeon Newton d 4 Aug 1874 ae 82y (G-9)
   Simeon N 2nd d 8 Oct 1901 ae 64y (D-34)
   Sophia K w/o William Esq d 4 Nov 1866 ae 82y (B-22)
   William Esq d 10 Aug 1844 ae 58y (B-22)
PHELPS, Abel d 30 Apr 1825 ae 53y (A-28)
   Abigail d/o Asahel & Sally d 9 June 1816 ae 3d (H-6)
   Amelia F s/o David & Rhoda d 11 Feb 1845 ae 21y (A-28)
   Asahel d 18 Jan 1820 ae 29y (H-5)
   David d 8 Sept 1843 ae 44y (A-28)
   Edward  d 15 Jan 1776 ae 46y --Lieut  (P-16)
   Eunice wid/o Abel d 22 Apr 1844 ae 72y (A-28)
   Martha w/o Edward d 2 Apr 1765 ae 28y (p-16)
   Rhoda d -- --- ---- (A-28)
PICKERING, CS b -- ---- 1857 d -- --- ---- (O-31)
   Mary F w/o CS b 1856 d 1912 (O-31)
PIERCE, Abigail w/o Samuel d 28 Feb 1777 ae 26y
   Asa d -- --- 1880 ae 77y (H-8)
   Asa d 13 Mar 1842 ae 66y (D-7)
   Augustus s/o Capt Thomas & Dolly d 27 Apr 1830 ae 31y (L-11)
   Deborah w/o Asa d 8 Dec 1818 ae 39y (D-6)
   Deborah d/o Asa & Daborah d 1 Apr 1824 ae 16y (D-7)
   Dolly d/o Capt Thomas S & Dolly d 23 Sept 1809 ae 17y (L-11)
   Dolly w/o Capt Thomas S d 20 Mar 1841 ae 73y (L-13)
   Dorlinda d/o Capt Thomas S & Dolly d 28 June 1828 ae
      22y (L-12)
   Elias d/o Joshua & Lydia d 25 Sept 1834 ae 50y (L-13)
   Eliza D d 20 Jan 1857 ae 51y (M-12)
   Franklin d 11 Sept 1887 ae 72y (D-7)
   George E s/o Sylvester & Abigail d 16 Apr 1836 ae 6w (I-31)
   James s/o Asa & Martha d 7 Dec 1831 ae 5y (D-7)
   Jonas d -- --- 1799 ae 1y (L-11)
   Joseph Bender s/o Doctor Nathaniel & Judith d 6 Mar
      1818 ae 9y (G-17)

Joshua d 4 Jan 1850 ae 80y (M-13)
Joshua d 5 Nov 1812 ae 71y -- Lieut REV (L-12)
Judith w/o Doctor Nathaniel d 29 May 1820 ae 42y (G-17)
Lydia wid/o Joshua d 25 Jan 1826 ae 85y (L-13)
Lydia d/o Thomas S & Dolly d 20 Sept 1857 ae 63y (L-13)
Martha w/o Asa d 15 Apr 1866 ae 76y (D-7)
Mira B d/o Asa & Martha d 28 Apr 1828 ae 5y (D-7)
Mira E b 2 Oct 1833 d 12 Aug 1908 (D-8)
Phineas d 20 June 1831 ae 57y (M-12)
Roxana w/o Joseph d 2 July 1836 ae 38y (I-33)
Rufus E s/o Asa & Martha d 2 July 1864 ae 34y (D-7)
Thomas s/o Capt Thomas & Dolly d 29 May 1821 ae 21y (L-11)
Thomas S s/o Joshua & Lydia d 26 June 1845 ae 78y (L-13)
POLLY, George A s/o Alvin M & Belinda d 6 June 1837 ae 3y (G-19)
PRENTISS, Caleb Mellen s/o Charles & Sophia ?grandson/o REV
    Francis Gardner d 16 Oct 1829 ae 27y (O-16)
    Charles s/o Rev Caleb b -- --- 1774 d 20 Oct 1820 (O-16)
    Sophia d/o Rev Caleb b -- --- 1778 d 8 Oct 1857 (O-17)
PRESCOTT, Lydia d 23 Dec 1872 ae 73y (H-13)
PRIEST, Joseph d 16 Mar 1824 ae 77y REV (A-23)
    Seviah d 20 Nov 1820 ae 62y (A-24)
PUTNAM, Albert A s/o Lydia d 30 Oct 1820 ae 21m (K-7)
PUTTER, Dorothy b -- --- 1804 d -- --- 1836 (H-32)
    Jacob b -- --- 1801 d -- --- 1880 (H-32)
    Martha b -- --- 1810 d -- --- 1910 (H-32)
RICE, Alvah s/o Forester & Rachel d 11 Sept 1819 ae 21y (D-25)
    Anne w/o John d 14 Nov 1860 ae 86y (J-32)
    Emory A s/o Forester & Rachel d 24 Apr 1826 ae 9m (D-25)
    Forester d 20 Oct 1854 ae 56y 10m (D-26)
    James B s/o Forester & Rachel d 9 Apr 1857 ae 20y (D-26)
    John d 17 Oct 1838 ae 68y (J-32)
    Mary d -- --- ---- (F-20)
    Rachel d 7 Dec 1851 ae 52y (D-26)
    Susan K d/o Forester & Rachel d 20 Feb 1831 ae 8d (D-25)
RICHARDSON, Abigail s/o Silas d 17 Jan 1829 ae 60y (D-30)
    Betsey d -- --- 1813 (R-15)
    Demarias w/o Lieut Luke d 18 Sept 1812 ae 74y (J-6)
    Eunice w/o John d 2 Mar 1831 ae 87y (H-16)
    Frances s/o John & Eunice d 6 Sept 1805 ae 36y (R-16)
    Green s/o John & Eunice d 9 June 1777 ae 1y (R-16)
    Horace d 1 Nov 1865 ae 70y (D-29)
    James d 10 June 1795 ae 67y -- Maj (H-9)
    John d 13 Feb 1814 ae 72y (H-16)
    Josiah b -- --- 1776 d -- --- 1863 (J-16)
    Luke d 2 Mar 1842 ae 78y (J-6)
    Luke d 27 Mar 1812 ae 77y --Lieut REV (E-38)
    Martha d -- --- 1819 ae 40y (R-15)
    Rebekah A d/o Horace & Sarah d 19 Mar 1840 ae 11y (D-29)
    Reliance C w/o Josiah b -- --- 1784 d -- --- 1862 (J-6)
    Relief w/o Luke d 8 Sept 1827 ae 60y (E-28)
    Sally w/o Abel d 22 June 1849 ae 74y (N-21)

Sarah w/o Horace d 4 Feb 1872 ae 78y (D-29)
Silas d 15 June 1833 ae 71y (D-29)
Sukey d/o John & Eunice d 5 Apr 1801 ae 26y (R-16)
William Crosby s/o Josiah & Reliance d 31 May 1817 ae
    3y (J-6)
ROBBINS, Elizabeth wid/o Thomas d 21 Oct 1823 ae 100y 6m 15d
    (D-24)
Julia d 19 July 1872 ae 78y 10m (D-23)
Laura d 22 Aug 1877 ae 75y (D-23)
Precilla d/o Thomas d 1 Mar 1834 ae 69y (D-24)
Thomas d 15 Aug 1843 ae 82y REV (D-23)
ROGERS, John First Minister d 6 Oct 1789 ae 77y (M-5)
Charles W b 2 Jan 1850 d 20 Nov 1902 (L-32)
ROLPH, Elsy w/o Solomon Jr d 4 Aug 1840 (F-30)
Eugene T s/o Nathan & Julia d 25 Sept 1840 ae 7m (L-32)
Frederick C s/o Nathan & Julia d 10 Sept 1840 ae 3y (L-32)
Julia A w/o Nathan d 4 Feb 1864 ae 53y (L-32)
Maria Louisa d/o Nathan & Julia d 10 Apr 1846 ae 1m
    (F-30)
Nathan d 3 Apr 1888 ae 75y (L-32)
RUGG, Benjamin d 15 Sept 1837 ae 52y 9m (N-31)
Catherine S w/o Benjamin d 28 Aug 1845 ae 56y (N-32)
Cecilia A d/o Benjamin & Catherine d 11 Jan 1844 ae 25y
    (N-31)
Clara Marie d -- --- ---- (A-34)
Elizabeth d -- --- 1799 (W-3)
SAMPSON, Mary C Jones w/o William C d 28 Feb 1869 ae 61y (F-26)
SHELDON, Charles A s/o Pelatiah & Lucy d 18 Oct 1849 ae 9y (A-18)
Edward s/o Pelatiah & Lucy d 7 Sept 1844 ae 7w (A-17)
Lucy w/o Pelatiah d 22 Aug 1872 ae 65y (A-17)
Lydia M d/o Pelatiah & Lydia d 5 Nov 1830 ae 1y (A-17)
Lydia w/o Pelatiah d 13 Nov 1835 ae 35y (A-18)
Pelatiah s/o Pelatiah & Lydia d 19 July 1832 ae 6m (A-17)
Pelatiah d 24 Nov 1871 ae 75y (A-17)
Sarah d/o Pelatiah & Lucy d 15 Aug 1847 ae 3m (A-18)
Warren s/o Pelatiah & Lucy d 25 Oct 1849 ae 11m (A-18)
SIMONDS, Ebenezer d 11 Dec 1844 ae 61y (I-13)
Hannah w/o John d 27 Feb 1819 ae 22y (D-10)
James d 11 Nov 1819 ae 28y War of 1812 (I-13)
John d 14 Oct 1823 ae 34y (D-10)
John Rt Worshipful d 17 Sept 1814 ae 68y John E s/o
    John & Sarah d 20 Apr 1821 ae 9w (I-13)
Mary w/o John d 13 Oct 1823 ae 68y (I-14)
Mary d -- --- 1842 ae 25y (D-19)
Sarah d/o John & Mary d 19 Jan 1812 ae 17y (I-13)
SIZER, Elizabeth d -- --- 1860 ae 26y (B-15)
SMITH, Hannah S d 2 Jan 1864 ae 83y (A-30)
Joseph d 30 Nov 1857 ae 74y (O-25)
Lucinda d -- --- 1840 ae 52y (L-14)
Martha d/o Joseph & Sarah R d 1 Mar 1878 ae 60y (O-26)
Nancy d 8 June 1880 ae 92y (D-6)

Samuel d 17 Feb 1816 ae 58y REV (D-6)

Sarah R w/o Joseph d 8 Jan 1850 ae 58y (O-25)

Sarah S consort of Samuel d 31 Oct 1833 ae 74y (D-7)

SNOW, Susan E d/o Lieut William & Betsey d 8 Dec 1816 ae 12y (E-19)

William d 27 Oct 1814 ae 32y -- Lieut (E-19)

SPAULDING, Asaph d 4 Jan 1843 ae 70y (G-27)

Elizabeth w/o Asaph d 29 July 1827 ae 48y (G-27)

Mira S d/o Asaph & Elizabeth d 20 Mar 1842 ae 40y (G-27)

STEARNS, Bettee d/o Thomas & Lydia d -- ---- 1778 ae 2y (R-18)

Caroline M d/o Thomas & Thirza b -- ---- 1813
d -- ---- 1911 (D-15)

Cecilia d/o Timothy & Polly d 24 Mar 1827 ae 18y (H-21)

Christiana d/o Timothy & Polly d 4 May 1826 ae 17y (H-21)

Daniel s/o Thomas & Lydia d -- ---- 1777 (W-4)

George s/o Thomas & Thirza d 19 Apr 1826 ae 5w (D-14)

George Otis s/o Otis & Lucy d 4 Sept 1822 ae 3y (F-6)

Justin s/o Thomothy & Mary d -- ----- 1794 ae 1y (F-8)

Lydia w/o Thomas d 26 Feb 1791 ae 72y (W-4)

Mary b 3 Apr 1785 d 21 Jan 1864 ae 79y (F-6)

Polly B d 7 Dec 1863 ae 71y (H-20)

Polly Kendall w/o Timothy d 27 Oct 1866 ae 73y (H-20)

Sarah d/o Thomas & Lydia d 30 Aug 1746 ae 21y (W-3)

Susan w/o Otis d 20 Sept 1813 ae 25y (F-6)

Susan K d/o Timothy & Polly d 13 Mar 1821 ae 10y (H-20)

Thirza B d -- ---- 1846 ae 18y (D-14)

Thirza Barrage w/o Thomas d 24 May 1819 ae 20y (D-14)

Thomas s/o Timothy & Mary d 18 Aug 1813 ae 23y (F-5)

Thomas d 15 Dec 1861 ae 67y (D-14)

Thomas d 5 Feb 1811 ae 94y (W-4)

Timothy d -- ---- 1811 ae 28y (H-20)

Timothy d 13 Sept 1795 ae 36y -- Lieut (F-5)

William A b -- ---- 1821 d -- ---- 1901 (D-14)

---- b -- ---- 1785 d -- ---- 1865 (F-6)

STILES, Sally w/o Zira d 22 Jan 1866 ae 64y (K-9)

Zira d 11 Oct 1822 ae 27y (K-9)

STUART, Ebenezer d 15 Aug 1778 ae 25y REV (M-22)

Huldah d 18 Jun 1850 ae 71y (M-22)

Julia M d -- ---- 1843 ae 24y (A-24)

John d -- ---- 1820 ae 36y War of 1812 (A-24)

SWAN, Mary d -- ---- 1769 ae 26y (N-10)

TAINTER, Betsey w/o William d 3 Sept 1819 ae 41y (K-15)

Elizabeth d/o William & Betsey d 28 Aug 1834 ae 20y (L-30)

Elizabeth d/o William & Betsey d 9 Dec 1811 ae 15m (K-15)

William d 1 Nov 1824 ae 52y (H-34)

TAYLOR, Anna w/o John d 8 Mar 1842 ae 73y (L-17)

John d 6 July 1844 ae 71y (L-17)

John s/o John & Anna d 3 June 1809 ae 15y (K-16)

Mary d 1 Sept 1849 ae 51y (K-16)

Robert d 22 Sept 1832 ae 31y (K-16)

TENNEY, Augustus s/o William & Betsy d 22 May 1832 ae 11y

(N-27)

Austin s/o William & Betsey d 8 Sept 1831 ae 8y (N-26)
Bartemous s/o Joseph & Ruth d 15 Sept 1799 ae 5y (M-8)
Betsey w/o William d 11 Oct 1860 ae 69y (N-27)
David d 10 May 1873 ae 72y (N-27)
David s/o Joseph & Ruth d Sept 1799 ae 2y (M-8)
Elizabeth d/o William & Betsey d 8 May 1832 ae 6y (N-26)
Elmira JP w/o David d 7 Sept 1884 ae 83y (M-27)
George A s/o David & Elmira d 14 May 1832 ae 2y (M-26)
Jane E b -- --- 1829 d -- --- 1865 (L-31)
Laura d -- --- 1836 ae 27y (M-24)
Ruth w/o Joseph d 26 Aug 1803 ae 50y (M-8)
Sophronia A d/o David & Elmira P d 18 Mar 1878 ae 52y (M-26)
William d 5 May 1863 ae 71y (N-27)
THURSTON, Elizabeth S d 5 Oct 1880 ae 70y (D-18)
Eunice G d 28 Sept 1862 (D-17)
Jerusha w/o Reverend Pearson d 10 Dec 1834 ae 70y (D-18)
Judith S d 29 Oct 1880 ae 80y (D-18)
Mary G w/o William P d 10 Aug 1849 ae 47y (D-17)
Pearson Rev d 15 Aug 1819 ae 57y
W H d -- --- ---- -- Capt CIV (D-18)
William Pm d 18 Mar 1847 (D-17)
TISDALE, Polly w/o Seth d 11 Sept 1813 ae 27y (J-13)
TYLER, Alice w/o Simeon d 8 Mar 1855 ae 77y (L-8)
Elizabeth w/o Phineas d 13 June 1820 ae 73y (M-6)
Hannah d 18 June 1813 ae 38y (L-5)
Harriet d 25 May 1833 ae 16y (E-24)
Ismena w/o Joshua d 7 May 1839 ae 83y
Joseph W d 11 Sept 1822 ae 3y (L-9)
Joshua d 27 Mar 1825 ae 78y
Mary w/o Simeon d 15 Oct 1814 ae 43y (L-9)
Mehitable d 27 Sept 1822 ae 32y (L-5)
Mira d 13 Sept 1812 ae 13m (L-9)
Nabby d 27 Mar 1814 ae 27y (L-5)
Phinehas d 6 Aug 1817 ae 81y (M-6)
Phineas d 21 Jan 1847 ae 82y (K-9)
Polly d/o Simeon & Mary d 21 Sept 1850 ae 55y (L-9)
Rodolphus s/o Daniel & Thirsa d 20 Oct 1822 ae 2y (K-4)
Sally d 1 Apr 1834 ae 12y (E-15)
Seth P d 21 Aug 1868 ae 77y (E-25)
Simeon d 12 Feb 1858 ae 86y (L-8)
Stephen s/o Phineas & Tabitha d 15 July 1806 ae 16y (K-10)
Susan P w/o Seth P d 12 July 1872 ae 84y (W-25)
Tabitha d 27 Sept 1850 ae 32y (K-10)
WALKER, Lawson d 19 Feb 1878 ae 89y War of 1812 (M-26)
Mary w/o Lawson d 28 Aug 1835 ae 46y (M-26)
Mary d/o Lovell & Elizabeth d 25 Sept 1837 ae 18y (M-26)
Nancy F d/o Lovell & Elizabeth d 26 Aug 1829 ae 22y (I-14)
Nathan s/o Lawson & Mary d 21 Jan 1849 ae 36y (M-25)
Relief s/o Lawson d 19 Sept 1865 ae 64y (M-26)
Sally w/o Lawson d 26 Nov 1850 ae 50y (M-26)

WARE, Abigail d 1 Jan 1866 ae 82y (F-34)
  Martha R d 3 Jan 1885 ae 65y (F-33)
  Samuel d 21 Sept 1840 ae 64y (F-34)
  Samuel B d 8 Dec 1831 ae 18y (F-34)
WARNER, Ephraim d 27 May 1832 ae 40y (J-24)
  Levi d 25 July 1813 ae 65y -- Capt REV (J-24)
WHEELER, Harriet d 2 Oct 1839 ae 21y (A-33)
WHITCOMB, Curtis s/o John & Betsey d 6 Sept 1831 ae 2y (A-22)
  Dorothy w/o Joseph & d/o Lieut Abiarthur Houghton b 28
      Aug 1787 d 1 Oct 1824 (E-21)
  Henry Houghton b 1 Sept 1810 d 26 July 1815 (E-21)
  Joseph b 27 Sept 1878 d 4 Jan 1834  War of 1812 (E-21)
  Josiah d 26 Nov 1833 ae 57y  War of 1812  (A-22)
  Sally w/o Capt Josiah d 10 Mar 1827 ae 40y (A-22)
WHITE, Ebenezer d 4 May 1807 ae 30y (L-10)
  Lucinda consort of Ebenezer d 14 Aug 1803 ae 23y (L-10)
WHITNEY, Horace M d 25 Oct 1837 ae 28y (M-27)
WILDER, Adeline d/o William & Mary d 15 May 1832 ae 13y (D-26)
  Catherine b 3 Aug 1815 d 21 Nov 1884 (N-31)
  Charles b 1 Mar 1813 d 28 May 1891 (N-31)
  David Deacon b 3 May 1778 d 21 Sept 1866 ae 88y (P-23)
  David d 5 Dec 1815 ae 75y  REV  (P-22)
  Dolly w/o Edward d 9 Oct 1815 ae 54y (E-5)
  Dolly d/o Edward & Dolly d 31 Dec 1784 ae 2m (S-6)
  Dorothy d/o Edward & Dolly d 23 Oct 1792 ae 1m (S-6)
  Edward d 16 Nov 1833 ae 73y REV (E-5)
  Edward s/o Edward & Dolly d 29 Aug 1791 ae 5y (S-6)
  Elisha d 2 May 1842 ae 78y (D-5)
  Elizabeth d/o Deac Gardner & Mary d 15 May 1761 ae 22y (T-7)
  Elizabeth d 10 Sept 1879 ae 85y (T-5)
  Emilia d/o Edward & Dolly d 21 June 1797 ae 4m (S-6)
  Ephraim d -- --- 1756 ae 4y (E-4)
  Esther d/o Deacon Gardner & Mary d 4 Oct 1756 ae 4y (?)
  Gardner Deacon d 19 Apr 1787 ae 76y (T-7)
  Greene s/o Edward Jr & Sarah T d 11 Feb 1833 ae 2y (J-31)
  Harriet d/o Josiah & Sarah d 27 Aug 1820 ae 12y (D-6)
  Henry M s/o David & Sally N d 10 Feb 1846 ae 31y (P-23)
  James s/o Deacon Gardner & Mary b 3 Apr 1742 d 3 Apr
      1742 (T-7)
  Lucy w/o Deacon David d 18 Nov 1796 ae 47y (P-22)
  Lucy d/o Lieut David & Lucy d 25 Aug 1772 ae 3y (P-22)
  Martha d/o David & Sally N d 22 Sept 1841 ae 21y
  Mary w/o William d 14 Nov 1831 ae 44y (D-27)
  Mary w/o Deacon Gardner d 21 Aug 1801 ae 83y (T-7)
  Mary H b 9 Aug 1843 d 11 May 1893 (N-31)
  Rebekah w/o Elisha d 27 Apr 1837 ae 58y (D-5)
  Roxanna w/o Edward d 13 Nov 1843 ae 68y (E-6)
  Sally B w/o Ephraim d 10 Apr 1850 ae 58y (E-4)
  Sally N d 21 Jan 1833 ae 46y (P-23)
  Sarah d/o Peter & Sarah d 22 May 1823 ae 20y (B-16)
  Thomas d 6 Jan 1802 ae 64y -- Capt  REV (H-12)

William d 26 Dec 1866 ae 79y (D-27)
WOOD, Artimus d 3 June 1812 ae 30y (Q-20)
    Caleb d 1834 ae 69y REV (O-17)
    Catherine w/o Artimus d 4 July 1812 ae 23y (Q-21)
    Elizabeth d -- --- 1797 ae 65y (P-19)
    Eunice d 25 Sept 1849 ae 57y (H-16)
    Eunice d -- --- 1833 ae 71y (O-17)
    Eunice d -- --- 1771 ae 11y (P-18)
    James d 16 July 1856 ae 60y (B-26)
    James Fry d -- --- 1801 ae 25y (O-17)
    John s/o John & Lydia d 8 Mar 1774 ae 13m (Q-19)
    John s/o John & Lydia d 27 Mar 1772 ae 5m 19d (Q-20)
    John d -- --- 1842 ae 66y (R-20)
    Joshua d -- --- 1803 ae 77y REV (P-18)
    Lillie d/o Franklin & Sarah M d 7 Sept 1851 ae 1y (D-28)
    Lydia d/o John & Lydia d 20 Mar 1798 ae 19y (Q-20)
    Lydia d -- --- 1819 ae 73y (P-20)
    Maria d/o James & Maria d 9 Apr 1834 ae 10y (B-25)
    Maria B w/o James d 8 June 1854 ae 57y (B-26)
    Maria C d 13 Mar 1858 ae 21y (B-25)
    Martha d 18 Dec 1884 ae 51y (B-25)
WOODBURY, Sophia Spaulding w/o Luke d 7 Apr 1867 ae 63y (G-27)
WOODCOCK, Brucy w/o Nathan d 9 Oct 1829 ae 61y (D-20)
    Elizabeth w/o Nathan d 28 June 1820 ae 49y
    Nathan d 30 Aug 1830 ae 64y (D-20)
WOODS, Abigail S d/o Selvester & Polly d 23 Dec 1824 ae 7m (D-13)
    Elisabeth w/o John d 27 Oct 1826 ae 88y (F-27)
    Lete d 19 Apr 1839 ae 56y (F-26)
    John d 4 Jan 1832 ae 87y (F-27)
    Joseph s/o Levi & Tamer d 7 June 1771 ae 2y (O-21)
    Joseph d 7 July 1843 ae 70y (F-26)
    Mary d 20 Jan 1825 ae 25y (D-13)
    Sarah d 16 Jan 1825 ae 47y (H-21)
    Sukey w/o Jospeh d 12 Jan 1834 ae 41y (F-27)
    Sylvester d 2 Aug 1822 ae 30y War of 1812 (D-13)
WYER, David Mrs w/o Capt David d 7 July 1823 ae 44y (L-10)


## EVERGREEN CEMETERY

In 1840, land was purchased on Main Street, one-fourth mile north of Pine Grove Cemetery. The new ground contained seven acres and ninety rods, and it was named Evergreen Cemetery. Additional land has been purchased several times. Today it contains over sixty acres.

A fountain was erected in Evergreen in 1875, followed by the gift of Haws Memorial Chapel in 1900, and the second mausoleum in Worcester County, named Evergren Abbey, opened in 1923. One hundred and forty eight years later Evergreen Cemetery in Leominster is the one public cemetery in use.

## ST. LEO'S PARISH CEMETERY

In June 1884, the Diocese of Springfield purchased of Joseph Collins twelve acres of land known as the James Burdett Place at 360 Lancaster Street for a parish cemetery.

The grounds were consecrated on October 28, 1874 by Bishop O'Riley of the Diocese of Springfield, assisted by Reverend Father Daniel O'Shiel, Pastor of St. Leo's Church.

The cemetery is used by the parishoners of both St. Leo's Church and St. Anna's Church.


## STE. CECILIA'S PARISH CEMETERY

In April 1900, the Diocese of Springfield purchased from Adolphe Houle thirty acres of land on Florence Street for a parish cemetery.

The land was consecrated by Bishop Thomas D. Beaven, D.D. of the Springfield Diocese, assisted by Reverend Father Wilfrid Balthasar, Pastor of the newly organized Ste. Cecilia's Church.

Abner W. Pollard    1840 - 1914

# STERLING

Originally a part of Lancaster, the area now known as Sterling was settled in 1720 as the "Second Precinct of Lancaster" and was also known at that time as "Woonksechoxsett" or "Chocksett." In 1781 it was incorporated as the Town of Sterling.

Sterling has six burial grounds/cemeteries: Chocksett Burial Ground (1736), Cookshire (1782), Fairbank (1760), Leg (1756), Oak Hill (1820), and Hillside (1953). Only the last two are in use today, although an occasional burial is made in Cookshire and Leg.

Death records and cemetery plot plans can be found at the Sterling Town Hall or at the Department of Public Works building on Worcester Road. The Sterling Historical Society and the Sterling Public Library also have a plot plan of Chocksett made in 1918 by Murray Trussell, a surveyor, which indicates the names and locations of graves, with a complete index to that date. Also on file are the records compiled in 1942 by Milton Cheever which list all persons buried in all Sterling cemeteries to 1942.

From 1983-1986 the Sterling Historical Society recorded and photographed all early gravestones pre-dating 1820. These photos and records are on file at their headquarters.

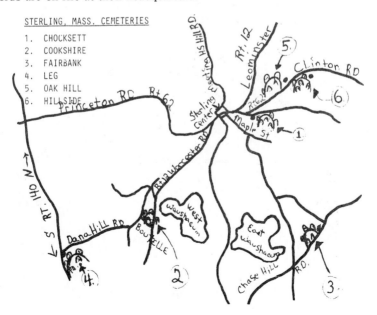

STERLING, MASS. CEMETERIES

1. CHOCKSETT
2. COOKSHIRE
3. FAIRBANK
4. LEG
5. OAK HILL
6. HILLSIDE

# LANCASTER–STERLING GRAVESTONES CARVERS

One carver of many of the 18th century gravestones in the Lancaster-Sterling cemeteries was James Wilder of Lancaster (1741-1794) who lived on Chace Hill Road, where he had a shop and worked with slate from a nearby quarry on Wilder land.

Approximately 225 gravestones have been attributed to him, and his tympanum style includes: 1) a skull, 2) a round young face with a cap of curls, 3) a longer face with ringlets at the sides, and 4) an older face with a straight rolled-back wig. Line drawings of Sterling gravestones are by Robbin DeVincentis.

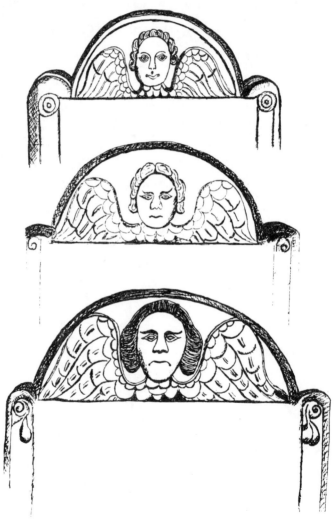

Another early stonecutter, Paul Colburn (1761–1825), came to Sterling from Hollis, New Hampshire in 1784 and worked here until 1806. Numerous stones carved by him can be found in Sterling cemeteries, as well as in area towns and southern New Hampshire.

Colburn moved to Holden in 1806/7 and shortly thereafter returned to New Hampshire. Then in 1815 he removed to Illinois where he died. His stonecutting shop was near the "Quag" (West Waushacum Lake) on Worcester Road. Two designs are prominent on his tympanums: 1) a face-with wings, and 2) an unadorned head in a niche or arch. He also carved stones with the urn and willow design. See following illustrations.

For more information on these two early stonecutters, refer to *James Wilder of Lancaster, Mass., Stonecutter, 1741–1794* by Chase & Gabel in NEHG Magazine, Vol. CXXXVII, April, 1983; and *The Colburn Connection, Hollis, N.H. Stonecutters, 1780–1820* also by Chase & Gabel, in Markers III, The Journal of the Association for Gravestone Studies, 1985.

## CHOCKSETT BURIAL GROUND
### (a.k.a. Old Village, or Kendall Hill Cemetery)

This, the oldest cemetery in Sterling, was set aside ca. 1736 as the burial ground for the "Second Precinct of Lancaster," or "Chocksett," as the Town was called before incorporation in 1781. It lies between Clinton Road (route 62) and Maple Street, almost in the center of the Town.

The first five settlers to Chocksett in 1720 are buried here: Gamaliel Beaman; Benjamin Houghton; Samuel Sawyer; the brothers David and Jonathan Osgood, as well as many of their descendants; and Colonel Asa Whitcomb, a Revolutionary War leader. Sadly, many of the graves are for very young children, often more than one of the same family, who died during epidemics which took many lives in the 1700's.

The Burial ground was enlarged in 1837 with the addition of two acres purchased from Augustine Holcomb. Burials continued into the late 1800's. The earliest section, facing on Clinton Road, contains more than 150 gravestones decorated with death's heads, skulls, and winged cherubs. These have recently been recorded and photographed by the Sterling Historical Society. Numerous other stones, dating after the 1800's carry the stylized urn and willow design, while some from the later 1800's are of white marble with lettering only and no designs.

The gates at both the Clinton Road and Maple Street entrances were a gift to the Town in memory of Nellie M. Reed (1843-1900).

Two tombs can be found in Section Q for the Allen-Parker and Fitch-Kilburn families. Records do not indicate who is buried in the Allen Parker tomb, but it is thought that Dr. Luther Allen, a physician in the Town in the early 1800's, and members of his family are interred there.

Capital letters in parens after each of the following entries indicate the location of the grave on the plot plan on the next page. "CW" indicates a Civil War veteran, "REV" one who fought in the Revolutionary War.

Inscriptions copied by Ruth Hopfmann & Barbara Dudley, 1983-1986. All burials to date are listed.

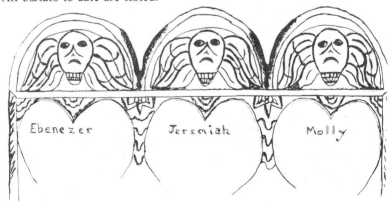

ABBOTT, Henry Augustus s/o Frederick A & Jane d 1 Jan 1850
    ae 4 (K)
  James W d 25 Jan 1859 ae 10 (K)
ADAMS, Mrs Harriet d 29 Dec 1851 ae 57 (F)
ALLEN, Israel d 8 Apr 1817 ae 60 (N)
ALLEN & PARKER TOMB, (no burial records) (Q)
ANDERSON, Lena (on Reed obelisk–sect I)
ANDREWS, William A d 1861 ae 48 (C)
ARNOLD, Rebekah (Willis) w/o Silas W d 23 Feb 1843 ae 55 (G)
  Silas W d 17 Oct 1844 ae 56 (G)
BAILEY, Abigail (Moore) w/o Benjamin d 31 Mar 1862 ae 82 (I)
  Alden s/o Benjamin & Abigail d 11 Jan 1852 ae 54 (I)
  Alma (Goss) w/o Joseph d 3 Oct 1858 ae 48 (E)
  Arabella E d/o Solon & Jane 1859–1861 ae 2 (C)
  Benjamin D 5 Jan 1843 ae 79 (I)
  Charles F s/o Paul Jr & Frinda d 10 Feb 1854 ae 18 (D)
  Cynthia (Fitch) 2d w/o Capt Paul d 12 July 1860 ae 78 (H)
  Elizabeth w/o Jonas d 6 June 1847 ae 90 (O)
  Elizabeth R d/o Benjamin & Abigail d 13 Sept 1896 ae 81 (I)
  F Sawyer s/o Joseph & Alma d 18 Mar 1859 ae 24 (E)
  Frinda (Murdock) w/o Paul Jr d 5 June 1896 ae 81 (D)
  George E s/o Sampson & Sophia d 2 July 1840 ae 25 (G)
  Jane E (Gaut) w/o Solon 1826–1924 (C)
  John E s/o Paul Jr & Frinda d 11 Oct 1863 ae 26 (D)
  Joseph d 26 June 1881 ae 77 (E)
  Jonas d 23 May 1841 ae 91 (O)  REV
  Jonathan d 1 Nov 1814 ae 81 (S)  REV
  Julia Eliza d/o Moses & Abigail d 2 Feb 1835 ae 1 (O)
  Laura A d/o Joseph & Alma d 15 Oct 1851 ae 23 (E)
  Martha Jane d/o Solon & Jane 1851–1861 (C)
  Moses s/o Moses & Abigail d 8 Oct 1835 ae 40 (O)
  Nathaniel M d 17 Sept 1833 ae 25 (N)
  Nathaniel Jr s/o Nathaniel & Betsey d 23 Feb 1807 ae 1 (W)
  Paul d 20 June 1851 ae 81 (H)  –– Capt
  Paul Jr d 20 Sept 1880 ae 72 (D)
  Sampson d 30 Nov 1859 ae 86 (H)
  Samuel S s/o Solon & Jane 1857–1861 (C)
  Shubael d 6 Apr 1824 ae 84 (O) REV
  Solon 1825–1893 (C)
  Sophia (Wilder) w/o Sampson d 9 Feb 1839 ae 53 (H)
  Sophronia E s/o Moses & Abigail d 8 Sept 1815 ae 21 (O)
BAYLEY, Anna d/o Samuel & Anna d 25 Feb 1756 ae 19 (S)
  Isaac s/o Samuel & Anna d 2 Nov 1750 ae 4 (S)
  Susanna d/o Samuel & Anna d 5 Oct 1750 ae 6 (S)
BARNARD, Elizabeth (Fairbank) w/o Dr John d 21 May 1809 ae 59 (E)
  John MD d 20 May 1825 ae 82 (E)
  Lucy d 29 Jan 1866 ae 87 (E)
  Mary Ann d 11 May 1871 ae 74 (E)
BARRON, Abigail Mary d/o William & Abigail d 1 June 1838 ae 9 (G)
  Charles A s/o Augustus & Elizabeth d 11 Oct 1854 ae 1 (G)

Charles H s/o Benjamin & Hepsey Ann d 9 Sept 1843 ae 19m (G)
Ellen M d/o Augustus & Elizabeth d 25 Dec 1861 ae 4 (G)
Helen M d/o Benjamin & Hepsy Ann d 24 Dec 1845 ae 17m (G)
BARTLETT, Andrew P s/o Perley & Persis d 20 Jan 1845 ae 8 (F)
Helen P d 20 Oct 1844 ae 5 (F)
Joseph W s/o Perley & Persis d 20 June 1878 ae 45 (F)
(buried New York City)
Mary w/o Thomas d 15 Sept 1880 ae 65 (C)
Perley d 27 Oct 1887 ae 80 (F)
Persis A (Wetherbee) w/o Perley d 19 Feb 1899 ae 89 (F)
Thomas d 5 Sept 1863 ae 51 (C) CW
BEAMAN, Dolly (Wilder) w/o Gideon d 14 Jan 1853 ae 84 (O)
Elizabeth D d/o Dea Ezra & Mary d 8 Dec 1841 ae 1 da (H)
Elory B d 30 Oct 1852 ae 42 (G)
Dea Ezra d 29 Mar 1847 ae 45 (H)
Gamaliel d 20 Oct 1745 ae 61 (W)
Gideon d 14 Jan 1833 ae 69 (O)  REV
Harriet W d/o Elory & Mary d 28 Nov 1850 ae 7 (G)
Joanna (White) w/o Phineas d 26 Jan 1799 ae 78 (W)
Mary N (Bruce) w/o Dea Ezra d 10 Feb 1861 ae 59 (H)
Mary P (Houghton) w/o Elory B d 11 Nov 1846 ae 33 (G)
Nabby (Brown) w/o Gideon Jr d 8 Nov 1828 ae 37 (N)
Phineas d 16 Mar 1803 ae 84 (W)
BELKNAP, Cyrus d 28 Mar 1855 ae 90 (O)
John s/o Cyrus & Mary d Apr 30 1842 ae 2 (O)
Lucy d/o Cyrus & Mary d 17 Nov 1881 ae 82 (O)
Mary (Woods) w/o Cyrus d 5 June 1837 ae 76 (O)
Mary d/o Cyrus & Mary d 26 Oct 1881 ae 82 (O)
Mary (Bullard) w/o William d 18 Apr 1865 ae 66 (O)
Mary B d/o William & Mary d 10 Dec 1868 ae 33 (O)
William d 4 Apr 1879 ae 89 (O)
BENNETT, Luke s/o Luke & Catherine d 4 Mar 1809 ae 11m (V)
BIRD, Bayley d 2 Feb 1857 ae 64 (F)
George s/o William & Mary d 22 Feb 1809 ae 17 (R)
Mary (Kilburn) w/o Bayley d 1 Oct 1844 ae 54 (F)
BLAKE, H G O (Harrison Gray Otis) b 10 Apr 1816 d 18 Apr
1898 (Conant lot sect F)
Nancy Pope (Conant) w/o HGO b 30 Nov 1828
d 16 Apr 1872 (F)
BLOOD, Amos s/o Reuben & Lucy d 1 Apr 1796 ae 2 (V)
Charles s/o Thomas & Polly d 13 June 1808 ae 10 (R)
Charles s/o Thomas & Polly d 21 Feb 1809 ae 3m (R)
Charles H s/o Thomas & Polly d 1826 ae 13 (R)
Louisa w/o Capt George d 1835 ae 34 (R)
Lucy (Ball) w/o Reuben d 1 Oct 1843 ae 73 (V)
Lucy d/o Reuben & Lucy d 11 Apr 1796 ae 14 da (V)
Mary C d/o Amos & Mary b 26 June 1843 d 7 May 1852 (R)
Melinda D 1st w/o Amos b 13 Aug 1819 d 27 July 1848 (R)
Polly w/o Thomas d 16 Mar 1850 ae 76 (R)
Reuben d 21 Feb 1842 ae 80 (V)
Thomas d 15 May 1848 ae 73 (R)

BOYNTON, Annah (Ross) w/o Zacheus d 5 May 1746 ae 30 (S)
  Ephraim d 21 Jan 1820 ae 37 (Y)
BRECK, Dea Amos W d 26 Aug 1891 ae 76 (G)
  Charles C d 10 Aug 1904 ae 93 (C)
  Eliab d 19 Mar 1855 ae 85 (C)
  Elizabeth d/o Eliab & Polly d 12 Aug 1811 ae 7 (C)
  Emeline B 1st w/o Dea Amos d 4 Nov 1864 ae 51 (G)
  John d 18 Mar 1824 ae 88 (C)  REV
BRECK, Julia A (Johnson) w/o Charles C d 5 June 1875 ae 58 (C)
  Mary (Hill) w/o John d 5 Feb 1829 ae 89 (C)
  Lovinia 2d w/o Dea Amos d 29 1867 ae 30 (G)
  Polly (Cheever) w/o Eliab d 13 Feb 1835 ae 61 (C)
  Sabra A (Barnes) 3d w/o Dea Amos 1822-1905 (G)
  Sarah M d/o Amos & Emeline d 1847 ae 3 (G)
  Sylvia d/o Eliab & Polly d 3 Feb 1890 ae 83 (C)
BRIGHAM, Eli Jr s/o Eli & Polly d 16 Sept 1824 ae 16 m (O)
  Eli Jr s/o Eli & Polly d 8 Mar 1832 ae 3 (O)
  Harriet Ann d/o ELi & Polly d 7 Mar 1837 ae 2 (O)
  Laura Ann d/o Eli & Polly d 24 June 1825 ae 5m (O)
BROOKS, Adaline A adopted d/o Ebenezer & Eliza d 4 Jan 1845
      ae 15m (J)
  Dolly (Kendall) 2d w/o Helon Brooks d 8 Mar 1835 ae 62 (N)
  Ebenezer Jr d 14 Mar 1840 ae 63 (J)
  John d 7 Nov 1824 ae 67 (X)  REV
  John s/o Sydney & Sally d 14 Nov 1789 ae 56 (R)
  Louisa A d/o William & Louisa d 30 June 1840 ae 13 (O)
  Lucinda d/o Ebenezer Jr & Tamer d 13 Oct 1821 ae 4 (O)
  Luthera d/o Ebenezer Jr & Tamer d 5 Oct 1821 ae 2 (O)
  Oren s/o Ebenezer Jr & Tamer d 30 Sept 1796 ae 10m (O)
  Phebe w/o John d 2 Nov 1821 ae 63 (X)
  Relief (Moores) w/o Ebenezer Sr d 11 Feb 1799 ae 52 (W)
  Sarapta d/o Ebenezer Jr & Tamer d 3 Oct 1827 ae 16 (O)
  Seth s/o Sydney & Sally d 16 Jan 1776 ae 23 (T)
  Solomon s/o John & Mary d 11 Sept 1786 ae 2 (Q)
  Sydney d 21 July 1827 ae 27 (S)
  Tamer d/o Ebenezer Jr & Tamer d 12 Oct 1821 ae 14 (O)
  Tamer w/o Ebenezer d 3 Dec 1849 ae 74 (J)
BROWN, Ann Elizabeth d/o Gilson & Sally d 12 June 1839 ae 1 (O)
  Emelie w/o Thomas d 11 Oct 1821 ae 22 (?)
  Francis R s/o Gilson & Sally d 20 Sept 1821 ae 2 (O)
  Genger (Hutchinson) w/o John d 11 Mar 1831 ae 82 (V)
  Gilson d 22 Dec 1834 ae 44 (O)
  James Tilden s/o Bartholomew & Betsy d 30 Mar 1809 ae 1 (V)
  John d 30 Aug 1820 ae 74 (V)
  John s/o John & Genger d 24 Feb 1781 ae 6 (V)
  Jonas s/o Samuel & Abigail d 10 Apr 1790 ae 2 (W)
  Josiah AM d 6 Feb 1773 ae 57 (W)
  Prudence (Prentice) relict of Josiah d 24 Feb 1795 ae 76 (W)
  Rebeckah d/o Josiah & Prudence d 11 Aug 1761 ae 5 (W)
  Sally (Holman) w/o Gilson d 31 Dec 1884 ae 92 (O)
  Samuel  d 20 June 1817 ae 57 (W)  REV

BUCK, Deborah (Beaman) w/o Silas d 19 July 1830 ae 38 (N)
  Mary 2d w/o Silas d 3 Dec 1873 ae 77 (N)
  Silas d 27 Sept 1863 ae 79 (N)
BURPEE, Abel d 12 Sept 1842 ae 42 (N)
  Abigail (Smith) 2d w/o Nathan Sr d 19 Aug 1828 ae 59 (O)
  Andrew s/o Jeremiah Jr & Molly d 18 July 1827 ae 24 (S)
  Asenath (Brooks) 3d w/o Jonathan d 24 Jan 1881
    ae 83 (buried Brooks lot J)
  Azuba (Osgood) w/o Nathan d 15 Sept 1756 ae 26 (W)
  Azuba d/o Samuel & Martha & w/o Abel Haild d 9 Dec 1804
    ae 37 (S)
  Betsey (Stevenson) w/o John d 27 Oct 1854 ae 57 (E)
BURPEE, Ebenezer s/o Jeremiah & Elizabeth d 31 Aug 1750 ae 4 (S)
  Elijah s/o Samuel & Elizabeth d 17 Nov 1750 ae 9 (T)
  Elijah s/o Nathan & Azuba d 20 Sept 1756 ae 3m (W)
  Elijah d 17 June 1836 ae 75 (K)  REV
  Elizabeth d/o Samuel & Elizabeth d 10 Oct 1749 ae 13 (T)
  Elizabeth (Harris) w/o Samuel d 27 Feb 1793 ae 91 (T)
  Elizabeth (Brockelbank) w/o Lt Jeremiah d 16 Dec 1800
    ae 74 (S)
  Elizabeth (Richardson) w/o Abel d 12 Nov 1819 ae 21 (N)
  Elizabeth 2d w/o Jeremiah Jr d 17 May 1835 ae 72 (S)
  Ellen M d/o George N & Harriet d 9 Feb 1851 ae 11 (F)
  Emmaline d/o John & Betsey d 10 Dec 1854 ae 29 (E)
  Fanny (Johnson) 1st w/o Jonathan d 31 Oct 1830 ae 43 (O)
  Hannah d/o Samuel & Elizabeth d 13 Oct 1756 ae 24 (S)
  Hannah (Wait) w/o Elijah d 27 Sept 1845 ae 84 (K)
  Harriet d/o Elijah & Hannah d 15 Sept 1822 ae 21 (K)
  Harriet E d/o Joel & Mary d 22 Dec 1841 ae 5 (J)
  Harriet N w/o George N d 16 Sept 1841 ae 24 (F)
  Harriet N d/o George N & Harriet d 3 Oct 1844 ae 3 (F)
  Jane d/o Newton & Myra d 25 Dec 1828 ae 10 wks (T)
  Jeremiah s/o Jeremiah & Elizabeth d 2 Sept 1756 ae 11 (S)
  Jeremiah d 20 Mar 1817 ae 92 (S)  -- Lt
  Jeremiah Jr d 7 Oct 1822 ae 62 (S)
  Joel d 6 Jan 1861 ae 62 (J)
  John d 6 Jan 1861 ae 73 (E)
  Jonathan d 13 Feb 1854 ae 66 (P)
  Luke s/o Abel & Nancy 1830-1906 (N)
  Martha w/o Samuel d 10 Sept 1810 ae 73 (S)
  Mary (Sargent) w/o Joel d 27 Jan 1875 ae 78 (J)
  Mary Elizabeth d/o Newton & Myra d 28 Oct 1821 ae 23m (T)
  Mary (Smith) 1st w/o CB Curtis 2d w/o Edward Burpee
    1824-1909 (C)
  Mary C d/o George N & Harriet d 15 Feb 1835 ae 9 da (F)
  Molly d/o Jeremiah & Elizabeth d 6 Sept 1756 ae 8 (S)
  Molly (Kendall) 1st w/o Jeremiah Jr d 7 Apr 1801 ae 33 (S)
  Moses d Nov 20 1827 ae 77 (O)  REV
  Myra (Roper) w/o Newton d 22 Aug 1831 ae 40 (T)
  Nathan Jr d 13 Sept 1856 ae 65 (O)
  Nathan d 30 Sept 1756 ae 25 (W)

Newton d 29 Mar 1864 ae 78 (T)
Polly (Gerry) w/o Newton Jr d 19 Apr 1831 ae 37 (O)
Polly (Wilder) 2d w/o Jonathan d 11 July 1838 ae 38 (O)
Polly A d/o Nathan Jr & Polly d 5 Oct 1832 ae 10 (O)
Samuel d 30 May 1810 ae 78 (S)
Samuel d 26 Oct 1791 ae 84 (T)
BUSS, Abigail d/o Ebenezer & Keziah d 13 May 1784 ae 29 (R)
Benjamin d 19 Jan 1836 ae 74 (O)
Dennice s/o John & Mehetabel d 28 Oct 1799 ae 1 (R)
Dea Ebenezer d 5 Mar 1833 ae 76 (O)  REV
Ebenezer Jr d 12 Mar 1868 ae 80 (O)
Dea Ebenezer d 1 July 1801 ae 78 (R)
Keziah (Houghton) w/o Dea Ebenezer d 20 Oct 1822 ae 94 (R)
Keziah d/o Ebenezer & Keziah d 10 Mar 1837 ae 85 (R)
Lucy Ellen d/o George Jr & Elizabeth d 22 Sept 1853 ae 4 (E)
Rebecca d/o Ebenezer & Keziah d 27 Mar 1854 ae 85 (R)
Rebecca H (Mason) w/o Benjamin d 11 Jan 1840 ae 74 (O)
BUSS, Ruhamah (Whitney) 2d w/o Ebenezer d 9 Oct 1840 ae 77 (O)
Ruhamah (Mason) 1st w/o Ebenezer d 25 Jan 1786
     ae 23 (Buried in Leg Cemetery)
Sally (Fairbank) w/o Capt Silas d 22 Apr 1860 ae 92 (O)
Sally (Moore) w/o Capt Silas Jr b 27 June 1801
     d 19 July 1887 (O)
Silas d 26 Mar 1827 ae 63 (O)  -- Capt
Silas Jr d 8 Oct 1871 ae 72 (O)  -- Capt
Sarah d/o Ebenezer & Ruhamah d 18 Mar 1865 ae 75 (O)
BUTTERICK, Abner d 17 Jan 1849 ae 66 Butterick obelisk (Q)
Elnathan d 15 Apr 1825 ae 44 Butterick obelisk (Q)
Hannah W (Sawyer) w/o Jonathan d 25 May 1829
     ae 86 Butterick obelisk (Q)
Hannah d 23 June 1847 ae 75 Butterick obelisk (Q)
Jane B d/o Francis & Mary d 18 Aug 1845 ae 1 (F)
Jane Gray d 29 July 1835 ae 23 Butterick obelisk (Q)
John d 6 July 1809 ae 21 Butterick obelisk (Q)
Jonathan d 23 July 1809 ae 73 Butterick obelisk (Q)
Jonathan d 11 Apr 1825 ae 44 Butterick obelisk (Q)
Josiah d 23 June 1867 ae 70 Butterick obelisk (Q)
Prudence d 10 Aug 1818 ae 32 Butterick obelisk (Q)
Thomas P d 30 July 1842 ae 20 Butterick obelisk (Q)
CARD, Christine E (Reed) w/o Edwin M d 19 Apr 1887 ae 27 (H)
CAREY, George R s/o Timothy & Mira 1823-1875 (R)
Ellen S d/o Timothy & Mira 1839-1841 (R)
Mary J d/o Timothy & Mira 1829-1830 (R)
Mira N 1st w/o Timothy d 9 Feb 1823 ae 16 (R)
Sarah L d/o Timothy & Mira 1836-1841 (R)
CHANDLER, Betsey (Nash) w/o Ozias d 23 Apr 1874 ae 89 (C)
Jane Maria w/o Benjamin d 10 May 1849 ae 21 (F)
Ozias d 11 Nov 1850 ae 82 (C)
CHURCHILL, Rebecca (Wilder) w/o Samuel d 2 June 1828 ae 81 (N)
Samuel d 24 Mar 1830 ae 80 (N)  REV
Samuel Jr s/o Samuel & Rebecca d 30 Jan 1827 ae 38 (N)

CLAP, Dea Joseph d 29 Jan 1799 ae 73 (R)
CLARK, Charles H 1857-1929 (E)
  Dorothy (Hovey) w/o Dea Samuel b 20 Dec 1744
      d 25 Aug 1831 (W)
  Herbert S 1890-1965 (E)
  Hovey s/o Samuel & Dorothy d 12 Feb 1812 ae 32 (W) -- Capt
  Ida M w/o Charles H 1871-1896 (E)
  Rebecca d/o Samuel & Dorothy b 14 May 1783
      d 12 Oct 1837 (W)
  Sally (Rice) w/o Jacob S d 13 Feb 1828 ae 28 (R)
  Dea Samuel b 3 Mar 1730 d 21 June 1816 (W)
  Sarah d/o Samuel & Dorothy d 19 June 1863 ae 80 (W)
CLIFFORD, Mary (Smith) w/o Young Squire Clifford d 2 Dec 1854
      ae 54 (S)
CONANT, Betsey (Pope) 2d w/o Jacob b 1 Feb 1788
      d 6 May 1867 (F)
  Elizabeth K d/o Jacob & Relief d 27 Dec 1816 ae 3 (X)
  Jacob b 13 Jan 1783 d 4 Sept 1839 (F)
  John s/o Samuel & Lydia d 7 Oct 1798 ae 3 (X)
  Lydia (Walker) w/o Samuel d 23 May 1796 ae 42 (X)
  Lydia d/o Samuel & Lydia d 23 Feb 1826 ae 38 (O)
  Mercy 2d w/o Samuel d 14 June 1840 ae 72 (F)
  Polly d/o Samuel & Lydia d 10 Nov 1814 ae 23 (X)
  Relief (Burpee) 1st w/o Jacob d 26 Dec 1814 ae 24 (X)
  Samuel d 2 Mar 1808 ae 58 (W)  REV
  Samuel Jr s/o Samuel & Lydia d 23 Oct 1824 ae 44 (X)
  Sophia (Burpee) w/o Samuel Jr d 29 Oct 1814 ae 26 (X)
COOLIDGE, Barak d 14 Apr 1851 ae 61 (C)
  Nancy (Harris) w/o Barak d 21 Feb 1880 ae 79 (C)
COOPER, Leonard s/o Moses & Ruth d 1 Sept 1750 ae 4 (S)
  Moses d 10 Jan 1793 ae 90 (V)
  Ruth (Johnson) w/o Moses d 21 July 1820 ae 97 (V)
  Ruth d/o Moses & Ruth d 27 Sept 1750 ae 6 (S)
COPELAND, Abbie T (Sawyer) w/o Frank b 8 Mar 1843
      d 9 Dec 1907 (H)
  Charles D s/o Elisha & Sophia d 1 Oct 1826 ae 1 (J)
  Elisha d 4 Oct 1882 ae 78 (K)
  Frank b 12 Aug 1833 d 10 Mar 1927 (H)
  George 1830-1912 (H)
  Hattie (Harriet) E (Raymond) w/o George 1835-1932 (H)
  Julia A d/o Elisha & Sophia d 24 Sept 1830 ae 1 (J)
  Sophia P (Willard) w/o Elisha d 27 Aug 1893 ae 90 (K)
  Maria H d/o Elisha & Sophia d 15 Aug 1855 ae 14 (K)
COREY, Willie H s/o Albert S & Elizabeth (Pratt) Corey
      d 17 Sept 1856 ae 5m (F)
CROSBY, Hannah (Wilder) w/o Jonathan d 4 Jan 1864
      ae 84 (Wilder lot F)
CURTIS, Benjamin F s/o Dea Jesse & Louisa d 14 Sept 1845
      ae 4m (C)
  Blanche (Densmore) w/o Charles A b 13 Aug 1850
      d 3 Jan 1913 (C)

Charles A b 10 Apr 1847 d 10 July 1879 (C)  CW
Dea Jesse d 3 Oct 1856 ae 64 (C)
Kenneth L s/o Charles A & Blanche 1877-1936 (C)
Louisa (Brigham) w/o Dea Jesse d 21 May 1891 ae 88 (C)
Marian d/o Dea Jesse & Louisa d at birth 29 Aug 1847 (C)
Mary (Smith) w/o Charles B Curtis 2d w/o Edward
    Burpee 1824-1909 buried Burpee lot (C)
CUTTING, Martha J d/o Silas & Susan 1870-1914 (D)
    Silas A 1836-1918 (D)
    Susan Maria (Dean) w/o Silas 1845-1918 (D)
DAVIDSON, Lucy (Patch) w/o Peter d 3 Dec 1882 ae 83 (H)
    Mary L w/o Thomas H d 23 Aug 1867 ae 24 (H)
    Peter d 25 Sept 1850 ae 57 (H)
    Thomas N d 27 Aug 1863 ae 28 (H)  CW
DAVIS, Mary P w/o Rev Samuel A d 20 Aug 1848 ae 38 (G)
DEAN, Charles A s/o John & Susan d 4 July 1843 ae 3m (D)
    John d 29 Apr 1876 ae 82 (D)
    Mary S d/o John & Susan d 12 Mar 1843 ae 2 d (D)
    Susan (Seaver) w/o John d 27 Feb 1874 ae 68 (D)
DORCHESTER, Jesse s/o Ismael & Peggy Dorchester
    d 10 Aug 1798 ae 2 (R)
DRAPER, Mrs Sarah B d 18 Mar 1864 ae 60 (G)
DRESSER, Aaron s/o Aaron & Mehitable d 20 Sept 1753 ae 1 hr (T)
    Hannah d/o Aaron & Mehitable d 18 Jan 1749 ae 12
        (Ftstone HD only) (T)
    Jedediah s/o Aaron & Mehitable d 30 Sept 1736 ae 2 (T)
    John s/o Aaron & Mehitable d 25 Feb 1737 ae 4 (T)
DUSTIN, Alexander d 24 Jan 1837 ae 60 (N)
    Sophia (Foster) w/o Alexander d 2 Dec 1862 ae 82 (N)
EAGER, Fortunatus Jr s/o Capt Fortunatus & Mehetabeel
        killed by a falling tree 18 Dec 1818 ae 22 (N)
    Mehetabeel (Bigelow) 1st w/o Capt Fortunatus Sr
        d 29 Mar 1759 ae 26 (R)
EDDY, Abigail (Allen) w/o Erastus d 3 Jan 1878 ae 73 (E)
    Erastus d 10 Nov 1867 ae 65 (E)
    E Webster (E - GS missing)
    Martha (E - GS missing)
FAIRBANK, Abijah d 19 June 1819 ae 70 (Y)  REV
    Nancy B (Kilburn) w/o Stephen d 14 Mar 1854 ae 56 (R)
    Polly d/o Stephen & Nancy d 10 Oct 1831 ae 4 (R-GS missing)
    Polly d 8 Dec 1854 ae 24 (R)
    Stephen d 7 Jan 1839 ae 46 (R)
    Vashti (Wilder) s/o Abijah d 8 July 1843 ae 79 (Y)
FAIRBANKS, Benjamin d 6 Oct 1849 ae 74 (K)
    Caroline L 1824-1909 (C)
    Lois (Whitcomb) w/o Benjamin d 6 June 1836 ae 60 (K)
    Jonathan s/o Jonathan & Thankful d 19 Oct 1747 ae 5 (S)
    Jonathan s/o Jonathan & Thankful d 4 Dec 1750 ae 2 (S)
    Joshua s/o Jonathan & Thankful 21 Oct 1747 ae 2 (S)
FINCH, Freddie M s/o William & Sally d 24 June 1870 ae 14 (C)
    Sally Ann (Mahan) w/o William d 2 July 1899 ae 76 (C)

William d 27 Oct 1894 ae 84 (C)
Willie E s/o William & Sally d 22 Mar 1861 ae 9 (C)
FITCH, Ebenezer d 26 Jan 1826 ae 76 (R) REV
 James W 1815-1893 Fitch-Kilburn tomb (Q)
 Luthera (Goodnough) w/o James W 1819-1914
   Fitch-Kilburn tomb (Q)
 Persis (Bush) w/o Ebenezer d 29 May 1816 ae 57 (R)
FLAGG, Caty (Brown) w/o Rufus b 31 Oct 1788 d 9 Jan 1869 (O)
 Rufus b 7 Oct 1778 d 9 Aug 1826 (O)
FRANCIS, Mary w/o Caleb d 20 Sept 1804 ae 38 (X)
 Phebe d/o Caleb & Polly d 20 Dec 1789 ae 6 hr (X)
 Phebe (Frost) w/o Nathaniel d 28 Dec 1806 ae 75 (X)
GATES, Ellen L d/o Capt Luther & Perney d 13 July 1830 ae 3 (R)
 Jane A d/o Capt Luther & Perney d 30 June 1830 ae 6 (R)
 Luther d 23 July 1847 ae 44 (R) -- Capt
 Mercy (Mrs) d 14 Feb 1756 ae 44 (X)
 Perney W (Geary) w/o Capt Luther d 24 Nov 1884 ae 84 (R)
GEARY, Joseph d 13 Apr 1781 ae 64 (R)
GERRY, Ezra d 26 July 1859 ae 72 (N)
 Henry C s/o Wilkes & Lydia d 24 Aug 1832 ae 2 (N)
 Hepsybath (Braybrook) w/o Jonathan d 28 Oct 1843 ae 86 (N)
 Jonathan d 3 Jan 1831 ae 80 (N) REV
 Mary w/o Ezra d 15 Oct 1849 ae 66 (N)
 Sally w/o Jonathan d 24 May 1857 ae 76 (S)
 Thomas d 26 Apr 1855 ae 54 (O)
GIBBS, Patty d/o William & Patty d 15 Dec 1793 ae 3 (V)
GLAZIER, Esther w/o John d 9 July 1753 ae 38 (S)
GODDARD, Mary W d 28 Nov 1871 ae 82 (F)
GOODELL, Nathan d 10 Sept 1762 ae 26 (S)
GOODNOW, Catherine (Goodnow) w/o Jonas B d 1 Sept 1892
   Waite-Goodnow obelisk (D)
 Harriet E d/o Jonas & Catherine d 12 Apr 1911
   Waite-Goodnow obelisk (D)
 Jonas B d 3 Jan 1848 ae 39 Waite-Goodnow obelisk (D)
 Kate A w/o Jonas & Catherine d 6 Mar 1909
   Waite-Goodnow obelisk (D)
GOSS, Abigail (Fairbanks) 1st w/o William d 24 Nov 1843 ae 42 (O)
 Asa d 18 Aug 1843 ae 67 (G)
 Caroline d/o William & Abigail d 28 Feb 1826 ae 2 (O)
 Caroline d/o William & Abigail d 16 Sept 1830 ae 2 (O)
 Charles d 15 June 1864 ae 27 (O) 21st Reg't MVM
   killed near Petersburg VA -- Capt CW
 Edwin s/o William & Abigail d 15 Dec 1857 ae 23 (O)
 Ella Blake d/o Frederick & Martha A d 30 Nov 1877 ae 17 (D)
 Francis s/o William & Abigail d 1 Sept 1831 ae 6 (O)
 Frederick b 23 Nov 1829 d 6 Sept 1905 (D)
 George d 12 Apr 1883 ae 62 (I) CW
 Hepsibeth (Fife) w/o Asa d 12 Aug 1870 ae 88 (no GS)
 Jane E 2nd w/o George d 27 Nov 1889 ae 65 (I)
 Josiah d 3 Apr 1821 ae 75 (P)
 Lucy d/o Josiah & Sarah d 10 Sept 1851 ae 79 (P)

Martha A 1st w/o Frederick d 24 Apr 1876 ae 42 (D)
Martha Ann 1st w/o George d 5 May 1851 ae 25 (I)
Mary (Johnson) 2nd w/o William d 10 Oct 1886 ae 85 (O)
Mary J (Quinn) 2nd w/o Frederick Goss m 2d Otis Nixon
    1852-1939 (D)
Peter s/o Asa & Hepsibeth d 19 Aug 1843 ae 40 (G)
Sarah w/o Josiah d 10 Aug 1817 ae 71 (P)
Sarah d/o Josiah & Sarah d 29 Sept 1786 ae 1 (P)
Sarah d/o Josiah & Sarah d 12 Sept 1843 ae 55 (P)
William d 17 Mar 1882 ae 85 (O)
GREENE, Harriet L (Wedge) w/o Dr Thomas L Greene
    m 2d John B Kendall d 21 May 1893 ae 59 buried
    Kendall lot (C)
GREENLEAF, Dorothy (Wilder Richardson) d 4 June 1790
    ae 76 burial unknown m 1st Josiah Richardson
    (D 1752 in W) m 2nd Dr Daniel Greenleaf
GRIFFIN, Charles s/o Jonathan & Zerviah d 12 Mar 1830 ae 27 (N)
HADLEY, Abel d 18 Sept 1827 ae 30 (N)
   Abraham d 10 Dec 1814 ae 56 (V) REV
   George s/o Abel & Lucy d 24 Jan 1824 ae 1m (N)
   Lucy Jane d/o Martin & Maria 1850-1860 (J)
   Maria (Hildreth) w/o Martin 1828-1900 (J)
   Martin 1817-1900 (J)
HAILD, Azuba (Burpee) w/o Abel d 9 Dec 1809 ae 37 (S)
HARRIS, Amaziah d 29 Mar 1847 ae 78 (G)
   Ann d/o William & Rebecca d 8 Feb 1778 ae 3 (W)
   Elizabeth (Burpee) w/o Amaziah d 31 Dec 1852 ae 78 (G)
   Foster d 15 Oct 1875 ae 74 (G)
   Mary (Richardson) w/o Foster d 10 Feb 1872 ae 69 (G)
   Rebecca (Mason) w/o William m 2d Benjamin Buss
     d 11 Jan 1840 ae 74 buried Buss lot (O)
   William d 30 Oct 1778 ae 34 (W) REV
   William s/o William & Rebecca d 16 Feb 1778 ae 5m (W)
HASTINGS, Aaron Sawyer s/o Stephen & Silence d 3 Oct 1805
    ae 8 (T)
HASTINGS, Silence (Sawyer) w/o Stephen d 26 June 1862 ae 87
   Hastings tomb (Q)
   Stephen d 3 Aug 1840 ae 69 Hastings tomb (Q) -- Col
HEADLEY, (see HADLEY)
HERSHEY, Abby A w/o Samuel S d 22 Nov 1850 ae 21 (H)
   Eugene C s/o Samuel & Abby d 10 Jan 1850 ae 1m (H)
HEYWOOD, Betsey (Palmer) w/o Rial d 27 Mar 1860 ae 69 (G)
   Harriet M d/o Rial & Betsey d 26 Nov 1845 ae 20 (G)
   John s/o Rial & Betsey d 10 Sept 1830 ae 1 (P)
   Luke d 2 Sept 1846 ae 60 (G)
   Martha A P d/o Luke & Zelida d 12 Jan 1857 ae 25 (G)
   Rial d 18 Jan 1856 ae 66 (G)
HILDRETH, Eunice (Sawyer) w/o Timothy d 2 Aug 1849 ae 68
   John H s/o Timothy & Eunice d 2 Sept 1830 ae 24 (J)
   Lucia d/o Richard & Lucy 1831-1887 (J)
   Lucinda (Miss) d 28 Apr 1844 ae 20 (J)

Lucy (Johnson) w/o Richard d ? (J)
Sarah A d/o Timothy & Eunice d 16 Sept 1843 ae 30 (J)
Timothy d 23 Apr 1817 ae 61 (Y) REV
Timothy Jr d 30 June 1825 ae 46 (T)
HILL, Asa d 25 Mar 1838 ae 35 (K)
Emelia (Beaman) w/o Asa d 16 Sept 1851 ae 51 (K)
HOLBROOK, Ann B Davis w/o Cyrus d 7 May 1873 ae 69 (F)
Cyrus d 1 Jan 1854 ae 57 (F)
Lydia B d/o Cyrus & Ann d 19 Oct 1831 ae 2 (F)
HOLCOMB, Abagail J d/o Augustine & Lucy d 24 Feb 1829 ae
5 wks (O)
Abigail J (Adams) Bush 2d w/o Rev Reuben Holcomb
d 21 Aug 1830 ae 70 (O)
Dea Augustine d 11 May 1837 ae 40 (O)
Helen d/o Augustine & Lucy d 13 May 1832 ae 3m (O)
Jane (Strong) 1st w/o Rev Reuben d 22 Apr 1822
ae 66 (W)
John (White) s/o Augustine & Lucy d 6 Nov 1835
ae 15m (O)
Rev Reuben d 18 Oct 1826 ae 75 (W)
Sukey d/o Rev Reuben & Jane d 10 July 1781 ae 4 (W)
William Frederick MD 1827-1904 (W)
HOLMAN, Alfreda Augusta d/o Porter & Persis d 4 Jan 1850
ae 8 (S) Also on the left are interred five other children
Joshua d 15 May 1886 ae 69 (S)
Persis (Reed) w/o Porter d 7 Jan 1880 ae 78 (S)
Porter d 14 Aug 1858 ae 65 (S)
Charles E (stone illegible) (C)
Frederick S (stone illegible) (C)
Mary J (stone illegible) (C)
Sarah A (stone illegible) (C)
Sarah J d/o Porter & Persis d 21 July 1855 ae 17 (S)
Nathaniel who was drowned d 15 Dec 1812 ae 23 (V)
HOLMES, William d 2 Apr 1807 ae 55 (Y) REV
HOUGHTON, Benjamin Jr d 25 Apr 1759 ae 27 (S)
Benjamin Sr d 28 Feb 1764 ae 74 (S)
Benjamin d 15 Feb 1819 ae 47 (N)
Bethesda d/o Josiah & Bethesda d 10 Apr 1756 ae 1 (S)
Bethesda (Braybrook) w/o Josiah d 20 Apr 1755 ae 37 (S)
Delia d/o Benjamin & Lucy d 10 Aug 1834 ae 31 (N)
Delia Sophia d/o Samuel & Eliza d 23 June 1836 ae 1 (N)
HOUGHTON, Dinah d/o Ezra & Dinah d 17 Oct 1756 ae 7 (S)
Dinah (Houghton) w/o Ezra d 1793 ae 66 (S)
Edward J 1854-1922 (D)
Eli d 30 Oct 1846 ae 39 (G)
Elijah Jr s/o Capt Elijah & Ruth d 2 June 1803 ae 8 (W)
Elijah d 18 Aug 1833 ae 60 (W) -- Capt
Eliza (Hinds) w/o Samuel d 26 Sept 1866 ae 69 (N)
Eliza J (Fish) w/o Edward 1858-1899 (D)
Eliza (Barnard) w/o Manasseh Jr 1806-1899 (J)
Elmer E s/o Edward & Eliza 1850-1850 (D)

Esther (Kendall) w/o Capt Nathaniel d 23 Aug 1842 ae 79 (H)
Eunice (Kendall) w/o Manasseh d 28 Feb 1857 ae 82 (K)
Ezra d 18 July 1789 ae 67 (S)
Fisk d 9 Oct 1837 ae 44 (N)
Heman s/o Manasseh & Eunice d 2 June 1824 ae 23 (K)
Hinds s/o Samuel & Eliza d 2 Feb 1822 ae 5m (N)
James  d ? (D – stone missing)  CW
Jonas d 20 July 1817 ae 39 (J)
Joshua d 1 Dec 1836 ae 83
Louisa Y w/o James d 10 Apr 1852 ae 33 (D)
Lucy (Willard) w/o Benjamin d 13 Oct 1827 ae 58 (N)
Manasseh d 4 July 1827 ae 57 (K)
Manasseh Jr 1804–1877 (K)
Maria d/o Capt Elijah & Ruth d 2 May 1883 ae 82 (W)
Mary d/o Ezra & Dinah d 12 Nov 1753 at birth (S)
Mary Ann d/o Samuel & Eliza d 2 Mar 1831 ae 7 (N)
Mary (Whitcomb) w/o Phineas d 7 Sept 1861 ae 75 (F)
Mary Ann (Kimball) w/o Eli 1807–1899 (G)
Miriam w/o Torry d ? (G – stone missing)
Nathaniel d 27 Jan 1839 ae 80 (H) -- Capt  REV
Phineas Jr s/o Phineas & Mary d 27 Dec 1843 ae 23 (F)
Phineas d 26 Nov 1874 ae 92 (F)
Ruth (Kilburn) w/o Joshua d 8 Nov 1825 ae 66 (N)
Ruth (Sawyer) w/o Jonas d 15 Oct 1857 ae 79 (J)
Ruth w/o Elijah d 28 Feb 1861 ae 90 (W)
Ruth Y d/o Edward & Eliza 1894–1916 (D)
Salmon d 24 May 1825 ae 62 (S)
Salmon s/o Benjamin & Lucy d 11 July 1825 ae 18 (N)
Samuel d 15 Dec 1866 ae 70 (N)
Sophia H (Greenleaf) w/o Fisk d 4 Mar 1850 ae 51 (N)
Susan d/o Manasseh & Eunice d 3 Feb 1835 ae 23 (K)
Torry d 5 Oct 1846 ae 33 (G)
Torry F only s/o Torry & Miriam d 14 Nov 1847 ae 14m (G)
HOUSE, Joshua d 8 Aug 1786 ae 62 (W)  REV
Joshua Jr s/o Joshua & Prudence d 4 Aug 1778 ae 20 (W)
HOWARD, Mary H d/o Edwin & Martha d 10 Oct 1850 ae 3 (H)
HOWE, Harriet M d/o Silas & Sally d 5 Oct 1843 ae 5 (G)
Josephine L (Bartlett) w/o Henry G Howe & d/o Perley &
        Persis  d 16 Jan 1867 ae 32 (F) Bartlett Obelisk
Otis s/o Silas & Submit d 23 Mar 1794 ae 2 (T)
Prudence (Kendall) 2d w/o Silas d 8 Apr 1850 ae 72 (D)
Sally (Hastings) w/o Capt Silas Jr d 6 Feb 1889 ae 90 (G)
Silas d 1 Apr 1867 ae 97 (D)
Silas H s/o Silas Jr & Sally d 9 Apr 1851 ae 25 (G)
Silas Jr d 14 Jan 1864 ae 70 (G) -- Capt
Sophia E (Hildreth) w/o Samuel 1819–1906 (J)
Submit (Sawyer) 1st w/o Silas d 2 Oct 1806 ae 36 (S)
Submit d/o Silas & Submit d 12 July 1801 ae 3wks (T)
William Nelson s/o Samuel & Sophia d 2 Nov 1869 ae 15 (J)
JENNISON, Hepsibeth (Fitch) w/o Martin d 15 Jan 1825 ae 41 (R)
JEWETT, Charlotte d/o Samuel & Lucy d 13 May 1846 ae 26 (D)

David d 21 Nov 1825 ae 76 (J)  -- Lt  REV
David Jr d 18 Feb 1825 ae 47 (J)
Esther (May) w/o David Jr d 16 May 1866 ae 78 (J)
Eunice R d/o Benjamin & Olive d y (K) (GS illegible)
Francis Abbott s/o Joshua & Hannah d 28 Mar 1841 ae 2 (G)
George s/o Benjamin & Olive d y (K) (GS illegible)
Hannah C w/o Joshua A d 29 Sept 1888 ae 83 (G)
Henry P d 4 July 1890 ae 75 (D)
Joshua d 26 June 1875 ae 74 (G)
Lucy (Rugg) w/o Samuel d 31 Aug 1835 ae 54 (D)
Margaret C d/o Solomon & Mary d 7 Dec 1860 ae 37 (H)
Mary Eliza d/o Solomon & Mary d y (stone illegible H)
Mary Holmes Kempton w/o Solomon d 29 Sept 1855 ae 65 (H)
Merrick d 26 Oct 1855 ae 47 (D)
Nathaniel S s/o Joshua & Hannah d 3 July 1892 ae 55 (G)
Olive (Townsend) w/o Benjamin d 24 Oct 1859 ae 68 (J)
Ruth (Sawyer) w/o Lt David d 14 Jan 1838 ae 84 (J)
Ruth Ann d/o Solomon & Mary d 12 Dec 1874 ae 47 (H)
Samuel d 30 Sept 1855 ae 83 (D)
Sarah W w/o Merrick d 10 Nov 1855 ae 33 (D)
Dea Solomon d 19 Nov 1806 ae 63 (W)
Solomon d 11 Aug 1873 ae 89 (H)
JOHNSON, Abel s/o Edward & Relief d 16 Oct 1799 ae 9 (W)
Asa  d 28 Oct 1801 ae 73 (W)  REV
Asa s/o Jonas & Damaris d 25 May 1790 ae 19 (Z)
Clarissa d/o Edward & Relief d 17 July 1801 ae 20 (W)
Edward s/o Edward & Relief d 10 July 1800 ae 1 (W)
Edward d 21 July 1828 ae 82 (O)  REV
Mary A w/o John B d 7 Feb 1880 ae 69 (D)
Oliver d 10 July 1857 ae 72 (O)
Peleg s/o Edward & Relief d 1 Sept 1822 ae 30 (W)
Relief w/o Edward d 11 Jan 1854 ae 87 (O)
Relief d/o Edward & Relief d 8 July 1878 ae 82 (O)
JOSLYN, Catherine E d/o Peter & Almira d 9 Oct 1833 ae 5 (K)
KELLETT, Thomas b Dublin Ireland d 15 May 1831 ae 29 (R)
Mary sister/o Thomas d 26 Aug 1828 ae 34 (R)
KENDALL, Abigail (Waldron) 1st w/o Ezekiel d 18 Dec 1804
        ae 37 (S)
Arrathusa (Houghton) w/o Ethan Jr d 3 Jan 1808 ae 34 (S)
Augustus s/o Capt Joel & Frances d 4 Nov 1833 ae 21 (J)
Augustus William s/o Edwin & Sarah d 16 June 1863 ae 3 (G)
Betsey (Jewett) w/o Ezra d 23 Feb 1865 ae 85 (J)
Charles d Apr 16 1903 ae 89 (C)
Charles B d 6 Aug 1876 ae 52 (O)
Charles W d 1905 ae 57 (C)
Dolly (Beaman) wid/o Isaac Willard & 2nd w/o Luther Kendall
        b  6 Nov 1793 d 3 July 1870 (J)
KENDALL, Edwin d 16 Jan 1860 ae 34 (G)
Elizabeth (Mason) w/o Maj James Jr d 30 Apr 1825 ae 86 (W)
Elizabeth (Wilder) 2d w/o Joseph d 9 Mar 1852 ae 89 (Q)
Elizabeth d/o Luther & Dolly 1830-1915 (E)

L Elizabeth d/o Harvey & Silba 1828-1852 (D)
Esther (Fairbanks) w/o George 1813-1886 (C)
Esther d/o Josiah & Tabatha d 10 Mar 1756 ae 4 (S)
Esther (Sawyer) w/o Josiah Jr d 13 Apr 1832 ae 94 (S)
Esther w/o Luther d 10 Nov 1868 ae 69 (S)
Ethan d 22 Sept 1834 ae 86 (S)  REV
Ethan Jr s/o Ethan Sr & Thankfull b 7 May 1772 d 4 Mar 1848 (S)
Ezekiel d 22 June 1824 ae 71 (S)
Ezra d 7 Oct 1828 ae 50 (J)
Ezra b 10 Sept 1800 d 8 Dec 1892 (J)
Frances (Newhall) w/o Capt Joel d 22 Sept 1867 ae 83 (C)
George 1811-1875 (C)
George A s/o Edwin & Sarah d 24 Feb 1858 ae 1m (G)
George Ezra s/o George & Esther 1850-1929 (C)
Gill s/o Joseph & Priscilla d 6 Jan 1798 ae 9m (O)
Harriett L (Wedge) wid/o Dr Thomas L Greene m 2d John
     B Kendall d 21 May 1893 ae 59 (C)
Harriett M d 25 Sept 1894 ae 58 (C)
Harrison s/o Josiah & Lucy d 21 July 1815 ae 15 (S)
Harvey 1797-1885 (D)
Henry E 1825-1935 (D)
Horace d 7 Nov 1853 ae 64 (C)
James d 25 Nov 1796 ae 87 (X)
James s/o Capt Joel & Frances d 21 Sept 1818 ae 2 (J)
James W s/o Edwin & Sarah d 27 July 1863 ae 7 (G)
James Wilder s/o Josiah & Sally d 19 Nov 1825 ae 2 (J)
Jane W (Smith) 2d w/o Henry E 1834-1916 (D)
Joel d 23 June 1844 ae 63 (C)  -- Capt
Joel Edward only s/o Charles & Susan d 29 Aug 1846 ae 2 (C)
John B d 30 Aug 1872 ae 44 (C)
John H s/o Harvey & Silba 1823-1879 (D)
John L s/o Horace & Mary d 9 Mar 1869 ae 9 (C)
Joseph d 27 Nov 1834 ae 86 (O)  REV
Josiah d 22 July 1785 ae 73 (S)
Josiah d 13 July 1826 ae 65 (S)  REV
Josiah d 19 Jan 1860 ae 67 (J)
Josiah Jr d 10 Jan 1816 ae 78 (S)  REV
Katherine (Edes) w/o Dr Pierson d 10 Oct 1835 ae 75 (K)
Lucinda (Kilburn) 1st w/o Dr Pierson T d 4 Oct 1827 ae 30 (O)
Lucy (Wright) w/o Josiah d 1 Nov 1823 ae 61 (S)
Luther d 1 Mar 1859 ae 64 (S)
Luther d 13 May 1859 ae 74 (J)
Luther Wilder s/o Josiah & Sally d 12 Oct 1835 ae 6 (J)
Mark s/o Josiah & Lucy d 12 Dec 1828 ae 37 (S) -- Ensign
Mary (Cogswell) w/o Horace d 14 Aug 1876 ae 77 (C)
Mary A (Richardson) wid/o Wm Burrage & 2d w/o Dr Pierson T
     d 23 June 1874 ae 72 (O)
Mary E (Safford) 1st w/o Henry E 1831-1851 (D)
Nancy (Wilder) w/o Ezra b 11 Sept 1800 d 7 Mar 1887 (J)
Nancy d/o Ethan Sr & Thankfull b 19 Aug 1783 d 8 Aug 1818 (S)
Peter s/o Joseph & Priscilla d 31 May 1786 ae 6 (O)

Pierson s/o James & Lydia d 22 Sept 1756 ae 9 (S)
Pierson MD d 3 May 1844 ae 78 (K)  REV
Pierson T MD d 11 Jan 1865 ae 72 (O)
Polly d 8 Dec 1854 ae 24 (R)
Priscilla (Thurston) 1st w/o Joseph d 28 May 1812 ae 60 (O)
Rebecca R w/o Ezekiel Jr d 9 July 1823 ae 31 (K)
Ruth (Mrs Ruth Calef) 2d w/o Ezekiel d 21 Dec 1846 ae 71 (S)
Sally (Wilder) w/o Josiah d 9 Mar 1863 ae 66 (J)
Sarah E d/o Josiah & Sally d 3 Oct 1835 ae 4 (J)
Silba (Bailey) w/o Harvey 1798-1882 (D)
Susan (Jewett) w/o Charles d 3 Nov 1882 ae 63 (C)
Susan L d/o Josiah & Sally d 23 Feb 1843 ae 9 (J)
Susan R (Colton) 1st w/o Luther d 2 Apr 1825 ae 37 (J)
Tabatha (Wyman) w/o Josiah d 22 Apr 1800 ae 87 (S)
Thankfull (Moores) w/o Ethan d 15 May 1807 ae 58 (S)
Wyman s/o Ethan Sr & Thankfull b 9 Apr 1774 d 8 Aug 1841 (S)
KEYES, Betsey (Pratt) w/o Ephraim d 23 Jan 1867 ae 79 (N)
Charlotte B d/o Ephraim & Betsey d 12 Mar 1826 ae 3 (N)
Ephraim P s/o Ephraim & Betsey d 20 Dec 1824 ae 8m (N)
KIDDER, Foster R s/o Jedediah & Miranda d 26 Jan 1827 ae 9m (R)
KILBURN, Cheney d 29 Sept 1873 ae 76 (K)  -- Col
Dea Joseph d 19 Nov 1789 ae 62 (S)
Joshua d 9 Jan 1833 ae 67 (R)  REV
Levi 1804-1891 (N)
Lucy Ann d/o Cheney & Sally d 24 Apr 1828 ae 5m (K)
Martha J (Sawyer) w/o Levi 1817-1838 (N)
Phebe (Brooks) w/o Joshua Kilburn m 2d Lt Joel Pratt
    d 10 Dec 1853 ae 84 (R)
Polly (Jewett) wid/o Sidney Roper w/o Levi Kilburn
    1797-1895 (J)
Sally w/o Col Cheney d 20 June 1879 ae 80 (K)
Samuel d 12 Mar 1858 ae 75 (C)
Susan (Fitch) w/o Timothy d (?) in Kilburn-Fitch tomb (Q)
Timothy d (?) (in Kilburn-Fitch tomb Q)
Timothy Jr s/o Col Timothy & Relief d 18 Aug 1801 ae 4 (Q)
KIMBALL, Abigail (Tyler) w/o Richard d 30 Dec 1831 ae 73 (N)
Lemuel s/o Richard & Abigail d 11 Feb 1856 ae 70 (D)
Richard d 31 Dec 1818 ae 64 (N)  REV
KNOWLTON, Almira M (Ross) w/o Joseph Henry 1850-1921
    (Ross lot-K)
LARKIN, Mattathias s/o Seth & Mary d 28 Oct 1790 ae 2 (Q)
LAWRENCE, Daniel H s/o Samuel & Susan d 23 Sept 1847 ae 10m (G)
Ella E d/o Samuel & Susan d 11 Mar 1857 ae 8 (G)
Samuel H d 28 Feb 1863 ae 48 (G)
Susan C (Hosmer) w/o Samuel d 31 Oct 1875 ae 53 (G)
LEAVITT, Mary 1st w/o Dr Josiah d 20 May 1778 ae 34 (Y)
LEGEYT, Melinda T d 17 Oct 1847 ae 37 (D)
LEWIS, Albert W s/o Dea Nathaniel & Betsey d 26 Sept 1837
    ae 1 (O)
Alvira M (Bradley) w/o Joseph Lewis & Isaac M Seaver
    1840-1923 (O)

Betsey w/o Nathaniel d 20 Sept 1881 ae 83 (O)

Betsey d/o Dea Nathaniel & Betsey d 15 July 1830 ae 3 (O)

LEWIS, Francis A s/o Nathaniel & Betsey killed at Gettysburg
      3 July 1863 ae 24 (O) CW Co A 15th Regt MVM

John d 5 Feb 1867 ae 46 (O)

Joseph P d 5 Jan 1882 ae 48 (O)

Josie s/o Joseph & Alvira d 4 Aug 1886 ae 4 (O)

Dea Nathaniel d 9 Nov 1859 ae 68 (O)

Thomas E d 15 Feb 1862 ae 37 (O)

LITTLEJOHN, Marah d/o Tilley & Hannah d 23 Mar 1776 ae 11 (Q)

Tilley d 1 Nov 1793 ae 58 (Q) Fr & Indian War

LORING, Franklin s/o Joseph & Mary d 26 Sept 1802 ae 1 (W)

Joseph F d 7 Oct 1815 ae 39 (F)

Mary (Polly) (Belknap) w/o Joseph d 25 Dec 1817 ae 52 (W)

Mary Jane d/o Joseph F & Abigail d 9 Apr 1861 ae 25 (F)

LYON Emma C d/o Emory & Mary d 4 June 1850 ae 6m (O)

Mary C w/o Emory d 23 Sept 1852 ae 27 (O)

MAHAN, Mrs Jane d 19 July 1878 ae 98 (Finch lot-C)

MAY, Henry d 29 Apr 1846 ae 39 (J)

Lucretia C (Davidson) w/o Edwin d 29 Oct 1855 ae 26 (H)

Lucretia d/o Edwin & Lucretia d 11 Aug 1855 ae 1 d (H)

Moses d 14 Oct 1843 ae 35 (J)

MAYNARD, Adeline w/o George C b 16 Jan 1824 d 17 Nov 1911 (E)

Calvin d 6 Oct 1827 ae 48 (E)

Cornelia (Smith) 2d w/o Calvin d 17 Jan 1868 ae 71 (E)

George C d 11 July 1866 ae 39 (E)

Hezekiah d 1 Oct 1863 ae 79 (E)

Olive (Whiting) 1st w/o Calvin d 11 July 1819 ae 30 (E)

MELLEN, Sophia d/o Rev John & Rebecca d 17 Dec 1778 ae 23 (W)

Thomas third s/o Rev John & Rebecca d 11 Aug 1766 ae 3 (W)

MOORE, Abigail (How) w/o Israel d 20 Dec 1759 ae 21 (S)

Abigail (Houghton) w/o Dea Oliver d 9 Mar 1800 ae 90 (S)

Dolly d/o Jonathan & Elizabeth d 22 Feb 1781 ae 4 (S)

Elizabeth (Richardson) w/o Jonathan d 27 Sept 1810 ae 60 (V)

Hannah d/o Oliver & Abigail d 1 Sept 1749 ae 3 (S)

Jonathan d 10 Apr 1816 ae 73 (W) REV

Dea Oliver d 23 Dec 1774 ae 67 (S)

Pitts s/o Jonathan & Elizabeth d 7 July 1786 ae 1 (S)

Prudence d 13 Feb 1807 ae 67 (S)

Prudy d/o Jonathan & Elizabeth d 6 Sept 1801 ae 26 (W)

MOORE, Calvin d 7 Feb 1841 ae 87 (O) REV

Calvin s/o Samuel & Phebe d 27 Feb 1831 ae 17 (O)

David d 31 Mar 1823 ae 53 (N)

Harriet d/o David & Harriet d 28 Feb 1821 ae 21 (N)

Rebecca d/o David & Harriet d 26 Sept 1845 ae 49 (N)

Susannah (Cutting) w/o Calvin d (GS missing) (O)

Tabitha w/o David d 31 Jan 1855 ae 89 (N)

MORSE, Alonzo d 15 Oct 1841 ae 26 (D)

Sophia d 13 June 1845 ae 33 (D)

NELSON, Dorothy w/o Jonathan d 17 Mar 1792 ae 76 (R)

Dea Ephraim d 13 Dec 1858 ae 73 (R)

Jonathan s/o Ephraim & Olive d 30 Aug 1819 ae 2 (R)
Jonathan d 12 Sept 1863 ae 25 (C) Co K 53d Regt MVM – CW
Kezia (Buss) 2d w/o Ephraim d 26 Feb 1859 ae 59 (R)
Kezia d/o Ephraim & Kezia d 9 Aug 1843 ae 6wks (R)
Marshall W s/o Cephas & Eunice d 3 Mar 1837 ae 3m (C)
Mary L d/o Cephas & Eunice d 10 Feb 1845 ae 4 (C)
Olive (Brown) 1st w/o Ephraim d 13 Aug 1819 ae 26 (R)
NEWHALL, Alice (Roper) w/o Samuel d 27 Aug 1890 ae 67 (F)
Cephas d 12 Aug 1865 ae 75 (F)
Ella J d/o Samuel & Alice d 31 Oct 1851 ae 10m (F)
Hattie E d/o Samuel & Alice d 30 June 1857 ae 11 (F)
Lucy Anne (Jewett) 2d w/o Cephas d 15 Feb 1877 ae 66 (F)
Ruth (Kilburn) 1st w/o Cephas d 22 Apr 1835 ae 42 (F)
Samuel C d 21 Sept 1884 ae 63 (F)
NEWTON, Nathan Goddard s/o Daniel & Martha d 29 Nov 1810
ae 11 m (V)
NICHOLS, H Josephine d/o William & Emily d 23 July 1846 ae 2 (G)
William R s/o William & Emily d 7 Sept 1851 ae 4 (G)
NIXON, Mary J (Quinn) wid/o Frederick Goss w/o C Otis Nixon
1852–1939 (D)
NOURSE, Edward J d 1864 (?) ae 12 (F)
Eunice H w/o Franklin 1813–1899 (F)
Franklin 1814–1879 (F)
Joseph W d 1864 (?) ae 15 (F)
Mary d 1864 ae 15 (F)
OSGOOD, Abigail (Whetcomb) w/o Jonathan Jr d 12 June 1759
ae 27 (W)
Anes (Church) 2d w/o Tyler P d 5 Feb 1829 ae 39 (J)
Asenath (Sawyer) w/o Dea Jonathan d 25 Feb 1753 ae 39 (W)
Asenath (Church) 3d w/o Tyler P d 2 Jan 1865 ae 85 (F)
Betsey (Stockwell) 1st w/o Tyler P d 13 Nov 1823 ae 50 (J)
David d 20 Feb 1771 ae 73 (W)
Eunice (Carter) w/o David d 16 Nov 1789 ae 85 (W)
Dea Jonathan d 10 Feb 1766 ae 70 (W)
Samuel d 31 Oct 1818 ae 80 (J) REV
Thankfull (Matthews) w/o Samuel d 14 May 1820 ae 80 (J)
Tyler P d 14 Apr 1851 ae 75 (J)
PALMER, Elizabeth H w/o John d 7 July 1803 ae 84 (V)
Elizabeth d/o John & Elizabeth d 24 Sept 1819 ae 59 (V)
Henry s/o William & Mary d 27 Mar 1854 ae 7 m (I)
Hitty w/o Dea Joseph d 6 Mar 1850 ae 90 (O)
Hitty d/o John & Elizabeth d 20 Sept 1800 ae 34 (V)
John d 21 Dec 1806 ae 78 (V)
John s/o Dea Joseph & Hitty d 12 Mar 1829 ae 30 (O)
Dea Joseph d 30 Jan 1832 ae 75 (O) REV
Joseph Jr d 1 Oct 1826 ae 38 (O)
Lucy 1st w/o William d 23 Sept 1842 ae 51 (I)
Mary E 2d w/o William d 13 Sept 1858 ae 42 (I)
Mary E d/o William & Mary d 13 Oct 1858 ae 5 m (I)
Sally d/o Dea Joseph & Hitty d 19 Oct 1861 ae 68 (O)
Sophia d/o Joseph & Hitty d 25 Dec 1801 ae 7 (V)

William d 23 Nov 1875 ae 73 (I)
PARKER & ALLEN TOMB (Q)
PARKER, Betsey (Seaver) w/o Maj Lewis d 5 Nov 1859 ae 76 (N)
 Evalina M d/o Lewis & Betsey d 7 June 1833 ae 21 (N)
 Lewis d 7 June 1834 ae 47 (N) -- Maj War of 1812
PATTEN, Elizabeth H d 20 Sept 1879 ae 62 (J)
 Emma D d 1 Oct 1867 ae 47 (J)
 Hannah (Hildreth) w/o James d 30 July 1838 ae 50 (J)
 James P d 22 Nov 1860 ae 77 (J)
PAYNE, Charlotte M d/o Oliver & Mary d 26 Mar 1862 ae 20 (C)
PAYNE Mary M w/o Oliver d 25 Aug 1891 ae 68 (C)
 Oliver d 4 Apr 1865 at Hampton VA ae 47 (C)
  Co C 34th Regt MVM CW
PIERCE, Benjamin d 13 Apr 1852 ae 60 (D)
 Louise (Newton) w/o Benjamin d 30 Mar 1885 ae 87 (D)
PHELPS, Abigail (Ross) w/o Clark d 30 June 1827 ae 29 (K)
 Catherine (Clark) w/o Josiah d 3 Apr 1855 ae 82 (G)
 Catherine d 17 May 1880 ae 82 (G)
 George s/o Clark & Abigail d 20 June 1827 ae 2 m (K)
 James d 28 July 1856 ae 56 (G)
 Josiah d 23 Aug 1825 ae 56 (W)
 Lewis s/o Josiah & Catherine d 27 Nov 1828 ae 21 (W)
 Mary Ann d 30 Oct 1840 ae 38 (G)
POPE, Ebenezer d 24 Mar 1825 ae 73 (R) REV
 Ebenezer d 11 Mar 1833 ae 49 (R) -- Col
 George H s/o Rev Rufus & Sarah d 12 Oct 1837 ae 5 m (G)
 Hannah (Shaw) w/o Joseph d 1 May 1798 ae 77 (R)
 Joseph d 27 May 1807 ae 91 (R)
 Joseph d 12 Aug 1814 ae 33 (R)
 Lucretia (Wilder) w/o Ebenezer d 24 Sept 1816 ae 55 (R)
PORTER, Augustus K s/o John & Mary d 28 Aug 1799 ae 1 (X)
 John d 21 Mar 1857 ae 87 (N) -- Capt REV
 Mary (Polly Kendall) w/o Capt John d 26 Feb 1836 ae 64 (N)
POWERS, Betsey (Kimball) w/o Ephraim d 11 Mar 1868 ae 78 (N)
 Charles d 4 Apr 1877 ae 72 (F)
 Charles Augustus s/o Charles & Ruth d 10 Aug 1839 ae 3 (F)
 Elizabeth H (Gregory) 2d w/o Charles d 1 Mar 1885 ae 76 (F)
 Ephraim d 4 Oct 1822 ae 40 (N) -- Maj
 Keziah (Sawyer) wid/o Capt Ezra Sawyer m 2d Ephraim
  Powers d 21 Oct 1824 ae 84 (W)
 Mary Augustus d/o Charles & Elizabeth d 16 Jan 1845 ae 2 (F)
 Rufus s/o Daniel & Mary d 27 Aug 1750 ae 10 (T)
 Ruth E 1st w/o Charles d 19 Apr 1836 ae 28 (F)
PRATT, Anna (Hildreth) w/o Maj J Wheelock b 29 Oct 1836
  d 11 Aug 1923 (F)
 Charlotte (Ball) 1st w/o Lt Joel d 12 Nov 1829 ae 67 (N?)
 Charlotte B d/o Col John & Elizabeth d 13 Aug 1862 ae 30 (F)
 Edward s/o William 1865-1866 (F)
 Elizabeth E (Wheelock) w/o Col John B d 4 Oct 1840 ae 40 (F)
 Ezra d 20 Oct 1837 ae 51 (J)
 Ezra Jr s/o Ezra & Polly d 22 Jan 1840 ae 24 (J)

Frank E s/o Emory & Rebecca (?) d 28 Sept 1862 ae 1 (C)
Hannah d/o Ezra & Polly d 22 Aug 1821 ae 16 m (J)
Henry Winthrop s/o J Wheelock & Anna 1865-1939 (F)
J Wheelock 1829-1866 Sgt US Engrs Maj 55th Regt USAVA
    (F) -- Maj CW
Jane B (Bird) 2d w/o Joel 3d d 11 Nov 1848 ae 27 (F)
Joel d 10 Nov 1844 ae 93 (N) -- Lt REV
Joel 3d b 30 July 1818 d 15 Nov 1843 ae 25 (F)
John Ball d 7 Feb 1855 ae 65 (F) -- Col
Mariah d/o Ezra & Polly d 18 May 1885 ae 53 (J)
Martha (Storey) w/o Emory d 2 Jan 1857 ae 29 (C)
Mary d/o Ezra & Polly d 18 Sept 1821 ae 8 (J)
Phebe (Brooks) wid/o of Joshua Kilburn 2d w/o
    Lt Joel Pratt d 10 Dec 1853 ae 84 (R)
PRATT, Polly (Bailey) w/o Ezra d 30 Apr 1883 ae 96 (J)
    Solomon s/o Ezra & Polly d 27 Aug 1821 ae 3 (J)
    Solomon s/o Ezra & Polly d 2 Nov 1835 ae 13 (J)
PROCTOR, Ann M W w/o Rev George d 9 Sept 1841 ae 25 (H)
    Ellen M d/o Rev George & Ann d 16 Sept 1841 ae 1 (H)
PROUTY, Jason G d 12 Mar 1828 ae 39 (P)
PUTNAM, Andrew s/o William 1755-1809 (D) REV
    Andrew Jr 1791-1845 (D)
    Charles 1795-1812 (D)
    Eliza 1805-1825 (D)
    Jerusha (Clap) w/o Andrew 1767-1834 (D)
    Samuel 1793-[815 (D)
    William 1730-1808 (D)
    William 1797-1814 (D)
RANGER, Amos s/o Samuel b May 1807 d Apr 1882 (I)
    Caroline F d/o Joel & Mary 1841-1844 (I)
    Ella d/o Joel & Mary 1847-1850 (I)
    Joel B d 18 May 1852 ae 49 (I)
    Mary (Rollins) w/o Joel d 18 July 1849 ae 42 (I)
    Samuel d 23 June 1842 ae 68 (I)
    Susanna (Adams) w/o Samuel d 5 May 1852 ae 79 (I)
RAYMOND, Hattie C d/o Joseph & Lucretia d 1855 ae 2 (G)
    Lucretia w/o Joseph d 17 Oct 1858 ae 46 (G)
    Mary J d/o Joseph & Lucretia d 1812 ae 3 m (G)
    Edward d -- --- ---- (footstone only E Raymond Esq V)
    Francis d 14 Mar 1873 ae 75 (K)
    Hannah (Burpee) w/o Francis d 1 Nov 1886 ae 87 (K)
    Hepsibah w/o Edward ? d -- --- ---- GS gone (V)
RAYMORE, Elizabeth (Loring) w/o James H d 27 Oct 1900 ae 88 (D)
    James H d 23 May 1879 ae 70 (D) CW
    Laura A d/o James H & Elizabeth d 8 Mar 1851 ae 11 (D)
REED, Almira (Burpee) w/o Samuel d 8 Feb 1844 ae 26 (F)
    Ann Mariah d 11 Dec 1836 ae 5 m (I)
    Betsey (Stewart) w/o Levi d 30 Dec 1863 ae 85 (C)
    Clerimond 1st w/o William Jr d 30 Mar 1841 ae 23 (N)
    Elbridge G d 28 June 1870 ae 70 (G)
    Elizabeth w/o Joel d 1 Feb 1845 ae 63 (D)

Emily d/o William & Polly 1818-1825 (W)
Harriet A d/o William & Susan d 23 Feb 1860 ae 13 (G)
Harriet E (Goodrich) 3d w/o William Jr d 24 Apr 1872
    ae 43 (G)
Haskell D b 3 Aug 1849 d 21 Apr 1862 (I)
Joel d 24 Sept 1864 ae 84 (D)
John Quincy b 7 June 1847 d 9 Feb 1911 (I)
Levi d 27 May 1855 ae 81 (C)
Lucretia K d 26 Apr 1855 ae 17 (I)
Marietta (Stuart) w/o Foster K d 10 Oct 1864 ae 35
    (Stuart obelisk)
Mary Ann (Rice) w/o Elbridge d 30 Dec 1880 ae 78 (G)
Mary Ann d/o Elbridge & Mary Ann d 5 Sept 1845 ae 15 (G)
Nathan d 28 June 1810 ae 43 (Y)
Nellie Maria d 9 Sept 1900 ae 57 (I) Cemetery gates in her
    memory
Peter K b 27 May 1811 d 21 Jan 1869 (I)
Polly (Gary) w/o William 1778-1826 (W)
REED, Roxanna (Reed) w/o Peter b 28 Oct 1811 d 16 Dec 1884 (I)
   Mrs Susan H d 11 Oct 1854 ae 32 (C)
   Susan P (Heywood) 2d w/o William Jr d 28 June 1851 ae 27 (G)
   William 1776-1851 (W)
   William Jr d 18 Jan 1878 ae 62 (G)
   William s/o William & Polly 1803-1815 (W)
REMINGTON, Phidello d 27 Apr 1886 ae 78 (G)
   Sarah (Wetherbee) w/o Phidello d 8 May 1883 ae 82 (G)
RICE, Philoma w/o John d 29 Jan 1872 ae 72 (G)
RICHARDSON, Josiah d 1 Sept 1752 ae 47 (W)
   Martha (Lewis) w/o Thurston d 23 Mar 1848 ae 25 (O)
   Mary J R w/o Samuel d 4 Mar 1842 ae 17 (F)
RILEY, Catherine A (Gates) w/o Thomas 1821-1896 (G)
   Harriet Heywood d/o Thomas & Catherine d 26 Apr 1849 ae 2 (G)
   Martha S (Howe) w/o ---- d/o Samuel & Sophia Howe
      1852-1920 (in Hildreth lot - J)
   Thomas d 2 Oct 1850 ae 36 (G)
ROBBINS, Daniel d 31 Mar 1755 ae 47 (S)
   Jacob d 21 May 1812 ae 62 (Z) REV
   John d 15 Nov 1833 ae 78 (J) Ftsone only "JR" REV
   Jude d 3 Sept 1807 ae 43 (Z)
   Lucy (Bush) w/o John d 16 June 1846 ae 85 (J) GS gone
   Lucy (Smith) w/o Roger d 26 May 1810 ae 83 (Z)
   Roger d 3 Feb 1787 ae 77 (Z)
ROPER, Asa s/o Jonas & Polly d 13 Apr 1826 ae 8 (R)
   Caroline (Burpee) w/o Ephraim d 1 Apr 1890 ae 74 (F)
   Catherine (Peirce) w/o Sylvester d 3 Nov 1841 ae 70 (G)
   Elizabeth (Burpee) w/o Silas d 2 Dec 1840 ae 80 (R)
   Ella d -- --- 1828 (N)
   Emily d/o Ephraim & Caroline d 14 Jan 1863 ae 13 (F)
   Ephraim d 5 Dec 1793 ae 78 (R) REV
   Ephraim d 23 June 1849 ae 43 (F)
   Henry s/o Ephraim & Michal d 28 Oct 1825 ae 32 (R)

Lizzie d 27 Jan 1890 ae 24 (G)

Lucy (Kendall) w/o Capt Silas d 1 July 1860 ae 74 (N)

Martha J (Houghton) 2d w/o Merrick d 3 Nov 1903 ae 77 (G)

Mary Ann (Ricard) 1st w/o Merrick d 24 Aug 1851 ae 30 (G)

Merrick d 17 Aug 1888 ae 79 (G)

Polly (Jewett) w/o Sidney Roper & Levi Kilburn
    1797–1895 (J)

Polly (King) w/o Asa d 11 June 1822 ae 63 (R)

Sidney 1801–1839 (J)

Silas d 7 Oct 1827 ae 73 (R)  REV

Silas d 21 Aug 1848 ae 65 (N) –– Capt

Silva d/o Silas & Elizabeth d 12 Apr 1799 ae 2 (R)

Sintha w/o Asa & Polly d 21 Sept 1794 ae 2 (R)

Sylvester d 2 Mar 1849 ae 86 (G)  REV

ROSE, William a native of Great Britain d 17 Feb 1824 ae 58 (P)

ROSS, Annie S d/o Nathaniel & Delicia 1860–1860 (K)

Betty d/o Thomas & Priscilla d 20 Sept 1796 ae 9 (S)

Betty 2d d/o Thomas & Priscilla d 4 Sept 1782 ae 5 (S)

Betsey d/o William & Tamer d 8 Oct 1790 ae 5 (O)

Betsey d/o Moses & Rebecca d 8 Feb 1792 ae 2 (S)

Calvin s/o Peter & Polly d 18 Mar 1824 ae 5 m (O)

Charles s/o William & Lucy d 1824 d y (F)

ROSS, Charlie N s/o Nathaniel & Delicia 1857–1858 (K)

Delicia A (Copeland) w/o Nathaniel 1827–1913 (K)

Ebenezer s/o Ebenezer & Achsah d 20 Apr 1772 ae 2 (S)

Eddie H s/o Nathaniel & Delicia 1864–1864 (K)

Elvira w/o Phineas 1825–1894 (G)

Harriet (Merriam) w/o William J d 22 Sept 1850 ae 22 (E)

Jonathan s/o Thomas & Mary d 10 Oct 1756 ae 1 (S)

Martin d 13 June 1817 ae 24 (S)

Mary w/o Thomas d 29 Nov 1765 ae 54 (S)

Mary D d/o Nathaniel & Delicia 1855–1855 (K)

Nathaniel 1820–1909 (K)

Phineas 1818–1906 (G)

Polly d/o Moses & Rebecca d 10 Nov 1806 ae 1 (S)

Priscilla G d/o Ebenezer & Achsah d 20 Apr 1776 ae 7 m (S)

Tamer (Johnson) w/o William d 10 June 1827 ae 73 (S)

William J May 1821–Apr 1887 (E)

William d 1 May 1815 ae 66 (S)

RUGG, Amos s/o Amos & Mary d 15 Sept 1746 ae 2 (T)

George Francis s/o Luther W & Mary d 6 Apr 1832 ae 8d (J)

Helen d/o Luther W & Ruth S d 2 Mar 1860 ae 10d (J)

John Abbott s/o Luther & Ruth d 25 July 1814 ae 4 (V)

Luther d 20 Oct 1863 ae 93 (E)

Luther Warren d 14 Dec 1859 ae 55 (J)

Martha d/o Reuben & Lydia d 1 Apr 1758 ae 26 (W)

Mary (Hager) 1st w/o Luther W d 3 Sept 1838 ae 28 (J)

Mason s/o Luther & Ruth d 7 Sept 1804 ae 1 (V)

Prudence d/o Reuben & Lydia d 20 May 1758 ae 19 (W)

Ruth (Jewett) w/o Luther d 10 Oct 1864 ae 89 (E)

Ruth S (Jewett) 2d w/o Luther W d 20 Apr 1891 ae 77 (J)

Solomon s/o Amos & Mary d 5 Nov 1756 ae 3 (T)
Stephen s/o Amos & Mary d 19 Oct 1756 ae 5 (T)
SANDICKY, Harriet w/o Dr D F b 26 Nov 1816 d 8 Mar 1844 (F)
SAWIN, Charles H s/o Josiah & Lucy A (Smith) d 7 June 1842
    ae 4 (?)
SAWYER, Aaron Sr d 15 Dec 1774 ae 42 (T)
  Abner d 6 Dec 1758 ae 47 (S)
  Abigail (Moor) w/o Aaron Sr d 19 July 1824 ae 86 (T)
  Abigail (White) w/o Thomas Jr d 26 Mar 1798 ae 87 (W)
  Abigail d/o Aaron & Abigail d 12 July 1788 ae 24 (S)
  Anna w/o Thomas d 5 Nov 1753 ae 74 (S)
  Azuba (Roper) 2d w/o Samuel d 22 Nov 1854 ae 70 (J)
  Betsey S (Wilder) w/o Moses d 3 Oct 1906 ae 86 (D)
  Deborah (Rugg) w/o Samuel d 17 Nov 1790 ae 80 (S)
  Dollee d/o Aaron & Abigail d 21 May 1782 ae 14 (S)
  Elizabeth (Houghton) w/o Capt Thomas d 18 May 1856
    ae 87 (N)
  Esther (Jewett) w/o Joshua d 21 Dec 1828 ae 83 (R)
  Esther d/o Joshua & Esther d 17 June 1841 ae 60 (R)
  Ezra d 23 Oct 1765 ae 63 (W)
  Ezra d 4 Mar 1776 ae 47 (W) -- Capt  REV
  Ezra 3d s/o Capt Ezra & Martha d 4 Oct 1806 ae 2 (W)
  Ezra Jr d 1 Feb 1828 ae 64 (N)  -- Capt
  Eunice (Buss) w/o Cornelius d 8 June 1821 ae 68 (W)
  Eunice (Houghton) 1st w/o Capt Ephraim d 24 June 1748
    ae 52 (W)
  Eunice d/o Joshua & Esther d 3 Dec 1800 ae 22 (R)
  Franklin s/o William & Nancy d 24 May 1812 ae 3 (S)
  Hepzibah (Thurston) 1st w/o Samuel d 31 July 1814 ae 43 (J)
  James s/o Thomas Jr & Abigail d 3 Oct 1756 ae 11 (S)
  Joshua d 4 Dec 1817 ae 75 (R)  REV
  Keziah (Sawyer) w/o Capt Ezra m 2d Ephraim Powers
    d 21 Oct 1824 ae 85 (W)
  Lucy (Richardson) w/o Maj Manasseh b 13 June 1749
    d 24 Feb 1821 (W)
  Manasseh b 30 June 1750 d 6 June 1801 ae 50 (W) -- Maj  REV
  Martha (Sawyer) w/o Capt Ezra d 1 Mar 1853 ae 80 (N)
  Mary W (Kendall) w/o ---- 1821-1846 (Kendall lot D)
  Moses d 23 June 1869 ae 55 (D)
  Moses d 4 Jan 1870 ae 85 (F)  -- Capt
  Moses Wilder s/o Moses & Betsey d 5 Oct 1844 ae 12d (D)
  Nancy w/o William d 21 July 1844 ae 67 (S)
  Nathaniel d 24 Mar 1835 ae 65 (N)
  Olive d/o Abner & Mary d 20 Oct 1756 ae 2 (S)
  Patty (Roper) w/o Samuel 2d d 10 May 1845 ae 55 (N)
  Phebe (Cooper) w/o Capt Samuel d 16 July 1820 ae 72 (V)
  Phebe d/o Capt Samuel & Phebe d 7 July 1793 ae 18 (V)
  Putnam d 11 Oct 1843 ae 67 (F)  -- Capt
  Rebekah (Whitcomb) w/o Ezra d 28 Jan 1792 ae 87 (W)
  Reuben H d 6 Nov 1847 ae 37 (G)
  Ruth d/o Samuel & Deborah d 9 Aug 1751 ae 17 (S)

Sally d/o Capt Samuel & Phebe d 7 Mar 1792 ae 5 (V)
Samuel d 13 June 1784 ae 87 (S)
Samuel d 12 July 1797 ae 58 (V) -- Capt  REV
Samuel 2d d 20 Sept 1826 ae 41 (N)
Samuel d 23 Nov 1848 ae 78 (J)
Samuel s/o Moses & Betsey d 21 Nov 1842 ae 26d (D)
Sarah d/o Thomas Jr & Abigail d 26 Sept 1756 ae 6 (S)
Susan H d/o Capt Thomas & Elizabeth b 20 Dec 1802
    d 11 Oct 1898 (N)
Thomas d 16 Aug 1825 ae 59 (N) -- Capt
Thomas Jr d 20 July 1787 ae 76 (W)
Thomas s/o Thomas Jr & Abigail d 28 Sept 1756 ae 17 (S)
William d 28 Mar 1827 ae 55 (S)
SCOOT/SCOTT, John d 16 Nov 1760 ae 80 (T) (father of Mrs Aaron
    (Mehitable) Dresser & grandfather to 3 young Dresser
    children buried nearby)
SEAVER, Abigail (Sawyer) w/o Joseph d 17 Nov 1844 ae 97 (N)
    Joseph d 14 Nov 1816 ae 70 (N) REV
    Olive (Moore) w/o James d 27 Mar 1867 ae 87 (D)
SHERMAN, Warren F d 15 Sept 1832 ae 16 (N)
SMITH, Abby H 2d w/o Sidney d 1 Mar 1880 ae 62 (D)
    Alexander s/o Moses & Martha d 2 Jan 1806 ae 1 (S)
    Betsey d/o Moses & Patty (Martha?) d 14 Nov 1791 ae 2 (S)
    Dea Elisha d 18 Aug 1862 ae 66 (D)
    Emma Thomas d/o Sidney & Harriet d 16 Oct 1848 ae 1 (D)
    Harriet 1st w/o Sidney d 6 Aug 1843 ae 35 (D)
    Helen S d/o Sidney & Abby d 26 Dec 1893 ae 40 (D)
    Martha (Bush) w/o Moses d 13 Sept 1837 ae 65 (S)
    Martha A d/o Elisha & Sarah d 5 Mar 1849 ae 16 (D)
    Moses (Town Clerk) d 29 July 1814 ae 51 (S)
SMITH, Nancy W d/o Moses & Martha d 12 Dec 1812 ae 7m (S)
    Nathan d 6 Feb 1851 ae 39 (G)
    Samuel Gibson s/o Sidney & Harriet d 21 June 1851 ae 1 (D)
    Sarah N w/o Dea Elisha d 27 Dec 1847 ae 44 (D)
    Sarah Ann d/o Elisha & Sarah d 27 Sept 1848 ae 18 (D)
    Sebastian d 24 Mar 1765 ae 73 (Q)
    Sidney d 19 May 1871 ae 72 (D)
    Susan F d/o Nathan & Cornelia d 2 Mar 1851 ae 3 m (G)
SNOW, Martha E (Bailey) w/o Henry C d 7 Sept 1867 ae 29 (E)
    Mrs Sarah d 30 Aug 1837 ae 83 (N)
SPENCER, Emma (Kendall) d/o Henry E & Jane w/o (?) 1856-1935
    buried in Kendall lot (D)
SPRINGER, Elizabeth (Barnard) w/o John d 9 June 1856
    ae 83 buried Barnard lot (E)
    John d 5 Feb 1866 ae 83 buried Barnard lot (E)
STEWART, Charles d 31 July 1750 ae 32 (S)
    Huldah d/o Charles & Sarah d 10 Aug 1750 ae 5 (S)
    Phebe d/o Charles & Sarah d 9 Aug 1750 ae 7 (S)
    Samuel s/o Charles & Sarah d 9 Aug 1750 ae 9 (S)
STUART, Benjamin d 4 June 1820 ae 63 (N)  REV
    Benjamin Jr d 19 Mar 1868 ae 75 (D)

Charles Wesley s/o Dea Levi & Jane d 15 Mar 1848
   ae 11 (H)
Corrissande d/o James & Sarah d 2 Sept 1823 ae 3 (J)
Damaris (Rice) w/o Benjamin d 11 Feb 1841 ae 79 (N)
Ellen M (Curtis) 2d w/o John H d 17 Mar 1924 ae 86 (D)
Eunice (Mirick) w/o Benjamin Jr d 6 Sept 1856 ae 63 (D)
George A s/o Benjamin & Eunice d 27 June 1830 ae 1 (N)
John H d 6 Apr 1893 ae 69 (D)
J H our baby s/o John H (D)
James s/o James & Sarah d 9 Mar 1822 ae 5 wks (J)
Jane (Ames) 1st w/o Dea Levi d 11 Sept 1856 ae 62 (H)
Dea Levi 1791-1875 buried in Oak Hill Cemetery
Louisa L (Curtis) 1st w/o John H d 22 Dec 1878 ae 52 (D)
Nancy (Mirick) w/o Ralph d Dec 1829 ae 39 (N)
Ralph d 2 Nov 1872 ae 77 (N)
William F s/o Benjamin & Eunice d 23 Sept 1830 ae 3 (N)
TAYLOR, Abigail (Seaver) w/o Edward d 3 July 1869 ae 89 (S)
Edward d 27 Mar 1859 ae 75 (S)
George E s/o Edward & Abigail d 29 Dec 1810 ae 6 m (S)
Harriet d/o Edward & Abigail d 14 May 1822 ae 2 m (S)
Jonathan S s/o Edward & Abigail d 23 Sept 1825 ae 2 (S)
Nathaniel b 15 Oct 1756 d 2 Mar 1842 ae 85 (F)  REV
Sally (Fuller) w/o Nathaniel d 18 Jan 1840 ae 84 (F)
THAYER, Deborah d/o Isaiah & Tamer d 24 Sept 1831 ae 39 (J)
Isaiah d 10 Nov 1827 ae 67 (J)
Sarah d 26 Sept 1869 ae 80 (C)
Sybil d/o Isaiah & Tamer d 14 Mar 1828 ae 41 (J)
Tamer (Bailey) w/o Isaiah d 29 Sept 1812 ae 55 (J)
THOMAS, Becca 1st w/o Moses d 7 July 1796 ae 17 (Y)
Becca d/o Moses & Rebecca d 22 Aug 1833 ae 34 (Y)
Frank s/o Moses & Rebecca d 22 July 1803 ae 15 m (Y)
Joshua  MD d 18 Sept 1820 ae 55 (Z)
Moses Esq d 12 Sept 1856 ae 89 (Z)
Nancy (Brown) 3d w/o Moses d 23 June 1840 ae 70 (Z)
Rebecca (Whiting) 2d w/o Moses d 28 Apr 1822 ae 53 (Y)
THOMAS, Sally d/o Moses & Rebecca d 30 June 1803 ae 27 m (Y)
THOMPSON, Abigail (Webb) w/o William d 28 Apr 1860 ae 47 (F)
Ebenezer s/o William & Abigail d 1 Oct 1844 ae 7 (F)
Lucy Ann d/o William & Abigail d 25 Jan 1842 ae 5 wks (F)
Mary E d/o Joseph & Phebe d 6 Oct 1853 ae 20 (C)
Sarah (Holden) w/o Thomas d 30 June 1847 ae 69 (C)
Thomas d 13 Apr 1845 ae 72 (C)
William d 17 May 1892 ae 79 (F)
THURSTON, Amy 3d w/o Silas d 15 Apr 1850 ae 88 (X)
Judith d/o Samuel & Priscilla d 20 June 1774 ae 18 (W)
Michal 2d w/o Silas d 25 Apr 1808 ae 47 (W)
Sally d/o Samuel & Priscilla d 16 June 1801 ae 34 (W)
Sally d/o Silas & Sarah d 21 Sept 1812 ae 21 (X)
Samuel d 8 Nov 1811 ae 82 (W)  REV
Sarah (Kendall) 1st w/o Silas d 20 Mar 1805 ae 45 (X)
Silas d 23 Mar 1840 ae 81 (X)  REV

TONEY, Simeon W d 12 Aug 1832 ae 47 (R)
TOWNSEND, Catherine C (Flagg) w/o Zimri b 28 Sept 1814
      d 16 Oct 1862 (D)
  Mary C d/o Zimri & Catherine b 19 July 1847 d 13 Sept 1849 (D)
  Zimri b 21 June 1813 d 17 Oct 1898 (D)
TUTTLE, Jedediah d 25 Nov 1849 ae 83 (E)
  Lydia (Porter) w/o Jedediah d 4 Jan 1856 ae 85 (E)
WAITE, Esther K d/o Nathan & Tabitha b 23 June 1811 d 8 Dec
      1872 (D)
  Lucy A d/o Nathan & Tabitha b 4 May 1818 d 24 Nov 1872 (D)
  Nathan d 20 Feb 1846 ae 83 (Waite-Goodnow obelisk) (D)
  Tabitha (Kendall) w/o Nathan d 29 May 1849 ae 73 (D)
WALLEY, Maryann (Gerry) w/o William d 15 Feb 1846 ae 28 (N)
  Susan d/o William & Maryann d 20 Jan 1821 ae 1 (N)
WARNER, Elizabeth C (Reed) w/o Tobias b 15 Feb 1813
      d 23 Jan 1847 (D)
WATERS, Lucy S d/o Rev George & Lucy b 8 June 1841
      d 18 Aug 1841 (J)
WELCH, Eliza Putnam (Kendall) w/o Silas A d 20 Mar 1858 ae 21 (J)
  Lucy A d/o Silas & Lucy d 27 Oct 1857 ae 22 (D)
  Lucy K (Gregory) w/o Silas d 27 Oct 1888 ae 79 (D)
  Lydia d/o Silas & Eliza d (?) (J)
  Silas d 7 Aug 1861 ae 57 (D)
  Sophia E d/o Silas & Lucy d 28 Sept 1857 ae 24 (D)
WHEELER, Lucy R (Stephenson) w/o David d 12 June 1864 ae 52 (E)
  Priscilla d 15 Sept 1853 ae 84 (F)
WHITCOMB, Asa d 16 Mar 1804 ae 85 (X)  -- Col  REV
  Ebenezer d 29 Jan 1799 ae 27 (O)
  Eunice (Sawyer) w/o Col Asa d 7 Sept 1760 ae 37 (X)
  Lyman s/o Ebenezer drowned Oct 26 1798 ae 2 (O)
  Mary J (Arnold) w/o William d 10 Aug 1845 ae 19 (G)
  Susan d/o William & Mary J d 29 Sept 1865 ae 47 (G)
WHITNEY, Amanda M (Wilder) w/o James d 17 Sept 1853 ae 19 (C)
  Anes (Church) w/o Jonathan d 6 Apr 1807 ae 75 (N)
  Caleb d 28 Mar 1822 ae 93 (N)  REV
  Caleb d 24 Jan 1847 ae 47 (K)
  Clara E d/o Joseph & Emma K d 28 June 1848 ae 2 (G)
WHITNEY, Emma K (Wilder) w/o Joseph d 28 Sept 1881 ae 67 (G)
  Jonathan d 18 Feb 1847 ae 78 (N)
  Joseph d 2 July 1883 ae 72 Whitney-Wilder monument (G)
  Lucy (Kendall) Smith w/o Jonathan d 2 Jan 1856 ae 84 (N)
WIGHT, Beulah (Smith) w/o John d 22 Sept 1857 ae 62 (D)
  Jabez d 10 Oct 1854 ae 89 (D)
  John d 19 Sept 1874 ae 83 (D)
  Jonas D d Troy N Y June 22 1856 ae 24 (G)
WILDER, Abigail (Temple) 1st w/o Sidney d 6 Apr 1847 ae 21 (D)
  Andrew J d 9 Mar 1864 ae 49 (H)
  Anna (Jones) 1st w/o Elihu d 14 July 1786 ae 22 (W)
  Arvine F d/o Fordyce & Emeline d 1 Apr 1858 ae 10 m (D)
  Asa d 28 Sept 1786 ae 56 (W) -- Lt REV
  Bailey s/o Phineas & Lucy d 1 June 1854 ae 50 (P)

Betsey (Roper) w/o Jonathan d 15 June 1874 ae 88 (N)
Bridget (Bailey) 2d w/o Phineas d 23 Nov 1801 ae 66 (X)
C---- (Kilburn) 2d w/o Calvin d 16 Aug 1860 ae 83 (G)
Calvin d 18 Dec 1852 ae 74 (G)
Calvin Jr s/o Calvin & Hannah d 29 July 1813 ae 2 (O)
Calvin N s/o Andrew J & Sarah d 22 Nov 1866 ae 18 (G)
Catherine R (Day) w/o Mirick d 29 Mar 1863 ae 54 (F)
Charles F s/o Fordyce & Emeline d 14 Mar 1853 ae 4 m (D)
Charlie L s/o Lewis & Lucretia d 21 Sept 1847 ae 1 (F)
Deborah (Sawyer) w/o Jonathan d 8 July 1790 ae 46 (V)
Dennis s/o Phineas & Lucy d 14 Sept 1798 ae 1 (P)
E K s/o Dea Silas & Katy d 28 Jan 1852 ae 21 (F)
Ebenezer s/o Elihu & Anna d 9 Dec 1785 ae 13 d (W)
Elihu d 18 June 1818 ae 58 (V)  REV
Elizabeth w/o Capt Samuel Jr d 6 Oct 1830 ae 31 (K)
Elizabeth d/o Capt Samuel Jr & Elizabeth d 22 Nov 1825
    ae 1 (K)
Elizabeth (Sawyer) w/o Silas d 5 Sept 1837 ae 86 (V)
Elizabeth d/o Capt Harrison & Keziah d 14 Aug 1882 ae 72 (G)
Emme w/o Silas d 23 Apr 1843 ae 67 (F)
Emory s/o Phineas & Lucy d 3 Feb 1825 ae 15 (P)
Ephraim d 29 Jan 1805 ae 71 (Q) -- Capt  REV
Eunice (Osgood) w/o Timothy d 25 July 1859 ae 90 (O)
Fordyce (GS missing) (D)
Harrison d 6 Mar 1854 ae 80 (G)  -- Capt
Isabella E d/o Dea Silas & Katy d 23 May 1848 ae 22 (F)
James d 16 June 1842 ae 79 (O) -- Col
Jonathan d 13 Jan 1794 ae 84 (V)
Jonathan d 7 May 1797 ae 53 (V)  REV
Jonathan Esq d 29 Dec 1853 ae 72 (N)
Joseph s/o Jonathan & Deborah d 31 Mar 1814 ae 21 (V)
Joseph d 7 Sept 1837 ae 20 (N)
Katy (Osgood) w/o Dea Silas d 29 Nov 1862 ae 65 (F)
Keziah (Powers) w/o Capt Harrison d 26 Feb 1859 ae 78 (G)
Lewis d 8 July 1854 ae 61 (P)
Lois (Brown) 1st w/o Phineas and 4 of their children
    no stones (X)
Lucretia (Lock) w/o Capt Ephraim d 29 Dec 1816 ae 83 (Q)
Lucy (Maynard) w/o Phineas d 11 Feb 1831 ae 62 (P)
Luther K s/o Andrew J & Sarah d 4 Apr 1851 ae 5 m (G)
Lydia (Rugg) w/o Lt Asa d 15 Aug 1803 ae ? (W)
Lydia P d/o Dea Sawyer & Hannah d 7 Feb 1823 ae 2 (N)
M Annie d/o Andrew J & Sarah d 9 Nov 1875 ae 21 (G)
Marcia Ann d/o Capt Harrison & Keziah d 2 Nov 1864 ae 57 (G)
Maria d/o Capt Harrison & Keziah d 29 July 1839 ae 35 (G)
Marshall d 30 Aug 1845 ae 57 (F)
Martha d/o John & Prudence d 28 Sept 1747 ae 5 (W)
Martha A w/o Sumner T d 1872 ae 22 (D)
Mary d/o Calvin & Hannah d 29 Apr 1825 ae 21 (O)
Mary w/o Samuel S d 23 Sept 1837 ae 20 (N)
Mrs Mercy (mother of Col James) d Apr 1827 ae 87 (O)

Mirick d 6 Nov 1859 ae 69 (F)
P W d (?) Calvin Wilder obelisk (G)
Philenia d/o Calvin & Hannah b 8 June 1816
    d 1 Aug 1889 Calvin Wilder obelisk (G)
Phinehas d 14 Aug 1803 ae 74 (X)  REV
Phineas d 16 Jan 1840 ae 78 (P)  REV
Prudence (Manning) 2d w/o Elihu d 21 Jan 1811 ae 52 (V)
Q F d (?) on Calvin Wilder obelisk (G)
Rebecca F d/o Calvin & Hannah b 16 Dec 1808 d 19 June 1878 (?)
Samuel Jr d 25 Feb 1830 ae 32 --- Capt (K)
Samuel B s/o Capt Samuel Jr & Elizabeth d 13 Aug 1841 ae 15 (K)
Samuel d 28 Sept 1804 ae 20 (V)
Samuel s/o Calvin & Hannah d 11 Oct 1807 ae 2 (O)
Sarah (Mirick) w/o Col James d 13 May 1836 ae 73 (O)
Sarah W (Jewett) w/o Andrew J b 22 Nov 1816 d 13 Feb 1911 (H)
Sarah Jane (Curtis) 1st w/o Fordyce d 14 Nov 1850 ae 22 (D)
Sarah Jane (Ricard) 2d w/o Sidney d 22 Jan 1894 ae 68 (D)
Dea Sawyer d 23 Aug 1837 ae 58 (N)
Sidney C s/o Sidney & Sarah J d 10 Oct 1877 ae 15 (D)
Sidney R d 11 Mar 1863 ae 40 Wilder-Whitney monument (D)
Silas d 19 Nov 1833 ae 85 (V)  REV
Silas d 18 Feb 1850 ae 79 (F)
Dea Silas d 31 May 1880 ae 81 (F)
Silvia d/o Jonathan & Betsey d 11 Oct 1821 ae 6 (N)
Timothy s/o Nathaniel & Lydia d 7 Oct 1756 ae 5 m (W)
Timothy  d 19 May 1831 ae 73 (O)  REV
Timothy Jr s/o Timothy & Eunice d 16 May 1850 ae 60 (O)
Zerviah (Houghton) w/o Jonathan d Nov 1804 ae 83 (V)
WILLARD, Ama (Houghton) w/o Aaron d 10 Apr 1795 ae 95 (V)
  Becca (Brooks) w/o Silas d 11 Nov 1832 ae 42 (N)
  Catherine sister of Manasseh d 22 Dec 1827 ae 37 (N)
  David d 6 Feb 1837 ae 81 (J)  REV
  David Jr d 1 Aug 1825 ae 46 (J)
  Dolly (Beaman) w/o Isaac m 2d Luther Kendall
      b 6 Nov 1793 d 3 July 1870 (J)
  Eliza A (Johnson) w/o Charles H d 10 Jan 1845 ae 43 (C)
  Eliza Millen d/o David Jr & Sophia d 6 Dec 1818 ae 1 d (J)
  Elizabeth S d/o Aaron & Ama d y 17 Mar -- (V) illegible
  Emeline A w/o ? 1822-1895 (J)
  Ephraim d 23 July 1821 ae 72 (N)  REV
  Francis Wright s/o Peter A & Hannah b 13 Nov 1833
      d 13 Sept 1836 (N)
  George B s/o Isaac H d 15 Aug 1821 ae 5 (J)
  Granville S s/o ---- & Emeline b 4 Aug 1849 d 27 Jan 1881 (J)
WILLARD H Francena d/o Peter A & Hannah b 11 Nov 1837 d 19
      May 1904 (N)
  Hannah (Wilder) w/o Peter A b 30 Jan 1807 d 24 Aug 1853 (N)
  Isaac d 21 Feb 1819 ae 33 (J)
  Isaac H d -- --- 1842 ae ? (?)
  Isaac H Jr s/o ---- & Emeline b 13 May 1848 d 4 July 1848 (J)
  Israel B s/o Isaac H d 10 Oct 1838 ae 20 (J)

Lois (Geary) w/o Ephraim d 22 Mar 1834 ae 80 (N)
Lorenzo B d/o David Jr & Sophia d 26 Oct 1825 ae 17 (J)
Lucha d/o Artemas & Mary d 16 Sept 1829 ae 4 m (T)
Luchous s/o Artemas & Mary d 16 Feb 1828 ae 3 (T)
Lucinda d/o Artemas & Mary d 20 June 1830 ae 2 (T)
Lucy Ann d/o Silas & Becca d 22 Jan 1829 ae 5 m (N)
Manasseh d 8 Mar 1836 ae 50 (N)
Manasseh D s/o Manasseh & Sarah d 8 Sept 1822 ae 18 m (N)
Peter A b 12 June 1796 d 11 June 1843 (N)
Polly d/o ---- & Zerviah d 28 Oct 1858 ae 66 (J)
Rhoda (Bunson) w/o David d 31 Aug 1855 ae 97 (J)
Rhoda d/o David Jr & Sophia d 6 Oct 1825 ae 13 (J)
Sophia (Bailey) w/o David Jr d 4 Aug 1865 ae 84 (J)
Walter K s/o ---- & Emeline b 30 Apr 1853
    d 17 Sept 1854 (J)
Mrs Zerviah d 8 Jan 1827 ae 64 (J)
WILSON, Ebenezer s/o Edward & Helen d 22 Apr 1791 ae 2 (S)
WRIGHT, Catherine d/o Col Thomas d 3 Apr 1875 ae 82 (O)
    Emory s/o Col Thomas d 24 Sept 1828 ae 26 (O)
    Ephraim s/o Thomas & Eunice d 2 Jan 1792 ae 3 m (W)
    Ephraim Jr 2d d?? y (W)
    Martha d/o Col Thomas d 3 May 1878 ae 80 (O)
    Thomas d 11 Nov 1813 ae 57 (W)  REV
    Thomas d 6 May 1858 ae 70 (O) -- Col

## COOKSHIRE CEMETERY

This cemetery, dating from 1782, is located at Sterling Junction, on Boutelle Road, just off Worcester Road (route 12).

The land was given by the family of Jonathan Fairbank, who was the first to be buried here on January 16, 1782. There are about 200 graves in this burial ground, mostly dating in the 1800's.

Iron gates were erected in 1881 with money donated by the families of those buried here, but later these had to be removed to allow the hearses to enter.

The name "Cookshire" was used for this district of the Town, and was said to have been so-called for a cobbler named Cook, who lived near the present Gates Road, and "who could tell time to the minute by the amount of work he had or had not done."

Six Revolutionary War patriots and five Civil War veterans are buried here.

Inscriptions copied by Barbara Dudley, 1986. All burials to this date have been listed.

ALLEN, Frederic L 1878-1948
    Lucy M (Staples) w/o Frederic L d -- ---- 1960
BLOOD, Eben P d 30 Sept 1879 ae 50y 7 m
    Eliza J (Dix) w/o Eben P d 12 July 1873 ae 52y 7 m
BOYNTON, George W CW C 25th MV d Fortress Monroe VA 7 Feb
    1862 ae 17y 4m

Mary A (Priest) 2d w/o Silas H 1846-1883
Phebe (Fairbanks) 1st w/o Silas H d 22 Nov 1861 ae 47y
Silas H d 13 Mar 1897 ae 84y 10m
CONANT, Hervey 1829-1896 CW Co A 15th MV
Martha (Upham) w/o Hervey 1829-1908
BURNHAM, Sarah J 1845-1921
DAVIDSON, ---- d 3 Sept 1726
DUNBAR, Marsilvia (Loring) w/o Henry K d 31 Dec 1851 ae 22y
EAGER, Ephraim d 12 Jan 1804 ae 42y
Ephraim d 27 Oct 1866 ae 53y 11m
Fortunatus d 24 Mar 1802 ae 67y -- Capt REV
Mehetabeel (Bigelow) 1st w/o Fortunatus (buried Chocksett)
Nancy (Fairbanks) w/o Uriah d 28 Mar 1880 ae 83y 3d
Nancy (Russell) w/o Ephraim d 18 Mar 1886 ae 64y 1m 1d
Polly d 29 Jan 1796 ae 18y
Tamar (Houghton) 2d w/o Fortunatus d 5 Apr 1806 ae 69y
Uriah d 10 Oct 1856 ae 74y
EDWARDS, Abigail D (Fairbank) w/o James 1815-1859
ELLIOTT, George C 1898-1972
Helen L 1894-1970
FAIRBANK, Charles F S s/o Harrison & Mary d 13 July 1875
ae 14y 2m
George F b 5 Mar 1863 d 30 Nov 1903
Hannah (Eager) w/o Jabez d 10 Oct 1847 ae 71y 3m
Harrison d 8 Nov 1873 ae 55y 6m
Hattie E d 13 Jan 1925 ae 73y 9m
Henry 1870-1944
Jabez Jr d 25 Feb 1843 ae 70y 9m
Jonathan d 18 Jan 1782 ae 66y
Keza (Houghton) w/o William d 14 Feb 1811 ae 52y
Mary A (Nichols) w/o Harrison 1832-1907
Mary L b 5 Nov 1825 d 26 Mar 1925
Sarah H (Fairbanks) w/o Uriah d 30 Aug 1891
ae 73y 1m 20d
Sumner s/o Jabez Jr & Hannah d 14 Mar 1874 ae 69y 10m
Thankful (Sawyer) w/o Jonathan d 1782 ae 66y
Uriah d 8 Jan 1871 ae 61y 11m 18d
William d 5 Mar 1810 ae 51y REV
William d 5 Mar 1840 ae 82y
FAIRBANKS, Sally (Holt) w/o Davis d 15 Feb 1852 ae 76y
GATES, John 1821-1903
Mary (Smith) w/o John 1820-1905
GOODNOW, Jennie L (Taylor) w/o Samuel E d 28 Dec 1929 ae 78y
Samuel E d 7 Jan 1913 ae 71y 2m 13d CW
a son of Samuel & Jennie L d 14 Nov 1884 ae 9d
GOSS, Joanne w/o Robert 1929-1982
HASTINGS, Charles A d 19 Jan 1905 ae 77y
John C 1819-1905
Martha C d 21 Sept 1876 ae 23y
Mary (Loring) w/o John C d 5 Aug 1874 ae 55y
HELLEBERG, Anders C 1904-1974

HODGENEY/HODGERNEY, Alice B (Burpee) 2d w/o John d (?)
 Arthur C Sr 1866-1938
 Arthur C Jr 1909-1958
 Capitola d 30 July 1872 ae 6m 13d
 Emma/Emily M (Coombs) 1st w/o John d 16 Aug 1865 ae 23y
 Emma M w/o John Jr 1879-1933
 Harry A d 22 Sept 1891 ae 17y 7m
 Herbert J 1899-1964
 John d 14 Feb 1909 CW Co D 26th MV
 John Jr d (?)
 John O 1907-1976
 Lillian (Cross) w/o Arthur C Jr d 1921
 Mabel M 1919-1985
HOLT, Arathusa (Fairbanks) w/o Tyler d 16 Aug 1837 ae 45y
 Harriet K d 30 Oct 1846 ae 25y
 Nancy F d 6 June 1842 ae 26y
 Tyler d 8 Nov 1866 ae 75y
HOUGHTON, Mary (Matthews) w/o Saul d 10 Apr 1802 ae 76y
JOHNSON, Gustaf R 1880-1961
KENT, Ridgley 1864-1947
 Lona (Hall) 1867-1944
KING, Marsilvia d/o Peres & Polly (Maynard) d -- Dec 1825
      ae 11y 10m
LEE, John H d 26 Oct 1888 ae 66y
LORD, Charles E d 9 Sept 1924
 Daniel P d 11 Mar 1919 ae 85y
 Mary F (Taylor) w/o Daniel d 5 Jan 1888 ae 47y
LORING, Becke d/o John & Elizabeth d 13 Oct 1786 ae 3y
 Betsey d/o John & Elizabeth d 24 Apr 1800 ae 21y
 Caty (Maynard) 1st w/o Daniel d 23 Oct 1815 ae 36y
 Charles H d 17 June 1900 ae 78y 10m
 Charles P d Nov 1889 ae 17y 7m 9d
 Daniel d 6 Jan 1864 ae 86y
 Elizabeth (Howe) w/o John d 6 Apr 1820 ae?
 Emily Maria (Jewett) w/o Henry A 1842-1898
 Georgiana (Porter) Pratt 3d w/o Charles H 1832-1903
 Henry A 1827-1895 CW
 Jessie M d 25 Aug 1885 ae 28y 9m 14d
 John d 17 Aug 1824 ae 81y REV
 John Hervey d 24 June 1850 ae 1y 27d
 Laura M 1851-1933
 Lydia d/o John & Elizabeth d 29 Oct 1858 ae 71y
 Maria (Bigelow) 2d w/o Charles H d 6 Feb 1862 ae 37y
 Mary S d 1813
 Maynard d 24 Nov 1871 ae 64y
 Melissa (Reed) 1st w/o Charles H d 16 Mar 1845 ae 20y
 Olive (Chace) w/o Maynard d 25 Mar 1879 ae 69y 7m
 Sabra (Maynard) 2d w/o Daniel d 30 Sept 1846 ae 61y
 Sarah Jane Burnham 1845-1921
LUNT, Elsie W 1875-1951
 Joseph M 1870-1947

MacGEOCH, Hazel 1895-1953
McKINLEY, Alfred F 1886-1955
MESSINGER, Celia E d 25 July 1853 ae 6m 17d
MILLER, Madalene (Carter) w/o Lewis 1895-1982
    Lewis 1893-1938  WWI
MOORE, Abigail/Nabby d 19 Jan 1860 ae 76y
    Oliver d 7 Sept 1828 ae 71y REV
    Rebecca (Fairbanks) w/o Oliver d 25 Jan 1833 ae 71y
MORTIMER, Ethel M (Buck) 1882-1904
    Ernest A 1882-1949
    Harriet P 1830-1907
    John 1826-1910
    John P 1871-1945
    Philip Buck 1904-1904
    Sarah (Perrett) w/o Stephen 1852-1935
    Stephen 1854-1943
MULROY, Edith E 1891-1966
    James R 1891-1964
NEILD, Wilhemina B 1863-1947
    Winifred 1904-1972
NICHOLS, Abigail Moore d/o Jonathan & Abigail (Moore)
        d 9 July 1830 ae 2y 1m
    Burton M s/o Luke & Hattie F 1865-1874
    Elizabeth T d/o Jonathan & Thankful (Keyes)
        d 1 Oct 1845 ae 7w
    Hattie F (Trow) w/o Luke 1841-1901
    Herbert E s/o Luke & Hattie 1862-1926
    Jonathan d 29 Oct 1876 ae 80y
    Luke W 1826-1908
    Thankful (Moore) 1st w/o Jonathan d 11 Jan 1843 ae 49y
    Thankful (Keyes) 2d w/o Jonathan 1809-1895
    William P s/o Luke & Hattie 1858-1889
NOEL, Carrington F 1909-1956
    James L 1882-1961
NOEL, Nettie 1881-1958
PLACE, John J 1871-1951
    Almira w/o John 1904-
PRIEST, Mary A d 1883
PRESCOTT, David s/o Jonathan Jr & Mary d 12 Sept 1786
        ae 5y 7m 14d
    Jonathan d 8 Mar 1810 ae 89y
    Jonathan Jr d 2 Nov 1805 ae 55y REV
    Mary (Brigham) w/o Jonathan Jr d 4 Jan 1834 ae 85y
    Vasthi (Houghton) w/o Jonathan d 10 Feb 1805 ae 78y
RANSOME, Myrtle 1930-1972
RENO, Chester 1912-1960
RUSHWORTH, Gladys w/o William R 1901-1981
    William R 1896-
SIMS, William H 1873-1944
SMITH, John d 23 Aug 1855 ae 75y
    Lephia (Kilburn) w/o John d 13 June 1867 ae 83y

Lucy B (Gary) w/o Manasseh d 8 Jan 1876 ae 89y 8m 28d
Manasseh d 24 Aug 1839 ae 63y 10m
STALEY, Ernest 1913-1970
Phyllis 1915-1973
ST JOHN, Emma 1881-1955
STONE, L Warner 1899-1955
TAFT, Ida I (Taylor) w/o E A Taft d 1876 ae 22y 8m
TAYLOR, Aaron W d 20 Apr 1867
Almira (Taylor) w/o Augustus C d 1 June 1886 ae 73y 3m
Augustus C d 26 Feb 1880 ae 66y 5m
Lucy (Fairbanks) w/o Luther d 22 Nov 1860 ae 79y
Lucy Ann d/o Luther & Lucy d 30 Oct 1821 ae 3y
Luther d 25 July 1825 ae 44y
Lydia E d/o Luther & Lucy d 13 Sept 1821 ae 16y
Sarah C d/o Luther & Lucy d 20 Oct 1821 ae 8m
TOWER, Debby Ann (Botton) 1st w/o Lendall d (?)
Henrietta (Braman) 2d w/o Lendall 1847-1921
Lendall Pratt 1833-1915
Marietta d/o Lendall & Debby Ann 1857-1916
TURNER, Abbie W (Fairbank) w/o John L 1893-1951
Florence E d/o George d 18 Sept 1972
John L 1870-1944
WAITE, Abigail (Brigham) w/o David d 15 Feb 1847 ae 88y
Abigail d/o David & Abigail d 6 Apr 1892 ae 97y
Catherine d/o David & Abigail d 4 Dec 1830 ae 42y
David 1752-1816 (no GS) REV
Patty d/o David & Abigail d 26 Apr 1802 ae 3y
WALDRON, Abigail 2d w/o Edward d 10 Feb 1791 ae 62y
7m 22d
Edward d 3 Feb 1822 ae 95y
Eunice d 3 Sept 1786
Hannah 1st w/o Edward d 11 Apr 1789 ae 37y
WHEELER, Betsey d/o Calvin & Lucy d 31 Aug 1825 ae 3y 10m
Calvin d 2 Jan 1860 ae 71y 4m 28d
George G s/o Calvin & Lucy d 14 Aug 1844 ae 9y 7d
Lucy (Whitney) w/o Calvin d 11 Apr 1871 ae 76y 11m
Lucy d/o Calvin & Lucy d 18 May 1837 ae 5y 6m 10d
Lydia A d/o Calvin & Lucy d 10 May 1837 ae 5y 6m 10d
Mary M d/o Calvin & Lucy d 14 Aug 1842 ae 28y 4m 4d
WILDER, Eunice (Osgood) w/o Abner d 14 Feb 1786 ae 60y
Josiah d 1 Mar 1782 ae 66y
a s/o Nathan & Susannah (Sawyer) Wilder d 1 Mar 1782 ae 10hrs
a s/o Nathan & Susannah (Sawyer) Wilder d 14 Jan 1788 15hrs


## FAIRBANK CEMETERY

This small private burial ground, located on Chace Hill Road in the "Squareshire District," contains 18 graves, which encompass three generations of the family of Deacon Thomas and Dorothy (Carter) Fairbank.

Their son Ephraim, who died of smallpox at the age of eighteen, was the first one buried here in 1760. Between then and 1859 seventeen more family members were interred in this small plot which lies on a small rise of land, and is surrounded by stone walls. This cemetery is now under the care of the Sterling DPW.

Deacon Thomas Fairbank was a soldier in the French and Indian Wars, and his two sons, Joseph and Oliver, served in the Revolutionary War.

Inscriptions copied by Ruth Hopfmann, 1985.

FAIRBANK, Amos s/o Joseph & Ann d 24 Dec 1785 ae 5y
  Ann (Dole) w/o Joseph d 14 Oct 1821 ae 83y
  Arathusa (Ross) 2d w/o Capt Paul d 2 Apr 1824 ae 32y
  Artemus s/o Oliver & Susanna d 15 Oct 1781 ae 4m
  Asenath d/o Capt Paul & Katy d 26 Oct 1834 ae 33y
  Dorothy (Carter) w/o Dea Thomas d 13 Sep 1784 ae 74y
  Ephraim s/o Dea Thomas & Dorothy d 19 Dec 1760 ae 18y
  Joseph (5) d 28 Aug 1813 ae 73y REV
  Katy (Phelps) 1st w/o Capt Paul d 9 June 1811 ae 30y
  Miriam d/o Benjamin & Lois d 1 Oct 1807 ae 4y
  Oliver (5) d 24 Apr 1829 ae 77y 7m REV
  Oliver Jr s/o Oliver & Susanna d 28 Jan 1786 ae 14y
  Patience (Richardson) 3d w/o Capt Paul d 23 Sep 1858 ae 76y
  Paul (6) d 12 July 1859 ae 78y -- Capt
  Sena d/o Oliver & Susanna d 29 Jan 1786 ae 10y
  Susa d/o Oliver & Susanna d 13 Jan 1786 ae 14y
  Susanna (Gates) w/o Oliver d 29 Jan 1827 ae 73y 10m
  Dea Thomas (4) d 10 Feb 1791 ae 85y

Why do we mourn departing friends
Or shake at deaths alarms:
Tis but the voice that Jesus sends
To call them to his arms

--Asenath Fairbank's epitaph

## LEG CEMETERY

This burial ground is located in West Sterling at the corner of Dana Hill Road and Route 140. It takes its name from the fact that this section of the Town, purchased from the Town of Shrewsbury ca. 1760, was "shaped like a leg."

Achariah Harvey gave the land for the cemetery and his young son, Daniel, was the first one buried here in 1756.

Although there is an occasional burial here, most gravestones date from the mid 1700's to the late 1800's. There are about three hundred graves here, including that of Robert B. Thomas (1766–1846), founder, editor, and publisher of the *Old Farmers' Almanac*. Captain Benjamin Richardson, the Town's first selectman, and the man credited with the naming of Sterling, is also buried here. All burials to date are listed.

Six Revolutionary War soldiers and seven Civil War veterans are interred here.

Inscriptions copied by Ruth Hopfmann & Barbara Dudley, 1986.

ALLEN, Daniel W d 7 Jan 1877 ae 77y
   George S b 10 Apr 1855 d 17 Sep 1938
   Martha Ann d/o Daniel W & Mehitable d 1 Sep 1831 ae 2y
   Mehitable (Child) 1st w/o Daniel W d 22 Jan 1891 ae 75y
   Otis D b 22 Feb 1840 d 13 Aug 1912
   Ruth (Whitaker) 2d w/o Daniel W d 22 Jan 1891 ae 75y
BABCOCK, Lydia (Hosmer) w/o Leonard b 21 Oct 1802 d 20 Apr 1835
BAILEY, Betsey (Eddy) w/o Capt Manasseh d 23 Apr 1821 ae 31
BAKER, (children of Vickery & Priscilla [Walker] Baker)
   Abigail d 1826
   Eliza Ann d 22 Oct 1833 ae 2
   James S d 14 Oct 1837 ae 19
   John W d 10 Oct 1833 ae 10m
   Vickery W d 22 Apr 1827 ae 1
BALDWIN, A Harriet (Broad) w/o William Jr d 30 Apr 1882 ae 36
   Abigail (Esty) w/o William d 20 Mar 1898 ae 90
   Charles d 2 Mar 1870 ae 32
   John d 2 May 1863 at New Orleans La ae 28 CW Co H 53d Regt MV
   Marcus M d 3 Oct 1864 ae 21
   William d 6 Aug 1889 ae 76
BIGELOW, Levi d 15 Sept 1845 ae 46
   Martha B (Howe) w/o Levi d 5 Feb 1879 ae 71
      She married 2d Samuel Lawrence Jr of West Boylston
BOYNTON, Elizabeth w/o John d 15 July 1762 ae 23
BREWER, Lucy (Whitaker) w/o Eber b 25 May 1814
      d 21 Mar 1898
BROAD, Albert s/o Erastus d 12 Mar 1849 ae 5m
   Augustus G (died Northboro)
   Charles s/o Erastus d 15 Sept 1840 ae 1
   Clarissa (Bailey) 1st w/o Erastus d 30 Sep 1836 ae 29
   Cora J d/o Augustus & Jerusha d 16 Dec 1862 ae 5m
   Ellen Maria d/o Augustus & Jerusha 1865–1917
   Erastus d 9 Jan 1878 ae 70
   Jerusha (Baldwin) w/o Augustus G d 12 Feb 1868 ae 28
   Lois (Fales) 2d w/o Erastus d 6 Apr 1863 ae 54
   Lois d/o Erastus & Lois d 26 Jan 1843 ae 1
BROOKS, Abigail (Whitaker) 1st w/o Samuel d 2 Jan 1826 ae 40
   Charlotte (Broad) 2d w/o Samuel d 14 Feb 1834 ae 31
   Samuel d Holden MA
   Thankfull (Fairbanks) w/o William d 5 Aug 1771 ae 19
   William d -- --- ----
BROWN, Addison L s/o Moses & Susan d 30 Sept 1839 ae 3m

Alfred s/o Moses & Susan d 21 Aug 1849 ae 3m
Almira A d 14 Sept 1873 ae 46
Almira twin d/o Samuel & Olive d 17 Jan 1822 ae 5m
Bethiah (Adams) w/o Samuel d 3 Jan 1837 ae 83
Betsey d/o Samuel & Olive d 24 Nov 1829 ae 13
Claricy d/o Benjamin & Caty d 18 Mar 1794 ae 8
George s/o Samuel & Olive d 29 Dec 1823 ae 5 wks
George s/o John Jr & Sarah d (burned) 15 Sept 1831 ae 9
Harriet Adaline (Howe) w/o Horace b 6 Sept 1830 d 9 Jan 1900
Horace b 6 Jan 1826 d 5 May 1887
John b Framingham 14 Aug 1765 d 15 Sept 1835
John Jr b Sterling 12 Mar 1798 d 11 Apr 1868
Mary twin d/o Samuel & Olive d 14 Aug 1821 5 wks
Mary A d/o Moses & Susan d 3 Apr 1833 ae 6m
Moses b 2 Jan 1810 d 6 Apr 1888
Olive (Fairbank) w/o Samuel d 2 Nov 1847 ae 57
Samuel b 1 Mar 1752 d 2 Nov 1834 ae 83  REV
Samuel d 6 Mar 1847 ae 61
Sarah (Babbs) w/o John Jr b 29 Mar 1795 d 23 Apr 1871
Susan (Fairbank) w/o Moses b 30 May 1812 d 11 Jan 1895
Elizabeth (Phillips) w/o John d 15 Sept 1833 ae 61
Thomas (of Concord) d 21 Nov 1799 ae 62 No GS (from church
    records First Church in Sterling)
Mehitable (Winch) w/o Thomas d Apr 1812 ae 77
    No GS (from church records First Church in Sterling)
BRUCE, Adaline (Holman) w/o Mark d 13 May 1868 ae 57
  Mark d 31 Dec 1883 ae 83
  Warren E s/o Mark & Adaline d 2 Mar 1837 ae 11m
BUCK, Isaac b 27 Sept 1757 d (?) REV
BUSS, Ruhamah (Mason) w/o Ebenezer Jr d 25 Jan 1786 ae 23
CALKINS, Adelaide A (Hosmer) w/o Dr Marshal 1831–1909 (Both are
    buried Springfield MA)
CHAPMAN, Esther T Mason w/o Robert T b 11 Aug 1821 d 11 Dec
1908
  Robert T 1821–1864 d Florence SC Co K 25th Regt MV CW
  Willie R s/o Robert & Esther 1860–1861
CHASE, Abigail G (Hapgood) w/o Leonard m 2d Luther Whitaker
    of Oakdale  d (?) (GS illegible)
  Leonard d 27 Nov 1842 ae 32
  William Henry s/o Leonard & Abigail d 22 Nov 1842 ae 5
CHENEY, Amelia A w/o Gustavus d 13 May 1889 ae 67
  Ebenezer b 29 June 1780 d 18 Jan 1839 ae 58
  Gustavus d 31 July 1860 in Boston (no GS)
CONANT, Caroline (Stone) w/o Silas d 8 Aug 1887 ae 85
  Silas d 8 Nov 1875 ae 74
DAVIS, Bloomy (Haskell) w/o John d 8 June 1824 ae 34
  Emily W w/o Thomas 1803–1870
  H Maria 1829–1897
  Harriet A (married Holmes) 1829–1922
  Henry A 1844–1864 d Covington KY Co E 21st Regt MV  CW
  John d 31 May 1843 ae 60  -- Capt

Martha R d/o John & Bloomy d 20 Jan 1823 ae 4
Thomas 1791-1861
EARLE, Anna (Brown?) d 1 Jan 1862 ae 80
EDDY, Amanda (Holt) w/o Luke d 15 May 1847 ae 19
Arthur L d 3 Mar 1848 ae 25
Barnet d 24 July 1835 ae 24
Benjamin F s/o Andrew & Rebecca d 31 July 1845 ae 5
Charles H Jr s/o Charles H & Emily d 5 Sept 1848 ae 5
Emily K w/o Charles H d 14 July 1854 ae 33
Henry s/o Joshua & Jemima d 7 Mar 1811 ae 18
Jemima (Robbins) w/o Joshua d 17 July 1819 ae 57
Jemima d/o Daniel & Tamer d 1 Apr 1826 ae 10
John d 14 July 1856 ae 30
Joshua d 12 Dec 1819 ae 70  REV
Lucretia d/o Joshua & Jemima d 12 Feb 1804 ae 3
Luke d 15 Feb 1848 ae 23
Polly d/o Joshua & Jemima d 16 Jan 1819 ae 24
Sally d/o Joshua & Jemima d 5 Jan 1819 ae 22
Tamer d 12 Mar 1818 ae 22
ELLIOT, Deborah (Taylor) 2d w/o Stephen A d 13 Aug 1849 ae 59
Polly 1st w/o Stephen A d 20 Nov 1816 ae 36
Stephen A d 23 Mar 1855 ae 78
FAIRBANK, Alpheus d 8 Oct 1832 ae 66
George W d 3 Nov 1841 ae 42
Mary (Willard) w/o Alpheus d 20 May 1836 ae 66
Polly d 23 Aug 1855 ae 62
FLAGG, Abraham 1820-1866
Lois R (Holman) w/o Abraham 1821-1856
Luther s/o Samuel & Lucy d 9 July 1818 ae 1
Mary J d/o Abraham & Lois 1848-1849
Rebecca (Dakin) w/o Solomon b 21 Nov 1770 d 15 Nov 1844
Sarah J d/o Abraham & Lois 1852-1857
Solomon b 1 Apr 1763 d 20 Jan 1841
FOSTER, Polly (Pearson) w/o Samuel d 23 Dec 1852 ae 70
GARRITY, John H  1848-1918 Co E 42d Regt MV Co G
61st Battery  CW
Mary (Johnston) w/o John H 1847-1926
GOODALE, Francis E d 28 Sept 1882 ae 52
Mary A (Mason) w/o Francis R d 5 Oct 1921 ae 91
Bertie & Gertie ch/o Francis & Mary d 19 & 21 Jan
ae 1 wk
GOULDING, Harriet (sister of Mary A. Goulding Houghton)
d 24 April 1857 ae 41
Joel (brother of Mary A Goulding Houghton) d 12 July 1870 ae 62
HARVEY, Daniel s/o Dr Zachariah & Anne d 4 Oct 1756 ae 4
HOLMAN, Elijah R d 13 May 1855 ae 55
Elijah R Jr s/o Elijah & Lucy d 1 Nov 1832 ae 2
Lucy (Tucker) w/o Elijah R d 31 Mar 1890 ae 91
Mary W d/o Elijah R Jr & Lucy d 20 Aug 1838 ae 3
Rufus d 28 Nov 1853 ae 77
Tryphenia (Rice) w/o Rufus d 5 July 1848 ae 73

HOSMER, Addison A s/o Ebenezer 1833-1902 Buried
Arlington National Cemetery -- Col CW
Arthur Dwight s/o Addison & Caroline d 20 Sept 1864 ae 9m
Caroline F (Buck) w/o Col Addison d 24 Aug 1863 ae 26
Daniel d 25 June 1820 ae 57
Daniel Jr b 22 Feb 1798 d 2 Oct 1879
Ebenezer d 29 Nov 1878 ae 77 -- Gen
Harry Mason s/o Addison & Caroline d 19 Feb 1878 ae 19
Marcia (Reed) 2d w/o Daniel Jr d 11 July 1859 ae 60
Maria (Beaman) 1st w/o Ebenezer d 28 Mar 1828 ae 23
Mary (Cheney) 2d w/o Ebenezer d 26 Feb 1883 ae 75
Sarah (Mason) w/o Daniel d 15 Jan 1834 ae 62
Susan (Child) 1st w/o Daniel Jr d 10 Nov 1822 ae 28
HOUGHTON, Abner d 21 Apr 1866 ae 90
Frank S d 30 July 1935 ae 82
Harriet E d 12 May 1900 ae 52
Keziah d/o Abner & Phebe d 21 Dec 1831 ae 9
Lucy L b 24 Sept 1848 d 18 Dec 1945
Mary A (Goulding) w/o Sawyer d 25 Sept 1889 ae 78
Phebe (Coolidge) w/o Abner d 20 Feb 1873 ae 90
Robert Coolidge b 24 Oct 1850 d 24 Dec 1945
Sawyer d 14 Oct 1884 ae 80
Silas G s/o Sawyer d 5 Nov 1896 ae 50
HOWE, Adoniram s/o Arad & Susannah d 10 Mar 1832 ae 8m
Susannah d/o Arad & Susannah d 3 Mar 1832 ae 7
Zara d 21 Feb 1875 ae 75
JOHNSTON, Caroline K d/o George & Johanna 1855-1856
George 1810-1890
Johanna (Kennedy) w/o George 1809-1888
Margaret A d/o George & Johanna 1848-1850
Robert s/o George & Johanna 1844-1920
KENDALL, Clarissa H (Wellington) 1st w/o Heman3
d 22 Dec 1842 ae 28
Heman d 9 June 1800 ae 61 REV
Heman2 d 28 Aug 1857 ae 74
Heman3 d 22 July 1883 ae 71
M Malvina d/o Heman & Clarissa d 7 Jan 1852 ae 13
Martha (Harris) 2d w/o Heman3 d 7 Aug 1881 ae 65
Mary (Fairbank) w/o Heman d (?)
Nathan s/o Heman & Submit d 9 Feb 1819 ae 2
Nathan H s/o Heman & Clarissa d 15 Apr 1860 ae 13
Peter d 8 Apr 1817 ae 30
Submit (Tuttle) w/o Heman2 d 22 Sept 1828 ae 44
Susanna (Keyes) w/o Peter d
KILBURN, Betsey w/o John Jr d 1 Jan 1805 ae 18
KRISTOFF, Eleanor Lillian (Miller) w/o Joseph P
b 23 Apr 1913 d 21 June 1980
Mary C w/o Samuel DeBoer b 26 Jan 1899 d 17 June 1982
Mary Elizabeth (Noone) w/o George W b 16 June 1910
d 26 Mar 1980
LAMSON, Nathaniel s/o Silas d Shelburne Falls MA

Philinda d/o Nathaniel & Sarah d 14 Sept 1830 ae 1
Sarah (Howe) w/o Nathaniel d 28 Feb 1832 ae 25
LARSON, Arthur L W 1886–1959
Dorothy M w/o Arthur 1894–
LAWRENCE, Bethiah (Hosmer) w/o Joseph d 27 Aug 1857 ae 68
Comfort B 1st w/o James B d 17 Feb 1847 ae 23
Jacob George drowned 2 Aug 1844 ae 21 (Changed his name
to George Washington before he died)
James Benjamin d 20 Feb 1854 ae 32
Joseph d 23 Apr 1854 ae 66
Sylinda P (Grant) 2d w/o James B d 6 June 1853 ae 33
Sylinda E d/o James B & Sylinda d 11 June 1853 ae 14d
LEE, Nelson M d 26 Apr 1862 ae 34
LYNCH, Thomas d 19 Jan 1820 (Killed by tree fall)
MANN, Daniel MD of Boston dentist death unknown (no GS)
Maria (Dimock) w/o Dr Daniel d 16 Feb 1892 ae 85 (no GS)
Nancy (Whittemore) Dimock w/o Rev Henry Dimock d 19 Jan 1859
ae 73 Parents of Maria (Dimock) Mann (no GS)
Alonzo K Dimock brother d 13 Sept 1888 ae 63 (no GS)
MASON, Azubah d/o Jonas & Submit d 12 Apr 1805 ae 27
D Waldo 1860–1940
Carrie (Jackson) w/o D Waldo 1864–1938
Daniel s/o Samuel & Hannah 1771–1815
Earl W s/o D Waldo & Carrie 1892–1893
Ebenezer s/o Jonas & Submit d Jan 1786 ae 21
Hannah (Whiting) 1st w/o Samuel 1751–1815
John s/o Samuel & Hannah 1779–1864
Dea Jonas d 18 May 1829 ae 91
Jonas Jr d (?) ae 2
Joseph of Northboro d 20 Apr 1944 ae ?
Lucy d/o Samuel & Hannah 1777–1863
Lucy E d/o William & Mary 1870–1903
Mary E d/o William & Mary 1868–1869
Mary S (Howe) w/o William H 1837–1905
Relief (Henry) w/o William d 27 June 1874 ae 81
Sally d/o William & Relief d 1 Nov 1819 ae 1
Samuel 1749–1839  REV
Samuel F b 5 July 1823 d 19 July 1915
Submit (Whittemore) w/o Jonas d 25 Jan 1820 ae 84
Thankfull (Cheney) 2d w/o Samuel 1760–1815
Warren s/o D Waldo & Carrie 1888–1891
William d 15 June 1853 ae 78
William H 1833–1918
MAY, Elizabeth (Fairbank) w/o Ezra d 6 Nov 1845 ae 75
Ezra d 4 Mar 1815 ae 43
Ezra Jr b 11 May 1802 d 10 Sept 1837
"My Mother" (Hannah Draper) b 14 Apr 1804 d 7 Nov 1856
Erected by C F May
MERRIAM, Adeline W (Foster) w/o William Jr d 1 June 1891
ae 70 Buried Oak Hill Cemetery
Mary A d/o William & Roxanna d 4 Apr 1834 ae 4

Mary A d/o William & Roxanna d 12 Mar 1839 ae 1
Roxanna (Foster) w/o William d 27 Jan 1892 ae 86
    She married 2d Dea Levi Stuart
Ruhamah 1837–1907
Sarah E d/o William & Roxanna d 30 May 1857 ae ?
William d 19 Nov 1851 ae 53
William Jr d 27 May 1880 ae 54
MERRILL, Charles Henry d 1916  CW
  Elizabeth (Scott) w/o Charles H d 8 Sept 1912 ae 72
  Florence (Flossie) d 11 July 1912 ae 37
  Herbert d 14 Sept 1893 ae 17 (Drowned)
MUNSON, Persis (Reed) w/o R S Munson d 6 Apr 1880 ae 33
NEWTON, Azubah d/o Ezekiel & Dorothy d 9 Aug 1779 ae 22
  Dorothy (Osgood) w/o Ezekiel d 24 Aug 1795 ae 68
  Ephraim s/o Ezekiel & Dorothy d 9 Sept 1756 ae 4
  Ezekiel d 11 Aug 1779 ae 54
  Samuel s/o Ezekiel & Dorothy d 28 Sept 1756 ae 28
NICHOLS, Anna (Rice) 2d w/o William d 12 Mar 1875 ae 76
  William d 29 Sept 1874 ae 79
  William F s/o William & Emily d 27 July 1844 ae 3
NIXON, Clarissa (Parmenter) w/o John d 24 Jan 1877 ae 77
  John d 21 Nov 1871 ae 86
PARMENTER, Esther (Mason) w/o Solomon 1773–1839
PEARSON, Catherine (Rice) w/o Nehemiah d 27 Oct 1884 ae 88
  Catherine d/o Nehemiah & Catherine d 1 Mar 1826 ae 3
  George A 1851–1938
  John s/o Joseph Jr & Rebecca d 16 Dec 1831 ae 6m
  John d 14 Mar 1862 ae 40
  John A d 4 Sept 1830 ae 1
  Joseph d 15 Aug 1840  ae 81 REV
  Mary (Farrar) 1st w/o Joseph d 3 Apr 1789 ae 28
  Mary Louisa (May) w/o John d 13 Mar 1856 ae 28
  Merrick d 24 Apr 1877 ae 40
  N Foster s/o Nehemiah & Catherine d 31 Jan 1871 ae 54
  Nehemiah d 28 Nov 1874 ae 85
PHELPS, Charlotte A d/o Jonas & Phidelia d 16 Oct 1850 ae 18
  Phidelia (Hosmer) w/o Jonas b 27 Feb 1807 d 17 Mar 1837
REDDING, Sally (Harrington) w/o Zebedee d 22 Jan 1816 ae 40
  Zebedee d 28 Feb 1856 ae 86
REED, Abigail d Apr 1836 ae 17
  Davis d 19 Apr 1843 ae 56
  Davis Jr d 15 Dec 1867 ae 42  Co K 25th MV  CW
  Maryette (Sargent) w/o Davis d 21 Jan 1858 ae 64
  Nancy (Houghton) Burpee 2d w/o Silas d 18 Oct 1875 ae 77
  Polly (Reed) 1st w/o Silas d 1 May 1846 ae 49
  Silas d 9 Feb 1874 ae 77
  Silas A d 17 Jan 1852 ae 31
  Francis Trowbridge d 3 Sept 1847 ae 29
RICE, Charles E d 31 Oct 1930 ae 80
  Emma E M (Chapman) w/o Charles E 1854–1920
  Esther d/o Charles & Emma d 30 June 1897 ae 1

Lorenze Tracey s/o Leonard & Mary C d 19 Oct 1849 ae 13m
RICHARDSON, Abigail (Whitcomb) French 2d w/o Benjamin
    d 1790 ae 43
  Abigail d/o Benjamin & Eunice d 1791 ae 31
  Artemas d 14 Aug 1828 ae 58
  Asa s/o Benjamin & Eunice d 1803 ae 33
  Benjamin d 8 June 1821 ae 89 -- Capt  REV
  Catherine d/o Benjamin & Eunice d 1792 ae 19
  Earl G s/o Sewell & Lefi d 14 Apr 1893 ae 1
  Elizabeth B d/o William B & Rebecca d 22 Nov 1862 ae 1
  Ethel C d/o Sewell & Lefi d 9 Dec 1887 at birth
  Eunice (Swan) 1st w/o Benjamin d June 1776 ae 35
  George H killed in battle at South Mountain MD
        11 Sept 1862 ae 28  CW
  Henry s/o William B & Rebecca d 6 Feb 1843 ae 9m
  Hubbard C s/o Thaddeus & Sarah d 19 Feb 1845 ae 22
  John s/o William B & Rebecca d 4 Feb 1837 ae 6m
  Lysander s/o William & Prudence d 12 Oct 1817 ae 2
  Maria d/o William B & Rebecca d 9 Oct 1832 ae 1
  Olive (Holman) 3d w/o Benjamin d Nov 1815 ae 70
  Prudence (Burpee) w/o William d 7 Feb 1879 ae 93
  Rebecca w/o William B d 8 Feb 1881 ae 74
  Vida L d/o Sewell & Lefi d 28 Oct 1889 ae 1
  William d 20 July 1828 ae 45
  William B d 27 Mar 1881 ae 72
SAWIN, Almina R (Sawin) w/o Porter G d 7 July 1872 ae 30
  Edgar W s/o Josiah & Lucy d 4 Nov 1851 ae 14m
  George E s/o Josiah & Lucy d 27 Oct 1851 ae 6
  Josiah William d 27 Apr 1882 ae 69
  Lucy Ann (Smith) w/o Josiah W d 14 Oct 1889 ae 76
  Porter G d 22 Nov 1863 ae 23
SMITH, Jacob d 16 Oct 1845 ae 70
STILES, Charles s/o John & Rebecca b 10 Nov 1810 d 25 Apr 1839
SNOW, Agnes Lucretia d/o Homes & Lucretia d 30 Sept 1857 ae 15m
STONE, Gracie B 1876-1878
  J Louis 1870-1897 Killed on RR
  John Elbridge 1832-1918
  Joseph 1879-1881
  Maud (Cougle) w/o John E 1881-1926
  John Elbridge 1880-
THOMAS, Aaron d 20 Mar 1833 ae 64
  Aaron M d 28 June 1840 ae 31
  Adaline (Darling) w/o Aaron M d 1 May 1836 ae 23
  Azubah (Goodale) 1st w/o William d 14 Jan 1781 ae 43
  Esther (Whitney) 2d w/o William d 27 Dec 1831 ae 88
  Hannah (Beaman) w/o Robert B d 28 Sept 1855 ae 81
  Lydia (Mason) w/o Aaron d 10 Nov 1833 ae 64
  Robert B d 19 May 1846 ae 80 Founder of Old Farmers Almanac
  William d 13 June 1810 ae 85
  ---- inf/o Aaron & Adaline Thomas d 20 July 1836 ae 3 das
THOMPSON, Martha (Howe) d/o Ara & Susanna 1841-1895

VOSE, Veline w/o John d 14 Nov 1864 ae 44
WALKER Edward P s/o Sylvanus & Caroline d 28 July 1837 ae 7m
   Jane E d/o Sylvanus & Caroline d 11 Sept 1841 ae 3m
   Leonard T s/o Sylvanus & Caroline d 3 Nov 1840 ae 10m
WARREN, Bethiah L (Lawrence) w/o Horace W d 26 Mar 1863 ae 36
WHALEN, E Eugene s/o John B & Jane d 4 Feb 1876 ae 1
   Ida L d/o John B & Jane d 30 Oct 1877 ae 10
   Jane M (Howe) w/o John B d 1 June 1879 ae 41
   John B b Boston 1839 res Ashland d (?) CW
WHITAKER, Almira d/o Sanderson & Betsey d 16 Apr 1827 ae 19
   Betsey (Howe) w/o Sanderson d 5 Apr 1833 ae 49
   David d 20 Oct 1847 ae 68
   Isaac d 8 Feb 1892 ae 79 His wife Mary Thayer died out West
   Polly/Mary (Chittenden) w/o David d 13 Dec 1849 ae 65
   Sanderson d 2 June 1829 ae 46
   Susan M d/o David & Polly d 19 Dec 1861 ae 31

## OAK HILL CEMETERY

The land for this cemetery was deeded to the Town of Sterling by Dr. Israel Allen in 1815. Additional acreage was acquired in 1858 and 1902. It is located on the north side of the road to Clinton, about one-half mile from the center, on an oak-studded hillside.

The stone wall along Clinton Road was built in 1829, and the stone watering trough was set in place at the entrance in 1898. At one time, an iron archway, set in granite posts, with the wording "1906 OAK HILL" graced the entrance. It was the gift of J. Edward Lynds of Minnesota. The arch was removed in the 1960's.

A very interesting cast iron fence, decorated with lambs and doves, surrounds the David & Emily Wilder lot.

Prior to the Civil War, there were only about twenty burials in this "new" cemetery, the earliest one in 1820.

Only the burials pre-dating 1860 are listed here.

Inscriptions copied by Ruth Hopfmann, 1986.

BENNETT, J H d 8 Dec 1846 ae 32y
BROOKS, Emily S (Goodrich) w/o Charles d 23 June 1858 ae 22y 8m
BUTTERICK, George 1821–1856
COLBURN, Maria O w/o Nicholas A d 15 Apr 1858
DAVIS, Lucy D 1st w/o Martin 1806–1857
FLAGG, Francis S 1841–1854
HASTINGS, Maria E d/o Rufus & Isabella d 31 Mar 1851 ae 14y 4m 4d
   Stephen s/o Rufus & Isabella d 3 July 1828 ae 4y 10m 2d
   William A H s/o Rufus & Isabella d 6 June 1835 ae 15d
KENDALL, Polly (Kilburn) 1st w/o Samuel d 18 June 1837 ae 43y
KEYES, Lucy (Hubbard) 1st w/o Dea Asa d Sep 1846
     ae 39y (buried in W Boylston)
PRATT, Sally (Richardson) 1st w/o Lt Joel 1795–1820
REED, Eliza (Burpee) w/o Joseph 1801–1860

RICE, John Atherton s/o Atherton Monroe & Mira Monroe Rice
     d 4 Jan 1817 ae 5y
  Nahum d @ Boston 1848 (buried Sterling)
SAWYER, George F s/o Solon & Nancy 1845-1845
STUART, Dolly S (Bailey) w/o Samuel Jr 1798-1827
  Jane (Ames) 1st w/o Dea Levi 1795-1856
  Samuel 1776-1829
WILDER, David 1792-1841
  Ruth J d/o Spencer & Harriet 1833-1854
  Susan B (Maynard) w/o Josiah 1818-1848
WILLARD, Abigail R (Wilder) w/o William P 1807-1842


## HILLSIDE CEMETERY

This is the newest cemetery in Sterling. It is located on the south side of Clinton Road, opposite and a little easterly of Oak Hill. The land was purchased from the Waters Family in 1931 and first put to use about 1953.

# BERLIN - OLD BURYING GROUND

The Old Burying Ground was deeded to the "Inhabitants of the Southerly part of Bolton" which had been "petitioned for a Precinct or District" and "in consideration of the love and good will we have for" said inhabitants by Samuel Jones and David Rice on May 9, 1768 "to be improved for a burying place ..." Bolton town records indicate that such a petition to separate the south part of Town was presented in 1766. The South Parish of Bolton was not incorporated until 1778. This became the District of Berlin in 1784 and received minor additions from Marlborough and Lancaster. Berlin became a town in 1812. Thus the burying ground was the Town's earliest piece of public property, acquired a decade earlier than its first incorporation.

The earliest burial was that of Samuel Jones, father of the donor, in 1769. There have been few burials in the Twentieth Century, the latest being William G. Sawyer, who died October 12, 1988.

In 1785 the District of Berlin voted to fence the burying field with a stone wall "four feet high and middling handsome ... as cheap as they can." In 1816 a twelve foot strip of land was added on the westerly side, given by Hollis Johnson to accommodate the hearse house, which had been built in 1805 on another site.

In 1905, the headstones were straightened and most of the cemetery graded and seeded to facilitate lawn mowing. It is believed that the footstones were removed at this time, many of them being placed in the stone wall built on the west side the following year. Others were used to line a drain constructed near that wall.

This listing was made by Katharine Ann Bacon and Jeanette Andrews in 1968, with current work by Barry Eager.

The listing begins in the west front corner.

BARNARD, Harry L 1838–1895
    Hannah w/o Lewis H d/o Luther & Lucy Carter d 16 May
        1851 ae 33y
    Lewis H s/o Josiah & Cati d 19 Jan 1851 ae 33y
MERRILL, Laura E (Carter) 1834–1866 w/o John A
    John A 1827–1916 CivWar
    Lorinda E (Mansfield) w/o John A 1844–1928
CARTER, Olive (Smith) w/o Ivory 1814–1887
    Ivory s/o Luther 1812–1850
    Lucy (Bigelow) w/o Luther 1788–1850

Luther 1790–1865
MOORE, Lovisa d/o Uriah d 4 Aug 1853 ae 60y 9m
HASTINGS, Almira (Puffer) w/o Ephraim d 10 July 1879 ae 86y
    Ephraim d 29 Aug 1855 ae 70y
3 tombs marked Sawyer, Howe, and Closed 1882
BARTLETT, Amory Adam 17 Apr 1822–14 Mar 1915 ae 93y
    Sarah Jane w/o Amory Adam 18 Jan 1824–6 Oct 1887 ae 63y
    Lewis Montgomery s/o Amory A & Sarah J d 11 July 1859
        ae 2y 3m 12d "Our Darling Montie"
BARTLETT, Mary w/o Dea John d 4 Jan 1877 ae 77y 10m 25d
    Deacon John d 6 Jul 1864 ae 67y
    Harriett d 23 Feb 1847 ae 52y
    Persis w/o Adam d 13 Jun 1861 ae 88y 1m 7d
    Adam d 22 Jul 1828 ae 74 RevWar
    Levi d 22 Aug 1875 ae 75y 19d
    Mary E w/o Jonathan Aug 1808–July 1887
    Jonathan Aug 1810–Mar 1890 -- Capt
    Susan Elizabeth d/o Jonathan & Mary 1835–1920
FELTON, Sylvester d 27 Sep 1851 ae 33y
    Lucinda w/o Jacob d 30 May 1865 ae 74
    Jacob d 23 Aug 1883 ae 92y 9m
white marble marker broken and illegible
WILLIAMS, George H s/o Samuel S & Abby d 9 Aug 1863
    ae 17y 8m
STARKEY, Martha M w/o Anthony S d 7 Jul 1850 ae 37y
BABCOCK, Dexter d 1 Jul 1860 ae 23y 4m
    Betsey w/o Josiah d 5 Mar 1889 ae 85y
    Josiah d 4 Dec 1859 ae 65y
    Lucy B d/o Josiah & Betsey d 4 May 1829 ae 1y 9m
    Elenor d/o Josiah & Betsey d 5 Dec 1826 ae 1y 2m
BRIGHAM, Ann w/o Thomas d 12 Sep 1876 ae 78y 3m
    Thomas Esq d 19 Jun 1855 ae 57y 8m
    Azubah d 1 Mar 1835 ae 25y 4m 25d
    Mrs Azubah w/o Thomas d 11 Oct 1847 ae 83y
    Thomas d 9 Mar 1821 ae 55y
    Paul d 24 Jun 1869 ae 73y -- Capt
BABCOCK, Wedwin s/o William & Hannah d 2 Nov 1825
    ae 10y 7m
    Abigail d/o William & Hannah d 2 Jun 1834 ae 21y 9m 6d
    Sarah d/o William & Hannah d 11 Apr 1839 ae 22y 1m 11d
    Mrs Hannah w/o William d 7 Jan 1845 ae 62y 30d
    William d 14 Sep 1861 ae 81y
BARNES, David d 7 May 1839 ae 74y
    Asenath Moore w/o David d 26 May 1847 ae 77y
    Welcome d 9 Nov 1830 ae 37y
    Hannah w/o Welcome d 20 Jul 1871 ae 78y
    Daniel d 6 Nov 1854 ae 59y 9m 15d
    Betsey Longley w/o Daniel d 13 Sep 1881 ae 82y
    3 illegible
HASTINGS, Johannah Obrian Bryant w/o Oliver Puffer Hastings
    Mary Agnes d/o Oliver & Johannah

WALLIS, Mary Jane d/o John & Susan d 23 Jul 1848 ae 26y
   William F s/o John & Susan d 8 May 1842 ae 24y
   Susan w/o John d 22 Jun 1860 ae 75y
   John d 29 Jan 1865 ae 82y 9m
BABCOCK, Patience w/o Abram d 29 Oct 1857 ae 63y 9m 24d
HOUGHTON, Susannah w/o Caleb d 20 Aug 1818 ae 36y 10m
   Caleb d 7 Aug 1823 ae 42y 10m
   Zilpher w/o Jonah d 3 Apr 1880 ae 81y
   Jonah d 2 Oct 1838 ae 46
   Mary w/o Dea Siras d 29 Aug 1838 ae 86y
   Dea Cyrus d 9 Jun 1834 ae 89
HOUGHTON, Henry T d 15 Dec 1839 ae 21y
   Amory d 9 Jun 1846 ae 24y
BARNARD, Caty w/o Josiah d 8 Nov 1825 ae 45y
   Josiah d 23 Dec 1831 ae 62y
LARKIN, Otis L d 27 Oct 1856 ae 31y 6m
BLISS, Mary w/o Gideon d 4 Sep 1856 ae 86y
FIFE, Sarah d/o Robert & Hepseybeth d 20 Sep 1803 ae 17
   Robart d 22 April 1787 ae 40 RevWar
BADCOCK, Sybel w/o William d 23 Jan 1790 ae 47y
   William d 31 Dec 1820 ae 79y RevWar
   Mrs Hepzibeth w/o William d 30 July 1826 ae 72y
HASTINGS, Nathaniel 1738-1820 RevWar
   Elizabeth Goodnow w/o Nathaniel 1743-1830
MOORE, Mary B d/o Warren & Hannah d 16 Oct 1828 ae 12y 5m
   Addison M s/o Warren & Hannah d 20 Apr 1825 ae 7m 7d
   Hannah w/o Warren d 23 Jul 1825 ae 33y
   Warren d 3 Jul 1827 ae 34y
   Mary w/o Isaac d 23 Feb 1825 ae 76y
   Isaac d 5 Jan 1825 ae 76y RevWar
STONE, Adaline w/o Willard former w/o Joseph Moore d 10 Dec 1863
MOORE, Joseph d 23 Nov 1854 ae 63y 3m 13d
   Betsey w/o Joseph d 25 Aug 1837 ae 43y
   Sarah w/o Joseph d/o Abijah & Hannah Pollard d 11 Nov 1816
     ae 29y
BARTLETT, Mrs Betsey B d 17 Feb 1854 ae 58y
BABCOCK, Hepzibah w/o Peter d 26 Aug 1822 ae 42y
   Peter d 30 Jan 1837 ae 54y
   2 marble stones illegible
BAILEY, Lucy w/o Benjamin former w/o Silas Houghton II
     d 17 Nov 1826 ae 49y
HOUGHTON, Silas d 16 Aug 1820 ae 43y
BAILEY, Alfred Townsend s/o Horace & Elisabeth d 6 Sep
     1831 ae 2y 10m
SAWYER, Henrietta E d/o Asa & Emma d 24 May 1834
     ae 4y 8m 21d
   Emma Bailey d/o Asa & Emma d 4 Sep 1831 ae 4y 9m 21d
   Fanny Woodbury d/o Asa & Emma d 18 Aug 1830
     ae 15y 1m 1d
   Asa d 23 May 1877 ae 81y 7m 28d
   Emma Bailey w/o Asa d 6 Apr 1880 ae 89y 5m 9d

HARTFORD, Susan M w/o Erastus G d 25 Aug 1859 ae 21y
   Susan d/o E G & S M d 24 Jun 1859 ae 11d
BRUCE, Sewell d 3 Nov 1846 ae 56y
   Eunice w/o Sewell d 11 Feb 1873 ae 88y
   Phidelia d 23 Sep 1832 ae 2y
FIFE, James d 21 Nov 1790 ae 31y RevWar
   Sarah d/o James & Patience d 29 Mar 1782 ae 16y
   Patience w/o James d 3 Mar 1816 ae 90y
   James d 25 Jun 1779 ae 60y RevWar
BABCOCK, Curtis s/o Ephraim & Eunice d 7 Nov 1830 ae 20y
   Abram s/o Ephraim & Eunice d 14 Sep 1803 ae 1y 4m
   Eunice d/o Ephraim & Eunice d 14 Sep 1803 ae 5y 3m
   Eunice w/o Ephraim d 10 Mar 1863 ae 88y 4m
   Ephraim d 15 Feb 1852 ae 80y 11m
HASTINGS, Thomas d 12 Jun 1813 ae 27y 5m 4d
POWERS, Henry R s/o John & Pamelia d 31 Oct 1860 ae 25y
BACON, Silas Herbert d 16 May 1968 ae 56y WWarII
   Katharine Ann w/o Silas d 23 Sep 1973 ae 63y
BAILEY, Elizabeth w/o Barnabas d 25 Apr 1818 ae 97y
   Barnabas d 23 May 1790 ae 75 RevWar
   Sarah E d/o Timothy & Sarah d 27 Jan 1837 ae 28y
   Sarah w/o Dea Timothy d 11 Apr 1843 ae 61y
   Dea Timothy d 3 Sep 1837 ae 57y
JOHNSON, Mary w/o Lewis H d 7 Dec 1886 ae 80y 11m
   Lewis H d 11 Aug 1866 ae 61y
   Hollis d 2 Nov 1858 ae 84y
   Abigail w/o Hollis d 6 Jun 1813 ae 33y
   Eunice w/o Hollis d 2 May 1846 ae 69y
   Catherine sister/o Hollis
   Hollis L s/o Lewis H & Mary killed at Bull Run battle
      30 Aug 1862 ae 24y CivWar
   Mary W d/o Hollis & Abigail d 11 Oct 1830 ae 21y
   Abigail G d/o Hollis & Abigail d 3 Dec 1837 ae 25y
SAWYER, Franklin d 10 Oct 1847 ae 38y
   Joseph s/o Amos & Persis d 30 Sep 1825 ae 16y
   Joseph s/o Amos & Persis d 3 Jul 1809 ae 7y 10m
   Franklin s/o Amos & Persis d 26 Jun 1809 ae 7y 9m 24d
   Persis w/o Dea Amos d 25 Sep 1850 ae 81y
   Dea Amos d 3 Oct 1842 ae 73y
   Hannah w/o William d 3 Feb 1830 ae 88y
   William d 28 Feb 1822 ae 81y RevWar
MARTYN, ---- w/o Docr Nathaniel d 24 Oct 1796 ae 53y
GODDARD, Maria d/o Eber & Lucy d 27 Sep 1805 ae 2y 1m 11d
SPOFFORD, Betsey Sawyer w/o Capt Samuel Jr 1805-1879
   Mary w/o Samuel d 21 Mar 1819 ae 21y
   ---- c/o Samuel & Mary d 3 Jan 1819 ae 2m 13d
   Samuel d 9 Apr 1858 ae 62y -- Capt
LARKIN, Catherine d/o John & Sarah d 12 Feb 1881
      ae 85y 6m
   John F d 17 Jan 1855 ae 58y
   Cynthia H w/o John F d 14 Jan 1847 ae 48y

SAWYER, Sophia R d 24 Oct 1873 ae 54y 1m
   Lewis b 2 Feb 1812 d 8 Feb 1856
   Saphira w/o Dea Oliver d 1 Sep 1841 ae 56y
   Lucy w/o Capt Oliver d 22 Apr 1804 ae 23y
   Dea Oliver d 15 Apr 1851 ae 78y
JOHNSON, Eleazer d 31 July 1791 ae 74y  RevWar
   Joshua d 25 Jan 1832 ae 86y  RevWar
   Jonas s/o Amos & Elizabeth b 16 Mar 1784 d 16 Mar 1784
   Maverick w/o Amos d 9 Jul 1852 ae 81y
BALL, James d 15 Sep 1784 ae 58y RevWar
JOHNSON, Elizabeth w/o Amos d 10 May 1813 ae 50y
   Amos d 12 Jul 1825 ae 74y 8m  RevWar
   Hannah w/o Joshua d 19 Dec 1810 ae 88y
   Joshua d 26 Jun 1784 ae 68y
   Mary w/o Capt Edward d 5 Jul 1810 ae 85y
   Edward d 29 Oct 1784 ae 70y -- Capt  RevWar
JOHNSON, Beulah w/o Nathan d 24 Feb 1830 ae 79y
   Nathan d 23 Dec 1832 ae 84y  RevWar
SAWYER, Sally w/o Thomas d 9 Feb 1833 ae 42y
   Thomas d 13 Jun 1864 ae 79y
   Abigail w/o Abraham d 7 Aug 1830 ae 39y
   Sarah w/o Silas d 26 Jun 1832 ae 65y
KEYES, Annah d 28 Jun 1857 ae 69y 2m
   Otis T s/o E S & C A d 13 Oct 1857 ae 8m 4d
   Amos E s/o E S & C A d 7 Feb 1860 ae 1y 3m
CARTER, Chloe d 27 Sep 1873 ae 61y 7m
   Hannah A w/o Sanderson d 9 Jul 1859 ae 91y 2m 29d
   Sanderson d 30 Aug 1841 ae 77y
JOHNSON, Susan
   Amelia
BAILEY, Algernon S s/o Dea Stephen & Sally b 11 May
       1782 d 26 May 1808 ae 26y
   Sally w/o Dea Stephen d 13 Oct 1812 ae 58y
   Dea Stephen d 12 Feb 1815 ae 61y  RevWar
LARKIN,  Lucy d/o John & Sally d 31 Mar 1815 ae 26y
   Peter 2nd s/o John & Sally d 26 Aug 1812 ae 25y
   John d 12 Apr 1811 ae 80y  RevWar
   Sarah R w/o John d 28 Jan 1813 ae 82y
   Azubah w/o Peter d 9 May 1805 ae 73y
   Peter d 13 Apr 1815 ae 88y  RevWar
SAWYER, Abigail w/o Ira d 24 Oct 1869 ae 81y 7m
   Ira d 30 Aug 1861 ae 73y 10m ·
BAILEY, Catherine w/o Col Silas d 6 April 1811 ae 74y
   Silas d 30 Oct 1793 ae 71y -- Col  RevWar
   Lucy w/o Col Silas d 5 Sep 1778 ae 52y
EGERY, Sibilla w/o Nathan d/o Benjamin Nurse d 18 Jan
       1803 ae 49y
BAILEY, Sibilla w/o Benjamin d 14 Oct 1803 ae 84y
   Benjamin d 13 Feb 1790 ae 79y  RevWar
HOLT, John T d 6 Feb 1872 ae 56y
   Eliza d/o Amasa & Hannah d 22 Oct 1838 ae 27y

Monument erected by Artemas Barnes in 1876 in memory of Lt.
Timothy Bailey, who died in Rhode Island during the Revolutionary
War. The monument records his death as being in 1777, but he was
recorded in Continental Army service in Rhode Island as late as 1781.

*Sketch by Audrey Gardner*

190

Eliza d/o Amasa & Nabby d 12 Sep 1805 ae 6y
Nabby w/o Amasa d 7 Jul 1807 ae 30y
Amasa d 3 Nov 1815 ae 43y
FANNING, Harriet M d 9 Jan 1841 ae 21y
George H d 3 Jan 1841 ae 17m
PIERCE, Joel d 10 Nov 1847 ae 80y
Lucy d 3 May 1851 ae 79y
BULLARD, Martha 1825-1898
Harriet H 1831-1875
Henry M 1826-1860
Judith B 1799-1864
Joel 1799-1850
Nathan d 21 May 1846 ae 84y RevWar
BIGELOW, Mary Eusebia d/o Abram & Eliza b 10 Mar 1831
d 7 May 1834
SAWYER, Hannah w/o Thomas d 21 May 1849 ae 72y
Rufus d 12 Apr 1865 ae 74y
Seraph w/o Rufus d 3 Dec 1863 ae 71y 1m 26d
MOORE, Lucinda w/o Isreal d 27 Nov 1840 ae 21y 2m 20d
STEARNS, Mary Adeline w/o Lorenzo d 20 May 1840 ae 25y
CARTER, Danforth d 8 Oct 1852 ae 50y 4m 19d
Louisa d 5 Oct 1853 ae 47y 8m 12d
Dolly E d 19 Jan 1854 ae 20y 11m 16d
KEYES, Angeline Clarissa d/o William P & Clarissa
d 26 Aug 1854 ae 5m 23d
Clarissa w/o William P d 16 Apr 1854 ae 32y
SAWYER, Lucy G w/o Abel d 8 Mar 1870 ae 53y
Abel d 16 Mar 1853 ae 39y
Lewis A d 23 Jul 1880 ae 24y
Lucinda B w/o Lewis A b -- --- 1853 d -- --- 1892
HOUGHTON, Rebeca w/o Benjamin d 12 Nov 1830 ae 75y
BRIDE, James M d 19 Feb 1823 ae 26y
William A d 25 Aug 1857 ae 11m 17d
BAILEY, Timothy d in R I in RevWar service bur RI
Silas s/o Amhurst & Lydia d 3 Oct 1797 ae 1y 7m
Lydia w/o Amherst d 14 Dec 1844 ae 77y 5m
Amherst (Bayley) d 9 Nov 1830 ae 70y RevWar
SAWYER, Charles F s/o Ira & Abigail d 26 Dec 1851 ae 29y 9m
Prudence w/o Capt Josiah d 13 July 1826 ae 66y
Josiah d 3 Jun 1808 ae 56y -- Capt RevWar
BAKER, Susanna w/o Samuel Baker d 14 Apr 1781 ae 62y
Samuel d 4 May 1795 ae 73y -- Capt RevWar
SAWYER, Mary w/o Dea Josiah d 25 Mar 1799 ae 71y
Dea Josiah d 13 Jul 1805 ae 90y 10m 18d RevWar
NURSE, Kate w/o Dr Benjamin d 14 Oct 1819 ae 62y
Docr Benjamin d 23 Apr 1804 ae 49y RevWar
Theophilus d 25 Oct 1824 ae 37y -- Capt
James Goddard d 19 Aug 1829 ae 19m s/o Theodore & Rebecca
James Goddard d 2 Apr 1834 ae 4y 2m 10d
s/o Theodore & Rebecca (Goddard)
FREEMAN, John S drowned 28 Jul 1850 ae 30y 4m

191

BRIGHAM, Betsy d 27 Sep 1841 ae 55y
   Sophia d 9 Apr 1827 ae 28y
CROSBY, Sarophine B w/o Josiah d 14 Feb 1870 ae 81y 8m
   Josiah d 15 Sep 1866 ae 84y
MOORE, Ellen F w/o Samuel b 29 Apr 1836 d 18 Oct 1863
FAY, Peter d -- --- 1851
BRIDE, Asa (McBride) 1771-1809
   Lucy 1773-1842
   Lucy 1804-1872
   Asa 1805-1872
   Caty 1806-1890
TAYLOR, Esther w/o David d 10 Jun 1801 ae 74y
   David d 30 Aug 1795 ae 72y  RevWar
JONES, Ichabod d (smallpox) 14 May 1778 ae 43y  RevWar
   Dorothy w/o Samuel d 25 Apr 1818
   Samuel d 23 Jan 1797 ae 71y  RevWar
   Susannah w/o Samuel of Marlborough d 17 Sep 1795
      ae 95y 11m 22d
   Samuel of Marlborough d 13 April 1769 ae 73y
   Timothy d 7 July 1822 ae 82y  -- Lt  RevWar
JEWETT, Lura Ann d/o Jesse & Mira d 13 Aug 1861 ae 41y
   Mira w/o Jesse d 16 Sep 1863 ae 68y
   Jesse d 8 Dec 1850 ae 58y
   Joshua s/o Jesse & Hannah d 4 Dec 1804 ae 22y 8m
   Hannah w/o Jesse d 26 Jan 1849 ae 95y
   Jesse d 5 Feb 1829 ae 76y  RevWar
PRIEST, Joseph d 31 Jul 1817 ae 85y  RevWar
   Hannah w/o Joseph d 6 Aug 1772 ae 88y
   Joseph d 30 Nov 1781 ae 88y
BAILEY, Clarissa d/o Jedediah & Clarissa d 15 Oct 1805 ae
    2y 10m
   Eliza d/o Jedediah & Clarissa d 12 Aug 1806 ae 5y 7m
SAWYER, Martha Chamberlain d/o George W & Mary A
    d 18 Jan 1844 ae 1y
   Mary Elizabeth d/o Geo W & Mary A d 6 Jan 1815 ae 3d
   William Hastings s/o Geo W & Mary A d 29 Sep 1864 ae
    18y 4m
   Martha Ann d/o Geo W & Mary A d 12 Oct 1864 ae 14y 5m
   Mary Ann w/o George W d 4 Jan 1892 ae 76y
   George W 10 Jun 1881 ae 69y 7m 29d
   Beatrice d/o Charles M & Ida J d 12 Dec 1906 ae 14y
BARTER, Mary Jane w/o Thomas S b 19 May 1822 d 1 Oct 1851
SAWYER, Chester A d 16 Dec 1917 ae 60y
SOUTHWICK, Addie A w/o George M d 26 July 1889 ae 32y
PETERS, Augusta E w/o Warren S d 2 Aug 1868 ae 22y
SAWYER, Lucina Frances d/o Amos & Sarah H d 15 Jan 1866
    ae 13y 8m 10d
   Clara Isabel d/o Amos & Sarah H d 15 Apr 1859 ae 5m
   Franklin A s/o Amos & Sarah H d 18 Mar 1856 ae 2y
   Frederick Amos s/o Amos & Sarah H b 28 Jul 1848
    d 30 Sep 1851

Joseph Marshall s/o Amos & Sarah H b 8 Nov 1841
d 28 Feb 1843
Sarah H w/o Amos d 21 Jul 1903 ae 85y
Amos d 15 Aug 1866 ae 58y
TEASDALE, Jane Elizabeth w/o James H d 11 Aug 1858 ae 76y
CONANT, Mary A w/o William F d 30 Jun 1855 ae 30y
William F b 14 Sep 1818 d 21 Aug 1882
Mary S w/o William F b 27 Aug 1837 d 15 Sep 1884
BRUCE, Limon s/o Sylvanus & Hannah d 7 Aug 1843 ae 17y 6m
Lewis B s/o Sylvanus & Hannah d 5 Jul 1853 ae 20y
Hannah w/o Sylvanus d 20 Mar 1880 ae 82y 6m
Sylvanus d 30 Jul 1879 ae 86y 8m
HOLT, Leslie O s/o O W & S G d 19 Sep 1871 ae 8y 7m
BRIGHAM, George A s/o Abraham & Hannah A d 26 Jan 1856
ae 14y 4m 18d
Abraham d 22 Nov 1857 ae 41y
Hannah A w/o Abraham d 26 Dec 1857 ae 35y
SEYMOUR, Gertie Louise d/o F & A L d 18 Sep 1871 ae 9m
HOWE, Warren S b 24 Aug 1848 d 17 May 1912
Lucy S 1st w/o Warren S b 13 Aug 1850 d 29 Jan 1884
Rudolph M s/o Warren & Lizzie E b & d 6 Jun 1889
Lizzie E w/o Warren b 9 Jun 1860 d 29 Dec 1941
STONE, Mary A w/o Isaac S d 29 Jan 1871 ae 68y
Martha A w/o Isaac S d 4 May 1855 ae 37y
Isaac S d 25 Mar 1883 ae 76y
HOLDER, Lucy F w/o Thomas d 14 Apr 1851 ae 53y
Thomas d 20 Oct 1856 ae 62y
BROWN, Abigail W w/o Henry d 19 Oct 1861 ae 73y 9m
Henry d 29 Oct 1848 ae 68y
LARKIN, Hepsybeth w/o Solomon d 11 Apr 1831 ae 39y
MOORE, Lucinda w/o Cummings d 8 Mar 1875 ae 85y 10m
Cummings d 9 July 1831 ae 41y 6m
CARTER, Amory d 10 Feb 1814 ae 30y
LONGLEY, Abigail w/o Nathaniel former w/o
Manaseh Fairbank d 4 May 1848 ae 82y
FAIRBANKS, Manaseh d 11 Mar 1806 ae 40y -- Capt
Persis d/o Manasseh & Abigail d 6 May 1837 ae 43y
MERRIAM, Mirick s/o Levi d 19 Oct 1797 ae 14m 15d
Abigail w/o Levi d 16 Feb 1832 ae 76y
Levi d 19 Mar 1812 ae 56y 24d RevWar
Dea Jonathan d 5 Jan 1823 ae 81y RevWar
Jonathan D d 13 Nov 1850 ae 61y
PRIEST, Ira s/o Silas & Persis d 3 Dec 1807 ae 1y 2m 14d
Silas d 10 Oct 1807 ae 34y
Prudence w/o Holman d 2 Jun 1817 ae 76y
Holman d 22 Jan 1831 ae 85y RevWar
Sally d/o Luther & Asanath d 10 Oct 1815 ae 20y 20d
Clarendon s/o Luther d 23 Apr 1816 ae 9m 10d
MOORE, Robert Parker d 26 Sep 1856 ae 20y
Oliver d 17 Jul 1848 ae 45y
CUTTING, Sarah L d/o George & Sarepta d 20 Jul 1851

ae 1y 1m 1w 1d

BARNES, Harriet A d/o John & Sarah d 1 Aug 1851 ae 12y

SPOFFORD, Caroline R d/o Benj E & Polly d 3 Nov 1842
    ae 18y
   Polly w/o Benj E d 25 Apr 1845 ae 47y

JOHNSON, Serena w/o Zenas d 25 Jun 1821 ae 32y 8m
    d/o Stephen & Prudence Shephard of Phillipston
   ---- an infant child
   Ann J w/o Zenas d 11 Oct 1828 ae 41y
   ---- an infant child
   Polly R w/o Zenas d 9 Sep 1856 ae 61y
   Zenas d 11 Nov 1850 ae 63y
   Francis S s/o Zenas & Ann d 14 Feb 1847 ae 21y

BARTLETT, William B d 9 Oct 1850 ae 30y
   Ezra K s/o William & Sarah d at Indianapolis
    10 Oct 1864 ae 19y CivWar
   Sarah w/o William d 13 Sep 1873 ae 69y 4m 3d
   William d 4 Jan 1874 ae 80y 9m 20d

MOORE, Elizabeth R w/o S J d 14 Jan 1892 ae 73y
   Samuel J b 30 Sep 1819 d 5 Sep 1896

POWERS, Eunice w/o Capt Henry d 23 Dec 1825 ae 60y

SPAFFORD, Samuel d 6 Nov 1809 ae 47y -- Capt RevWar

GODDARD, Keziah w/o William Goddard d 10 Mar 1794 ae 90y
   Hannah w/o Dea James d 21 Mar 1807 ae 72y 6m 28d
   Dea James Sr d 13 Jan 1815 ae 84y RevWar

SPOFFORD, James Richardson s/o Capt Samuel & Eunice
    d 3 Mar 1815 ae 6y 7m
   Hannah d/o C Saml & Eunice d 5 Oct 1809 ae 14y
   a pair of twins of Capt Samuel & Eunice
   Job Spafford s/o Samuel & Eunice d 9 Jul 1801 ae 3y
   James Spafford s/o Samuel & Eunice d 15 Apr 1790
    ae 5m 8d

SMITH, Calvin d 5 Dec 1883 ae 79y 4m 2d
   Rebecca w/o Calvin d 6 Dec 1879 ae 78y
   Angenette d/o Calvin & Rebecca d 19 Nov 1876 ae 33y
   Charles s/o Calvin & Rebecca d 24 May 1851 ae 5y 5d
   Eusebia w/o Calvin Jr d 5 Dec 1841 ae 37y 7m

BRAITHWAITE, Christiana W Goddard Carter w/o
    J Braithwaite d 24 Jun 1902 ae 78y 2m

CARTER, D H d 22 Sep 1872 ae 58y 8m

GODDARD, Benj Franklin d 24 Jul 1860 ae 24y 1m 12d
   Catherine R S d/o James & Betsy b 5 Apr 1825 d 11 Nov
    1838 ae 13y
   Betsey w/o James d 2 Oct 1857 ae 53y 10m 29d
   Betsey d/o James & Keziah d 10 Mar 1808 ae 20y 5m
   William s/o James & Keziah d 18 Jan 1808 ae 19y
   Jabez s/o James & Keziah d 10 Aug 1807 ae 9y
   Kezia d/o James & Kezia d 27 Feb 1796 ae 8m
   James 3rd s/o James & Keziah d 14 Nov 1801 ae 16y
   Keziah w/o James d 19 Jul 1848 ae 85y
   James b 15 Apr 1763 d 19 Jan 1842 ae 78y RevWar

BRUCE, Hugh b 5 Aug 1770 d 11 Sep 1821
  Sally w/o Hugh b 10 Dec 1776 d 28 May 1840
  Rixina d/o Hugh & Sally d 7 Aug 1804 ae 4y 5m 15d
GODDARD, Wm d 23 Mar 1834 ae 21y
  Jacob d 19 Jun 1870 ae 79y
  Mary w/o Jacob d 13 Feb 1873 ae 80y
  Abigail w/o Jacob d 10 Oct 1814 ae 23y 3m
BIGELOW, Rhoda w/o Christopher B d 8 Aug 1850 ae 84y
  Christopher B d 7 April 1830 ae 65y
FOSGATE, Gilbert d 25 Jul 1811 ae 28y
  Naomi w/o Joel d 1 Oct 1839 ae 82y
  Joel d 24 Mar 1824 ae 78y  RevWar
  Mary Susan d/o Luke & Mary d 19 Oct 1845 ae 12y
HOUGHTON, Lucy Ann w/o Levi b 8 Oct 1816 d 14 Jan 1896
CONANT, Harriet N d/o Josiah & Lucy H d 19 Apr 1884
        ae 69y 6m
  ---- d/o Josiah & Lucy H d 4 Sep 1813
  Josiah d 10 Jun 1848 ae 57y 3m
  Lucy H w/o Josiah d 17 Jul 1875 ae 85y 10m
BARNES, Fortunatus b 25 Sep 1738 d 9 Nov 1807
        ae 69y  RevWar
  Persis Hosmer w/o Fortunatus b 19 Apr 1739
        Concord d 16 Sep 1821 ae 82y
  William b 5 Apr 1773 d 26 Oct 1853 ae 80y
  Betsey w/o William d 6 Jan 1863 b 9 Mar 1774
  Martha Washington d/o William & Betsey d 1 Aug 1814
        b 11 Apr 1811
  Sarah d/o William & Betsey b 5 May 1808 d 3 Oct 1894
  Hannah d/o William & Betsey b 18 Sep 1801 d 8 Jun 1864
BRIGHAM, Persis Baker d/o Dr Daniel & Anna d 28 Oct 1808
        ae25y
TEMPLE, Lucy w/o Isaac d 26 Jan 1834 ae 37y
  Isaac d 6 Oct 1831 ae 39y
WILDER, Lucretia d/o Nathaniel & Lucy d 29 Aug 1826
        ae 1y 12d
BRIGHAM, George L d 23 Mar 1837 ae 1y 3m s/o
        Ira & Betsey
  Louisa E d/o Ira & Betsey d 21 Nov 1840 ae 2y 9m
BARNES, Alice w/o Artemas d 16 Nov 1849 ae 54y 7m 23d
  Nancy w/o Artemas d 16 Jul 1832 ae 30y 4m 11d
  Artemas b 7 Jun 1796 d 2 Feb 1877
JONES, Martha w/o Capt Samuel d 7 Oct 1831 ae 73y
  Samuel d 22 Sep 1811 ae 55y   -- Capt  RevWar
PARK, Charlotte d/o James R & Anna d 12 Sep 1796
        ae 2y 1m 2d
  Anna w/o James R d 4 May 1838 ae 80y 10m
  James R d 13 Jul 1813 ae 52y 10m  RevWar
JONES, Sally d/o Capt Samuel & Martha d 27 Aug 1798
        ae 2y 7m 11d
PUFFER, Phebe M d/o Rev Reuben & Phebe d 8 Oct 1833
        ae 18y 8m 25d

Sarah d/o Rev Reuben & Hannah d 19 Jan 1822 ae 20y
Reuben s/o Rev Reuben & Hannah d 7 Sep 1792 ae 5w
Oliver s/o Rev Reuben & Hannah d 20 Jan 1799
    ae 16m 12d
Phebe w/o Rev Reuben d 12 Jan 1856 ae 84y
Hannah w/o Rev Reuben d 5 Jan 1812 ae 51y
Rev Reuben d 9 April 1829 ae 74y
PARK, Bulah L d/o Joseph d 21 Jun 1834 ae 26y
    Melissa d/o Joseph & Hannah d 28 Nov 1851 ae 39y
    Lawson s/o Col Joseph & Hannah d 15 Mar 1821 ae 5y 6m
    Hannah w/o Col Joseph d 7 Dec 1825 ae 39y
    Eliza w/o Col Joseph d 2 Oct 1842 ae 58y
    Joseph b 11 Nov 1787 d 24 Nov 1879 -- Col
JONES, Abigail d/o Samuel & Abigail d 11 Oct 1803
    ae 1y 10m 19d
JOHNSON, Anna w/o Edward d 27 Aug 1848 ae 58y
    Edward d 15 Nov 1827 ae 42y
    John N P d in service 20 May 1865 ae 46y CivWar
CARTER, Chandler b 7 Oct 1808 d 1 Feb 1891
    Nancy w/o Chandler d 7 Mar 1851 ae 40y
    Leah H w/o Chandler d 16 Aug 1879 ae 57y
BABCOCK, Martha A d 23 May 1851 ae 20y
BIGELOW, Persis w/o Henry d 6 July 1848 ae 27y 20d d/o
    Paltiah & Persis Jones
JONES, Persis w/o Paltiah d 2 Mar 1860 ae 80y 9m 28d
    Pelatiah d 14 Mar 1864 ae 77y
HOWE, Solomon 1777-1830
    Sarah Stowe w/o Solomon 1783-1831
PETERS, Lydia Howe w/o Luther 1811-1882
HASTINGS, Isabella Howe 1804-1876 bur Westboro
HOWE, William A 1806-1863 bur Mt Auburn
    Sarah 1809-1826
HOUGHTON, Mary Grace Howe 1815-1882 bur South Berlin
HOWE, Solomon Henry 1821-1879
ROBBINS, Sarah w/o Jonas d 24 Nov 1863 ae 76y 8m
    Jonas d 17 Dec 1846 ae 51y
CARTER, Mary W d/o Rufus & Sarah d 28 Dec 1876 ae 42y
SAWYER, Sarah E w/o Eli former w/o Rufus Carter
    d 4 Nov 1855 ae 45y
CARTER, Rufus d 9 Nov 1842 ae 38y
GAGE, Samuel S s/o Samuel d 15 Oct 1829 ae 19y
WILDER, Mary w/o John d 20 Jan 1824 ae 69y
MAYNARD, Mary w/o Capt Barnabas d 16 Sep 1814 ae 72y
    Barnabas d 23 Sep 1828 ae 81y -- Capt
FAY, Dexter W d 25 Jun 1843 ae 26y
    Zilpah w/o Dea Dexter d 7 Aug 1872 ae 88y 10m
    Dea Dexter d 31 Dec 1851 ae 71y
HOWE, Sarah d/o Solomon & Sarah d 29 Jan 1826 ae 17y
    Sarah w/o Solomon d 2 Sep 1831 ae 48y
    Solomon d 29 Jul 1830 ae 53y
CARTER, Jonas B d 13 Sep 1834 ae 2y

Ann G w/o Leonard d 29 Sep 1874 ae 75y
Persis w/o Leonard d 18 Jun 1827 ae 34y
Leonard d 18 Sep 1849 ae 57y
Dolly w/o Daniel d 11 Dec 1853 ae 88y
Daniel d 29 July 1824 ae 62y  RevWar
SPAFFORD, Job s/o Lt Job & Esther d 21 Dec 1791 ae 7y
Esther w/o Dea Job d 15 May 1849 ae 90y
Dea Job d 5 Apr 1840 ae 87y  RevWar
TAYLOR, Miss Hannah d 13 Mar 1823 ae 62y
SAWYER, Lockhart s/o Uriah & Sally d 1 Sep 1830 ae 22y
SPAFFORD, ---- s/ Dea Job & Esther d 7 Oct 1822 ae 39y
FAY, Betty w/o David of Northborough d 13 Apr 1821 ae 78y
BOWMAN, Betsy w/o Simeon d 4 Jun 1822 ae 58y
Persis w/o Simeon d/o John & Elizabeth Gibson d 10 Apr
1833 ae 48y
Simeon d 23 Nov 1845 ae 75y
POLLARD, Deborough w/o Thomas d 13 Oct 1827 ae 87y
Thomas d 2 Oct 1827 ae 84y  RevWar
Ezra R s/o Stephen & Betsey b 21 Nov 1823 d 5 Dec 1850
Abigail d/o Stephen d 25 Nov 1888 ae 70y 5m 15d
Betsey H w/o Stephen b 17 Jul 1787 d 23 Jul 1851
Stephen b 29 Jan 1780 d 22 May 1853
Rebecah d/o Luther & Matilda d 11 Jun 1843 ae 32y

Markers recorded in 1830s no longer present

BADCOCK, Wheeler s/o Wm & Sybel ae 4 1/2y d 4 Oct 1778
BAILEY, Betty d/o Silas & Levinah d 3 J-- 1789 ae 4m 26d
SPAFFORD, a pair of twins of Capt Samuel & Eunice
JONES, Jonathan s/o Capt Samuel & Martha d 25 Sep 1802
ae 1y 3m
SAWYER, Sarah w/o Alvan d 14 Nov 1806 ae 35y
JONES, ---- s/o Timothy & Sally d 1 Aug 1810 ae 5d

Marker in South Cemetery moved there after 1857

JONES, ---- s/o Timothy & Sally d 1 Aug 1810 ae 5d
Charles s/o Timothy & Sally d 18 Aug 1816 ae 9y 8m

## MOUNT VERNON CEMETERY, WEST BOYLSTON
### (Includes Beaman Cemetery)

The Wachusett Reservoir took much of the original Town of West Boylston. On March 2, 1901 a new site for the Beaman Cemetery at the rear of Mount Vernon Cemetery was approved. In March 1901 Mr. Charles Bray and Mr. William Wood directed the relocation of the sixty graves.

Inscriptions copied by Edgar A. Whitcomb II.

BEMAN, Jabez d 22 Sep 1757 ae 53y
   Persis w/o Ezra d 7 Nov 1788 ae 50y
   Ezra d 4 Jun 1811 ae 74y
   Mary w/o Ezery d 6 Jun 1813 ae 62y
BIGELOW, Levina d 13 Jan 1849 ae 89y
BEAMAN,Ezra d 25 Jul 1863 ae 92y
NEWTON, Silas d 3 Feb 1836 ae 66y
   Eunice d 18 Jul 1864 ae 90y
   Alfred s/o S & E Newton d 22 Apr 1822 ae 6y 8m
RICE, Luther d 21 Nov 1818 ae 63y
   Betsey w/o Luther d 16 Apr 1836 ae 69y
   Ezra B s/o L & B d 28 Sep 1822 ae 23y
REED, Joseph A d 3 Mar 1867 ae 75y
   Mary B w/o Joseph d 28 Jul 1822 ae 25y
   Tamer w/o Joseph d 20 Apr 1846 ae 51y
NEWTON, Jabez B d 12 Oct 1888 ae 79y
   Mandana W d 25 Aug 1868 ae 25y
   Isabel Rice w/o Jabez d 30 Mar 1901 ae 86y
   Eunice I d/o J & I d 28 Sep 1857 ae 8m 26d
   Ezra B s/o J & I Newton d 8 Jan 1848 ae 1y 28d
   Caroline I d/o J & I Newton d 10 Aug 1848 2m 25d
   Mary Ann w/o Jabez d 9 Aug 1844 ae 34y
DAVIS, Elias d 20 Sep 1869 ae 85y
   Mary Bigelow w/o Elias d 8 Feb 1857 ae 72y
   Thomas Boylston s/o E & M d 12 May 1838 ae 31y
EAMES, William 1788 – 1835
   Persis Rice w/o William 1789 – 1852
   Levi 1782 – 1869
   Betsey Rice w/o Levi 1786 – 1853
   William 1809 – 1893
   Mary R 1822 – 1898
NEWTON, Betsey Beaman 1819 – 1892

FORBUSH, Anna Newton 1844 - 1922
KING, George Edward s/o M & L King d 25 Mar 1834 ae 6m 23d
   Ellen Eliza d/o M & L King d 22 Nov 1836 ae 1y 2m 4d
   Henry T s/o M & L King d 28 Jan 1847 ae 18m
KING, George s/o M & L King d 8 Oct 1849 ae 6y 4m
   Mary B d/o M & L King d 29 Jul 1850 ae 1y 7m
   Ella d/o M & L King d 15 Sep 1853 ae 2y
JOHNSON, Zoath d 5 Apr 1765 ae 25y
DANA, Jesse d 25 Sep 1831 ae 64y
   Tamer d 9 Dec 1851 ae 83y
   Sarah E d 18 Jan 1823
   Phinches P d 25 Mar 1835 ae 37y
   Tamer B w/o Ebenezer d 22 Jul 1835 ae 45y
BEAMAN, Ephriam d 25 Mar 1805 ae 62y
   Tamer w/o Ephriam d 18 Mar 1824 ae 81y
   Jabez d 21 Mar 1812 ae 47y
   Mary w/o Jabez d 25 Mar 1788 ae 21y
   Silas d 24 Mar 1811 ae 46y
   Persis W w/o Silas d 17 Jun 1815 ae 48y
   Ephriam s/o S & P Beaman d 24 May 1790 ae 8m 20d
   Persis d/o S & P Beaman d 12 Jan 1795 ae 1y 5m
   Betsey d/o S & P Beaman d 5 Oct 1797 ae 6y 5m
   Jonathan d 10 Apr 1771 ae 78y
   Dinah w/o Jonathan d 5 Dec 1774 ae 60y

*Mount Vernon Cemetery*

**Town Meeting, 9 April 1894**: Article 2. To see if the Town will accept of the Mortuary Chapel, and Receiving Toomb as built on the Old Common, from donations from Mr. Charles Nash, Mrs. S.C. Rawson and Mrs. A.H. Rice, with the following provisos: That it shall be kept in repair and be opened free to any one who may desire to have funeral services held there, and for no other purposes, except that it may be opened any Memorial Day, during services held in this, and the adjoining cemetery; Furthermore, that the Furniture shall not be loaned or removed! **Voted**: that the Chapel and Toomb be accepted under the provisos made by the donors. The vote was passed by a large and full vote. Sketch by Grace Howe Klar.

200

Mount Vernon Cemetery of West Boylston is located on the east side of the Town Common and is separated from it by a stone wall running the length of the east side of the Common.

Earliest indications from gravestones in the cemetery appear to coincide with the building of the first Meeting House, its dedication on 1 January 1795 and the establishment of this area as the Second Precinct of Boylston, Sterling and Holden in June 1796. Earliest gravestones show dates of 1795 – 1798.

Early records using the name of Mount Vernon Cemetery show land acquisitions to expand the cemetery dated 1852.

At the annual meeting of the Mount Vernon Cemetery Association on 5 May 1931 it was unanimously voted to convey and transfer the real and personal property of the Mount Vernon Cemetery to the Town of West Boylston.

## HOLBROOK MEMORIAL CHAPEL

Erected in 1892 on the site of the Town Pound by the heirs of the Holbrook family in memory of Eli W. Holbrook, mill owner, and also in memory of Rev. William Nash, first settled minister in town.

Two other cemeteries that exist today in West Boylston, namely High Plains in Oakdale Village and St. Luke's off Lancaster Street, are not included in this listing because they came into existence after the 1850's.

BEAMAN – Front Section starting at west wall (L to R)

ROW 1

BANNING, Charles M 1851 – 1883
   Mary Jane w/o Charles 1852 – 1922
   Harry 1878 – 1961 s/o C & M J
   Mary M d 20 Apr 1881 ae 5y
BURINGAME, Fred 1869 – 1929
   Ada E w/o Fred 1872 – 1941
VINTON, Sarah Elizabeth 1879 – 1917
BURLINGAME, Joyce Shirley 1942 – 1960
   Harold 1901 – 1984
   Florence M 1911 – 1979
ALLEN, Frederick W 1871 – 1959
   Josephine G w/o Frederick 1878 – 1962
SIMMONS, Robert W 1907 – 1909
MERROW, George W 1885 – 1921
   Ernest W 1899 – 1929
   George E 1889 – 1891
   Harry E 1892 – 1897
GAMMEL, Louise E 1885 – 1889
LORD, Ada L 1867 – 1958

GAMMEL, Vera M 1889 – ?
  Clarence B 1888 – 1953
KNIGHT, Amos F 1811 – 1898
  Persis Fay w/o Amos 1818 – 1888
BOND, Percy H 1866 – 1920  Odd Fellows symbol
HARDING, Freeman d 21 Nov 1886 ae 79y  Masonic symbol
  Jane M 2nd w/o Freeman d 3 Nov 1892 ae 82y
BOND, Benjamin F 1837 – 1910 Co H 17th Regt Marine Vols
  Harriet F w/o Benjamin 1835 – 1905


ROW 2


TOOMBS, Joseph E 1834 – 1917
  Adeline P w/o Joseph 1883 – 1921
  Charles Olney 1844 – 1917 Co C 18th Regt Conn Vols
  Eva F w/o Charles 1869 – 1942
RYAN, Michael H 1849 – 1917
  Pauline C w/o Michael 1851 – 1932
  Etta M d/o M & P Ryan 1873 – 1905
  Corrine d/o M & P Ryan 1887 – 1981
HALE, Seymour E 1883 – 1948
  Lillian G w/o Seymour 1880 – 1962
BOWEN, Andrew 1846 – 1918
  Mary 1860 – 1947
  Cora 1882 – 1904
  Lena 1894 – 1924
  Walter 1882 – 1964
MAXWELL, Samuel K 1858 – 1939
  Mary E 1864 – 1953
HIGGINS, Eugene 1838 – 1918
  Ellen M w/o Eugene 1833 – 1883
HOLT, Sanford d 22 Oct 1886 ae 71y
  Fidelia w/o Sanford d 15 Nov 1886 ae 66y
  Alfred ?
  Charles M d 10 Feb 1892 ae 48y
  Mary A w/o Charles d 11 Jul 1858 ae 35y
  Mabel E d/o C & M Holt d 1 Jan ----
CASWELL, Florence
  George


ROW 3


BARTON, John W d 18 Nov 1817 ae 40y
TILTON, Nathan d 18 May 1866 ae 82y
  Sally R wid/o John Barton w/o Nathan d1865 ae 73y
PROUTY, Mary w/o Adam Prouty d 23 Feb 1828 ae 20y
O A ----
HINDS, Rebeckah d 21 Feb 1806 ae 26d

ROW 4

WHITCOMB, John d 11 Sep 1820 ae 50y
AMES, Luther d 21 Oct 1867 ae 79y
   Hannah w/o Luther d 2 May 1868
   John W s/o L & H Ames d 21 Sep 1833 ae 2y 11m
   Polly d 30 Oct 1870 ae 50y
   George W 1823 – 1898
WORCESTER, Sampson d 19 May 1845 ae 41y
   Betsey T w/o Sampson d 12 Mar 1839 ae 32y
   Mary B w/o Sampson d 29 Jan 1890 ae 81y
   Mary Elizabeth d 30 Aug 1862 ae 18y
   Thomas Adams d 15 Jul 1842 ae 4m 5d
RICE, Ezra Beaman 1825 – 1912
   Almira F Worcester w/o Ezra 1829 – 1864
   Susan L Wood w/o Ezra 1834 – 1868

ROW 5

GOODELL, Susan P d 3 Nov 1899 ae 4y 4m 5d
DARLING, Eunice Goodell w/o Samuel D Darling 1809 – 1837
SHAW, A M w/o John Shaw d1833 ae 28y
GOODALE, Abel d 8 Nov 1853
   Mehitable w/o Deacon Abel d 23 Mar 1867
   Grace w/o Abel d 26 Dec 1819
MERRIFIELD, Asaph d 29 Aug 1820 ae 79y
   Mercy w/o Asaph d 31 Jul 1845 ae 89y

ROW 6

WHITTEMORE, Eunice w/o Jonathan d 23 Dec 1842 ae 70y
DAVENPORT, Isaac N d 21 Apr 1882 ae 79y
   Elizabeth D w/o Isaac d 8 May 1867 ae 65y
   Orissa d/o I & E Davenport d 22 Jul 1836 ae 10m
   Warren N s/o I & E Davenport d 15 Aug 1848 ae 9y
   Sarah w/o Ebenezer d 15 Mar 1845 ae 73y
---- Lucy w/o Andrew J d 6 Sep 1818 ae 39y
KEYES, Asa d 27 Dec 1850 ae 82y
   Tamer w/o Asa d 29 Dec 1854 ae 80y
   Asa Jr d 21 Dec 1844 ae 2y 11m
   Susan Mehitable d/o Asa d 11 Mar 1813 ae 11m
GOODALE, Eli s/o A & M Goodale
CHENEY, Artemas s/o J & S Cheney d 2 Mar 1826 ae 8y

ROW 7

FAIRBANK, Aramus d 8 Jan 1850 ae 52y
   Isaac d 22 Sep 1841 ae 50y
   Prudence G w/o Isaac d 7 Feb 1871 ae 75y
   Seth d 31 Dec 1833 ae 78y
   Releif w/o Seth d 10 Jun 1839 ae 80y

ROW 8

COXEN, George William s/o W & R Coxen d 30 Nov 1835 ae 11y
   Sarah w/o Richard d 28 Nov 1838 ae 23y
PARKER, Jane A 1810 – 1878
   Abigail w/o Timothy d 4 May 1827 ae 46y
   Mrs Timothy d 8 Apr 1826 ae 46y
PEIRCE, Oliver 1746 – 1813  Cady's Mass Det Rev War
   Hollis d 25 May 1833 ae 58y
   Lucinda w/o Hollis d 21 Jan 1820 ae 30y
HOSMER, Theo M Co E 134 Ill Inf GAR Vet
   Lot L Sgt 134 Ill Inf GAR Vet
PRESCOTT, D D 1805 – 1880
   Lucy C w/o D D 1803 – 1876
   Marrietta A 1848 – 1908
MORGAN, Elizabeth Phelps w/o Francis D d 18 Feb 1844 ae 25y
   Cordelia d 11 Feb 1812 ae 16y
   Calvin Jr d 31 Oct 1836 ae 29y
DUNSMORE, Susan d/o G & C M Dunsmore d 10 Oct 1837 ae 5y
MORSE, Mindwell w/o William d 19 Jul 1839 ae 44y

ROW 9

PEIRCE, Dorothy A d/o J & S Peirce d 7 Nov 1814 ae 5y
FAIRBANK, Alexander s/o B & S Fairbank d 23 Dec 1813 ae 4m
WINTER, Eliza w/o Aaron E d 25 Apr 1830 ae 22y
PEIRCE, Lucinda d 27 Mar 1863 ae 54y
   Joseph W d 28 Apr 1857 ae 42y
PIERCE, Heneretta d 30 Jul 1871 ae 24y
   Louisa M w/o Joseph W d 19 Feb 1891 ae 76y
BRIANT, Rebecca w/o Lyman d 27 Apr 1825 ae 19y
SMITH, Isad 1755 – 1827  Sgt Col Keyes Regt Rev War

ROW 10

HOWARD, Charles B s/o B & B Howard d 9 Sep 1833 ae 19y
CARPENTER, Mary T w/o Albian d 19 Apr 1811 ae 29y
WINTER, Carrie E d/o A & D Winter d 6 Nov 1858 ae 1y 8m 2d
MORSE, Henry Eugene s/o D & E Morse d 18 Feb 1866
WINTER, Herbie A s/o A & D Winter d 11 Sep 1853
   Willie H s/o A & D Winter d 6 Apr 1817 ae 1y 9d
STILES, Sarah F d/o J C Stiles d 12 Sep 1810 ae 1y 11m 6d
   Frank s/o J C Stiles d 15 Feb 1845 ae 14m 3d
PRESCOTT, D F 1836 – 1913
   Lauretta K w/o D F Prescott 1837 – 1897
FAIRBANK, Lillah V 1859 – 1953
   Netina E 1881 – 1972
FISHER, Evelyn E 1861 – 1912
ROSS, Alexander 1812 – 1890
   Milton D s/o A & H Ross d 7 Oct 1875 ae 20y
   A Dillon d 9 Oct 1854 ae 1y 8m 20d

MARTIN, Thomas d 13 Mar 1889 ae 67y
  Mary E 1861 – 1940
MOORE, Jacob d 29 Nov 1881 ae 30y


ROW 11

VINTON, Boylston d 11 Oct 1860 ae 80y
  Lydia w/o Boylston


ROW 12

ELDREDGE, Storrs d 19 Nov 1860 ae 80y
WHEELER, John d 31 Jul 1873 ae 21y
  Dinah W w/o John d 25 Oct 1876 ae 67y
  John C s/o J & D Wheeler d 9 Aug 1819 ae 8m
  William D s/o J & D Wheeler d 20 Jun 1811 ae 1m
  Mary T d/o J & D Wheeler d 30 Dec 1850 ae 11y
WHITE, Joseph d 9 Nov 1861 ae 72y
  Matilda w/o Joseph d 23 Sep 1880 ae 84y
  Hannah Mandana d 24 Jan 1843 ae 17y
  Joseph E s/o J & M White d 16 Feb 1832 ae 7m
BROWN, Charles d 29 Jul 1856 ae 29y
WHITE, Thomas d 21 Feb 1881 ae 84y
  Lois M w/o Thomas d 3 Dec 1868 ae 58y
  Deliah w/o Thomas Jr d 12 Sep 1837 ae 37y
WHITE, Delia d/o T & D White d 6 Sep 1837 ae 17d
  Laura M d/o T & L White d 30 Aug 1846 ae 23d
  Laura A w/o Thomas White Jr d 10 Apr 1847 ae 44y
NEWTON, Lemeul D 1805 – 1895
  Sarah L w/o Lemeul 1805 – 1889
  Hattie
NEWELL, Harriet d/o L & S Newton d 23 Feb 1867 ae 26y
SOMMER, Maria Tusan w/o Henry Sommer 1826 – 1893
  Henry 1821 – 1899
  Margaret A 1851 – 1854
  Willie M 1859 – 1863
SMITH, Sibley Putnam s/o G & L Smith d 12 Jun 1825 ae 2y
  George S d 1 Nov 1853 ae 52y
  Lucinda w/o George d 1 Sep 1837 ae 30y
  Matilda J w/o George d 16 Jan 1864 ae 64y
  Agnes d/o G & L Smith d 18 May 1857 ae 27y


ROW 13

PARMENTER, Harriet 1804 – 1881
  Hannah w/o Jonas d 25 Nov 1851 ae 90y
DAVIS, Stephan H s/o F & E Davis d 25 Dec 1838 ae 3m
  George P s/o F & M Davis d 24 Oct 1828 ae 6m
  Francis d 16 Oct 1838 ae 14y
  Mary P w/o Francis d 7 Sep 1828 ae 33y
  Eunice P w/o Francis d 17 Oct 1861 ae 63y

Mary R d 16 Jul 1850 ae 31y
Francis W d 6 Jul 1851 ae 26y
Abby B w/o Francis W d 12 Jan 1856
SANBORN, Caroline L w/o Levi E d 15 Jun 1874 ae 51y
Levi E d 18 Aug 1899 ae 79y
WHITE, Thomas d 20 Jul 1849 ae 91y
Hanna H w/o Thomas d 25 Jul 1830 ae 68y
Windsor N d 16 Nov 1871 ae 48y
Elizabeth A w/o Windsor 1835 – 1925
Miriam w/o Windsor d 12 Feb 1861 ae 36y
Joseph Nelson s/o W & M White d 19 Jan 1817 ae 17m 19d
Mandana Matilda d/o W & M d 12 Aug 1848 ae 16m 18d
Thomas s/o W & M 1850 – 1916
Newton Day s/o W & E White d 29 Apr 186– ae 2y 9m
Polly d 30 Jan 1850 ae 64y
RICHARDS, Leander d 13 Jun 1891 ae 81y  Co I Mass R A
Elizabeth C w/o Leander d 3 Nov 1888 ae 83y
Hiram A s/o L & E Richards d 19 Jan 1845 ae 7y
Francis A s/o L & E d 31 Aug 1817 ae 12y
HOWARD, Eliza A d/o L & E Richards d 6 Oct 1856 ae 23y
MURDOCK, Carrie H 1855 – 1934
Carolina w/o Rev William 1817 – 1891
MURDOCK, William (Rev) d 13 Nov 1879 ae 66y


ROW 14

WINTER, Luther
Abigail B w/o Luther 1809 – 1862
Nancy Abigail 1829 – 1829
Edward Payson 1831 – 1852
Charles Adolphus 1837 – 1863
Susan Abigail 1844 – 1853
A R 1810 – 1900
Susan Cordelia d/o W & M Winter d 17 Mar 1857 ae 1y 9m 13d
Calvin d 25 Nov 1839 ae 63y
Lucy w/o Calvin d ---- ae 81y

ROW 15

HOWE, Harriot d/o H & O Howe d 15 Sep 1813 ae 4y 5m 11d
Olive d/o H & O Howe d 8 Aug 1808 ae 11y
ALDRICH, Olive w/o George d 25 Oct 1841 ae 29y
HOWE, Hiram d 13 Aug 1829 ae 51y
Olive w/o Hiram d 2 Dec 1852 ae 78y
KNIGHT, ---- d 24 Mar 1829 ae 82y
Polly w/o Isaac d 16 Jan 1839
KILBURN, Levi d 23 Jan 1812 ae 20y
Katy w/o Levi d 16 Nov 1830 ae 59y
FAIRBANK, Lemuel d 4 Jul 1819 ae 68y  Rev War Vet
Phebe w/o Lemuel d 19 Dec 1824 ae 73y
Baruck B d 9 Jan 1824 ae 45y

Sally w/o Baruck B d 8 Feb 1847 ae 67y
Emily d/o B & S Fairbank d 3 Aug 1823 ae 4y 2m
Persis B d 2 May 1825 ae 14y
FAIRBANKS, Delina d/o J & S Fairbanks d 30 Mar 1833 ae 24y
PROUTY, Joshua d 17 Apr 1853 ae 71y
WILDER, Thankful w/o Reuben Wilder d 28 Jan 1855 ae 80y
PROUTY, Phebe w/o Joshua 1785 – 1870
FAIRBANK, Esther d 10 Jun 1871 ae 83y
WIITE, Seth Alonzo s/o S & L White d 11 Oct 1825 ae 2y 11m
GILL, Polly w/o John d 21 Mar 1826 ae 39y
Mary Ann d/o J & P Gill d 15 Oct 1821 ae 9y
---- one s/o and one d/o d 8 Mar 1826 in infancy
GALE, Oliver d 25 Nov 1824 ae 53y
FISK, Capt Ebenezer d 25 Sep 1830 ae 23y
EARLE, Eunice w/o Emory Earle d 22 Nov 1828 ae 42y
WELLINGTON, Charlotte d 17 Jul 1830 ae 31y
WILLINGTON, Ebenezer d 21 Apr 1833 ae 67y


ROW 16

GOODNOW, Elijah (Capt) d 19 May 1821 ae 53y
Eunice w/o Elijah d 5 Aug 1828 ae 56y
Otis s/o E & E Goodnow d 17 Oct 1805 ae 1y 11m 9d
GOODNOW, Julia Ann d/o E & E Goodnow d 9 Sep 1813 ae 17m 10d
Persis d/o E & E d 25 Aug 1820 ae 13y
LOVELL, Amos d 6 Nov 1815 ae 62y  Rev War Vet
Mary w/o Amos d 13 Feb 1833 ae 76y
BALL, Samuel d 17 Mar 1806 ae 77y
Persis d 9 Jan 1821 ae 67y
LOVELL, Hannah F w/o Addison d 26 Jul 1838 ae 29y
---- Lottie w/o Amos Lovell d 5 May 1837 ae 59y
Betsey Darling d 13 Feb 1841 ae 25y
WOOD, Nath G d 1 Aug 1836 ae 72y
Levina w/o Nath d 14 Feb 1819 ae 46y
Merrill d 4 Nov 1873 ae 79y
Betlinda w/o Merrill d 17 Dec 1813 ae 41y
Mary E w/o Merrill d 21 May 1879 ae 73
MURDOCK, Artemas d 21 Jun 1855 ae 28y
Keziah w/o Attemas d 24 Jul 1818 ae 18y
Mary S w/o Artemas Murdock Jr d 3 Oct 1834 ae 23y
Judia Ann d/o A & K Murdock d 18 Oct 1821 ae 13m 21d
George H s/o A & K Murdock d 7 Dec 1834 ae 4m 10d
Martha M w/o C M Murdock 1816 – 1875
A M (Lieut) d 25 Mar 1865 ae 19y  GAR


ROW 17

GLAZIER, Emmons J s/o J & S Glazier d 3 Jul 1851 ae 29y
EAMES, Luther R 1826 – 1901
Auguste W w/o Luther 1828 – 1894
Allira B 1856 – 1871


207

Canley Denard 1857 – 1928
Emma S Miller w/o Canley 1869 – 1953
Zalius C 1860 – 1871
Kenneth Reid 1897 – 1949
Claire Auguste 1899 – 1984
Luther Rice 1906 – 1973
LITTLE, Lucy 1815
WORCESTER, Sampson d 5 May 1821 ae 53y
Phebe w/o Sampson d 1 Oct 1837 ae 63y
Benjamin E s/o S & P Worcester d 17 Mar 1819 ae 14m
PENNIMAN, Susan A Murdock w/o H H Penniman 1841 – 1910
MURDOCK, David C d 15 Oct 1886 ae 80y
Adeline King w/o David d 30 Jun 1887 ae 78y
Julia A d 6 Nov 1818 ae 10y
Angeline B d 4 Nov 1840 ae 1y 4d
Mary C d 24 Jan 1847 ae 1y 3m
Clara A d 30 Aug 1850 ae 2y


ROW 18

STILES, Oliver d 9 Aug 1854 ae 42y
Lucy R w/o Oliver d 8 Feb 1852 ae 43y
STILES, Harriet N d/o O & L Stiles d 1 Mar 1852 ae 6y

ROW 19

JOHNSON, George E 1851 – 1884
Mary E w/o George 1856 – 1915
Edwin S 1824 – 1900
Martha K w/o Edwin 1826 – 1864
Martha L d/o E & M Johnson 1860 – 1861
HOLBROOK, E W d 26 Nov 1888 ae 75y
Adaline w/o E W d 5 Feb 1887 ae 75y
Levi 1815 – 1884
Rebecca w/o Levi 1814 – 1907
Myron Holly s/o L & R Holbrook 1845
Sarah Electa d/o L & R Holbrook 1843 – 1848
James d 31 May 1839 ae 59y
Sarah Wheeler w/o James d 21 Oct 1827 ae 48y
Sarah d/o J & S Holbrook d 18 Feb 1827 ae 14y
Elizabeth d/o J & S Holbrook d 26 Dec 1822 ae 22y
Reuben W d 7 May 1886
CROFUT, Harriet R d/o L & R Holbrook 1854 – 1929


ROW 20

HOLT, Nancy d 7 Apr 1836 ae 19y
NEWTON, Dinah d/o W & S Newton d 2 Dec 1820 ae 18y
SARGENT, Thomas 1805 – 1863
Clarissa G w/o Thomas 1804 – 1877
Angeline A 1841 – 1842

Martha A 1845 – 1853
Edgar A 1851 – 1933
Sarah w/o John T Lovell d 29 Apr 1842 ae 17y
Elizabeth 1826 – 1827
Thomas Jr 1828 – 1831
Levi 1836 – 1837

ROW 21

NEWTON, Charles H 1846 – 1918  Co B 57 Mass Reg
   Silas 1844 – 1922  Co F 42 Mass Vol
   Ella C Nelson w/o Silas Newton 1850 – 1928
   Alta Christine 1884 – 1893
   Tracey L 1867 – 1933
   Mary Elsie 1890 – 1918
   Grace L 1869 – 1953
CLARK, Richard N 1925 – 1944  PFC Co I 377 Reg 95 Div
RICE, Francis Beaman 1864 – 1946
   Lillian Blanche w/o Francis 1866 – 1933
   Paul Beaman 1902 – 1967
   Marion Anner w/o Paul 1906 – 1977
NASH, Rev William 1768 – 1829
   Charles 1806 – 1896
NASH, Elizabeth S 1812 – 1891
   Mary G w/o Dr Thompson 1808 – ?
   William Henry 1804 – 1809
ANDERSON, J Emerson 1833 – 1896  Sgt Co D 2nd Mass Inf
   Lucy A Wheeler w/o J Emerson 1835 – 1900
   Isabella d/o J & L 1869 – 1938

ROW 22

PARKER, Rev William Wheeler d 22 Sep 1894 ae 70y
   Emily W w/o William 1826 – 1926
   William E 1880 – 1927
   Luna F w/o William E 1857 – 1944

ROW 23

WINN, Maria J w/o Peter S 1837 – 1917
GRANT, Fredrick A 1873 – ?
   Sarah J w/o Fredrick 1864 – 1939
ANDERSON, Frederick A 1920 – 1982 LCDR US Navy WW2

ROW 24

BUSS, Fred 1850 – 1901
   Ellen E Salisbury w/o Fred 1856 – 1896
   Alice M 1886 – 1890
   Gladys C 1895 – 1971
   Herbert S 1890 – 1968

COLBURN, George W 1893 – 1973
    Myrtle M w/o George 1894 – 1976

ROW 25

TAYLOR, Millard C 1905 – 1968
    Mary Louise 1896 – 1908 d/o Arthur & Harriet
    ---- Albert 1875 – 1919

+ + + + + +

MOUNT VERNON – Front Section, right of roadway

ROW 1

DAY, Provose W 1873 – ?
    Sarah A 1875 – 1930
    Clarence W s/o Wm & M L d 12 Aug 1881 ae 9y 4m
COOK, Benjamin F 1840 – 1914
    Ellen M Barnes w/o Benjamin 1839 – 1881
    Cranson 1819 – 1898
    Hepsibah B w/o Cranson 1818 – 1888
    Herbert F 1863 – 1923
    Mary E Buck w/o Herbert 1856 – 1943
    Chester H 1886 – 1906
EARLE, Susan B d 16 Apr 1891 ae 65y 3m
DAY, William 1848 – 1923
    Mary L 1852 – 1937
HOWE, Rufus E 1847 – 1935
    Rosie A 1854 – 1938
WHEELER, Albert A 1849 – 1936
WHEELER, Ella L 1853 – 1931
    A Harry 1873 – 1950
    Helen M Bonzey w/o A Harry 1882 – 1974
GILLETTE, Albert H 1864 – 1925
    Ida M Sumner w/o Albert 1864 – 1928
ANTINARELLA, Daniel 1883 – 1973
    Angela C DiSilvo w/o Daniel 1888 – 1966
    Pauline 1911 – 1917
    George 1912 – ?
    Sabino 1921 – ?
STEWART, Augustus 1868 – 1954
    Elizabeth 1882 – 1951
BRIGHAM, John B Co B Mass Inf GAR
    Ann M Gleason w/o John 1841 – 1908
AUREN, Phillip C 1886 – 1968
    Edyth M 1893 – 1944
SMITH, George F 1882 – 1953
    S Marguerite w/o George 1873 – 1957
    Louise E 1879 – 1930
    Mary V 1887 – 1944

210

Clifford Austin 1877 - 1905
MYERS, ----
CLARK, Edward B 1848 - 1896
   Andrew P 1838 - 1918
   Henrietta F 1846 - 1930
   George B 1854 - ?
NEWTON, Eleanor F MD 1845 - 1901
MORTON, E A 1877
   F W 1896
   M E 1896
HIGGINS, Sparrow 1834 - 1913
   E F 1870 - 1941
   E W 1871 - 1932


ROW 2

MITCHELL, Harriet w/o Richard d 18 Nov 1829 ae 79y 9m 18d
HARTHAN, Corp Lyman Co E 49th Mass Inf GAR
   Harriot Morse w/o W B d 25 Sep 1847 ae 38y
   Charles s/o W B & H d 29 Aug 1839 ae 3y
   George B s/o W B & H d 31 May 1843 ae 13y
   Emely A d/o W B & H d 31 Oct 1845 ae 2y
FULLER, Charles S GAR 1860 - 1933
   Lydia A w/o Charles d 4 Oct 1882 ae 52y 11m
   Charles H 1860 - 1933
   Ella
   Jenny
ROSS, William W d 26 Jan 1885 ae 43y Sgt Co F 4 Bn Mass Vol
   Lydia M Child Haskins w/o William 1843 - 1912
   Harry
ANDERSON, Herberte 1862 - 1924
   Mabel O Ross w/o Herberte 1868 - 1921
FLETCHER, Halsey L 1822 - 1901
STUART, George W 1823 - 1915
   Mary D Tilton w/o George 1830 - 1903
   Cora L d/o G & M 1861 - 1863
   George W 1868 - 1927
   Flora A May 1866 - 1953
   Charlotte V 1871 -
HOUGHTON, Corp George M 1840 - 1911  Co K 53 Reg Mass Vol
   Abbie F Bruce w/o George 1848 - 1907
WHITTUM, Charles E 1847 - 1917
   Sarah E Houghton w/o Charles 1847 - 1932
RECORD, J Frank 1851 - 1913
   Clara E w/o J Frank 1858 - 1944
   Everett C 1893 - 1917
CLAYTON, Harry V 1872 - ?
   Louise S w/o Harry 1870 - 1943
   Dorothy K 1906 - ?
GRAY, Samuel S 1838 - 1904
   Marilla S Merrow w/o Samuel 1847 - 1911

RICHARDS, Justin F 1857 – 1939
  Elizabeth P w/o Justin 1856 – 1925
  George A s/o J F & E P d 29 Sep 1903 ae 18y 10m 29d
ENGEL, Phillip B 1887 – 1964
  Ida M Richards w/o Phillip
LUCE, Newman Brown 1843 – 1912
  Lucretia Jane Harthan w/o Newman 1841 – 1903
  George B 1864 – 1911
  Sarah F w/o George 1870 – 1950
  Lucretia M d/o G B & S F b&d 1903
PRATT, William T 1836 – 1900
  Sarah A w/o William 1840 – 1931
  Albert W 1871 – 1925
  Mary D Gardner 1869 – 1955
DODGE, Joanna D 1804 – 1875
FARLEY, Benjamin F 1808 – 1892
  Mary E White w/o Benjamin 1818 – 1904
  Mary L 1841 – 1905
  Gardner 1848 – 1856
  Herbert M Lang 1848 – 1918
  L Frances Lang 1844 – 1931
HUBBARD, Cyrus 1824 – 1892
  Sarah H Fiske w/o Cyrus 1829 – 1919


ROW 3


COOKE, James A 1901 – 1980  Lt USAF
COOKE, Doris L Prescott w/o James 1898 – 1983
CHILD, Amos d 17 Nov 1839 ae 72y
  Dorcas w/o Amos d 13 May 1822 ae 56y
  Nancy R w/o Amos d 3 Apr 1881 ae 85y
  David d 16 Jun 1851 ae 22y
  Mehitable w/o David d 8 Dec 1894 ae 79y
  Mary Ann P d 28 Aug 1828 ae 1y 4m
  Jonathan R d 8 Aug 1830 ae 8d
  David d 4 Aug 1803 ae 92y
  Amos d 2 Jan 1869 ae 65y 3m
  Eunice w/o Amos d 10 Feb 1849 ae 47y 26d
  Ellen M d/o Amos & Eunice d 16 Jul 1860 ae 17y 22d
  Ellen L d/o Amos & Eunice d 9 Aug 1842 ae 1y 10m
  Lyman G s/o Amos & Eunice d 2 Mar 1840 ae 6y 11m
  Eunice d/o Amos & Eunice d 8 Oct 1831 ae 2y 11m
  Otis M s/o Amos & Eunice d 4 Aug 1836 ae 1y 4m
MOORE, Israel d 26 Aug 1811
  Katherine w/o Israel d 14 Jun 1802 ae 60y
SEVERY, Caleb d 22 Apr 1815 ae 28y 8m
LEE, Benjamin ae 90y 11m 2d
  Eunice w/o Benjamin d 30 May 1838 ae 54y
  Bezaleel s/o Benjamin & Eunice 1806 – 1821
DWELLY, Mary w/o Joseph d 29 Sep 1832 ae 72y 10m 14d
PIERCE, Abajah d 18 Apr 1822 ae 56y

RICE, Asa d 27 Feb 1856 ae 64y
  Harriet w/o Asa d 7 Jun 1832 ae 33y
  Harriet M d/o Asa & Harriet d 21 May 1836 ae 14y
DAVIS, Catherine R w/o Asa Rice & Jonas Brooks d 1899
READ, Capt John d 8 May 1838 ae 68y VET
----, Emerson M
----, Clarinda d 18 Aug 1829
CLEAVLAND, Hannah w/o Loren d 17 Oct 1840 ae 38y
NIXON, Dr Nahum d 22 Aug 1850 ae 62y
  Jane E d/o Nahum & Harriet d 12 Feb 1856 ae 22y
BOND, George E d 1 Oct 1913 ae 83y 19d
  Caroline J w/o George E d 18 Feb 1919 ae 88y 2m 10d
  Hattie A d/o G E & C J d 6 Dec 1893 ae 27y 7m 23d
  Sarah S d/o G E & C J d 8 Oct 1873 ae 15y
ODIE, Emma J d/o G E & C J Bond d 17 Oct 1950 ae 93y 11m

ROW 4

SPOFFORD, Emerson d 30 May 1862 ae 58y
  Mary B w/o Emerson d 28 Apr 1881 ae 88y 8m
HASKINS, Robert W s/o Robert & Rebecca d 8 Jan 1881 ae 76y1m20d
CHILD, Zachariah d 19 Sep 1845 ae 81y 10m  Rev War Vet
  Lydia consort of Zachariah d 19 Dec 1849 ae 85y 2m
  Dolly d/o Zachariah d 11 Nov 1811 ae 23y 8m
CHILD, Lydia d/o Zachariah d 25 Aug 1878 ae 80y 2m 22d
ANDROS, Susan H d/o Zachariah Child d 25 May 1855 ae 55y 6m
BIGELOW, Cynthia G d/o Zachariah Child d 1 Aug 1820 ae 35y 7m
HASKINS, Lucretia d/o Zachariah Child d 15 Jun 1848 ae 43y 2m
JONES, Olivia w/o John C d 28 Apr 1825 ae 36y
  Frances Olivia d/o John & Olivia d 14 Nov 1846 ae 22y 7m 29d
KENNAN, Ephraim 1791 – 1872
  Thankful B 1797 – 1863
  Marsha Maria d/o E & T d 22 Dec 1832 ae 1y 10m 13d
  Alonzo
SHERMAN, Sarah Ann w/o Charles H
FLAGG, Silas d 25 Aug 1818 ae 28y
HOLT, Jonas d 9 Apr 1853 ae 73y 5m
  Anna w/o Jonas d 6 Aug 1845 ae 65y 5m
  Marcell Shed s/o J S & A d 14 Sep 1822 ae 2y 24d
  Anna d/o J S & A d 2 Sep 1808 ae 2y 9m
  Russell d 12 Jun 1875 ae 70y 10m 7d
  Emeline P w/o Russell d 21 Dec 1846 ae 30y
  Sarah w/o Russell d 3 Apr 1897 ae 74y 10m 14d
BURNHAM, Ella L 1853 – 1905
LOVELL, Jonathan d -- Oct 1817 ae 73y
  Mercy w/o Jonathan d 16 Jul 1829 ae 81y
KNIGHT, Elijah d 1 Aug 1843 ae 63y
  Eunice w/o Elijah d 1 Dec 1865 ae 85y
  Jona Lovell s/o E & E d 16 Feb 1823 ae 3y 1m 16d
TEMPLE, Isaac d 9 Aug 1832 ae 48y
  Hannah S w/o Isaac d 11 Feb 1839 ae 52y

DAVIS, Celina T w/o Gardiner d 20 Jan 1842 ae 35y
   George E s/o G & C T d 6 Aug 1835 ae 3d
TEMPLE, Jonas H d 2 May 1845 ae 35y
GOODWIN, Anna w/o Anraziah d 5 Oct 1846 ae 19y 2m 28d
UNDERWOOD, Parney (Mrs) w/o Joseph Underwood d 31 Mar 1844
   ae 66y
TEMPLE, John 1762 – 1841  Rev War Vet
   Persis w/o John 1762 – 1832
   Polly w/o John d 19 Jun 1856


ROW 5


DIKE, Capt Benj d 29 May 1873 ae 87y  Mex War Vet
   Lucy w/o Benjamin d 8 Feb 1853 ae 67y
   Charles E s/o B & L d 18 Aug 1852 ae 21y
   Benjamin d 29 Apr 1878 ae 58y
KING, Catherine L d/o Perez & Mary d 30 Apr 1844 ae 28y
BIGELOW, Asa 1794 – 1876
   Lois H w/o Asa d 27 Dec 1839 ae 46y 1m 21d
   Abel d 14 Oct 1821 ae 67y
   Capt Joseph d 30 Nov 1800 ae 75y REV
   Olive w/o Joseph d 26 Jun 1810 ae 76y
MORSE, Joseph d 10 Jan 1826 ae 68y
   Sophia w/o Joseph d 26 Oct 1831 ae 72y 9m
   Silvanus d 5 Feb 1813 ae 66y
GLAZIER, Nancy w/o John d 11 Jul 1813 ae 20y 10m
   ---- an infant
   Lydia d/o Oliver & Rachel d 1 Oct 1798 ae 10m 19d
GOODALE, Peter d 14 May 1834 ae 82y
   Abigail w/o Peter d 10 Jan 1809 ae 56y
   Rachel w/o Peter d 14 Sep 1828 ae 62y
   Elizabeth d/o Peter & Abigail d 22 Aug 1799 ae 23y
   Benjamin s/o Peter & Abigail d 10 Feb 1810 ae 33y
   Peter s/o Peter & Abigail d -- Sep 1812 ae 29y
   Junia s/o Peter & Abigail d 30 Mar 1819 ae 30y
HAZELTON, Betty w/o John d 12 Aug 1809 ae 61y 4m 20d
LOVEL, Deacon Asa d 9 Oct 1814 ae 63y
BIGELOW, Luther d 7 Dec 1885 ae 80y 1m 7d
   Isabella H w/o Luther d 24 Oct 1894 ae 83y 1m 2d
   Sarah E d 17 Feb 1916 ae 75y 11m
   Hannah w/o Luther d 11 Nov 1838 ae 34y
   Eleanor d/o L & H d 23 Nov 1838 ae 3m
   Sarah B w/o Luther d 17 Sep 1840 ae 25y
BROWN, Chloe w/o Nathan d 22 Aug 1838 ae 53y
GOODALE, Ezra d 18 Oct 1861 ae 71y
   Sena Perry w/o Ezra d 1 Mar 1876 ae 88y
GOODELL, Jane Amanda 1821 – 1903
PERRY, Moses d 17 Dec 1813 ae 85y
   Hannah w/o Moses d 22 Mar 1813 ae 84y
GOODELL, R B T d 1 Oct 1880 ae 57y 11m
   Jane Rice w/o R B T d 10 Feb 1893 ae 69y 5m 10d

PIERCE, Susan E d/o Jonathan & Fidelia d 15 Dec 1811 ae 2y 2m
   Theodore F s/o Jonathan & Fidelia d 8 Nov 1811 ae 3m
TOOMBS, Robert C 1804 – 1869
   Louisa w/o Robert 1804 – 1897
   Eunice P d/o R C & L 1832 – 1902
WHITE, William 1831 – 1892
   Ellen A w/o William 1829 – 1911
ROSS, Maria L w/o William J d 26 Apr 1884 ae 67y
PIERCE, Wm A d 15 Dec 1848 ae 36y


ROW 5 1/2 (Right of road to Beaman Cemetery near chapel)


WHITE, Addie A d/o T H White d 21 Feb 1839 ae 15y 9m
   Jane E d/o T H d 26 Jul 1869 ae 19y 9m
   Sarah d 28 Feb 1819 ae 27y
   Louisa M w/o Tarbel H d 13 Oct 1850
   Sarah Louisa d/o Tarbel & Adeline d 10 Apr 1853 ae 16m
   ---- inf/s/o Tarbel & Louisa d 26 Jul 1818
   Charles T s/o Tarbel d 20 Feb 1898
GREGSON, Jane d/o Robert & Mary d 12 Nov 1857 ae 9m
   John E Gregson 1863 – 1931
   Mother – father


ROW 6


GOODALE, Paul d 19 Oct 1847 ae 69y
   Azubah N w/o Paul d 11 Apr 1849 ae 66y
GARFIELD, Hiram B d 8 Nov 1897 ae 72y
   Clarissa T Goodale w/o Hiram d 3 Apr 1890 ae 71y 3m 9d
GOODALE, Mary Ann d/o Levi & Abigail d 10 Nov 1822 ae 16y
   Tirza H d 28 Oct 1814 ae 24y
   Paul d 4 Dec 1828 ae 81y  Rev War Vet
   Eunice w/o Paul d 3 Aug 1824 ae 77y
   Moses d 28 Mar 1815 ae 75y 6m
   Sarah H w/o Edward d 7 Mar 1810 ae 96y
   Aaron d 17 Aug 1817 ae 75y Vet Rev War
   Eunice w/o Aaron d 17 Jan 1832 ae 83y
MORSE, Benjamin d 12 May 1830 ae 48y
   Harvey s/o Joseph & Sofia d 14 Mar 1803 ae 2y 2m 14d
   Sofia Bigelow d/o Joseph & Sofia d 30 Oct 1811 ae 16y
MERRIFIELD, Phebe w/o Louis d 18 Mar 1839 ae 60y 9m
   Silvanus M s/o Louis & Phebe d 17 Jan 1807 ae 10w
   Hannah d/o Louis & Phebe d 30 Jul 1820 ae 17y 8m
   Melinda K d/o Louis & Phebe d 4 Feb 1830 ae 14y 5m 13d
WARREN, Ira d 31 Aug 1875 ae 70y
   Abiail Merrifield w/o Ira d 5 Mar 1887 ae 89y
WHITE, Sally M d/o Peter & Sally d 20 Jan 1798 ae 1y 11d
COOK, Joseph H d 6 Aug 1824 ae 48y
DUNSMOOR, Olive d 19 Nov 1831 ae 15y
TILTON, Aaron d 31 Jul 1876 ae 77y 3m
   Polly D w/o Aaron d 10 Jun 1830 ae 29y

Harriet F w/o Aaron d 22 Jul 1850 ae 42y
Phebe Worcester w/o Aaron d 5 Jul 1887 ae 81y 11m 5d
Our Angel Cora
HOWE, Joel d 3 Jan 1842
Sofie w/o Joel d 4 Jun 1852 ae 63y
PIERCE, Frances E d/o Wm & E H d 6 Sep 1848 ae 2y
HARTHAN, Capt Dennis 1796 – 1876  Mex War Vet
Anna H w/o Dennis 1798 – 1891
Hannah B d/o Dennis & Anna d 2 Sep 1850 ae 25y
Eveline T d/o Dennis & Anna d 1 Jun 1846 ae 15y
Dennis M s/o Dennis & Anna d 24 Jul 1828 ae 1y 5m 22d
FELTON, Lyman S d 29 Sep 1883 ae 67y 7m 17d
Sarah E Bruce w/o Lyman d 2 Aug 1910 ae 80y 3m 27d


ROW 7


DAVIS, Abigale B d/o Barnabas & Marcy d 10 Sep 1807 ae 15m 17d
Abigale B d/o Barnabas & Mary d 17 Oct 1810
DAVIS, Persis w/o Simon d 30 Jul 1800 ae 33y
Ezra s/o Simon & Persis d 9 Dec 1796 ae 4y 8m 22d
---- s/o Simon & Persis stillborn 1791
BELLOWS, Marcy w/o Lieut Ezekiel d 30 Jul 1811  ae 60y
SNOW, Mary A d/o R Winthrop & Abigale d 29 Sep 1834 ae 11m 4d
GOODALE, Aaron d 6 Nov 1840 ae 62y
Mehittable w/o Aaron d 26 Jul 1858 ae 76y
Gardner s/o Aaron & Hitta d 25 Aug 1818 ae 4y 2m
Franklin s/o A & H d 27 Aug 1818 ae 5y 8m
KITREDGE, Melvin S s/o Otis & Maria d 1 Mar 1839 ae 8m 17d
HARTHAN, David d 8 Aug 1823 ae 59y
Prudence w/o David d 28 Feb 1840 ae 76y
Prudy d/o D & P d 24 Sep 1800 ae 13m
Silas s/o D & P d 25 Nov 1813 ae 22y
Antipas d 17 Mar 1815 ae 26y
BRUSH, Ira S 1852 – 1949
Mary E Sawyer w/o Ira 1854 – 1928
SAWYER, Henry d 18 Jun 1876 ae 78y
Cornelia S Wilder w/o Henry d 25 Mar 1883 ae 62y
TILTON, Luke B d 21 Dec 1863 ae 55y 10m
Amanda w/o Luke d 24 Nov 1876 ae 70y 5m 13d
ALDRICH, William H d 18 Dec 1851 ae 27y 3m
WOOD, Samuell d 7 Jan 1819 ae 30y
Clarissa d/o Samuell d 30 Aug 1811 ae 2m 20d
Samuell W s/o Samuell d 11 Aug 1818 ae 6m 8d


ROW 8


DAVIS, Addison d 14 Dec 1839 ae 49y
John A d 3 Nov 1838 ae 40y
FOSS, Mary Ann d/o Robert & Lydia d 3 Dec 1824 ae 10m 18d
Robert s/o Robert & Lydia d 14 Nov 1826 ae 1y 1m 12d
ESTABROOK, Samuel Jr 1747 – 1816 Rev War Vet

KYES, Thomas Jr d 30 Oct 1831 ae 29y
   Eveline w/o Thomas Jr d 22 Sep 1828 ae 24y 6m
   Thomas d 25 Jun 1856 ae 89y
   Lydia w/o Thomas d 25 Oct 1824 ae 59y 8m 7d
   Betsy d/o Thomas & Lydia d 11 May 1839 ae 42y
   Sarah d/o Asa & Sarah d 12 Dec 1830 ae 29y
ANDERSON, Allen s/o Allen & Esther d 27 Nov 1797 ae 20d
DENSMORE, Reuben d 25 Feb 1821 ae 49y
   Polly w/o Reuben d 9 Apr 1856 ae 80y
GLAZIER, Emeline E d/o Ezra & Mary d 15 Oct 1842 ae 11y 6m
NUTTELL, Nelson s/o Edmund & Melba d 9 Apr 1819 ae 3y 6m


ROW 9

PAINE, Rev Elijah H d 14 Sep 1836 ae 38y
   Charles G s/o Elijah d 21 May 1837
BRIGHAM, Edmund d 13 Apr 1840 ae 71y
BRIGHAM, Mary w/o Edmund d 15 May 1817 ae 40y
   Eunice w/o Edmund d 1 Nov 1857 ae 69y
   Stephen B d 6 Jun 1856 ae 44y 10m 18d
   Betsy w/o Stephen d 20 Aug 1902 ae 79y 9m 8d
HOLT Asa d 10 Aug 1847 ae 72y
   Nancy w/o Asa d 10 Sep 1863 ae 80y
   Nancy d/o Asa & Nancy d 29 May 1829 ae 24y
   Emerline d/o Asa & Nancy d 7 Mar 1851 ae 32
MURDOCK, William d 25 Oct 1829 ae 1y 2m 25d
   John Quincy d 20 Feb 1838 ae 4m 8d
PRESCOTT, David d 1 Nov 1814 ae 23y
   Harriet B d/o David & Lucy d 16 Nov 1830 ae 2y 6m 12d
   John d 21 Aug 1848 ae 63y
   Dorinda d/o John & Eunice d 8 Feb 1811 ae 1d
   John s/o John & Eunice d 9 Apr 1816 ae 2d
   John B s/o John & Eunice d 20 Sep 1839 ae 16y 4m
HASTINGS, Nahum d 21 Mar 1819 ae 69y 6m
SMITH, Amos d 16 Nov 1829 ae 40y
FOSSETT, Benjamin s/o Abel & Lois d 3 Jun 1795 ae 1m 3d
   Francis Benjamin s/o Abel & Lois d 5 Oct 1800 ae 2y 2m 13d
GIBBS, Louisa S 1834 – 1910
WINN, John d 28 Nov 1843 ae 83y Rev War Vet
   Abigail w/o John d 18 Apr 1853 ae 89y
WOODWARD, E d 29 Dec 1818
   Eunice d 20 Sep 1847
KEYES, Lyman d 27 Aug 1845 ae 31y
   Dennis D d 21 Oct 1866 ae 54y 7m 15d
WHITMORE, James 1823 – 1880
   Chloe Elizabeth w/o James 1831 – 1889
WALKER, Sarah A d -- May 1888 ae 77y
SEAVER, Nathan A d -- Jun 1894 ae 74y
CHENEY, Joseph d -- Feb 1856 ae 76y
   Sally d -- Feb 1853 ae 20y
WOODS, Mabel Estelle d/o G H & F d 13 Feb 1877 ae 2y 8m 26d

ROW 10

MAHAN, E W Co C 34th Mass Inf
KEYES, Hannah w/o Artemas d 5 Jan 1832 ae 29y
   Hervey s/o Artemas & Hannah d 9 Mar 1832 ae 5y
   Mary w/o Artemas d 27 Jan 1837 ae 42y
   Mary H d/o A & M d 26 Jan 1837 ae 14d
   Benjamin d 6 Jun 1821 ae 53y
   Anise w/o Benjamin d 2 Aug 1845 ae 77y
HILLS, Eli d 9 Mar 1884 ae 53y
   Martha Jane w/o Eli d 13 Jul 1866 ae 33y
HOLT, Parkman d 23 Jun 1841 ae 32y
   Ephraim
BEAMAN, Lemuel s/o Lemuel & Prudence d 16 Dec 1790 ae 20y
   Phinehas s/o Josiah & Elizabeth d 16 Sep 1795 ae 19y
WOOD Daniel Simon s/o Silas & Rebeckah d 14 Jul 1856 ae 5y 5m
BLUNT, George F s/o Joseph & Abigail d 6 Feb 1845 ae 15m 21d
RICE, Josephine d/o Asa & Catherine d 11 Jan 1856 ae 4y 7m
JOHNSON, William H 1819 – 1878
   Alsamena M w/o William 1823 – 1860
   Anna B w/o William 1836 – 1862
   Willie s/o W H & A M b&d 1849
   Maria T d/o W H & A M b&d 1854
   Charles B s/o W H & A M 1850 – 1858
KENDALL, Charles S d 17 May 1864 ae 53y 10m
   Mary W w/o Charles d 24 Dec 1847 ae 38y 7m
   Fannie Jane w/o Robert d 13 Jun 1866 ae 20y 24d

ROW 11

LOVELL, Abigail d/o Johnathan d 12 Sep 1812 ae 16y
HARTWELL, Edmund d 25 Oct 1856 ae 71y 9m 14d
   Olive L d/o Edmund & Olive d 17 Jan 1833 ae 9y
DANA, George 1804 – 1881
   Melinda Newton w/o George 1806 – 1889
   Waldo E s/o George & Orra d 27 Mar 1856 ae 19y 1m
   Sarah O d/o George & Melinda d 8 Aug 1811 ae 4y
BROWN, Sarah P w/o James d 18 Feb 1851 ae 38y 11m
   John F s/o James & Sarah d 24 Aug 1811 ae 8m 10d
BUTLER, Lorenzo 1818 – 1899
   Catherine Flagg w/o Lorenzo 1824 – 1863
   Ellen Hathaway w/o Lorenzo 1831 – 1885

ROW 12

WILCOX, Roxana Adams w/o David d 24 Aug 1880 ae 76y 5m
   Mary Ann d/o David & Roxana d 17 Mar 1845 ae 16y
   Oliver B MD d 17 Jul 185- ae 85y 9m 10d
NEWTON, Ella A d 2 Nov 1877 ae 11d
PEIRCE, Levi d 24 Mar 1867 ae 72y
   Polly w/o Levi d 21 Dec 1841 ae 46y

DAVIS, Richard Harris 1907 - 1962 WW II Vet
DANA, Mary Ann d/o Silvanus & Sally d 8 Feb 1827 ae 5y 21d
HOUGH, Rev Alling d 14 Aug 1824 ae 32y
FLAGG, Lambert s/o Samuel & Lucy d 22 Dec 1822 ae 1y 1m 8d
    Orrin s/o Samuel & Lucy d 8 Dec 1822 ae 4y 11m 29d
    Samuel L s/o Samuel & Lucy d 6 Dec 1828 ae 11m 7d
    Leander s/o Samuel & Lucy d 13 Mar 1826 ae 10m 17d
FAIRBANK, Artemas d 15 Dec 1836 ae 44y
    Clarissa d 29 Aug 1867 ae 72y
KNIGHT, Emily T d 18 Mar 1889 ae 73y
    Elijah Jr d 31 Jul 1868 ae 63y 5m


ROW 13


HOLMES, Thomas d 3 Aug 1848 ae 59y 8m
HOLMES, Sally w/o Thomas d 27 Aug 1857 ae 72y
    Thomas II s/o Thomas & Sally d 30 Jul 1818 ae 2y 8m
    Mary Jane d/o Thomas & Sally d 7 Nov 1837 ae 10y
DAVIS, Hannah w/o Charles d 2 Apr 1862 ae 81y
BRUCE, Ira 1814 - 1881
    Phebe Sawin w/o Ira 1813 - 1877
    Ellen P d/o Ira & Phebe 1840 - 1861
    Myron Ira s/o Ira & Phebe 1844 - 1845
    John 1781 - 1865
    Prudence Priest w/o John 1785 - 1854
HARRIS, Thomas H 1825 - 1906
    Phebe S w/o Thomas 1828 - 1924
    Ruth E d/o Thomas & Phebe 1847 - 1848
    Waty H s/o Thomas & Phebe 1849 - 1852
MOORE, William s/o William & Mary Ann
    Mary Ann w/o J David d 1 Jul 1847 ae 18y


ROW 14


BAKER, Caleb S s/o Bezaled & Mary d 12 Nov 1840 ae 9d
HAPGOOD, Joseph d 24 Nov 1861 ae 77y
    Susanah w/o Joseph d 1 Apr 1860 ae 75y
MOSHER, Ann w/o Isaac d 8 Mar 1857 ae 31y
HOWE, George A s/o Charles & Clorina d 26 Apr 1819 ae 2y 1m


ROW 15


LEWIS, Fred A 1865 - ?
    S Annie w/o Fred 1869 - 1940
MORSE, John G 1789 - ?
    Amay w/o John d 3 Jun 1848 ae 62y
FISHER, Alpheus d 21 Oct 1851 ae 66y 11m
    Sylvia w/o Alpheus d 25 Jul 1877 ae 92y 7m 29d
PAINE, Ebenezer d 27 Aug 1847 ae 70y
    Lydia w/o Ebenezer d 25 Feb 1825 ae 49y
    Cynthia w/o Ebenezer d 13 Jun 1849 ae 64y 11m

Susannah d/o E & L d 24 Mar 1813 ae 9y 9m
---- inf/s d 13 Jun 1813 ae 1d
Ebenezer s/o E & L d 15 Aug 1813 ae 4y 11m 11d
Richard Ivory 1907 - 1923
BOLTON, Henry E d 29 Oct 1880 ae 44y 6m 2d GAR marker
PRESCOTT, William M 1821 - 1900
   Patience C w/o William 1830 - 1915
   Albert 1857 - 1914
   Alfred C 1869 - 1939
   Clarence E 1850 - 1850
   Amanda 1851 - 1872
   Levi 1855 - 1856
   Henry 1860 - 1860
   Anna 1864 - 1864
PRATT, Charles L 1797 - 1871
   Nancy Stratton w/o Charles 1802 - 1892
   Stephen S d 6 Dec 1849 ae 23y 9m
   Charles W s/o Stephen d 4 Aug 1848 ae 1y
   George D d 2 Mar 1875 ae 58y
   Sarah B w/o George d 21 Jun 1894 ae 74y
BOND, Isaac d 19 Jan 1859 ae 65y
   Hannah H d 13 Jun 1885 ae 80y
   Albert A s/o Isaac & Hannah d 11 Aug 1850 ae 17y 4m
   Andrew S d 26 Aug 1898 ae 63y 2m 3d GAR marker
   Francis L Barker w/o Andrew d 30 Mar 1867 ae 43y
   Annie M d/o A S & F L d 29 Dcc 1900 ae 45y


ROW 16
SHEPARD, George T 1848 - 1931
   Mary J Patt w/o George 1852 - 1947
   G Bertram s/o George & Mary 1876 - 1953
   Mary A Moody w/o G Bertram 1876 - 1960
   Barbara d/o G B & M A 1919 - 1944
SMITH, John S d 19 Apr 1855 ae 81y 8m
   Martha w/o John d 10 Aug 1862 ae 84y 4m
   Fidelia d/o J & M d 14 Dec 1807 ae 1y 7m
   Stephen H s/o J & M d 20 Dec 1807 ae 3y 7m
   Sarah C d/o J & M d 28 Mar 1826 ae 2y 7d
   Betsey A d/o J & M d 12 Feb 1848 ae 25y 7m
   Ermina d/o J & M d 3 Sep 1855 ae 36y 6m
   Lucy Hastings d/o J & M d 30 Aug 1884 ae 70y 11m
   Fidelia d/o J & M d 10 Oct 1897 ae 89y 1m
BASSETT, Oliver C 1808 - 1891
   Louisa S 1811 - 1902
   George O 1838 - 1911
CUNLIFFE, John 1830 - ?
   Margaret w/o John 1836 - 1885
   Elizabeth M d/o J & M 1861 - 1896
   Cora B d/o J & M 1867 - 1902
---- Keziah w/o ---- ae 77y
MCINTIRE, Seth d 16 Mar 1857 ae 77y

TOOMBS, Daniel d 5 Jun 1839 ae 24y
HASTINGS, Francis A s/o Lewis & Margaret d 9 Aug 1848 ae 2y 7m
ILLEGIBLE MARKER
HEALY, Herbert H s/o George & ---- d 18 Oct 1838 ae 4y 6d
---- Jonas R s/o George & Mary ---- d 12 Jan ----
---- Lauraette d/o ---- d 10 Jun 1817 ae 17d
PARKER, Joel 1807 - 1880
   Obra w/o Joel 1809 - 1893


ROW 17


HOWE, LaForest D 1862 - 1948
   Carrie w/o LaForest 1863 - 1933
HOWE, Harry R s/o L & C 1888 - 1927  Capt QM Corps USA
   Robert M s/o Harry b&d 1927
   George B d 21 May 1876 ae 69y
   George C d 1 Nov 1887 ae 47y 6m 25d
   Nancy D w/o George C d 23 Nov 1879 ae 37y 4m 12d
   Amanda Hinds w/o George C d 7 Dec 1883 ae 85y
   Hanson s/o George d 8 Nov 1844 ae 2y 9m 24d
   Amanda J d/o George & Amanda d 30 Jan 1852 ae 15y 7m 13d
NEWTON, Alice G Howe w/o Tracy d 31 Oct 1893 ae 21y 5m 6d
HINDS, Jacob d 28 Oct 1852 ae 85y
   Cicero d 8 May 1856 ae 57y 7m
CHASE, Elwin I 1854 - 1930
   I Adelia Foster w/o Elwin 1854 - 1906
CONKLIN, Frances A 1889 - 1941
WHITAKER, O Elizabeth w/o Isaac d 24 Jul 1854 ae 27y 28d
   Mauris H s/o Isaac & O E d 24 Mar 1854 ae 3y 6m 19d
HENRY, Anna d/o John & Ruth d 15 Mar 1842 ae 12y 7m 16d
JEWETT, Hervey S d 11 Nov 1832 ae 56y 3m 24d
   Sally w/o Hervey
   Charles H s/o Hervey & Sally d 1 Nov 1852 ae 2m 13d
BALHELDER, A B 36 Mass Inf
CURRIER, Eunice A w/o John W d 30 Apr 1882 ae 36y
BIGELOW, Joseph d -- Jul 1885 ae 86y 6m
   Betsey w/o Joseph d 14 Nov 1857 ae 58y 10m
   Elizabeth F w/o Joseph d 5 Feb 1869 ae 56y
   Charles F 1840 - 1864 24th Reg Mass Vol
   Angeline A d/o Otis & Millia d 7 Feb 1851 ae 19d
   Elmira M d/o Otis & Millia d 8 Feb 1852 ae 6w
KILGOUR, John R s/o Wm & Margaret d 10 Jan 1862 ae 1y 10m
REID, Thomas d 4 Jan 1885 ae 83y 2m
   Magdalena w/o Thomas d 1 May 1851 ae 57y 10m
   Mary w/o Thomas d 20 Aug 1856 ae 51y


ROW 18

KERSHAW, James H 1852 - 1920
   Sarah Dawson 1849 - 1911
DAWSON, Martha 1821 - 1896

HELLEWELL Harriet D 1844 - 1928
FRANCE, William 1842 - 1926
   Betty w/o William 1841 - 1901
MERRILL, Charles S 1867 - 1937
   Martha F w/o Charles 1874 - 1958
   Ralph D 1906 - 1908
BEACH, William 1844 - 1930
   Abbie J w/o William 1848 - 1931
   Harry W 1878 - 1969
   Agnes K w/o Harry 1871 - 1940
BEACH, Gertrude 1916 - 1917
ADAMS, Andrew W 1864 - 1929
   Edith L w/o Andrew 1870 - 1957
KELLOGG, Annette 1869 - 1952
ROBBINS, James W 1852 - 1921
   Emma E Mansfield w/o James 1857 - 1919
   Roy P 1894 - 1895
   Blanche M 1889 - 1957
   May E 1883 - 1963
   Walter 1881 - 1966
   Hattie L Goodale w/o Walter 1883 - 1963
AUSTIN, Malcolm W 1911 - 1985
   Adele R 1914 - ?
LUNDGREN, Per A 1853 - 1921
   Anna A w/o Per 1852 - 1921
   Charles A 1874 - 1925
LUNDQUIST, Anna K 1825 - 1892
SHARRON, David Stephen 1968 - 1969
JOHNSON, Charles F 1894 - 1969
   Madelyne 1897 - 1967
CHRISTIANSEN, Fred 1893 - 1942 Sgt 4 Co 151 Dep Brig W W I
   Dorothy B 1899 - 1938
BLACKWELL, William 1850 - 1951
   F Elizabeth 1891 - 1974
WHITMORE, Sadie May 1866 - 1940


ROW 19


WALKER, Joel 1798 - 1896
   Deidamia Stone w/o Joel 1795 - 1878
   Raymond J 1834 - 1914
   Roxanna Miriam w/o Raymond 1836 - 1912
   Willie R s/o R J & R d 3 Apr 1863 ae 3w 3d
   Josie L d/o R J & R d 2 Jan 1866 ae 1y 1m 5d
HURD, Louisa Walker w/o H G d 9 Jan 1889
PRESCOTT, Frank Nelson 1866 - 1902
   Angie F Sawyer w/o Frank 1871 - 1943
LUCE, Francis N 1895 - 1977  Maj US Army W W I & II
   Mildred F Prescott w/o Francis 1894 - 1957
   Winnie E Spidle w/o Francis 1909 -
BUCK, George B 1826 - 1914

Lucy Allen w/o George 1840 – 1907
Mary Elizabeth 1865 – 1896
Ella Augusta 1862 – 1953
PICKERING, James H 1872 – 1962
Ruth Buck 1867 – 1957


ROW 20

TROW, Frank Hamant 1871 – 1944
Sadie L Sawyer w/o Frank 1875 – 1951
JEWELL, Emma M 1843 – 1901
Susie E 1867 – 1941
FISHER, Frank E 1854 – 1932
Adam w/o Frank 1861 – 1893
Bernice E w/o Frank 1874 – 1926
Zeta Bell d/o Frank & Bernice b&d 1907
Jeremiah 1831 – 1913
Harriet F w/o Jeremiah 1831 – 1913
Susie G d/o J & H 1861 – 1907
Herbert J 1853 –
Ada E Wilcox w/o Herbert 1857 – 1914
SEELEY, John F 1868 – 1943
Mabel E Fisher w/o John 1870 – 1938
OVENDEN, William G 1856 – 1921
Ella M w/o William 1860 – 1932
Louie Felton 1885 – 1887
Grace Marion b&d 1893
WHITMORE, George E 1862 – 1918
HOWE, William Waldo 1865 – 1950
Nellie Fillebrawer 1866 – 1893
Emily Consitt 1864 – 1964
Wilfred Consitt 1899 – 1986
Dorothee Giddens 1904 –
CUTLER, E P C 1887 – 1968 (footstone #1)
M P C 1863 – 1946 (footstone #2)
E W C 1866 – 1919 (footstone #3)
BURATH, Eduardo d 9 Feb 1923 ae 1y 11m
Binito 1888 – 1923
FALLAVOLLITA, Angelina 1890 – 1947
Mildred 1927 – 1928
MASCITTI, Anna b&d 1927
Mary b&d 1928


+ + + + + +

REAR OF CHAPEL

ROW 1

CAMPBELL, Mary J d 25 Jun 1892 ae 65y
MAGUE, Thomas 1813 – 1899

Laura A Campbell w/o Thomas 1818 – 1897
Henry T s/o Thomas & Laura d 21 May 1882 ae 35y 9m 24d
Laura Estella 1851 – 1912
Edwin G 1854 – 1918
Nellie Morin w/o Edwin G 1870 – 1947
PRESCOTT, Thomas H 1831 – 1884 GAR
Eunice w/o Thomas 1844 – 1891
––––, Lucius S 1880 – 1944
––––, Rena C 1882 – 1966
CHEEVER, Herbert M 1880 – 1960 11th US Inf


ROW 2

HARRIS, Charles Morris 1851 – 1892
Ella Jeanette w/o Charles
Florence May d/o Charles & Jeanette 1880 – 1881
Clara Augusta 1852 – 1934
George L 1879 – 1949
LANDY, Clarence E 1896 – 1936 AS USNRF
G Ethel w/o Clarence 1896 –
Charles C 1859 – 1923
D M w/o Charles 1865 –
Ralph E s/o C C & D M d 16 Oct 1900 ae 1y 3m 25d
HALL, Stephen C 1843 – 1903 Co D 25 Mass Vols
Laura A Putnam w/o Stephen 1848 – 1917
Robert T 1875 – 1915
Charles C 1878 – 1959
Gertrude R 1885 – 1919
Stanley S 1907 – 1962
Arthur C 1873 – 1948
Lena R Hirtle w/o Arthur 1877 – 1960
Ralph M 1905 – 1967
Mary McDonald w/o Ralph 1906 –
Harold C 1914 –
Julie L Hilbert w/o Harold 1918 –
Madelyn b&d 1916
Jason Hirtle b&d 1912
Arthur Carroll 1899 – 1911


ROW 3

BATHRICK, Thomas K
Dorothy Phelps w/o Thomas
BEANE, Augustus W
Amelia Bathrick w/o Augustus
Charles H
William A 1876 – 1963
DAVIS, Ida M F
RHODES, Gerald M
Bertha J Beane w/o Gerald
BUTLER, Winsor T 1847 – 1918

Mary F Pearson w/o Winsor 1848 - 1945
Mable E 1874 - 1955
Charles Merrick 1884 - 1894
LADD, George H 1832 - 1900 Corp Co F 42 Mass Vols
Mary M 1833 - 1930
Alfred W 1860 - 1926
Henry C 1864 - 1925
Gertrude w/o Henry 1871 - 1926
PEIRCE, Ezekiel d 13 Aug 1865 ae 77y
Ruth P d 10 Sep 1869 ae 77y
Estes d 18 Mar 1889 ae 77y
Catherine Loring w/o Estes d 16 May 18-- ae 84y
Henry 1826 - 1899
Theresa M Adams w/o Henry d 10 Jan 1867 ae 38y
Caroline E Holt w/o Henry 1846 - 1912
Flora M 1864 - 1936
H Dillon s/o Henry & Theresa d 5 Sep 1852 ae 5m 12d
HOWE, George Francis 1825 - 1899
Julia Ann Child w/o George 1825 - 1892
HOLT, Henry Keyes d 8 Sep 1828 ae 40y 2m 6d
Lydia Fairbank w/o Henry d 23 Feb 1875 ae 86y 5m 4d
Lucius K 1822 - 1894
Rebeccah w/o Lucius 1820 - 1888
Lucius Milton s/o L K & R M d ae 3y 3m
Henry K s/o L K & R M d ae 7y 5m
Henry F d 23 Dec 1882 ae 66y 28d
Martha L Wood w/o Henry d 9 May 1903 ae 83y 26d
John Milton s/o H F & M L d 30 Jan 1879 ae 2y 4m
HOBBS, William H 1841 - 1915  Co C 6th Mass Vol
Martha L Holt w/o William 1846 - 1906
Katharine 1871 - 1943
LOVELL, Harrison (broken marker)
Patty w/o Harrison d 18 Jan 1841 ae 32y
Martha E d/o Harrison & Patty d 15 Jul 1860 ae 20y 7m 11d
Helen Elizabeth d/o Harrison & Patty d 20 Nov 1838 ae 1y 26d
Ahline d/o Harrison & Pedia d 8 Sep 1844 ae 11m
Lucy A d/o Harrison & Pedia d 13 Jul 1847 ae 22m 13d
Clara I d/o Harrison & Pedia d 19 Jun 1851 ae 10m 3d
Ella J d/o Harrison & Pedia d 11 May 1854 ae 6y 5m 11d
David d 30 Jan 1863 ae 76y 2m 2d
Susan Bigelow w/o David d 4 Dec 1849 ae 61y 8m
Mary B d 10 Jan 1904 ae 80y 4m 25d
Alice O d 29 Mar 1860 ae 11m
Louisa A d 22 Sep 1870 ae 14y 6d
Albert d 27 Jan 1915 ae 86y 11m 13d
Susan C Stowe w/o Albert d 26 Apr 1909 ae 84y 10m 2d
Levi B d 13 Mar 1877 ae 66y 7m 15d
Mary w/o L B d 21 May 1863 ae 52y 2m 10d
Levi B Jr d 19 Jul 1848 ae 14y 10m 3d
ALMSTROM, Howard E 1918 -
Doris H Goodale 1915 - 1948

FAIRBANKS, Washington 1815 - 1891
  Sophia E Harris w/o Washington 1817 - 1893
  Sabelle K d/o W & S E 1845 - 1845
  George W s/o W & S E 1847 - 1849
  Wilson H s/o W & S E 1850 - 1878
  Edwin C 1852 - 1929
  Lelia W Lovell w/o Edwin 1859 - 1940
DOLBEARE, Florence E Fairbanks 1883 - 1959
SCARLETT, Andrew J 1849 - 1935
  Clara B 1858 - 1930
  W Clifford 1880 - 1910
  Clarence B 1901 - 1902


ROW 4


PIERCE, Albert B 1848 - 1932
  Mary A Whiteside 1852 - 1910
WHITESIDE, Robert 1827 - 1899  Co E 42 Mass Vols
  Mary Nuttle w/o Robert 1829 - 1903
PEIRCE, James E 1834 - 1903  Masonic emblem
  Eliza Lovell w/o James 1866 - 1888
  William O 1864 - 1928
  Carrie L Stratton w/o William 1877 - 1957
GLOVER, Mary L Peirce 1862 - 1920
JOHNSON, Marcia E w/o Rollin d 10 May 1887 ae 35y 3m
POTTER, Charles 1866 - 1955
  Alice B 1872 - 1927
BROWN, Norman G 1892 - 1962  Masonic emblem
  Helen E w/o Norman 1893 -
HERMAN, Charles H 1817 - 1888
  Elizabeth 1819 - 1898
WALKER, Maida


RIGHT OF MAIN ENTRANCE SECTION 1


COWEE, Edward Arron 1857 - 1912
  Hattie L Cutler w/o Edward 1860 - 1930
  Howard W 1884 - 1966
  Elsie Kirschner w/o Howard 1879 - 1957
WOOD, Franklin 1911 -
  Barbara Cowee w/o Franklin 1918 - 1970
CUTLER, Oliver Blake 1827 - 1894
  Harriet Rebecca Cutting w/o Oliver 1831 - 1918
KIRSCHNER, Lydia L 1879 - 1957
MERRIFIELD, Charles E 1852 - 1915
  Abbie F w/o Charles 1855 - 1928
  Emily P d 17 Jul 1893 ae 79y
  Charles d 23 Nov 1888 ae 77y
HARRINGTON, James 1842 - 1927
  Josephine Merrifield w/o James 1844 - 1919
  Charles s/o James & Josephine d 11 Aug 1874 ae 8w

SMITH, Jarvis d 8 Nov 1891 ae 79y 8m 4d
   Susan M w/o Jarvis d 24 May 1898 ae 78y 1m 1d
   Hanson d 9 Feb 1851 ae 4m 13d
   Carrie 1846 - 1888
   Albert 1879 - 1949
   Alice M Keefe w/o Albert 1881 - 1970
ALLEN, Florence Smith w/o Leo J d 19 Mar 1957
WINTER, Aaron E 1804 - 1886
   Eliza Pierce w/o Aaron 1808 - 1830
   Dorina Dinsmore w/o Aaron 1811 - 1898
   Willie H s/o A E & D D 1846 - 1847
   Herbie A s/o A E & D D 1851 - 1853
   Carrie E d/o A E & D D 1854 - 1858
JACKSON, Henry
   Eugenia F w/o Henry
   Henry W s/o Henry & Eugenia 1874 - 1955
BUSHONG, J Chester 1870 - 1936
   Kathryn P 1878 - 1965


## SECTION 2 - REAR OF OLGC CHURCH

RICE, Francis H 1849 - 1916
   Addie H 1853 - 1918
HILDRETH, George F 1838 - 1914
   Mary Cowee w/o George 1839 - 1923
MUZZY, Cephas d 11 Dec 1861 ae 76y 2m 13d
   Miriam M N w/o Cephas d 6 Nov 1871 ae 43y 10d
   Nancy C d 15 Jun 1855 ae 62y 11m
   John s/o Aaron G d 5 Dec 1854 ae 18y 11m 5d
   Lucy M d/o Aaron G d 23 May 1855 ae 22y 6m 15d
CLEVELAND, Charles M d 23 Feb 1866 ae 41y 5m 8d
   Nancy Muzzy w/o Charles 1823- 1899
   Hattie M d/o C M & M J d 2 Dec 1874 ae 21y 1m 24d
   J Milton s/o C M & M J d 23 Aug 1849 ae 2y 7m
   Lotan d 1875 ae 78y 10m 8d
   Hannah d 17 Oct 1840 ae 35y 28d
   Mary A d 10 Nov 1860 ae 12y
   Elizabeth M d -- Aug ---- ae 43y
PHELPS, John d 30 Mar 1859 ae 48y 9m
   Angeline P d/o John & S A d 20 Mar 1857 ae 19y 4m
   Ellen L d/o John & S A d 13 Nov 1863 ae 17y 7m
DAVIS, E Carrie d 25 Jul 1893 ae 50y 11m
LAMSON, D L 1806 - 1866
   Mary Smith w/o D L 1806 - 1880
   Madeline M 1846 - 1886
HOLT, Stephen 1820 - 1887
   Mary M w/o Stephen d 23 Mar 1883 ae 59y 11m 4d
   Sarah A 1828 - 1915
LOVELL, Ephraim 1811 - 1869
LOVELL, Dorothy C w/o Ephraim 1808 - 1893
   Lucy 1811 - 1814

Amos 1841 – 1853
Susan A 1848 – 1865
Freeman 1843 – 1868
E Lester 1850 – 1904
Augustus 1846 – 1921
Nellie M w/o Augustus 1860 – 1956
Addison 1809 – 1888
Jane M Greenwood w/o Addison 1813 – 1892
Alfred s/o Addison & Jane 1851 – 1939
Angeline Warner w/o Alfred 1856 – 1947
BOLSTER, Clarence W 1869 – 1945
Bertha Mabel Smith w/o Clarence 1884 – 1960
GREEN, Rose J Lovell w/o Geo S 1845 – 1874
WALKER, Ruth E 1884 – 1949
Ernest s/o Erastus & Fanny Lovell 1881 – 1881
GOODALE, Aaron d 25 Apr 1898 ae 75y 2m 24d
Elizabeth w/o Aaron d 23 Aug 1891 ae 65y 11m 12d
Lucretia d/o Aaron & Elizabeth d 14 Nov 1847 ae 2y 9m 28d
Caroline E d/o A & E d 27 May 1859 ae 1m 20d
Caroline Jane d/o A & E d 27 Jul 1889 ae 25y 4m 12d
Aaron d 17 Aug 1911 ae 69y 8m 17d
Nellie G Merriam w/o Aaron d 20 Jun 1936 ae 82y 2m 26d
Aaron 1889 – 1978
Annie B Converse w/o Aaron d 3 Sep 1917 ae 28y 10m 28d
Velma G Smith w/o Aaron 1893 – 1980
Charles d 16 Apr 1883 ae 75y
Sarah Burdett w/o Charles d 13 Aug 1888 ae 82y
Angeline A d/o Charles & Sarah d 30 Aug 1850 ae 19y
WARNER, Mandana G d/o C & S Goodale d 23 May 1877 ae 41y
Etta J Rice w/o Charles S d 18 Oct 1899 ae 39y
NEWTON, Agnes w/o Silas d 17 Jan 1878 ae 36y
Philip inf/s/o Silas & Agnes d 15 Aug 1875


## SECTION 1A – ALONG BROW OF HILL

BULLARD, Charles P 1829 – 1913
Abigail w/o Charles 1833 – 1916
Lillian A d/o Charles & Abigail 1868 – 1869
Frank G s/o Charles & Abigail 1861 – 1902
CARPENTER, Dennis 1853 –
Fannie E w/o Dennis 1854 – 1913
GAMMELL, Warren E 1831 – 1918
Elmina S Barrus w/o Warren 1837 – 1908
SHAW, Caroline A d 6 Nov 1877
LANDY, James d 26 Aug 1890 ae 62y 3m 24d
Alvah d 17 Feb 1905 ae 32y 10m 27d
LANDY, Flora E d/o J & J E d 11 Apr 1885 ae 21y 5m 3d
George M s/o J & J E d 19 Mar 1878 ae 6y 7m 14d
ALLEN, Alma G d/o A W & G R 1878 – 1878
Frank L s/o A W & G R 1881 – 1882
Etta M d/o A W & G R 1879 – 1885

228

PRESCOTT, Chas K   Co 1 42 Mass Inf GAR marker
LUCE, Francis N 1835 - 1879
    Mehitable Allen w/o Francis 1836 - 1900
    Charles F 1858 - 1930
    Iva M Eagles 1874 - 1954
    William D 1866 - 1931
    Cecelia W w/o William 1866 - 1961
KAVEN, James M 1820 - 1914
    Harriet Barnfield w/o James 1831 - 1921
    Moses B 1864 - 1937
    Helen M Kidder w/o Moses 1857 - 1935
BAKER, John E 1874 - 1915
    Martha E 1845 - 1929
HADLEY, Charles W 1862 - 1932
    Allie E w/o Charles 1875 - 1954

SECTION 3 - RIGHT OF OLGC RECTORY DRIVE

HOWE, Milton K 1827 - 1907
    Mary L w/o Milton d 30 Sep 1862 ae 28y 7m 6d
    Sarah A w/o Milton 1839 - 1908
    Walter A s/o Milton & Mary d 6 Apr 1863 ae 4y 5m
    Mamie L d/o Milton & Sarah d 6 Sep 1869 ae 10m 10d
    Edgar P 1855 - 1908
WALKER, Eli d 9 Jun 1886 ae 84y 6m
    Louisa Parker w/o Eli d 24 Feb 1884 ae 77y 2m 11d
    Melville s/o Edgar d 21 Mar 1829 ae 3m 7d
    Harriot S d 18 Jan 1850 ae 18y
BALL, Fordice B d 7 Feb 1855 ae 22y 6m
    Eliza w/o Jonas d 1 Oct 1854 ae 44y 4m
----, Illegible marker of GAR Vet
GRAVELINE, George A 1883 - 1970
    Permelia V 1883 - 1979
ALGER, Martha A w/o Amasa d 16 Jan 1855 ae 23y
    Maria w/o Amasa d 31 Oct 1864 ae 32y
    Carrie Lucia d/o Amasa & Maria d 4 Sep 1863 ae 4m 7d
LARSON, Hilmar C 1910 -
    Florence M Kelly w/o Hilmar 1913 - 1965
CIOCIOLO, Antonio 1895 - 1976
    Antoinette 1903 -
    Matthew G 1925 - 1960  Mass AMM3 USNR WW II
BRIGHAM, Chester I 1876 - 1937
    Mary E McQuillan 1880 - 1969
BRIGHAM, Lillian E d/o Chester & Mary 1915 -
LEONE, Angelo J 1910 - 1979  PFC U S Army WW II
    Mary C 1909 -
PIERCE, Ezra B d 16 Dec 1884 ae 78y
    Mary w/o Ezra d 20 Jul 1901 ae 81y
    Marion
    Mary
HENNESSEY, Abraham T 1849 - 1922

DAMON, Frank E 1845 – 1894
   Angie M Goodrich w/o Frank 1854 – 1936
   Everett E 1874 – 1922
   Emma Jane 1878 – 1879
LANE, Edward F 1859 – 1926
GOODRICH, Oney B 1850 – 1950
   Ida M w/o Oney 1861 – 1936
HARRIS, Whipple B 1832 – 1920
   Melissa J w/o Whipple 1831 – 1901
   David W 1851 – 1865
   Lillian I 1863 – 1865
PARKER, Harry B 1856 – 1893
   Whipple H 1891 – 1918  Lt Co C 316 Inf d in France
   Louise Dent w/o Whipple 1893 – 1918
WALKER, David 1805 – 1840
   Bathsheba Chase w/o David 1811 – 1899
   Harris d 10 Feb 1888
PEDINI, Victor 1904 – 1965  American Legion marker
KENNEDY, William R 1901 – 1967
   Cecelia 1903 –

Inscriptions read by:   Shirley Cameron, Doris Chartier, Laura Drown, Alva Erickson, Constance Esonis, Margaret Hennessey, Grace Klar, Pauline McCarthy, Dorothy Meanor, Doris Nutter, Doris Shepard, Marjorie Smith, Gwendolyn Soule, Elsie Swenson, Mary Urquhart, Edgar Whitcomb.

# MAIN STREET CEMETERY, HUDSON

Hudson was formerly part of Marlborough and was called New City from 1800-1828; it was called Feltonville from 1828-1866, when it was incorporated and then renamed Hudson for Charles Hudson, who gave twenty-five years of public service and had a career as a minister and author.

At their March 1825 annual meeting, the Town of Marlborough voted to purchase one acre of land for a cemetery from Benjamin Priest for fifteen dollars. This lot was "on the northerly side of a county road leading from the town of Berlin towards Boston," deeded May 21, 1825.

During the next fifty-seven years, parcels of land were added, completing the present 4 1/2 acres.

     1863 -- 27 rods purchased by the town of Marlborough
     1865 -- 2 56/100 acres bought
     1866 -- 4 more rods
     1870 -- unspecified amount deeded
     1882 -- 16 1/2 rods deeded

The deterioration of gravestones and burial grounds is becoming very serious. Weathering, sulphur pollution, acid rain, poor maintenance, and vandalism all contribute to their decay.

Alfred M. Braga, chairman of the Hudson Historical Commission in 1982, contacted the Cemetery Commissioners and the Public Works Department and found that they did not have the names of lot owners on the existing plot plan of the oldest section of the Main Street Cemetery, dating from 1825--the southeast corner.

In 1982-3, members of the Hudson Historical Commission--Richard McQuiggan; John Gillis; and Alfred Braga, chairman, researched this material from the tombstones in order that a permanent record might be made for future reference. Mr. Braga's wife, Eloise, and two grandsons, Christopher and Daniel Marques, also assisted in this inventory.

The following five persons were the first to be buried in the Main Street Cemetery:

     George Goodnow s/o Silas d 11 May 1826 ae 4y
     George Stratton s/o Daniel d 18 Oct 1826 ae 4y
     Sally w/o Silas Goodnow m/o George d 9 July 1827 ae 27y
     George Pope d 8 Feb 1828

Sarah Wilkins w/o Edward Wilkins d 17 Jan 1829 ae 72y

## THE FALLEN COMRADES

Following is a limited roster of Comrades of the Army and Navy
buried in Hudson, or who having enlisted in the Feltonville quota are
buried elsewhere: Main Street Cemetery

(May 31, 1884 *Hudson Pioneer*)

Joseph Francis, enlisted Aug. 17, 1861, private in Co. A.,
    1st Mass. Infy; killed in action at Williamsburg, May 5, 1862.
Eugene Smith, enlisted Dec. 12, 1863, private Co. K., 1st
    Heavy Artillery. Discharged on account of disability;
    died Mar. 30, 1862 of consumption.
H. H. Brown, enlisted May 23, 1861, private Co. B. 1st
    Mass. Infy. Died in Hudson of wounds.
A. A. Powers, commissioned Sept. 10, 1862, 1st Lieutenant,
    Co. I. 5th Mass. Infy. Discharged as Capt. May 16,
    1864; died May 8, 1873.
Isaac Stratton, enlisted Sept. 1862, private Co. I. 5th
    Infy. Discharged May 16, 1864.
Geo. E. Hartwell, enlisted July 16, 1861 as private, Co. F.,
    13th Mass. Infy. Discharged for disability July 18, 1862.
W. W. Claflin, commissioned Asst. Surgeon, 13th Mass. Infy.
    April 29, 1862. Resigned Dec. 1, 1862.
C. S. Bennett, enlisted private, July 16, 1861, Co. F. 13th
    Infy. Discharged for disability July 25, 1862.
James Gibson, enlisted July 16, 1861, was made Sergt.
    Co. F., 13th Mass. and discharged July 30, 1865 as
    1st Lieut., 57 Mass. Infy.
Abel H. Pope, commissioned 1st Lieut. Co. F., 13th Infy.
    July 16, 1861. Discharged as Capt. Aug. 3, 1863.
Gilbert Robinson, enlisted July 16, 1861 private Co. B.,
    13th Infy. Discharged Aug. 1, 1864.
Eugene A. Holyoke, enlisted July 16, 1861, private Co. I.
    13th Infy., in June 1864, wounded in leg at Petersburg.
    Discharged Nov 17, 1864, died Sept. 4. 1873.
Chas Allen, record unknown.
W. F. Brigham, commissioned Capt. Co. L. 36th Infy. Aug. 22
    1862. Discharged for disability Jan. 20, 1865. Died in
    hospital Annapolis, Md. Feb. 6, 1865.
George A. Nourse, enlisted Aug. 22, 1863, private Co. I.
    36th Infy., killed in action 1864.
Ephraim W. Hunt, enlisted April 2, 1864, private Co. I. 59th
    Infy. Discharged July 30, 1865.

PRIEST, Grace E Manson d/o F & J Manson b 18 Sept 1860
  d 1 Dec 1881 ae 21
  Silas b 29 June 1800 d 30 Mar 1886 Lot 108
  Sarah w/o Silas d 7 Mar 1857 ae 49
  Silas H s/o Silas & Sarah d 24 Mar 1852 ae 21
  ---- w/o Silas d 8 July 1875 ae 14y
POWERS, A A d 8 May 1873 ae 43 Lot 109   -- Maj
  Sarah A w/o Maj Powers 1832-1917
  Charles S s/o A A Powers ae 9y
  Edward L 1849-1920
  M Lizzie w/o Edward 1851-1937
RICE & LOCKE, Warren F 1830-1900  Lot 110
  Isabell w/o Warren 1839-1908
  Abigail C Woodard 1833-1910
  Frank D 1860-1934
  Carrie L w/o 1865-1949
  Jessie L 1890 1891
  Bessie M 1891-1905
  G F Rice d 17 Sept 1865 ae 46
  Lucilla w/o G F Rice d 6 Apr 1867 ae 44
  George Franklin s/o G F Rice d 5 Apr 1817 ae 2m
  Jabez Rice (father) d 23 Oct 1868 ae 82y
  Mother d 31 --- 18-- 59y
  Elizabeth d/o Jabez Rice d 26 --- 18-- ae 21y
  Abbie d -- --- ----
  Warren F d -- --- ----
  Isabell D d -- --- ----
  Abigail C -- --- ----
  Bessie M -- --- ----
  Frank d -- --- ----
  Jessie d/o F D Locke b 7 June 1890 d 20 Apr 1891
  Carrie d -- --- ----
BROOKS & HARRIMAN, James B Brooks b 12 Feb 1828
     d 27 May 1867 Lot 111
  Eliza A w/o James b 20 Aug 1831 d 26 Mar 1921
  James L Harriman MD b 11 May 1833 d 28 Dec 1905
  Mary w/o James b 8 Apr 1836 d 12 Sept 1890
  William Bradford Brooks b -- --- 1859 d -- --- 1938
  Caroline Ricard Brooks b -- --- 1863 d -- --- 1936
  Ricard Brooks b -- --- 1894 d -- --- 1954
  George Reardon b 12 May 1861 d 4 May 1924
  Blanche Harriman w/o George b 14 June 1867 d 23 Dec 1963
  Bertha Harriman d/o George b 4 July 1865 d -- Sept 1865
HAYWARD & COOLIDGE, Otis H Hayward d 19 Mar 1882 ae 90y
       Lot 112
  L--- w/o Otis d -- Sept 1870 ae 72y
  Otis F s/o Otis H d -- May 18--
  Maria d 26 Sept 1865
  Ada M Coolidge d -- --- ----
  Henry Coolidge d -- --- ----
  Anna w/o Henry d -- --- ----

FAIRBANKS, Silas d -- --- ----  Lot 113
   Mary P w/o Silas d -- --- ----
   Annie L d -- --- ----
   F W Ruggles d -- --- ----
   Jessie L w/o F W Ruggles d -- --- ----
   George P d -- --- ----
   Nellie w/o George d -- --- ----
   Bertie S d -- --- ----
   Freddie S d -- --- ----
   Nestor S d -- --- ----
   Susan R w/o Nestor d -- --- ----
   Alice L d -- --- ----
   Mary S d -- --- ----
   Charles C d -- --- ----
   Ida w/o Charles d -- --- ----
   Edith d -- --- ----
BRUCE & WITT, Edwind Bruce d -- --- ---- Lot 115
   Alice M Bruce d -- --- ----
   Mary M Bruce mother d -- --- ----
   Charles Allen d -- --- ----
HASTINGS, Charles d -- --- ---- Lot 116
   Ann w/o Charles d -- --- ----
WITT, Ebenezer d -- --- ---- Lot 117
   Adeline Bigelow w/o Ebenezer d -- --- ----
   Eliza A d/o Ebenezer d -- --- ----
MERRILL, George d -- --- ---- Lot 119
   Guy Merrill d -- --- ----
BURGESS, Charles H d -- --- ---- Lot 120
   John F d -- --- ----
   George E d -- --- ----
   Cora L d/o J J & Lea--- d 19 Sept 1866 ae 6w
HOUGHTON, Moses d 16 July 1866 ae 70y Lot 121
   Annah w/o Moses d 5 Apr 1868 ae 68y
   Nancy d/o Moses d 2 Oct 1838 ae 11y
HOUGHTON, Jonas T 1833-1900 Lot 122
   Lucinda H Ross w/o Jonas 1836-1866
   Willard 1828-1897
   Jane Wilkins w/o Willard 1828-1867
   Willie E 1858-1859
   Albert R 1862-1863
   Effie M 1856-1874
CLAFIN, William Webster MD 1833-1864 Lot 124
   Julia M 1839-1875
   Fred H 1860-1918
   Willie W 1862-1862
   Webster W 1887-1888
   Marjorie W 1890-1890
LAFOREST, Edward A d 23 Jan 1876 ae 72y Lot 125
   Adeline w/o Edward d 22 Apr 1860 ae 42y
AYER & HORTON, Harry W 1863-1911 Lot 126
   Levitta E w/o Harry d -- --- 1867

Lucetta b 21 Apr 1853 d 16 June 185–
Elvia A b 11 May 1838 d 9 July 1860
William Horton s/o W H Horton b 23 May 18--
    d -- --- ----
Joanna w/o William b 11 Dec 18-- d -- --- ----
WALCOTT, Freeman d 27 Mar 1881 Lot 127
    Lurena W w/o Freeman d 1 Mar 1887
    Clifford P 1850-1930
    Mary Alice w/o Clifford 1851-1942
    Ruth A 1884-1972
HAPGOOD, Ruben d 7 Aug 1890 ae 77y Lot 128
    Ruth G w/o Ruben d 16 May 1873 ae 51
    Elvira A d/o Ruben d 10 May 1883
    Edmund A s/o Ruben d 7 Apr 1855 ae 5m
RANDALL, Cyrus C d 13 May 1865 ae 33y Lot 129
    Eliza B w/o Cyrus d 16 Mar 1857 ae 22y
    Lilla Florence d/o Cyrus d 25 Oct 1857 ae 7m
    Sarah A w/o Cyrus d 5 Aug 1865 ae 25y
    Paul Randall d 6 July 1812 ae 57  -- Capt
    Betsy C w/o Paul d 28 Nov 1864 ae 77
STOWE, Edmund M b 23 Sept 1828 d 28 Sept 1905  Lot 130
    Henrietta G w/o Edmund b 23 Oct 1831 d 5 Mar 1899
    Herbert R d 24 Jan 1851 ae 1y
    Mary Ella d 27 July 1861 ae 1y
    Charlie E d 3 Aug 1864 ae 2y
    Clarence H d 16 Oct 1864 ae 2y
OSGOOD, Hannah 1781-1865  Lot 131
    Henry A 1811-1888
    Mary A 1810-1901
    John I Taylor 1816-1890
    Abigail R Taylor 1819-1888
    Abby M Taylor 1855-1855
    John I Taylor Jr 1859-1867
    George W Taylor 1850-1868
MAYNARD, Alvin L 1815-1900 Lot 132
    Mary A 1819-1852
    Mary B 1815-1865
    Mary M 1830-1916
BRIGHAM, Francis D d 7 Mar 1883 ae 74y  Lot 133
    Sarah P w/o Francis d -- --- ----
    Charles A s/o Francis d 5 Dec 1860 ae 23y
    George D s/o Francis d 19 Apr 1838 ae 8m
    Ella F d/o Francis d 10 July 1853 ae 20m
    George A s/o of Francis d 24 July 1834 22 m
    Charles D s/o of Francis d 14 Oct 1836 ae 16m
RANDALL, Charles C 1 Oct 1847-10 Feb 1906 Lot 134
    Henrietta C w/o Charles 17 July 1848-25 July 1950
    Jonathan 25 Oct 1817-6 Aug 1853
    Elizabeth R w/o Jonathan 1 Dec 1820-16 Sept 1897
    Harriet Brigham 3 Oct 1802-18 Sept 1890
BRODEUR, Mitchell 1843-1908 Lot 135

Emma J w/o Mitchell 1856-1923
Elizabeth I 1868-1947
Howard M 1897-1960
WHEELER, Caroline E d -- --- ---- Lot 137
VINAL, Charles T 1835-1927 Lot 138
Mary E w/o Charles 1840-1874
Harry 1874-1945
Alice M 1901-1931
Clarence C 1868-1946
Lurena W w/o Clarence 1871-1935
LORING, Thomas C d 22 Mar 1881 ae 56y  Lot 139
Thomas C s/o Thomas 4 June 1859-14 Apr 1896
Parker G W -- --- 1928
Phoebe Loring w/o of G W -- --- 1950
DARLING, Mary 2 July 1868 ae 87y Lot 140
Alvin Sawyer h/o Mary d 2 Oct 1868 ae 61
BRIGHAM, Francis 7 Dec 1880 ae 67y Lot 141  -- Capt
Persis E d 22 June 1886 ae 68y
William F b 9 Apr 1839 d 6 Feb 1865  -- Capt
Wilbur F b 9 Apr 1839 d 13 Nov 1901
William F -- --- ----
Sophia d 30 Aug 1815 ae 41y
Francis D s/o Francis d 20 Sept 1836 ae 10m
Emily M d 6 Dec 1855 ae 35y
---- s/o Francis d 7 Jan 1853 ae 4w
DAVIS, Fred Alton 1866-1928 Lot 142
Susan Campbell w/o Fred 1872-1958
Annie V Davis Woods -- --- 1897
Alton E 1902-1906
Paul Spencer 1898-1924
Charles Royal Woods 1878-1960
BEATON, Arline 1900-1900 Lot 143
John L B 1914-1915
COCHRAN, Maria S w/o Wm N 10 Sept 1841 18 Jan 1878
ae 36y Lot 148
JOHNSON, Dexter W 2 Jan 1878 ae 52y Lot 149
Susan J d/o Dexter d 12 Dec 1858 ae 3y
LAFOREST, Anna Bigham m/o Margaret LaForest 21 June 1858
Lot 150
Emily G Hallett d 18 Aug 1853 15y
Eliza w/o John LaForest d 24 Jan 1867 ae 72y
Margaret w/o John d 2 Oct 1844 ae 44y
Joseph Rena Aubin s/o John & Jan Laforest 19 Apr 1839
ae 4y
HOWE, Elsie w/o Dana Howe d 3 Mar 1890 Lot 151
Lucy w/o Dana d 25 Aug 1858 ae 47
Jabez M d 27 Mar 1875 ae 23y
TRULL, Fred F 1856-1925 Lot 152
Mary Adella w/o Fred 1855-1931
Mehitable C w/o John d 28 Mar 1880 ae 59y
John d 18 Mar 1887 ae 85y

Joel A d 17 Apr 1879 ae 38y
Edward B d 17 May 1916 ae 70y
HOLDEN, (TOMB) 1879 Lot 154
John C d 31 Jan 1899 ae 46y
Fran B d 5 Feb 1927 ae 79
G E C d 2 Jan 1911 ae 76
Ida B d 17 Feb 1929 ae 74y
Asa W  d 15 Jan 1879 ae 72
Carrie B d 17 Sept 1899 ae 51
Flora A M d 24 May 1885 ae 35y
Frances M d 11 Nov 1891 ae 53y
Lucy R C d 25 Mar 1904 ae 94y
Alice d 26 Jan 1879
Isabel A d 10 Feb 1933 ae 74
Blanche May Bell d -- --- 1878 ae 12
Sarah J R d 8 Apr 184- ae 15y
Frances A d 31 Jan 1845 ae 5y
Raymond C d 23 Sept 1902 ae 22y
BIGELOW, (TOMB) 1880  Lot 154
Warren H d 21 Feb 1950 ae 83
Adin D d 24 Dec 1868 ae 4m
H Bigelow d -- --- ----
M Lizzie 29 July 1886 ae 28
Elizabeth L 6 Sept 1891 ae 66y
Henry d 12 Sept 1891 ae 77y
COX, Rufus d 20 Nov 1860 ae 37  Lot 155
Louisa D d/o Loring & Alina d 1 June 1833 ae 7y
Edwin s/o Loring & Alma d 16 Nov 1844 ae 13y
COX, Rufus d 28 Apr 1856 ae 61 Lot 156
Rufus Jr d 29 Nov 1826 ae 1y
William d 19 Jan 1836 ae 6y
Elisha d -- --- 1851 ae 81y
Mary w/o Elisha d 4 Mar 1866 ae 94y
COX, ---- d -- --- ---- ae 5y Lot 157
COX, Willard d 19 June 1875 ae 79y Lot 158
Susan b 22 Apr 1802 d 18 July 1887
THOMAS, Children of George H & Laura C Thomas Lot 159
Gaira I d 17 Oct 1861 ae 9y
Alta F d 29 Oct 1861
BRUCE, Elmira w/o Walter d 24 Feb 1851 ae 34y  Lot 160
George W c/o Walter & Elmira d 20 Mar 1842 ae 13y
HAPGOOD, Silas d 18 Sept 1861 ae 42y Lot 162
Susan w/o Silas d 28 Aug 1832 ae 33y
William H s/o Silas d 8 Aug 1853 ae 1m
WALCOTT, Truman 14 July 1807–18 Aug 1884 Lot 163
Charlotte B w/o Truman 10 Jan 1812–23 Feb 1854
Aurelia M w/o Truman 10 June 1823–7 Sept 1888
Louise T d/o Truman 10 Mar 1846–31 Mar 1851
Henrietta N d/o Truman 13 Feb 1854–8 Sept 1855
Henry K s/o Truman 13 Feb 1854–3 Mar 1856
JONES, Levi d 15 Aug 1877 ae 66y Lot 164

Sally M w/o Levi 1814–1893
Lucy A d 24 June 1860 ae 16y
Mary E d/o Levi 19 Aug 1839 ae 3m
Hannah C 10 Sept 1871 ae 51y
HOWE, Willard 1820–1866 Lot 165
Almira w/o Willard 1823–1901
Edna J 1854–1917
RANDALL, Charles M 1823–1895 Lot 166
Mary E w/o Charles 1823–1917
Alla A d/o Charles d 28 Nov 1880 ae 28y
HASTINGS, John d 17 Mar 1831 ae 25 Lot 167
WILKINS, Edward d 17 May 1837 ae 80 Lot 168
Sarah w/o Edward d 17 Jan 1829 ae 72y
WOOD, Sopronia d/o Capt Jedediah & Betsy
    d 13 Aug 1829 ae 17 Lot 169
WOOD, Frederick A s/o Moses Wood d 17 May 1833 ae 11y
    Lot 171
MAYNARD, William G s/o Calvin & Judith d 30 Aug 1817
    ae 1y Lot 173
William G d 10 June 1833 ae 16y s/o Calvin
Calvin d 13 Mar 1834 ae 5y s/o Calvin
Calvin d 13 --- 1816 ae 53y
Judith W w/o Calvin d 25 May 1870 ae 76
FRYE, Kate d -- --- ---- Lot 174
Richard 28 July 1809–25 Oct 1879
Caroline 16 Dec 1814–13 Mar 1901
DUDLEY, Mary Ann d/o Isaac d 31 Aug 1834 ae 2y Lot 175
Susan M mother 1818–1881
PRENTICE Benjamin (slave) b 4 Feb 1760 d 20 Mar 1857
    ae 97y Lot 177
WILSON, ---- d -- --- ---- Lot 178
MURDOCK, Julia w/o Charles d 20 June 1873 ae 32y Lot 179
BEMIS, Ephraim S d 29 July 1870 ae 51y Lot 181
Lucy Ann w/o Ephraim d 17 July 1851 ae 30y
Catherine w/o Ephraim d 14 Aug 185- ae 29y
Addie Louisa d/o ES & C M d 6 Feb 1858 ae 2y
Addie Louisa d/o of ES & CM d 4 July 1867 ae 7m
Frank W d 8 May 1875 ae 21y
Charles E d 20 May 1881 ae 35y
M Melvin d 18 Oct 1891 ae 44y
Ellen R w/o M Melvin 1851–1944
WITT, George Dana 1826–1869 Lot 182
Ruth Ann w/o George 1825–1907
FILONDON Seabury T 1884–1924
FILONDON Gertrude W 1885–19--
WHITTEMORE Everard 1858–1937
WHITTEMORE Grace Witt 1861–1937
BADGER, Joseph Co D 1st Battn Mass HA Lot 183
COX, (TOMB) Elisha d 5 Mar 1855 ae 62y Lot 184
CROWL, Dolly w/o Joel d 25 July 1882 ae 75y Lot 185
CRANSTON, Joel Hon d 22 Oct 1835 ae 73 Lot 186

238

Lucretia w/o Joel d 20 July 1846 ae 81

PRIEST, Ann Jeanette d/o Benjamin d 1 July 1833 ae 6y
 Lot 187

 Elmira w/o Benjamin d 29 Mar 1868 ae 68y

 Benjamin d 23 June 1862 ae 64y

HAPGOOD, Phebe d/o Jonathan & Betsy Hapgood d 18 Sept
 1853 ae 30y Lot 187

 Jonathan d 13 Feb 1830 ae 43y

 Betsy w/o Jonathan d 13 Aug 1879 ae 90y

SMITH, Jedthuan d 2 Mar 1834 or 7 ae 60y Lot 188

 Christina w/o Jedthuan d 1 July 1853 ae 78y

 RUSSELL James s/o G Russell d 12 Aug 1871 ae 7m

WOLCOTT, Josiah d 18 Oct 1870 ae 70y Lot 189

 Betsy w/o Josiah d 23 June 1859 ae 69y

MORSE, Zerulah w/o Elijah d 29 July 1836 ae 81 Lot 191

 SMITH David d 23 Oct 1848 ae 70y

 Abigail w/o David d 4 Jan 1832 ae 54

 BRUCE Nathaniel d 6 July 1834 ae 82

 Mary w/o Nathaniel d 18 Oct 1829 ae 82y

 Moses d 16 Nov 1835 ae 55y

 Susannah w/o Moses d 14 Sept 1848 ae 72

HAPGOOD, Dea Jonathan d 12 Apr 1849 ae 90 Lot 193

 Jerusha w/o Jonathan d 2 Mar 1842 ae 80

 David s/o Moses & Sally Hapgood d 22 Jan 1835 ae 13m

 David 1 June 1788–13 Oct 1830

 Lydia 26 Mar 1768–22 Dec 1850

KEITH, Albion A 1850–1912 Lot 193A

VALENTINE, Bessie M w/o Albian 1856–1912

WILKINS, Edward d 21 Mar 1866 ae 72 Lot 194

 Mary w/o Edward d 18 May 1876 ae 73y

 Daniel d 26 Sept 1830 ae 1y

 Mary d 12 May 1833 ae 6y

 Caroline d 19 Aug 1833 ae 2y

 Emerson d 18 Sept 1810 ae 2y s/o Edward

 Edward d 12 Sept 1867 ae 25y

COOLIDGE, Helen M d/o Nathan & Helen d 24 Sept 1836
 ae 2y Lot 198

ANDREWS, Lucy w/o John d 21 Jan 1838 ae 26 Lot 200

COX, Lore d 4 July 1887 ae 72y Lot 204

 Mary A d 11 Sept 1899 ae 83y

 HOWE Jabez d 21 Apr 1851 ae 61y

 Roxanna w/o Jabez d 5 May 1851 ae 57y

 Sidney A d 15 Aug 1838 ae 21y

HOWE, Elijah 5 Aug 1826–3 Oct 1913 Lot 204

 Emeline L w/o Elijah 21 June 1831–16 Apr 1907

 Albert S s/o Elijah d 18 Oct 1878 ae 26y

 Alfred H 10 Dec 1859–3 Aug 1912

ROBINSON, Susan C w/o William d 9 June 1865 ae 20y Lot 205

BALL, Sophronia w/o Warren d 16 Feb 1846 ae 27y Lot 206

 Sydney A s/o Warren d 17 Dec 1845 ae 5m

WILSON, Hannah P d/o Daniel & Hannah d 6 Oct 1854

ae 28y Lot 207
MAYNARD, Abigail R w/o John C d 7 July 1862 ae 55y Lot 209
  John C d 4 Aug 1845 ae 43y
  Mariah N d/o John d 8 Sept 1841 ae 1y
  Corrinda A d/o John d 19 Apr 1843 ae 9m
BENNETT, Charles S 1830-1865 Lot 213
  Mary J w/o Charles 1837-1881
  Charles E 1860-1911
CHAROUX, Edward 1861-1894 Lot 215
  Alice 1863-1934
  DUPREE Jerrie 1869-1942
  Alice w/o Edward 1863-1934
  DUPREE Jerrie 1869-1942
  Lona M w/o Jerrie 1871-1965
  Lester Dupree 1893-----
  Mabel w/o Lester 1888-1976
  HAPGOOD Burt E 1874-1936
  Leona F 1877-1905
JONES, Frank 8 Apr 1830-4 Aug 1907 Lot 216
  Harriet A Vannevar 26 July 1833-30 June 1899
  Frank Elwyn 8 May 1855-28 Nov 1855
  Ethel Vannevar 16 Mar 1870- 8 Jan 1888
  Harry S 1852-1915
POPE, George s/o Stephen & Sally d 8 Feb 1828 ae ---11m
      Lot 217
BLANCHARD, Edward B 1845-1897 Lot 218
  Charlie 1882-1882
STRONG, Mary L Mother 1851-1927
  Ethel M d/o Mary 1877-1942
  Mabel L d/o Mary 1884-1969
  Bertha S d/o Mary 1888 -----
  Franklin F Co K Mass Inf
HOWE, George H s/o Louisa Hildreth d 5 Jan 1895 ae 63y Lot 219
  Louisa Hildreth d 4 June 1881 ae 75y
  Jonas & wife Lydia
FARNSWORTH, C Rebecca w/o G W d 10 Apr 1884 ae 37y Lot 220
  Barker G d 19 Jan 1865 ae 23y
  Ira B s/o Daniel & Olive d 6 Mar 1834 ae 7m
  Olive w/o David d 10 Aug 1833 ae 23
  L W Farnsworth 1806-1891 Mother
  D Farnsworth 1805-1882 Father
HOWE, Lewis T 1843-1894 Lot 220
  Mary E 1846-1925
WOLCOTT, George K d 29 June 1842 ae 27 Lot 224
  Mariette d/o George K Emeline d 3 Apr 1843 ae 2y
RICE, Obed 1810-1890 Lot 225
  Sarah M w/o Obed 1816-1895
  Carrie M 1837-1894
WOLCOTT, Lorenzo d 7 Nov 1858 ae 31y Lot 225
HASKELL, Phineas d 24 Oct 1843 ae 44y Lot 226
  Betsey d 17 Sept 1883 ae 83y

Susan M d 13 Apr 1851 ae 22y
Roena d 1 Jan 1853 ae 16y
Nathan L d 29 Mar 1844 ae 9m
Sarah R d 24 Dec 1815 ae 23y
DURST, Joseph d 5 Apr 1909 Lot 226
HASKELL, Arethusa w/o Joseph d 20 Jan 1923 ae 83y
William d 27 Oct 1851 ae 26
WHITNEY, Mother Ann w/o James B d 27 Nov 1880 ae 54y Lot 228
WHITNEY, Charles M s/o George W & Sarah B d 23 Jan 1862 ae 20y
Mother Sarah B w/o George W d 15 Aug 1873 ae 61y
Father George W d 22 Feb 1872 ae 61y
Mother Ann w/o James B d 27 Nov 1880 ae 54y
PETERS, John G Lot 230
Irene 1838-1922
Luther 1806-1895
Abigail 1812-1847
Maria 1820-1855
Edwin 1853-1855
MAYNARD, Orrin d 25 Apr 1872 ae 56y Lot 231
S Adeline 17 Aug 1863-31 Dec 1947
Marietta A d/o C & MAS d 28 Aug 1854 ae 3y
STEARNS, Mary A w/o Orrin Maynard d 3 Apr 1916 ae 94y Lot 231
WHITE, Martha L w/o George Stearns 1884 Lot 231
STICKNEY, Phebe d 9 Mar 1851 ae 65y Lot 232
IAZELL, Roxana relict/o Joseph d 9 Oct 1842 ae 46y
RANDALL, Paul 1820-1895 Lot 234
Abbie A w/o Paul 1816-1852
Louisa w/o Paul 1816-1852
M Louisa d/o Paul 1844-1905
BRIGHAM, Charles 1815-1899 Lot 235
Sarah H w/o Charles 1820-1880
Harriett H 1850-1960
Horace 1857-1861
Caleb B 1852-1924
Ella B w/o Caleb 1854-1920
Ivory 1765-1853
Sally w/o Ivory 1779-1849
Bethiah 1756-1848
KENNEDY, Raymond Co K 17 Mass Inf Lot 236
Isaac S 1844-1909
Willie ---------
BRIGHAM, Mary Ann w/o George d 25 Nov 1878 ae 65y Lot 237
George d 6 Apr 1889 ae 80y
Ellen S 1842-1915
George W s/o George d 23 June 1843 ae 2y
PULSIFER, ---- Lot 238
WITT, Lot 238
GOODNOW, Silas d Aug 1854 ae 75y Lot 239
Hannah w/o Silas d 18 Jan 1814 ae 29
Sally w/o Silas d -- --- 1827 ae 37y
Solomon s/o Silas d 9 1833 ae 13y

Lindsey d 22 Aug 1838 ae 17y
George s/o Silas 11 May 1825 ae 4y
Rufus s/o Silas 24 Aug 1841 ae 20y
Nancy E d 3 Nov 1919 ae 87y
BRUCE, Mary C 1823-1897 Lot 241
Charles A 1849-1851
NEWTON, ---- Lot 244
BRUCE, Abby S d 15 Aug 1869 ae 58y Lot 246
Eleanor d 21 Aug 1889 ae 57y
Calvin d Sept 1848 ae 60y
KNOX, William d 6 Nov 1890 ae 73y Lot 247
Elizabeth w/o William d 11 Oct 1889 ae 70y
ADAMS, Otis -- --- ---- Lot 248
Lena d/o Lucy & Otis -- --- ----
CRAWFORD, John A d 17 Apr 1877 B 3 Reg't Mass 1 GAR Post 9
Lot 249
McVEY, James J father d 16 Nov 1872 ae 66y Lot 251
WILKINS, Hepzibah w/o Levi d 4 Mar 1838 ae 78 Lot 254
c/o Stephen d 23 Oct 18-- 14y
Stephen 1788-1858
Relief 1792-1882
GOODNOW, Alma W w/o W J d 27 May 1864 ae 43y Lot 255
Annan w/o Silas d 6 Apr 1835 ae 45
Silas d 14 June 1851 ae 65y
ROWE, George Co L 23 Mass Inf
COOLIDGE, Phebe H d/o David d 15 Sept 1838 ae 10m Lot 256
Phebe H d/o David d 2 Oct 1836 ae 11m
Rhoda w/o David d 5 Aug 1839 ae 25y
David d 14 Nov 1879 ae 72y
Harriott H w/o David d 12 Sept 1877 ae 67y
BRIGHAM, William d 22 Jan 1839 ae 35y Lot 256 -- Col
William s/o Col William & Marriott d 24 Mar 1833
SPURR, Sarah w/o Eliphalet d 9 Sept 1842 ae 67y Lot 257
PRIEST, S E 1827-1882 Lot 258
Lucy A 1840-1890
Annah F w/o S Emerson d 9 Aug 1857 ae 21y
Annah F d/o S Emerson d 1 Sept 1857 ae 3w
Harriet B w/o S E d 17 July 1878 ae 47y
William d 7 May 1849 ae 29
Abraham d 29 Jan 1855 ae 58y
Louisa w/o Abraham d 5 Feb 1855 ae 62y
WILSON, Harriet Maria d/o James d 5 Oct ---- ae 8m Lot 259
BRUCE, Francis M d 10 Nov 1862 ae 34y Lot 260
Mary J d 4 Feb 1851 ae 14y
Laura w/o George d 17 Feb 1847 ae 41
WETHERBEE, Susan d/o Phineas d 22 Mar 1844 ae 25y Lot 261
Phineas d 22 Jan 1856 ae 78y
Sally w/o Phineas d 15 Dec 1854 ae 72
Ari d 20 July 1841 ae 38
Ari P s/o Ari & Caroline d 13 Dec 1841 ae 3m
BURDEN, Rev John d 27 July 1875 ae 67y Lot 262

Catherine C w/o Rev John d 12 May 1889 ae 69y
BRUCE, (Tomb) E -- --- 1845 Lot 263
POPE, (Tomb) S -- --- 1845 Lot 264
PRIEST, Betsy w/o Gilman 24 Oct 1819–20 Dec 1899 Lot 265
    Gilman 28 Aug 1813–9 Sept 1895
    Phebe w/o Benjamin d 4 Mar 1855 ae 87y
    Benjamin d 22 Oct 1853 ae 90
BRUCE, Francis L d 26 Dec 1863 ae 23y Lot 265
HAPGOOD, George d 11 Feb 1890 ae 68y Lot 266
    Harrieta w/o George d 17 Feb 1888 ae 62
    Lucy E d 26 Sept 1887 ae 38y
    Myron L d 30 Aug 1851 ae 4m
WHITNEY, Hattie F 1854–1896 Lot 266
RANDALL, William 17 Nov 1814–28 July 1849 Lot 267
WARREN, Marshall A Co A L Ind Cav --Sgt
RAWSON, George S d 4 Mar 1875 ae 53
    S Ethel 1863–1943
    Annie Mabel w/o Herbert E d 24 Apr 1896
    Herbert E d 28 Mar 1936 ae 84
    Aimee B 1877–1893
    S Ethel d/o George & Sarah 1863–1943
    Sarah d/o Harry Spofford 4 Aug 1924
BURNHAM, Sarah w/o George Rawson d 6 Apr 1875 ae 49y
WOOD, Clifford H d 9 Nov 1889 ae 29y
BURNHAM, Rachel S w/o John Burnham d 26 Apr 1870 ae 70 Lot 269
    John d 5 June 1866 ae 78y
BRUCE, Lavina S mother 1839–1902 Lot 271
    Philo father 1826–1895
MOSCROP, Richard 1852–1935 Lot 272
    Mary Abbie w/o Richard 1858–1911
OSTERHOUT, Robert S 1869–1942 Lot 272
    Cassie E w/o Robert 1870–1958
STONE, Esther M w/o Charles H Robbins 1869–1895 Lot 273
    Lydia M w/o William H Stone 1832–1898
BRUCE, Elmira d/o John & Sarah d 9 June 1857 ae 20y Lot 274
    Sarah w/o John d 20 Oct 1855 ae 49y
    John d 15 Feb 1889 ae 89y
WHITNEY, Sarah E w/o F H d 6 Oct 1856 ae 32 Lot 274
    Henry F d 18 Nov 1873 ae 20y
    Georgie s/o FH & ME d 9 Sept 187- ae 2y
    Melly E s/o FH & ME d 5 Dec 1864 ae 3y
    Mary E w/o Francis 30 Nov 1842–20 Dec 1922
    Francis H 26 May 1824–5 Aug 1901
WILKINS, Rufus father 1825–1898  Lot 275
    Abigail I mother 1825–1895
    Charlie d 9 Mar 1850 ae 1y
    Lizzie d 20 Oct 1861 ae 4m
    Mary A mother 1849–1933
    H Warren father 1851–1914
    Gracia d/o Warren H d 1 Mar 1885 ae 7y
WILKINS, William H d -- --- 1860 ae 1y s/o Harry

Abby w/o Henry d 29 July 1856 ae 24y
William d 1 Aug 1869 ae 68y
JOHNSON, William N 24 Nov 1812-23 July 1891 Lot 277
WHITNEY, William E d 22 Oct 1895 ae 68y Lot 277
Sally w/o Israel Whitney d 27 Jan 1871 ae 87y
Israel d 12 Feb 1849 ae 67y
WARFIELD, George W 1818-1894  Lot 279
Maria L w/o George 1825-1848
Arabella w/o George 1828-1907
Charles E 1861-1862
Freddie G 1872-1872
Maria L w/o George W d 1 Aug 1818 ae 23y
ARNOLD, Sophronia d/o Samuel & Betsy 4 Sept 1831-4 Sept 1854
ae 23 Lot 279
Betsy w/o Samuel d 7 Apr 1828 ae 24y
Samuel d 2 Sept 1812 ae 18y
STRATTON, Daniel d 14 1837 ae 60y Lot 280
Sally w/o Daniel d 31 Aug 1857 ae 78y
George s/o D & S d 18 Oct 1826 ae 4y
Martha d 2 May 1884
Daniel 1817-1890
Tryghena R w/o Daniel 1819-1904
Albert L s/o Daniel 1846-1846
Barker s/o Rufus & Clarrinda d 29 Sept 1839 ae 14m
BURGESS, Lucy J d May 1895 Lot 280
NOLAN, Howard J 1858-1942 Lot 282
BENNETT, Ida w/o Howard J Nolan 1872-1913 Lot 282
Charlotte Priest 1845-1927
Henry Foster 1831-1915
Little Herbert ---------
Little Frank ---------
HATCH, Mary Bennett ---------
TYLER, Abram 1815-1898 Lot 283
Mary E w/o Abram 1828-1908
A Tyler ---------
Elizabeth B ---------
Josephine d 25 Dec 18--
Jenney A d 29 Aug 1858
Willie A d -- Dec 1855
Frank A d 20 Dec 1856
KENDALL, Lucy J w/o John d 30 June 1854 ae 69  Lot 283
John d 12 Oct 1847
PAGE, Ella Tyler 1846-1924 Lot 283
Harry Carleton 1878-1901
CLARK, H Lewis 1855-1892 Lot 284
Sarah L w/o H Lewis 1862-1946
Karl A 1887-1968
C Louise 1886-1980
HOUGHTON, George d 23 Mar 1896 ae 73 Lot 136
Sophia w/o George d 29 Nov 1857 ae 34y
Clarinda w/o George d 10 June 1876 ae 44y

George E d 5 Aug 1864 ae 16y
Willie Alonzo s/o G & C Houghton d 15 Dec 1862 ae 1y
Franklin S s/o G & C Houghton d 9 Feb 1868 ae 9m
Clarinda d -- --- ---- ae 4m
Hattie I d 28 June 1887 ae 23y
Lizzie G d 23 Oct 1888 ae 17y
Herbert A 8 Sept 1869-2 July 1906
BARKER, Augusta Ann w/o William 5 Jan 1826-10 Sept 1914
    Lot 146
PETERS, John M d 13 Jan 1842 ae 3y Lot 147
    John H d 10 May 1887 ae 67y
    Lucy W 12 Jan 1857 ae 37y
    Zilpah H 1841-1932
    Father 1820-1887
    John Melville s/o J & L Peters 22 Sept 1842-13 Jan 1847
NOURSE, Stedman W 1817-1896 Lot 278
    Elizabeth P w/o Stedman 1811-1891
    Corp George s/o SW & EP killed 6 May 1861 ae 19y -- Corp
    John C s/o SW & E P d 6 Nov 1852 ae 4y


## THE HUNTER-POOR FARM BURIAL GROUND

In the autumn of 1988 a long-forgotten burial ground was discovered in the Town of Hudson. This was partly accidental and partly the result of a lengthy search by Richard McQuiggan, chairman of the Historical Commission of Hudson, assisted by Alfred Braga, Town Historian. A title searcher was looking for a right-of-way to a landlocked parcel of land owned by a client; McQuiggan was seeking the right-of-way to the cemetery of the Town Poor Farm. Each had found the right-of-way desired by the other; finally, they got together and exchanged information to their mutual advantage.

Hudson was incorporated in 1866 and before that date had been a part of the Town of Marlborough. When Hudson was incorporated it acquired the Marlborough Poor Farm, which Hudson continued to use until its sale in 1942. One of the new owners divided the land into lots of varying sizes. One of these lots contained thirty-four acres, which does not border on the road, but has a right-of-way some 150 feet long which goes from the road to the former cemetery. Old time residents recall seeing a grave stone or two many years ago. None are visible today, although Mr. McQuiggan has found grave stone fragments of good size.

The first owners of the property, which was originally two hundred acres or more, were the Hunter family, prominent in the early days of Marlborough. The earliest date on any record of the family is the record of the birth in 1745 of Elizabeth d/o Edward and Tabitha Hunter. The Hunter farm was more than four miles from the center of Marlborough, and it is thought that the family established the burial ground on their farm because the early burial ground at Spring Hill (to the rear of the present Congregational Church) was too far away. Several of the Hunter family were in the American Revolution and tradition says that they were interred in their family burial ground. Marlborough paupers who died at the Poor Farm, if their bodies were unclaimed by relatives, were buried in the Poor Farm burial ground. The Town furnished grave stones for them. There is no record of the burial ground having been used after 1866 when that area become the Town of Hudson.

The Massachusetts Historical Commission has been contacted and has agreed to give the Town of Hudson professional help in the restoration of this burial ground.

# ADDENDUM

## Lancaster, Massachusetts

## THE NORTH BURIAL GROUND

At a Town Meeting in April 1800, it was voted to buy "a piece of land at the north part of Town where a number of persons are buried." A deed from Eiijah Wilds conveyed to the Town of Lancaster 144 rods of land.

The road to this yard is now "abandoned" and it is nearly surrounded by the firing range of the Fort Devens Reservation. Large trees obscure it from view and many of the stones are on the ground and broken.

Three Revolutionary soldiers are buried there.

ALEXANDER, Rebecca w/o Nathaniel d 7 Nov 1843 ae 61y 6m
BACON,  Jacob R d 3 Nov 1845 ae 25y
BARNES,  Jeremiah d 27 July 1845 ae 34y
BARRETT,  Reuben Jr d 26 July 1816 ae 34y
   Moses  d 4 Aug 1846 ae 62y
   Rebecca d 27 Sept 1847 ae 85y 4m
   Samuel P d 23 Sept 1847 ae 2y 6m
   lnfant Child
BLANCHARD,  Elizabeth d/o William & Elizabeth d 19 Dec
      1807 ae 10m
   William d 13 Nov 1818 ae 56y
BUTLER, Nancy d/o Samuel & Nancy d 11 July 1827
     ae 20y 4m
   Samuel d 27 Mar 1828 ae 44y
   Nancy w/o Samuel d 11 Aug 1849 ae 64y
   Sally d/o Samuel & Nancy d 25 Dec 1831 ae 20y
   Sarah w/o Abel 16 Mar 1800 – 14 July 1830
COOK, Aaron Jr s/o Aaron & Betsy d 3 July 1803 ae 2y 4m
   Harriet d/o Aaron & Betsy d 12 Oct 1807 ae 12y
   Betsy d/o Aaron & Betsy d 20 Feb 1830 ae 33y
   Aaron d 20 Oct 1845 ae 74y
   Elizabeth w/o Aaron d 17 Jan 1842 ae 67y
   Susan d/o Aaron & Elizabeth d 17 Feb 1844 ae 26y
COWDRY, Ruthy w/o lsaac d 19 Jan 1828 ae 50y
CUTLER,  Rebeckah relict of James d 9 July 1840 in 69y
DYAR, Susan w/o Jeremiah d 16 Feb 1824 ae 47y

247

FARWELL, Ann Elizabeth d/o Capt Joseph & Sarah d 31 Aug 1842
ae 17y 2m

Josoph d 17 Sept 1834 ae 75y - A SOLDIER OF THE
REVOLUTION

Sarah w/o Leonard d 1 June 1809 in 51y

Leonard b 2 Oct 1760 d Milton, NY Oct 1822 ae 62y REV

Mary w/o Lucius L d 7 Nov 1845 ae 50y

Mary I d/o Lucius & Mary d 5 Aug 1846 ae 9m 4d

GIBBS, William s/o Joseph & Lucy d 6 Mar 1832 ae 7y

HASKELL, Elias d 2 July 1811 ae 76y

JOHNSON, Luther d 22 Apr 1822 ae 33y

Aaron d 6 Feb 1820 ae 79y REV

Sewell s/o Calvin & Abigail d 22 Nov 1845 ae 28y

Abigail w/o Calvin d 13 Feb 1845 ae 54y

Harrison d 13 Oct 1842 ae 28y

NICHOLS, Abijah s/o Joseph & Anna d 19 Aug 1801 ae 23y

SANDERSON. Elisha d 14 Mar 1843 ae 81y

Mary w/o Elisha d 18 Dec 1829 ae 65y

Martha d/o Elisha & Mary d 1 Mar 1829 ae 20y

THOMAS, Anna w/o Dr Joshua of Boston d 18 June 1799 ae 47y

Joshua 14 Mar 1745 - 4 Feb 1831

Mary w/o Joshua d 25 May 1808 ae 67y

WILLARD, Sarah w/o William d 2 June 1803 in 36y

Paul Esq d 2 Aug 1817 ae 52y

Martha w/o Paul d 22 May 1808 in 34y

Mary d/o Paul & Martha d 4 Oct 1803 ae 2y 1m

Lucia d/o Paul Esq d 14 Nov 1818 ae 15y

Dexter s/o Paul Esq d 6 July 1810 ae 17y

Sarah F w/o Dr Amory 6 Feb 1787 - 9 July 1834

S Josephine d/o Dr A & SF 24 Jan 1825 - 24 Apr 1830

Luke d 17 Sept 1813 ae 20y

William d 18 May 1837 ae 70y

Lucy w/o William d 27 June 1819 ae 41y

Henry d 11 June 1847 ae 37y

Mary Ann w/o Henry d 20 Feb 1847 ae 41y

Abigail w/o Benjamin d 12 Oct 1848 ae 74y

WORSTER, Mary d/o Samuel & Rebecca d 10 Oct 1815 (no age)

Elizabeth d 31 May 1818 ae 1y 8m

# INDEX

ANTINARELLA (continued)
Daniel 210 George 210
Pauline 210 Sabino 210
ARNOLD, Betsy 244 Mary J 166
Rebekah 143 Samuel 244 Silas
W 143 Sophronia 244
ATHERION, Eliakim 86
ATHERTON, Adeline 35 Adeliza
37 Amos 4 Annes 32 Arathusa
F 45 Benjamin 85 90 106 C
Lowell 106 Caroline 34
Charles 32 David 4 45 46 Ebon
45 Edward F 103 Elizabeth 4
33 45 Esther 45 46 Eunice 90
Experience 45 Franklin 103
Fred A 45 George 45 James H
45 Joseph 46 47 Lucretia 106
Lucy 45 Martha 33 Martin 46
Mary 45 46 103 Oliver 33
Oliver H 35 Otis R 34 Peter 45
Philemon 33 Rachel 33 Sarah
46 Simon T 77 Sylvia 74 Wil-
liam 35 William M 45
AUREN, Edyth M 210 Phillip C
210
AUSTIN, Adele R 222 Malcolm W
222
AYER, 234
BABBETT, Maria 79
BABBIT, Abiather 74 Eliza 76
Polly 73
BABBITT, Abbott 26 Abigail 74
79 Anna 79 Betty 78 Cora Bell
26 Elizabeth 74 Hannah 79
Henry S 76 Mary 79 Seth 77
Susan 74 Tabitha 79
BABBS, Sarah 176
BABCOCK, Abigail 186 Abram
187 188 Bessie E 113 Betsey
186 Charles J 112 Curtis 188
David 112 Dexter 186 Elenor
186 Elizabeth 109 110 111
Elizabeth Wolcott 112 Ellen
113 Ellen E 113 Ephraim 188
Eunice 188 Hannah 186 Hep-
zibah 187 Hepzibeth 187 Jesse
113 Jesse W 113 Josiah 110
111 186 Josiah C 110 111
Katie E 113 Leonard 175 Lucy
B 186 Lydia 175 Maria M 110
111 Marjorie J 112 Martha A
196 Nathan 112 Patience 187

BABCOCK (continued)
Peter 187 Sarah 186 Sarah W
112 Sybel 187 Wedwin 186
William 186 187
BACON, Alma E 30 C E 41
Caroline Elizabeth 41
Elizabeth C 40 Elizabeth D 41
Elizabeth George 40 H 41
Hezekiah 40 J W 41 J Willard
41 Jacob R 23 247 Katharine
Ann 188 Lizzie 41 Lucia H 30
Luther Austin 30 Lydia L 41 M
41 Mary 40 Nancy F 30 S E 30
S N 30 Samuel 30 Samuel A 40
Sarah 40 Silas 188 Silas Her-
bert 188 Sophia A 30
BADCOCK, Sybel 197 Wheeler
197 Wm 197
BADGER, Joseph 238
BAGLEY, Curtis 102 Lizzia S 102
Sarah 102
BAGSTER, Mary J 36 Sophia C 36
Thomas 36
BAILEY, Abigail 143 Adeline C
Burt 59 Alden 143 Alfred
Townsend 187 Algernon S 189
Alma 143 Amherst 191
Amhurst 191 Andrew 101
Arabella E 143 Barnabas 188
Benjamin 89 143 187 189 Ben-
jamin D 143 Betsey 143 175
Betsy 31 Betsy B 101 Betty
197 Bridget 167 Catherine 189
Charles F 143 Clarissa 175
192 Cynthia 143 Daniel 59
Dexter 101 Dolly S 183
Elisabeth 187 Eliza 101 192
Eliza Sophia 101 Elizabeth 143
188 Elizabeth R 143 Emma
187 F Sawyer 143 Frinda 143
George E 143 Horace 187 Ira
94 Jane 143 Jane E 143
Jedediah 192 John E 143 Jonas
143 Jonathan 143 Joseph 143
Julia Eliza 143 Laura A 143
Levi 31 Levinah 197 Lucy 28
187 189 Lusinda 89 Luther 94
Luther W Houghton 94 Lydia
191 Manasseh 175 Martha E
164 Martha Jane 143 Moses
143 Nathaniel 143 Nathaniel Jr
143 Nathaniel M 143 Orson 101

BAILEY (continued)
Paul 143 Paul Jr 143 Polly
160 Sally 189 Sampson 143
Samuel S 143 188 Sarah E 94
188 Shubael 143 Sibilla 189
Silas 189 191 197 Silba 156
Solon 143 Sophia 143 169
Sophronia 94 Sophronia E 143
Stephen 189 Tamer 165
Timothy 188 190 191
BAKER, Abigail 175 Bezaled 219
Caleb S 219 Eliza Ann 175
Elizabeth Woodbury 117
James S 175 John E 229 John
W 175 Martha E 229 Mary 219
Priscilla 175 Reuben 117 Sally
95 Samuel 191 Susanna 191
Thomas G 95 Vickery 175
Vickery W 175
BALCH, Dorcas A 117 Er 117
John H 117 Susan 117
BALCOM, C 102 Charles B 102
Chas 102 E 102 Edgar P 102
Edmund W 102 Electa W 102
Eliza 102 Emma F 102 Evelyn
S 102 Ezra A 102 Francis L
102 Henry L 102 Lyman 102
Lyman H 102 Mary E 102
Rebecca P 102 Sara E
Stoughton 102
BALDWIN, A Harriet 175 Abigail
175 Charles 175 Jerusha 175
John 175 Lucy 10 Marcus M
175 Oliver 10 William 175
William C W 70 William Jr
175
BALHELDER, A B 221
BALL, Abby A 105 Albert W 105
Charles E 105 Charlotte 159
Edward E 105 Eliza 229 Emer-
son 105 Emily S 11 Fordice B
229 George 117 James 189
Jonas 229 Levi 11 Lucinda 11
Lucy 144 Micah 117 Persis
207 Samuel 207 Sarah 105
Sarah E 105 Sophronia 239
Sydney A 239 Warren 239
BALLARD, Abigail 3 11 18 Anna
3 11 Anna G 11 Charles 11
Eliphas 11 Elsey 10 Henry 11
18 Jeremiah 11 John 3 11 John
Augustus 11 Josiah 11

BALLARD (continued)
Josiah Jr 3 Lucy 11 Molly 11
Nancy 11 Nancy Whitney 11
Rebecca 11 Sally 11 Sarah 11
Sarah Augusta 11 Sarah
Elizabeth 11 Sophia 11
Sophronia 11 Thomas 3 11
William 10 William A 10
BALLENTINE, Jane K 50
BALTHASAR, Wilfrid 138
BANCROFT, Ann 10 L T 10
Lorey F 10 Luther T 10 S J 10
BANNING, C 201 Charles 201
Charles M 201 Harry 201 M J
201 Mary Jane 201 Mary M 201
BARBER, Daniel 37 Darius 37
Rebecca 37
BARKER, Augusta Ann 245 Fran-
cis L 220 John 117 William
245
BARNARD, Abigail 107 Abner 59
Albert Willard 40 Alice 68 Ann
Willard 40 Annas 11 An-
toinette 68 Asenath F 59
Augustus E 68 Benijah 11
Benjamin 32 56 Benjamin K 59
Benjamin Keep 59 Betsy W 44
Caleb 10 Cati 185 Caty 187
Charles 59 Charles P 68
Charles Wesley 59 Charlotte
68 Charlotte E 68 Daniel 28
David 35 Dorothy F 68 Eliza
152 Eliza Robinson 32
Elizabeth 68 143 164 Emeline
68 Emory 39 40 Emory L 39
Ephraim 57 68 Ephraim Jr 57
Francis 35 George Edward 28
Hannah 28 57 185 Harriet V A
40 Harry L 185 Jemima 56
Joab 107 Joel 101 107 John 28
69 143 Jonathan 10 11 Joseph
32 Josiah 40 185 187 Jotham
56 Julia 10 Levi 56 68 Lewis
H 185 Lucy 56 143 Luther A 68
Mary 32 35 107 Mary Ann 143
Mary Eliza 101 Mary H 35
Mary Hager 59 Maud 69 Phebe
10 Phineas 44 Rebecah 56
Rebecca E 59 Reuben T 32
Sally 35 Sam'l 28 Sarah B 44
Susan G 39 Waldo G 68 Wil-
liam 10 Winsor 10

BARNES, Adelaide A 106 Alice
195 Artemas 190 195 Asenath
Moore 186 Betsey 195 Betsey
Longley 186 C 106 Daniel 186
David 186 Ellen M 210 For-
tunatus 195 Hannah 186 195
Harriet A 194 Jeremiah 23 247
John 194 Joseph P 106 Martha
Washington 195 Nancy 195
Persis Hosmer 195 S 106 Sabra
A 145 Sarah 194 195 Welcome
186 William 195
BARNFIELD, Harriet 229
BARRAGE, Thirza 134
BARRETT, Asa 99 100 Bertie 99
100 Ella V 99 100 Frankie 99
100 Helen 99 100 Jabez 99 100
Joel Sawyer 99 100 John 99
Joseph 10 Levi 90 Lucy 10 99
Lydia 10 Moses 23 247 Oliver
93 99 R 25 Rebecca 23 108 247
Reuben Jr 23 247 Roswell 99
100 S 25 Samuel P 23 247
Sarah 78 90 99 100 Sarah J 99
100
BARRON, Abigail 143 Abigail
Mary 143 Augustus 143 144
Benjamin 143 144 Charles A
143 Charles H 143 144
Elizabeth 143 144 Ellen M 143
144 Helen M 143 144 Hepsey
Ann 143 144 Hepsy Ann 143
144 William 143
BARRUS Elmina S 228
BARRY, Benjamin W A 102 Jane
102 Sarah 102 Simeon 102
Simeon Chamberlin 102
BARTER, Mary Jane 192 Thomas
S 192
BARTLES, Marble 111
BARTLETT, Adam 186 Amory
Adam 186 Andrew P 144 Bet-
sey B 187 Ezra K 194 Harriett
186 Helen P 144 John 186
Jonathan 186 Joseph W 144
Josephine L 153 Levi 186
Lewis Montgomery 186 Luther
117 Mary 144 186 Mary E 186
Perley 144 153 Persis 144 153
186 Persis A 144 Sarah 194
Sarah J 186 Sarah Jane 186
Susan Elizabeth 186

BARTLETT (continued)
Thomas 144 William 194 Wil-
liam B 194
BARTLEY, A Elmira 111
BARTON, John 202 John W 202
Sally R 202
BASSETT, George O 220 Louisa S
220 Oliver C 220
BATEMAN, Andrew P 39 Carleton
B 39 Charles C 39 Clara M 39
Eliza Abiah 39 Elizabeth 41
Ellen Clara 39 Francis A 39
Frederick William 39 George
39 George Henry 39 Harriet 39
Harriet F 39 Horatio 39 John F
C 39 Jonas 39 41 L H 39
Louisa H 39 Mary 39 Sarah E
39 Silas C 39 W F 39 William
F 39
BATES, Emorancy 104 Nancy 11
Stephen 11
BATHRIC, Eunice 75
BATHRICK, Amelia 224 Dorothy
224 Thomas 224 Thomas K
224
BAYLEY, Amherst 191 Anna 143
Isaac 143 Samuel 143 Susanna
143
BEACH, Abbie J 222 Agnes K 222
Gertrude 222 Harry 222 Harry
W 222 William 222
BEAMAN, Betsey 200 Deborah
146 Dinah 200 Dolly 144 154
168 Elizabeth 218 Elizabeth D
144 Elory 144 Elory B 144
Emelia 152 Ephriam 200 Ezra
144 199 Gamaliel 142 144
Gideon 144 Gideon Jr 144 Han-
nah 10 181 Harriet W 144
Jabez 200 Joanna 144 Jonathan
200 Joseph 10 Josiah 218
Lemuel 218 Maria 178 Mary
144 200 Mary N 144 Mary P
144 Nabby 144 P 200 Persis
200 Persis W 200 Phineas 144
Phinehas 218 Prudence 218 S
200 Silas 200 Tamer 200
BEAN, Javan E 53 Mary S 54
Spencer D 54 Willie Louis 54
BEANE, Amelia 224 Augustus
224 Augustus W 224 Bertha J
224 Charles H 224

BEANE (continued)
William A 224

BEARD, Abigail 36 Eldad 36 Ezra
K 36 Jonathan 36 Jonathan Jr
36 Judith 36 Susan 36

BEARNARD, Alfred 118

BEATON, Arline 236 John L 236

BEAVEN, Thomas D 138

BECKWITH, A 25

BELKNAP, Cyrus 144 John 144
Lucy 144 Mary 144 157 Mary B
144 Polly 157 William 144

BELL, James 102 Rebecca Weston 102 Rhoda P 10 William
10

BELLOWS, Ezekiel 216 Marcy
216

BEMAN, Ezery 199 Ezra 199
Jabez 199 John 5 Mary 199
Persis 199 Priscilla 5

BEMIS, Abigail 42 Addie Louisa
238 C M 238 Catherine 238
Charles E 238 E S 238 Ellen R
238 Ephraim 238 Ephraim S
238 Frank W 238 Lucy Ann
238 M Melvin 238 Rejoice
Wetherbee 42 Sarah 73

BEMIS Sophronia Chapin 42
Stephen 42 Susan Chaplin 42
William 42

BENDER, Abigail 99 Peter 90
Sarah 90

BENNET, Jotham 116

BENNETT, Bathsheba 117 C S
232 Catherine 11 144 Charles
240 Charles E 240 Charles S
240 Charlotte Priest 244
Elisha 11 Elizabeth 46 127
Eunice 11 Frank 244 Henry
Foster 244 Herbert 244 Ida 244
J H 182 John 10 117 Luke 11
144 Mary J 240 Nancy 11
Nathan 11 117 Salome Pratt 10

BENNIT, Bathsheba 2 John 2
Samuel 2

BIGELOW, Abel 214 Abijah 117
Abram 191 Adeline 234 Adin D
237 Angeline A 221 Asa 214
Betsey 221 Charles F 221
Christopher B 195 Cynthia G
213 Daniel 53 Eleanor 214
Eliza 191 Elizabeth 51 63

BIGELOW (continued)
Elizabeth F 221 Elizabeth L
237 Elmira M 221 H 214 237
Hannah 103 117 214 Henry 196
237 Isaac 117 Isabella H 214
James G 102 Jason 43 Joseph
214 221 L 214 Letitia 102 Levi
175 Levina 199 Lois H 214
Lucy 185 Luther 214 M Lizzie
237 Maria 171 Martha B 175
Mary 199 Mary Alice 102 Mary
Eusebia 191 Mehetabeel 149
170 Millia 221 Nancy 117
Nancy B 103 Olive 214 Otis
221 Persis 196 Rhoda 195
Rogers 51 Sarah 43 Sarah B
214 Sarah E 43 214 Susan 225
W H 102 Warren H 237 Wil-
liam 103

BIGHAM, Anna 236

BILLINGS, Alonzo 10 Benjamin
M 104 Hannah 10 Josiah 10
Nancy 10

BIRD, Bayley 144 George 144
Jane B 160 Mary 144 William
144

BIRGHAM, Laura Ann 145

BLACKWELL, F Elizabeth 222
William 222

BLAKE, Harrison Gray Otis 144
Nancy Pope 144

BLANCHARD, Abel 32 Abigail 33
60 78 Asenath 73 Betsy 33
Charlie 240 Edward 60 Edward
B 240 Elizabeth 23 247 Emma
A 111 Grove B 78 I H T 30
Jemima 79 John 33 60 Lucy 32
Margaret Bromfield 30
Nathaniel 60 Olive 78 Pamelia
33 Seth 77 William 23 247

BLANEY, Ambrose 87 Sarah 87

BLISS, Cyrus 10 Gideon 187 L
112 Lydia 112 Lydia Elizabeth
112 Martha Jane 10 Mary 187
Mary W 112 Minerva Chadwick
112 R 112 Roswell 112 Susan
10

BLOOD Alfred 43, Alfred S 43
Amos 144 Augustus 96
Caroline A 96 Catherine 43
Catherine S 43 Charles 71 144
Charles H 144 Eben P 169

BLOOD (continued)
Eliza J 169 Emma Maria 43
Frankey C 71 George 144 Harriet 71 Heman L 55 Henry Albert 43 Herbert Eugene 43
Kezia 74 Louisa 144 Lucretia
98 Lucy 144 Lucy A 55 Lyman
R 55 Mary 144 Mary C 144
Mary E 43 108 Melinda D 144
Nancy M 58 Oliver 58 Polly
144 Reuben 144 Samuel 76 98
Thomas 144

BLUNT, Abigail 218 George F
218 Joseph 218

BODGER, Parmelia 26

BOLSTER, Bertha Mabel 228
Clarence 228 Clarence W 228
Persis E 98

BOLTON, Edward 26 Henry E 220

BOND, A S 220 Albert A 220
Andrew 220 Andrew S 220
Annie M 220 Benjamin 202
Benjamin F 202 C J 213
Caroline J 213 Emma J 213 F
L 220 Francis L 220 G E 213
George E 213 Hannah 220 Hannah H 220 Harriet F 202 Hattie
A 213 Isaac 86 220 Percy H
202 Sarah S 213 Susannah 86

BONZEY, Helen M 210

BOOKS, Catherine R 213

BOTTON, Debby Ann 173

BOUTELL Abigail 117 Artemas
117 Dorothy 117 Eliza A 117
Enock 117 George W 117
James 117 John 117 Josiah
117 Judith 117 Loring 117 118
Martha 117 118 Martha Jane
117 118 Philinda T 117 118
Rachel 117 118 Rachiel 117
118 Relief 117 118 Sarah 117
118 Sarah F 117 118 Timothy
117 118 Timothy T 117 118
William 117 118

BOUTELLE, Abigail 117 Artemas
117 Dorothy 117 Eliza A 117
Enock 117 George W 117
James 117 John 117 Josiah
117 Judith 117 Loring 117 118
Martha 117 118 Martha Jane
117 118 Philinda T 117 118
Rachel 117 118

BOUTELLE, (continued)
Rachiel 117 118 Relief 117 118
Sarah 117 118 Sarah F 117 118
Timothy 117 118 Timothy T
117 118 William 117 118

BOWARS, John 3

BOWEN, Andrew 202 Cora 202
Lena 202 Mary 202 Walter 202

BOWER, Elizabeth 26

BOWERS, Cephas H 61 Charlotte
A 53 Francis 61 Jerahmeal 118
Joel 53 61 63 Josiah 10
Lavinia 63 Lucy Ann 53 Mary
Houghton 118 Phebe 118
Rebecca 10 63 Rebeckah 61
Rebekah 118 Samuel 118

BOWLES, Anna 31 Elizabeth 31
John 31 Josiah 71 Mary 31
Nathaniel 31 Sarah 31 Stephen
31 William 31

BOWMAN, Betsy 197 Clara E 94
Elsie G 94 Herbert L 94 John
94 John W Houghton 94
Jonathan 10 94 Persis 197
Samuel W 10 Sarah 10 Sarah B
94 Simeon 197

BOYNTON, Annah 145 Elizabeth
175 Ephraim 145 George W
169 John 175 Mary A 169 170
Phebe 169 170 Silas H 169 170
Zacheus 145

BRABOOK, Charles 118 Elizabeth
H 118 Ezra 118 Ezra H 118
Hollis 118 Joanna 118 Levi
118 Nancy 118 Sophia 118
William 118

BRADFORD, Adelaide R 100
Frank 100 J E 100 J K 100
Luzana 39 Winslow 39

BRADLEY, Alvira M 156 Franklin
10 M P 10 R M 10 Robert M 10

BRAGA, Alfred 231 245 Alfred M
231 Eloise 231

BRAGG, Ebenezer 10 Horatio C
10 Martha 10

BRAITHWAITE, Christiana W
Goddard Carter 194 J 194

BRAMAN, Henrietta 173

BRAY, Charles 199

BRAYBROOK, Bethesda 152 Hepsybath 150

BRECK, Amos 145 Amos W 145

BRECK (continued)
Charles C 145 Eliab 145
Elizabeth 145 Emeline 145
Emeline B 145 John 145 Julia
A 145 Lovinia 145 Mary 145
Polly 145 Sabra A 145 Sarah M
145 Sylvia 145
BREWER, Eber 175 Lucy 175
BRIANT, Lyman 204 Rebecca 204
BRIDE, Asa 192 Caty 192 James
M 191 Lucy 192 William A
191
BRIDGE, Abigail 11 Abigail C 53
Annes S 52 Annis 52 Caroline
11 Ebenezer 52 53 54 Eirene
10 Elizabeth 32 Franklin 11
George 11 Henry 11 Isaac 32
James 11 John A 52 John H 53
Josiah 10 Mehitable 54 Polly
52 Sarah 10 Solomon 11 Sophia
11 Susan 11 53 Susan Hartwell
53 Thomas H 53 William 11
BRIDGES, Hannah 77 James 98
Jonathan 77 Persis 78 Rachel
79
BRIGHAM, ---- 36 Abigail 173
Abraham 193 Addie L 94 Ann
186 Ann M 210 Anna 195 Anna
W 105 Azubah 186 Bethiah 241
Betsey 195 Betsy 192 217
Caleb 241 Caleb B 241 Charles
241 Charles A 235 Charles D
235 Chester I 229 Daniel 195
Edmund 217 Eli 145 Eli Jr 145
Elizabeth 118 Ella B 241 Ella
F 235 Ellen S 241 Emily M
236 Eunice 217 Francis 235
236 Francis D 235 236 George
241 George A 193 235 George
D 235 George H 105 George L
105 195 George W 241 Hannah
A 193 Harriet 235 Harriet Ann
145 Harriett H 241 Helen M
105 Horace 241 Ira 195 Ivory
241 Jennie M 105 Joel 118
John 210 John B 210 Legrand
L 94 Lillian E 229 Louisa 149
Louisa E 195 Marriott 242
Mary 172 217 229 Mary Ann
241 Mary C K 105 Mary E 229
Mary E McQuillan 229 Paul
186 Persis Baker 195

BRIGHAM (continued)
Persis E 236 Polly 145 Sally
118 241 Sarah H 241 Sarah P
235 Sophia 192 236 Stephen
217 Stephen B 217 Thomas 186
W F 232 Wilbur F 236 Wil-
liam 242 William F 236 Wil-
liam H 105 William M 105
BRIGHAN, Chester 229 Jotham 10
Lucy 10
BROAD, A Harriet 175 Albert 175
Augustus G 175 Charles 175
Charlotte 175 Clarissa 175
Cora J 175 Ellen Maria 175
Erastus 175 Jerusha 175 Lois
175
BROCKELBANK, Elizabeth 146
Asa 25 M 25
BRODEUR, Elizabeth I 235 236
Emma J 235 236 Howard M
235 236 Mitchell 235 236
BROMFIELD, Henry 38 Margaret
30
BROOKS, 233 Abigail 175 Adaline
A 145 Asenath 146 Becca 168
Betsy 32 Caroline Ricard 233
Charles 182 Charlotte 175
Dolly 145 Ebenezer 145
Ebenezer Jr 145 Ebenezer Sr
145 Eliza 145 Emily S 182
Helon 145 James 233 James B
233 John 145 Jonas 213 Louisa
145 Louisa A 145 Lucinda 145
Luthera 145 Mary 145 Mary O
98 Nathan 93 98 99 Oren 145
Phebe 145 156 160 Relief 145
Ricard 233 Sally 145 Samuel
32 175 Sarah 87 Sarapta 145
Seth 145 Solomon 145 Sydney
145 Tamer 145 Thankfull 175
William 145 175 William
Bradford 233
BROWN, Aaron 91 Abigail 91 145
Abigail S 118 Abigail W 193
Abijah 95 Addison L 175
Alfred 175 176 Almira A 175
176 Ann Elizabeth 145 Anna
177 Arad 91 Bartholomew 145
Belinda S 62 Benjamin 175 176
Bethiah 175 176 Betsey 175
176 Betsy 145 Caleb 56 Caty
150 175 176 Charles 205

BROWN (continued)
Charles H 97 Chloe 214
Claricy 175 176 Clarissa P
Shannon 69 Elizabeth 56 Ellen
Brown Winde 69 Elmer E 95
Emelie 145 Francis R 145
Genger 145 George 175 176
George W 62 76 Gilson 145
Gladys M 95 H H 232 Harriet
Adaline 175 176 Helen E 226
Henry 193 Hepzabeth 56
Horace 175 176 James 218
James Tilden 145 Jerusha D
97 John 11 145 175 176 John F
218 John Jr 175 176 Jonas 145
Josiah 145 Josiah A M 145
Josiah Jr 97 Lewis B 97 Lillie
A 97 Lois 72 167 Lucy A 95
Martha 91 Mary 11 65 175 176
Mary A 175 176 Mary Brown
Houghton 69 Mehitable 175 176
Moses 175 176 Nabby 144
Nancy 97 165 Nathan 214 Nor-
man 226 Norman G 226 Olive
158 175 176 Polly 11 Prudence
145 Rebeckah 145 Reuben 69
Reuben F 69 Sally 145 Samuel
91 145 175 176 Sarah 175 176
218 Sarah P 218 Stephen B 65
Susan 175 176 Thomas 145 175
176 Thos H 97 Timothy 118
Warren 96 William H 69
BROWNELL, Lizzie A 112
BRUCE, 234 Abbie F 211 Abby S
242 Adaline 176 Alice M 234
Calvin 242 Catharine 10
Charles A 242 E 243 Edwind
234 Eleanor 242 Ella B 98 El-
len P 219 Elmira 237 243
Eunice 188 Ezra T 55 Francis
L 243 Francis M 242 George
242 George H 55 George W 237
Hannah 193 Hugh 195 Ira 219
John 219 243 Jonathan 10
Laura 242 Lavina S 243 Lewis
B 193 Limon 193 Mark 176
Mary 239 Mary C 242 Mary J
242 Mary M 234 Mary N 144
Mary O 113 Myron Ira 219
Nathaniel 239 Paulina C 55
Phebe 219 Phidelia 188 Philo
243 Prudence 219 Rixina 195

BRUCE (continued)
Sally 195 Sarah 90 243 Sarah E
216 Sewell 188 Simeon 113
Susannah 239 Sylvanus 193
Walter 237 Warren 176 Wil-
liam 90
BRUSH, Ira 216 Ira S 216 Mary E
216
BRYANT, Amos 96 Emma R 96
Geo Albert 96 Ida E 96 Johan-
nah Obrian 186 Mary H 96
Mary I 96 Sarah 96 Sarah C 96
Sarah S 96
BUCK, Caroline F 178 Deborah
146 Ella Augusta 222 223
Ethel M 172 George 222 223
George B 222 Isaac 176 Lucy
222 223 Mary 146 Mary E 210
Mary Elizabeth 222 223 Silas
146
BULL, Abbie L 66 Abby Delia 29
Abby Wetherbee 29 Annie
Francis 29 Eliza M 66 Hannah
66 Harriet E 29 Josephs 29
Julia Gertrude 29 Louisa H 66
Mercy Sawyer 66 Merrit 66
Sidney 66 Sidney H 66 Trum-
ball 29 William Albert 29
BULLARD, Abigail 228 Charles
228 Charles P 228 Frank G 228
Harriet H 191 Henry M 191
Joel 191 Judith B 191 Lillian
A 228 Marcia M 77 Martha 191
Mary 144 Nathan 191
BUNSON, Rhoda 169
BURATH, Binito 223 Eduardo 223
BURDEN, Catherine C 242 243
John 242 243
BURDETT, Abigail 118 Augustus
P 118 Betsey 118 Edwin J 118
Hervey 118 James 118 138
John 118 Lucinda 118 Lydia
118 Mary E 118 Mary
Elizabeth 118 Mary T 118
Nathan 118 Phinehas S 118
Polly 118 Sarah 228 Sarah Jane
118 William 118
BURDIT, Abigail 118 Augustus P
118 Betsey 118 Edwin J 118
Hervey 118 James 118 John
118 Lucinda 118 Lydia 118
Mary E 118

BURDIT (continued)
Mary Elizabeth 118 Mary T
118 Nathan 118 Phinehas S 118
Polly 118 Sarah Jane 118 William 118

BURDITT, Abigail 118 Augustus
P 118 Betsey 118 Betsy S 18
Charles A 10 Edwin J 118 F
Wentworth 10 Franklin C 10
Hervey 17 118 James 18 118
John 10 118 Lucinda 17 118
Lydia 118 Margaret 10 Mary E
118 Mary Elizabeth 118 Mary
T 118 Nathan 10 118 Phinehas
S 118 Polly 118 Sally 10 Sarah
B 10 Sarah Jane 118 Thomas
10 William 118

BURGES, Abigail 32 Ebenezer 32
Ephraim 32 Hannah Hazen 32
Josiah 32 Loami 32 Marret 32
Mary 32 Nancy 32 Rachel 32
Sarah 32

BURGESS, Abi 36 Asa 36 Asa
Simeon 36 Charles H 234 Cora
L 234 Ebenezer 56 Eunice 101
Frank A 36 George E 234 Han-
nah 56 Isaac 37 J J 234 Jane
Maria 36 John F 234 Josiah
Nelson 101 Lea 234 Lucy J
244 Lydia Ann 36 Lydia W 36
Nathaniel 101 Roxalana 37
Sylvia P 36 William 56

BURINGAME, Ada E 201 Fred
201

BURLINGAME, Florence M 201
Harold 201 Joyce Shirley 201

BURNAM, Lemuel 96 Lemuel Jr
96 Lucinda 96 Reuben 96
Roxanna W 95 Sarah 96

BURNHAM, Ella L 213 Hannah 33
John 243 Moses 33 Rachel S
243 Sarah 243 Sarah J 170

BURNS, John 48 Martha 48 Mary
Ann 26 Sally 26

BURPEE, Abel 146 Abigail 146
Alice B 171 Almira 160
Andrew 146 Asenath 146 Azuba
146 151 Betsey 146 Caroline
161 Ebenezer 146 Edward 146
149 Elijah 146 Eliza 182
Elizabeth 146 151 161 Ellen M
146 Emmaline 146 Fanny 146

BURPEE, (continued)
George N 146 Hannah 146 160
Harriet 146 Harriet E 146 Har-
riet N 146 Jane 146 Jeremiah
146 Jeremiah Jr 146 Joel 146
John 146 Jonathan 146 147
Luke 146 Lydia 10 Martha 146
Martin 10 Mary 146 149 Mary
C 146 Mary Elizabeth 146
Molly 146 Moses 146 Myra 146
Nancy 146 180 Nathan 146
Nathan Jr 146 147 Nathan Sr
146 Newton 146 147 Newton Jr
146 147 Polly 146 147 Polly A
146 147 Prudence 181 Relief
148 Samuel 146 147

BURRAGE, Abigail 118 Asenath
118 Caroline 118 Dana Bassett
118 Henry Augustine 118 119
Henry Waldo 118 119 John 118
Joseph 118 119 Mary 118 119
Mary A 155 Mary Jane 118 119
Molly 118 119 Patty 118 119
Phebe 118 119 Polly 118 119
Roxana 118 119 Roxanna 118
119 Sarah 118 119 Thomas 118
119 William 118 119 155 Wil-
liam Sr 118 119

BURT, Adeline 58 Adeline C 59 B
25 Daniel 58 Emeline E 58
Eva 58 59 Eva H 59 Flora 59
George E 58 Hannah 52 John
52 Molly 52 O 25 William 52

BUSH, Abigail J 152 Lucy 161
Martha 164 Persis 150

BUSHONG, J Chester 227 Kathryn
P 227

BUSS, Abigail 147 Alice M 209
Asaph 119 Asaph C 119 Asaph
E 119 Benjamin 147 151 Bet-
sey 125 Betsy 125 Dennice 147
Ebenezer 147 Ebenezer Jr 147
176 Elizabeth 119 147
Elizabeth T 119 Ellen E 209
Ephraim 119 Eunice 163 Fred
209 George Jr 147 Gladys C
209 Hannah 2 Herbert S 209
John 2 119 147 John Jr 119
Lucy Ellen 147 Mary E 119
Mehetabel 147 Prudence 119
Rebecca 147 151 Rebecca H
147 Ruhamah 147 176

CLAFIN (continued)
Webster W 234 William
Webster 234 Willie W 234 W
W 232
CLAP, Jerusha 160 Joseph 148
CLARK, Andrew P 211 Anna 97
Arad 91 C Louise 244
Catherine 159 Charles H 148
Clarissa P 97 Dorothy 148 Edward B 211 Elizabeth 91
Elizabeth D 91 Ella F Robinson 109 Emma C 109 Eunice
51 Francis A 97 George B 211
H Lewis 244 Hannah 51 79
Harriet E 29 Henrietta F 211
Herbert S 148 Hovey 148 Ida M
148 Jacob S 148 John 2
Jonathan P 97 Judah 51 Karl A
244 Lucy 74 Lucy Ellen 109
Lucy G 76 Mary 2 Mary E 97
Mary J 97 Mathew 2 Mercy 74
Peter 91 Phineas 97 Rebecca
148 Richard N 209 Robert 109
Robert F 109 S 26 Sally 148
Samuel 148 Samuel B 91 Sarah
2 148 Sarah J 97 Sarah L 244
Susan J 67 William 26
CLAYTON, Dorothy K 211 Harry
V 211 Louise S 211
CLEAVLAND, Hannah 213 Loren
213
CLEVELAND, C M 227 Charles
227 Charles M 227 Elizabeth
M 227 Hannah 227 Hattie M
227 J Milton 227 Joseph Hiller
7 Lotan 227 M J 227 Mary 7
Mary A 227 Nancy 227 William 7
CLEVERLY, Rachel 40
CLIFFORD, Mary 148 Young
Squire 148
CLOUTMAN, John 76
COBURN, Catherine 89 William
89
COCHRAN, Maria S 236 Wm N
236
COFFRAN, Joseph 104
COGSWELL, Mary 155
COLBURN, Abigail 101 121 Anna
Darby 121 Betsey 121 Betsy
121 Caroline Matilda 121
Charles S 121 Deborah H 121

COLBURN (continued)
Elijah 12 Elisha 121 George
210 George W 210 John 121
Joseph 121 Lorenzo Theodore
121 Maria O 182 Mary F 73
Myrtle M 210 Nathaniel 101
Nicholas A 182 Oliver 121
Paul 141 Relief 121 Sally 12
Sarah Ann 121
COLE, Jedediah 55 Jonathan 55
Judith 55 Martha 55 Mary 55
COLLINS, Abel 109 Abel J 112
Amos 109 Amos W 112 Daniel
121 Dorcas 121 Hannah 121
James 121 Jedidiah 121
Joseph 138 Lucy F 112
COLTON, Susan R 156
COMBS, Emily M 171
CONANT, ---- 195 Abel 121
Abigail 32 Abigail D 32 Antonette 121 Betsey 148 Betsy
35 Caroline 176 Elizabeth K
148 Ellen Sophia 36 Harriet N
195 Hervey 170 Huldah 58
Jacob 148 John 148 Joseph 121
Joshua Josiah 195 Levi 32
Lucy H 195 Lydia 55 148
Maria 36 Maria R 121 Martha
170 Mary A 193 Mercy 148
Nancy Pope 144 Patience 121
Polly 148 Rebecca 121 Relief
148 Reuben 55 Samuel 148
Samuel Jr 148 Sarah 58 Sewall
32 Sherman G 36 Silas 176
Susan 35 William 35 William
F 193
CONKLIN, Frances A 221
CONN, George 30 Mary 30 Rosannah 82
CONNELL, John E 98
CONQUERETTE, Mary 12
CONVERSE, Annie B 228
COOK, 169 Aaron 23 247 Aaron Jr
23 247 Abigail D 26 Benjamin
F 210 Betsy 23 247 Calvin 121
Calvin B 121 Chester H 210
Cranson 210 Elizabeth 23 247
Ellen M 210 Hannah 66 Harriet
247 Harriot 23 Henrietta 76
Hepsibah B 210 Herbert 210
Herbert F 210 Joseph H 215
Mary E 210 Meriam 121

COOK (continued)
    Miriam 121 Roger 66 Susan 23
    247 Theodore 121
COOKE, Doris L 212 James 212
    James A 212
COOLEDGE, Albert 113 Charles
    Edward 113 Judith 113 Silas
    113
COOLIDGE, 233 Abigail S 113
    Ada M 233 Anna 121 122 233
    Barak 148 Culy 26 David 242
    Elisha 121 122 Eliza 121 Han-
    nah 63 Harriott H 242 Helen
    239 Helen M 239 Henry 233
    Lucy J 113 Martha 121 Mary
    Ann 121 122 Mary W 36 Nancy
    148 Nathan 239 Phebe 178
    Phebe H 242 Rebecah 121 122
    Rhoda 242 Sarah 52 Silas 113
    William 101
COOMBS, Emma M 171
COOPER, Abigail 74 Bulah 79
    Deliverance 78 Eleanor 73
    Francis 73 Leonard 148 Moses
    148 Phebe 163 Ruth 148 Sarah
    73 Solomon 77
COPELAND, Abbie T 148 Charles
    D 148 Delicia A 162 Elisha
    148 Frank 148 George 148 Har-
    riet E 148 Hattie E 148 Julia A
    148 Maria H 148 Sophia 148
    Sophia P 148
COREY, Albert S 148 Elizabeth
    148 Rebecca 12 Stephen 12
    Triphena 12 Willie H 148
COTTING, Daniel 91 Martha 91
COUGLE, Maud 181
COWDRY, Isaac 23 247 Ruthy 23
    247
COWEE, Barbara 226 Edward 226
    Edward Arron 226 Elsie 226
    Hattie L 226 Howard 226
    Howard W 226 Mary 227
COX, ---- 237 Alina 237 Edwin
    237 Eisha 237 Elisha 238 Lore
    239 Loring 237 Louisa D 237
    Lydia 78 Mary 237 Mary A 239
    Roxanna 239 Rufus 237 Rufus
    Jr 237 Sidney A 239 Susan 237
    Willard 237 William 237
COXEN, George William 204 R
    204 Richard 204 Sarah 204

COXEN (continued)
    W 204
CRAGG, Georgia Baker 103
    Richard 103 Sarah Ann 103
CRAGGS, Annie 56 Elizabeth E
    70 James 70 John R 70 Mary
    Ann 70 William 56
CRANSTON, Joel 238 239
    Lucretia 238 239
CRAWFORD, John A 242
CROFUT, Harriet R 208
CROOK, Elizabeth Boothby 104
CROOKER, Peleg 31
CROSBY, Hannah 148 Jonathan
    148 Josiah 192 Sarophine B
    192
CROSS, Lillian 171
CROSSMAN, Ellen Maria 91
    Evelina 91 John 91
CROUCH, Caleb 77 David 26 73
    Elizabeth 74 Enoch 37 George
    70 Harriet C 37 Jonathan 77
    Lucinda E 70 Martha 76 77
    Mary 74 Mary E 78 Mehitable
    75 Moses 77 Patience 79 Sarah
    37 79
CUMMINGS, Abigail 122 Anna
    Maria 11 Charles F 104
    Charles H 41 Emeline 122
    Emma 41 F L T 41 Helen S 41
    Jonathan 122 Joseph 58 Mary
    11 Mehitable T 41 Rufus K 122
    Sarah T Wetherbee 41 Thomas
    41 Timothy S 122 Wright 11
CUNLIFFE, Cora B 220 Elizabeth
    M 220 J 220 John 220 M 220
    Margaret 220
CUNNINGHAM, Sarah F 57
CURRIER, Eunice A 221 John W
    221
CURTIS, Benjamin F 148 Blanche
    148 149 C B 146 Charles A 148
    149 Charles B 148 149 Ellen M
    165 Jesse 148 149 Kenneth L
    148 149 Louisa 148 149 Louisa
    L 165 Marian 148 149 Mary
    146 148 149 Sarah Jane 168
CUTLER, E P C 223 E W C 223
    Harriet Rebecca 226 Hattie L
    226 James 23 247 M P C 223
    Oliver 226 Oliver Blake 226
    Rebeckah 23 247

CUTTING, George 104 193 Harriet
Rebecca 226 Leonard 93 Martha J 149 Sarah L 193 Sarepta
193 Silas 149 Silas A 149
Surepta 104 Susan 149 Susan
Maria 149 Susannah 157
DABY, Abbie 71 72 Adeline 53 71
72 Anna 122 Asa 47 71 Asa
Whitcomb 47 Deliverance 122
Elizabeth 45 Esther 47 Ethan
71 72 Hannah 45 John 45
Judith 47 Lucy H 71 72 Lurena
47 Lurenia 71 72 Mary
Symonds 47 Simon 47 Susannah 74
DADMUN, Abbie A Haskell 61
Addie Sophia 61 Charles
Ruggles 33 Charlotte Haskell
33 E F 61 Elizabeth 63
Elizabeth Bigelow 63
Elizabeth F 61 Elizabeth Jane
63 J F 61 James F 61 Joanna
33 Joseph 63 Mary Hannah 33
Polly A 63 William 33 Wm 33
DAKIN, Betsy 100 Herbert J 102
Joel 100 Joseph H 102
Rebecca 177
DAMON, Abigail 13 Angie M 230
Emma Jane 230 Everett E 230
Frank 230 Frank E 230 Jonas
M 13 Margaret 13 Margaret
Ann 13 Rebecah 13 Samuel 13
William 13
DANA, Ebenezer 200 George 218
Jesse 200 Mary Ann 219
Melinda 218 Orra 218 Phinches
P 200 Sarah E 200 Sarah O 218
Tamer 200 Tamer B 200
Waldo E 218
DANFORTH, Elias 12 F 13 Lucy
12 Sarah 13 Sarah Ann 12
DANIELS, Ella D 37 James R 37
M Josephine 37 Sarah A 36
DARBY, Anna 121 Dinah 27 John
27
DARLING, Adaline 181 Cassius
Augusta 122 Charles 122
Eunice 203 Granville 122
Joseph 122 Joseph Frank 122
Joseph Granville 122 Joseph S
122 Mary 122 236 Mary M 122
Mary Richardson 122

DARLING (continued)
Samuel D 203
DARNUM, Asa 78
DAVENPORT, E 203 Ebenezer
203 Elizabeth D 203 I 203
Isaac 203 Isaac N 203 Orissa
203 Sarah 203 Warren N 203
DAVIDSON, ---- 170 Lucretia C
157 Lucy 149 Mary L 149
Peter 149 Thomas H 149
Thomas N 149 William 76
DAVIS, Aaron 48 Abby B 205 206
Abigail 28 45 Abigale B 216
Addison 216 Alfred 48 Alton E
236 Alvin 48 Ann B 152 Annie
V 236 Austin 13 Barnabas 216
Bloomy 176 177 C T 214
Caroline S 58 Catherine R 213
Celina T 214 Charles 219
Charles Royal Woods 236
Cummings E 58 Daniel 48
Drusilla 44 E 199 205 E Carrie
227 Eleazer 45 Elias 199 Eliza
H 44 Ellen M 55 Emily W 176
Emma 13 Eunice 44 Eunice P
205 Ezra 216 F 205 Flint 28
Francis 205 Francis W 205
206 Fred 236 Fred Alton 236 G
214 Gardiner 214 George E 214
George P 205 H F 68 H Fessenden 68 H Maria 176 Hannah
13 219 Hannah Giles 54 Hannah J 44 Harriet A 176 Henry
54 Henry A 176 Hollis 13
Hosea 44 Hulda P 68 Ida M F
224 John 48 176 177 John A
216 Jonas 57 Lucy D 182
Lydia 30 M 199 205 Marcy 216
Martha R 176 177 Martin 182
Mary 199 216 Mary Davis
Stone 58 Mary P 149 205 Mary
R 205 206 Nancy N S T 122
Paul Spencer 236 Persis 216
Phineas 30 Rebecca 48
Rebecca T 44 Richard Harris
219 Ruth 48 Sally 13 Samuel A
149 Sarah 45 Simon 216
Stephan H 205 Susan 236
Thomas 176 177 Thomas
Boylston 199 Walter Austin 13
William 44 48 112 122
DAWSON, Martha 221

DWINELS (continued)
Sarah 35 Sarah E 35
DWINNELLS, Anna 96 Asa P 95
Benj 96 Frances A 96 Horace
96 Mary Ann 96
DYAR, Albert 55 56 Albert A 55
Albert F 55 Arethusa 55 56
Arethusa P 55 Arethusa W 55
Charles G 56 Charles H 55
Guildford D 56 Jeremiah 23
247 John F 55 Louisa 56 Mary
55 Susan 23 247
DYER, Jeremiah 34 Lucy 34
EAGER, Althina 13 Caroline 13
Ephraim 170 Farwell 13 For-
tunatus 149 170 Fortunatus Jr
149 Fortunatus Sr 149 Hannah
170 Mehetabeel 149 170 Nancy
170 Polly 170 Sarah A 13
Tamar 170 Uriah 170
EAMES, Allira B 207 Auguste W
207 Betsey 199 Canley 207 208
Canley Denard 207 208 Claire
Auguste 207 208 Emma S 207
208 Kenneth Reid 207 208 Levi
199 Luther R 207 Luther Rice
207 208 Mary R 199 Persis 199
William 199 Zalius C 207 208
EARLE, Anna 177 Clark 93
Emory 207 Eunice 207 Matilda
93 Susan B 210
EATON, Alma E 30 Jacob S 30
Lucy 13 Nathaniel 13
EDDY, Abiather 77 Abigail 149
Amanda 177 Andrew 177 Arthur
L 177 Barnet 177 Benjamin F
177 Betsey 175 Charles H 177
Charles H Jr 177 Daniel 177 E
Webster 149 Emily 177 Emily
K 177 Erastus 149 Hannah 75
Henry 177 Jemima 177 John
177 Joshua 177 Lucretia 177
Luke 177 Martha 149 Polly 177
Rebecca 177 Sally 177 Tamer
177
EDES, Catherine O 108 E L 108
Edward L 108 F C 108 Francis
C 108 Katherine 155 Miriam B
Sprague 108
EDGERLY, Abigail 56 Addison 56
Edward Gardner 56 George 56
George G 56 Mary 56

EDGERTON, Benjamin 13
Maryann 13 Sarah 13
EDMANDS, S 25
EDSON, Charles 75 Hiram 75
Hosea 75 Polly 74 Relief 74
EDWARDS, Abigail D 170
EGERY, Nathan 189 Sibilla 189
ELDREDGE, Storrs 205
ELLENWOOD, Arah 122 Eliza P
122 Ellen L 122 Emily M 122
Luicrelia 122
ELLINWOOD, Nathan 96 Sarah 96
ELLIOT, Deborah 177 Polly 177
Stephen A 177
ELLIOTT, George C 170 Helen L
170
ELLIS, Joseph S 66
ELLSWORTH, Henry 75
EMERSON, Abigail Knight 60
Abigail R 60 Alfred B 60
Catherine R 60 Dorothy 31 Ed-
ward P 60 Elias 13 Eunice
Wright 7 Francis P 7
Frederick B 60 Hannah 28 Har-
riet E Porter 60 Hazen 7 Jacob
31 Joseph 13 Judith Kelley 7
Lucy 28 Lydia Carleton 7 Mary
13 28 31 Moses 7 Moses K 7
Peter 28 31 Phebe 13 Sally 30
Sally C 7 Sally Carleton 7
Sarah 28 Sarah A 60 William
60 William B 60
EMMES, Esther 98 John 98
Stephen 98
ENGEL, Ida M 212 Phillip 212
Phillip B 212
ESTABROOK, Samuel Jr 216
ESTERBROOK, Mehitabel 123
Nathaniel C 123
ESTY, Abigail 175
EVANS, Amos Jr 111 Elizabeth
109 111 Frederick B 109 John
123 Josiah 109 Mary 123
Nathaniel 123 Samuel 123
FAIRBANK, Abbie W 173 Abigail
51 193 Abigail D 170 Abijah
149 Achsah 87 Alexander 204
Alpheus 177 Amos 54 174 Ann
174 Anna 4 Aramus 203
Arathusa 174 Artemas 219 Ar-
temus 50 174 Asenath 174 B
204 206 207 Baruck B 206 207

FAIRBANK (continued)
Benjamin 174 Betsy 31 50
Charles F S 170 Clarissa 219
Clark 38 Cyrus 4 14 50 53
Dorothy 173 174 Eddie 50 Edwin Symonds 38 Elijah 123
Eliza 31 Elizabeth 4 14 51 143
179 Ellen Louisa 38 Emily 206
207 Ephm 87 Ephraim 4 51 89
105 173 174 Esther 207 George
C 38 George F 170 George W
177 Grace 4 Grase 4 Hannah 4
50 170 Harrison 170 Harry
Gardner 38 Hattie E 170 Henry
50 170 Hepzibah 89 Horatio
107 Isaac 203 Jabez 4 34 53 89
170 Jabez Jr 170 Jacob 40
Jane K Ballentine 50 Jane S 38
John 72 Jonas 4 14 Jonathan 4
7 50 169 170 Joseph 4 31 50 51
174 Joseph Jr 48 51 Katy 174
Keza 170 Keziah 53 Lemuel
206 Lillah V 204 Lois 174
Lucy 4 54 Lucy A 38 Lydia 65
225 Manaseh 193 Manasseh 53
Margaret Blanchard 41 Martha
7 Mary 4 14 50 51 53 170 177
178 Mary A 170 Mary L 170
Mercy 54 Miriam 174 Nahum
50 Nancy 149 Nancy B 149
Netina E 204 Olive 176 Oliver
173 Oliver Jr 174 Omar 50
Patience 174 Paul 174 Persis
B 206 207 Phebe 206 Phineas
107 Phineas J 107 Phinehas 53
56 65 Polly 149 177 Prudence
G 203 Rachel Houghton 50
Rachel Sophia 50 Releif 203 S
204 206 207 Sally 4 147 206
207 Sarah 40 53 56 65 Sarah H
170 Sena 174 Seth 203 Silas 7
Sophia 50 Stephen 149 Sumner
170 Susa 174 Susan 107 176
Susan Robinson 107 Susanna
174 Thankful 4 7 170 Thomas
51 173 174 Uriah 170 Vashti
149 Waldo 107 Walter H 38
Warren N 50 William 170
FAIRBANKS, Abigail 150 193 Addison 70 Albert W 62 Alice L
234 Amos 37 Annie L 234
Arathusa 171 Benjamin 149

FAIRBANKS (continued)
Bertie S 234 Caroline L 149
Charles 234 Charles C 234
Charlotte 86 Clark 62 Davis
170 Delina 207 Edith 234 Edwin 226 Edwin C 226 Elizabeth
B 62 Ellen J 62 Emeline Talmage 70 Emma Della 70 Esther 154 155 F W Ruggles 234
Freddie S 234 G 62 George 234
George P 234 George W 226
Hannah 62 Ida 234 J 207 J W
62 Jessie L 234 Joel W 62
John O 70 Jonathan 62 149
Jonathan H 62 Joshua 149
Lelia W 226 Levi 62 Lois 149
Lucy 173 Lydia 62 Manaseh
193 Manasseh 193 Margaret B
62 Mary P 234 Mary S 234
Nancy 170 Nancy S 73 Nellie
234 Nestor 234 Nestor S 234
Persis 193 Phebe 170 Phineas
86 Rebecca 37 172 S 207 S E
226 Sabelle K 226 Sally 62 170
Sarah H 170 Silas 234 Sophia E
226 Susan R 234 Thankful 149
Thankfull 175 Thomas 62 W
226 Washington 226 Wilson H
226
FALES, Amy 13 Ellen Louise 37
George G 37 Jeremiah 13 Lois
175 Louise J 37 Sophia 13
Warren 13
FALLAS, Charity 7 William 7
FALLAVOLLITA, Angelina 223
Mildred 223
FANNING, George H 191 Harriet
M 191
FARLEY, Benjamin 212 Benjamin F 212 Gardner 212 Herbert M Lang 212 L Frances
Lang 212 Mary E 212 Mary L
212
FARMER, Almeda P 60 Elizabeth
60 Ella C 60 Emroy 60 Luke
60 Luke W 60 Lydia 65 Martha
60 Mary 60 Mary A P 60
Sophia Raymond 60 Warren A
60
FARNSWORTH, Abel 38 62
Abigail 105 Andrew 13 Asa D
14 57 Barker G 240

FARNSWORTH (continued)
Benjamin 14 Benjamin 2nd 14
Betsy 14 44 Betsy S 57 C
Rebecca 240 Caroline C 38
Catharine M 13 Charles C 105
Charles L 105 D 240 Daniel
240 Davis 240 Dorcas 14 Ed-
ward E 14 Edwin A 54
Elizabeth 62 Eunice 47
Franklin 105 G W 240 Ira 39
Ira B 240 James 14 Jerome 52
Jerome Jr 52 John A 57 L W
240 Laura 54 Lewis F 105
Lewis H 105 Lucy 38 Lydia 35
52 Lydia B 105 Mark 54
Mehitable 39 Nathaniel 47
Obidiah 105 Olive 240 Rebecca
38 Sally 14 Samuel 35 Sarah F
Cunningham 57 William 44
William A 38
FARNWORTH, Ephraim 7
FARR, Asa 36 Ezannah 36 Fran-
cis 36 61 George R 38
Jonathan 61 Lucia E 38 Lydia
61 Maria 36 Martha E 38 Mary
C 78 Sarah 61 Thomas 61 Wil-
liam 61
FARRAR, Martha 79 Mary 180
FARWELL, Abby Maria 45 Alice
E 67 Andrew 67 Ann Elizabeth
23 248 Arathusa 31 32 45
Augusta M 36 Bethia W 48
Clarisa 31 Daniel 48 David 48
Emeline 45 Eunice 48 Hannah
48 Harriet N 67 James 13 John
31 32 45 47 48 Joseph 23 248
Leonard 23 248 Louisa 45
Lucius 23 248 Lucius L 248
Luther 48 Lydia 48 Mary 13 23
248 Mary Emeline 45 Mary I
23 248 Mary R Fisher 67
Maurice 45 Sally 48 Sarah 23
48 248 Sarah H 45 Sewall 48
Stedman 48 William 45
FAULKNER, Abigail F 8 Emily 8
Emory Jr 112 Eunice 8 Hannah
8 Horace 8 Mary 112 Paul 8
FAY, Baxter 113 Betsy 42 Betsy
A 47 Betty 197 David 197 Dex-
ter 196 Dexter W 196 John 47
Josiah 14 Mary E 47 Nancy F
14 Peter 192 Warren 42

FAY (continued)
Zilpah 196
FELTON, Jacob 186 Lucinda 186
Lyman S 216 Sarah E 216 Syl-
vester 186
FIELD, Elizabeth 104
FIFE, Abigail 7 Deliverance 7
Hepsibeth 150 Hespseybeth
187 James 188 Joseph 7 FIFE
Patience 188 Robart 187
Robert 187 Sarah 187 188 Wil-
liam 7
FILONDON, Gertrude W 238
Seabury T 238
FINCH, Freddie M 149 Sally 149
150 Sally Ann 149 William 149
150 Willie E 149 150
FISH, Eliza J 152
FISHER, Ada E 223 Adam 223
Alpheus 219 Betsy 14 Brnice E
223 Charles 14 Charles Luther
29 Elizabeth 14 Elizabeth S 29
Ephraim 14 Evelyn E 204
Frank 223 Frank E 223 George
29 H 223 Harriet F 223 Herbert
223 Herbert J 223 J 223 Jacob
14 Jeremiah 223 Mabel E 223
Mary H 29 Mary R 67 Nancy 14
Sarah 14 Sophromia 14 Susie G
223 219 Zeta Bell 223
FISK, Ebenezer 207 James 123
Jonas 123 Louis 123
FISKE, Elisha 29 Mary H 29
Sarah H 212
FITCH, 142 Cynthia 143 Ebenezer
150 George 13 Hepsibeth 153
James W 150 Johnnie 13
Luthera 150 Persis 150
Sophronia 13 Susan 156 Torrey
13
FLAGG, Abraham 177 Catherine
218 Catherine C 166 Caty 150
Dolly 14 Francis S 182 Ger-
shom 8 Hannah 8 Josiah 14
Lambert 219 Leander 219 Lois
177 Lois R 177 Lucy 177 219
Luther 177 Mary J 177 Orrin
219 Rebecca 177 Rufus 150
Samuel 177 219 Samuel L 219
Sarah J 177 Silas 213 Solomon
177
FLETCHER, Albert 71

266

GARDNER (continued)
Francis 123 126 Francis H 41
Harry C 109 Henry 123 Jerome
33 41 John 123 Joseph 123
Joseph H 109 Lucinda 123
Lucy Anne 99 Moses 33 Moses
Jr 31 S 99 Sally B 33 Sally T
41 Sarah 123 126 Sarah E
Jones 99 Sarah T 41 Stephen P
99 Susanna 123 Theodore 99
Walter L 41
GARFIELD, Clarissa T 215
Hiram 215 Hiram B 215
GARRITY, John H 177 Mary 177
GARY, Lucy B 173 Polly 161
GATES, Abigail 4 14 18 Abraham
47 Amos 4 Ann 123 124 Ann
Maria 123 Ann Mariah 123 124
Anna 3 109 123 124 Artemus C
123 124 Calvin 112 Carter 123
124 Catherine A 161 Charles
123 124 David 95 Elias 123
124 Elizabeth 48 Ellen L 150
Gardner R 123 124 Henry 123
124 Hezekiah 3 Isaac 48 Jacob
48 James C 123 124 Jane A
150 John 4 170 Jonas 123 124
Jonas J 123 124 Jonas Jr 123
124 Jonathan 47 Lois 123 124
Lucy 4 Luke 123 124 Luther
150 Lydia 112 123 124 Marcy
123 124 Martha 123 124 Mary
47 123 124 170 Mary C 123 124
Mercy 150 Molly 123 124
Nancy 3 Perney 150 Perney W
150 Polly 123 124 Reuben 123
124 Sarah 48 87 Sarah E 123
124 Silas 123 124 Sophia 123
124 Submit 48 Susanna 174
Thomas 4 14 18 Vashti 123
124 Wilder 4
GAUT, Jane E 143
GEARY, Joseph 150 Lois 168 169
Nathaniel 57 Perney W 150
Susannah 57
GERRY, Adeline 69 Betsy 62
Caleb S 44 Elbridge 44
Elbridge G 62 Elizabeth R 44
Ella E 44 Ezra 150 Fisher 59
George 40 Helen M 68 Henry C
150 Hepsybath 150 Jesse K 40
John 59 68 69 Jonathan 150

GERRY (continued)
Luther T 59 Lydia 150 Mary
150 Maryann 166 Nathaniel 62
Polly 146 147 Rebecca 59 S B
44 S C 44 Sabra 40 Sabra A 40
Sally 59 69 150 Sally Knight 68
Sarah B 44 Sarah Elizabeth 69
Susan R 59 Thomas 150 Ward
S 59 Wilkes 150
GETCHELL, Frederick 35 Sarah
Hartwell 35 William 35
GIBBS, Elizabeth 90 Hezekiah 90
Joseph 248 Louisa S 217 Lucy
248 Patty 150 Sarah 90 Wil-
liam 150 248
GIBSON, Adelia M 124 Avery 124
Bezaleet 124 Charles A 124
Elizabeth 197 Ellen 124 James
124 232 John 197 Lucinda 124
Lucy P 124 Persis 197
GIDDINGS, Sussan 75
GILBERT, Abigail 33 Jude 33
GILES, Hannah 54
GILL, ---- 207 J 207 John 207
Mary Ann 207 P 207 Polly 207
GILLETTE, Albert 210 Albert H
210 Ida M 210 Lottie Tremper
75
GILLIS, John 231
GILSON, Martha 14 Martha Ann
14 Varnum 14
GLAZIER, ---- 214 Emeline E
217 Emmons J 207 Esther 150
Ezra 217 J 207 John 150 Lydia
214 Mary 217 Nancy 214 Oliver
214 Rachel 214 S 207
GLEASON, Ann M 210
GLOVER, Betsy 124 Mary Ann
124 Mary L 226 William 124
GODDARD, Abigail 195 Benj
Franklin 194 Betsy 194
Catherine R S 194 Eber 14 188
Hannah 86 194 Jabez 194
Jacob 86 195 James 86 194
James Sr 194 Keziah 194 Lucy
188 Maria 188 Mary 195 Mary
W 150 Rebecca 191 William
86 194 195
GODDEN, Henry 75
GODFREY, Amelia S 38 Annie C
26 George E R 38 Levi 2
Lucretia M 26 Lucy 26

GODFREY (continued)
Mary 37 Rebecah 2 Salmon 2
Zechariah T 38
GOLDSMITH, Charles 47 Charles
Theodore 47 Hannah 110 John
28 Mary 61 Mercy 47 Moriah
28 Perley Dunsmore 110
Rachel 28 Richard 28 Salla 28
Sarah 28 Sherman 28 Theodore
47 Timothy 28
GOODALE, A 203 216 228 Aaron
215 216 228 Abel 203 Abigail
214 215 Angeline A 228 Annie
B 228 Azubah 181 Azubah N
215 Benjamin 214 Bertie 177 C
228 Caroline E 228 Caroline
Jane 228 Charles 228 E 228
Edward 215 Eli 203 Elizabeth
214 228 Eunice 215 Francis E
177 Francis R 177 Franklin
216 Gardner 216 Gertie 177
Grace 203 H 216 Hattie L 222
216 Junia 214 Levi 215
Lucretia 228 M 203 Mandana G
228 Mary 177 Mary A 177 Mary
Ann 215 Mehitable 203 Mehitt-
table 216 Moses 215 Nellie G
228 Paul 215 Peter 214 Rachel
214 S 228 Sarah 228 Sarah H
215 Tirza H 215 Velma G 228
GOODELL, Eunice 203 Jane 214
Jane Amanda 214 Nathan 150
R B T 214 Susan P 203
GOODING, Margaret 79
GOODNOUGH, Luthera 150
GOODNOW, Alma W 242 Annan
242 Catherine 150 E 207 Elijah
207 Elizabeth 187 Eunice 207
George 231 241 242 Hannah
241 Harriet E 150 Jennie L 170
Jonas B 150 Julia Ann 207
Kate A 150 Lindsey 241 242
Nancy E 241 242 Otis 207 Per-
sis 207 Rufus 241 242 Sally
231 241 Samuel E 170 Silas
231 241 242 Slias 241 Solomon
241 W 242
GOODRICH, Angie M 230 Emily S
182 Harriet E 161 Ida M 230
Oney 230 Oney B 230
GOODRIDGE, Asaph 63 Lavinia
63 Lois 124

GOODSPEED, Daniel 14
Elizabeth 14 Elizabeth Rugg
14
GOODWIN, Anna 214 Anraziah
214 Bathsheba 14 Harriet M 14
James 14 John 14 124 Rebecca
14 Susan 124 Susan E 124
GOOS, John 8
GOSS, Abigail 150 Alma 143 Anna
3 Asa 150 151 Caroline 150
Charles 150 Daniel 3 14 Daniel
Jr 14 Ebenezer 14 Edwin 150
Ella Blake 150 Eunice 3 14
Francis 150 Frederick 150 151
158 George 150 151 Henry 14
Henry Lawton 14 Hepsibeth
150 151 James 8 Jane E 150
Joanne 170 John 8 14 John Jr 8
Jonas 3 14 21 Joseph 8 Joseph
F 97 Josiah 150 151 Judith 14
Lucy 150 Martha A 150 151
Martha Ann 150 151 Mary 150
151 Mary J 150 151 158 Mary
W 8 Nancy 14 Peter 150 151
Philip 4 Rebecca 14 Robert
170 Sarah 14 150 151 Sarah E
21 Thomas 92 William 150
151
GOUDLING, Joel 177
GOULD, Benjamin 14 Edward E
14 Elizabeth 14 Harriet 14 15
James 14 15 Jane 48 Joseph
48 Lydia 14 Marshall E 14
Sally 57 Sarah 14 William 14
William Jr 14
GOULDING, Harriet 177 Mary A
177 178
GOWING, Esther 124 130 Thomas
124
GRACE, Sarah 73
GRAHAM, Asenath 124 Samuel
124 Warren 124
GRANT, Fredrick 209 Fredrick A
209 L A 40 S Augusta Hartwell
40 Sarah J 209 Sylinda P 179
GRASSIE, Alexander 104 Eliza A
H 104 Elizabeth 104 Elizabeth
Field 104 George B 104 Sibby
Ann 104
GRAVELINE, George A 229 Per-
melia V 229
GRAY, Bella 60

GRAY (continued)
Charles Francis 60 Emma
Cleone 60 Marilla S 211
Samuel 211 Samuel S 211
GREEN, -- A 65 Andrew 65
Andrew Fairbank 65 Catherine
A 65 Ellen 77 Ethel A 65 Geo
S 228 Kitte 65 Lizzie Etts 46
Louisa E 77 Martha 47 82
Peter 47 82 Rose J 228 Simeon
46 Susan Elizabeth 46 Warren
65 Warren H 65
GREENE, Harriet L 151 Harriett
L 155 Thomas L 151 155
GREENLEAF, Asa 90 Becke 90
Calvin 90 Daniel 90 151 Daniel
Jr 90 Dolly 90 Dorothy 151 Ex-
perience 90 John 90 Laban 90
Lorin 90 Moses 90 Sarah 90
Silence 90 Sophia H 153
GREENWOOD, Jane M 228
GREGORY, Elizabeth H 159 Lucy
K 166
GREGSON, Jane 215 John E 215
Mary 215 Robert 215
GRIFFIN, Charles 151 Jonathan
151 Zerviah 151
GROSVENOR, Augustus H 76
Ebenezer 42 77 Elizabeth 42
Lucy 42 Mary 78 Nancy 42
GROTON, Anna 81 John 81
GROUT, Charissa A 124 Charles
124 Eliza P 124 Louisa E 124
Lucinda 124
GROVER, 25 Benjamin 39
Caroline W 39 Charles H 39
Charles W 39 Charlotte Ann 39
Elizabeth E 75 Hiram S 39
Martha L 39 Mary 39 Olive M
39 William 39 76
GUTTERSON, Jacob 51 52 Lucy
51 52
HADLEY, Abel 151 Abraham 151
Allie E 229 Charles 229
Charles W 229 George 151
Lucy 151 Lucy Jane 151 Maria
151 Martin 151
HAGER, Mary 162
HAILD, Abel 151 Azuba 151
HALE, Benjamin 54 C B 15 Cal-
vin 124 125 Catherine 124
Eleanor 124 Elias 124

HALE (continued)
Eliner 124 Elizabeth 124 125
Esther 124 125 Father 124 125
Hannah 124 125 Hepzibah 124
125 Lillian G 202 Mary 54 124
125 Mother 124 125 Oliver 124
125 P 124 125 Phebe 124 125
Polly 124 125 Rebecca 15
Sally 124 125 Samuel 124 125
Sarah 124 125 Seymour 202
Seymour E 202 Sintha 124 125
Thomas 124 125
HALL, Abigail 125 Arthur 224 Ar-
thur Carroll 224 Bailey 125
Betsy M 75 Catherine 77
Charles C 224 Eliza 125
Gertrude R 224 Hannah 74
Harold 224 Harold C 224 Helen
H 78 Henry 57 Henry M 57
Jason Hirtle 224 Jerusha 57
Jerusha Smith 57 John 56 Julie
L 224 Laura A 224 Lena R 224
Lona 171 Madelyn 224 Mary
224 Ralph 224 Ralph M 224
Robert T 224 Sally 56 HALL
Sarah 56 Stanley S 224 Stephen
224 Stephen C 224 Timothy 56
William 56 77 William H 57
HAMLEN, Asia 62 Eleazar 62
Sarah 62
HAMLIN, Africa 36 Lydia 36
Rebecca 73 Sophronia 36
HAMMOND, Bennjamin F 77
David 58 Elmira 58 Elmira A
58 G 25 H L 58 John 58 Joseph
26 Lizzie 58 Lucy A 75 Mary
75 Mary A 79 Ruby L 58 S H
58 Sarah 78 Simon H 58
Thomas 76 Thomas Sr 75
HANNUM, Sarah 74
HANSCOM, 107
HAPGOOD, Abigail G 176 Adella
46 Andrew 33 Asa 47 Augusta
P 35 Betsy 239 Burt E 240
Charles B 67 Charles Butler 67
Charles D 46 Charles H 35
Charlotte Mead 63 Clara C 36
Cleora 35 David 239 Dolly
Mosman 67 Edmund A 235
Elizabeth 34 35 47 Elizabeth
Bennett 46 Ella 46 Elvira A
235 Fannie Augusta Foster 67

HAPGOOD (continued)
George 33 34 35 243 Harrieta
243 Henry 35 Hiram 67 J
Gardner 59 Jabez 34 Jerusha
239 Joel 63 John 33 36 John Jr
33 Jonathan 67 239 Jonathan
Fairbank 67 Joseph 219 Lucy
34 Lucy E 243 Lydia 239
Lydia H 35 M Adelaide 59
Marcy 87 Martha Ann 67 Mary
33 46 Mary Ann 36 Mary
Elizabeth 67 Mary Josephine
46 Matilda 35 Moses 239
Myron L 243 Nancy 34
Nathaniel 87 Peter D 33 Phebe
239 Ruben 235 Ruth G 235
Sally 63 239 Sarah Mosman 67
Shadrach 34 47 Silas 237 Susan
237 Susan Wetherbee 67
Susanah 219 Susannah 34 Susie
46 Theodore Goldsmith 67
Warren E 67 William H 237
HARBACK, Elizabeth 125
Thomas 125
HARDING, Freeman 202 Jane M
202
HARDY, Albert 71 Albert E 71
Carrie 70 Charles O 71 E S 70
Eliza 71 Eliza B 71 Emerson
71 Emerson G 71 Sarah E 71
Sarah W 71
HARLOW, Abbie R Fletcher 29
Ada F 29 Adeline S 30 Anna E
29 Carrie S 30 Charles 33
Charles E 29 Dorcasina 33 El-
lis 29 33 George H 29 John B
29 30 Mary W 29 Miriam A 29
Nancy H 29 P Holden 29
Pauline 30 Phebe K 29 Sarah
33 Sarah Ann 33 Sarah R 29
Susie M 29 William 29 33
HARRIMAN, 233 Bertha 233
Blanche 233 George 233 James
L 233
HARRINGTON, Anna 2 Charles
226 James 226 Josephine 226
Sally 180 Timothy 2
HARRIS, Amaziah 151 Ann 151
Asahel 15 Charles 224 Charles
Morris 224 Clara Augusta 224
David W 230 Eliza H 15
Elizabeth 146 151

HARRIS (continued)
Ella Jeanette 224 Emory 15
Florence May 224 Foster 151
Frederick W 37 George 15
George L 224 Hezediah 15 Joel
37 Lillian I 230 Martha 178
Mary 37 151 Melissa J 230
Nancy 148 Phebe S 219
Rebecca 151 Ruth E 219
Sophia E 226 Thomas 219
Thomas H 219 Waty H 219
Whipple 230 Whipple B 230
William 151
HARRISS, Amos 4 Edmond 4
Elizabeth 4
HARROD, Ann Maria 66 Charles
E 66 Edward 30 Eusebia 30
Fredric A 30 George 66 James
65 Mary E 65 Mary R 65 Noah
30 Rebecca 30 37 William H
30
HART, Harriet P 75
HARTFORD, E G 188 Erastus G
188 S M 188 Susan 188 Susan
M 188
HARTHAN, Anna 216 Anna H 216
Antipas 216 Charles 211 D 216
David 216 Dennis 216 Dennis
M 216 Emely A 211 Eveline T
216 George B 211 H 211 Han-
nah B 216 Harriot 211 Lucretia
Jane 212 Lyman 211 P 216
Prudence 216 Prudy 216 Silas
216 W B 211
HARTONE, Harry 70
HARTSHORN, Fanny E 71 Nellie
T 71 Stephen M 71
HARTWELL, Abigail P 41
Abigail T 41 Daniel 40 41
David 41 David W 41 Edmund
218 Elizabeth 50 Ethan 41 Geo
E 232 George 35 Josiah 35
Lucinda 41 Lucinda F 41 Lucy
E 41 Margaret A 35 Mary 62
Nathan 62 Olive 218 Olive L
218 S Augusta 40 Sarah 35
Sarah C 40 Susan 35 53
HARVEY, Achariah 174 Anne 177
Daniel 174 177 John 125 John
P 125 Sally 125 Sally R 125
Sarah Ann 125 Zachariah 177
HASKELL, 72 Abbie A 61

HASKELL (continued)
Abigail 50 Adolphus 61 Anna
45 59 Arethusa 241 Asa 59
Betsey 240 Bloomy 176
Catherine 67 Charles C 59
Charles H 59 Charlotte 33
Cynthia 59 Edward 59 Eleanor
B 59 Elias 24 248 Eliza 67
Elizabeth F 61 Elvira 59
Emma Josephine 67 Eugene
Ormond 67 Eunice 45 Flora
Burt 59 George 67 Hannah 31
Henry 2 23 51 Jacob 35 James
59 John 15 John E 15 Joseph
47 50 59 241 Joseph F 61
Josiah 48 Josiah W 35 Judith
B 59 Lucius 59 Lydia 59 Mary
47 48 71 Moses 45 Nathan L
240 241 Phineas 240 Roena
240 241 Ruth 51 Sally 35 Sally
Preston 35 Samuel 51 Sarah 15
51 67 Sarah R 240 241 Susan
35 Susan M 240 241 Sybel 51
William 241
HASKINS, Lydia M Child 211
Mary C 78 Rebecca 213 Robert
213 Robert W 213
HASTINGS, Aaron Sawyer 151
Almira 186 Ann 234 Benjamin
15 Benjamin Jr 15 Charles 234
Charles A 170 Daniel 82
Deborah A 90 Elizabeth 187
Ephraim 186 Experience 15
Francis A 221 Isabella 182
Johannah 186 Johannah Obrian
Bryant 186 John 91 238 John C
170 Maria E 182 Martha C 170
Mary 90 170 Mary A 90 Mary
Agnes 186 Nahum 217
Nathaniel 187 Olive 15 Oliver
186 Oliver Puffer 186 Rufus
182 Sally 153 Samuel 15 Sarah
Abby 15 Silence 151 Stephen
151 182 Submit 91 Thomas 15
188 William 90 William A H
182
HATCH, Eliza 114 John 114 John
P 114 Mary Bennett 244 Olive
26 75 Rebecca B 114
HATHAWAY, Ellen 218
HAVEN, Horris 106 Jubal 106
Lucy 106 Nancy 106

HAVEN (continued)
Richard 106 Sally 106
HAWKES, John 15
HAWKS, Benjamin 125 Mary 125
HAYDEN, Benjamin 46 Charlotte
61 Daniel 125 Edmund 61
Fanny 46 Frances J 52
Frederick 125 Honora 70
James N 61 Levi 52 Lewis T
52 Ruth 46 Sally 52 Sarah 52
70 Susan P 52 Warren 70
HAYNES, Amanda 79 Caroline
106 Charles D 109 Elizabeth
109 Francis 109 H F 109 Henry
109 Henry F 109 John C 109
Mary E 109 Nathan 91 Rebecca
91 Rebeckah 91 Samuel 91
Samuel S 106
HAYWARD, 233 Amos 101 L 25
L--- 233 M 25 Otis 233 Otis F
233 Otis H 233 Sally 101
HAZARD, Allen 55 Allen H 55
Catherine F 55 James T 55
Lucy W 55 Martha 55 Martha
A 55 R B 55 Tower 55 Warren
T S 55 Winfield 55
HAZELTON, Betty 214 John 214
HAZEN, Hannah 32
HEADLEY, (see HADLEY) 151
Abby 151 Samuel 151
HEALD, Ann A 125
HEALY, George 221 Herbert H
221
HELLEBERG, Anders C 170
HELLEWELL, Harriet D 222
HENDERSON, John 125 Margret
125
HENNESSEY, Abraham T 229
HENRY, Anna 221 John 221
Relief 179 Ruth 221
HERMAN, Charles H 226
Elizabeth 226
HERRIFIELD, Mercy 203
HERSEY, ---- 72 Charles 46
Emila 46 Hannah 72 Thomas
72
HERSHEY, Abby A 151 Eugene C
151 Samuel S 151
HEYWOOD, Betsey 151 Harriet M
151 John 151 Luke 151 Martha
A P 151 Rial 151 Susan P 161
Zelida 151

HICKS, Frances V 108 Jesse B
108 John S Veal 108
HIGGINS, Albert F 105 E F 211 E
W 211 Ellen N 202 Eugene 202
Robert F 105 Sparrow 211
HILBERT, Julie L 224
HILDRETH, Abigail 98 Adaline
98 Amos 52 Anna 159 Augus-
tus S 37 Carrie 37 Dolly 52 E
N 37 Eunice 151 152 George
227 George F 227 Hannah 98
99 159 J H 102 John H 151
Joseph 98 Joseph S 98 Julia
Ann 98 Louisa 240 Lucia 151
Lucinda 151 Lucy 52 78 151
152 Lydia 52 Maria 151 Mary
52 227 Nancy 15 Persis 98
Richard 151 Sarah A 151 152
Sophia E 153 Susan 52
Timothy 98 99 151 152
Timothy Jr 151 152
HILL, Asa 152 Augustus Gran-
ville 61 Betsy 67 Emelia 152
John 54 57 67 Martha Sawyer
61 Mary 31 145 Mary
Goldsmith 61 Mary R 76
Minerva 79 Oliver 61 Roxalana
79 Sam'l 28 Sherman G 61
HILLER, Joseph 7
HILLS, Albert 125 Belinda 125
Betsey 125 Betsy Buss 125
Charles 125 Charles A 125
Christinia 125 Dennis 125
Dolly B 125 Dorothy B 125 Eli
218 John 125 126 Josephine A
125 Josiah J 125 Martha Jane
218 Nancy W 125 Sally 125
126 Smith 125 126 Thomas 125
126 Volney 125 126
HINDS, Amanda 221 Charles
Henry 33 Cicero 221 Eliza 152
Elizabeth 31 Henry 33 Jacob
221 John 31 Pamelia 33
Rebeckah 202
HIRTLE, Lena R 224
HOBBS, Katharine 225 Martha L
225 William 225 William H
225
HODGENEY, Alice B 171 Arthur
C Jr 171 Arthur C Sr 171
Capitola 171 Emily M 171
Emma M 171 Harry A 171

HODGENEY (continued)
Herbert J 171 John 171 John Jr
171 John O 171 Lillian 171
Mabel M 171
HODGERNEY, Alice B 171 Arthur
C Jr 171 Arthur C Sr 171
Capitola 171 Emily M 171
Emma M 171 Harry A 171 Her-
bert J 171 John 171 John O 171
Lillian 171 Mabel M 171
HOGHTON, Hepzabah 87 John 87
HOLBROOK, Adaline 208 Ann 152
Ann B Davis 152 Cyrus 152 E
W 208 Eli W 201 Elizabeth
208 Harriet R 208 J 208 James
208 L 208 Levi 208 Lydia B
152 Myron Holly 208 R 208
Rebecca 208 Reuben W 208 S
208 Sarah 208 Sarah Electa 208
HOLCOMB, Abagail J 152 Augus-
tine 142 152 Helen 152 Jane
152 John 152 Lucy 152 Reuben
152 Sukey 152 William
Frederick 152
HOLDEN, Alice 237 Asa W 237
Betsey 48 Blanche May Bell
237 Carrie B 237 Flora A M
237 Fran B 237 Frances A 237
Frances M 237 G E C 237 Ida
B 237 Isabel A 237 John C 237
John Farwell 48 Lucy R C 237
Raymond C 237 Sarah 165
Sarah J R 237
HOLDER, Christopher 110 David
110 David G 111 Deborah D
111 Geo W 110 Hannah S 110
Isaac B 110 Joseph 111 Lois
W 110 Lucy F 193 Lunette E
110 Lydia B 113 Rachel F 111
Ruth 110 Thomas 193 William
P 110
HOLLAND, Elizabeth 15
HOLMAN, Abigail 86 90 107 108
Abraham 86 94 99 Abraham 3rd
86 Abraham Jr 86 Abram 93
Adaline 176 Alfreda Augusta
152 Alice 29 Amory 86 93 99
Asa 90 Azuba 94 Becca 90
Betsy 95 Charles E 152 Char-
lotte Louisa 69 E A 29
Eliakim 29 Eliakim A 29
Elijah R 177 Elijah R Jr 177

273

HOLMAN (continued)
Elizabeth 86 Emory 69 Eunice
86 F E 29 Francis Eugene 29
Frederick S 152 Grace 29 Harry
Atherton 29 John 15 Jonas 69
107 108 Jonas W 107 Jonathan
86 Joshua 152 Katharine 86
Levi 90 Lois R 177 Lucinda 29
Lucy 69 177 M S 29 Margaret
Stebbins 29 Mary J 152 Mary
W 177 Nancy 69 Nancy T 69
Nancy W 15 Nathaniel 90 152
Olive 181 Oliver 86 Persis 152
Porter 152 Roxana 69 Rufus
177 Sally 145 Samuel Kendall
93 99 Sarah A 152 Sarah J 152
Silas 69 86 95 Silas W 69
Sophia Whitcomb 29 Susan 107
108 Susan C 29 Tryphenia 177
HOLMES, Harriet A 176 Mary 154
Mary Jane 219 Sally 219
Thomas 219 Thomas II 219
William 152
HOLT, A 213 Alfred 202 Amanda
177 Amasa 189 191 Anna 213
Arathusa 171 Asa 217 C 202
Caroline E 225 Charles 202
Charles M 202 Eliza 189 191
Emeline P 213 Emerline 217
Ephraim 218 Fidelia 202 H F
225 Hannah 189 Harriet K 171
Henry 225 Henry F 225 Henry
Keyes 225 J S 213 John Milton
225 John T 189 Jonas 213 L K
225 Leslie O 193 Lucius 225
Lucius K 225 Lucius Milton
225 Lydia 225 M 202 M L 225
Mabel E 202 Marcell Shed 213
Martha L 225 Mary 89 Mary A
202 Mary M 227 Nabby 189 191
Nancy 208 217 Nancy F 171 O
W 193 Parkman 218 R M 225
Rebeccah 225 Russell 213 S G
193 Sally 170 Sanford 202
Sarah 213 Sarah A 227 Stephen
227 Susanna 26 Thomas 89
Tyler 171 Uriah 8
HOLYOKE, Eugene A 232
HOMER, Harriet F 53 Jacob 53
Sarah L 53 Sarah Wetherbee 53
HOOKER, Thomas 8
HOOPER, Edward 15 Emily 15

HORGAN, Edward 24 25 Edward R
25 26
HORTON, 234 Joanna 235 W H
235 William 235
HOSLEY, David 15 Luceba 15
HOSMER, Addison 178 Addison A
178 Adelaide A 176 Arthur
Dwight 178 Bethiah 179
Caroline 178 Caroline F 178
Daniel 178 Daniel Jr 178
Ebenezer 178 Eli 65 Eli W 65
Harry Mason 178 Lucy 65
Lydia 175 Marcia 178 Maria
178 Mary 178 Myra E H 63 64
Olive R 65 Persis 195 Phidelia
180 S Augusta 65 Sally B 63 64
Samuel 63 64 Sarah 178 Susan
178 Susan C 156 Sylvanus G 63
64 Theo M 204
HOUGH, Alling 219
HOUGHTON, ---- Ellen 95 Abbie
F 211 Abbie F Draper 96 Abby
G 69 Abel 32 Abiarthur 136
Abigail 2 15 90 126 157 Abner
178 Abraham 38 Adelaide E
Dudley 96 Albert R 234 Allice
15 Ama 168 Amory 187 Andrew
J 94 Ann 108 Anna 64 90 Anna
Gertrude 54 Annah 234 Anne 90
Arrathusa 154 Asa 51 Asenath
90 Azor 106 B S 100 Benjamin
15 32 142 152 153 191 Ben-
jamin Jr 152 Benjamin Sr 152
Bethesda 152 Betsy 32 56 69
Betsy W 32 72 Betsy
Wetherbee 69 C 244 245 Caleb
187 Calista 126 Caroline L 28
Carrie 71 Catherine 69 Cephas
72 97 108 Charles W 69
Clarinda 244 245 Cyrus 48 187
Damforth 90 Daniel 69 Daniel
P 69 Daniel W 107 David 126
Delia 152 Delia Sophia 152
Dinah 8 152 153 Dorothy 136 E
106 E H 42 E W 28 Ebenezer
126 Edward 152 153 Edward E
95 Edward J 152 Edward War-
ren 54 Effie M 234 Eli 152 153
Elijah 15 50 56 152 153 Elijah
Jr 152 Eliza 152 153 Eliza J
152 Elizabeth 38 51 55 63 163
Elizabeth Violetta 69

274

HOWE, 186 Adeliza B 102
Adoniram 178 Albert S 239
Alfred H 239 Alice 221 Almira
238 Amanda 221 Amanda J 221
Arad 178 Betsey 182 C 221
Carrie 221 Charles 219 Charles
A 101 Clorina 219 Dana 236
Dorothee Giddens 223 Edgar P
229 Edna J 238 Elijah 239
Elizabeth 171 Elsie 236
Emeline L 239 Emily Consitt
223 Eunice B 96 97 Francis 96
97 Freddie 96 97 George 221
225 George A 219 George B
221 George C 221 George
Francis 225 George H 240 H
206 Hanson 221 Harriet
Adaline 176 Harriet M 153
Harriot 206 Harry 221 Harry R
221 Henry G 153 Hiram 206
Jabez 239 Jabez M 236 Jane M
182 Joel 216 Jonas 102 240
Josephine L 153 Julia Ann 225
L 221 LaForest 221 LaForest
D 221 Lewis T 240 Lillie 96
97 Lizzie 193 Louisa 240
Lovilla S 96 97 Lucy 236 Lucy
S 193 Lydia 102 196 240
Maggie A 101 Mamie L 229
Martha 181 Martha B 175 Mar-
tha S 161 Mary 229 Mary E 240
Mary L 229 Mary S 179 Milton
229 Milton K 229 Moses 96 97
Nahum 102 Nancy D 221 Nellie
Fillebrawer 223 O 206 Olive
206 Otis 153 Prudence 153
Robert M 221 Rosie A 210
Roxanna 239 Rudolph M 193
Rufus E 210 Sally 153 Samuel
153 161 Sarah 102 179 196 229
Sarah A 229 Silas 153 Silas H
153 Silas Jr 153 Sofie 216
Solomon 196 Solomon Henry
196 Sophia 96 97 153 161
Sophia E 153 Submit 153 Susan
102 Susan E 102 Susannah 178
Walter A 229 Warren S 193
Wilfred Consitt 223 Willard
238 William Nelson 153 Wil-
liam Waldo 223 Zara 178
HOYT, Abbie 50 Elizabeth T 50
John 50

HUBBARD, Calvin P 35 Cyrus
212 Eliza 21 Lucy 182
Rosewell 21 Sarah H 212
HUDSON, Charles 231
HUGHTON, Sanderson 89
HUNT, Arrethusa 15 Ephraim W
232 Maria 15 Otis 15 Otis Jr
15 Samuel 51 Tabitha 51
HUNTER, Edward 245 Elizabeth
245 Tabitha 245
HURD, H G 222 Louisa 222 Wil-
liam 76
HURLBUT, Cora A Jacobs 102
James 102 James D 102 Lucy
S 102
HUSE, Charlotte 34 Denison 38
Enoch 34 Enoch Jr 34 Esther
W 34 James W 38 John 34
John D 34 Lucy 34 Mary B 38
Rebecca 34 Stephen 34
HUTCHINS, Bethia 45 William 45
HUTCHINSON, Genger 145
HYNES, Christie Sawyer 66
Franklyn 66 Franklyn M 66
IAZELL, Joseph 241 Roxana 241
JACKSON, Ann 44 Carrie 179
Eugenia 227 Eugenia F 227
Henry 227 Henry W 227
JACOBS, Arthur 113 Caroline 113
George C 113 George E 113
George S 113 Gertrude 113
Helen C 113 Ira 112 Rachel F
112 Urena R 113 William 113
JEFFERSON, Sarah 77
JENKS, Mary 8 Phebe 8 William
8
JENNISON, Hepsibeth 153 Martin
153
JEWELL, Emma M 223 Susie E
223
JEWETT, Aaron 77 Abel 77 Benj
87 Benjamin 153 154 Betsey
154 Caroline A Moore 106
Charles H 221 Charlotte 153
Daniel 78 David 153 154 David
Jr 153 154 Elizabeth 79 Emily
Maria 171 Esther 153 154 163
Eunice 87 89 Eunice R 153 154
Francis Abbott 153 154 Hannah
153 154 192 Hannah C 153 154
Henry 109 Henry P 153 154
Hervey 221 Hervey S 221

JEWETT (continued)
Jesse 192 John 89 Jonathan
106 Joshua 153 154 192 Joshua
A 153 154 Keziah 91 Lucy 153
154 Lucy Anne 158 Lura Ann
192 Lydia 89 Margaret 153 154
Mary 74 109 153 154 Mary C
109 Mary Eliza 153 154 Mary
Holmes Kempton 153 154 Mer-
rick 153 154 Mira 192
Nathaniel S 153 154 Olive 87
153 154 Oliver 91 Polly 156
162 Ruth 153 154 162 Ruth Ann
153 154 Ruth S 162 Sally 221
Samuel 153 154 Sarah 75 80 89
91 Sarah W 153 154 168
Solomon 153 154 Susan 156
JILSON, Josephine 24
JOHNSON, ---- 194 A M 218
Aaron 24 248 Abel 154 Abigail
24 188 248 Abigail G 188 Al-
samena M 218 Amelia 126 189
Amos 189 Ann 194 Ann J 194
Anna 196 Anna B 218 Artimas
R 126 Asa 154 Belinda 126
Belinda H 126 Benjamin 126
Betsey 126 Betsy 44 Beulah
189 Calvin 24 248 Catherine
188 Charles B 218 Charles F
222 Charles S 126 Clarissa 154
Damaris 154 Daniel 27 44
Dexter 236 Dexter W 236 E
208 Edward 154 189 196 Edwin
208 Edwin S 208 Eleazer 189
Eliza A 168 Elizabeth 189
Emily Porter 126 Ephraim 116
126 Eunice 188 Fanny 146
Francis S 194 George 208
George E 208 Gustaf R 171
Hannah 189 Harrison 24 248
Hollis 185 188 Hollis L 188
Huldah 126 Jane 126 John B
154 John N P 196 John P 126
Jonas 126 154 189 Joseph 126
Joshua 189 Josiah 126 Jotham
126 Julia A 145 Levi 126
Lewis H 188 Lucy 152 Luke
116 Luther 24 248 M 126 208
Madelyn 222 Marcia E 226
Maria T 218 Martha K 208
Martha L 208 Mary 119 120
126 151 188 189 Mary A 154

JOHNSON (continued)
Mary E 208 Mary W 126
Maverick 189 Mrs Frederick F
116 Nathan 126 189 Nathan Jr
126 Oliver 154 Pearle W 116
Peleg 154 Polly R 194
Prudence 126 Relief 154 Rhoda
126 Rollin 226 Ruth 148 Sally
Ann 126 Sarah 126 Sarah
Adelia 126 Serena 194 Sewell
24 248 Sophia 126 Sophronia
126 Susan 189 Susan J 236
Tamer 162 W H 218 William
H 218 William N 244 Willie
218 Zenas 193 Zoath 200
JOHNSTON Caroline K 178
George 178 Johanna 178 Mar-
garet A 178 Mary 177 Robert
178
JONES, ---- 197 Aaron 15
Abigail 196 Amasa 126 127
Anna 166 Benjamin F 15 Betsy
112 Charles 197 Charlotte 16
David 26 Dorothy 192 Edwin 15
Ethel Vannevar 240 Frances
Olivia 213 Frank 240 Frank
Elwyn 240 Frederick 126 127
Frederick W 126 127 Hannah C
237 238 Harriet A Vannevar
240 Harry S 240 Ichabod 192
James 71 John 213 John C 213
Jonathan 197 Levi 237 238
Lucy A 237 238 Luther 16
Marcus L 16 Martha 126 127
195 197 Mary Ann 15 Mary C
133 Mary E 237 238 Moses 15
Olivia 213 Paltiah 196 Pattie
126 127 Pelatiah 196 Persis
196 Phebe 126 127 Robert 76
Sally 15 126 127 195 197 Sally
M 237 238 Samantha 71
Samuel 126 127 185 192 195
196 197 Sarah E 99 Sarah
Elizabeth H 74 Sarah J 16
Solon 15 Submit 15 Submittee
15 Sullivan 15 Susannah 192
Timothy 192 197
JOSLIN, Abigail R 127 Betsey
127 Calvin 127 Caroline 127
Dorothy 5 Elias 115 127 Elias
Jr 116 Elizabeth 127 George W
127 Hannah 5 James 127

JOSLIN (continued)
Joanna 5 Joel 127 John 127
John Jr 116 Joseph 127 Lorin
127 Luke 127 Martha 5
Nathaniel 5 Patience 127 Peter
5 127 Polly 127 Priscilla 127
Prudence 127 Sally 127 Sarah
127 William 127
JOSLYN, Abigail 16 Abigail
Wilder 18 Almira 154
Catherine E 154 Jonas 16 Mar-
tha 7 Mary 16 Nathaniel 16
Peter 7 16 154 Samuel 15 16
18
JOY, Hiram 68 Seraphinia P 68
KAVEN, Harriet 229 Helen M 229
James 229 James M 229
Moses 229 Moses B 229
KEEFE, Alice M 227
KEEP, Elizabeth 78 Jabez 42
Phebe 73 74 Rachel 78 Ruth 73
Sarah 78
KEITH, Albion A 239
KELLETT, Mary 154 Thomas 154
KELLEY, Charles N 77 Mary A
76
KELLOGG, Annette 222
KELLY, Florence M 229
KEMPTON, Mary 154
KENDALL, Abel 127 Abigail 3
154 Annas 127 Arrathusa 154
Augustus 154 Augustus Wil-
liam 154 Betsey 154 Charles
154 155 156 218 Charles B 154
Charles S 218 Charles W 154
Claressa 127 Clarissa 178
Clarissa H 178 David 127
Dolly 145 154 168 Edwin 154
155 Eliza Putnam 166
Elizabeth 154 Elizabeth Ben-
nett 127 Emma 164 Enoch 61
Esther 153 154 155 Ethan 154
155 156 Ethan Jr 154 155
Ethan Sr 154 155 156 Eunice
153 Ezekiel 154 155 Ezekiel Jr
154 155 156 Ezra 154 155
Fannie Jane 218 Fanny 61
Frances 154 155 George 154
155 George A 154 155 George
Ezra 154 155 Gill 154 155
Hanna 127 Hannah 78 Harriet L
151 Harriett L 154 155

KENDALL, (continued)
Harriett M 154 155 Harrison
154 155 Harvey 154 155 156
Heman 178 Heman 2nd 178
Heman 3rd 178 Henry E 154
155 Horace 154 155 James 61
154 155 156 James Jr 154
James W 154 155 James
Wilder 154 155 Jane W 154
155 Joel 154 155 Joel Edward
154 155 John 244 John B 151
154 155 John H 154 155 John
Jr 127 John L 154 155 Jonas
127 Joseph 154 155 156 Josiah
154 155 156 Josiah Jr 154 155
Katherine 154 155 L Elizabeth
154 155 Lucinda 154 155 Lucy
127 154 155 162 166 Lucy J
244 Luke 61 127 Luther 154
155 156 168 Luther Wilder 154
155 Lydia 154 155 156 M Malvina 178 Mark 154 155 Martha
178 Mary 154 155 178 Mary A
154 155 Mary E 154 155 Mary
W 112 163 218 Molly 146
Nancy 154 155 Nathan 178
Nathan H 178 Otis A 112 Peter
154 155 178 Pierson 154 155
156 Pierson T 154 155 156
Polly 127 134 154 155 156 159
182 Priscilla 154 155 156
Prudence 127 153 Rebecca R
154 155 156 Robert 218 Ruth
154 155 156 Sally 154 155 156
Samuel 182 Sarah 78 127 154
155 165 Sarah E 154 155 156
Silba 154 155 156 Submit 178
Susan 154 155 156 Susan G 75
Susan L 154 155 156 Susan R
154 156 156 Susanna 178 Sybel
61 Tabatha 154 155 156
Tabitha 166 Thankfull 154 155
156 Thomas 3 William 61 77
Wyman 154 155 156
KENDELL, Nathan 77
KENNAN, Alonzo 213 E 213
Ephraim 213 Marsha Maria 213
KENNAN T 213 Thankful B
213
KENNEDY, Cecelia 230 Isaac S
241 Johanna 178 Raymond 241
William R 230 Willie 241

LAFOREST, Adeline 234 Anna
Bigham 236 Edward 234 Ed-
ward A 234 Eliza 236 Emily G
Hallett 236 Jan 236 John 236
Joseph Rena Aubin 236 Mar-
garet 236
LAKEMAN, Eben H 62 Ebenezer
60 Lindie A 62 Mary 60
Selenda S 62
LAMB, Adeline 127 Albert 127
Charles Albert 127 Charles
Francis 41 Mary Gardner 41
LAMSON, D L 227 Madeline M
227 Mary 227 Nathaniel 178
179 Philinda 178 179 Sarah 178
179 Silas 178
LANDY, C C 224 Charles 224
Charles C 224 Clarence 224
Clarence E 224 D M 224 G
Ethel 224 George M 228 J 228
J E 228 James 228 Ralph E
224
LANE, Benjamin R 37 Edward F
230 Edwin 36 Jane W 36
LARKIN, Azubah 189 Catherine
188 Cynthia H 188 Hepsybeth
193 John 188 189 John F 188
Lucy 189 Mary 156 Mattathias
156 Otis 187 Peter 189 Sally
189 Sarah 188 Sarah R 189 Seth
156 Solomon 193
LARSON, Arthur 179 Arthur L W
179 Dorothy M 179 Florence M
229 Hilmar 229 Hilmar C 229
LATHE, Anna 74 Eunice 73 Ezra
74
LAUGHTON, Artemas 16 Clarissa
16 Ephraim 16 Jeremiah 42
John 16 42 John Jr 16 Lucy
Ann 16 Martha B 16 Mary Ann
16 Nancy 16 Olivea 42 Rachel
42 Sarah 42 Stephen 16
LAWRENCE, Abbott 70 Abel 50
Abijah 28 95 107 Abijah Jr 107
Abraham 70 Alvarus 46 Andrew
70 Benjamin 62 Bethiah 179
Bethiah L 182 Betsy 28 Brad-
ley V 70 C H 70 Caroline 39
Comfort B 179 Daniel H 156
Deborah W 49 Delia 46 Delia
Maria 46 Edmund 16 Eliza 49
Ella E 156 Esther W 49

LAWRENCE (continued)
Francis 46 George E 70 George
Washington 179 Henry 49
Horace A 70 Horace R 70
Jacob George 179 James B 179
James Benjamin 179 John K
60 Jonathan 70 Joseph 179
Katherine L 70 Kimball 39
Laura Ann 70 Lewis D 70
Lucinda Maria 70 Lucy 49 106
Lucy B 49 Lucy Folger 49
Martha B 175 Mary Ann 95
Mary H 49 Millicent 107 Oliver
W 70 Phebe 50 Rhoda 49
Rhoda Wood 70 Rollin H 70 S
S 70 Sally 16 Samuel 156
Samuel H 156 Samuel Jr 175
Sarah 39 Sarah A Williston 70
Sarah Jane 39 Stephen 49
Stephen Jr 49 Susan 156 Susan
C 156 Susie J 70 Sylinda 179
Sylinda E 179 Sylinda P 179
Tryphena 50 William 49
LEACH, Abigail 16 Collins 16
Eliab 16 Joanna P 34 Joseph
16 Rebecca 16 Susannah 16
William S 34
LEAVITT, Josiah 156 Mary 156
LEE, B 16 Benjamin 212
Bezaleel 212 Eunice 212 John
H 171 L 16 Nelson M 179
LEGEYT, Melinda T 156
LEGGATT, Elizabeth Dorothy
Evered 127 Mary 127 128
Thomas 127 128
LELAND, John 128
LEONARD, William 76
LEONE, Angelo J 229 Mary C 229
LEWIS, Albert W 156 Alvira 157
Alvira M 156 Betsey 156 157
Fanny 27 Francis A 157 Fred
219 Fred A 219 John 157
Joseph 156 Joseph P 157 Josie
157 Martha 161 Nathaniel 156
157 S Annie 219 Sarah 27
Thomas E 157 William 16 27
LINCOLN, Abigail F 128 Augusta
128 Caleb 16 Chloe 16 Cum-
mins 16 David 128 Elizabeth
128 Ephraim 128 Eunice 128
Jacob 16 Laura 128 Luke 128
Lydia 128 Mark 128

281

MCLEAN, Almyra E 77
MCQUIGGAN, Richard 231 245
MCVEY, James J 242
MEAD, Charlotte 63 Hannah 32
Samuel 31 32
MEED, Mercy 42 Samuel 42
MEEDS, Lydia 65 Lydia Priest 65
Reuben 65
MEEHAN, Sally 76
MELLEN, John 157 Rebecca 157
Sophia 157 Thomas 157
MELVIN, Lucy D 129
MERIAM, Amos 129 Clarissa 129
Delia 129 Elizabeth 129
Frances 58 Jonas 58 Jonathan
129 Jonathan Jr 129 Luther 129
Luther S 129 Mary 129 Nathan
129 Polly 129 Rachel 58 129
Sarah 58 William 58
MERRIAM, Abigail 193 Adelne W
179 Amos 87 129 Asaph 105
Clarissa 129 Delia 129
Elizabeth 129 Hannah 87 Har-
riet 162 Jonathan 129 193
Jonathan D 193 Jonathan Jr
129 Levi 193 Luther 129
Luther S 129 Mary 129 Mary A
179 180 Mirick 193 Nathan 129
Nellie G 228 Phebe 91 Polly
129 Rachel J 129 Roxanna 179
180 Ruhamah 179 180 Sarah 27
Sarah E 179 180 Simon 91
William 179 180 William Jr
179 180
MERRIFIELD, Abbie F 226
Abiail 215 Asaph 203 Charles
226 Charles E 226 Emily P
226 Hannah 215 Josephine 226
Louis 215 Melinda K 215
Phebe 215 Silvanus M 215
MERRILL, Charles H 180 Charles
Henry 180 Charles S 222
Elizabeth 180 Florence 180
Flossie 180 George 234 Guy
234 Herbert 180 J D 111 John
A 185 John D 111 Laura E 185
Martha F 222 Mary Hattie 111
Mellissa 111 Ralph D 222
MERROW, Ernest W 201 George
E 201 George W 201 Harry E
201 Marilla S 211
MESSINGER, Celia E 172

MILES, Betsy 33 Catherine 17
Nancy Maria 33 Ruth 17
Thomas 17 Wm 33
MILLER, Charles 17 Eleanor Lil-
lian 178 Emma 76 Emma S
208 Joseph T 17 Lewis 172
Madalene 172 Matilda 17 Os-
car M 17
MINER, Alvin B 98 Arthur B 98
Aurilla 98
MIRICK, Eunice 165 Nancy 165
Sarah 168
MITCHELL, Eliza 73 Harriet 211
Richard 211
MIXTER, Elizabeth 73
MONROE, Delia C 36 Eliza A 36
John 36 Joseph 36 Polly 36
MOODY, Mary A 220
MOOR, Abigail 163 Achsah 88
Betsy 88 Eliza 88 John 89
John Jr 85 Levi 88 Peter 88
Phineas 89 Ruth 89
MOORE, Abigail 143 157 172
Abraham 88 Achsah 9 90
Adaline 187 Addison M 187
Asenath 186 Betsey 187 C G
86 Caleb 90 Calvin 157
Charles 90 Christopher C 90
Cornelius 104 Cummings 193
David 157 Dolly 157 Elizabeth
157 Elizabeth R 194 Elizabeth
Wood 129 Ellen F 192 Emma
C 116 129 Freeman B 106
Hannah 88 104 157 187 Harriet
9 157 Helen F 109 Henry 9 88
Henry O 106 Isaac 88 187 Is-
rael 157 191 212 J David 219
Jacob 88 205 Jonadab 88
Jonathan 88 157 Joseph 187
Joshua 90 Katherine 212 L 86
Levi 129 Lovisa 186 Lucinda
191 193 Lucy Lawrence 106
Luther 88 Lydia Richardson 90
Marius 129 Marshall 88 Mary 2
187 Mary Ann 219 Mary B 187
Nabby 172 Olive 164 Oliver
157 172 193 Parney 129 Phebe
157 Phineas 89 Pitts 157
Prudence 157 Prudy 157
Rebecca 157 172 Robert Parker
193 Ruth 88 Sally 147 Samuel
157 192 Samuel J 194

MOORE (continued)
Sarah 88 89 187 Silence 88
Susannah 157 Tabitha 157
Thankful 172 Uriah 186 Warren
187 Wilbur E 129 William 219
MOORES, Relief 145 Thankful
156
MOORS, Cathorign 8 Edward A 17
Ephraim 8 Eunice 91 Hannah 8
Jacob 8 Jeremiah 17 Joseph 8
Lucy 8 Margaret Ann 17 Mary
17 Mary Ann 91 Rebeckah 8
Rebekah 8 Thomas 91
MORGAN, Bertha E 95 Calvin Jr
204 Cordelia 204 Elizabeth 204
Francis D 204
MORIN, Nellie 224
MORRIS, Charles 128 Mary 128
MORSE, Abigail 239 Alonzo 157
Amay 219 Benjamin 103 215 D
204 E 204 Elijah 239 Eliza 103
Harriot 21 Harvey 215 Henry
Eugene 204 John 219 John G
219 Joseph 24 129 214 215
Lucy 24 Lydia 103 Mary 239
Mary R 26 Mindwell 204
Moses 239 Sally 103 Silvanus
214 Sofia 215 Sofia Bigelow
215 Sophia 157 214 Susan 129
Susannah 103 239 William 204
William Gibbs 24 Zerulah 239
MORTIMER, Ernest A 172 Ethel
M 172 Harriet P 172 John 172
John P 172 Philip Buck 172
Sarah 172 Stephen 172
MORTON, E A 211 F W 211 M E
211
MOSCROP, Mary Abbie 243
Richard 243
MOSHER, Ann 219 Isaac 219
MOSMAN, Dolly 67
MOTHER, Ab--- 60
MOULTON, Aaron 91 John 91
MULROY, Edith E 172 James R
172
MUNDAY, William 75
MUNROE, Aaron 17 Ephraim 41
Mercy 41
MUNSON, Persis 180 R S 180
MURDOCK, A 207 A M 207 Abel
129 Adeline 208 Albert H 129
Angeline B 208 Artemas 207

MURDOCK (continued)
Artemas Jr 207 Attemas 207 C
M 207 Carolina 206 Carrie H
206 Charles 238 Charlotte D
129 Clara A 208 David 208
David C 208 Edward F 129
Frinda 143 George H 207 John
Quincy 217 Judia Ann 207
Julia 238 Julia A 208 K 207
Keziah 207 Laura Jane 129
Margarette 129 Martha M 207
Mary C 208 Mary S 207 Susan
A 208 William 206 217
MUSSEY, Chas 49 Eddie 49
Emily 49 I 49 Minnie 49 P 49
MUZZY, Aaron G 227 Cephas 227
John 227 Lucy M 227 Miriam
M N 227 Nancy 227 Nancy C
227
MYCALL, John 27 Mary 27
MYERS, ---- 211
MYRICK, Daniel 76 Elijah 77
Eliza 79 Elizabeth 79 Isaac 76
Jesse 75 77 Joseph M 77 Lucy
79 Sally 79 Samuel H 77 Susan
K 79
NASH, Betsey 147 Charles 200
209 Elizabeth S 209 Mary G
209 Thompson 209 William
201 209 William Henry 209
NASON, Maria 72 Nancy 72 Seth
71
NATHAN, Prudence 126
NEAL, Annie Craggs 56
NEELAND, Joseph 53 Merriam 53
NEILD, Wilhemina B 172
Winifred 172
NELSON, Cephas 157 158 Dorothy
157 Ella C 209 Ephraim 157
158 Eunice 157 158 Jonathan
157 158 Kezia 157 158 Mar-
shall W 157 158 Mary L 157
158 Olive 157 158
NEWELL, Adeline 35 Harriet 205
L 205 N N 35 Norman N 35 S
205
NEWHALL, Alice 158 Asa J 129
Ella J 158 Elmira 26 Frances
155 George W 129 Hattie E
158 Jane J 129 Lucy Anne 158
Mary M 129 Michael 129 Patty
17 Pliney 17 Ruth 158

NEWHALL (continued)
Samuel 158 Samuel C 158
Susanna 129
NEWMAN, Abbie D 59 Abby
Davis 58 Abigail 58 Caroline
M 17 Gowen 17 Gowen B 17
James Homer 17 Lucy 17 Mary
Homer 58 Nancy 58 Robert E
58
NEWTON, ---- 242 Agnes 228
Alfred 100 Alice G 221 Alta
Christine 209 Azubah 180 Bet-
sey Beaman 199 Betsy 101
Caroline I 199 Charles E 94
Charles H 209 Daniel 158
Dinah 208 Dorothy 180 E 199
Edward S 94 Eleanor F 211
Ella A 218 Ella C 209 Emily S
94 Emma F 108 Ephraim 180
Eunice 199 Eunice I 199
Ezekiel 180 Ezra B 76 199
Fidelia 108 Francis M 91
George B 108 Grace L 209
Grace M Powers 108 H B 108
Hannah Ann 101 Hattie 205
Haven 101 Helen C 108 Henry
B 108 Horatio 108 I 199 Isabel
199 J 199 Jabez 199 Jabez B
199 Keizer 108 Lemeul 205
Lemeul D 205 Louise 159 M J
106 107 M L 108 Mandana W
199 Martha 158 Mary Ann 199
Mary Elsie 209 Mary L 108
Mary L Sampson 108 Melinda
218 Mercy S Soule 108 Nathan
Goddard 158 Olive M 91 Orien
H 101 Philip 228 Prudentia 94
Rebecca Barrett 108 Reuben 94
S 199 208 Samuel 180 Sarah
101 Sarah L 205 Silas 199 209
228 Tracey L 209 Tracy 221 W
208 W E 106
NICHOLS Abigail 172 Abigail
Moore 172 Abijah 24 248 Anna
24 180 248 Artemas J 129 Bar-
timas 129 Betsy 129 Burton M
172 Charles C 129 130 Desire
129 130 Edmund H 129 130
Eleanor 129 130 Eleanor B 129
130 Elinor 129 130 Elizabeth T
172 Emily 129 130 158 180
Ephraim 129 130

NICHOLS (continued)
Esrail 129 130 Esther 129 130
Esther Gowing 129 130 H
Josephine 158 Harriet 129 130
Hattie F 172 Herbert E 172 Is-
rael 129 130 Israel T 129 130
John 129 130 John S 129 130
Jonathan 172 Joseph 24 248
Laura 129 130 Levi 129 130
Luke 172 Luke W 172 Mary
129 130 Mary A 170 Roger 3
Ruth 129 130 Thankful 172
Thirza 129 130 Thomas 129
130 Thomas G 129 130 Wil-
liam 129 130 158 180 William
A 129 130 William F 180 William P 172 William R 158
NICKOLS, Artemas J 129 Bar-
timas 129 Betsy 129 Charles C
129 130 Desire 129 130 Edmund H 129 130 Eleanor 129
130 Eleanor B 129 130 Elinor
129 130 Emily 129 130
Ephraim 129 130 Esrail 129
130 Esther 129 130 Esther
Gowing 129 130 Harriet 129
130 Israel 129 130 Israel T 129
130 John 129 130 John S 129
130 Laura 129 130 Levi 129
130 Mary 129 130 Ruth 129 130
Thirza 129 130 Thomas 129
130 Thomas G 129 130 Wil-
liam 129 130 William A 129
130
NILANT, Nathaniel 78
NILES, Sophia S 75
NIXON, C Otis 158 Clarissa 180
Harriet 213 Jane E 213 John
180 Mary J 158 Nahum 213
NOBLE, Gideon C 60 Matthew 60
Nancy Perkins 60
NOEL, Carrington F 172 James L
172 Nettie 172
NOLAN, Howard J 244 Ida 244
NOONE, Mary Elizabeth 178
NORCROSS, Alma 67 H N 67 M A
67
NOURSE, 105 A H 93 Abby A 99
Andrew L 103 Arthur Henry 104
Asa W 101 Barnard 99 Bertha
E Morgan 95 Caleb 93 99
Caleb E 99 Calvin 100

PAINE (continued)
   L 219 220 Lydia 219 Mary 110
   Richard Ivory 219 220 Susan-
   nah 219 220 Tyler 110
   Winthrop 106
PALMER, Betsey 151 Edward T
   105 Elizabeth H 158 Ellizabeth
   158
PALMER, Henry 158 Hitty 158
   John 158 Joseph 158 Joseph Jr
   158 Lucy 158 Mary 158 Mary E
   158 Sally 158 Sophia 158 Wil-
   liam 158 159
PARK, Abigail 43 Andrew 53
   Anna 195 Benjamin K 53 Ben-
   jamin Kimble 83 Betsy 130
   Bulah L 196 Charlotte 195
   Eliza 130 196 Eunice 53 83
   Hannah 196 Hannah Fisher 43
   James 27 James R 195 Jane
   53 83 John 27 53 82 83 84 John
   3rd 83 John Jr 83 Joseph 196
   Lawson 196 Margaret 27 Maria
   Stetson 43 Melissa 196 Nabby
   53 Richard 130 Rosannah 27 28
   82 Rufus 83 Sally 53 Stuart
   James 43 Susan Hayward 43
   Thomas 27 28 43 81 82 83
   William 43 53 81 82 83 Wil-
   liam 2nd 83
PARKER, 142 143 Abigail 130
   204 Amos 98 Amos M D 98
   Augustus 56 Augustus D 56
   Betsey 159 Blanche W 56 E E
   D 57 Elizabeth 98 Elizabeth L
   B 98 Emily W 209 Emma J
   Weld 67 Essie 57 Esther E
   Dudley 57 Ethel 67 Eva B 56
   Evalina M 159 Granville M 38
   Harriet F 67 Harry B 230 Hep-
   sibah R 130 J O 57 J Oliver 57
   J S 130 James 130 131 James
   S 130 131 Jane A 204 Joel 221
   John 38 Joseph 76 Lewis 159
   Lottie D 57 Louisa 229 Louisa
   Jane 98 Louise 230 Lucy 38
   Luna F 209 Lydia 38 130 131
   Mabel L 56 Margaret 58 Mary
   49 Mary Edna Willard 56 Moss
   58 Mrs Timothy 204 Norman F
   49 Obra 221 Oliver 57 Orville
   C 56 Timothy 204 Whipple 230

PARKER (continued)
   Whipple H 230 Willard 130
   131 Willard Jr 131 William 38
   130 131 209 William A 67
   William E 209 William
   Wheeler 209
PARKHURST, Eliza E 75 Fanny
   47 Mary M 79 Sarah 47 Silas
   47 Sophia 43 Theophilas 43
PARMENTER, Clarissa 180 Han-
   nah 205 Harriet 205 Jonas 205
PARSONS, Ann E 75 Leander A
   26
PATCH, Abbie S Rahn 71 Adel-
   bert H 60 Albert B 71 Andrew
   60 Andrew Warren 60 Clarence
   M 71 David 76 Eliza 89 John
   71 John Herbert 60 John W 71
   Joshua 89 Lucy 149 Maria M
   60 Maria Mead 60 Mary Has-
   kell 71 Rebecka 89
PATRICK, Eliza B 101 Henry 101
   Samuel 101
PATT, Mary J 220
PATTEN, Elizabeth H 159 Emma
   D 159 Hannah 159 James P
   159
PATTERSON, Asa 52 John 131
   Lemuel 52 Susan 52
PAYNE, Charlotte M 159 Eloise
   Richards 9 Mary 159 Mary M
   159 Oliver 159
PEACOCK, Elizabeth 18
PEARCE, Gad 51 Marcy 51 Wil-
   liam 51
PEARSON, Abigail B 30
   Catherine 180 Edwin A 30
   Eliphalet 30 George A 180
   Henry 30 Henry B 30 John 180
   John A 180 Joseph 180 Joseph
   Jr 180 Julia E 26 Margaret 30
   Mary 180 Mary E 30 Mary F
   225 Mary Louisa 180 Merrick
   180 N Foster 180 Nehemiah
   180 P Holyoke 30 Polly 177
   Rebecca 180 S Bromfield 30
PEASLEE, Moses 18
PECKHAM, Alfred N 70 Betsy
   Houghton 69 Chandler Adams
   69 Honora 70 Honora Hayden
   70 Horace L 69 Horace Lyman
   69 Nellie O 70 Samuel H 70 71

287

PEDINI, Victor 230
PEIRCE, Caroline E 225 Carrie L
226 Catherine 161 225 Dorothy
A 204 Eliza 226 Estes 225
Ezekiel 225 Flora M 225 H
Dillon 225 Henry 225 Hollis
204 J 204 James 226 James E
226 Joseph W 204 Levi 218
Louisa M 204 Lucinda 204
Mary L 226 Oliver 204 Polly
218 Ruth P 225 S 204 Theresa
225 Theresa M 225 William
226 William O 226
PENNIMAN, H H 208 Susan A 208
PERHAM, Dolly 79
PERKINS, Benjamin 131 Enoch
45 Francis 45 Julia A 45 Lydia
131 Mary 45 Mary Adeline 45
PERRETT, Sarah 172
PERRY, Catherine 131 Delia J
131 Elizabeth 131 Evelina 131
Evelina Parker 131 Hannah 131
214 Henry 131 Icabod 131
Ichabod 131 Jane Eliza 131
John 75 Josephine 131 Lavina
131 Martin 131 Mary 75 Moses
214 Simeon N 2nd 131 Simeon
Newton 131 Sophia K 131 Wil-
liam 131
PERSONS, Elizabeth 76 George
25 Matilda S 76
PETERS Abigail 241 Augusta E
192 Edwin 241 Irene 241 J 245
John  M 245 John G 241 John
H 245 John Melville 245 L 245
Lucy W 245 Luther 196 241
Lydia 196 Maria 241 Warren S
192 Zilpah H 245
PHELPS, Aaron 9 Abel 131 Abiel
S 9 Abigail 131 159 Abijah 18
Amelia F 131 Angeline P 227
Asahel 131 Catherine 159
Charlotte A 180 Clark 159
David 131 Dolly 18 Dorothy
224 Edward 131 Elizabeth 204
Ellen L 227 Ephraim 18 Ester
18 Eunice 131 Father 18
George 159 Henry 18 Hezekiah
18 James 159 Joel 4 17 John 6
9 227 Jonas 180 Joseph 18
Joshua 76 Josiah 159 Julia L
17 Katy 174 Lewis 159

PHELPS (continued)
Lorinda 17 Martha 131 Mary 18
Mary Ann 18 159 Mary E 18
Meriel 18 Mother 18 Peter 9
Phidelia 180 Phinehas 4
Prudence 4 Relief 37 Rhoda
131 Robert 18 S A 227 Sally 9
131 Sarah 4 Sylvester 4 18
Zipporah 6
PHILLIPS, Bathshebe 1 Edward 1
Elizabeth 176 John 1 Jonathan
1 Lydia 1 Philip 105 Rebecca
1 Ruth W Schoellkopf 105
Samuel 1
PHINNEY, Elizabeth 74
PICKERING, C S 131 James H
223 Mary F 131 Ruth Buck 223
PIERCE, Abajah 212 Abigail 131
Albert B 226 Amy 108 Annah L
108 Asa 131 132 Augustus 131
Benjamin 159 Bertie 108 Char-
lotte S 108 Daborah 131
Deborah 131 Dinah 37 Dolly
131 132 Dorlinda 131 E 25 E H
216 Elias 131 Eliza 37 227
Eliza D 131 Ezra B 229
Fidelia 215 Frances E 216
Franklin 131 Fred A Cutler 94
George E 131 Helen B 108
James 104 131 James W 108
Joel 191 John 37 Jonas 131
Jonathan 57 215 Joseph 131
132 Joseph Bender 131 Joshua
131 132 Judith 131 132 Louise
159 Lucy 191 Lucy S 94 Lydia
131 132 Marion 229 Martha 104
131 132 Martha W 104 Mary
229 Mary A Whiteside 226
Mira B 131 132 Mira E 131 132
Nathaniel 131 132 Phineas 131
132 Ralph 108 Roxana 131 132
Rufus E 131 132 S H 108
Samuel 131 Sarah 57 Susan E
215 Sylvester 131 Theodore F
215 Thomas 131 Thomas S 131
132 Warren 108 William 216
William A 215 William S 108
PINDER, Sarah 39
PITTS, Betsy 18 Betsy S 18
Hiram W 18 James 17 18
Lewis Hiram 18 Lucinda 17
PLACE, Almira 172 John 172

288

PRENTISS (continued)
Francis Gardner 132 Sophia
132
PRESCOTT, Abigail 18 Albert
220 Alfred C 220 Amanda 220
Angie F 222 Anna 220 Bethia
74 Chas K 229 Clarence E 220
D D 204 D F 204 David 172
217 Dorinda 217 Doris L 212
Dorothy 5 Eunice 217 224 Ex-
perience 5 Frank 222 Frank
Nelson 222 Harriet B 217
Henry 220 Jabez 18 John 4 5
217 John B 217 Jonathan 5 172
Jonathan Jr 172 Lauretta K 204
Levi 220 Lucy 217 Lucy C 204
Lydia 132 Marrietta A 204
Mary 5 172 Mildred F 222
Patience C 220 Thomas H 224
Vasthi 172 William 220 Wil-
liam M 220
PRESTON, Sally 35
PREVOT, Ellin G 25
PRIEST, ---- 233 Abigail 9
Abraham 242 Andrew 31 Ann
62 Ann Jeanette 239 Ann P 67
Anna 9 Annah F 242 Asanath
193 Benjamin 231 239 243
Benjamin J 31 Betsy 243 Cal-
vin 54 Caroline S 52 Charles F
79 Charlotte 75 244 Clarendon
193 Daniel 53 David 62 E 25
Edward H 52 Eliza 67
Elizabeth 52 Elizaeth 53 Ellen
E 67 Elmira 239 Francis W 71
Gabriel 51 Gilman 243 Grace E
233 Hannah 51 192 Harriet B
242 Hazadiah 53 Henry A 52
Holman 193 Ira 193 J Rogene
71 Jabez 54 72 Jacob 28 44
Jacob 3rd 44 Jacob Jr 44
Jeremiah 61 John 9 28 54 John
F 52 Jonathan 9 52 Joseph 132
192 Lois 28 Louisa 242 Lucy
A 242 Luther 193 Mary 28 54
Mary A 170 172 Mary E 52
Milly 68 Oliver 28 Persis 193
Phebe 243 Philemon 28 67
Philemon Jr 62 67 Prudence
193 219 Rachel 54 Relief 54
Rhoda 28 44 65 S E 242 S
Emerson 242 Sally 28 44 193

PRIEST (continued)
Sara C 31 Sarah 28 54 106 233
Sarah A 31 Sarah E 31 Seviah
132 Silas 193 233 Silas H 233
Sophia 52 William 242 Zimri
44
PROCTER, Rebecca 79
PROCTOR, Adelaide R 100 Amos
47 100 Amos P 100 Ann M W
160 E A 98 Elizabeth 47 Ellen
M 160 Emery A 98 George 160
Jemimah K 100 Job 47 Joel
101 Jonathan 47 Lutie E 98
May H 98 Pamelia A 101
Rebecca M 100 Ruby E 98
PROUTY, 26 Adam 202 Jason G
160 Joshua 207 M 26 Mary 202
Phebe 207
PUFFER, Abigail 18 57 Almira
186 Hannah 195 196 Jonathan
57 Jonathan Jr 57 Molly 57
Nathan 18 Oliver 195 196
Phebe 195 196 Phebe M 195
Reuben 195 196 Sarah 195 196
William A 59
PULSIFER, ---- 241
PURRINGTON, Anna 26
PUTNAM, Albert A 132 Andrew
160 Andrew Jr 160 Charles 160
Eliza 160 Emma R 96 Irvin 96
Jerusha 160 Laura A 224
Samuel 160 William 160 Lydia
130
PUTTER, Dorothy 132 Jacob 132
Martha 132
QUINCY, Ann 9 Josiah 9
QUINN, Mary J 151 158
RAHN, Abbie S 71
RAMSEY, Burl 102
RAND, Abigail 51 Clarissa B 36
Eleazer 78 Ellen Maria 18
Harry 18 Jonathan 51 Jonathan
Jr 59 Josiah 36 Lucy 18 Mary
E 30 Nancy E 18 Nancy
Elizabeth 18 Nathaniel 18
Silas 51
RANDALL, David 65 Sarah 65
Stephen 65
RANDALL, Abbie A 241 Alla A
238 Anna A 112 Betsy C 235
Charles 235 238 Charles C 235
Charles M 238 Cyrus 235

RANDALL (continued)
Cyrus C 235 Eliza B 235
Elizabeth R 235 Harriet 235
Henrietta C 235 Jonathan 235
Joseph 111 Joseph J 112 Lilla
Florence 235 Louisa 241 M
Louisa 241 Martha 111 Martha
T 111 Mary A 111 Mary E 238
Paul 235 241 Reuben 111 Ruth
30 Ruth W 111 Sarah A 235
Sarah E 111 Stephen 111
Stephen A 111 William 243
RANGER Amos 160 Caroline F
160 Ella 160 Joel 160 Joel B
160 Mary 160 Samuel 160
Susanna 160
RANSOME, Myrtle 172
RATHBUN, Francis E 112 Hannah
112 Hannah M D 112 Solomon
112 Solomon H 112
RAWSON, Aimee B 243 Annie
Mabel 243 George 243 George
S 243 Herbert E 243 Mrs S C
200 S Ethel 243 Sarah 243
RAY, David 91
RAYMOND, Charles 63 Edward
160 Elizabeth D 73 Francis
160 Hannah 160 Harriet E 148
Hattie C 160 Hattie E 148
Hepsibah 160 Joseph 160
Lucretia 160 Mary J 160 Mira
W Dwinell 63 Sophia 60
Stillman W 63
RAYMORE, Elizabeth 160 James
H 160 Laura A 160
READ, Abigail 65 John 213
REARDON, Blanche 233 George
233
RECORD, Clara E 211 Everett C
211 J Frank 211
REDDING, Sally 180 Zebedee 180
REED, 143 Abigail 180 Almira
160 Ann Mariah 160 Betsey
160 Charles F 64 Christine E
147 Clerimond 160 Davis 180
Davis Jr 180 Elbridge 161
Elbridge G 160 Elihu 104 Eliza
182 Elizabeth 160 166 Emily
160 161 Etta H 64 Foster K
160 161 Francis Trowbridge
180 George Francis 18 Harriet
A 160 161 Harriet E 160 161

REED (continued)
Haskell D 160 161 Israel 59
Isreal 83 Joel 160 161 John
104 John Quincy 160 161
Jonathan 33 Joseph 182 199
Joseph A 199 Levi 33 160 161
Lois 33 Lucretia K 160 161
Marcia 178 Marietta 160 161
Mary Ann 160 161 Mary B 199
Mary Elizabeth 18 Maryette
180 Melissa 171 Nancy 180
Nathan 160 161 Nellie Maria
160 161 Persis 152 180 Peter
161 Peter K 160 161 Polly 160
161 180 Rachel 104 Roxanna
161 Sabra 104 Samuel 160
Sarah Sawyer 104 Silas 180
Silas A 180 Sophia 33 Susan
160 161 Susan H 161 Susan P
161 Tamer 199 Thomas R 59
60 William 104 160 161 Wil-
liam Jr 160 161
REID, Magdalena 221 Mary 221
Thomas 221
REMINGTON, Phidello 161 Sarah
161
RENO, Chester 172
REUSE, Lissie 73
RHODES, Bertha J 224 Gerald 224
Gerald M 224
RICARD, Mary Ann 162 Sarah
Jane 168
RICE, 233 A A 96 Addie H 227
Almira F 203 Alvah 132 Anna
180 Anne 132 Asa 213 218
Atherton Monroe 183 B 199
Betsey 199 Betsy 18 Carrie M
240 Catherine 180 218
Catherine R 213 Charles 180
Charles E 180 Damaris 165 E I
96 E J 96 E Maud 96 Elizabeth
233 Emily 18 Emma 180
Emma E M 180 Emory A 132
Esther 180 Etta J 228 Ezra 203
Ezra B 199 Ezra Beaman 203
Forester 132 Francis 209
Francis Beaman 209 Francis H
227 Frederick A 96 G F 233
George A 95 George Franklin
233 H Frank 96 Harold F 96
Harriet 213 Harriet M 213
Isabel 199 Jabez 233

RICE (continued)
James B 132 Jane 214 John
132 161 Joseph 17 18 Joseph
Atherton 183 Josephine 218 L
199 Leonard 180 181 Lillian
Blanche 209 Lorenze Tracey
180 181 Lucilla 233 Luther 199
Marion Anner 209 Mary 132
Mary Ann 18 161 Mary C 180
181 Mary E 96 Mary L 96 Mira
Monroe 183 Mrs A H 200
Nahum 183 Obed 240 Paul 209
Paul Beaman 209 Persis 199
Philoma 161 Rachel 132 Sally
148 Sarah 240 Sarah M 240
Susan K 132 Susan L 203
Tryphenia 177
RICH, Isaac 76 Nellie P 32
Obediah 75
RICHARDS, E 206 E P 212 Eliza
A 206 Elizabeth C 206
Elizabeth P 212 Florence E
107 Francis A 206 George A
212 Gerald R 107 Hiram A 206
Ida M 212 J F 212 Justin 212
Justin F 212 L 206 Leander
206
RICHARDSON, Abel 132 Abigail
132 181 Achsah 89 Artemas
181 Asa 181 Benjamin 175 181
Betsey 132 Caleb 89 Catherine
181 Charlotte 9 David 18
Demarias 132 Dorothy 151 Earl
G 181 Elizabeth 89 146 157
Elizabeth B 181 Elizabeth G
109 Elizabeth Ruggles 89
Ephraim 9 Ethel C 181 Eunice
9 132 133 181 Frances 132
George H 181 Green 132 Henry
181 Horace 132 133 Hubbard C
181 Isadora 26 James 89 132
John 132 133 181 Joshua 89
Josiah 132 133 151 161 Lefi
181 Lucy 163 Luke 132 Lydia
89 Lysander 181 Maria 181
Martha 132 161 Mary 151 161
Mary A 155 Mary J R 161
Olive 181 Patience 174
Prudence 181 Rebecca 181
Rebekah A 132 Reliance 132
133 Reliance C 132 Relief 132
Robert 89 Sally 132 182

RICHARDSON (continued)
Samuel 161 Sarah 132 133 181
Sewell 181 Silas 132 133 Sukey
132 133 Thaddeus 181
Thurston 161 Vida L 181 Wil-
liam 181 William B 181 Wil-
liam Crosby 132 133
RICHMOND, Sally 60 Sylvester 60
RILEY, Catherine 161 Catherine
A 161 Harriet Heywood 161
Martha S 161 Thomas 161
RIVERS, A G 107 Sarah A 107
ROBBINS, Anna 78 Azana 74
Bathsheba 1 Blanche M 222
Charles H 243 Charlotte 34
Daniel 34 161 Daniel M 76
Edward 1 Elizabeth 133 Emma
E 222 Esther M 243 Hattie L
222 Henry 64 Jacob 161 James
222 James W 222 Jemima 177
John 64 65 161 Jonas 196
Jotham 1 Jude 161 Julia 133
Laura 133 Lucy 64 65 161
Lucy Whitney 64 65 Martha 64
65 Mary 75 May E 222 Precilla
133 Prudence 18 R 25 Rebecca
74 Roger 161 Roy P 222 Ruth
74 Sally 74 78 Salny M 64
Sarah 79 196 Sarah A 74 Sarah
Ann 78 Silas 75 Thomas 77
133 Walter 222 Willlam 77
ROBERTS, Aaron 102 Polly 102
ROBERTSON, David Steuart 9
John 9
ROBINS, Anna 64 Augustus 64
Benjamin 51 Caroline 63
Ephraim Whitcomb 64 Jacob
64 James 51 Juliana W 64
Lydia 51 Olive 64 Olive S 64
Peter 64 Sally 51 Suky 51
Susannah 64
ROBINSON, Abby D 45 Anna
Gates 109 Arna 109 Arna W
109 Aseneth 33 Edna L 109
Elizabeth 75 Ella F 109
Fannie H 94 G W 109 George
33 George C 45 Gilbert 232
John E 109 Lucy A 109 Martha
33 Mary E 109 Myra W 109
Oliver 77 Roxalania 33 Sarah
37 Susan 107 Susan C 239 Wm
109 239 Wm A 109 Wm W 94

ROGERS, Charles W 133 John
133
ROLLINS, Mary 160
ROLPH, Elsy 133 Eugene T 133
Frederick C 133 Julia 133
Julia A 133 Maria Louisa 133
Nathan 133 Solomon Jr 133
ROPER, Alice 158 Asa 161 162
Azuba 163 Betsey 167 Caroline
161 Catherine 161 Elizabeth
161 162 Ella 161 Emily 161
Ephraim 161 Henry 161 Jonas
161 Lizzie 161 162 Lucy 161
162 Martha J 161 162 Mary
Ann 161 162 Merrick 161 162
Michal 161 Myra 146 Patty 163
Polly 156 161 162 Sidney 156
161 162 Silas 161 162 Silva
161 162 Sintha 161 162 Syl-
vester 161 162
ROSE, William 162
ROSS, A 204 A Dillon 204 Abigail
19 105 159 Achsah 162
Alexander 204 Almira M 156
Annah 145 Annie S 162
Arathusa 174 B A 108 ROSS
Betsey 162 Betty 162 Calvin
162 Charles 162 Charles P 105
Charlie N 162 David 105
Deborah 105 Delicia 162
Delicia A 162 Ebenezer 162
Eddie H 162 Ellen M 105 El-
vira 162 H 204 Harriet 162
Harry 211 Jonathan 162 Josiah
19 Lucinda H 234 Lucy 162
Lydia M Child Haskins 211
Mabel O 211 Maria H 108
Maria L 215 Martin 162 Mary
162 Mary D 162 Milton D 204
Moses 162 Nathaniel 162 Peter
162 Phineas 162 Polly 162
Priscilla 162 Priscilla G 162
Rebecca 105 162 Seth 19
Tamer 162 Thomas 162 Wil-
liam 105 162 William J 162
215 William Jr 105 William
W 211
ROWE, Catherine Davison 107
Edith S 107 Eliot E 107
Everett B 107 George 242
Helen Woodbury 107 Miriam
Brownold 107 S Goodrich 107

ROYAL, A T 30 Austin G 30 H B
30 Herbert B 71
RUGG, A M L 19 Aaron 18 Abel
19 Abigail 55 Abijah 18 Abram
55 Addison E 19 Amos 162 163
Bathsheba 18 19 Benjamin 133
Betsey 18 Catherine S 133
Cecilia A 133 Clara Marie 133
Daniel 18 Deborah 163 Elisha
19 Elizabeth 18 133 Ephraim
18 Francis 19 George Francis
162 Hannah Jones 19 Helen
162 Isaac 4 18 James 19 Joel
18 19 Joel I 18 John 5 John
Abbott 162 Katharine 19 Lucy
19 154 Luther 162 Luther W
162 Luther Warren 162 Lydia 5
162 167 Martha 162 Martin 19
Mary 19 162 163 Mason 162
Prudence 18 162 Rebekah 5 18
Relief 55 Reuben 162 Ruth 162
Ruth S 162 Samuel 18 Sarah
Wilder 18 Solomon 162 163
Stephen 18 162 163 Submit 19
Susanna 18
RUGGLES, Elizabeth 89 F W 234
RUSHWORTH, Gladys 172 Wil-
liam R 172
RUSS, Sally 18
RUSSEL, Elizabeth 51 Jason 51
Parker 51
RUSSELL, Amos 49 Deborah 49 G
239 James 239 Nancy 170
RYAN, Corrine 202 Etta M 202 M
202 Michael 202 Michael H
202 P 202 Pauline C 202
SAFFORD, Augustus 40 Catharine
9 Charles 19 Elizabeth 9
George 19 John 30 Julia 19
Martha 30 Martha Ann 40 Mary
19 Mary E 155 Priscilla 30
Sarah 25 Sarah Julia 19
Thomas 9 Ward 30
SALISBURY, Ellen E 209
ST JOHN, Emma 173
SAMON, Abraham 13
SAMPSON, John 57 Mary C Jones
133 Mary L 108 Stephen 51
William C 133
SAMSON, Abisha 37 Eleanor 37
James Manning 37 Mehitable
37 Thomas H 37

SANBORN, Caroline L 206 Levi E
206
SANDERSON, Elisha 24 248
Eunice 65 Isaac 65 Martha 24
248 Mary 24 248
SANDICKY, D 163 Harriet 163
SANFORD, Garry C 19
SARGEANT, Aaron 20 Ann 20
Elizabeth 20 Hannah 20 John
20 Seth 20
SARGENT, Angeline A 208 An-
geline E 46 Clarissa G 208
Curtis 19 Edgar A 208 209
Elizabeth 45 208 209 Huldah
19 Julia Ann 19 Levi 208 209
Martha A 19 208 209 Mary 146
Maryette 180 Merick 19
Rebecca 19 Sarah 73 208 209
Thomas 208 Thomas Jr 208
209 Winfield P 19
SAUNDERS, Washington 70
SAVAGE, Annie W Thacher 69
Charles T 69 Frederick 60
Frederick S 67 Harold G 67
Philemon 67 Sarah Barnard
Puffer 59 Susan J Clark 67
Virginia 60 Walter W 67 Wil-
liam 69 William H 69
SAWIN, Aaron 20 Almira R 181
Charles H 163 Edgar W 181
Ellen C 20 George E 181
Josiah 163 181 Josiah W 181
Josiah William 181 Lucy 181
Lucy A 163 Lucy Ann 181
Phebe 20 219 Porter G 181
SAWTELLE, J D 50 Susan 50
SAWYER, 186 A 94 A D 97 A G
97 A J 63 Aaron 163 Aaron Sr
163 Abbie G Smith 63 Abbie T
148 Abby B 19 Abel 191
Abigail 4 49 94 163 164 189
191 Abigail Bender 99 Abigail
G Shedd 94 Abner 46 163
Abraham 189 Achsah 46 94
Adaline 62 Agatha H 31 Alfred
62 Alfred A 62 Alice J 99
Alma 31 Alvan 197 Alvin 236
Amory Pollard 99 Amos 4 5 9
188 192 193 Angie F 222 Ann
Genette 97 Anna 163 Arad 62
187 Asenath 158 Augustus J 63
Azuba 94 163 Beatrice 192

SAWYER (continued)
Benjamin 92 Betsey 163 164
188 Betsey S 163 Betsy 21
Betty 89 Bezaleel 3 Caleb 51
52 53 Calvin 94 Caroline L 61
Cephas 46 Charles 19 94
Charles A 94 Charles F 19 191
Charles J 94 Charles M 192
Chester A 192 Christie 66
Clara Isabel 192 Cornelia S
216 Cornelius 163 Daniel 19 94
Darius 4 David 89 Deborah 4
163 167 Dinah 9 Dollee 163
Eben 19 Elbridge 101 Eli 196
Elias 9 19 Elijah 9 89 Eliza 19
62 Elizabeth 9 19 20 86 163
164 167 Ellen E 99 100 Elmer
J 62 Emma 62 187 Emma
Bailey 187 Ephraim 163 Esther
155 163 Esther C 101 Eunice 3
86 99 151 163 166 Ezra 19 159
163 Ezra 3d 163 Ezra Jr 163
Fanny Woodbury 187 Francena
19 Francis A 19 Francis W 97
Frank 99 100 Frank J 99 100
Franklin 163 188 Franklin A
192 Frederick Amos 192
Frederick H 19 G L 62 George
94 95 George F 183 George L
62 George W 99 192 Guy F 62
H Mabel Windram 94 H W C
63 Hannah 88 89 99 188 191
Hannah Coolidge 63 Hannah W
147 Hellen M 99 100 Henrietta
E 187 Henrietta H 94 Henry
216 Henry H 19 Hepzibah 163
Hooker 86 Ida J 192 Ira 189
191 J 93 94 99 J E 101 J S 99
Jabez 89 94 100 James 31 163
James M 94 John 9 49 89 92
94 John F 92 94 John P 61
Jonathan 52 62 Jonathan Jr 52
Joseph 5 49 95 99 188 Joseph
Henry 99 Joseph Marshall 192
193 Joshua 101 163 Josiah 31
89 191 Keziah 159 163 L 99
Lavinia 89 Lemuel 49 Levi 89
99 Lewis 189 Lewis A 191
Lockhart 197 Louisa A 19
Lucina Frences 192 Lucinda B
191 Lucy 89 99 163 189 Lucy
Ann 19 Lucy F 62 Lucy G 191

294

SAWYER (continued)
Lucy H 94 Luke 46 61 Lusena
21 Luther 46 Lydia 9 56 M F
62 Manassah 56 Manasseh 42
163 Manasseh Jr 42 Marcia
Frost 62 Martha 5 61 163 Mar-
tha Ann 192 Martha Chamber-
lain 192 Martha J 156 Martha S
19 Martyn A 61 Mary 5 19 49
52 63 86 89 163 191 236 Mary
A 192 Mary Ann 19 Mary E 216
Mary E Wilson 95 Mary
Elizabeth 192 Mary L H 61
Mary W 163 Mercy 42 50 61 66
Mercy B 61 Minnie L 99
Moses 5 9 19 20 21 163 164
Moses Wilder 163 N 93 99
Nahum 46 Nancy 19 163 183
Naomi 31 Nathan Corey 99
Nathaniel 163 Nellie F 94
Olive 163 Oliver 93 94 189
Patty 163 Paul 5 Persis 188
Peter 88 101 Phebe 163 164
Prudence 5 191 Putnam 163
Rachel 94 Rebecca 62 Rebekah
163 Relief 53 86 Reuben H 163
Rhoda 89 Rufus 191 Ruth 9 95
153 154 163 S Konisky 99
Sadie L 223 Sally 19 163 164
189 197 Samuel 142 163 164
Saphira 189 Sarah 5 9 51 52 88
95 101 104 163 164 189 197
Sarah B 99 Sarah E 19 196
Sarah H 192 193 Sarah Whitney
94 Seraph 191 Seth 9 51 Seth A
61 Silas 19 189 Silence 151
Solon 183 Sophia 46 Sophia R
189 Submit 153 Susan 101 163
164 Susan H 163 164 Susannah
173 Symmes 19 Thankful 170
Thomas 3 5 9 19 86 163 164
189 191 Thomas Jr 163 164
Uriah 197 Wesley 52 Wilbur
63 Wilbur F 63 William 85 88
89 163 164 188 William Corey
95 William G 185 William
Hastings 192 Zilpah 95
SCARLETT, Andrew J 226 Clara
B 226 Clarence B 226 W Clifford 226
SCHOELLKOPF, Ruth W 105
SCOOT, John 164 Mehitable 164

SCOTT, Abraham 51 Elizabeth
180 John 164 Mary 51
Mehitable 164
SEARS, Elizabeth 75 Hulda 51
SEAVER, Abigail 164 165 Betsey
159 Isaac M 156 James 164
Joseph 164 Nathan A 217 Olive
164 Susan 149
SEELEY, John 223 John F 223
Mabel E 223
SENTER, Mary 38
SERS, Anna 2
SETZER, Judith Ann 102
SEVERY, Caleb 212
SEYMOUR, A L 193 F 193 Gertie
Louise 193
SHANNON, Clarissa P 69
SHARRON, David Stephen 222
SHATTUCK, Elizabeth 73
Thomas 73
SHAW, A M 203 Caroline A 228
Hannah 159 John 203
SHEDD, Abigail G 94
SHELDON, Charles A 133 Edward
133 Lucy 133 Lydia 133 Lydia
M 133 Pelatiah 133 Sarah 133
Warren 133
SHEPARD, Barbara 220 G B 220
G Bertram 220 George 220
George T 220 M A 220 Mary
220 Mary A 220 Mary J 220
Prudence 194 Serena 194
Stephen 194
SHERER, Mary C 79
SHERMAN, Alfred 34 Charles H
213 Lydia Ann 34 Sarah Ann
213 Sarah E 34 Warren F 164
SIBLEY, Amelia 58 Ann Adelia
58 Clark 58 Ellen Amelia 58
Emily Adams 58 Henry C 58
Jerusha Adams 58
SIMMONS, Robert W 201
SIMONDS, Ebenezer 133 Hannah
133 James 133 John 133 Mary
133 Sarah 133
SIMS, William H 172
SIZER, Elizabeth 133
SKILLINGS, Adelima Beane 63 J
G 63 W P 63 William P 63
SMART, H M 107 Haynie 107
R H 107
SMITH, Abbie G 63 Abby 164

SMITH (continued)
Abby H 164 Abigail 20 146
239 Agnes 205 Albert 227
Alexander 164 Alice M 227
Amos 217 Angenette 194 Bertha Mabel 228 Betsey 164 Betsey A 220 Beulah 166 Calvin
194 Calvin Jr 194 Carrie 227
Charles 194 Charles Henry 20
Christina 239 Clifford Austin
210 211 Cornelia 157 164
David 93 239 David A 93
Elisha 164 Emma Thomas 164
Ermina 220 Eugene 232
Eusebia 194 Fidelia 220
Florence 227 G 205 George 205
George F 210 George S 205
Hannah S 133 Hanson 227 Harriet 164 Helen R 108 Helen S
164 Howell 19 Isad 204 J 220
Jacob 181 Jane W 155 Jarvis
227 Jedthuan 239 Jerusha 57
John 172 220 John S 220
Joseph 133 134 L 205 Léphia
172 Louise E 210 Lucinda 133
205 Lucy 161 166 Lucy A 163
Lucy Ann 181 Lucy B 172 173
Lucy Hastings 220 M 220
Manasseh 172 173 Martha 133
164 220 Martha A 164 Mary
146 148 149 170 227 Mary V
2100 Matilda J 205 Moses 20
164 Nancy 133 Nancy W 164
Nathan 164 Olive 185 Patty
164 Rebecca 194 Richard R 93
Roena B 95 S Marguerite 210
Sally 19 Samuel 46 134 Samuel
Gibson 164 Sarah 20 164 Sarah
Ann 164 Sarah C 220 Sarah N
164 Sarah R 134 Sarah S 134
Sebastian 164 Sibley Putnam
205 Sidney 164 Stephen H 220
Susan F 164 Susan M 227
Velma G 228
SNOW, Abigale 216 Agnes
Lucretia 181 Betsey 134 Henry
C 164 Homes 181 Lucretia 181
Martha E 164 Mary A 216 R
Winthrop 216 Sarah 164 Susan
E 134 William 134
SOLLENDINE, Deborah 19
Manasseh 19

SOMMER, Henry 205 Margaret A
205 Maria 205 Willie M 205
SOUTHWICK, Addie A 192
George M 110 192 Jerusha B
110 Jonathan D 110 Mary 110
Silas 90 Sophia H 111 Stephen
H 111 Stephen S 110 Willard
111
SPAFFORD, ---- 197 Esther 197
Eunice 197 James 194 Job 194
197 Samuel 194 197
SPARHAWK, Calphurna 96 Dexter
95 Harrietta 96 Mary Abbie 101
Rufus S 101 Thomas 96 William E 95
SPARROW, Betsy F 79 Godfrey
76 Martha H 76 Mary 74
SPAULDING, Asaph 134
Elizabeth 134 Mira S 134
Sophia 137
SPENCER, Emma 164 Henry E
164 Jane 164
SPIDLE, Winnie E 222
SPOFFORD, ---- 188 Benj E 193
Betsey 188 Caroline R 194
Emerson 213 Eunice 194 Hannah 194 Harry 243 James 194
James Richardson 194 Job 194
Mary 188 Mary B 213 Polly
194 Samuel 188 194 Samuel Jr
188 Sarah 243
SPRAGUE Ann 5 Elizabeth
Hartwell 50 John 5 9 Katharine
5 Laura 27 Lowell 50 Lydia 27
Mary E Blood 108 Miriam B
108 Nathan 34 Sam'l 27
Samuel John 5 Walter 108
Walter L 108
SPRINGER, Elizabeth 164 John
164
SPURR, Eliphalet 242 Sarah 242
STACY, E Waldo 59 George 60
John 60 Lucy W 59 Nathaniel
59
STALEY Ernest 173 Phyllis 173
STANHOPE, Abigail 74
STAPLES, Lucy M 169
STARKEY, Anthony S 186 Martha
M 186
STEARNS, ---- 134 Abby E 63
Anna 63 Augustus 19 Bettee
134 Caroline M 134 Cecilia

STEARNS (continued)
134 Christiana 134 Daniel 20
134 Deborah 20 Eli 19 George
134 241 George Otis 134 Jonas
63 Justin 134 Lorenzo 191
Lucy 134 Lydia 134 Martha L
241 Mary 134 Mary A 241 Mary
Adeline 191 Mary Whitney 19
Otis 134 Polly 134 Polly B 134
Polly Kendall 134 Sarah 134
Susan 134 Susan K 134 Thirza
134 Thirza B 134 Thirza Bar-
rage 134 Thomas 134
Thomothy 134 Timothy 134
William 134 Winslow B 63
STEBBINS, Margaret 29
STEDMAN, Almy 20 Christopher
E 20 Mary Ann 20 N Thayer 20
William 20 William Jr 20
STEELE, A 60 Elizabeth G 60
STEPHENSON, Lucy R 166 Lydia
20
STERNS, Ruth 75
STETSON, Elizabeth 36 Jane 36
Sarah A 36 Thomas 36
STEVENS, John 74
STEVENSON, Betsey 146 Lydia
19 Martin 19
STEWART, Augustus 210 Betsey
160 Charles 164 Elizabeth 210
Huldah 164 Phebe 164 Samuel
164 Sarah 164
STICKNEY, Phebe 241
STILES, Charles 181 Frank 204
Harriet N 208 J C 204 John 181
L 208 Lucy R 208 O 208 Oliver
208 Rebecca 181 Sally 134
Sarah F 204 Zira 134
STOCKWELL, Betsey 158
STONE, Adaline 187 Agnes M 71
Ame 49 Anna 48 Benjamin 43
Caroline 176 Charles Newton
43 Charles Timothy 43 Cynthia
D 43 Deborah 51 Deidamia 222
E D 71 E E 71 Elisha D 71
Eliza 71 Emeline 43 Emeline
E 71 Ephraim 48 49 80 Esther
M 243 Eunice 48 83 Gracie B
181 Hannah 71 Isaac 43 Isaac
N 43 Isaac S 193 J C 71 J
Louis 181 James 51 John E
181 John Elbridge 181 Joseph

STONE (continued)
32 181 Joseph C 71 L Warner
173 Louis C 71 Lucy 43 Lucy
D 43 Lydia M 243 Maria 32
Martha A 193 Mary 55 Mary A
193 Mary Godfrey 37 Maud 181
Micah 55 Moriah 48 Oliver 48
Rachel 32 Samuel F 37 Sarah
Robinson 37 Simon 48 80
Sophia 71 Willard 187 William
71 William H 243
STOREY, Martha 160
STOW, Abigail 28 Abigail H 9
Benjamin 28 Benjamin D 28
Dorcas 28 Luke 9 Sally 28
STOWE, Charlie E 235 Clarence
H 235 Edmund 235 Edmund M
235 Henrietta G 235 Herbert R
235 Mary Ella 235 Sarah 196
Susan C 225
STRATTON, Albert L 244 Barker
244 Carrie L 226 Clarrinda 244
D 244 Daniel 231 244 Dolly 99
Elizabeth 99 George 19 231
244 Isaac 99 232 Lucinda 19
Lydia Ann 19 Martha 244 Mary
99 Mary Harlow 99 Nahum 99
Nancy 220 Rufus 244 S 244
Sally 244 Tryghena R 244
STREETER, Eliza H 20 Vernis 20
STRONG, Bertha S 240 Ethel M
240 Franklin F 240 Jane 152
Mabel L 240 Mary 240 Mary L
240
STUART, Benjamin 164 165 Ben-
jamin Jr 164 165 Charles
Wesley 164 165 Charlotte V
211 Cora L 211 Corrissande
164 165 Damaris 164 165 Dolly
S 183 Ebenezer 134 Ellen M
164 165 Eunice 164 165 Flora
A May 211 G 211 George A 164
165 George W 211 Huldah 134
J H 164 165 James 164 165
Jane 164 165 183 John 134
John H 164 165 Julia M 134
Levi 164 165 183 Louisa L 164
165 M 211 Marietta 161 Mary
D 211 Nancy 164 165 Ralph
165 Samuel 183 Samuel Jr 183
Sarah 164 165 William F 164
165

TIFFANY, Daniel 78
TILTON, Aaron 215 Amanda 216
    Luke B 216 Mary D 211 Nathan
    202 Polly D 215 Sally R 202
TISDALE, Polly 135 Seth 135
TOMBS, Lewis 105 Polly 105
TOMPKINS, Lemuel 77
TONEY, Simeon W 166
TOOMBS, Adeline P 202 Charles
    202 Charles Olney 202 Daniel
    221 Eunice P 215 Eva F 202
    Joseph 202 Joseph E 202 L
    215 Louisa 215 R C 215 Robert
    C 215
TORREY, Roger Clapp 37
TOWER, Asahel 21 Debby Ann
    173 Henrietta 173 Lendall 173
    Lendall Pratt 173 Marietta 173
    Meliscent 21
TOWNSEND, Abigail H 20 Alfred
    87 Almira 20 Betsy 15 20 21
    Betsy Townsend 21 Caleb 3
    Caroline P 21 Catherine 166
    Catherine C 166 Elizabeth 9
    Elvira 21 Hannah 87 104 Henry
    20 James 87 104 John 21
    Joshua 9 Lucinda 87 Martha 20
    Mary C 166 Nancy 104 Nancy
    W 15 Olive 87 154 Robert 15
    20 21 Ruth 21 Sarah 87 104
    Warren 20 William 20 Zimri
    166
TRASK, Selah 78
TROW, Frank 223 Frank Hamant
    223 Hattie F 172 Saide L 223
TRULL, Edward B 236 237 Fred
    236 Fred F 236 Joel A 236 237
    John 236 Mary Adella 236
    Mehitable C 236
TRUSSELL, Murray 139
TUCKER, Elizabeth 37 Joshua 37
    Lucy 177
TUFTS, Sarah 104
TURNER, Abbie D Newman 59
    Abbie W 173 Abigail 37 52
    Adeliza Atherton 37 B T 20
    Bethia 42 Betsy 32 Charlotte E
    20 Charlotte M 58 D N 59 Ed-
    ward O 37 Elisha 32 Ellen P
    37 Ezra 74 Florence E 173
    George 37 173 Harriet 37
    Horatio 52 John L 173 Lurenia

TURNER (continued)
    J 20 Luther 37 52 Luther G 37
    Nabby 40 Oliver W 37 Prince
    32 Rebecca 32 Rebecca Harrod
    37 S H 20 Simeon 42 T J 59 T
    Jackson 59 Thomas J 59
    Washington 65
TUSAN, Maria 205
TUTTLE, Eunice Emily 20
    George 20 George C 20
    Jedediah 166 Lydia 166 Lydia
    B 20 Submit 178
TYLER, A 244 Abigail 61 156
    Abram 244 Alice 135 Alma E
    30 Benjamin 21 Daniel 135
    Edward 61 Eliza 21 Elizabeth
    135 Elizabeth B 244 Ella 244
    Ellis 61 Frank A 244 Hannah
    135 Harriet 135 Ismena 135
    James R 61 Jenney A 244 John
    61 Joseph 135 Josephine 244
    Joshua 135 Mary 21 32 135
    Mary E 244 Mehitable 135
    Mira 135 Moses 32 Nabby 135
    Phineas 135 Phinehas 135
    Polly 135 Rodolphus 135 Sally
    135 Seth P 135 Simeon 135
    Stephen 135 Susan P 135
    Tabitha 135 Thirsa 135 Willie
    A 244
UNDERWOOD, Joseph 214 Par-
    ney 214
UPHAM, Lysander 54 Martha 170
    Mercy F 54
UPTON, Joseph 21 Phebe 21
VALENTINE, Albian 239 Bessie
    M 239
VANNEVAR, Harriet A 240
VINAL, Alice M 236 Charles 236
    Charles T 236 Clarence 236
    Clarence C 236 Harry 236
    Lurena W 236 Mary E 236
VINTON, Boylston 205 Lydia 205
    Sarah Elizabeth 201
VOSE, Ann 5 Ann Austin 5 Ed-
    ward Henry 5 Francis Henry 5
    John 182 Peter 5 Peter
    Thacher 5 Samuel Sprague 5
    Veline 182
WADE, Charlotte O 22 Deborah
    22 Snell 22
WAIT, Hannah 146 150

WAIT (continued)
Abigail 173 Catherine 173
David 173 Deborah H 21 Esther
K 166 George 21 Joel 21 Lucy
A 166 Nathan 166 Patty 173
Tabitha 166

WALCOTT, Aurelia M 237 Char-
lotte B 237 Clifford 235 Clif-
ford P 235 Freeman 235 Hen-
rietta N 237 Henry K 237
Joshua B 111 Louise T 237
Lurena W 235 Mary Alice 235
Mary B 111 Ruth A 235
Truman 237

WALDRON, Abigail 154 173 Edward 173 Eunice 173 Hannah
173

WALES, Elizabeth 22 Joseph 22

WALKER, Annie L 75 Bathsheba
230 Caroline 182 Catheirne 75
David 230 Deidamia 222 Edgar
229 Edward P 182 Eli 229
Elizabeth 135 Ernest 228 Har-
riet 43 Harriot S 229 Harris 230
Jane E 182 Joel 222 Josie L
222 Lawson 135 Leonard T 182
Louisa 222 229 Lovell 135
Lydia 148 Maida 226 Mary 135
Mary F 43 Melville 229 Nancy
F 135 Nathan 135 Priscilla 175
R 222 R J 222 Raymond 222
Raymond J 222 Relief 135
Roxanna Miriam 222 Ruth E
228 Sally 135 Samuel S 43
Sarah A 217 Sylvanus 182
Willie R 222

WALLACE, Cleora Ann 21 David
21 Sarah 21

WALLEY, Maryann 166 Susan
166 William 166

WALLIS, John 187 Mary Jane 187
Susan 187 William F 187

WALTON, Eliza 22 George Henry
22 Jotham 22

WARD, Dolly 21 Lucretia Murray
21 Samuel 21 Samuel Jr 21
Sarah Hall 21

WARE, Abigail D 136 Martha R
136 Samuel 136 Samuel B 136

WARFIELD, Arabella 244
Charles E 244 Freddie G 244 G
244 George W 244 Maria L 244

WARNAR, John 2

WARNER, Aaron 50 54 64 Abigail
61 Albert 64 Angeline 228
Anna 64 Asa 21 Benjamin F 57
Betsy 38 C 40 Caleb 38 Caleb
Jr 38 Calvin 62 64 Catherine B
38 Charles 54 Charles S 228
Dorothy 64 Edwin S 40 Elias
61 95 Elias Jr 95 Elijah 77
Eliza 57 Elizabeth 50
Elizabeth C 166 Ephraim 50
136 Etta J 228 Francis 26
George H 95 Hannah 54 64
Harriet S 40 John 7 57 58 78
Levi 77 136 Louisa 38 Lovisa
64 Lucinda 50 Luke 64 Lydia
62 Mandana G 228 Martha M
95 Mary A 95 Mary Ann 95
Mary Ann Lawrence 95 Mercy
50 Nathan 64 Nathaniel 21 P
25 Percis 25 Phinehas 50
Polly 21 Quincy A 95 Rebekah
7 Roena B 95 Sally 21 57 58
Sally Gould 57 Samuel 54 64
Sarah 7 64 Sarah I 60 Sarah J
95 Susan C 95 Tobias 166 W
40 Zerviah 64 Zopher 60

WARREN, Abiail 215 Bethiah L
182 Horace W 182 Ira 215
Marshall A 243

WATERS, 183 George 166 Jacob
1 Lucy 166 Lucy S 166

WATSON, Alexander 52 Sarah 52

WEBB, Abigail 165 James A 70

WEDGE, Harriet L 151 Harriett L
155

WELCH, Eliza Putnam 166 Lucy
166 Lucy A 166 Lucy K 166
Lydia 166 Silas A 166 Sophia
E 166

WELD, Emma J 67

WELLINGTON, Ann Maria 22
Charlotte 207 Clarissa H 178
Lucy 22 Thomas 22

WELSH, Guildford 103 Lovisa
109 Mary 109 Rebecca 103
Silas 103 109 Silas Jr 103
Sophia Ann 103 Thomas 103
109 Zilpah 103

WEST, Ann 90 Annie G 113 Harry
A 113 Howard E 113 Mary 90

WESTON, Rebecca 102

WETHERBEE, Abby 29 Anna 51
Ari 242 Ari P 242 Arne 38
Betsy 47 69 Caroline 242
Catherine 47 Elizabeth Sargent
45 Ethan 47 Ethan D 53 Ezra
52 53 Ezra Z 53 Francis W 53
George W 29 Harriet E 29 John
51 Jonathan 50 Josiah 57 Julia
Ann 52 Katrina 67 Lucy 67
Malinda 31 Mary 38 Mary G 50
Micah 51 Nahum 47 Persis A
144 Phineas 242 Rachel 52 53
Rejoice 42 Sally 28 53 242
Sarah 34 161 Sarah Coolidge 52
Stillman 45 Susan 67 242 Syl-
vanus 67 William 26 Zophar
52
WETHERBY, Europe 100
Rebeckah 100 Reuben 100
WHALEN, E Eugene 182 Ida L
182 Jane 182 Jane M 182 John
B 182
WHEELER, A Harry 210 Aaron
113 Abbie 110 Abigail 110 111
Abigail K 102 Adeline Kent
110 Albert A 210 Albert Buf-
fum 112 Amasa J Gilbert 112
Amos 21 Amos Augustus 21
Anna 97 Asa 110 Asa A 110
Asa W 110 Bessie M 111 Bet-
sey 173 Betsy Jones 112 Buf-
fum W 110 Caleb 97 Calvin
173 Caroline A 110 Caroline E
236 Chester M 111 D 205
Daniel 111 David 166
Deliverance 49 Dinah W 205
Dolly 97 Elizabeth 111 Ella L
210 Elonor E 113 Elwood O
111 F A 107 110 Florence A
107 Francis A 110 Frank A 107
Franklin G 113 Frederick W
110 George G 173 Gertrude E
102 H A 102 Hannah 110 Han-
nah D 111 Harriet 136 Harriet
A 102 Helen M 210 Henry H
110 J 205 J D 111 J K 102
James Lincoln 102 Jane F 110
Jarvis 111 Jemima D 111
Jennie H Manchester 110
Jennie S 107 Jerusha D 97
Jesse A 111 John 112 205 John
C 205 Jonathan 97 111

WHEELER (continued)
Jonathan F 111 Joseph 27
Josiah 7 Levi 27 Lilla G 111
Louisa 110 Lucy 173 Lucy A
209 Lucy R 166 Lydia A 173
Mariam 113 Marilla Emora 111
Martha 7 Mary 27 49 Mary B
111 Mary Lovisa 112 Mary T
110 205 Merriam 110 Miriam
111 Phebe K 111 Priscilla 166
Prudence 21 Reuben 110
Reuben A 110 Roena 110
Rosella E 102 Roxanne 21
Sabra 110 Samuel 97 102 Sarah
208 Sarah H 110 Susan C 111
Thomas A 111 Thomas Jr 49
Thomas W 110 W K 102 Wil-
liam 110 William D 205 Wil-
liam W 110
WHEELOCK, A 26 C A 106
Elizabeth E 159
WHETCOMB, Abigail 158 David
7 Hezekiah 7 Josiah 6 Lucy 87
Mary 7 William 87
WHIPPLE, Hannah 21
WHISKINS, William 75
WHITAKER, Abigail 175 Abigail
G 176 Almira 182 Betsey 182
David 182 Isaac 182 221 Lucy
175 Luther 176 Mary 182
Mauris H 221 O E 221 O
Elizabeth 221 Polly 182 Ruth
175 Sanderson 182 Susan M
182
WHITCOMB, A F 72 Abby F 72
Abel 53 95 96 Abigail 100 181
Achsah 86 87 88 Adeline 97
Adeline A 97 Adella Asenath
96 Asa 86 87 97 142 166 Azuba
86 Becke 87 Becky 42 Betsey
136 Boulder 98 Caroline 97
Carrie S 97 Catherine 103
Charles 44 98 Charles H 98
Charlie 103 Clarissa 87 Curtis
136 David 88 Doritha 87
Dorothy 136 E A 98 Ebenezer
166 Edwin A 98 Elizabeth 87
95 Emeline Barnard 68 Etta M
103 Eunice 166 Francis 86 87
Frank H 97 Frank Oscar 97
George L 98 George William
96 Hannah 37 53 72 88 Hattie

301

WHITCOMB (continued)
May 103 Henrietta 103 Henry
G 86 87 Henry Houghton 136
Hepzabah 87 Horatio F 95
James 51 53 James Jr 51 Joel
100 John 86 87 136 203 John P
72 John Post 72 Jona 86 87 88
Jonas 88 Jonathan 42 51 86 87
88 Joseph 98 136 Josiah 87
136 Leonard 37 Lois 53 149
Louisa D 72 Lucy 51 87 Luke
98 Lydia 53 Lyman 166 Maria
M 97 Martha L 96 Mary 53 86
87 153 Mary Agnes 97 Mary G
98 Mary Gardner 98 Mary J 166
Mercy 72 Molley 51 Nabby 87
Nancy 98 Paul 87 111 Persis H
98 Peter 53 R 72 Rebecca 87
Rebekah 163 Reuben 72 103
Reuben Jr 72 Reuben M 103
Richard 88 Ruhamah 87 Sally
87 136 Sally M 49 Sarah 49 51
53 86 87 88 Sarah F 44 Sarah
M 96 Silas 86 87 Simon 87 Son
72 Sophia 86 95 111 Sophia H
111 Susan 166 Susannah Bond
86 Thomas 87 Vandola E 68
William 49
WHITE, ———— 215 Abel 22 Abigail
163 Addie A 215 Adeline 215
Charles H 105 Charles T 215 D
205 Deliah 205 E 206 E G 22 E
H 22 Ebenezer 136 Elizabeth 2
Elizabeth A 206 Ellen A 215
Fred W 105 Hanna H 206 Han-
nah Mandana 205 J 205 Jane E
215 Joanna 144 John 152
Joseph 22 205 Joseph C 22
Joseph E 205 Joseph Nelson
206 Josiah Jr 116 L 205 207
Laura A 205 Laura M 205 Lois
M 205 Louisa 215 Louisa M
215 Lucinda 136 Lucy C 22 M
205 206 Mandana Matilda 206
Marietta E 105 Martha L 241
Mary Ann 96 Mary E 212
Matilda 205 Miriam 206 New-
ton Day 206 Peter 215 Polly
206 S 207 S F 22 S S 22 Sally
215 Sally M 215 Samuel F 22
Sarah 215 Sarah Emory 22
Sarah Louisa 215 Seth Alonzo

WHITE (continued)
207 T 205 T H 215 Tarbel H
215 Thomas 205 206 Thomas
Jr 205 W 106 William 215
Windsor N 206
WHITESIDE, Mary 226 Mary A
226 Robert 226
WHITING, Abigail 7 Dorcasina B
29
WHITING, Fabius 22 Hannah 179
John 2 22 Julia 22 Lydia 7
Olive 157 Orpha 22 Rebecca
165 Sarah 76 Timothy 7 Wil-
liam H 29
WHITMAN, Abbie Pollard 95 96
Davis 22 Hannah 22 Nathaniel
95 Sarah H 95 Susanne 108
WHITMORE, Chloe Elizabeth 217
George E 223 James 217 Sadie
May 222
WHITNEY, 168 A 68 Aaron 43 44
Abel 44 63 Abigail 31 42 58
Abigail H 21 Abigail Knight 58
Abraham 26 31 63 Adeline 66
Adeline P 66 Agnes 55 Alas 53
Alice 53 89 Amanda M 166
Amos 30 31 Anes 53 166 Ann
68 241 Anna 44 Anna Danforth
44 Anna E 103 Asena 51 B F
49 Benjamin F 49 Benjamin
Franklin 49 Bertha Laura Bull
29 Betsy 52 103 Caleb 53 55
166 Caroline W 31 66 Carrie
W Wright 49 Charles Edward
49 Charles H 66 Charles L 49
Charles M 241 Charlotte 58
Charlotte M Turner 58 Clara E
166 Clara Sophia 41 Claricy 31
Cyrene Adelia 46 Cyrus 48 51
Daniel 30 Daniel H 43 David
103 Elias 55 Elijah 55 89
Eliza 63 103 Eliza H 103
Elizabeth 54 68 Emma 103
Emma K 166 Ephraim 22 Es-
tella G Scattergood 41 181 Eva
H Burt 59 Everlina 55 F H 243
Fanny 22 Frances Alice 49
Francis 31 243 Francis H 243
Francis W 71 George 30
George B 66 George F 59
George W 241 Georgie 243
Hannah 31 54 55 71 Hannah

WHITNEY (continued)
Haskell 31 Harriet E 29 Harriet E Wetherbee Clark 29
Harriet Lucy 49 Hattie F 243
Hazel 55 Henry 31 Henry B 66
Henry F 243 Hepzibah 44
Hezekiah 53 Hiram 68 Horace
M 136 Horatio Turner 58 Isaac
31 32 35 48 Isaiah 30 31 48 49
71 91 Israel 31 244 J L 68 J
Milton 47 Jacob 54 James 54
166 James B 241 James L 68
Jane J 59 Jerome G 41 John 63
72 89 90 John Marshall 66
Jonas 22 44 Jonathan 2 22 53
55 166 Joseph 63 103 166
Joseph Addison 49 Joshua 53
Josiah 59 63 Lauretta 49 Levi
55 Lois 89 Lottie C Wilder 49
Louisa 49 Lucy 22 31 32 37 44
53 54 65 166 173 Luke 31 35
58 Luther 31 Lydia 71 Lydia H
Hapgood 35 M E 243 Malinda
Wetherbee 31 Maria 67 Maria
S 66 Marshall 66 Martha 103
Martha A 68 Martha Ann 54
Mary 2 31 48 50 54 65 Mary
Ann 72 Mary E 243 Mary Hill
31 Mary Jane 59 Mary Louisa
49 Mary P Sherman 47
Mehitable 55 Melly E 243
Mercy 44 66 Mercy F 54 Milley 90 Milly 66 68 Miriam 44
Moses 44 Naby 31 Nancy 46 63
Nathan 46 Oliver 42 Percis 49
Phebe 31 Phinehas 71 Rachel
54 Rebbeca 55 Rebekah 63
Reuben 54 66 Reuben F 66
Rhoda 89 Richard 44 54 57 68
Robert 21 Ruhamah 147 Ruth
30 Sally 43 57 68 244 Salmon
44 Samuel 41 89 Sarah 31 41
44 53 55 59 89 90 94 Sarah A
Bull 29 Sarah B 241 Sarah E
243 Sarah Louisa 49 Sarah T
Gardner 41 Simon 50 63 65
Simri 66 Solon Franklin 49
Solon W 29 Sophia A 68 Susan
44 57 68 Susan H 43 Susanna
35 Susannah 91 Susia L 68
Wetherbee 64 William 22 55
Wm E 244 Wm F 59 Z 22 44

WHITON, Henry L 80
WHITTAKER, Genevieve 98 Gordon 98
WHITTEMORE, Amelia 22 Asa
Dunbar 22 Deliverance 78
Eunice 203 Everard 238
Florence 55 Grace Witt 238
Henry 55 Jonathan 203 Lydia
22 Mary 22 Mary M 22 Nancy
179 Nathaniel 22 57 Nathaniel
Jr 22 Raymond G 55 Submit
179 Susanna 26
WHITTUM, Charles 211 Charles
E 211 Sarah E 211
WHOTCOMB, William 166
WIGHT, Beulah 166 Jabez 166
John 166 Jonas D 166
WILCOX, Ada E 223 David 218
Mary Ann 218 Oliver B 218
Roxana 218
WILD, E 25
WILDER, 115 Abigail 6 18 166
Abigail R 183 Abigail Smith 6
Abner 173 Abraham 100
Adeline 136 Amanda M 166
Andrew 1 Andrew J 166 167
168 Anna 3 6 166 167 Anna
Maria 6 Arvine F 166 Asa 166
167 Asaph 6 Bailey 166 Becca
100 Betsey 166 167 168 Betsey
S 163 Bridget 166 167 C 166
167 Caleb 6 Calvin 21 166 167
168 Calvin Jr 166 167 Calvin N
166 167 Catherine 22 136
Catherine R 166 167 Charles
136 Charles F 166 167 Charles
J 22 Charlie L 166 167 Charlotte 21 22 67 Cornelia S 216
Daniel 22 Daniel K 21 David 6
136 182 183 Deborah 1 5 166
167 Dennis 166 167 Dolly 136
144 Dorothy 136 151 E K 166
167 Ebenezer 6 21 166 167
Edward 22 136 Edward Jr 136
Electa 6 Elihu 166 167 168
Elijah 21 Elisha 136 Eliza C
22 Elizabeth 1 3 136 154 166
167 168 Emeline 166 167
Emilia 136 Emily 182 Emma
K 166 Emme 166 167 Emory
166 167 Enos 22 Ephraim 3 6
22 136 166 167 Ephraim Jr 3

WILDER (continued)
Ephriam 2 Esther 136 Eunice
6 166 167 168 173 Fordyce 166
167 168 Francina Melanie 6
Francis 21 Gardner 2 17 22 136
George 67 George W 22 Greene
136 Hannah 6 148 166 167 168
Harriet 136 183 Harrison 166
167 Henry M 136 Holman 22
Isaac A 100 Isabella E 166 167
James 6 22 116 136 140 141
166 167 168 Joel 21 22 Joel
Thomas 22 John 5 6 22 166
167 196 Jonas 21 Jonathan 6
166 167 168 Joseph 1 2 5 6 21
166 167 Josephus 22 Josiah 6
136 173 183 Katharine 6 Katy
166 167 Keziah 166 167 Levi 6
Lewis 166 167 Lois 166 167
Lucinda 100 Lucretia 2 159
166 167 195 6 136 166 167 195
Luke 22 Lusena 21 Luther K
166 167 Lydia 22 166 167 168
Lydia P 166 167 M Annie 166
167 Manasseh 6 Marcia Ann
166 167 Maria 166 167 Mar-
shall 166 167 Martha 2 6 17 21
136 166 167 Martha A 166 167
Mary 2 6 22 136 166 167 196
Mary H 100 136 Mary M 21
Mercy 166 167 Mirick 166 167
168 Moses 100 Nancy 155
Nathan 173 Nathaniel 166 168
195 Oliver 2 P W 166 168
Peter 5 136 Philenia 166 168
Phineas 166 167 168 Phinehas
166 168 Polly 146 147
Prudence 6 166 167 168 Q F
166 168 Rebecca 2 147
Rebecca F 166 168 Rebeccah 2
Rebekah 22 136 Reuben 207
Roxanna 136 Rufus 6 Ruth 1 6
Ruth J 183 Ruth Prescott 6 S V
S 6 Sally 22 156 Sally B 136
Sally N 136 Sampson Vryling
Stoddard 6 Samuel 21 166 167
168 Samuel B 166 168 Samuel
Jr 166 167 168 Sarah 6 166 167
168 Sarah J 166 168 Sarah T
136 Sarah Vryling Stoddard 6
Sarah W 166 168 Sarah Jane
166 168 Sawyer 166 167 168

WILDER (continued)
Seraphinia 67 Sidney 166 168
Sidney C 166 168 Sidney R 166
168 Silas 166 167 168 Silvia
166 168 Sophia 21 143 Spencer
183 Sumner T 166 167 Susan B
183 Susanna 21 Susannah 6 173
Thankful 207 Thomas 6 136
Timothy 166 167 168 Timothy
Jr 166 168 Titus 6 Vashti 149
Volney 21 22 William 21 136
137 Zerviah 166 168 Zipporah
6
WILDS, Elijah 247 Eunice 79 I 25
WILES, Elijah 23
WILKINS, Abby 243 244 Abigail I
243 Caroline 239 Charlie 243
Daniel 239 Edward 232 238 239
Emerson 239 Gracia 243 H
Warren 243 Harry 243 Henry
243 244 Hepzibah 242 Jane 234
Levi 242 Lizzie 243 Mary 239
Mary A 243 Relief 242 Rufus
243 Sarah 232 238 Stephen 242
William 243 244
WILLARD, ---- 168 169 A 24
248 A W 34 Aaron 7 168 Abbie
Sophia 40 Abel 34 54 55 Abiah
W 34 Abigail 24 34 248
Abigail R 183 Abijah 5 22
Abijah Jr 5 Adelle Gerry 64
Alfred R 28 Alice 37 Alonzo 64
Alpheus R 36 Ama 168 Amasa
22 Amory 24 248 Andrew L 64
Ann 47 Anna 5 Arabella 41 71
Artemas 48 168 169 Augusta M
Farwell 36 Augustus G 56 Be-
cca 168 169 Benjamin 24 248
Bethiah 78 Betsy 22 44 Betsy
R 40 C L 64 Carrie Ellsworth
64 Catherine 5 168 Charles 32
Charles A 32 33 65 Charles H
168 Christopher 64 Clarence C
R 38 Clarissa Malvina 32
David 168 169 David Jr 168
169 Dexter 24 248 Dolly 154
168 Dorcasina 64 Dorothy 7 E
R 34 Ebenezer 32 65 Ebenezer
C 63 Eleanor B 34 Eliza A 168
Eliza Millen 168 Eliza S 34
Elizabeth 5 7 22 34 42 44 47
Elizabeth S 168 Ellen 47 54

WILLARD (continued)
Ellen M Davis 55 Ellen R
Dudley 34 Elliott 54 Emeline
168 169 Emeline A 168
Emeline Augusta 40 Ephraim
168 169 Ephraim S 40 Esther C
55 Etta H 64 Fanny 22 Frances
M 63 Francis 28 Francis
Wright 168 Frederick A 41
Gardner 40 George 37 George B
168 Grace M 57 Granville S
168 H Francena 168 Hannah 37
168 Helen M Gerry 68 Henry
248 Henry C 63 Hosea 37 38
Hosea 2nd 37 Hosea Edwin 55
Howland 36 Isaac 154 168
Isaac H 168 Isaac H Jr 168 Is-
rael B 168 Ithamar 40 Jerome
22 Joel 48 John 5 47 John B 41
John Jr 47 Joseph 34 47
Joseph K 34 Joseph Kendall 34
Josiah R 38 Julia A 65
Katharine 5 L 34 Lemuel 42
Levi 5 34 Lois 168 169
Lorenzo B 168 169 Lucha 168
169 Luchous 168 169 Lucia 24
248 Lucinda 168 169 Lucy 24
40 153 248 Lucy Ann 168 169
Lucy Melvina 37 Luke 24 248
Luther 34 41 Luther D 34
Luther Jr 41 Luther R 41 M H
64 Manasseh 168 169 Manas-
seh D 168 169 Maria P 33
Martha 24 32 248 Mary 7 22 24
41 48 168 169 177 248 Mary
Ann 24 248 Mary B 28 Mary
Davis 41 Mary E 39 Mary Edna
56 Mary G 41 71 Mary J 65
Melissa A 36 Melissa O 36 N
25 Nabby 42 Nancy 38 Nancy B
28 Nathanial 7 Nellie P Rich
32 Patience 48 Paul 24 248
Peter A 168 169 Polly 168 169
Rebecca 39 Rhoda 168 169
Robert 28 S F 24 248 S
Josephine 24 248 Salley 34
Sally 28 Samuel 4 Sarah 24 41
168 169 248 Sarah B 39 Sarah
E 32 Sarah Esther 64 Sarah F
24 248 Sarah Wetherbee 34
Silas 168 169 Simeon 42 Simon
22 Sophia 168 169 S P 148

WILLARD (continued)
Susan 32 34 65 Susan M 63 65
Susanna A 34 Tarbell 47
Theodorah 5 Timothy 44 W B
33 34 Walter K 168 169 War-
ren O 68 William 24 39 47 48
248 William B 55 William P
183 Willie 57 Wright 7 Zer-
viah 168 169
WILLIAMS, Abby 186 Deborah 74
Elizabeth 73 Esther P 101
George H 186 Hannah 73 R 26
Samuel S 186
WILLINGTON, Ebenezer 207
WILLIS, Abbie H 67 Albert E 67
Daniel 67 George W 67
Josephine R 67 Maria Whitney
67 Marilla E 67 Rebekah 143
Victoria A 67
WILLISTON, Sarah A 70
WILLSON, Benjamin 6 Jeremiah
6 Nathaniel 6 Rebecca 6 Rhoda
6
WILSON, ---- 238 Daniel 239
Ebenezer 169 Eliza Ann 21
Hannah 239 Hannah P 239 Har-
riet Maria 242 Hepsebah 115
James 36 242 John 21
Jonathan 115 Lucy 36 Mary E
95
WINCH, Mehitable 176
WINCHESTER, Bathsheba 74
Benjamin 76 Elhanan 73
Elizabeth 79 Elvira 78
Frederick 77 Lydia 75 Polly 79
Samuel 21 Sarah 21 Selah 79
Susan 79
WINDE, Ellen Brown 69
WINDITT, J W Jr 21 John 21 M
E 21 Mary E 21 Phebe 21
Sarah 21 Sarah A 21
WINN, Abigail 217 John 217
Maria J 209 Peter S 209
WINTER, A 204 A E 227 A R 206
Aaron E 204 227 Abigail B 206
Calvin 206 Carrie E 204 227
Charles Adolphus 206 D 204 D
D 227 Dorina 227 Edward
Payson 206 Eliza 204 227
Herbie A 204 227 Lucy 206
Luther 206 M 206 Nancy
Abigail 206 Susan Abigail 206

305

WRIGHT (continued)
    Thomas 169
WYER, David 137 David Mrs 137
WYETH, Joseph 75
WYMAN, Benjamin 22 Elizabeth
    2 Ephraim 1 Fanny 23 Jonas

WYMAN (continued)
    23 Martha Joslin 23 Mary 2
    Nathaniel 2 Submit 2 Tabatha
    156 William 23 Zaccheus 23
WYTHE, Eunice 74
YOUNG, Charlotte 67 Samuel 67
    68 Seraphinia 67 68 Stephen 76